CLOSING CASES

APPENDIX CASES

WEBSITE HIGHLIGHTS

Country Market Report

Hyperlinks for

  IMF (International Monetary Fund)

  WTO (World Trade Organization)

  NAFTA (North Atlantic Free Trade Association)

  EU (European Union)

  Export Promotion

  Current Travel Warnings

  U.S. Trade Sanctions and Embargoes

  Public Citizen: Global Trade Watch

  OPIC (Overseas Private Investment Corporation)

  Government Tenders

  Country Corruption Scores

  Online Sources of Secondary Data

  Safe Harbor

  International Trade Fairs

  U.S. Government

  Japanese Government

  Travel Information

  Regional Groups

  International Franchise Association

  U.S. Federal Trade Commission

  ISO (International Standards Organization)

  ANSI (American National Standards Institute)

  Anti-Counterfeiting

GLOBAL MARKETING

SECOND EDITION

Kate Gillespie

University of Texas at Austin

Jean-Pierre Jeannet

Babson College, Wellesley, Massachusetts
International Institute for Management
Development (IMD)
Lausanne, Switzerland

H. David Hennessey

Babson College, Wellesley, Massachusetts
Ashridge Management College
Berkhamsted, United Kingdom

HOUGHTON MIFFLIN COMPANY

BOSTON   NEW YORK

Publisher: George T. Hoffman
Associate Sponsoring Editor: Joanne Dauksewicz
Project Editor: Paula Kmetz
Senior Art and Design Coordinator: Jill Haber
Senior Photo Editor: Jennifer Meyer Dare
Composition Buyer: Chuck Dutton
Senior Manufacturing Buyer: Renee Ostrowski
Marketing Manager: Mike Schenk
Marketing Specialist: Lisa E. Boden

Cover image: © Ben Shakirov/Images.com

Printed in the U.S.A.

Library of Congress Control Number: 2005936529

Instructor's exam copy:
ISBN 13: 978-0-618-73147-3
ISBN 10: 0-618-73147-4

For orders, use student text ISBNs:
ISBN 13: 978-0-618-65953-1
ISBN 10: 0-618-65953-6

123456789–QT–09 08 07 06 05

BRIEF CONTENTS

CONTENTS

CHAPTER 4

POLITICAL AND REGULATORY CLIMATE   94

CHAPTER 11
GLOBAL STRATEGIES FOR SERVICES, BRANDS, AND SOCIAL MARKETING 334

CHAPTER 12
PRICING FOR INTERNATIONAL AND GLOBAL MARKETS 364

CHAPTER 13
MANAGING GLOBAL DISTRIBUTION CHANNELS 396

PREFACE

Today, virtually every major firm must compete in a global marketplace. Buyers can comprise ordinary consumers or local businesses in international markets, multinational corporations, or foreign governments. Competitors can be local firms or global firms. Although some consumer needs and wants may be converging across national markets and multilateral agreements seek to bring order to the international economic and legal environment, global marketers must still navigate among varied cultures where unexpected rules apply. Addressing this varied and increasingly competitive marketplace and developing strategies that are both efficient and effective are the tasks that face the global marketer.

Whether they oversee foreign markets or face international competitors at home, every student who plans to enter marketing as a profession will need to understand and apply the essentials of global marketing. This text prepares them for that challenge.

Why This Book?

There are a number of global marketing texts on the market. Our approach differs from that of other books in several ways.

A Dual Focus: International Buyers and Global Competition. Whereas most texts envisage global marketing as an understanding of international buyers, we envisage it as *competing* for those buyers. Immediately following our chapter on global markets and buyers we present the student with a chapter on global and local competitors. From then on we keep students focused on both buyers and competitors throughout the book.

A Global View Combined with a Strong Appreciation for Cultural Differences. Some global marketing texts downplay culture. Others make cultural differences their focus. Our approach is to recognize that cultural differences do exist and influence global marketing in a plethora of ways. To this end, we introduce the student early to cultural issues and ways of analyzing culture that are reinforced throughout the book. But we also present students with a global view of managing cultural differences. For example, if you know you are going to sell a new product in seventy countries, why not consider this when you first design the product? What is the best design that will allow for necessary adaptations with the least effort and cost?

Regional Balance. For a text to be true guide to global marketing, it must present students with a regional balance. Most texts concentrate on the markets of United States, Europe, and Japan. Some briefly discuss markets in Latin America or the Pacific Rim. Our book delivers a balance of developed and developing markets including insights into the often-overlooked markets of Africa and the Middle East. We also encourage students to think of competitors as coming from all countries, including developing countries such as India, Korea, and Mexico.

Current Coverage Across a Wide Variety of Topics. Our combined research and consulting experience allows us to speak with enthusiasm and conviction across the many areas covered by a global marketing text, including global strategy, cross-cultural consumer behavior, and marketing organization as well as the effects government policy can have on international markets and global marketing. Our text combines recent academic research along with in-the-news corporate stories.

Gender Representation. We have taken care to present examples of women as well as men in roles of global marketers. This is apparent in our end-of-chapter cases as well as the current vignettes in our *World Beat* boxed inserts.

An Interactive Approach. Because the field of global marketing changes so quickly, perhaps no subject is better suited to take advantage of Internet technology. The Internet now offers a variety of respected sites that allow students to do research and formulate preliminary marketing plans. Our goal is to familiarize each student with these tools that are available to the global marketer.

Application Opportunities. To help students better internalize their knowledge of global marketing, this text offers various opportunities to apply knowledge of global marketing concepts and skills to business situations. These opportunities include full-length cases, shorter end-of-chapter cases, and an online Country Market Report guide. This guide assists students in assessing whether a firm should enter a foreign market. For example, should Marriott hotels enter Uzbekistan? Should Yoshinoya, a Japanese casual dining chain, enter Brazil? The guide walks students through subsequent marketing mix questions such as what adaptations would a U.S.-based dating service have to make if it were to enter the French market. What pricing, promotion, and distribution strategies should it employ?

Why This New Edition?

Updated Coverage of Evolving Issues in Global Marketing. Global marketing doesn't stand still! The new edition of this text includes insights and frameworks from recent academic and consulting research. Just some of the new questions addressed include:

▶ How do consumers in different countries respond to global brands? New segmentation helps marketers better understand who hates them and who loves them—and why.

▶ What suggestions do experienced global marketers propose for implementing successful global account programs?

▶ Born-global firms are new to the world marketplace. What do we now know about their strengths and weaknesses?

▶ Outsourcing is considered essential for global competitiveness in many industries. Why do some countries win (and others lose) in these multifaceted and highly politicized transactions?

▶ Rethinking country of origin: What threat to global marketers does consumer animosity pose?

▶ How does a myriad of national laws make it so difficult (but not always impossible) to shut down parallel importers by taking them to court?

▶ How can service marketers globalize and localize at the same time?

▶ What makes global social marketing the same as—and different from—commercial global marketing?

Even More End-of-Chapter Cases. New cases are provided to capture recent developments in global marketing. They include:

▶ *Textile Trauma* Can textile and clothing manufacturers in countries as diverse as Mexico, Turkey, Bangladesh, and Mauritius still compete against China after world textile quotas were lifted in 2005? If so, how?

▶ *The Global Baby Bust* From France to Japan, Russia to South Korea, China to Mexico—world population growth is in decline and the world population is heading for an implosion. What implications to global marketers do these surprising new demographic trends pose?

▶ *The New Cola Wars* Watch out Coke and Pepsi! New challengers from Europe and Latin America are determined to dislodge these giant competitors. How real is the threat?

▶ *Gamali Air* A marketing team must respond to a countertrade proposal from a prospective customer. Can they come up with a counterproposal that both sides can live with?

▶ *Fighting AIDS in Asia* A former global product manager in packaged foods has turned social marketer and must prioritize markets and programs to help alleviate the spread of AIDS in Asia. Can her skills in global marketing be put to use in this new context?

Expanded Test Bank with Both Factual and Problem-Oriented Questions. We now provide more than 1,500 questions in the test bank. Approximately 450 are application-oriented questions.

Content and Organization of the Book

Chapter 1 presents an introduction to global marketing. In this chapter we describe the development of global marketing and the importance of global marketing to both firms and the managers of the future. We explore the need for a global mindset and set forth the structure of the book.

Part 1 is entitled "Understanding the Global Marketing Environment." In this early section we investigate the key ways that the macro environment can affect global marketers. Although the concepts may be macro, we constantly show how they apply to a variety of firms trying to succeed in a vibrant international marketplace. In Chapter 2, "The Global Economy," we present the student with basic theories of trade, explain how exchange rates work, and explore issues of protectionism and trade restrictions as well as economic integration and the challenges of outsourcing. In Chapter 3, "Cultural and Social Forces," we explore the impact on marketing of factors such as religion, family structure, education, and attitudes toward time. We describe the Hofstede measures of culture and present ratings for nearly seventy countries—ratings that can be used time and again when analyzing cultural underpinnings of marketing dilemmas later in the book. The chapter continues with a discussion of issues relating to language and communication such as the difference between high- and low-context cultures and the social acceptability (or not) of showing emotion. We conclude with insights into overcoming the language barriers and dealing with culture shock. In Chapter 4, "Political and Regulatory Climate," we begin by asking the question, "What do governments want?" We then explore the varied ways that both host and home countries can impact global marketers. We describe how legal systems and attitudes toward rules vary around the world. We continue by explaining the difference to the global marketer between the task of forecasting and managing regulatory change and the task of managing political risk, and we offer concrete ideas on how to do both. The chapter concludes with a discussion of how terrorism impacts global marketing.

Part 2 concentrates on "Analyzing Global Opportunities." Beginning with Chapter 5, "Global Markets," we introduce students to global concerns and cross-cultural aspects of consumer, business, and government markets, including a discussion of bribery and international contracts. Chapter 6, "Global Competitors," introduces students to both issues of global firm versus global firm as well as global firm versus local firm. In particular, we present ways in which one global firm can successfully engage another as well as ways in which a local firm can respond to an encroaching global firm—including going global itself. We then explore cultural attitudes toward competition that can help explain why government regulation of corporate behavior varies around the world and why firms from different countries can be expected to behave differently. We describe how home countries' actions can affect the global competitiveness of their firms. In addition to discussing firms from the developed world—the United States, Europe, and Japan—we devote a separate section to better understanding firms from the emerging markets of the developing world. We conclude by examining the country-of-origin advantage (or sometimes disadvantage) that affects global competition, and we discuss the increasingly visible phenomenon of consumer animosity toward firms from particular countries. In Chapter 7, "Global Marketing Research," we present issues of research design and organization in a global setting and discuss the collection of secondary and primary data across cultures.

Part 3, "Developing Global Participation Strategies," examines the key decisions of determining where and how to compete and how to enter foreign markets. In Chapter 8, "Global Market Participation," we look at traditional patterns of how firms internationalize as well as the more recent phenomenon of born-global firms that enter foreign markets from their inception. We identify the pros and cons of geographic market choices such as targeting developed versus developing economies and explore the concepts of standalone attractive markets and strategically important markets. We then provide a format for country selection. In Chapter 9, "Global Market Entry Strategies," we cover the varied options of how to enter (and sometimes leave) a foreign market, including production and ownership decisions, portal or e-business entry options, and when to consider exiting markets.

Part 4, "Designing Global Marketing Programs," covers the global management of the marketing mix and the cross-cultural challenges involved in decisions concerning products, pricing, distribution, and promotion. Chapter 10, "Global Product Strategies," explores necessary and desirable product (including packaging and warranty) adaptations for international markets, and it explains the importance of managing a global product line. We examine a new paradigm—designing a product with multiple national markets in mind. We also explore the decision to design (rather than adapt) a product for an important foreign market. We identify different sources for new products, whether developed in-house or outsourced, and conclude with an examination of global rollouts for new products. In Chapter 11, "Global Strategies for Services, Brands, and Social Marketing," we present the particular cross-cultural challenges of services marketing and discuss branding decisions, including issues of brand protection. The chapter concludes with a discussion of the possibilities and challenges of applying global marketing concepts to social marketing internationally. In Chapter 12, "Pricing for International and Global Markets," we examine how cost and market factors as well as environmental factors such as exchange rate movements and inflation can affect pricing in international markets. We then explore managerial issues such as determining transfer prices, quoting prices in foreign currencies, dealing with parallel imports, and deciding when and how to participate in countertrade arrangements.

Part 4 continues with Chapter 13, "Managing Global Distribution Channels." This chapter reviews global channels and logistics and introduces the potential differences that exist among local channels, with special emphasis on accessing and managing these channels. Recent trends are examined, including the globalization of retail chains and the growth of direct marketing worldwide, as well as the peculiar challenges of smuggling and the increasing presence of organized crime in the global movement of consumer goods. Chapter 14, "Global Promotion Strategies," begins by exploring global selling and cross-cultural differences in local selling and sales force management. It continues with a discussion of international sports sponsorship and public relations, as well as cross-cultural differences in sales promotions, product placement, and managing word of mouth. Part 3 concludes with Chapter 15, "Managing Global Advertising," which explores issues of global versus local advertising as well as global media strategies and agency selection.

Chapter 16, "Organizing for Global Marketing," in Part 5 identifies the elements that will determine the most appropriate organization for a firm's global marketing and outlines the characteristics of various organizational options. The chapter examines issues of control as well and discusses the particular problem of conflict between headquarters and national subsidiaries. We conclude with a discussion of global marketing as a career.

Pedagogical Advantages

Our book has incorporated several features to help students learn about global marketing.

Chapter-Opening Stories. Each chapter begins a short recap of a recent marketing experience that illustrates key issues from the chapter that follows. This helps students grasp immediately the real-life relevance and importance of issues presented in the chapter.

Chapter Outlines and Learning Objectives. At the beginning of each chapter we present both a chapter outline and a list of clear learning objectives to help focus students on the understanding they can expect to take away from of the chapter.

"World Beat" Boxed Inserts. Numerous and timely examples of market challenges from around the world help students further explore international issues.

Internet Icons. Throughout the text we draw the student's attention to readings, exercises, or hyperlinks provided on our website that have particular relevance to the subject under discussion.

Pictures and Full-Color Text and Graphics. We believe that engaging the student visually enhances the learning experience.

Discussion Questions. We provide discussion questions at the end of each chapter that challenge a student's creativity to stretch beyond the chapter.

Short but Evocative End-of-Chapter Cases. We believe cases can be short but conceptually dense. We have included two or three such cases at the end of each chapter. These cases were written or chosen to work with the chapter content. The end-of-case questions often refer specifically to chapter content in order to test a student's ability to apply the chapter to the case.

Longer Cases for More In-Depth Analysis. We are aware that some instructors like to augment shorter cases with several longer ones, either throughout the course or at the end of a course. For these instructors, we have provided several longer cases that challenge students to apply and synthesize their knowledge.

An Internet-Based Country Market Report. This exercise presents students with an opportunity to apply concepts from the chapters in the book as well as introduces them to Internet sites that are useful to global marketers.

Complete Teaching Package

A variety of ancillary materials are designed to assist the instructor in the classroom.

Online Instructor's Resource Manual. An instructor's manual provides ideas pertaining to discussion questions and teaching notes for both the end-of-chapter cases and the longer cases presented at the end of the book. Suggestions for assigning the Country Market Report are also provided. A test bank provides multiple-choice, true/false, and fill-in questions for each chapter. Questions are both factual and application oriented.

Test Bank. The Test Bank has been completely updated and expanded to include over 1,500 questions with over 450 application-type questions. The test bank includes true/false, multiple-choice, fill-in-the-blank, and essay questions, complete with answers and text-page references.

Online Teaching Center. The center provides instructors with lecture notes, answers to end-of-chapter questions, teaching notes for the end-of-chapter and appendix cases, basic and premium PowerPoint slides, sample syllabi, and "Kate's Updates," news clips about current events updating in-text examples, published for the fall and spring semesters.

HMTesting. The computerized version of the Test Bank allows instructors to select, edit, and add questions, or generate randomly selected questions to produce a test master for easy duplication. Online Testing and Gradebook functions allow instructors to administer tests via their local area network or the Web, set up classes, record grades from tests or assignments, analyze grades, and compile class and individual statistics. This program can be used on both PCs and Macintosh computers.

Videos. The video package highlights global companies and corresponds with the concepts and topics highlighted in the text. The video guide provides teaching notes to help prepare for each video and to provide in-class discussion ideas.

PowerPoint. This classroom presentation package (downloadable from the Web) comes in basic and premium versions, including over twenty-five slides per chapter combining clear, concise text and art to create a total presentation package. Instructors who have access to PowerPoint can edit slides to customize them for their presentations. Slides can also be printed as lecture notes for class distribution. In addition to slides covering textbook content, the premium version of the program provides examples and data that supplement what is in the text. These slides come with additional notes for instructors.

Call-in Test Service. This service lets instructors select items from the Test Bank and call our toll-free faculty services number (800-733-1717) to order printed tests.

The student package includes:

Online Study Center. This especially rich resource for students includes Internet links that allow students to further explore global marketing issues and resources, a flashcard glossary, ACE study questions, and step-by-step guidance for completing a comprehensive Country Market Report.

Wall Street Journal Subscription Offer. This offer is available with this textbook. Students whose instructors have adopted the *WSJ* with Gillespie/Jeannet/ Hennessey will receive, shrink-wrapped with their book, a registration card for the 10-week print and online subscription to the *WSJ*. Students must fill out and return the registration card found in the text to initiate the subscription privileges. The text package will also include a copy of the *Wall Street Journal Student Subscriber Handbook*, which explains how to use both print and online versions of the newspaper. This is only sold as a package with new textbooks. *WSJ* subscriptions cannot be sold as a standalone item.

Acknowledgments

We very much appreciate the contributions of cases studies from Anna Andriasova, Juliet Burdet-Taylor, William Carner, Jaeseok Jeong, Kamran Kashani, Martha Lanning, Michael Magers, Sam Perkins, Liesl Riddle, K. B. Saji, and Valerie VinCola. We are also especially thankful to Liesl Riddle for her help with the supplements and with testing a number of our cases in her international marketing classes at The George Washington University.

In addition, we are grateful to the following reviewers for their insights and guidance:

Sally Andrews, *Linn-Benton Community College*

David Andrus, *Kansas State University*

Walter H. Beck, Sr., *Reinhardt College*

Gloria Christian, *Butter County Community College*

Joyce A. Claterbos, *University of Kansas*

Tevfic Dalgic, *University of Texas, Dallas*

Darrell Goudge, *University of Central Oklahoma*

Paul Herbig, *Tri State University*

Glen Johns, *Cedar Crest College*

Theodore Jula, *Stonehill College*

William Lesch, *University of North Dakota*

Marilyn Liebrenz-Himes, *The George Washington University*

Steven Lysonski, *Marquette University*

Michell Marette, *Northern Virginia Community College*

Maria McConnell, *Lorain County Community College*

Sanjay Mehta, *Sam Houston State University*

Mark Mitchell, *University of Southern California*

Fred Pragasam, *University of North Florida*

Alfred Quinton, *The College of New Jersey*

H. Rika Houston, *California State University–Los Angeles*

Liesl Riddle, *The George Washington University*

Fred Tennant, *Webster University*

Frank Tian Xie, *Drexel University*

Michael Weinstein, *Brooklyn College*

GLOBAL MARKETING

1 INTRODUCTION TO GLOBAL MARKETING

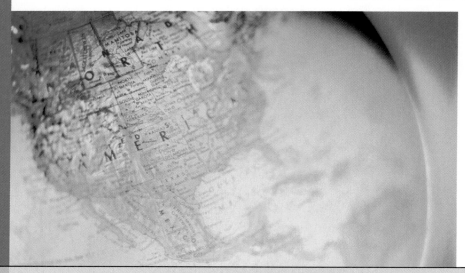

WHEN MTV first went international, it aired the same videos it used in the United States, essentially blaring Michael Jackson at the world. In Europe, this strategy worked well in attracting the top two hundred largest pan-European advertisers. But to reach other advertisers, MTV had to adopt a more national approach, tailoring music and programming to local tastes and languages. However, over time the rising costs of production ($200,000–$350,000 per half-hour episode) caused MTV to reevaluate its multidomestic strategy. Now local subsidiaries are encouraged to create products that will play across regions or even globally. For example, *Famous Last Minutes,* a parody imagining the deaths of rock stars, was thought up by MTV Germany but would have been too expensive to produce solely for the German market.[1]

Global firms must constantly balance the unique needs of national markets with global imperatives. Global marketers must address different cultures and regulatory environments. The demands of local consumers are multifaceted and often changing. Global marketers must also exploit economies of scale in order to deliver quality and value in a competitive global marketplace. Competition increasingly occurs across markets, and competitive moves cross national borders at an alarmingly fast rate. Aided by technology, local consumers are more and more aware of products and prices

LEARNING OBJECTIVES

After studying this chapter, you should be able to

▶ Describe the development of global marketing.

▶ Explain the importance of global marketing and the need for a global mindset.

CHAPTER OUTLINE

from around the world, and large retailers and multinational firms have become powerful global buyers that demand special attention. National markets remain unique but are increasingly interdependent. All these challenges are at the heart of global marketing.

This first chapter introduces you to the field of global marketing. Initially, we explore why companies seek global markets and examine the differences among domestic, international, multinational, and global types of marketing. We then explain why mastering global marketing skills can be valuable to your future career. A conceptual outline of the book concludes the chapter.

THE IMPORTANCE OF GLOBAL MARKETS

Global markets are expanding rapidly. The combined value of merchandise exports has exceeded $7 trillion. Exports of commercial services account for nearly another $2 trillion. For many years, international trade has grown faster than domestic economies, further contributing to the ever-increasing pace of globalization.[2]

Furthermore, international trade statistics do not reflect a substantial portion of international marketing operations. In particular, overseas sales of locally manufactured and locally sold products produced by foreign investors are not included in world trade figures. Consequently, the total volume of international marketing far exceeds the volume of total world trade. Sales of overseas subsidiaries for U.S. companies are estimated at three times the value of these companies' exports. Although no detailed statistics are available, this pattern suggests that the overall volume of international marketing amounts to a multiple of the world trade volume.

The scope of global marketing includes many industries and many business activities. Boeing, the world's largest commercial airline manufacturer, engages in global marketing when it sells its aircraft to airlines across the world. Likewise, Ford Motor Company, which operates automobile manufacturing plants in many countries, engages in global marketing, even though a major part of Ford's output is sold in the country where it is manufactured. Large retail chains, such as Kmart and Wal-Mart, search for new products abroad to sell in the United States. As major global buyers, they too participate in global marketing.

Headquartered on the shores of Lake Geneva, Swiss-based Nestlé is the world's largest foods company. Its products are sold in virtually every country.

A whole range of service industries are involved in global marketing. Major advertising agencies, banks, investment bankers, accounting firms, consulting companies, hotel chains, airlines, and even law firms now market their services worldwide. Leading orchestras from Vienna, Berlin, New York, and Philadelphia command as much as $150,000 per concert. Booking performances all over the world, they compete with new global entrants from St. Petersburg and Moscow.

Why Companies Seek Global Markets

Companies become involved in international markets for a variety of reasons. Some firms simply respond to orders from abroad without making any organized efforts of their own. Most companies take a more active role. Many firms enter foreign markets to increase sales and profits. Some companies pursue opportunities abroad when their domestic market has reached maturity. For example, Coca-Cola, the market leader worldwide in the soft-drinks business, finds that on a per-capita basis, most foreign consumers drink only a fraction of the cola that Americans drink. Consequently, Coca-Cola sees enormous growth potential in international markets.

Sometimes a domestic competitive shock provides the impetus to globalize. After Mexico joined the North American Free Trade Association (NAFTA), Mexican companies realized that they would face increased competition from U.S. firms. Bimbo, Mexico's market leader in packaged foods, entered the U.S. market to better understand the competition it would inevitably face back home in Mexico.[3]

Other firms launch their international marketing operations by following customers who move abroad. Major U.S. banks have opened branches in key financial centers around the world to serve their U.S. clients better. Similarly, advertising agencies in the United States have created networks to serve the interests of their multinational clients. When Japanese automobile manufacturers opened plants in the United States, many of their component suppliers followed and built operations nearby. Failing to accommodate these important clients could result in the loss not only of foreign sales but of domestic sales as well.

For some firms, however, the reason to become involved in global marketing has its roots in pure economics. Producers of television shows in Hollywood can spend $1.5 million to produce a single show for a typical series. Networks in the United States pay only about $1 million to air a single show, and the series producers rely on international markets to cover the difference. Without the opportunity to market globally, they would not even be able to produce the shows for the U.S. market.

THE DEVELOPMENT OF GLOBAL MARKETING

The term *global marketing* has been in use only since the 1980s. Before that decade, *international marketing* and *multinational marketing* were the terms used most often to describe international marketing activities. Global marketing is not just a new label for an old phenomenon, however. Global marketing provides a new vision for international marketing. Before we explain global marketing in detail, let us first look at the historical development of international marketing as a field in order to gain a better understanding of the phases through which it has passed (see Figure 1.1).

Domestic Marketing

Domestic marketing marketing activities aimed at a firm's domestic market

Marketing that is aimed at a single market, the firm's domestic market, is known as **domestic marketing**. In domestic marketing, the firm faces only one set of competitive, economic, and market issues. It essentially deals with only one set of national customers, although the company may serve several segments in this one market.

Export Marketing

Export marketing marketing activities undertaken when a firm sells its products abroad and when those products are shipped from one country to another

Export marketing covers marketing activities that are involved when a firm sells its products outside its domestic base of operation and when products are physically shipped from one country to another. The major challenges of export marketing are the selection of appropriate markets or countries through marketing research, the determination of appropriate product modifications to meet the demand requirements of export markets, and the development of export channels through which the company can market its products abroad. In export marketing, the firm may concentrate mostly on product modifications, running its export operations as a welcome and profitable byproduct of its domestic strategy. Other aspects of marketing strategy such as pricing, channel management, and promotion may be outsourced either to foreign

FIGURE 1.1
International and Global Marketing

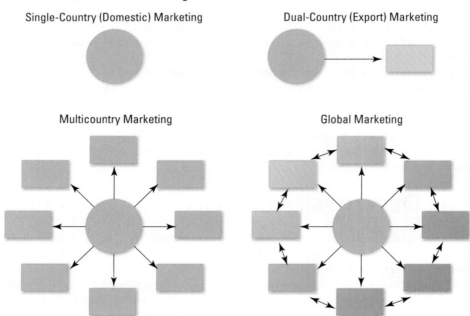

Single-Country (Domestic) Marketing

Dual-Country (Export) Marketing

Multicountry Marketing

Global Marketing

agents or distributors or to specialist export management companies located in the firm's home country. Although export marketing probably represents the most traditional and least complicated form of nondomestic marketing, it remains an important feature for many firms.

International Marketing

A company that practices **international marketing** goes beyond exporting and becomes much more directly involved in the local marketing environment within a given country. The firm is likely to have its own sales subsidiaries and will participate in and develop entire marketing strategies for foreign markets. At this point, the necessary adaptations to the firm's domestic marketing strategies become of greater concern. Companies need to decide how to adjust an entire marketing strategy, including how they sell, advertise, and distribute products, in order to fit new market demands. Understanding different cultural, economic, and political environments becomes increasingly necessary for success.

International marketing marketing activities undertaken when a company becomes significantly involved in local marketing environments in foreign countries

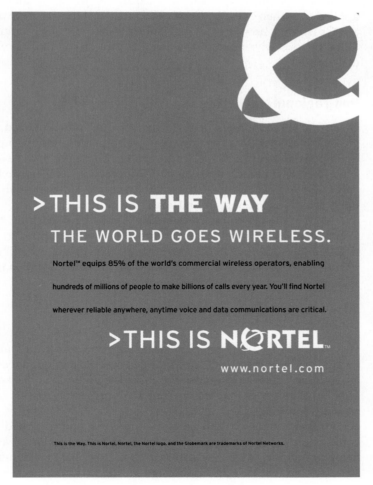

Global reach: Nortel equips 85 percent of the world's commercial wireless operators.

Typically, much of the field of international marketing has been devoted to making the environment understandable and helping managers navigate the differences.

Multinational Marketing

Multinational corporation (MNC) a company that possesses extensive investments in assets abroad and operates in a number of foreign countries as though it were a local company

Multidomestic strategy a strategy pursued by a multinational firm in which various marketing strategies are developed, each tailored to a particular local market

The focus on multinational marketing came as a result of the development of the **multinational corporation (MNC)**. These companies, characterized by extensive investments in assets abroad, operate in a number of foreign countries as though they were local companies. Multinationals traditionally pursue a **multidomestic strategy**, wherein the multinational firm competes by applying many different strategies, each one tailored to a particular local market. Often, MNCs attempt to appear "local" wherever they compete. The major challenge confronting the multinational marketer is to find the best possible adaptation of a complete marketing strategy to each individual country. This more extreme approach to international marketing leads to a maximum amount of localization and to a large variety of marketing strategies. Ironically, the traditional multidomestic strategies of MNCs failed to take advantage of the global reach of these firms. Lessons learned in one domestic market were often not applied elsewhere. Good ideas in product development or promotions were not always shared among national subsidiaries. Similarly, multinationals often failed to take advantage of their global size in negotiating with suppliers and distributors.

Pan-regional Marketing

Given the diseconomies of scale that plague individualized marketing strategies, each tailored to a specific local environment, many companies have begun to emphasize strategies for larger regions. These regional strategies encompass a number of markets, such as pan-European strategies for Europe, and have come about as a result of regional economic and political integration. Such integration is also apparent in North America, where the United States, Canada, and Mexico have committed themselves to the far-reaching NAFTA trade pact. Companies considering regional strategies seek synergies in marketing operations in one region with the aim of achieving increased efficiency. Many firms are presently working on such solutions, moving from many multidomestic strategies toward selected pan-regional strategies.

Global Marketing

Global marketing strategy a single transnational strategy for a product, service, or business that nonetheless incorporates flexibility for local adaptation

Over the years, academics and international companies alike have become aware that opportunities for economies of scale and enhanced competitiveness are greater if firms can manage to integrate and create marketing strategies on a global scale. A **global marketing strategy** involves the creation of a single strategy for a product, service, or company for the entire global market. It encompasses many countries simultaneously and is aimed at leveraging the commonalities across many markets. Rather than tailoring a strategy perfectly to any individual market, a firm that pursues global marketing settles on a basic strategy that can be applied throughout the world market, all the while maintaining flexibility to adapt to local market requirements where necessary. Such strategies are inspired by the fact that many markets appear increasingly similar in environmental and customer requirements. The management challenges are to design marketing strategies that work well across multiple markets, while remaining alert to the possible adaptations that may be advisable on a market-to-market basis.

Even though global marketers face the unique challenge of finding marketing strategies that fit many countries, the skills and concepts that have been critical since the earliest stages in the history of marketing remain important and continue to be needed. Firms that pursue global strategies must also be adept at international marketing because designing one global strategy does not mean ignoring national differences. Instead, a global strategy must reflect a sound understanding of the cultural, economic, and political environment of many countries. Few global marketing strategies can exist without local tailoring, which is the hallmark of multinational marketing. Managing global marketing is the last in a series of skills that managers must acquire to be successful in the global marketplace.

WHY STUDY GLOBAL MARKETING?

You have probably asked yourself why you should study global marketing. Each year multinational companies hire large numbers of marketing professionals. As these firms become increasingly globalized, competence in global marketing will become even more important in the future—and many marketing executives will be pursuing global marketing as a career. Other career opportunities exist with a large number of exporters, where job candidates will require international marketing skills. Even newly formed companies are now entering foreign markets at a young age.

With the service sector becoming increasingly globalized, many graduates joining service industries find themselves confronted with international opportunities at early stages of their careers. Today, consulting engineers, bankers, brokers, public accountants, medical services executives, and e-commerce specialists all need global marketing skills to compete in a rapidly changing environment. Consequently, a solid understanding and appreciation of global marketing will benefit the careers of most business students, regardless of the field or industry they choose to enter.

A Need for Global Mindsets

The Swedish firm IKEA is today one of the world's largest furniture retailing chains. IKEA entered the important U.S. market and quickly become a dominant player. IKEA's success was largely attributable to a new concept that it introduced to the United States: setting up large stores where consumers could browse, buy, and take furniture home in disassembled form at the end of their visit. IKEA is but one example of an international global competitor entering a previously "safe" market with new ideas, bringing global competition to the doorstep of strictly domestic companies.

Few firms can avoid the impact of global competition today. Foreign competition has made enormous inroads into the manufacture of apparel, textiles, shoes, electronic equipment, and steel. Although foreign competition for many consumer goods has been evident for years, inroads by foreign firms into the industrial and capital goods markets have been equally spectacular.

The need to become more competitive in a global economy will force many changes on the typical company. Firms will have to compete in global markets to defend their own domestic markets and to keep up with global competitors based in other countries. These firms will need an increasing cadre of managers who can adopt a global perspective. This requires not only a knowledge of other countries, economies, and cultures but also a clear understanding of how the global economy works. Managers with a global perspective will also have to integrate actions taken in one national market with actions in another national market. This means that global marketers will be required to use ideas and experiences from a number of other countries so that the best products can be marketed the most efficiently and effectively. Managers with a global mindset will need to deal with new strategies that were not part of the domestic or older international business scenes.

To compete successfully in today's global marketplace, companies and their management must master certain areas. *Environmental competence* is needed to navigate the global economy. This area of expertise includes a knowledge of the dynamics of the world economy, of major national markets, and of political, social, and cultural environments. *Analytic competence* is necessary to pull together a vast array of information concerning global markets and competitors. *Strategic competence* helps executives focus on the where, why, and how of global market participation. A global marketer must also possess *functional competence,* or a thorough background in all areas of marketing such as product development, channel management, pricing, and promotion. *Managerial competence* is the ability to implement programs and to organize effectively on a global scale. In addition to these basic competencies, global marketers must attain an overarching **global competence** or the ability to balance local market needs with the demands of global efficiency and the opportunities of global synergies.

Global competence the ability to balance local market needs with the demands of global efficiency and the opportunities of global synergies

Organization of This Book

This text is structured around the basic requirements for making sound global marketing decisions, as depicted in Figure 1.2.

Part 1, Chapters 2 through 4, is concerned with the global marketing environment. Special emphasis is placed on the economic, cultural, political, and legal environments that companies must address in order to be successful.

Part 2, Chapters 5 through 7, concentrates on global market opportunity analysis. Chapters in this section discuss global buyers, competitors, and the research methods that are necessary to apply in order to understand marketing opportunities globally.

Chapters 8 and 9, which make up Part 3, deal with global market participation. Chapter 8 introduces key issues relating to market choices. Chapter 9 describes the various modes of entry that companies can employ once they decide to enter a foreign market.

Part 4, which comprises Chapters 10 through 15, aims at developing competence in designing global marketing programs consistent with a global strat-

COMPETENCE LEVEL	DECISION AREA	
ENVIRONMENTAL COMPETENCE	UNDERSTANDING THE GLOBAL MARKETING ENVIRONMENT	
	CH 2	THE GLOBAL ECONOMY
	CH 3	CULTURAL AND SOCIAL FORCES
	CH 4	POLITICAL AND REGULATORY CLIMATE
ANALYTIC COMPETENCE	ANALYZING GLOBAL OPPORTUNITIES	
	CH 5	GLOBAL MARKETS
	CH 6	GLOBAL COMPETITORS
	CH 7	GLOBAL MARKETING RESEARCH
STRATEGIC COMPETENCE	DEVELOPING GLOBAL PARTICIPATION STRATEGIES	
	CH 8	GLOBAL MARKET PARTICIPATION
	CH 9	GLOBAL MARKET ENTRY STRATEGIES
FUNCTIONAL COMPETENCE	DESIGNING GLOBAL MARKETING PROGRAMS	
	CH 10	GLOBAL PRODUCT STRATEGIES
	CH 11	GLOBAL STRATEGIES FOR SERVICES, BRANDS, AND SOCIAL MARKETING
	CH 12	PRICING FOR INTERNATIONAL AND GLOBAL MARKETS
	CH 13	MANAGING GLOBAL DISTRIBUTION CHANNELS
	CH 14	GLOBAL PROMOTION STRATEGIES
	CH 15	MANAGING GLOBAL ADVERTISING
MANAGERIAL COMPETENCE	MANAGING THE GLOBAL MARKETING EFFORT	
	CH 16	ORGANIZING FOR GLOBAL MARKETING

FIGURE 1.2
Global Marketing Management

egy. The chapters in this section cover product and service strategies, global branding, social marketing, pricing, channel management, promotion, and advertising.

The text concludes with Part 5, which consists of Chapter 16. Here the emphasis is on building managerial competence in a global environment. Chapter 16 discusses how firms organize for effective global marketing and also explores career issues of concern to the global marketer.

At the end of each of Chapters 2 through 16, two or three short cases are included to help you think concretely about global marketing and apply concepts from the chapter. At the end of the book, we have placed several longer, capstone cases that will give you a chance to synthesize what you have learned across chapters. For those of you wishing to put your knowledge to immediate use, the book website provides you with a guide to developing a Country Market

GLOBAL MARKETING AT FORD

"In order to run a successful global enterprise you must deliver a high quality product in a timely and cost efficient manner. To effectively market products on the global stage your brand strategy must be flexible enough to connect in a real way with customers in all your markets. To reach emerging markets, you can't just serve up warmed over marketing strategies utilized in the more developed countries. That is a recipe for disaster. In my 23 years with Ford Motor Company, I have traveled around the globe, and this I understand: To effectively manage a global enterprise you must spend time in your markets to listen to the unfiltered voice of the customer."

Randy Ortiz
General Sales Manager, Lincoln Mercury

"I began my international assignment with Ford as director of marketing for Ford of Mexico. I was responsible for advertising, communication, brand management, strategy, product planning, and marketing research. That assignment gave me a greater appreciation for international business, because marketing cars in Mexico isn't the same as in the United States. Even with my fluency in Spanish, there were lessons to be learned in the arts of communication and relationship building. I find that each person can contribute a uniquely different perspective which is formed partially from one's cultural background but also from one's personal experiences and skill sets."

Lisa Bacus
Executive Director of Global Consumer Insights

"I began my career with Ford's International Operations as Executive Director of Marketing, Sales and Service for the Asia-Pacific and Africa regions. It was a fantastic assignment that required me to understand market dynamics and customers in twelve unique markets. The assignment has also provided me a greater appreciation of Ford's diversity in people and has heightened my understanding of cultural differences and their impact on business. More recently, I have taken on bigger responsibilities as president of Ford Thailand. I have learned that effective leadership requires an open-mind, respect, two-way communication and the ability to see beyond our differences to discover what works best."

John Felice
President of Ford Thailand

Report (complete with numerous Web links) to help you evaluate a national market for a product or service and determine the best form of market entry. Subsequently, the guide leads you through the steps to determine how your product or service should be adapted for the local market, what location or distribution channel is most appropriate, what price you should charge, and what promotional strategy you should pursue.

CONCLUSION

As a separate activity of business, global marketing is of great importance to nations, to individual companies, and to prospective managers. With markets and industries becoming increasingly globalized, most companies must become active participants in global marketing. The competitive positions of most companies, both abroad and in their domestic markets, rest on their ability to succeed in global markets. At the same time, the economies of entire countries depend on the global marketing skills of managers. The standard of living of many people will be governed by how well local industry performs in the global marketplace. These forces will place a premium on executive talent that is able to direct marketing operations from a global perspective. Clearly, many business professionals will need to understand the global dimension of the marketing function if they are to progress in their careers.

Although the need to develop a global competence may be clear, the circumstances that determine successful marketing practices for foreign markets are far less clear. The foreign marketing environment is characterized by a wide range of variables not typically encountered by domestic firms. This makes the job of global marketing extremely difficult. Despite the complexities involved, there are concepts and analytic tools that can help global marketers. By learning to use these concepts and tools, you can enhance your own global marketing competence. As a result, you will be able to contribute to the marketing operations of a wide range of firms, both domestic and foreign.

QUESTIONS FOR DISCUSSION

1. How is global marketing as a field related to your future career? How would you expect to come into contact with global marketing activities?

2. What do you think are the essential skills of a successful "global marketer"?

3. Which important skills make up an effective "global mindset"?

4. List ten things that are important to you that you hope to be able to understand or accomplish after studying this book.

NOTES

1. Charles Goldsmith, "MTV Seeks Global Appeal," *Wall Street Journal*, July 21, 2003, p. B1.
2. *WTO International Trade Statistics 2004* at www.wto.org.
3. David Gregorcyk, "Internationalization of Conglomerates from Emerging Markets," Teresa Lozano Long Institute of Latin American Studies, The University of Texas at Austin, May 2005.

UNDERSTANDING THE GLOBAL MARKETING ENVIRONMENT

PART 1

2 THE GLOBAL ECONOMY

WHEN EuroDisney Opened outside Paris, French attendance at the theme park was disappointing. Some attributed low ticket sales to a cultural snub of this American icon. Others noted a particularly wet and cold season. Still others blamed the strength of the franc against the U.S. dollar. French consumers could buy—and spend—dollars at bargain prices. If the French wanted Disney, they could catch a plane to Florida's Disney World for not much more than they would pay for a weekend at EuroDisney.

The global economy constantly affects international marketing. Billions of dollars of goods and services are traded among nations each day. Currency exchange rates fluctuate, affecting sales and profits. Businesses establish operations and borrow funds in locations throughout the world. Banks lend and arbitrage currencies worldwide. When these transactions are interrupted or threatened, we can truly appreciate the scope and significance of the international economy.

This chapter introduces the important aspects of world trade and finance. We begin by explaining the concept of comparative advantage, the basis for international trade. Then we explain the international system to

LEARNING OBJECTIVES

After studying this chapter, you should be able to

▶ Distinguish among the basic theories of world trade: absolute advantage, comparative advantage, and competitive advantage.

▶ Discuss the pros and cons of global outsourcing.

▶ List and explain the principal parts of the balance-of-payments statement.

▶ Describe how and why exchange rates fluctuate.

▶ List and describe the major agencies that promote world trade, as well as those that promote economic and monetary stability.

▶ Describe common trade restrictions and explain their impact on international marketers.

▶ Compare the four different forms of economic integration.

monitor world trade, particularly the balance-of-payments measurement system. From this base, we describe the workings of the foreign exchange market and the causes of exchange rate movements. We discuss the international agencies that promote economic and monetary stability, as well as the strategies that countries use to protect their own economies. We conclude with a look at economic integration as a means of promoting trade.

17

International Trade: An Overview

Few individuals in the world are totally self-sufficient. Why should they be? Restricting consumption to self-made goods lowers living standards by narrowing the range and reducing the quality of the goods we consume. For this reason, few nations have economies independent from the rest of the world, and it would be difficult to find a national leader willing or able to impose such an economic hardship on a country.

International Dependence of Nations

Peter Johnson, a student, is awakened in the morning by his Sony clock radio. After showering, he puts on an Italian-made jacket. At breakfast, he has a cup of Brazilian coffee, a bowl of cereal made from U.S.-grown wheat, and a Colombian banana. A quick glance at his Swiss watch shows him that he will have to hurry if he wants to be on time for his first class. He drives to campus in a Toyota, stopping on the way to fill the tank with gas refined from Saudi Arabian oil. Once in class, he rushes to take a seat with the other students, 30 percent of whom hold non-U.S. passports.

Foreign goods are central to the living standards of all nations. But as Table 2.1 shows, countries vary widely in their reliance on foreign trade. Imports are less than 9 percent of the gross domestic product (GDP) of Japan, whereas Switzerland and Mexico have import-to-GDP ratios of 31 and 28 percent, respectively. Even in countries that seemingly do not have a great reliance on imports, such as the United States where imports are 12 percent of the GDP and exports are 7 percent, world trade in goods and services plays an important role.

The figures given in Table 2.1 are useful for identifying the international dependence of nations, but they should be viewed as rough indicators only. In any widespread disruption of international trade, there is little doubt that the United States would be harmed much less than the Netherlands. Yet this is not to say a disruption of trade would not be harmful to countries with large domestic markets such as the United States and Japan, which both depend heavily on world trade for growth. In the United States, $1 billion of exports supports the creation, on average, of about 11,500 jobs.[1]

The Growth in World Trade

After its stock market crash of 1929, the United States turned its back on free trade. Fearing losses of jobs at home, this country tried to assist local industries by sharply increasing taxes on imports from other countries. Unfortunately, other countries retaliated with similar measures. In less than a year, world trade collapsed, sending the world into a global depression. Two hard-hit countries were Germany and Japan. Many believe that this severe economic downturn encouraged the militaristic regimes that precipitated World War II. After the war, the United States and other industrialized nations were eager for world trade to be promoted and to expand.

Their vision has certainly come to pass. World trade has increased over 22-fold since 1950, far outstripping the growth in world GDP. This growth has been fueled by the continued opening of markets around the world. The Bretton

TABLE 2.1 IMPORTS AND EXPORTS AS A PERCENTAGE OF GDP (IN BILLIONS OF DOLLARS)					
	GDP	IMPORTS	IMPORTS/GDP	EXPORTS	EXPORTS/GDP
INDUSTRIAL COUNTRIES					
France	1700.0	388	23%	385	22%
Germany	2400.0	602	25	748	31
Canada	834.4	246	30	272	32
Japan	4300.0	383	9	472	11
Italy	1500.0	289	19	290	19
Switzerland	309.5	96	31	101	33
United Kingdom	1800.0	388	21	304	17
United States	10900.0	1306	12	724	7
DEVELOPING COUNTRIES					
Argentina	129.7	14	11%	29	22%
Brazil	492.3	51	10	73	15
China	1400.0	413	29	438	31
India	599.0	70	12	55	9
Mexico	626.1	179	28	165	26
Russian Federation	433.5	74	17	135	31
South Africa	159.9	38	24	38	23

SOURCES: Adapted from WTO Report 2004, the Economist Unit (www.eiu.com), and World Bank Group, Data Profiles, (www.worldbank.org).

Woods conference of world leaders in 1944 led to the establishment of the General Agreement on Tariffs and Trade (GATT), which we will discuss in detail later. GATT, and subsequently the World Trade Organization (WTO), helped to reduce import tariffs from 40 percent in 1947 to an estimated 4 percent today. The principle of free trade has led to the building of market interdependencies. International trade has grown much more rapidly than world GDP output, demonstrating that national economies are becoming much more closely linked and interdependent via their exports and imports.

Foreign direct investment, another indication of global integration, increased over 100 percent in a single decade, and services are an important and growing part of the world's economy. Industries such as banking, telecommunications, insurance, construction, transportation, tourism, and consulting make up over half the national income of many rich economies. A country's **invisible exports** include services, transfers from workers abroad, and income earned on overseas investments.

Invisible exports a country's earnings abroad from intangibles such as services, remittances, and income earned on overseas investments

THE BASIC THEORIES OF WORLD TRADE: ABSOLUTE, COMPARATIVE, AND COMPETITIVE ADVANTAGE

Internationally traded goods and services are important to most countries, as shown in Table 2.1. Because jobs and standard of living seem to be so closely tied to these inflows and outflows, there is much debate about why a particular country finds its comparative advantages in certain goods and services and not in others.

The past 20 years have witnessed not only a dramatic rise in the volume of trade but also numerous changes in its patterns. Countries that once exported vast amounts of steel, such as the United States, are now net importers of the metal. Other nations, such as Japan, once known for producing inexpensive, handmade trinkets, now compete globally in high-tech products. What caused these changes in trade patterns? Why do countries that are able to produce virtually any product choose to specialize in certain goods? Where do international cost advantages originate? As the twenty-first century continues, will we still think of Indonesia and China as having the greatest advantage in handmade goods, or will they come to be like Japan and Taiwan are today?

The early work of Adam Smith provides the foundation for understanding trade today. Smith saw trade as a way to promote efficiency because it fostered competition, led to specialization, and resulted in economies of scale. Specialization supports the concept of absolute advantage—that is, sell to other countries the goods that utilize your special skills and resources, and buy the rest from those who have some other advantage. This theory of selling what you are best at producing is known as *absolute advantage*. But what if you have no advantages? Will all your manufacturers be driven out of business? David Ricardo, in his 1817 work *Principles of Political Economy*, offered his theory of *comparative advantage*. This theory maintains that it is still possible to produce profitably what one is best at producing, even if someone else is better. The following sections further develop the concepts of absolute and comparative advantage, the economic basis of free trade and hence of all global trade.

Absolute Advantage

Although many variables may be listed as the primary determinants of international trade, productivity differences rank high on the list. Take, for example, two countries—Vietnam and Germany. Suppose the average Vietnamese worker can produce either 400 machines or 1,600 tons of tomatoes in one year. Over the same time period, the average German worker can produce either 500 machines or 500 tons of tomatoes. (See example 1 in Table 2.2.) In this case, German workers can produce more machinery, absolutely, than Vietnamese workers can, whereas Vietnamese workers can produce more tomatoes, absolutely, than can their German counterparts. Given these figures, Vietnam is the obvious low-cost producer of tomatoes and should export them to Germany. Similarly, Germany is the low-cost producer of machines and should export them to Vietnam.

Currently China has an absolute advantage in garlic production. Chinese farm labor receives $1 per day versus $5 in Mexico and $8.50 an hour in California. Garlic has a shelf life of up to nine months and can be easily shipped. Not unexpectedly, the California producers have been devastated.[2]

Comparative Advantage

We should not conclude from the previous examples that absolute differences in production capabilities are necessary for trade to occur. Consider the same two countries in the first example—Vietnam and Germany. Now assume that

TABLE 2.2 ABSOLUTE VERSUS COMPARATIVE ADVANTAGE: WORKER PRODUCTIVITY EXAMPLES		
	VIETNAM	GERMANY
EXAMPLE 1		
Yearly output per worker		
Machinery	400	500
Tomatoes	1,600 tons	500 tons
Absolute advantage	Tomatoes	Machinery
EXAMPLE 2		
Yearly output per worker		
Machinery	200	500
Tomatoes	800 tons	1,000 tons
Opportunity costs of production	1 machine costs 4 tons tomatoes *or* 1 ton tomatoes costs 0.25 machine	1 machine costs 2 tons tomatoes *or* 1 ton tomatoes costs 0.50 machine
Absolute advantage	None	Tomatoes Machinery
Comparative advantage	Tomatoes	Machinery

the average Vietnamese worker can produce either 200 machines or 800 tons of tomatoes each year, whereas the average German worker can produce either 500 machines or 1,000 tons of tomatoes (see example 2 in Table 2.2). Germany has an absolute advantage in both goods, and it appears that Vietnam will benefit from trade because it can buy from Germany cheaper goods than Vietnam can make for itself. Even here, however, the basis for mutually advantageous trade is present. The reason lies in the concept of comparative advantage.

Comparative advantage measures a product's cost of production not in monetary terms but in terms of the forgone opportunity to produce something else. It focuses on tradeoffs. To illustrate, the production of machines means that resources cannot be devoted to the production of tomatoes. In Germany, the worker who produces 500 machines will not be able to grow 1,000 tons of tomatoes. The cost can be stated as follows: Each ton of tomatoes costs 0.5 machine, or 1 machine costs 2 tons of tomatoes. In Vietnam, producing 200 machines forces the sacrifice of 800 tons of tomatoes. Alternatively, this means that 1 ton of tomatoes costs 0.25 machine, or 1 machine costs 4 tons of tomatoes.

From this example, we see that even though Vietnam has an absolute disadvantage in both commodities, it still has a comparative advantage in tomatoes. For Vietnam the cost of producing 1 ton of tomatoes is 0.25 machine, whereas for Germany the cost is 0.5 machine. Similarly, even though Germany has an absolute advantage in both products, it has a comparative cost advantage only in machines. It costs Germany only 2 tons of tomatoes to produce a single machine, whereas in Vietnam the cost is 4 tons of tomatoes.

The last step in examining the concept of comparative advantage is to choose a mutually advantageous trading ratio and show how it can benefit both countries. Any trading ratio between 1 machine = 2 tons of tomatoes

(Germany's domestic trading ratio) and 1 machine = 4 tons of tomatoes (Vietnam's domestic trading ratio) will benefit both nations (see Table 2.3). Suppose we choose 1 machine = 3 tons of tomatoes. Because Germany will be exporting machinery, it gains by getting 3 tons of tomatoes rather than the 2 tons it would have produced domestically. Likewise, because Vietnam will be exporting tomatoes, it gains because one machine can be imported for the sacrifice of only 3 tons of tomatoes, rather than the 4 tons it would have to sacrifice if it made the machine in Vietnam.

Our discussion of comparative advantage illustrates that relative rather than absolute differences in productivity can form a determining basis for international trade. Although the concept of comparative advantage provides a powerful tool for explaining the rationale for mutually advantageous trade, it gives little insight into the source of the differences in relative productivity. Specifically, why does a country find its comparative advantage in one good or service rather than in another? Is it by chance that the United States is a net exporter of aircraft, machinery, and chemicals but a net importer of steel, textiles, and consumer electronic products? Or can we find some systematic explanations for this pattern?

The notion of comparative advantage requires that nations make intensive use of those factors they possess in abundance—in particular, land, labor, natural resources, and capital. Thus Hungary, with its low labor cost of US$1 per hour, will export labor-intensive goods such as unsophisticated chest freezers and table linen, whereas Sweden, with its high-quality iron ore deposits, will export high-grade steel.

Competitive Advantage

Michael Porter argues that even though the theory of comparative advantage has appeal, it is limited by its traditional focus on land, labor, natural resources, and capital. His study of ten trading nations that account for 50 percent of world exports and one hundred industries resulted in a new and expanded theory.[3] This theory postulates that whether a country will have a significant impact on the competitive advantage of an industry depends on the following factors:

▶ The elements of production
▶ The nature of domestic demand
▶ The presence of appropriate suppliers or related industries
▶ The conditions in the country that govern how companies are created, organized, and managed, as well as the nature of domestic rivalry

TABLE 2.3 MUTUALLY ADVANTAGEOUS TRADING RATIOS

TOMATOES	MACHINES
Germany, 1 ton tomatoes = 0.50 machine	Vietnam, 1 machine = 4 tons tomatoes
Germany, 1 machine = 2 tons tomatoes	Vietnam, 1 ton tomatoes = 0.20 machine

Porter argues that strong local competition often benefits a national industry in the global marketplace. Firms in a competitive environment are forced to produce quality products efficiently. Demanding consumers in the home market and pressing local needs can also stimulate firms to solve problems and develop proprietary knowledge before foreign competitors do.

A good example of a country that enjoys a competitive advantage in digital products is South Korea. South Koreans are among the most "wired" people on earth. More than half of Korea's households have broadband service, and more than 60 percent of Koreans own cell phones. Seventy percent of share trades in the Korean securities market are done online. Korean companies can use entire urban populations in their home market as test markets for their latest digital ideas. This in turn gives these Korean companies an advantage when they want to export new products or know-how abroad.[4]

GLOBAL OUTSOURCING

For two hundred years, most economists have agreed with the theory of comparative advantage: Nations gain if they trade with each other and specialize in what they do best. However, advances in telecommunications, such as broadband and the Internet, have created for the first time a global market for skilled workers that threatens traditional ideas of national specialization. According to comparative advantage, India, with its vast numbers of low-paid, low-skilled workers, should specialize in low-wage standardized products. Yet the country competes successfully in a global market for white-collar workers, undercutting the wages of highly skilled Americans and Europeans.[5] Increasingly, information technology (IT) jobs and back-office services (such as credit collection, benefits and pension administration, insurance claims processing, and tax accounting) are outsourced to cheaper labor in developing countries.[6]

A study published by the McKinsey Global Institute on the national impact of outsourcing back-office services and IT jobs to India reveals that outsourcing need not be a zero-sum game. This is not to say there are not national winners and losers.[7] To date, as depicted in Table 2.4, the United States and India would appear to be net winners, while Germany would be a loser.

TABLE 2.4 NATIONAL NET GAINS FOR EACH U.S. DOLLAR SPENT IN INDIA ON OUTSOURCING BACK-OFFICE SERVICES AND IT FUNCTIONS			
	INDIA	USA	GERMANY
Outsourced wages, profits, taxes	$ .33	—	—
Cost savings	—	$ .58	$ .52
New revenues from India	—	.05	.03
Repatriated earnings	—	.04	—
Redeployment of workers	—	.46	.25
Total	$ .33	$1.13	$ .80

Global outsourcing has created a political backlash in the United States.

Direct benefits of outsourcing are captured by India, such as wages, profits to local firms, and taxes collected by the Indian government. Indian workers in the back-office services and IT fields, who are usually college educated and proficient in English, have seen their wages soar in recent years—though not enough to stop the outsourcing to India. However, new revenues and repatriated earnings from multinationals selling to firms in India are captured in Germany and the United States. Because U.S. multinationals have a larger presence in the Indian market than do German multinationals, the United States captures more of these particular benefits than does Germany. Cost savings from outsourcing is an important benefit as well. Again, this benefit is lower for Germany than the United States because Indian businesses in these areas operate in English. This raises the relative coordination costs for German companies working with Indian firms. The biggest advantage in realized benefits for the United States over Germany lies in the redeployment of workers (particularly to higher-value-added jobs). Workers in the United States who are displaced by outsourcing are more likely to find new jobs, and find them more quickly, than are similar workers in Germany.

However, even if the United States currently gains as a whole from global outsourcing, the losses and benefits of outsourcing accrue differently to different groups. For this reason global outsourcing remains very controversial and politically explosive. New revenues from India and repatriated earnings accrue primarily to investors, not workers. How the cost savings from outsourcing are distributed depends on the relative power of the different groups—investors, labor, and buyers. As labor in the United States loses its bargaining power in the new global labor market, most of the savings are likely again to accrue to investors, not labor.

If white-collar job losses rise to 6 percent in the United States, the wages for remaining workers could be depressed by 2 to 3 percent. This is similar to the wage-level losses due to earlier outsourcing in manufacturing. Another concern is whether the United States can continue to realize gains from redeployment of labor as the type of job outsourced becomes increasingly sophisticated. Despite the greater worker mobility in the United States, only about 30 percent of laid-off workers earn the same or more after three years. When only manufacturing jobs moved to developing countries, about 25 percent of the U.S. labor force was affected. With the addition of professional jobs at risk to outsourcing, a majority of American workers could lose more from job losses and the depression of wages than they gain from lower prices of goods.[8]

BALANCE OF PAYMENTS

Newspapers, magazines, and nightly TV news programs are filled with stories related to aspects of international business. Often, media coverage centers on the implications of a nation's trade deficit or surplus or on the economic consequences of an undervalued or overvalued currency. What are trade deficits? What factors will cause a currency's international value to change? The first step in answering these questions is to gain a clear understanding of the contents and meaning of a nation's balance of payments.

The **balance of payments (BOP)** is an accounting record of the transactions between the residents of one country and the residents of the rest of the world over a given period of time. Transactions in which domestic residents either purchase assets (goods and services) from abroad or reduce foreign liabilities are considered *outflows of funds*, because payments abroad must be made. Similarly, transactions in which domestic residents either sell assets to foreign residents or increase their liabilities to foreigners are *inflows of funds*, because payments from abroad are received.

Listed in Table 2.5 are the principal parts of the balance-of-payments statement: the current account, the capital account, and the official transactions account. There are three items under the **current account**. The **goods category** states the monetary values of a nation's international transactions in physical goods. The **services category** shows the values of a wide variety of transactions, such as transportation services, consulting, travel, passenger fares, fees, royalties, rent, and investment income. Finally, **unilateral transfers** include all transactions for which there is no quid pro quo. Private remittances, personal gifts, philanthropic donations, relief, and aid are included within this

Balance of payments (BOP) an accounting record of the transactions between the residents of one country and the residents of the rest of the world over a given period of time

Current account a principal part of the balance of payments statement that includes the key subaccounts of goods, services, and unilateral transfers

Goods or merchandise account BOP account stating the monetary value of a country's international transactions in physical goods

Services account BOP account stating a country's international transactions in intangibles such as transportation services, consulting, royalties on intellectual property, and dividends on foreign investment

Unilateral transfers all the transactions for which there is no quid pro quo, such as private remittances, personal gifts, philanthropic donations, and aid

TABLE 2.5 BALANCE OF PAYMENTS	USES OF FUNDS	SOURCES OF FUNDS
CURRENT ACCOUNT		
1. Goods	Imports	Exports
2. Services	Imports	Exports
3. Unilateral transfers	Paid abroad	From abroad
CAPITAL ACCOUNT		
1. Short-term investment	Made abroad	From abroad
2. Long-term investments	Made abroad	From abroad
a. Portfolio investment		
b. Direct investment		
OFFICIAL TRANSACTIONS ACCOUNT		
Official reserve changes	Gained	Lost

account. Unilateral transfers have less impact on the U.S. market but are important to markets elsewhere. For example, remittances from workers abroad have fueled demand for consumer products in many developing countries such as Egypt, Mexico, and the Philippines.

The **capital account** is divided into two parts on the basis of time. *Short-term transactions* refer to maturities less than or equal to one year, and *long-term transactions* refer to maturities longer than one year. Purchases of Treasury bills, certificates of deposit, foreign exchange, and commercial paper are typical short-term investments. Long-term investments are separated further into portfolio investments and direct investments.

In general, the purchaser of a **portfolio investment** holds no management control over the foreign investment. Debt securities such as notes and bonds are included under this heading. **Foreign direct investments** are long-term ownership interests, such as business capital outlays in foreign subsidiaries and branches. Stock purchases are included as well, but only if such ownership entails substantial control over the foreign company. Countries differ in the percentage of total outstanding stock an individual must hold in order for an investment to be considered a direct investment in the balance-of-payment statements. These values range from 10 percent to 25 percent.

Because it is recorded in double-entry bookkeeping form, the balance of payments as a whole must always have its inflows (sources of funds) equal its outflows (uses of funds). Therefore, the concept of a deficit or surplus refers only to selected parts of the entire statement. A deficit occurs when the particular outflows (uses of funds) exceed the particular inflows (sources of funds). A surplus occurs when the inflows considered exceed the corresponding outflows. In this sense, a nation's surplus or deficit is similar to that of individuals or businesses. If we spend more than we earn, we are in a deficit position. If we earn more than we spend, we are running a surplus.

The most widely used measure of a nation's international payments position is the statement of balance on current account. It shows whether a nation is living

Capital account principal BOP account that records a country's international financial assets and liabilities over the BOP period

Portfolio investments investments, such as the purchase of stocks and bonds, over which investors assume no direct management control

Foreign direct investments foreign investments over which investors assume some if not all direct management control

within or beyond its means. Because this statement includes unilateral transfers, deficits (in the absence of government intervention) must be financed by international borrowing or by selling foreign investments. Therefore, the measure is considered to be a reflection of a nation's financial claims on other countries.

Exchange Rates

The purchase of a foreign good or service can be thought of as involving two sequential transactions: the purchase of the foreign currency, followed by the purchase of the foreign item itself. If the cost of buying either the foreign currency or the foreign item rises, the price to the importer increases. A ratio that measures the value of one currency in terms of another currency is called an **exchange rate**. An exchange rate makes it possible to compare domestic and foreign prices.

When a currency rises in value against another currency, it is said to **appreciate**. When it falls in value, it is said to **depreciate**. Therefore, a change in the value of the U.S. dollar exchange rate from 0.50 British pound to 0.65 British pound is an appreciation of the dollar and a depreciation of the pound. The dollar now buys more pounds, whereas a greater number of pounds must be spent to purchase 1 dollar.

Exchange rate the ratio that measures the value of one currency in terms of another currency

Appreciation an increase in value or price of a currency

Depreciation a decrease in value or price of a currency

The Foreign Exchange Market

Foreign exchange transactions are handled on an over-the-counter market, largely by phone or e-mail. Private and commercial customers as well as banks, brokers, and central banks conduct millions of transactions on this worldwide market daily.

A poster advertises money exchange in Seoul, South Korea. When the Korean won increases in value against the U.S. dollar, American products can become less expensive and more appealing to Korean buyers. But Korean products become more costly in the U.S. marketplace.

As Figure 2.1 shows, the foreign exchange market has a hierarchical structure. Private customers deal mainly with banks in the retail market, and banks stand ready either to buy or to sell foreign exchange as long as a free and active market for the currency exists. Banks that have foreign exchange departments trade with private commercial customers on the retail market, but they also deal with other banks (domestic or foreign) and brokers on the wholesale market. Generally, these wholesale transactions are for amounts of $US1 million dollars or more. Not all banks participate directly in the foreign exchange market. Smaller banks may handle customers' business through correspondent banks.

Central banks play a key role in the foreign exchange markets because they are the ultimate controllers of domestic money supplies. When they enter the market to influence the exchange rate directly, they deal mainly with brokers and large money market banks. Their trading is done not to make a profit but to attain some macroeconomic goal, such as altering the exchange rate value, reducing inflation, or changing domestic interest rates. In general, even if central banks do not intervene in the foreign exchange markets, their actions influence exchange rate values because large increases in a nation's money supply increase its inflation rate and lower the international value of its currency.

Causes of Exchange Rate Movements

Exchange rates are among the most closely watched and politically sensitive economic variables. Regardless of which way the rates move, some groups are hurt and other groups are helped. When a currency's value rises, domestic busi-

FIGURE 2.1
Structure of the Foreign Exchange Market

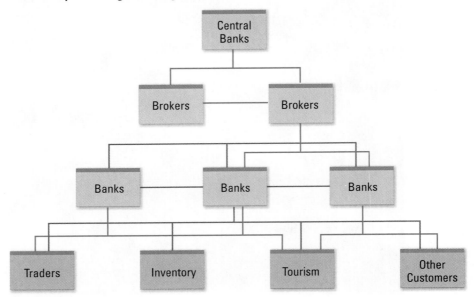

nesses find it more difficult to compete internationally, and the domestic unemployment rate may rise. When the value of a currency falls, foreign goods become more expensive, the cost of living increases, and domestically produced goods become cheaper to foreign buyers. What are the causes of these exchange rate movements, and to what extent can governments influence them?

Most major currencies are **freely floating**. Their exchange rates are determined by the forces of supply and demand. Consumers in different countries can affect the supply and demand for these national currencies. An increase in a nation's GDP gives consumers in that country the wherewithal to purchase more goods and services. Because many of the newly purchased goods are likely to be foreign, increases in GDP will raise the demand for foreign products and therefore raise the demand for foreign currencies.

Similarly, a relatively high inflation rate can shift consumer demand and weaken a currency. If the U.S. inflation rate exceeds that of Japan, then U.S. goods will become progressively more expensive than Japanese goods. Consequently, U.S. consumers will begin to demand more Japanese goods, thereby increasing the supply of dollars to the foreign exchange market while increasing the demand for Japanese yen. For the same reason, Japanese consumers will reduce their demand for dollars (that is, reduce their supply of yen) as they purchase fewer U.S. goods. Therefore, inflation in the United States will cause the international value of the dollar to fall and the value of other currencies to rise.

Supply and demand for currencies are also affected by investors and speculators. If, for example, Japanese interest rates were greater than U.S. interest rates (adjusted for such things as risk, taxes, and maturity), then investors would have an incentive to sell dollars and purchase yen in order to place their funds where they earned the highest return—in Japan. Speculators buy and sell currencies in anticipation of changing future values. If there were a widespread expectation that the Japanese yen would rise in value relative to the dollar, speculators would try to purchase yen now (that is, sell dollars) in anticipation of that change.

Finally, governments affect foreign exchange markets in a variety of ways. Because governments exercise strong and direct controls over domestic money supplies, their activities affect inflation rates and interest rates, which, in turn, affect the exchange rates of their currencies. Perhaps the most pronounced impact governments have is as buyers and sellers in foreign exchange markets. Suppose the United States and Japan agreed to lower the dollar's value relative to the yen. For this to occur, dollars would have to be supplied—and yen demanded—in the foreign exchange markets. For the United States, this would mean putting upward pressure on the domestic money supply as newly created dollars were exchanged for circulating Japanese yen. For Japan, this type of intervention would mean putting downward pressure on its money supply as dollar reserves were used to take yen off the market.

Freely floating currency a currency whose exchange rate is determined by the market forces of supply and demand

Impact on Global Marketers

Intuitively, citizens may be proud of a strong national currency. It can, however, present challenges to international marketers and particularly to firms that export products manufactured in their home country. The strengthening of a domestic currency against the currency of the country's trading partners can have a negative effect on exporters.

When the U.S. dollar reached a 16-year high against most foreign currencies, the cost of American-made products (translated into those foreign currencies) soared. This forced U.S. manufacturers to find creative ways to compete overseas as well as to protect their own home market from foreign competitors that enjoyed a cost advantage. Automatic Feed Company of Ohio embarked on its most extensive product redesign in its 52-year history trying to offset the cost advantage of its foreign competitors. Angell Manufacturing Company established its first manufacturing operation outside the United States in order to supply less expensive car parts to clients in Germany. Other companies discovered that they needed to invest in more salespeople and market research in order to deliver better value to customers.[9]

Not long after the dollar hit its high, it began to collapse against the currencies of its major trading partners in Europe and Canada. Many Canadian exporters were hurt, especially since 85 percent of Canadian merchandise exports go to the United States. However, some Canadian exporters weathered the revaluation of the Canadian currency better because they had U.S. manufacturing operations or they imported large amounts of U.S. products as inputs into their manufactured goods.[10]

As costs of exports rise due to a strengthening currency, a major managerial question is how much of the higher costs of goods or services should be passed on to the buyer versus how much should come out of the exporters' own margins. It is tempting to raise prices, but raising prices can discourage consumption and lose buyers to competitors. In 2004, the U.S. dollar was tumbling against the euro just as Americans were planning their spring and summer trips to Europe. Hermes, a European firm that sells expensive scarves and ties, marked up its entire U.S. line by 5 percent.[11] However, a number of European hotels offered to let tourists lock in at current exchange rates. Hotel Gratti Palace in Venice agreed to keep a deluxe room price at US$465 throughout the season if booked by July 1.[12]

Managed Currencies

Soft currency a currency that attracts little global demand

Pegged currency a currency whose price is fixed by its government to another currency or basket of currencies

The foreign exchange market just described is not applicable to all currencies. Small, less developed countries often have currencies that attract little global demand. No effective international markets develop for these **soft currencies**. Also, until recently, most foreign exchange rates in developing countries were set by the government. This is still true in many countries today. Managed currencies are usually **pegged** to the currency of a developed country that is a major trading partner. Many are pegged to the U.S. dollar. The value of the local currency is sometimes kept stable and other times allowed to fluctuate a few percentage points based on market demand.

Pegged currencies are not immune to the forces of supply and demand. Defending a peg from devaluation requires keeping a relatively strong demand for the local currency in line with the price set by the government. If domestic inflation is higher than that of trading partners, local goods can quickly become too overpriced to sell on export markets. Governments cannot indefinitely prop up currencies if there is little demand for them because of such factors as low levels of export earnings or low levels of inward bound foreign investment.

WORLD BEAT 2.1

Ecuador Dollarizes

THE ANDEAN NATION OF ECUADOR was a mess. It had defaulted on its public debt, banks had collapsed, and a president had been overthrown. Real wages were declining and 56 percent of Ecuadorians earned less than $42 a month. Two years later, however, Ecuador's economy was on a rebound with a growth rate of 5.4 percent—the highest in Latin America.

Joyce de Ginatta, a grandmother of twelve, had pushed to have the local currency, the sucre, replaced by the U.S. dollar. Ms. de Ginatta had been an importer of toilets and sinks from American Standard but saw her products become too expensive as the dollar gained 300 percent against the sucre from 1991 to 1997. Tired of dealing with a national currency that was always losing value against the dollar, she sold her business and began her relentless media campaign to be done with the sucre once and for all. She arranged news conferences and held public forums.

But things kept getting worse for the sucre. It was battered by low prices for oil, a major export for Ecuador, as well as by shrimp disease that hit another key export. A financial crisis in Asia discouraged foreign investors from putting money in any developing country. By June 1999, the sucre was selling for 12,000 to the dollar. On January 9, 2000, newly elected President Mahuad shocked both Ecuadorians and the United States by announcing that the dollar would replace the sucre.

President Mahuad was ousted 2 weeks after taking office by a military-backed coup, but his successor continued with dollarization. On March 13, 2000, a fixed exchange rate was set (25,000 sucres to the dollar), and the government proceeded to remove 98 percent of the old national currency from circulation.

But was dollarization the cause of Ecuador's economic improvement? Part of the improvement could be attributed to a rise in oil prices. Oil export earnings jumped 63 percent in 2000. Also, 400,000 Ecuadorians working abroad helped the economy by sending home remittances. These remittances had become the country's second-largest source of foreign exchange earnings. Analysts also warned that dollarization robbed Ecuador of any flexibility in monetary or foreign exchange policy that could help buffer the country from external shocks such as a decline in oil prices. Most important, a dollarized economy requires a constant source of dollars, and this means exports and fiscal responsibility.

Sources: Stephen Wisnefski, "One Year After, Jury Still Out on Ecuador Dollarization," *Dow Jones International News*, March 14, 2001; Marc Lifsher, "As Argentina Teeters, the Ecuadorean Success Story Looms," *Wall Street Journal*, November 29, 2001, p. A14; and "Mixed Blessings," *Economist.com* (posted January 24, 2002).

Trying to defend a peg too long can result in sudden large devaluations in developing countries instead of more gradual ones.

For example, Venezuela experienced depressed export earnings because of continued low prices on oil, its major export. The Venezuelan bolivar plunged against the U.S. dollar in 2002 after the Venezuelan government relinquished its 6-year-old system to keep the bolivar steady with the dollar. Even with the collapse of the bolivar, Venezuela experienced capital flight as people hurried to exchange bolivars for dollars. Although few currencies today are nonconvertible, Venezuela was forced to establish currency controls to restrict access to foreign exchange. This caused problems for foreign firms in the country such as General Motors, Ford, and Procter & Gamble. These firms waited months for the government to approve requests to change local currency into U.S. dollars for purposes of paying foreign suppliers.[13]

Although it has evolved into a major currency in world trade, the Chinese yuan doesn't trade freely but has been kept pegged primarily to the U.S. dollar by the Chinese government. Between 2003 and 2005, neighboring Asian countries saw their currencies appreciate against a weakening U.S. dollar. Manufacturers in Korea, Thailand, and Taiwan had to decide whether to raise prices in the United States or cut into their already thin margins at home. This put manufacturers in these countries at a disadvantage compared with manufacturers in China. For example, 30 to 40 percent of Korean exports compete directly with Chinese exports. A yuan that remained constant against the dollar didn't help U.S. exports, either, since the declining dollar didn't decrease the cost position in yuan of U.S. manufacturers trying to export to China.[14] Consequently, a major debate has emerged regarding managed and floating currencies. Is an exchange rate system in which currencies like the Chinese yuan are pegged but the euro and the yen float freely the best way to balance the world's trade and capital flows?[15]

INTERNATIONAL AGENCIES FOR PROMOTING ECONOMIC AND MONETARY STABILITY

Stability in the international economy is a prerequisite for worldwide peace and prosperity. It was for this reason that at the end of World War II, representatives from several countries met at Bretton Woods, New Hampshire, and formed both the International Monetary Fund and the World Bank (the International Bank for Reconstruction and Development). With headquarters in Washington, DC, these two agencies continue to play major roles on the international scene.

International Monetary Fund (IMF)

The core mission of the International Monetary Fund (IMF) is to help stabilize an increasingly global economy. The IMF's original goals were to promote orderly and stable foreign exchange markets, restore free convertibility among the currencies of member nations, reduce international impediments to trade, and provide assistance to countries that experienced temporary balance-of-payments deficits.

Over the years, the IMF has shifted its focus from exchange rate relations among industrialized countries to the prevention of economic instability in developing countries and countries from the former Eastern European bloc. The Mexican economic crisis in 1994 prompted an unprecedented bailout of $47 billion and launched the recent trend of providing rescue packages to major economies in the developing world. In the past several years, the IMF approved a $19 billion rescue package for Turkey and led a $17.2 billion rescue for Thailand, a $42 billion package for Indonesia, and a $41.5 billion deal for Brazil. South Korea got a whopping $58.4 billion when it was on the verge of bankruptcy. These rescue packages helped stabilize the respective economies and avoid total economic collapse of the countries involved.

To qualify for assistance, the Fund may require that countries take drastic economic steps, such as reducing tariff barriers, privatizing state-owned enterprises, curbing domestic inflation, and cutting government expenditures. Although many nations have resented such intervention, banks worldwide have used the IMF as a screening device for their private loans to many developing countries. If countries qualify for IMF loans, they are considered for private credit.

Want to know more about the IMF? Check out the link on our website (college.hmco.com/ business/).

World Bank

The World Bank (International Bank for Reconstruction and Development) acts as an intermediary between the private capital markets and the developing nations. It makes long-term loans (usually 15 or 25 years) carrying rates that reflect prevailing market conditions. By virtue of its AAA credit rating, the bank is able to borrow private funds at relatively low market rates and pass the savings along to the developing nations. However, because it must borrow to obtain capital and is not funded by members' contributions, the World Bank must raise lending rates when its costs (that is, market interest rates) rise. Table 2.6 lists typical projects that the World Bank finances.

When private funds were pouring into developing economies, some critics questioned the future role of the World Bank. However, a pan-Asian economic crisis caused the flow of private funds to developing countries to drop by more than $100 billion in 1998. The World Bank has expanded its role from mostly loans to partial guarantees of government bonds for investment projects. In Thailand, the World Bank partially guaranteed the Electricity Generating Authority of Thailand. The guarantee attracted investors and spawned interest in similar programs in South Korea and the Philippines. In addition, the bank is encouraging governments to improve financial supervision and reduce red tape.

Group of Seven

The world's leading industrial nations have established a Group of Seven, which meets regularly to discuss the world economy. Finance ministers and central bank governors from the United States, Japan, Germany, France, Britain, Italy, and Canada make up this group, which is often referred to as the G7. (When Russia joins the talks, the group calls itself the G8.) The members work together informally to help stabilize the world economy and reduce extreme disruptions. For example, the G7 developed proposals to reduce the debt of thirty-three impoverished nations, mostly in Africa, by 70 percent. The G8 agreed to help rebuild the Balkans, including Serbia if it continued to demonstrate a full commitment to economic and democratic reforms.

European Monetary System

In the early 1970s, a group of European countries established the European Joint Float agreement. The values of the currencies were fixed against one another in a narrow range of plus or minus 2.25 percent. This early system was

TABLE 2.6 SELECTED WORLD BANK PROJECTS

COUNTRY	PROJECT
Albania	Water Resources Management
Azerbaijan	Economic Development Support
Bangladesh	Economic Management Technical Assistance Program
Bulgaria	Wood Residue to Energy
Cambodia	Rural Electrification and Transmission
China	Inner Mongolia Highway and Trade Corridor
Colombia	Integrated Mass Transit Systems
Croatia	Coastal Citites Pollution Control
Ethiopia	Private Sector Development Capacity Building
India	Lucknow Muzaffarpur National Highway
Indonesia	Government Financial Management and Revenue Administration Program
Kenya	Energy Sector Recovery
Mexico	Housing and Urban Technical Cooperation
Morocco	Basic Education Reform Support Program
Nigeria	Sustainable Management of Mineral Resources
Pakistan	Tax Administration Reform
Peru	Poechos Hydropower
Poland	Energy Efficiency
Senegal	Casamance Emergency Reconstruction Support
Russia	E-learning Support
Ukraine	Development of the State Statistics System for Monitoring the Social and Economic Transformation
West Bank/Gaza	Northern Gaza Emergency Sewage Treatment
Yemen, Republic of	Basic Education Development

later replaced by the European Monetary System (EMS), which included the fifteen members of the European Union (EU). The EMS included measures to force member countries to regulate their economies so that their currencies stayed within 2.25 percent of the central rates. For example, a country could be required to increase or lower interest rates to stay in line with the other currencies.

Beginning in January 1999, the new EU single currency, the euro, replaced eleven national currencies in Europe. These countries used national currencies for notes and coins until 2002, when the euro replaced the national currencies for these applications as well. The European Central Bank (ECB) has complete control over the euro and is obliged to maintain price stability and avoid inflation or deflation.

The changeover to the euro was not easy, however. One study showed that a vending machine in France that dispensed coffee for two French francs could not charge the equivalent in euros. The conversion rate turned out to be .3049. The coffee could be repriced at .30 euro, causing the vendor to lose 1.5 percent of gross revenue. Alternatively, the vending machine could be expensively reconfigured to dribble out slightly less coffee.[16]

Nonetheless, supporters of the euro believed it would reduce transaction costs and foreign exchange risk within Europe and provide a strong viable currency alternative to the dollar. To date, their faith appears to be justified. A report by eleven economists estimates that trade among the euro-zone members increased by 30 percent in the first 4 years alone. Britain didn't adopt the euro, and UK trade with the euro zone rose by only 13 percent.[17]

PROTECTIONISM AND TRADE RESTRICTIONS

It is a fact of life that like virtually all changes, free trade creates both beneficiaries and victims. By increasing competition, free trade lowers the price of imported goods and raises the overseas demand for efficiently produced domestic goods. In these newly stimulated export industries, sales will increase, profits will rise, and stock prices will climb. Clearly, consumers of the imported good and producers of the exported good benefit from these new conditions. However, it is equally clear that other groups are harmed. Domestic producers of the import-competing goods are one of the most visible of such groups. They experience noticeable declines in market share, falling profits, and deteriorating stock prices.

Herein lies the major reason for protectionist legislation. The victims of free trade are highly visible and their losses quantifiable. Governments use

Although trade restrictions have decreased worldwide, there remains a market for home-grown products such as those promoted on this Made in the USA search engine.

protectionism as a means of lessening the harm done to these easily identified groups. Conversely, the individuals who are helped by free trade tend to be dispersed throughout the nation rather than concentrated in a specific region.

Protectionist legislation tends to take the form of tariffs, quotas, or qualitative trade restrictions. This section describes these barriers and their economic effects.

Tariffs

Tariff a tax on goods or services moving across an economic or political boundary

Tariffs are taxes on goods moving across an economic or political boundary. They can be imposed on imports, exports, or goods in transit through a country on their way to some other destination. In the United States, *export tariffs* are constitutionally prohibited, but in other parts of the world they are quite common. Of course, the most common type of tariff is the *import tariff*, and it is on this tariff that we focus our attention.

Import tariffs have a dual economic effect. First, they tend to raise the price of imported goods and thereby protect domestic industries from foreign competition. Second, they generate tax revenues for the governments imposing them. Regardless of what the goals are, tariffs may not be the most direct or effective means of attaining them. For example, foreign sellers may lower their prices to offset any tariff increase. The net effect is for the consumer-paid price to differ only slightly, if at all, from the price before the tariff was imposed. Consequently, the nation has greater tariff revenues but little additional protection for the domestic producers.

When tariffs do raise the price of an imported good, consumers are put at a disadvantage, whereas the import-competing industries are helped. However, tariffs can have wider implications. For example, when the U.S. Department of Commerce imposed a high duty on advanced flat screens used on laptop computers, the duty helped some small U.S. screen manufacturers. But it hurt computer companies such as Apple, Compaq, and IBM, who argued that the high duty inflated the cost of their products, undermined their ability to compete abroad, and would force them to shift production to other countries.

Quotas

Quota a physical limit on the amount of goods that can be imported into or, less commonly, exported from a country

Quotas are physical limits on the amount of goods that can be imported into a country. Unlike tariffs, which restrict trade by directly increasing prices, quotas increase prices by directly restricting trade. Naturally, to have such an effect, imports must be restricted to levels below the free-trade level.

For domestic producers, quotas are a much surer means of protection. Once the limit has been reached, imports cease to enter the domestic market, regardless of whether foreign exporters lower their prices. Consumers have the most to lose with the imposition of quotas. Not only are their product choices limited and the prices increased, but the goods that foreign exporters choose to ship often carry the highest profit margins. Restrictions on imported automobiles, for instance, result in the import of more luxury models with high-cost accessories. Because foreign producers are restricted in the number of cars they can sell, they seek the highest margin per car.

Orderly Marketing Arrangements and Voluntary Export Restrictions

An **orderly marketing arrangement** or **voluntary export restriction** is an agreement between countries to share markets by limiting foreign export sales. Usually, these arrangements have a set duration and provide for some annual increase in foreign sales to the domestic market. The euphemistic terms are intended to give the impression of fairness. After all, who can be against anything that is orderly or voluntary?

Scratch the surface of these so-called negotiated settlements, however, and a different image appears. First, the negotiations are initiated by the importing country with the implicit threat that unless concessions are made, stronger unilateral sanctions will be imposed. They are really neither orderly nor voluntary. They are quotas in the guise of negotiated agreements. For example, the U.S. Commerce Department reached an agreement whereby Russia would voluntarily limit its steel imports into the United States to 750,000 tons per year, compared with 3,500,000 tons in the prior year. If Russia had not agreed to the limits, the Commerce Department was prepared to announce duties of 71 to 218 percent on Russian steel.[18]

The Omnibus Trade and Competitiveness Act of 1988 gave presidents of the United States the right to negotiate orderly marketing arrangements and set countervailing duties to deal with the problems of trade deficits, protected markets, and dumping. The use of these voluntary export restraints (VERs) has spread to textiles, clothing, steel, cars, shoes, machinery, and consumer electronics. There are approximately three hundred VERs worldwide, most protecting the United States and Europe. More than fifty agreements affect exports from Japan, and another thirty-five affect South Korea.

A study conducted by the Institute for International Economics in Washington revealed that import restrictions, tariffs, and voluntary restraints in Europe cost the European consumer dearly. For example, banana import restrictions cost European consumers $2.0 billion, or 55 cents per kilo; beef tariffs, local subsidies, and bans on hormone-treated beef cost consumers $14.6 billion, or $1.60 per kilo. The total costs of protection in Europe on fruits, cars, steel, textiles, video recorders, beef, milk, cheese, telecoms, airlines, and more is estimated to be $43 billion. Research by the Institute for International Economics suggests that these restrictions save approximately 200,000 jobs in Europe at a cost of $215,000 per job saved, or enough to buy each lucky worker a new Rolls-Royce each year![19]

> **Orderly marketing arrangement** (or **voluntary export restriction**) an agreement between countries in which one country agrees to limit its exports to the other

Nontariff Trade Barriers

The final category of trade restrictions is perhaps the most problematic and certainly the least quantifiable. **Nontariff barriers** include a wide range of charges, requirements, and restrictions, such as surcharges at border crossings, licensing regulations, performance requirements, government subsidies, health and safety regulations, packaging and labeling regulations, and size and weight requirements. Not all of these barriers are discriminatory and protectionist. Restrictions dealing with public health and safety are certainly legitimate, but the line between social well-being and protection is a fine one.

> **Nontariff barriers** nonmonetary restrictions on trade

At what point do consular fees, import restrictions, packaging regulations, performance requirements, licensing rules, and government procurement procedures discriminate against foreign producers? Is a French tax on automobile horsepower targeted against powerful U.S. cars, or is it simply a tax on inefficiency and pollution? Are U.S. automobile safety standards unfair to German, Japanese, and other foreign car manufacturers? Does a French ban on advertising bourbon and Scotch (but not cognac) serve the public's best interest?

Sometimes, nontariff barriers can have considerable impact on foreign competition. For decades, West German authorities forbade the sale of beer in Germany unless it was brewed from barley malt, hops, yeast, and water. If any other additives were used—a common practice elsewhere—German authorities denied foreign brewers the right to label their products as beer. The law was eventually struck down by the European Court of Justice.

Nevertheless, many nontariff barriers continue in many creative ways. For example, under China's WTO commitments, quotas for imported cars were to be abolished by 2006. However, a Chinese policy paper that outlines China's plan to become a major car manufacturer suggests a number of nontariff ideas to support the local automobile industry, such as restricting the number of ports where foreign imports can be offloaded and requiring Chinese-made and foreign-made automobiles to use different sales outlets. The latter would increase the cost of introducing new brands and effectively slow imports.[20]

General Agreement on Tariffs and Trade (GATT)

Because of the harmful effects of protectionism, which were most painfully felt during the Great Depression of the 1930s, twenty-three nations banded together in 1947 to form the General Agreement on Tariffs and Trade (GATT). Over its life, GATT has been a major forum for the liberalization and promotion of nondiscriminatory international trade between participating nations.

The principles of a world economy embodied in the articles of GATT are reciprocity, nondiscrimination, and transparency. The idea of *reciprocity* is simple. If one country lowers its tariffs against another's exports, then it should expect the other country to do the same. *Nondiscrimination* means that one country should not give one member or group of members preferential treatment over other members of the group. This principle is embodied in the **most favored nation (MFN) status**. MFN does not mean that one country is most favored, but rather that it receives no less favorable treatment than any other. *Transparency* refers to the GATT policy that nations make any trade restrictions overt, such as replacing nontariff barriers with tariffs. Through these principles, trade restrictions have been effectively reduced.

Although its most notable gains have been in considerably reducing tariff and quota barriers on many goods, GATT has also helped to simplify and homogenize trade documentation procedures, discourage government subsidies, and curtail dumping (that is, selling abroad at a cost lower than the cost of production).

The Uruguay Round of GATT talks, which lasted 7 years, was finally completed in late 1993. This agreement covered several controversial areas, such as patents and national protection of agriculture and the textile and clothing industry.

Most favored nation (MFN) status a guarantee in a trade agreement between countries binding signatories to extend trade benefits to each other equal to those accorded any third state

World Trade Organization (WTO)

The final act of GATT was to replace itself with the World Trade Organization in 1996. The WTO continues to pursue reductions in tariffs on manufactured goods as well as liberalization of trade in agriculture and services. With 148 member countries in 2005, the WTO is the global watchdog for free trade. Even China became part of the WTO in 2001 after 14 years of negotiations concerning its vast semiplanned economy, with its formidable array of import quotas, trade licenses, and import inspections. Since its inception the WTO has established an agreement on tariff-free trade in information technology among forty countries, as well as a financial services agreement that covers 95 percent of trade in banking and insurance. An agreement on intellectual property covering patents, trademarks, and copyrights has also been negotiated.

A major advantage that the WTO offers over GATT involves the resolution of disputes. Under GATT, any member could veto the outcome of a panel ruling on a dispute. WTO panels are stricter. They must report their decisions in 9 months and can be overturned only by consensus. Countries that break the rules must pay compensation, mend their ways, or face trade sanctions.

The use of quotas and voluntary export restrictions is declining with the strengthening of the WTO and with increased compliance by its member countries. Whereas GATT presided over three hundred disputes over its lifetime (1947–1994), the WTO dealt with over three hundred complaints in its first 8 years. The WTO has not been used by the big countries solely to control the smaller ones, as some feared. Costa Rica, for example, asked the WTO to rule against American barriers to its export of men's underwear. It won the case, and the United States was forced to change its import rules.

The WTO's current concerns focus on several challenges. First, the WTO continues to push for liberalization of foreign investment. Other challenges comprise the "new issues" of trade policy such as competition policy, labor standards, and even censorship. Taiwan, for example, has a strong modern dance culture that is accepting of nudity onstage. Mainland Chinese authorities consider this pornographic. Did joining the WTO mean that China could no longer ban performing arts from Taiwan that it considered offensive?[21]

Want to know more about the WTO? Check out the WTO link on our website (college.hmco.com/business/).

ECONOMIC INTEGRATION AS A MEANS OF PROMOTING TRADE

Another important issue facing the WTO is the spread of regional trading agreements. The WTO exempts members of regional trade agreements from the MFN principle. In other words, the United States could extend Israel a lower tariff rate under a free-trade agreement that it would not have to extend to other countries under the MFN principle expected by WTO membership. Recently there has been a significant increase in the number of such agreements. There are nearly 250 regional agreements between countries granting preferential access to each other's markets. Nearly all members of the WTO belong to at least one regional pact. Table 2.7 lists examples of such agreements.

Some believe that the increase in these bilateral agreements (very much in favor with the United States) will undermine the multilateral vision of the WTO.

TABLE 2.7 SELECTED INTEGRATION AGREEMENTS

AGREEMENT	COUNTRIES	FOUNDING DATE	AGREEMENT TYPE
NAFTA (NORTH AMERICAN FREE TRADE AGREEMENT)	Canada, Mexico, United States	1994	Free-trade area
EU (EUROPEAN UNION)	Austria, Belgium, Cyprus, Czech Republic, Denmark, Estonia, Finland, France, Germany, Greece, Hungary, Ireland, Italy, Latvia, Lithuania, Luxembourg, Malta, Netherlands, Poland, Portugal, Slovak Republic, Slovenia, Spain, Sweden, United Kingdom	1951	Common market
AFTA (ASEAN FREE TRADE AREA)	Brunei Darussalam, Cambodia, Indonesia, Laos, Malaysia, Myanmar, Philippines, Singapore, Thailand, Vietnam	1992	Free-trade area
MERCOSUR (SOUTHERN COMMON MARKET)	Argentina, Brazil, Paraguay, Uruguay	1991	Customs union
CAN (ANDEAN COMMUNITY)	Bolivia, Colombia, Ecuador, Peru, Venezuela	1969	Customs union
CIS (COMMONWEALTH OF INDEPENDENT STATES)	Azerbaijan, Armenia, Belarus, Georgia, Moldova, Kazakhstan, Russian, Federation, Ukraine, Uzbekistan, Tajikistan, Kyrgyz Republic	1999	Free-trade area
GCC (GULF COOPERATION COUNCIL)	Bahrain, Kuwait, Oman, Qatar, Saudi Arabia, United Arab Emirates	1981	Customs union (as of 2003)
EFTA (EUROPEAN FREE TRADE ASSOCIATION)	Iceland, Liechtenstein, Norway, Switzerland	1960	Free-trade area
CACM (CENTRAL AMERICAN COMMON MARKET)	Costa Rica, El Salvador, Guatemala, Honduras, Nicaragua	1960	Customs union

By dangling access to its large market, the United States has special negotiating power over smaller, developing countries. Furthermore, bilateral deals fragment negotiating power of coalitions of smaller markets.[22]

Although the degree of economic integration can vary considerably from one organization to another, four major types of integration can be identified: free-trade areas, customs unions, common markets, and monetary unions.

Free-Trade Areas

Free-trade area two or more countries that formally sign an agreement to drop trade barriers among themselves but to allow each member country to maintain independent trade relations with nonmember countries

The simplest form of integration is a free-trade area. The most famous is the North American Free Trade Association (NAFTA), which includes the United States, Canada, and Mexico. Within a **free-trade area**, nations agree to drop trade barriers among themselves, but each nation is permitted to maintain independent trade relations with countries outside the group. There is little attempt at this level to coordinate such things as domestic tax rates, environmental regulations, and commercial codes. Generally such areas do not permit resources (that is, labor and capital) to flow freely across national borders. Moreover, because each country has autonomy over its money supply, exchange rates can fluctuate relative to both member and nonmember countries.

Despite the apparent simplicity of this form of economic integration, unexpected complications can arise. When NAFTA was being negotiated, U.S. business groups demanded that foreign investors be protected, noting that the Mexican government had a history of nationalizing U.S. assets. Consequently, arbitration procedures established by the World Bank ensure that governments in the United States, Mexico, and Canada will pay compensation to any foreign investor whose property is seized. Arbitration panels cannot make new law. However, they can interpret law, and their rulings cannot be appealed. One NAFTA panel issued its own interpretation of the Mexican constitution and awarded $16.7 million to a California waste disposal company after the governor of the state of San Luis Potosi and a town council refused to honor the company's permit to open a toxic-waste site. The idea that NAFTA law may give foreign investors privileges over those enjoyed by local companies has many concerned in all NAFTA countries.[23]

Free-trade areas have been less successful among many developing countries. A case in point is the Asian Free Trade Area (AFTA). AFTA was envisaged to create a regional free-trade zone by slashing tariffs. However, the actual free trade that ensued has fallen far short of the rhetoric. For example, Malaysia refused to remove protective tariffs for its auto industry. Furthermore, the association's member countries represent widely disparate development levels, political institutions, and economic philosophies. Some countries are democracies, others military dictatorships.[24] While trade within NAFTA grew by 17 percent in its first 7 years, interregional trade in AFTA dropped 19 percent in the same amount of time. Some of the key problems that persist are different product standards across countries and unpredictable policy implementation.[25]

Want to know more about NAFTA? Check out the NAFTA links on our website (college.hmco.com/business/).

Customs Unions

Customs unions, a more advanced form of economic integration, possess the characteristics of a free-trade area but with the added feature of a common external tariff/trade barrier for the member nations. Individual countries relinquish the right to set trade agreements outside the group independently. Instead, a supranational policymaking committee makes these decisions.

Customs union two or more countries that formally sign an agreement to drop trade barriers among themselves and to establish common external barriers between member and nonmember countries

Common Markets

The third level of economic integration is a **common market**. This arrangement has all the characteristics of a customs union, but the organization also encourages the free flow of resources (labor and capital) among the member nations. For example, if jobs are plentiful in Germany but scarce in Italy, workers can move from Italy to Germany without having to worry about severe immigration restrictions. In a common market, there is usually an attempt to coordinate tax codes, social welfare systems, and other legislation that

Common market a form of economic integration with all the characteristics of a customs union and in which the free flow of resources, such as labor and capital, is encouraged among member nations influences resource allocation. Finally, although each nation still has the right to print and coin its own money, exchange rates among nations often are fixed or are permitted to fluctuate only within a narrow range. The most notable example of a common market is the European Union. The EU has been an active organization for trade liberalization and continues to increase its membership size.

When Vicente Fox was elected president of Mexico, he called for expanding NAFTA into a common market. He admitted, however, that this would be a long-term project that would gradually evolve over 20 to 40 years. As an initial step, however, he wanted the United States to accept more Mexican labor, expanding its temporary-worker program so that 300,000 or more Mexicans a year could be legally employed in the United States.[26]

Want to know more about the EU? Check out the link on our website (college.hmco.com/business/).

Monetary Unions

The highest form of economic integration is a monetary union. A monetary union is a common market in which member countries no longer regulate their own currencies. Rather, member-country currencies are replaced by a common currency regulated by a supranational central bank. With the passage of the Maastricht Treaty by EU members, the European Monetary System became the first monetary union in January 1999.

THE GLOBALIZATION CONTROVERSY

In December 1999, groups representing organized labor, human rights, and environmental interests confronted the WTO in what has come to be known as the Battle of Seattle. The WTO had convened in the American city for a new round of negotiations to reduce trade barriers. Thirty thousand protesters from around the world, angered by what they believed was a failure of the WTO to properly address their concerns relating to poverty, labor conditions, and the environment, blocked traffic and in a few cases engaged in vandalism and violence. The police responded with tear gas and rubber bullets. The next meeting of the WTO was subsequently scheduled in the Arab Gulf state of Qatar, described by a U.S. State Department report as a country that "severely limits freedom of assembly and prohibits workers from organizing unions."[27]

Clearly a final challenge facing the WTO is how to handle an increasingly global and organized opposition to its agenda. Some parties believe that the globalization fostered by the WTO favors developed countries seeking to sell to developing countries and not vice versa. For example, the United States, Japan, and Europe maintain some of their highest tariffs on agricultural products, which account for a large portion of exports from the developing world. Agricultural subsidies in the developed world further undermine the ability of developing countries to compete in the global marketplace. Developing countries also claim that food safety standards imposed by developed countries are often discriminatory. Thailand sued Australia for requiring chicken parts to be precooked at such a high temperature that it renders the product inedible.[28]

Other opposition to globalization comes from traditional labor unions in industrialized countries as well as new groups opposed to the outsourcing of

WORLD BEAT 2.2

The Furniture Advantage

LACQUER CRAFT MANUFACTURING COMPANY is one of China's largest furniture exporters. Established in 1992, the company exports hundreds of millions of dollars of furniture a year primarily to the United States. U.S. furniture companies have found it hard to compete against such efficient firms and their lower labor costs. Workers in China get paid about US$100 a month. In just over 2 years, 34,000 jobs were lost in the U.S. furniture industry. The Chinese don't plan to stay in the low-end market, either. Investing in better design and higher quality, Chinese furniture manufacturers are moving into high-end furniture as well.

Is there any way U.S. rivals can compete? Customization and speed could be the answer. Furniture from Asia shipped by boat takes 5 to 6 weeks to arrive. A number of major U.S. producers are decreasing their product lines but increasing their inventory to be able to respond to orders more quickly. Others are offering custom orders filled in only a few weeks. One key to a quick turnaround: Replace assembly-line manufacturing with a flexible team that works on the piece of furniture from beginning to end. Surprisingly, many companies report that this is not only turning out to be faster but more efficient as well, since workers feel more invested in their work when they are involved in the whole process.

Sources: Cheryl Lu-Lien Tan, "U.S. Response: Speedier Delivery," *Wall Street Journal*, November 18, 2004, p. D1; Jon E. Hilsenrath and Peter Wonacott, "Imports Hammer Furniture Makers," *Wall Street Journal*, September 20, 2002, p. A2; "U.S. Furniture Makers Seek Protection from China Imports," *Dow Jones Business News*, July 14, 2003; and Dan Morse, "Chinese Furniture Goes Upscale," *Wall Street Journal*, November 18, 2004, p. D1.

professional jobs. Both conservatives and liberals in developed and developing countries are concerned that the WTO usurps sovereignty from governments. For example, the state of Utah outlawed gambling for 110 years, and this prohibition was later extended to Internet gambling. The government of the tiny Caribbean country of Antigua and Baruda brought a complaint to the WTO charging that Utah shut out Internet gambling operations based in its country. The WTO ruled that Utah did indeed discriminate against foreign providers of "recreational services." Such rulings fuel the fears of those who believe that the WTO is an attempt to impose a one-world government.[29]

Is globalization bad or good? As we saw with the case of global outsourcing, this depends on who you are. The distribution of income in the United States reflects increased inequality over the past 25 years. Geoffrey Garret argues that this pattern can also be observed at a national level. Twenty years of increased globalization appears to have been more advantageous to industrialized countries and the world's poorest countries. However, countries that comprise the economic middle—many of which are located in Asia and South America—have not fared as well. Real per-capita income grew by less than 20 percent in these countries in the last two decades of the twentieth century. This was less than half the growth rate in upper-income countries and less than one-eighth the growth in the low-income countries. Middle-income countries appear to face the possibility of being squeezed out of the world economy. They do not have the political institutions or as educated a workforce to compete with the upper-income countries, so they are forced to compete with countries such as China and India in the production of more standardized products. However, this may be a losing battle as well, because these low-income countries have considerably lower wage rates.[30]

CONCLUSION

The global economy is in a state of transition from a set of strong national economies to a set of interlinked trading groups. This transition has accelerated over the past few years with the collapse of communism, the coalescing of the European trading nations into a single market, and the expansion of membership in the WTO. The investment by Europeans, Japanese, and Americans in one another's economies is unprecedented. In much of the developing world, trade and investment liberalization has accelerated as well.

There is no doubt that the world has been moving toward a single global economy. Information technology, telecommunications, and the Internet have made worldwide information on prices, products, and profits available globally and instantaneously. With markets more transparent, buyers, sellers, and investors can access better opportunities, lowering costs and ensuring that resources are allocated to their most efficient use. Past changes have helped some groups and hurt others, and it remains unclear what the future of globalization will be. Successful companies will be able to anticipate trends and respond to them quickly. Less successful companies will miss the changes going on around them and wake up one day to a different marketplace governed by new rules.

PUT THIS CHAPTER TO USE:
Check out *Country Market Report* on our website (college.hmco.com/business/).

QUESTIONS FOR DISCUSSION

1. Suppose that Brazil can produce, with an equal amount of resources, either 100 units of steel or 10 computers. At the same time, Germany can produce either 150 units of steel or 10 computers. Explain which nation has a comparative advantage in the production of computers. Choose a mutually advantageous trading ratio and explain why this ratio increases the welfare of both nations.

2. Why would a government want to place export tariffs on products leaving its country? What problems could export tariffs cause?

3. Do you agree with the protesters who claim that the WTO has excessive power over national governments? Will free trade widen the gap between rich and poor? Why or why not?

4. Should the WTO force China to accept nudity onstage? Should the WTO force Utah to accept gambling?

5. What makes regional integration more difficult for developing countries?

CASE 2.1

Banana Wars

For nearly a decade, the European Union (EU) and the United States were engaged in a heated trade dispute over bananas. The EU had introduced tariffs and quotas that discriminated in favor of bananas grown in former European colonies and dependencies located in the Caribbean and Africa. The new rules were favorable to the European-based banana companies, whose production was heavily located in these preferred regions. However, the new rules were disadvantageous to the U.S.-based companies, such as Chiquita and Dole, that owned banana plantations in Latin America.

Dole responded to the crisis by shifting more banana production to West Africa. Over the next few years, Dole's market share in European bananas actually increased. Chiquita, however, asked the U.S. government to bring a complaint against the EU under GATT. The United States won two subsequent suits, but the EU used its veto power under GATT to avoid compliance. However, these veto rights were rescinded under the WTO.

The WTO then ruled on the case again in favor of the United States, calling Europe's quota system blatantly discriminatory. This time the United States was allowed to employ sanctions against the EU if it failed to comply. The EU proceeded to make what most observers believed to be cosmetic, ineffectual changes to its banana importation rules. In retaliation, the United States announced that it would levy 100 percent tariffs on seventeen categories of European goods, including printed cards, cashmere clothing, coral jewelry, and chandeliers.

EU officials objected, claiming that the United States was not authorized to determine whether the EU's actions were insufficient and thus was required to take the case back to the WTO. The U.S. government believed this was a delaying tactic that the EU could employ again and again. The WTO supported the U.S. position and approved the retaliatory actions.

In Europe, the U.S. sanctions were called "silly" and a "return to the Middle Ages." Many EU manufacturers were angry that they were made to suffer over a trade issue that did not concern them. For example, thousands of jobs were at risk in the Belgian biscuit industry, where some companies exported 20 percent of their production to the United States. The sanctions also threatened Asian investors in Europe such as the British battery subsidiary of the Japanese Yuasa Corporation, which had only recently developed export sales to the United States. Now that effort would be for nothing. Only products from Denmark and the Netherlands escaped sanctions because these countries had lobbied the EU for compliance with the banana decision.

Some questioned why the United States was pursuing the banana case so vehemently. After all, no jobs were at risk in the United States. Still, Chiquita's lobbying efforts paid off. The head of Chiquita was a major donor to both the Republican and Democratic parties in the United States. A lobbyist for Greek feta cheese was less successful in his efforts to keep feta off the sanction list, despite his argument that the pain would be borne by Greek Americans, for whom feta was a dietary staple.

The United States insisted that the issue at stake in the banana wars was nothing less than the credibility of the WTO. Europe could not flaunt a WTO decision. Ironically, the U.S. trade representative had angered Europeans five years earlier by stating that WTO membership would not obligate America to obey its rules. The United States could defy WTO rules and accept retaliation from an injured party. After all, few countries would wish to initiate a trade war with the United States. Despite this rhetoric, the United States had complied with WTO rulings against it, such as one concerning U.S. restrictions affecting the import of oil from Brazil and Venezuela.

The United States was not alone in its attempts to receive redress for losses in the EU banana market. The WTO arbitration panel allowed Ecuador to impose over $200 million in sanctions, an amount equivalent to its banana exports shut out of EU markets. However, Ecuador annually imported products worth only $62 million from the EU, and these imports were mainly medicines. Consequently, the WTO authorized Ecuador to impose punitive tariffs on service providers and copyrighted material, including compact discs, from the EU. The EU trade ambassador announced that the EU would monitor Ecuador's penalties and challenge them if they were excessive.

Discussion Questions

1. Who are the winners and the losers in the banana wars?
2. Is the U.S. response silly?
3. What potential threats to the WTO are illustrated by the banana wars?

Sources: Michael M. Weinstein, "The Banana War between the United States and Europe Is More Than a Trivial Trade Spat," *New York Times,* December 24, 1998, p. 2; Helen Coopers, "Curdish War," *Wall Street Journal,* March 1, 1999, p. A1; Brian Kenety, "Trade: Banana Producers Fear Tariff Solution to EU-US Trade War," Inter Press Service, March 16, 2000; and Elizabeth Olsen, "WTO Allows Ecuador to Impose Tariffs on EU in Banana Dispute," *International Herald Tribune,* p. 13.

CASE 2.2

Trouble in Mercosur

Since its inception Mercosur had become Latin America's most successful integration agreement. Among its members were Latin America's largest economy, Brazil (GDP = US$1,035 billion), and its third-largest economy, Argentina (GDP = US$374 billion). From 1991 to 1998, trade between Brazil and Argentina increased 500 percent to $15 billion. However, in 1999, Mercosur trade volume fell 20 percent. Argentina and Brazil were both experiencing recessions and disagreed on which foreign exchange policy to follow. This disagreement threatened the future of Mercosur.

Argentina's Convertibility Plan pegged its peso to the U.S. dollar and banned the printing of unbacked currency. By restricting its money supply and curbing government spending, Argentina reduced inflation from 5,000 percent in 1989 to 1 percent by the year 2000. Through the early and mid-1990s, Argentina experienced an economic boom attributed to its trade liberalization, monetary and foreign exchange stability, and the privatization of previously state-owned companies.

Similarly, Brazil's Real Plan initially pegged the Brazilian real to the U.S. dollar. Inflation fell from 2,500 percent in 1993 to 2.5 percent in 1998. Trade and investment liberalization encour-

aged investment in Brazil, but pent-up demand for capital and consumer goods caused the country's merchandise balance to drop from a surplus of US$10.5 billion in 1994 to a deficit of US$6.3 billion in 1998. The Asian financial crisis in mid-1997 caused foreign investors to worry about the future of other developing countries. Foreign capital fled Brazil, and the country's balance of payments (BOP) deteriorated. A subsequent recession, augmented by the failure of the Brazilian Congress to pass key spending reforms, further eroded investor confidence in the country. Brazil's foreign exchange reserves continued to dwindle. The government responded by announcing a change to the free float of the real. The real plummeted against the dollar and consequently plummeted against the Argentine peso.

Still, the Argentine government remained committed to foreign exchange stability. Argentina even began discussing with the U.S. Treasury the possibility of formally dollarizing its economy. The idea was feasible. Panama had adopted the U.S. dollar as its currency in 1904. Already over half of the bank deposits and loans in Argentina were in dollars. Automated teller machines dispensed both pesos and dollars. The U.S. Federal

Reserve shipped tons of dollar-denominated bills overseas every year. Nearly two-thirds of the almost $500 billion in U.S. currency circulated outside the United States.

Nonetheless, dollarization would be practically irreversible. Argentina would give up control over its money supply to the U.S. Federal Reserve. Critics argued that the U.S. Federal Reserve set policy to assist the U.S. economy, which had little in common with the Argentine economy. Even talking about dollarization would undermine confidence in the peso. Others noted that the alternative of allowing the peso to float freely like the real would be likely to erode confidence even more, resulting in a devaluation of the peso.

Nonetheless, costs of doing business in Brazil were soon 30 percent below those in Argentina. Argentina saw its trade surplus with Brazil disappear. The placing of quotas on certain products imported from Brazil, the first quotas in Mercosur history, had alarmed Brazil, which was investigating legal means to have them lifted. Many Argentine companies and multinational corporations, such as Philips Electronics NV and Goodyear Tire and Rubber Company, had shifted production from Argentina to Brazil. Argentina claimed to have lost 250,000 jobs since the devaluation in Brazil. Unemployed workers marched with signs saying "Made in Brazil—No!" The state governor of Buenos Aires summed up the anti-Brazilian feeling: "The Brazilians are like bad neighbors that come into our house to steal the furniture."

In December 2001, the Argentine government temporarily set limits on the amount of money that Argentines could withdraw from banks or transfer abroad. In the previous year, 20 percent of bank deposits in the country had been converted by their owners into dollars and moved to overseas accounts. Banks were concerned about how long dollar reserves would last in the country at the rate of one peso to one dollar. Rumors of a possible devaluation of the peso were rife by early 2002. But devaluation remained problematic. Many debts and contracts in Argentina were denominated in dollars. A devaluation of the peso would increase the cost in pesos of meeting those dollar obligations. This situation in turn could cause a banking crisis.

Discussion Questions

1. What foreign exchange regime should Argentina adopt: dollarization, a freely floating peso, the status quo, or another? Why?
2. Which foreign exchange regime would you prefer to see in Argentina if you were a U.S. exporter of heavy machinery? A European exporter of cosmetics? A Brazilian exporter of automobiles? Why?
3. What problems related to regional integration agreements are illustrated in this case?

Sources: David Wessel and Craig Torres, "Passing the Buck," *Wall Street Journal*, January 18, 1999, p. A1; Craig Torres and Matt Moffet, "Neighbor-Bashing," *Wall Street Journal*, May 2, 2000, p. A1; U.S. Department of State, FY 2000 Country Commercial Guides: Argentina and Brazil; and Michelle Wallin, "Analysts Warn That a Free-Floating Peso Is Only Part of the Fix That Argentina Needs," *Wall Street Journal*, February 8, 2002, p. A16.

CASE 2.3

Textile Trauma

When the General Agreement on Tariffs and Trade (GATT) was first signed, the textile and apparel industries were too controversial to be included within its scope. Employment in these industries was still high in Europe and the United States, and developed countries feared significant unemployment if protective measures were not continued against new producers from developing economies. As a result, textile trade was negotiated bilaterally and governed for 20 years by the rules of a separate international agreement, the Multifibre Arrangement (MFA), which allowed for the emergence of an international quota system regulating world trade in textiles and clothing.

Despite these protectionist measures, employment in these industries continued to decline in the developed world as manufacturers closed facilities or relocated production in lower-cost countries. And textile and apparel quotas were not immune from politics. After the terrorist attacks of September 11, 2001, on New York and Washington, DC, Pakistan was recruited to the U.S. war on terror. The country was extended US$143 million in new textile quotas by the United States, and the European Union increased Pakistan's quota by 15 percent.

The MFA was later replaced by the WTO Agreement on Textiles and Clothing, which set out a transitional process for the ultimate removal of these quotas by January 1, 2005. Tariffs would remain. These were generally higher in developing countries, ranging from 5 to 30 percent in Malaysia (depending on the category), 13 to 35 percent in Mexico, and up to 44 percent in Turkey. Among developed countries, tariffs were highest in Australia, Canada, and the United States, where they ranged between 0 and 15 percent.

The end of quotas was expected to create big winners and losers. For example, sources at the WTO estimated that India's share of U.S. clothing imports would rise from 4 percent before to 15 percent after the lifting of quotas, and China's share of imports would rise from 16 percent before to 50 percent after the lifting of quotas. China was also expected to see a large increase in its position in the European Union. Estimates put that share at 29 percent of total imports the first year quotas were lifted, threatening currently strong regional producers such as Turkey. In fact, many expected China to attain a 50 percent share of world market within only a few years.

China's textile and apparel industries had several advantages over those in other developing countries. Chinese labor was often cheaper and usually more productive, which was a particular advantage in the labor-intensive apparel industry. Huge factories attained substantial economies of scale, and China provided a good transportation infrastructure with especially quick turnaround times for ships in Chinese ports. Locally pro-duced inputs such as cotton also helped keep costs low. Productive Chinese textile mills provided cheap cloth to Chinese garment manufacturers. In addition, opponents accused China of unfairly gaining advantage by pegging its currency too low and not allowing it to revalue based on market demand. China was also notorious for massive software pirating, including software used in the textile and apparel industries, resulting in savings from the avoidance of paying royalties on the intellectual property of others. Critics argued that many Chinese manufacturers were government owned and thereby received unfair subsidization.

However, others were less sure about the ability of China to attain and sustain its projected gains in market share. Besides the possibility that its currency could be revalued, the Chinese economy showed signs of overheating and the government might decide to tighten credit to textile mills. As many foreign clothing manufacturers moved production to China, prices for materials and labor could increase. Already, clothing factories in China's more developed coastal cities were experiencing difficulty in recruiting new labor. As China's rural incomes rose, fewer Chinese migrated to its cities. Many international producers—as well as global buyers—were considering the risk (both political and economic) of relying too heavily on a single source such as China. Also, the large increases in market share predicted for China were based on actual experience in Australia, where quotas had been removed several years earlier. But some analysts believed that supplier countries near to major markets could partially defend their positions if they focused on "replenishment" products—fashion-oriented products whose buyers (such as Wal-Mart) were sensitive to a supplier's ability to fill reorders very quickly and reliably.

Still, China presented a very real threat to the textile and apparel industries in most other countries. One report projected Mexico's share of the U.S. market to fall from 10 percent to only 3 percent, and the market share for the rest of the Americas to fall from 16 percent to 5 percent. U.S. manufacturers would suffer both directly and indirectly, as many U.S. firms supplied inputs to apparel manufactures in Latin American and the Caribbean. Also of concern was whether bilateral trade agreements between the United States and Latin American countries would allow Latin American clothing manufacturers to use Chinese textiles in clothing exports that received lower tariff rates from the United States. Even if the use of Chinese textiles were to be prohibited or penalized, many believed that Chinese textiles could be smuggled easily into Mexico or Central America due to lax customs procedures. Therefore, enforcing such a rule would be difficult.

The lifting of textile and apparel quotas threatened the economies of developing countries more than it did those of the United States or Europe. Cambodia, for example, expected its economic growth rate to be halved by expected losses in its garment sector. A system originally designed to protect jobs in Europe and the United States had become the vehicle by which many countries in the developing world could receive guaranteed, if limited, access to these developed markets. For example, if Wal-Mart sought to source a large amount of T-shirts, its preferred supplier in China might not be able to deliver the full amount due to a U.S. quota on T-shirts from China. Wal-Mart could be forced to seek additional suppliers in other developing countries, even if the output from those manufacturers was more costly and of lower quality than that of the preferred Chinese supplier.

But guaranteed market access for less-efficient developing countries was now disappearing. In response, a coalition consisting of U.S. manufacturers and those from twenty-four developing countries convened a Summit on Fair Trade in Brussels and issued a communiqué warning the WTO that thirty million jobs were at risk in the developing world with the passing of the Multifibre Arrangement. Not everyone was sympathetic. The executive director of the U.S. Association of Importers of Textiles and Apparel, sent a letter to the trade representatives at Brussels scoffing, "There is no 'crisis' other than the one created by those who did not prepare or who are unwilling to compete without the crutch of protection."

One of the early promoters of the summit was Mauritius, a tiny island state located off the coast of East Africa. Its population was largely ethnic Indians, many bilingual in French and English. A stable, business-friendly government had offered tax incentives to export-oriented industries, and large amounts of foreign investment in clothing manufacture had poured into the country. The garment industry grew to employ one in five working Mauritians, producing products for such global brands as Calvin Klein and Gap. As a result, the median household income of the country had doubled in 10 years to US$4,560, making it one of the highest-income countries in Africa. However, the entry of China into the world market had already resulted in the closing of garment factories on the island, and unemployment had risen from 3 percent to 10 percent.

Bangladesh, a mostly Muslim country of 140 million, was another case in point. Its garment industry employed half the country's industrial workforce and supplied 80 percent of its hard-currency earnings, Bangladesh was one of the poorest countries in Asia and had been designated the most corrupt country in the world by watchdog organization Transparency International. Political tension was pervasive, and Muslim fundamentalist parties were expanding their control in parliament. Some rural areas had become essentially ungovernable harbors of militant Islamic extremists who were opposed to the neighboring governments of India and Myanmar.

Bangladesh ranked low in basic infrastructure such as transportation and communications, and delays and strikes at its ports often forced garment exporters to employ expensive air-cargo space in order to meet order deadlines. While its garment workers earned less than half of what Chinese garment workers earned, its garment factories had never attained the economies of a scale found in China. Unlike China, its apparel industry had no homegrown source of cotton and remained dependent on imported fabrics. Nonetheless, under the MFA Bangladesh had become a major supplier of apparel to both the United States and Europe.

Now experts estimated that over half of the jobs in the Bangladesh apparel industry would disappear. In addition, fifteen million jobs in related industries would be lost as well. As in Mauritius, factory closings had already begun.

The burden of this unemployment would fall on both men and women, as over half the workers in the industry were female. An earlier increase in female employment (attributed to the garment industry) had resulted in improvements in women's lives, such as increased enrollments in primary education. Also, studies had linked a decline in domestic violence against women in developing countries with a woman's ability to earn cash outside the home.

As the end of textile and apparel quotas approached, both the EU and the United States prepared to apply temporary restrictions on certain Chinese imports that would threaten their own manufacturers. The ability to employ such temporary restrictions had been previously negotiated as part of the agreement for China to join the WTO. However, just two weeks before quotas were due to be lifted, China announced that it would impose export duties on its garment industry. The duties would be levied by item rather than by value and would amount to somewhere between 2.4 and 6 cents per piece. Some industry observers predicted that the duties would be painful to Chinese producers without being crippling. Others believed that the impact would be negligible. Nonetheless, Chinese officials insisted that the export tariffs represented a serious attempt to limit the Chinese threat to other developing countries, such as Cambodia and Bangladesh.

Discussion Questions

1. What factors contribute to a country's success as an apparel exporter?
2. Which theory best explains a nation's success in this industry post MFA—the theory of comparative advantage or the theory of competitive advantage? Explain.
3. How will temporary restrictions help U.S. manufacturers?
4. What actions would you suggest for textile and garment producers in Mexico and Turkey?
5. Why do you think the Chinese government has imposed export tariffs on its industry?
6. Is there hope for Mauritius and Bangladesh in the global economy? What advice would you give these countries?

Sources: Farhan Bokhari, "US Rejects Pakistan Pleas on Textile Quotas," *Financial Times*, August 13, 2003, p. 8; Carlos Tejada, "Paradise Lost," *Wall Street Journal*, August 14, 2003, p. A1; Neil King Jr. and Dan Morse, "Bush Set Quotas on Some Imports of Chinese Goods," *Wall Street Journal*, November 19, 2003, p. A1; Peter Fritsch, "Looming Trouble," *Wall Street Journal*, November 20, 2003, p. A1; Rebecca Buckman, "Navigating China's Textile Trade," *Wall Street Journal*, September 10, 2004, p. A10; Greg Hitt, "American Textile Makers Mobilize Alliance of Rivals to Counter China's Share," *Wall Street Journal*, December 14, 2004, p. A2; Andrew Browne, "China Discloses Details of Its Textile Duties," *Wall Street Journal*, December 28, 2004, p. A2; Ind*ustrial Tariff Liberalization and the Doha Development Agenda*, World Trade Organization, 2003; and Greg Hitt, "Latin Trade Deal Has Chinese Flavor," *Wall Street Journal*, January 26, 2005, p. A4.

NOTES

1. Bob Donath, "Don't Miss Opportunities in Global Market," *Marketing News*, July 21, 2003, p. 7.
2. "Garlic Wars," CBSNEWS.com (accessed July 23, 2003).
3. Michael E. Porter, *The Competitive Advantage of Nations* (New York: Macmillan, 1990), pp. 69–175.
4. Moon Ihlwan, "A Nation of Digital Guinea Pigs," *Business Week*, February 4, 2002, p. 50.
5. Aaron Bernstein, "Shaking Up Trade Theory," *Business Week*, December 6, 2004, pp. 116–120.
6. Christopher B. Clott, "Perspectives on Global Outsourcing and the Changing Nature of Work," *Business and Society Review* 109, no. 2 (2004), pp. 153–170.
7. Diana Farrell, "How Germany Can Win From Outsourcing," *McKinsey Quarterly*, 2004, No. 4.
8. Bernstein, pp. 118, 120.
9. Timothy Aeppel, "Survival Tactics," *Wall Street Journal*, January 22, 2002, p. A1.
10. Christopher J. Chipello and Mark Heinzl, "As Canada's Dollar Surges, the Country's Exporters Pay a Steep Price," *Wall Street Journal*, June 14, 2003, p. A14.
11. Katy McLaughlin, "The Rising Cost of Being Fabulous," *Wall Street Journal*, May 13, 2003, p. D1.
12. Eleena De Lisser, "Europe Steps Up the Travel Deals," *Wall Street Journal*, March 25, 2004, p. D1.
13. Marc Lifsher, "Venezuela's Ills Confound Foreigners," *Wall Street Journal*, June 23, 2003, p. A13.
14. Phillip Day, "Yuan's Drop Propels China's Export Powerhouse," *Wall Street Journal*, May 28, 2003, p. A11.
15. Marcus Walker, "Exchange-Rate Policy Gains Currency as an Urgent Global Issue," *Wall Street Journal*, February 1, 2005, p. A11.
16. Thomas T. Semon, "Euro Currency's Ripple Effects Are Far, Wide," *Marketing News*, February 18, 2002, p. 7.

17. Marc Champion, "Euro-Zone Debate Keeps Britain Abuzz," *Wall Street Journal*, May 21, 2003, p. A1.

18. Helene Cooper, "Russia Agrees to Limit Steel Shipments," *Wall Street Journal*, February 23, 1999, p. A8.

19. "Trade: Europe's Burden," *The Economist*, May 22, 1999, p. 12.

20. David Murphy, "Car Makers Worry China Is Planning a U-Turn," *Wall Street Journal*, July 31, 2003, p. A14.

21. Ken Smith, "Eye on Beijing: Can China Liberalize Its Culture Industry?" *Wall Street Journal*, March 28, 2002, p. A18.

22. Jagdish Bhagwati and Arvind Panagariya, "Bilateral Trade Treaties Are a Sham," *Financial Times*, July 14, 2003, p. 17.

23. Paul Magnusson, "The Highest Court You've Never Heard Of," *Business Week*, April 1, 2002, pp. 76–77.

24. Andrew Marshall, "Southeast Asia Talks Free Trade, But Progress Slow," *Reuters English News Service*, April 5, 2002.

25. Adam Schwarz and Roland Villinger, "Integrating Southeast Asia's Economies," *McKinsey Quarterly*, 2004, No.1.

26. Geri Smith and Paul Magnusson, "Fox's Dream," *Business Week*, August 14, 2000, p. 56.

27. Paul Blustein, "A Quiet Round in Qatar?" *Washington Post*, January 30, 2001.

28. William Drozdiak, "Poor Nations May Not Buy Trade Talks," *Washington Post*, May 15, 2001.

29. Paul Magnusson, "States' Rights vs. Free Trade," *Business Week*, March 7, 2005, pp.102, 104.

30. Geoffrey Garrett, "Globalization's Missing Middle," *Foreign Affairs* 83, no. 6 (November/December 2004), pp. 84–97.

3 CULTURAL AND SOCIAL FORCES

McDonald's Operates in over a hundred countries and is the world's largest user of beef. The U.S.-based fast-food chain was drawn to India with its population of 1,000 million, even though the majority of Indians were Hindus and did not eat beef. At the McDonald's in Delhi a sign reads, "No beef or beef products sold at this restaurant." Pork is also omitted to avoid offending India's Muslims. Food on the menu is strictly divided into vegetarian and nonvegetarian lines. Even the mayonnaise has no egg in it. Despite the cultural sensitivity shown by many fast-food chains that have established themselves in India, many Indians consider these foreign-based businesses to be an assault on their culture. Kentucky Fried Chicken found its restaurant in the city of Bangalore under siege from farmers and antiglobalization protesters. A mob vandalized the restaurant, and KFC abandoned the Indian market.[1]

In Chapter 1 we noted that the complexities of international marketing are partially caused by societal and cultural forces. In Chapter 3 we describe some of these cultural and societal influences in more detail. However, because it

LEARNING OBJECTIVES

After studying this chapter, you should be able to

▶ Define what *culture* is and demonstrate how various components of culture affect marketing.

▶ Explain how different world religions affect marketing.

▶ Describe how family structure can vary and explain its impact on marketing.

▶ Illustrate ways in which the educational system of a country can affect marketers.

▶ Differentiate between monochronic and polychronic cultures and explain the three temporal orientations.

▶ List and describe Hofstede's four dimensions of culture.

▶ Explain why language can be important in gaining true understanding of a culture.

▶ Identify ways of adapting to cultural differences.

is not possible to list all of them—or even to describe the major cultures of the world—only some of the more critical forces are highlighted. Figure 3.1 shows the components of culture that are described in this chapter. Rather than identifying all the cultural or societal factors that might affect international marketers, we concentrate on analytic processes that marketers can use to identify and monitor any of the numerous cultural influences they will encounter around the globe.

FIGURE 3.1
Cultural Analysis

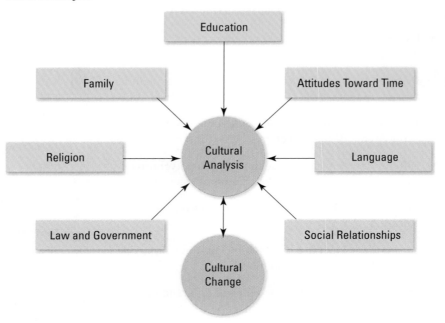

A DEFINITION OF CULTURE

Anthropology is the study of human behavior. Cultural anthropology examines all learned human behaviors, including social, linguistic, and family behaviors. **Culture** encompasses the entire heritage of a society transmitted orally, via literature, or in any other form. It includes all traditions, morals, habits, religion, art, and language. Children born anywhere in the world have the same essential needs for food, shelter, and clothing. But as they mature, children experience desires for nonessential things. *How these wants develop* and *what relative importance the individual assigns to them* are based on messages from families and peers. This socialization process reflects each person's culture.

For example, eating habits and tastes vary greatly around the world, but few of these variations reflect physiological differences among people. Instead, food is extremely culture-bound. One exception relates to milk products. Many people in China lack the enzymes to digest milk products. But like many things Western, milk is becoming increasingly popular in China among a new generation more socialized to Western products. To bridge the gap—in taste and enzymes—many dairy producers in China are selling yogurt-based drinks, which many Chinese find easier to digest.[2]

The role and influence of culture in modern society are evolving as more and more economies become interlinked. Samuel Huntington identifies the cultures of the world as Western (the United States, Western Europe, Australia), Orthodox (the former Soviet republics, Central Europe), Confucian (China,

Culture all human knowledge, beliefs, behavior, and institutions transmitted from one generation to another

Southeast Asia), Islamic (the Middle East), Buddhist (Thailand), Hindu (India), Latin American, African, and Japanese.[3] He argues that conflict in the post-cold-war era will occur between the major cultures of the world rather than between nations. Francis Fukuyama disagrees that cultural differences will necessarily be the source of conflict. Instead, he foresees that increasing interaction between cultures will lead to cross-stimulation and creative change.[4] In any case, understanding cultures helps marketers avoid costly mistakes in the marketplace today.

Cultural Influences on Marketing

The function of marketing is to earn profits from the satisfaction of human wants and needs. To understand and influence consumers' wants and needs, we must understand their culture. Cultural understanding is also necessary when international marketers interact with foreign competitors, distributors, suppliers, and government officials.

Figure 3.2 is a diagram of how culture affects human behavior. As the figure shows, culture is embedded in such elements of the society as religion, language, history, and education. These aspects of the society send direct and indirect messages to consumers regarding the selection of goods and services. The culture we live in answers such questions as the following: Is tea or coffee the preferred drink? Is black or white worn at a funeral? What type of food is eaten for breakfast?

Isolating Cultural Influences

One of the most difficult tasks for global marketers is assessing the cultural influences that affect their operations. In the actual marketplace, several factors are always working simultaneously, and it is extremely difficult to isolate any one factor. Frequently, cultural differences have been held accountable for any noticeable differences among countries. But do these differences result from underlying religious beliefs, from the prevailing social structure, or simply from different sets of laws? In this chapter we will examine the cultural influences of religion, the family, education, attitudes toward time, social interactions, and language. The cultural factors of government and law will be discussed in Chapter 4.

FIGURE 3.2
Cultural Influences on Buyer Behavior

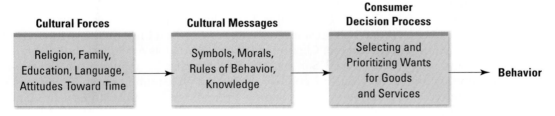

RELIGION

Many businesspeople ignore the influence religion may have on the marketing environment. Religion can have a profound impact on societies. It helps determine attitudes toward social structure and economic development. Its traditions and rules may dictate what goods and services are purchased, when they are purchased, and by whom. For example, the Shinto religion encourages the Japanese people to cultivate a strong patriotic attitude, which may in part account for Japan's excellent economic performance. Alcoholic beverages are banned in Saudi Arabia on religious principles, and El Al, the national airline of Israel, does not fly on Saturday, the Jewish Sabbath.

Table 3.1 lists the leading religions for selected countries. It is beyond the scope of this text to provide a complete description of all world religions and their implications for marketing. By briefly examining several of the world's major religions, however, we can illustrate their potential impact.

Marketing and Western Religions

Historically, the religious tradition in the United States, based on Christianity and Judaism, has emphasized hard work, thrift, and a simple lifestyle. These religious values have certainly evolved over time; many of our modern marketing activities would not exist if these older values had persisted. Thrift, for instance, presumes that a person will save hard-earned wages and use these savings for purchases later on. Today, Americans take full advantage of the ample credit facilities that are available to them. The credit card is such a vital part of the American lifestyle that saving before buying seems archaic. Most Americans feel no guilt in driving a big SUV or generously heating a large house.

Christmas is one Christian tradition that remains an important event for many consumer goods industries in all Christian countries. Retailers have their largest sales around that time. However, Christmas is a good illustration of the substantial differences that still exist among even predominantly Christian societies. A large U.S.-based retailer of consumer electronics discovered these differences the hard way when it opened its first retail outlet in the Netherlands. The company planned the opening to coincide with the start of the Christmas selling season and bought advertising space accordingly for late November and December, as retailers do in the United States. The results proved less than satisfactory. Major gift giving in Holland takes place not around December 25, Christmas Day, but on St. Nicholas Day, December 6. Therefore, the opening of the company's retail operation was late and missed the major buying season.

From a marketing point of view, Christmas has increasingly become a global phenomenon. Christmas fever is catching the imagination of China's growing urban middle classes. Fashionable bars charge up to $25 for entrance on Christmas Eve, and hotel restaurants charge $180 for a Christmas Eve function. For many young Chinese, Christmas is not regarded as a religious holiday but simply represents "fun."[5] Santa Claus is increasing in popularity in the predominantly Sunni Muslim country of Turkey. In Istanbul shopping centers, children stand in line to sit on Santa's lap and ask for gifts. Stores sell Santa suits and statues.[6]

TABLE 3.1 LEADING RELIGIONS OF SELECTED COUNTRIES

COUNTRY	RELIGION[a]		
AFRICA			
Cameroon	Muslim	Christian	Animist
Congo	Christian	Animist	Muslim
Ethiopia	Orthodox Christian	Muslim	Protestant
Ghana	Christian	Animist	Muslim
Kenya	Protestant	Catholic	Animist
Mauritius	Hindu	Christian	Muslim
Nigeria	Christian	Muslim	Animist
South Africa	Christian	Animist	Secular
Zambia	Christian	Hindu	Muslim
Zimbabwe	Christian	Animist	Secular
ASIA			
China	Secular	Buddhist	Taoist
India	Hindu	Muslim	Christian
Indonesia	Muslim	Christian	Hindu
Japan	Shintoist	Buddhist	Christian
Malaysia	Muslim	Buddhist	Hindu
Pakistan	Muslim	Hindu	Christian
Philippines	Catholic	Muslim	—
Singapore	Buddhist	Muslim	Secular
South Korea	Christian	Buddhist	—
Thailand	Buddhist	Muslim	Traditional
EUROPE			
Denmark	Catholic	Protestant	Muslim
France	Catholic	Muslim	Jewish
Germany	Protestant	Catholic	Secular
Italy	Catholic	Protestant	Jewish
Netherlands	Catholic	Protestant	Muslim
Norway	Protestant	Secular	Catholic
Poland	Catholic	Secular	Orthodox Christian
Portugal	Catholic	Secular	Protestant
Russia	Orthodox Christian	Muslim	Secular
Spain	Catholic	Protestant	Secular
Switzerland	Catholic	Protestant	Secular
United Kingdom	Christian	Muslim	Sikh

(*continued*)

TABLE 3.1 (CONTINUED)

COUNTRY	RELIGION[a]		
MIDDLE EAST/CENTRAL ASIA			
Armenia	Orthodox	Muslim	Secular
Egypt	Muslim	Christian	—
Israel	Jewish	Muslim	Secular
Jordan	Muslim	Christian	Secular
Kazakhstan	Muslim	Orthodox Christian	Catholic
Morocco	Muslim	Jewish	Christian
Saudi Arabia	Muslim	—	—
Tunisian	Muslim	Jewish	Christian
Turkey	Muslim	Christian	Jewish
Turkmenistan	Secular	Muslim	Orthodox Christian
NORTH AMERICA			
Canada	Catholic	Protestant	Orthodox Christian
United States	Protestant	Catholic	Secular
LATIN AMERICA/ CARIBBEAN			
Brazil	Catholic	Traditional	Protestant
Chile	Catholic	Protestant	Jewish
Colombia	Catholic	Protestant	Secular
Cuba	Secular	Catholic	Protestant
Jamaica	Protestant	Traditional	Catholic
Mexico	Catholic	Protestant	Secular
Peru	Catholic	Protestant	Traditional
Uruguay	Catholic	Protestant	Jewish
Venezuela	Catholic	Jewish	Muslim

[a]As reported by countries and in descending order left to right.
SOURCE: Adapted from *Cultural Practices and Heritage: Leading Religions*, UNESCO.

Another Christian holiday, Saint Valentine's Day, has become popular in Iran despite disapproval of conservative Muslim clerics who view the holiday dedicated to love as decadent and immoral. Its popularity is spawned by young people who hear about it via satellite television and the Internet and respond by throwing parties and buying Valentine's Day gifts. Stores note sales in the week prior to Valentine's Day are now similar to those before *Norouz*, the traditional Iranian New Year's Day. Valentine paraphernalia is both imported (from China!) and produced locally.[7]

Kosher conforming to Jewish dietary laws

The **kosher** diets of Orthodox Jews present certain marketers with both challenges and opportunities. For example, eating pork is forbidden, and meat and milk may not be eaten together. Many processed foods containing meat products have come under increased scrutiny. These include cereals, such as Kellogg's Frosted Mini Wheats, that are traditionally eaten with milk.[8]

The rigorously Orthodox make up about 12 percent of Israel's 4.7 million Jews, but their numbers are growing more rapidly than those of the rest of the population. As a result, Israeli food manufacturers have expanded their lines of strictly kosher products and have employed packaging and advertising in keeping with the more traditional sensitivities of Israel's Orthodox communities. Elite, a chocolate manufacturer, ran a contest for Orthodox children in which chocolate wrappers could be exchanged for cards showing prominent rabbis or religious teachers. The company also offered lottery prizes, including a trip abroad to tombs of revered Jewish sages. Coca-Cola ran a separate line of advertisements aimed at Orthodox consumers in Israel. These ads depicted Coke drinkers in conservative dress instead of the scantily clad young people used in advertisements aimed at the Israeli public in general.[9]

Recently, U.S. manufacturers and Israeli exporters have been battling over the U.S. market for matzo, the unleavened bread eaten during the Jewish holiday of Passover. Symbolic of the bread baked during the exodus of the Hebrew slaves from Egypt, matzo is now a $90 million market in the United States. The U.S. manufacturers were not worried when the Israelis entered the market in the early 1990s, offering matzo at much lower prices than the American competitors. They believed that consumers bought matzo on the basis of tradition and were unlikely to switch to the new Israeli brands that competed on price. By 2001, however, Israeli matzo had captured 35–40 percent of the U.S. market.[10]

Marketing and Islam

Islam is the religion of nearly 20 percent of the world's population. It is an important cultural force not only in the Middle East but in Asia and Africa as well. In fact, some of the world's largest Muslim populations live in China, Indonesia, and Malaysia.

The prophet Mohammed established Islam in Mecca, located in modern-day Saudi Arabia, in the year 610. By the time of the prophet's death in 632, the holy book of Islam, the **Koran**, had been completely revealed. Muslims believe it contains God's own words. The Koran was supplemented by the **Hadith** and the **Sunna**, which contain the reported words and actions of the prophet Mohammed. These works are the primary sources of guidance for all Muslims on all aspects of life.

Koran the sacred text of Islam

Hadith an authoritative collection of the sayings and reported practices of Muhammad

Sunna a way of life prescribed for Muslims based on the practices of Muhammad and scholarly interpretations of the Koran

Islam affects marketers in a number of ways (see Table 3.2). For example, Islam prohibits the paying or collecting of interest. In most Muslim countries, commercial banks must compete with Islamic banks, which do not offer savings accounts that pay interest. Although these accounts are not attractive to all, many devout Muslims prefer to keep their money in these banks. Islamic banks have also developed a unique product to compete with interest-bearing accounts at other banks. The profit-loss account allows customers to invest their savings in businesses that the bank preselects. Annual profits from the businesses are distributed into the shareholders' accounts.

Islam also prescribes a number of rules concerning food consumption and personal cleanliness. Greater awareness of these Islamic traditions can create new business opportunities. For example, Kohilal is a small business catering

TABLE 3.2 MARKETING IN AN ISLAMIC FRAMEWORK

ELEMENTS	IMPLICATIONS FOR MARKETING
FUNDAMENTAL ISLAMIC CONCEPTS	
A. *Unity*—Concept of centrality, oneness of God, harmony in life.	Product standardization, mass media techniques, central balance, unity in advertising copy and layout, strong brand loyalties, a smaller evoked size set, loyalty to company, opportunities for brand extension strategies.
B. *Legitimacy*—Fair dealings, reasonable level of profits.	Less formal product warranties, need for institutional advertising and/or advocacy advertising, especially by foreign firms, and a switch from a profit-maximizing to a profit-satisficing strategy.
C. *Zakat*—2.5 percent per annum compulsory tax binding on all classified as "not poor."	Use of "excessive" profits, if any, for charitable acts; corporate donations for charity, institutional advertising.
D. *Usury*—Cannot charge interest on loans. A general interpretation of this law defines "excessive interest" charged on loans as not permissible.	Avoid direct use of credit as a marketing tool; establish a consumer policy of paying cash for low-value products; for high-value products, offer discounts for cash payments and raise prices of products on an installment basis; sometimes possible to conduct interest transactions between local/ foreign firms in other non-Islamic countries; banks in some Islamic countries take equity in financing ventures, sharing resultant profits (and losses).
E. *Supremacy of human life*—Compared with other forms of life, objects, human life is of supreme importance.	Pet food and/or products less important; avoid use of statues, busts—interpreted as forms of idolatry; symbols in advertising and/or promotion should reflect high human values; use floral designs and artwork in advertising as representation of aesthetic values.
F. *Community*—All Muslims should strive to achieve universal brotherhood—with allegiance to the "one God." One way of expressing community is the required pilgrimage to Mecca for all Muslims at least once in their lifetime, if able to do so.	Formation of an Islamic economic community—development of an "Islamic consumer" served with Islamic-oriented products and services ("kosher" meat packages, gifts exchanged at Muslim festivals, and so forth); development of community services—need for marketing of nonprofit organizations and skills.
G. *Equality of peoples*	Participative communication systems; roles and authority structures may be rigidly defined, but accessibility at any level relatively easy.
H. *Abstinence*—During the month of Ramadan, Muslims are required to fast without food or drink from the first streak of dawn to sunset— a reminder to those who are more fortunate to be kind to the less fortunate and as an exercise in self-control.	Products that are nutritious, cool, and digested easily can be formulated for Sehr and Iftar (beginning and end of the fast).
Consumption of alcohol and pork is forbidden; so is gambling.	Opportunities for developing nonalcoholic items and beverages (for example, soft drinks, ice cream, milk shakes, fruit juices) and nonchance social games, such as Scrabble; food products should use vegetable or beef shortening.

(continued)

TABLE 3.2 (CONTINUED)

ELEMENTS	IMPLICATIONS FOR MARKETING
I. *Environmentalism*—The universe created by God was pure. Consequently, the land, air, and water should be held as sacred elements.	Anticipate environmental, antipollution acts; opportunities for companies involved in maintaining a clean environment; easier acceptance of pollution control devices in the community (for example, recent efforts in Turkey have been well received by the local communities).
J. *Worship*—Five times a day; timing of prayers varies.	Need to take into account the variability and shift in prayer timings in planning sales calls, work schedules, business hours, customer traffic, and so forth.

ISLAMIC CULTURE

A. *Obligation to family and tribal traditions*	Importance of respected members in the family or tribe as opinion leaders; word-of-mouth communication, customer referrals may be critical; social or clan allegiances, affiliations, and associations may be possible surrogates for reference groups; advertising home-oriented products stressing family roles may be highly effective—for example, electronic games.
B. *Obligations toward parents are sacred*	The image of functional products should be enhanced with advertisements that stress parental advice or approval; even with children's products, there should be less emphasis on children as decision makers.
C. *Obligation to extend hospitality to both insiders and outsiders*	Product designs that are symbols of hospitality, outwardly open in expression; rate of new product acceptance may be accelerated and eased by appeals based on community.
D. *Obligation to conform to codes of sexual conduct and social interaction*—These may include the following:	
1. Modest dress for women in public.	More colorful clothing and accessories are worn by women at home, so promotion of products for use in private homes could be more intimate—such audiences could be reached effectively through women's magazines; avoid use of immodest exposure and sexual implications in public settings.
2. Separation of male and female audiences (in some cases).	Access to female consumers can often be gained only through women as selling agents, salespersons, catalogues, home demonstrations, and women's specialty shops.
E. *Obligations to religious occasions*—For example, two major religious observances are celebrated—Eid-ul-Fitr, Eid-ul-Adha.	Tied to purchase of new shoes, clothing, and sweets and preparation of food items for family reunions, Muslim gatherings. There has been a practice of giving money in place of gifts. Increasingly, however, a shift is taking place to more gift giving; because of lunar calendar, dates are not fixed.

SOURCE: Mushtaq Luqmani, Zahir A. Quraeshi, and Linda Delene, "Marketing in Islamic Countries: A Viewpoint," *MSU Business Topics* (Summer 1980), pp. 20–21. Reprinted by permission.

A Dairy Queen in Bahrain offers a half-price Deluxe Double Cheeseburger as a special Ramadan promotion. During the month of Ramadan, observant Muslims abstain from eating or drinking between sunrise and sunset as part of a spiritual fast.

Halal permitted under Islamic law

to traditional Muslims in Malaysia. The company markets, among other items, a soap made of palm oil that is free of animal fats. Its products contain no forbidden ingredients such as pork products and alcohol and are thus **halal** (acceptable under Islamic teaching).

The world market for Muslim halal food is estimated at $80 billion, and even fast-food companies such as McDonald's and Kentucky Fried Chicken have obtained halal certificates to serve the Muslim market. In Malaysia, a government agency certifies that products are halal. Products must be free of forbidden foods, and production facilities must meet standards of cleanliness and proper storage. Every product sold by Nestlé Malaysia is certified halal. Even Singapore, where only 14 percent of the 3 million population is Muslim, has established its own halal certification body. Indonesia has a Muslim population of nearly 200 million. In response to consumer demand, the Indonesian government also established halal certification. When it was discovered that the Japanese food company Ajinomoto was using a pork-based enzyme in its halal seasoning products in Indonesia, the company had to pull tons of product off the shelves. The company not only faced possible legal action but also suffered a loss of consumer trust.[11]

In many Muslim countries such as Indonesia, Ramadan (the month in which Muslims fast from dawn to dusk) is the major annual shopping season.

Coca-Cola developed an advertisement to be played during Ramadan. Developed by McCann-Erickson Malaysia, the commercial included a small boy and his mother going with gifts to an orphanage, the mother with a rug and basket of food, the boy with his cherished bottle of Coca-Cola. After sunset the little boy leaves his house to go back to the orphanage to break fast and share the Coca-Cola with his new friends. The ad ends with the slogan "Always in good spirit. Always Coca-Cola." It appealed to religious sentiment across national boundaries and was scheduled to air in twenty countries.[12]

Marketing and Eastern Religions

Asia is a major market today for many international firms, and global marketers must take into account the possible impact of the Eastern religious and philosophical traditions of Hinduism, Buddhism, Confucianism, and Shintoism. Hinduism and Buddhism are the two largest Eastern religions. Hinduism is professed by about 450 million people, most of whom live in India, where Hindus constitute nearly 85 percent of the population. Hindu theology varies among believers but is generally polytheistic, with different groups showing a preference for one or several gods. In India, October and November are full of traditional holidays. As such, the two months are the Indian equivalent of the Christmas shopping season in Europe and the United States—a time for gift giving and major purchases.[13]

Hinduism includes a doctrine of rebirth into conditions determined by a person's prior life. A person can be reborn as a human, an animal, or a celestial being. Hinduism also encompasses a hereditary caste system that requires Hindus to marry within their own caste. Many Hindus are vegetarian, and eating beef is particularly taboo. Buddhism also began in India but rejected many of Hinduism's hierarchical structures. Today it is influential predominantly in East and Southeast Asia.

In India, Hyundai respects local beliefs when it launches new car models on auspicious days selected from the Hindu calendar.[14] A Seattle-based company showed far less sensitivity when it launched a line of toilet seats. The Sacred Seat Collection depicted images of Hindu gods such as Ganesh, the elephant god of learning. Several Indian politicians joined members of the large U.S. Hindu population in condemning the company.[15]

Confucianism is not a religion, but its founder Confucius is regarded as the greatest of China's sages and his impact is still greatly felt. Confucius taught respect for one's parents and for education, values common among Chinese today. Confucius' name has also proved valuable to marketers in China. Kong Demao was one of the two surviving members of the seventy-seventh generation of the family of Confucius. Since the early 1990s she had been the nominal chair of three distillers in the Qufu region of China, the ancestral home of Confucius. When all three distillers took the Confucius family name for their products in the mid-1980s, sales soared. In the 1990s, two of the distillers went to court over who really owned the name. Although the case remained unsettled, all three distillers decided it would be wise to contact Kong and pay a stipend for the use of her name. She was also named "Lifetime Honorary President" of the Confucius International Travel Agency.[16]

Japan has been heavily influenced both by Buddhism from Korea and by Confucianism from China. In the late nineteenth century, Japan's earlier Shinto religion was revived as the patriotic symbol of Japan, the emperor being exalted as the descendant of the sun goddess. Shinto rituals were performed at state occasions. State Shinto was abolished after World War II, but popular cults persist. When the first Starbucks abroad opened in Tokyo, Shinto priests offered prayers at the opening ceremony.[17] One enterprising tour group brings foreign tourists to Japan to view Shinto processions during October, a festival month in a number of Japanese cities.[18]

Global marketers require a keen awareness of how religion can influence business. They need to search actively for influences that may not be readily apparent. Showing respect for local religious traditions is an important part of cultural sensitivity.

THE FAMILY

The role of the family varies greatly among cultures, as do the roles that the various family members play. Across cultures, we find differences in family size, in the employment of women, and in many other factors of interest to marketers. Companies familiar with family interactions in Western society cannot assume that they will find the same patterns elsewhere.

In the United States, there has been a trend toward the dissolution of the traditional nuclear family. With people marrying later and divorcing more often, the "typical" family of father, mother, and children living in one dwelling has become far less common than in the past. More recently, a similar trend in Western Europe has resulted in an increase in the number of households even in countries where the overall population is decreasing. This outcome has in turn increased demand for many consumer durables, such as washing machines and ovens, whose sales correlate with number of households rather than with population. Also, an increasing number of women are working outside the home (see Table 3.3), a situation that boosts demand for frozen dinners and child-care centers.

Marketers should not expect to find the same type of family structure in all countries. In many societies, particularly in Asia and Latin America, the role of the male as head of the household remains pronounced. Some cultures still encourage the bearing of male rather than female children. In most cultures, 105 boys are born for every 100 girls, but in China the figure for boys is 118.5 and in South Korea, 116. In some areas of South Korea, boy births outnumber girls 125 to 100, indicating that female fetuses may be being aborted.[19] This male dominance coincides with a lower rate of participation by women in the labor force outside the home. This situation results in a lower average family income. The number of children per family also varies substantially by country or culture. In many Eastern European countries and in Germany, one child per family is fast becoming the rule, whereas families in many developing countries are still large by Western standards.

Extended Families

So far we have discussed only the nuclear family. However, for many cultures, the extended family—including grandparents, in-laws, aunts, uncles, and so

TABLE 3.3 FAMILY STATISTICS OF SELECTED COUNTRIES (IN PERCENTAGES)

COUNTRY	POPULATION GROWTH RATES[a]	FEMALE POPULATION IN LABOR FORCE[b]
Australia	0.96	55.9
Austria	0.05	50.5
Belgium	0.21	39.8
Brazil	1.24	54.1
Canada	0.77	60.7
Chile	1.23	35.7
China	0.73	51.6
Denmark	0.24	73.0
Egypt	1.99	20.2
France	0.47	49.2
Germany	0.07	49.3
Greece	0.14	37.7
Hungary	−0.46	46.9
India	1.51	—
Indonesia	1.26	51.5
Italy	−0.10	37.1
Japan	0.14	48.4
Malaysia	1.93	46.7
Mexico	1.45	38.1
Netherlands	0.50	55.9
Nigeria	2.53	—
Norway	0.43	69.0
Pakistan	2.44	16.2
Russian Federation	−0.57	59.2
Singapore	1.69	55.5
South Africa	0.59	47.8
Spain	0.21	43.3
Sweden	0.09	76.2
Switzerland	−0.05	59.4
Thailand	1.01	65.0
Turkey	1.42	26.6
United Kingdom	0.31	55.3
United States	1.03	59.5
Venezuela	1.86	54.7

[a]Average annual population growth rate between 2000 and 2005.
[b]Percentage of adult women in the workforce.
SOURCE: Adapted from *Indicators on Population and Indicators on Income and Economic Activity*, United Nations Statistics Division (wwww.un.org).

on—is of considerable importance. In the United States, older parents usually live alone, whether in individually owned housing, in multiple housing for the elderly, or in nursing homes (for those who can no longer care for themselves). In countries with lower income levels and in rural areas, the extended family still plays a major role, further increasing the size of the average household. In China, 67 percent of parents with grown children live with one of their children, and 80 percent of such parents have contact with their children at least once a week.[20]

Extended families or clans play an important role among overseas Chinese as well. Driven by poverty and political upheaval, waves of families fled China to other countries in Asia during the past two hundred years. They developed dense networks of thrifty, self-reliant communities united by their Chinese ethnicity. These Chinese communities have flourished in both commerce and industry. For example, ethnic Chinese make up 1 percent of the population and 20 percent of the economy in Vietnam, 1 percent and 40 percent in the Philippines, 4 percent and 50 percent in Indonesia, and 32 percent and 60 percent in Malaysia.[21] Ironically, the Chinese homeland has followed a one-child policy during the past generation in an attempt to curb its population growth. This policy is having an immediate impact on the younger generation's ability to form the traditional Chinese family business. Young entrepreneurs in China report that they establish business relationships with fellow students from high school or university instead of with siblings and cousins.

Beyond the Family

Most societies appreciate and promote a strong family unit. However, Francis Fukuyama argues that a culture can suffer from too great an emphasis on family values. Some cultures, such as that of southern Italy, emphasize nuclear family relationships to the exclusion of all others. It has been said that adults are not persons in southern Italy; they're only parents. In this **low-trust society**, trust is extended only to immediate family members.[22]

Low-trust society a society in which trust is extended only to immediate family members

Yet business relationships depend on trust. Even with contracts and law courts, businesses could not survive if managers spent all their time in litigation. If trust is not extended beyond the family, business dealings must stay within the family. This practice stymies the growth of modern large-scale enterprises and impedes development. For this reason, southern Italy remains one of the poorest regions in Western Europe. Most of the developing world qualifies as relatively low-trust, according to Fukuyama's paradigm. Comparatively few large corporations in the private sector evolved outside North America, Europe, and Japan. Those that did retained their family ties much longer than firms in developed countries.

High-trust society a society in which trust is extended to persons beyond the immediate family, encouraging the emergence of various voluntary organizations such as civic groups and modern corporations

Germany, Japan, and the United States are all very different in many aspects of culture. However, Fukuyama notes that these three countries are **high-trust societies**. They all share a history of voluntary associations—civic, religious, and business—that extend beyond the family. This history of associating with nonfamily members to accomplish common goals taught people that they could trust others who were not blood relations. This experience paved the way for large, publicly owned corporations to emerge, because family businesses could

WORLD BEAT 3.1

Who'll Clean the House?

PROFESSIONAL HOUSECLEANERS are becoming more common in Japan. For decades, housecleaning was considered the job of the Japanese housewives, and even well-to-do families didn't hire strangers to clean their houses. But Japanese society is experiencing a redefinition of gender roles as women enter the workforce in record numbers.

Nonetheless, the industry faces a number of challenges—not least of which is the high cost of delivering services in Japan. The country discourages immigration and labor costs remain high. The Duskin Company, a pioneer in Japan's housecleaning market, charges 15,000 yen ($113) to clean a single toilet bowl and a minimum of $420 to do spring cleaning of a two-bedroom apartment. Another company ran a half-price sale on week-

days promoting the idea that guilty housewives could keep their outsourcing secret from their husbands.

Cleaning entrepreneurs aren't discouraged. The Japan Housecleaning Organization, a volunteer group with sixty members, offers a 10-day training course for novices—mainly middle-aged men who have lost their corporate jobs during Japan's extended economic recession. Housecleaners even have their own section in the yellow pages. But they're listed under the English word *housecleaning*, which is preferred over the Japanese word *soji*.

Sources: Yumiko Ono, "Japan's Distress Prompts an Odd Career Transition," *Wall Street Journal*, April 1, 2002, p. B1; and Anthony Faiola, "Japanese Women Live, and Like It, on Their Own," *Washington Post*, 31 August 2004, p. A01.

feel secure in raising money outside the family, and stockholders could eventually trust their investments in the hands of professional managers. Marketers who compete in high-trust countries usually must contend with these large corporate competitors. However, the history of associations can also be exploited by savvy marketers. Marketers of credit cards in Japan discovered that consumers took quickly to credit cards cobranded with associations and clubs, because the typical Japanese was proud to belong to civic groups.

EDUCATION

Education shapes people's outlooks, desires, and motivations. To the extent that educational systems differ among countries, we can expect differences among consumers. However, education not only affects potential consumers; it also shapes potential employees for foreign companies and for the business community at large.

Levels of Participation

In the United States, compulsory education ends at age sixteen. Virtually all students who obtain a high school diploma stay in school until age eighteen. In high school, about 25 percent take vocational training courses. After high school, students either attend college or find a job. About half of all high school graduates go on to some type of college.

This pattern is not shared by all countries. Many students in Europe go to school only until age sixteen. Then they join an apprenticeship program. This is particularly the case in Germany, where formal apprenticeship programs exist for about 450 job categories. These programs are under tight government supervision and typically last three years. They include on-the-job training, with one day a week of full-time school. About 70 percent of young Germans enter such a program after compulsory full-time education.[23] During the first year, they can expect to earn about 25 percent of the wages earned by fully trained craftspeople in their field. Only about 30 percent of young Germans finish university schooling. In Great Britain, the majority of young people take a job directly in industry and receive only informal on-the-job training. In a study of frontline employees in German, Japanese, and U.S. companies, the U.S. employees received the least training once employed.[24]

Even with similar levels of participation in secondary education, attitudes toward the quantity and quality of education can differ. For example, Japanese high school students attend class more days than students in the United States, where the school year is only 180 days long. Because students in other countries also spend a higher percentage of their school day on core academic subjects, the differences in hours spent on mathematics, science, and history are great: 1,460 total hours for high school students in the United States, 3,170 in Japan, 3,280 in France, and 3,528 in Germany.[25] It is not surprising that among twenty-one countries studied, U.S. high school seniors ranked near the bottom in these fields, behind all their European counterparts and 6 percent below the international average.[26]

A study of reading comprehension in eight countries, conducted by the Organization for Economic Cooperation and Development (OECD), found that the United States outperformed only Poland. One out of five Americans surveyed did not understand the directions on an aspirin bottle. Why, then, is the United States economy so productive? A study by McKinsey Consulting found that differences in basic skills were not a large factor in productivity. Management talent, labor rules, and regulatory environment were more important—all areas in which the United States does well.[27] The OECD study also found a definite link between the percentage of students staying in school beyond the minimum leaving age and a country's economic well-being. Countries such as Japan, Holland, Germany, Austria, and the United States get a high return on their educational expenses because so many young people stay in school, in either traditional or vocational schools. Portugal, Spain, Britain, and New Zealand get a poor return on their educational expenses because so few young people continue their education. On average, each additional year of formal schooling results in a return of anywhere from 5 to15 percent per year in additional earnings.[28]

Impact on Consumers and Employees

The extent and quality of education in a society affect marketing on two levels: the consumer level and the employee level. In societies where the average level of participation in the educational process is low, one typically finds a low level of literacy. Basic literacy levels can vary widely across countries (see Table 3.4). This variation in reading ability not only affects the earning potential of consumers, and thus the level of consumption, but also determines the communication options for marketing programs, as we will see in Chapters 14 and 15. Another concern is how much young people earn. In countries such as Germany, where many of its youth have considerable earnings by age twenty, the value and potential of the youth market is quite different from those in the United States, where a substantial number of young people do not enter the job market until age twenty-one or twenty-two.

TABLE 3.4 ADULT ILLITERACY RATES FOR SELECTED COUNTRIES (IN PERCENTAGES)

COUNTRY	MALE	FEMALE
Algeria	22.0	40.4
Argentina	3.0	3.0
Armenia	0.3	0.8
Bangladesh	49.7	68.6
Bolivia	6.9	19.3
Brazil	13.8	13.5
Bulgaria	0.9	1.9
Cambodia	19.2	40.7
Cameroon	23.0	40.2
Chile	4.2	4.4
China	4.9	13.5
Egypt	32.8	56.4
Ethiopia	50.8	66.2
Ghana	37.1	54.3
Hungary	0.6	0.7
Indonesia	7.5	16.6
Iran	16.5	29.6
Israel	2.7	6.6
Mexico	7.4	11.3
Morocco	36.7	61.7
Peru	8.7	19.7
Qatar	15.1	17.7
Russian Federation	0.3	0.5
Saudi Arabia	15.9	30.5
South Africa	15.9	19.1
Thailand	5.1	9.5
Turkey	5.6	21.5
Vietnam	6.1	13.1

SOURCE: Adapted from *Indicators on Illiteracy*, United Nations Statistics Division (www.un.org), January 28, 2005.

The educational system also affects employee skills and executive talent. In the United States, the sales organizations of many large companies are staffed strictly with university graduates. In many other countries, sales as a profession has a lower status and attracts fewer university graduates. The typical career path of an American executive involves a 4-year college program and, in many cases, a master's degree in business administration (MBA) program. This format for executive education is less common in other countries, despite the fact that MBA programs have proliferated around the world in the past 20 years. For example, large corporations in Korea hire fewer MBAs than their American counterparts, but they import top management educators to teach in their in-house executive programs.

Thus different countries have substantially different ideas about education in general and about management education in particular. Traditional European education emphasizes the mastery of a subject through knowledge acquisition. In contrast, the U.S. approach emphasizes analytic ability and an understanding of concepts. Students passing through the two educational systems probably develop different thinking patterns and attitudes. It requires a considerable amount of cultural sensitivity for an international manager to understand these differences and to make the best use of the human resources that are available.

ATTITUDES TOWARD TIME

In Poland, decisions are usually made quickly. In Kazakhstan, canceling a meeting at the last minute is common, whereas punctuality is strictly observed in Romania.[29] These are all examples of behaviors that reflect cultural attitudes toward time. In the United States, time is seen as having economic value. It is a commodity to be planned for and used wisely. Schedules are set and appointment times are interpreted precisely. If a meeting is scheduled at 3:00 p.m., participants are expected to arrive at 3:00 p.m. In many other countries, such as Costa Rica and Saudi Arabia, meetings rarely begin on time. An American arriving at a meeting in Saudi Arabia can wait quite a while for others to show up. Faced with this phenomenon, the American is likely to be annoyed. Time is being wasted!

Monochronic versus Polychronic Cultures and Temporal Orientation

Monochronic culture a culture in which activities are undertaken one at a time and people respect schedules and agendas

Polychronic culture a culture in which multitasking is common, schedules and agendas bend to the needs of people, and interruptions are common

The United States is basically a **monochronic culture.** Activities are undertaken one at a time. People respect schedules and agendas. In **polychronic cultures,** expectations are different.[30] At any one time, a manager is expected to be managing multiple tasks. Schedules and agendas must bend to the needs of people, and interruptions are not the exception but the rule. It is not unusual for a high-ranking Indian manager to stop work to listen to an employee's family problems. In Brazil, it would be impolite to abruptly cut off a conversation with one group to attend a prearranged meeting with another group. Salespeople from monochronic cultures who travel to polychronic cultures should expect to be kept waiting and should not interpret their clients' tardiness as lack of interest or disrespect.

In many countries, such as Turkey, the traditional and the modern coexist—presenting marketers with both challenges and opportunities.

Temporal orientations also vary by culture. Some cultures, such as Mexico and Brazil, are oriented to the present: Life is enjoyed for the moment. One Mexican ceramics manufacturer noted that as soon as his employees made enough money for the week, they stopped coming to work. The United States is a future-oriented culture, where efforts are focused more on working to achieve a future goal. European and Middle Eastern cultures are more oriented to the past, placing a greater emphasis on historical achievements and relationships. When Israel and Egypt signed a peace treaty 30 years ago, it ended a war that had been going on for nearly 30 years. The U.S. government, which had assisted in the peace process, expected business relations to blossom between the two countries. Today, Israeli firms have barely begun to penetrate the Egyptian market. Egyptians—consumers, distributors, potential partners, and government officials—are still highly aware of the 30 years of war that preceded the peace.

Temporal orientation a society's predominant time focus—either on the past, the present, or the future

Work and Leisure Time

Different societies have different views about the amounts of time it is appropriate to spend at work and in leisure pursuits. In most economically developed countries, leisure has become a major aspect of life. In such countries, the development of the leisure industries is an indication that play and relaxation can be as intensely consumed as any other products.

Society significantly influences work and leisure through statutory vacation allowances and public holidays. Traditionally, European statutes have required companies to give employees 25–30 days of vacation annually, whereas many workers in the United States, Japan, Mexico, and the Philippines enjoy only 5–10 vacation days. These differences result in lower working hours per year in Europe than in the United States, Japan, and Mexico.

These differences in the use of leisure time reflect, to some degree, differences in attitudes toward work (see Table 3.5). An OECD study found that in Germany, the United Kingdom, and Japan, working hours declined over a period of about 20 years, whereas in the United States, working hours increased.[31] Management concepts such as performance-related pay, reengineering, and outsourcing also support longer working hours in the United States. Nonetheless, a study by Robert Half International found that two-thirds of U.S. workers would like shorter hours even if the cutback meant lower wages.[32]

Increasingly, globalization may force a convergence in work hours. For example, on average, German employees work about 25 percent fewer hours than their counterparts in the United States. For the past 25 years, German unions have successfully pushed for a shorter workweek in hopes of creating more jobs. However, this has resulted in German labor costs becoming the highest in the world, and German companies are now shifting jobs out of Germany in order to remain globally competitive. The recent addition of Eastern European countries to the EU is expected to accelerate this trend.[33] Facing the threat of job losses, French workers at a car components factory owned by Bosch voted to work longer hours for the same pay. Some saw this vote as the beginning of a de facto rollback of France's 35-hour legal workweek.[34]

THE HOFSTEDE MEASURES OF CULTURE

Geert Hofstede developed a four-dimensional framework by which to measure several key attributes of cultures. This framework emerged as a result of his research on IBM employees and has since attracted considerable interest among business scholars.[35] The research involved over 116,000 questionnaires and incorporated seventy-two different national subsidiaries, twenty languages, and thirty-eight occupations. Hofstede's insights can be very useful to international marketers. The four dimensions are power distance, individualism-collectivism, masculinity-femininity, and uncertainty avoidance. The scores for sixty-nine countries and regions are listed in Table 3.6. Although Hofstede's four dimensions do not, of course, fully describe national cultures, they are a useful place to begin.

Power Distance

Power distance a measure of culture capturing the extent to which the less powerful members within a society accept that power is distributed unevenly

Power distance is the extent to which the less powerful members within a society accept that power is distributed unevenly. Geert Hofstede tells the story of a clash of cultures between the high-power-distance culture of France and the low-power-distance culture of Sweden:

The nobles of Sweden in 1809 deposed King Gustav IV, whom they considered incompetent, and surprisingly invited Jean Baptiste Bernadotte, a French general who had served under their enemy Napoleon, to become King of Sweden.

TABLE 3.5 VALUES OF SELECTED COUNTRIES

COUNTRY	AVERAGE NUMBER OF WORKING HOURS PER YEAR[a]	EXTENT TO WHICH VALUES OF SOCIETY SUPPORT COMPETITIVENESS[b]	MANAGERS' SENSE OF ENTREPRENEURSHIP[c]
Australia	1,757	7.82	6.58
Austria	1,696	6.22	6.53
Belgium	1,722	5.90	5.77
Brazil	1,869	6.29	6.13
Canada	1,869	7.07	6.79
Chile	2,195	7.13	6.75
China	1,958	6.56	5.35
Denmark	1,658	6.36	5.88
Finland	1,714	7.38	5.63
France	1.561	4.54	5.57
Germany	1,674	5.03	4.92
Greece	1,744	6.07	5.82
Hungary	2,012	5.64	5.03
India	2,347	6.68	6.51
Indonesia	2,175	3.85	4.72
Ireland	1,779	7.19	6.43
Italy	1,764	4.86	5.01
Japan	1,864	5.92	4.15
Korea	2,270	6.79	6.09
Malaysia	2,152	7.53	6.94
Mexico	2,281	4.65	4.58
Netherlands	1,741	6.30	5.90
New Zealand	2,022	6.28	6.52
Norway	1,703	4.72	4.74
Philippines	2,301	4.97	5.47
Portugal	1,804	5.12	4.55
Singapore	2,056	7.81	5.90
South Africa	1,910	5.36	5.70
Spain	1,763	5.56	5.43
Sweden	1,775	5.62	5.56
Switzerland	1,884	6.00	5.64
Taiwan	2,327	7.48	7.36
Thailand	2,184	6.45	6.27
Turkey	2,154	6.89	5.91
United Kingdom	1,787	6.16	5.30
United States	1,895	8.44	7.47
Venezuela	1,989	4.57	4.81

[a]Average number of working hours per year.
[b]Where 0 equals "do not support competitiveness" and 10 equals "supports competitiveness." Average reported from 4,160 executives from 47 countries.
[c]Where 0 equals "a lack of entrepreneurship" and 10 equals "a sense of entrepreneurship." Average reported from 4,160 executives from 47 countries.
SOURCE: Adapted from *The World Competitiveness Report 2004,* Figures 3.5.05, 3.5.06, and 3.5.07.

TABLE 3.6 VALUES OF HOFSTEDE'S CULTURAL DIMENSIONS FOR 69 COUNTRIES OR REGIONS

COUNTRY/REGION	POWER DISTANCE	INDIVIDUALISM-COLLECTIVISM	MASCULINITY-FEMININITY	UNCERTAINTY AVOIDANCE
Arabic countries[a]	80	38	53	68
Argentina	49	46	56	86
Australia	36	90	61	51
Austria	11	55	79	70
Bangladesh	80	20	55	60
Belgium	65	75	54	94
Brazil	69	38	49	76
Bulgaria	70	30	40	85
Canada	39	80	52	48
Chile	63	23	28	86
China	80	20	66	30
Colombia	67	13	64	80
Costa Rica	35	15	21	86
Czech Republic	57	58	57	74
Denmark	18	74	16	23
East African region[b]	64	27	41	52
Ecuador	78	8	63	67
Estonia	40	60	30	60
Finland	33	63	26	59
France	68	71	43	86
Germany	35	67	66	65
Greece	60	35	57	112
Guatemala	95	6	37	101
Hong Kong	68	25	57	29
Hungary	46	80	88	82
India	77	48	56	40
Indonesia	78	14	46	48
Iran	58	41	43	59
Ireland	28	70	68	35
Israel	13	54	47	81
Italy	50	76	70	75
Jamaica	45	39	68	13
Japan	54	46	95	92
Luxembourg	40	60	50	70
Malaysia	104	26	50	36
Malta	56	59	47	96
Mexico	81	30	69	82

(*continued*)

TABLE 3.6 (CONTINUED)

COUNTRY/REGION	POWER DISTANCE	INDIVIDUALISM-COLLECTIVISM	MASCULINITY-FEMININITY	UNCERTAINTY AVOIDANCE
Morocco	70	46	53	68
Netherlands	38	80	14	53
New Zealand	22	79	58	49
Norway	31	69	8	50
Pakistan	55	14	50	70
Panama	95	11	44	86
Peru	64	16	42	87
Philippines	94	32	64	44
Poland	68	60	64	93
Portugal	63	27	31	104
Romania	90	30	42	90
Russia	93	39	36	95
Salvador	66	19	40	94
Singapore	74	20	48	8
Slovakia	104	52	110	51
South Africa	49	65	63	49
South Korea	60	18	39	85
Spain	57	51	42	86
Surinam	85	47	37	92
Sweden	31	71	5	29
Switzerland	34	68	70	58
Taiwan	58	17	45	69
Thailand	64	20	34	64
Trinidad	47	16	58	55
Turkey	66	37	45	85
United Kingdom	35	89	66	35
United States	40	91	62	46
Uruguay	61	36	38	100
Venezuela	81	12	73	76
Vietnam	70	20	40	30
West African region[c]	77	20	46	54
Yugoslavia	76	27	21	88

[a]Egypt, Iraq, Kuwait, Lebanon, Libya, Saudi Arabia, and United Arab Emirates.
[b]Ethiopia, Kenya, Tanzania, and Zambia.
[c]Ghana, Nigeria, and Sierra Leone.
SOURCES: Geert Hofstede, *Cultures and Organizations: Software of the Mind* (New York: McGraw-Hill, 1991), pp. 53, 68, 84, and 113; Geert Hofstede, *Culture's Consequences* (Thousand Oaks, CA: Sage, 2001), p. 502.

Bernadotte accepted and he became King Charles XVI; his descendents occupy the Swedish throne to this day. When the new king was installed, he addressed the Swedish Parliament in their language. His broken Swedish amused the Swedes, and they roared with laughter. The Frenchman who had become king was so upset that he never tried to speak Swedish again.[36]

As a French general, Bernadotte was used to deference from those below him in the hierarchy. Members of Parliament would never laugh at a king in France or criticize him to his face. Even today, France has a high-power-distance score compared with other Western European countries. Nearly all the top jobs in the French public and private sectors are held by graduates of two elite institutions—the École Nationale d'Administration and the École Polytechnique.

Beginning in the family, children in high-power-distance cultures are expected to be obedient to their parents. Respect for parents and elders is considered a virtue. In low-power-distance countries, children learn to say no at a young age and are encouraged to attain personal independence from the family. In these societies, subordinates are less dependent on their bosses and are more comfortable approaching their bosses and contradicting them.

Individualism-Collectivism

Individualism-collectivism
a measure of culture capturing the extent to which a society evaluates a person as an individual rather than as a member of group

Hofstede's second dimension of culture is the **individualism-collectivism** dimension. The United States rates very high on individualism. However, most of the world is far more collectivist. In collectivist societies, the good of the group prevails over the good of the individual. From birth, individuals are integrated into strong, cohesive groups. They are identified in terms of their group allegiance and their group role.

The collectivist worldview tends to divide people into in-groups and out-groups. In other words, people do not simply choose which in-group to join. Often one has to be born into an in-group, such as a family, an ethnic group, or a nationality. Collectivist societies tend to be more suspicious of outsiders, whereas individualistic societies are more welcoming of them. For example, only one of an individual's parents needs to be an American for the individual to qualify as an American citizen. Furthermore, one can be an American citizen simply by virtue of having been born in the United States, even of foreign parents. And if one does not qualify by birth, immigration is a possibility. Each year hundreds of thousands of immigrants request and are granted American citizenship. More collectivist societies, on the other hand, do not bestow citizenship so freely. For one to qualify as an Egyptian citizen, both of one's parents should be Egyptian, and naturalization is virtually unknown in this country.

Individuals in collectivist societies are more dependent on their group and more loyal to it than members of individualistic societies. Group members are expected to take care of one another. In turn, they tend to follow group norms and to avoid deviating from the group in opinions or behavior. This group cohesiveness may transfer to groups joined later in life, such as friends from high school and college or corporate colleagues.

Outsiders may come to be trusted in collectivist societies, but only after they have invested much time and effort. Many firms relate a common experience in

Saudi Arabia: A manager is sent to Saudi Arabia to establish business relations. After a long time, the potential Saudi client agrees to do business with the firm, but only if the manager who originally established the relationship stays and manages the relationship. In other words, the trusted outsider must be a person, not a firm.[37]

Masculinity-Femininity

Hofstede's third dimension of culture is **masculinity-femininity**. This was (not surprisingly) the only dimension identified in the IBM study in which male and female respondents' scores were significantly different. Nonetheless, some countries were rated more masculine overall, including their women, and some more feminine overall, including their men. Masculinity is associated with assertiveness. Femininity is associated with modesty and nurturance. Masculine societies value ambition, competitiveness, and high earnings. Feminine societies are concerned with public welfare. For example, the percentage of gross national product (GNP) that a state allocates for aid to poor countries does not correlate with wealth but does correlate with femininity.

In Denmark, a feminine country, students tend to prepare a résumé that underplays their achievements. Interviewers know that they must ask probing questions to elicit an account of these achievements in the interview. Students in more masculine societies, such as the United States, tend to construct their résumés to broadcast any achievements. In this regard, Hofstede noted that Americans look like braggarts to Danes and that Danes look like suckers to Americans.

> **Masculinity-femininity** a measure of culture relating to assertiveness/modesty and competitiveness/nurturance

Uncertainty Avoidance

Uncertainty avoidance is the state of being uneasy or worried about what may happen in the future. It is not the same as being averse to risk. People who are risk-averse are afraid that something specific might happen—for example, that an inflated stock market might crash or that they might fail their final exams because they haven't studied hard. People who are uncertainty-avoidant are *anxious in general*. Exams always make them anxious, even if they have studied hard and have done well in the past. The future is uncertain for all of us. Typical persons from low-uncertainty-avoidance societies accept this fact and are confident that they can deal with whatever might arise. In other words, they are comfortable "rolling with the punches." Typical persons from high-uncertainty-avoidance societies try to control and minimize future uncertainty. They have a tendency to work hard or at least to feel more comfortable if they are busy doing something.

Uncertainty-avoidant cultures don't like ambiguity. Events should be clearly understandable and as predictable as possible. Teachers in these cultures are expected always to have the answers. In low-uncertainty-avoidance cultures, on the other hand, teachers are allowed to say, "I don't know." High-uncertainty-avoidance cultures have an emotional need for formal and informal rules. Low-uncertainty-avoidance cultures dislike rules. What rules they do employ, however, are generally more respected than are the many rules of uncertainty-avoidant cultures.

> **Uncertainty avoidance** a measure of culture relating to general worry about the future

High-uncertainty-avoidance cultures tend to think that what is different is potentially dangerous. This fear may make such cultures less innovative than low-uncertainty-avoidance cultures, because radically new ideas are suspect to them. However, they can prove outstanding at implementing the ideas of others. As Hofstede noted, Britain (a low uncertainty-avoidance culture) has produced more Nobel Prize winners than Japan (a high uncertainty-avoidance culture), but Japan has brought more new products to the world market.[38]

Uses and Limitations of the Hofstede Measures

The Hofstede measures are an excellent way to identify quickly those areas where significant cultural differences exist. Americans dealing with distributors in Guatemala must remember that their agents come from a very different culture. Guatemala scores much higher on power distance and uncertainty avoidance. It is a very collectivist society, whereas the United States is a very individualistic one. If we send a young American manager to negotiate terms with Guatemalan distributors, our American manager must be careful to show proper respect and deference to any older distributors. Our manager should expect the distributors to ask for clear and detailed contracts. In turn, our manager should take care that the distributors belong to the right in-group. For example, do their group ties allow them to reach the right retailers and to access preferential financing? Have the potential distributors conformed to group norms, and have they established themselves as trustworthy within their group?

We must remember that all these scores are relative. Depending on the reference point, Japan can appear collectivist or individualistic. American culture is more individualistic than Japanese culture, but Japanese culture is more individualistic than South Korean culture. When a multinational company sends American managers to deal with Japanese customers, these managers must adjust to a more collectivist culture. When the multinational sends South Korean managers to deal with the same Japanese customers, they must adjust to a more individualistic culture.

Hofstede's framework is the culture framework that has received by far the most interest by business researchers.[39] Yet, the framework has a number of limitations. Not all countries were included in the original IBM study. Because IBM had no subsidiaries in Russia or Eastern Europe in the late 1970s, with the exception of Yugoslavia we have no original scores for these markets. Luckily, new studies have added to the list. Still, for reasons of sample size, some countries in both Africa and the Middle East were grouped together despite probable cultural differences between them. We must also keep in mind that ethnic groups and regional populations within a country can vary significantly from the national average.[40] Also, the Hofstede measures should not be used for stereotyping people. They do present us with central tendencies or averages for a culture, but they cannot be used to describe any one person who might come from that culture. Some individual Swedes will behave in a more "masculine" manner than some Japanese, even though Sweden as a whole is a feminine culture and Japan as a whole is a masculine one.

Finally, although the Hofstede measures are useful for identifying cultural differences and suggesting potential cross-cultural problems that international marketers may face, they do not capture or elucidate all aspects of a culture. Britain and the United States appear nearly similar across all the Hofstede measures. Still, they differ in many aspects of culture. For example, Britain exhibits greater class consciousness than is found in the United States, and the United States scores higher on religiosity, as exhibited, for example, in church attendance. People in the United States are more outgoing in expressing their emotions while the British are more reserved. We cannot hope to capture a complete culture in four numeric measures. They are a great place to start, but they are only a start.

Cultural Change

How quickly does culture change? Are the Hofstede measures valid after 30 years? Will they be valid 30 years from now? Culture does change, but most writers on culture agree that it changes very slowly. In the 1920s, the Ottoman Empire that ruled Turkey was ousted in a military uprising. A new charismatic leader, Ataturk, attempted in various ways to distance Turkey from its culture of the past and force Turks to adopt more European ways. A major assault was made on collectivism. Voluntary organizations such as political parties and business associations were required by law to be open to all. Ethnic affiliations that had played a major role in the politics of the Ottoman Empire were discouraged under Ataturk. Citizens were socialized to think of themselves simply as Turks. Physical emblems of religious affiliations, such as the veil worn by Muslim women and the fez worn by Muslim men, were outlawed. Eighty years later, much has changed in Turkey, and Ataturk enjoys hero status among nearly all Turks. Yet his attempt to defeat collectivism has failed. Modern Turkey struggles with the Kurdish ethnic question in the east, Islamic political parties win elections, and Turkey scores only 37 on Hofstede's individualism-collectivism measure.

It is true that most developing countries rate high on power distance and collectivism (see Figure 3.3), and the average religiosity of a country's population tends to decline with increased economic development. These observations have led some to conclude that as economies develop, all societies will someday converge in a single, modern culture. Americans in particular tend to believe that this modern culture will resemble American culture. Yet, ironically, the United States remains an outlier regarding the religiosity rule. Despite enjoying one of the highest per-capita incomes in the world, Americans remain one of the world's most religious societies.[41] Also, Americans rate higher on the traditional value of national pride than do citizens in other developed countries. Based on these observed patterns of social development, Sweden and the Netherlands are arguably better examples of modernity than is the United States.[42]

It is important to remember that cultures in the world today vary greatly. With global media, Internet connection, and human migration, virtually all cultures are affected by other cultures. All societies are evolving. In a hundred years, Indonesia will undergo cultural change, but it won't become America. In a hundred years, America will undergo cultural change as well. Marketing managers from all nations will continue to deal with the cultural differences that make all nations unique.

FIGURE 3.3
The Positions of Fifty Countries and Three Regions on Power Distance and Individualism-Collectivism Dimensions[a]

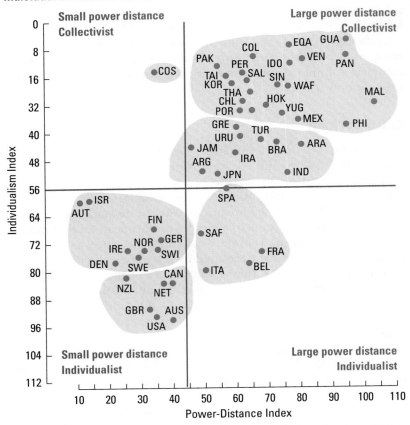

[a] ARA, Arabic-speaking countries (Egypt, Iraq, Kuwait, Lebanon, Libya, Saudi Arabia, United Arab Emirates); ARG, Argentina; AUS, Australia; AUT, Austria; BEL, Belgium; BRA, Brazil; CAN, Canada; CHL, Chile; COL, Colombia; COS, Costa Rica; DEN, Denmark; EAF, East Africa (Ethiopia, Kenya, Tanzania, Zambia); EQA, Ecuador; FIN, Finland; FRA, France; GBR, Great Britain; GER, Germany F.R.; GRE, Greece; GUA, Guatemala; HOK, Hong Kong; IDO, Indonesia; IND, India; IRA, Iran; IRE, Ireland (Republic of); ISR, Israel; ITA, Italy; JAM, Jamaica; JPN, Japan; KOR, South Korea; MAL, Malaysia, MEX, Mexico; NET, Netherlands; NOR, Norway; NZL, New Zealand; PAK, Pakistan; PAN, Panama; PER, Peru; PHI, Philippines; POR, Portugal; SAF, South Africa; SAL, Salvador; SIN, Singapore; SPA, Spain; SWE, Sweden; SWI, Switzerland; TAI, Taiwan; THA, Thailand; TUR, Turkey; URU, Uruguay; USA, United States; VEN, Venezuela; WAF, West Africa (Ghana, Nigeria, Sierra Leone); YUG, Yugoslavia.
SOURCE: Geert Hofstede, *Cultures and Organizations* (New York:McGraw-Hill, 1991), pp. 23, 51, 83, and 111. Reprinted with permission of the author.

LANGUAGE AND COMMUNICATION

Knowing the language of a society can become the key to understanding its culture. Language is not merely a collection of words or terms. Language expresses the thinking pattern of a culture—and to some extent even forms the thinking itself. Linguists have found that cultures with more primitive languages or a limited range of expression are more likely to be limited in their thought patterns. Some languages cannot accommodate modern technological or business concepts, forcing the cultural elite to work in a different language.

The French are particularly sensitive about their language as an embodiment of their culture and seek to protect it from outside influence. The French government has proposed legal action to limit further incursions by other languages, especially by English. For example, *le airbag* is called *coussin gonflable de protection* and *fast food* is *restauration rapide*. France persuaded the European Community that 40 percent of TV programming should be produced domestically. Cinema tickets in France are taxed and the funds used to support the French film industry as protection against the U.S. film industry, which has come to dominate the European film market.

Table 3.7 lists the official languages of selected countries. Note that some countries have more than one official language. India has nineteen, although the most commonly spoken language is Hindi. South Africa has eleven official languages. A very few countries, such as the United States, do not designate an official language. African countries with diverse tribal languages often adopt a colonial European language as their official language. However, the use of this official language may be restricted to elites. Similarly, Spanish is one of the official languages of Bolivia, but two native Indian languages are also official. Certain languages are associated with certain regions of the world, but key markets in these regions may speak a different language. For example, Arabic is associated with the Middle East, but Persian (Farsi) is spoken in Iran, and Turkish in Turkey. Spanish is associated with Latin America, but Portuguese is spoken in Brazil.

Forms of Address

The English language has one form of address: All persons are addressed with the pronoun *you*. This is not the case in many other languages. The Germanic, Romance, and Slavic languages always have two forms of address, the personal and the formal. Japanese has three forms. A Japanese person will use a different form of address with a superior, a colleague, or a subordinate, and there are different forms for male and female in many expressions. These differences in language represent different ways of interacting. English, particularly as it is spoken in the United States, is much less formal than Japanese. Americans often address their bosses and customers by their first names. In Japan this practice could be considered rude. Consequently, knowing the Japanese language gives a foreigner a better understanding of cultural mores regarding social status and authority.

The Context of Language

When an American executive says "yes" in a negotiation, this usually means "Yes, I accept the terms." However, *yes* in Asian countries can have a variety of meanings. It can mean that your hearers recognize that you are talking to them but not necessarily that they understand what you are saying. It can mean that they understood you but disagree with you. It can mean that they understand your proposal and will consult with others about it. Or, finally, it can indicate total agreement.

TABLE 3.7 OFFICIAL LANGUAGES OF SELECTED COUNTRIES

COUNTRY	LANGUAGE(S)	COUNTRY	LANGUAGE(S)	COUNTRY	LANGUAGE(S)
AFRICA		**AMERICAS**		**ASIA**	
Angola	Portuguese	Argentina	Spanish	Pakistan	Urdu, English
Cameroon	French, English	Belize	English	Sri Lanka	English, Sinhala, Tamil
Chad	French, Arabic	Bolivia	Aymara, Quechua, Spanish		
Ethiopia	Amharic			Japan	Japanese
Kenya	Swahili	Brazil	Portuguese	Malaysia	Malay
Mozambique	Portuguese	Canada	English, French	Philippines	Tagalog, English
Niger	French	Chile	Spanish	Singapore	Chinese, English, Malay, Tamil
Nigeria	English	Haiti	French, Creole		
Rwanda	French, Kinyarwanda	Jamaica	English	South Korea	Korean
		Mexico	Spanish	Thailand	Thai
Somalia	Somali	Peru	Spanish		
		Venezuela	Spanish		
EUROPE		**MIDDLE EAST**			
Belgium	Dutch, French, German	Egypt	Arabic, English, French		
Finland	Finnish, Swedish	Iraq	Arabic		
France	French	Iran	Farsi		
Germany	German	Israel	Hebrew, Arabic		
Italy	Italian	Lebanon	Arabic, French		
Netherlands	Dutch, Frisian	Turkey	Turkish		
Russian Federation	Russian				
Spain	Spanish				
Switzerland	French, German, Italian, Romansh				
United Kingdom	English, Welsh				

SOURCE: Adapted from *Cultural Practices and Heritage: Leading Languages,* UNESCO Cultural Policy Resources (www.unesco.org).

Low-context culture a culture in which communication is explicit and words tend to retain their meaning in all situations

High-context culture a culture in which communication is more implicit and the meanings of words change depending on who is speaking to whom, where that person is speaking, and under what circumstances he or she is speaking

The simple term *yes* is a good example of how some languages can be affected by social milieu or context. In **low-context cultures** such as the United States, communication is explicit and words tend to retain their meaning in all situations. In Asian **high-context cultures**, meanings are more implicit. The meanings of words change depending on who is speaking to whom, where that person is speaking, and under what circumstances. These subtleties make communication all the more difficult for persons who were not born and raised in those cultures.[43] Not surprisingly, collectivist cultures tend to be high-context cultures.

Before beginning a conversation or a negotiation in high-context cultures, the parties involved need to take part in preliminary chats in order to place one another in the correct social context. For example, do both parties come from the same social background, or is one an outsider? Do both negotiators possess the status required to make a final decision on their own, or will they need to consult with others? In high-context cultures, these questions would never be asked or answered directly. Instead, people are socialized to pick up on the right cues, such as where someone went to school or how long that person has been employed with his or her company. "Placing each other" helps negotiators determine how they will interact and interpret each other's statements.

Also, *how* something is said may be considered as important, or even more important, than what is said. When U.S. Secretary of State James Baker told the Iraqis that the United States would attack Iraq if they did not get out of Kuwait, the high-context Iraqis understood that the Americans would not attack them. Baker spoke calmly and did not seem angry. Therefore, the Iraqis concluded that they needn't take the threat seriously.[44]

Body Language

As important as understanding a verbal foreign language is, it is only part of the challenge. The use of nonverbal communications, or **body language**, is also important. Body language includes such elements as touching, making arm and hand gestures, and keeping the proper distance between speakers. Mexicans happily come within 16–18 inches of a stranger for a business discussion. For Latins, Arabs, and Africans, proximity is a sign of confidence. Asians, Nordics, Anglo-Saxons, and Germanic people consider space within 1 yard or meter as personal space. When a Mexican moves closer than this to an English person, the English person feels invaded and steps back, giving the Mexican the incorrect message that he or she does not want to do business.[45] The appropriateness of eye contact varies with culture as well. Americans consider making eye contact while speaking a sign of trustworthiness. Many Asian cultures, such as that of Korea, can consider it a sign of disrespect.

Body language nonverbal communications, including touching, making arm and hand gestures, and keeping a proper distance between speakers

Showing Emotion

Another way in which cultures vary in their communication style is the degree to which they exhibit emotion. In **affective cultures**, such as Italy, the United States, and Arab countries, speakers are allowed—even expected—to express emotions more than in nonaffective or **neutral cultures**, such as China, Korea, and Japan. If upset or even excited, a speaker is allowed to speak louder and gesticulate. This is not to say that Americans and Italians feel emotions more strongly than Koreans but merely that Koreans are expected not to *show* emotions. Persons from affective cultures can unnerve those from neutral cultures with their displays of emotion. On the other hand, persons from neutral cultures can appear inscrutable to those from affective cultures.

Despite their nonaffective culture, Japanese marketers are reconsidering the power of a smile. Some retail and service businesses are sending employees to newly opened smile schools that consider "importing joviality" to be their

Affective culture a culture in which speakers are allowed—even expected—to express emotions

Neutral culture a culture that discourages a show of emotion

Students at a Japanese smiling school.

corporate mission. Yoshihiko Kadokawa, author of *A Laughing Face*, believes that smiling at customers increases sales and boosts employee morale. However, teachers at Japan's smile schools concede that smiling excessively is still controversial in Japan, where it is thought to reflect suicidal tendencies, especially among males.[46]

OVERCOMING THE LANGUAGE BARRIER

International marketing communications are heavily affected by the existence of different languages. Advertising has to be adjusted to each language, and personal contacts are made difficult by the language barrier. To overcome this language barrier, businesspeople all over the world have relied on three approaches: the translation of written material, the use of interpreters, and the acquisition of foreign-language skills.

Translating and Translators

Translations are needed for a wide range of documents, including sales literature, catalogues, advertisements, and contracts. Some companies send all correspondence through a translation firm. For a company that does not have a local subsidiary in a foreign market, competent translation agencies are available in most countries. The largest translation staff in the world belongs to the European Union, which has 1,500 people translating 1.2 million pages of text per year into its three working languages: English, French, and German. EU bureaucrats also use machine translation to provide rough translations used for e-mail and other less official communications.

Traveling with executives and attending meetings, personal translators can perform a very useful function when a complete language barrier exists. They are best used for a limited time only. Realistically, they cannot overcome long-term communication problems. When one is traveling in Asia, it is tempting to use senior subsidiary managers, who are usually bilingual, as translators. However, this pratice should be avoided. Translators are considered low-level staff members in Asia, and senior managers employed in this manner would be looked down on.

Translation Problems

Both translation services and translators work by translating one language into another. In certain situations, however, it is almost impossible to translate a given meaning accurately and fully into a second language. When the original idea, or thought, is not part of the second culture, for example, the translation may be meaningless. When China first liberalized its economy after years of strict communism, Chinese translators had difficulty translating basic English business terms such as *profit* and *loss*, because these concepts were unknown in the communist-planned economy.

Translation problems abound with the use of brand names in various markets. Brand names can be particularly affected by language, because they are not normally translated but are merely transliterated. Consequently, a company may get into trouble using a product name in a foreign country, even though its advertising message is properly translated. Coca-Cola's launch in China was complicated by the fact that, when spoken aloud, its brand name sounds like "bite the wax tadpole" in Chinese.

Today, global companies tend to choose product names carefully and test them in advance to ensure that the meaning in all major languages is neutral and positive. They also make sure that the name can be easily pronounced. Language differences may have caused many blunders, but careful translations have now reduced the number of international marketing mistakes. Still, the language barrier remains, and companies that make a conscientious effort to overcome this barrier frequently achieve better results than those that do not.

Which Language to Learn?

One can draw two major conclusions about the impact of language on international marketing. First, a firm must adjust its communication program and design communications to include the languages used by its customers. Second, the firm must be aware that a foreign language may reflect different thinking patterns or indicate varying motivations on the part of prospective clients and partners. To the extent that such differences occur, the simple mechanical translation of messages will not suffice. Multinational firms require marketing managers with foreign-language abilities. Still, managers cannot be expected to speak all languages. Global marketers are increasingly united by the use of English as a global business language. Chile inaugurated a nationwide campaign to ensure that all high school students became fluent in English. The objective: to make Chile a world-class exporter.[47]

English has the advantage of being a noncontextual language that many consider relatively easy to learn. Its influence in international commerce was established first by the British Empire and later by the influence of the United States and U.S. multinational firms. According to a study by the OECD in Paris, 78 percent of all websites and 91 percent of secure websites are in English.[48]

The widespread use of English has even allowed U.S. firms to outsource customer service tasks to call centers based in India. These centers tap into a large pool of English-speaking labor to answer calls from U.S. consumers concerning anything from late credit card payments to problems with software. Indian service personnel call themselves by American names—Barbara, not Bhavana—and learn to speak with an American accent. Customers on the line have no idea they're talking to someone on the other side of the world.[49]

Matsushita, the world's largest seller of consumer electronics, issued a controversial directive in 2000: Managers must pass an English-competency test in order to be promoted. Other Japanese companies that have tied promotions to the ability to speak English include Toyota, NEC, Hitachi, Komatsu, and IBM Japan. In 2000, only students in Afghanistan, Laos, and Cambodia scored lower on English standardized tests than did students in Japan, despite a heavy emphasis on English-language learning in Japanese schools. Matsushita believes that its company's mentality has remained monocultural and monolingual even though half its revenues and half its employees are non-Japanese. It hopes to globalize the mindset of managers by requiring them to think occasionally in a foreign language.[50]

Although English has become the language of commerce and electronic communications, a marketing manager's personal relationships will often benefit from the manager's having achieved language skill in a customer's native tongue. Both Philips Electronics NV, the Dutch consumer giant, and U.S.-based General Electric have adopted English as their corporate language, and managers are not required to speak a local language to run a subsidiary. However, both companies appreciate multilingual managers and consider languages skills to be an advantage.[51] In fact, cultural empathy may best be developed by learning a foreign language, and learning any language will help develop cultural sensitivity. By learning even one foreign language, a student can gain a better appreciation of all different cultures.

ADAPTING TO CULTURAL DIFFERENCES

Some companies make special efforts to adapt their products or services to various cultural environments. Even when a firm tries hard to understand the culture of a new market, however, it is easy to make mistakes. When Disney, the U.S-based entertainment giant, decided to open a theme park in Europe, it had almost no direct overseas experience. Tokyo Disneyland had proved successful, but it had been developed and run by a local Japanese partner. When

EuroDisney opened in France, management had already incorporated changes in its successful models from California and Florida. To accommodate the cooler, damper climate in France, more indoor attractions were developed and more covered walkways were installed. Multilingual telephone operators and guides were hired to assist visitors from different European countries. Kennels were built for the many French families who would never think of going on vacation without the family dog. Estimates of restaurant traffic took into consideration the fact that Europeans like to linger over their food and are far less tolerant of standing in lines than Americans.

Still, for the first year of operations, EuroDisney refused to sell alcohol on its premises because this practice clashed with its American idea of family entertainment. The management also refused to cut prices during off-season months, despite a time-honored European tradition of doing this at vacation destinations. The first year of operation was disappointing. Disney then bowed to cultural realities and adopted wine, beer, and differentiated prices. Adapting to European culture paid off. By 2002, EuroDisney was Europe's top tourist attraction—even more popular than the Eiffel Tower.[52]

As the story of EuroDisney illustrates, the influence of culture is particularly important for food products. However, quite a few food firms have overcome cultural barriers. One such celebrated case is McDonald's, the U.S. fast-food franchise operator. Sixty percent of McDonald's sales and all of its top ten restaurants, measured in terms of sales and profits, are now overseas. Leading stores are in Moscow, Paris, and Rome, hardly markets where one would expect the typical U.S.-style hamburgers to do well. In general, McDonald's restaurants overseas have sales about 25 percent higher than the average U.S. outlet. In fact, one of the company's stores in Poland holds the world record for first-day sales, having served 33,000 customers on its opening day.[53]

Still, there are some countries where the McDonald's hamburger menu does not do well. In Japan, McDonald's had to substantially adapt its original U.S.-style menu. It introduced McChao, a Chinese fried rice dish. This dish proved to be a good idea in a country where 90 percent of the population eats rice daily. The results were astounding. Sales climbed 30 percent after the McChao was introduced. McDonald's continues to innovate in Japan with the Teriyaki McBurger and Chicken Tatsuta.[54]

Similar adjustments were made by Domino's Pizza, one of the many pizza franchises active in Japan. The types of pizza favored by Japanese consumers are quite different from those favored in the United States. Although Domino's advertises its pizza as "from the U.S.A.," it offers such toppings as teriyaki gourmet, consisting of Japanese-style grilled chicken, spinach, onion, and corn. In addition, Domino's offers squid and tuna toppings, as well as corn salad.[55]

When Big Boy, a U.S.-based hamburger chain, opened in Bangkok, the franchisee in Thailand also discovered that he needed to make adaptations to the menu to suit Thai tastes. However, those were not the only cultural surprises. Many Thai consumers were at a loss about what to make of the chain's giant statue of a boy in checkered overalls. Some Thais left bowls of rice and incense at the feet of the statue as though it were a religious icon. Other Thais said the statue spooked them. In addition, the restaurant employees would not eat on shifts but insisted on eating together, all at the same time.[56]

WORLD BEAT 3.2

Cinema Sensitivities

WHEN WALT DISNEY STUDIOS opened its Hollywood Studio complex at its theme park outside Paris, the new attraction came complete with palm trees and a 1940s Hollywood Boulevard. Starlets pose for cameras, and producers recruit visitors as actors.

But Disney is careful to pay homage to European culture and filmmaking traditions. One show celebrating the history of animation depicts Disney characters speaking in six different languages. Another documentary reminds visitors of the European roots of Disney's animated classics. Cinderella weeps in French, and Pinocchio cries for help in Italian. A stunt show features cars and motorcycles racing through a village modeled after the French resort town of Saint Tropez.

For nearly 20 years, the French government has spent hundreds of millions of dollars to save EuroDisney from bankruptcy. Is this a sign that Disney's cultural sensitivity is paying off? Maybe. But Disney's main attraction for the French government is the 43,000 jobs it provides—making it among the largest employers in the Paris area.

Sources: Paulo Prada and Bruce Orwall, "A Certain 'Je Ne Sais Quoi' at Disney's New Park," *Wall Street Journal*, March 12, 2002, p. B1; Angela Doland, "EuroDisney Opens New Cinema Theme Park Outside Paris," *Associated Press Newswires*, March 15, 2002; Richard Verrier, "Disney Looking for Boost in Paris Entertainment," *Los Angeles Times*, March 15, 2002, p. C1; and Jo Wrighton and Bruce Orwall, "Mutual Attraction," *Wall Street Journal*, January 26, 2005, p. A1.

Culture Shock

Interbrew, the Belgian brewing giant, entered the Korean market by purchasing 50 percent of Korea's Oriental Brewing Company. Both sides experienced a degree of culture shock when managers from Belgium and the United States arrived in Korea. The Western managers insisted that the staff speak their minds. The Korean managers, on the other hand, were used to a hierarchical relationship based on respect and unswerving loyalty to the boss. Still, after a bumpy start, the blend of two cultures turned out to be a good thing for the company.[57]

Marketing managers who enter different cultures must learn to cope with a vast array of new cultural cues and expectations as well as to identify which old ones no longer work. Often they experience stress and tension as a result. This effect is commonly called **culture shock**. The authors of *Managing Cultural Differences* offer the following ten tips to deflate the stress and tension of cultural shock:

Culture shock stress and tension resulting from coping with new cultural cues and expectations

- ▶ Be culturally prepared.
- ▶ Be aware of local communication complexities.
- ▶ Mix with the host nationals.
- ▶ Be creative and experimental.
- ▶ Be culturally sensitive.

- ▶ Recognize complexities in host cultures.
- ▶ See yourself as a culture bearer.
- ▶ Be patient, understanding, and accepting of yourself and your hosts.
- ▶ Be realistic in your expectations.
- ▶ Accept the challenge of intercultural experiences.[58]

CONCLUSION

In this chapter, we explored a small sample of the wide variety of cultural and social influences that can affect international marketing operations.

It is essential for international marketers to avoid cultural bias in dealing with business operations in more than one culture. As the president of a large industrial company in Osaka, Japan, once noted, our cultures are 80 percent identical and 20 percent different. The successful businessperson is the one who can identify the differences and deal with them. Of course, this is a very difficult task, and few executives ever reach the stage where they can claim to be completely sensitive to cultural differences.

How do cultural considerations affect your marketing plans? Continue with your *Country Market Report* on our website (college.hmco.com/business/).

QUESTIONS FOR DISCUSSION

1. How might the educational systems of the United States, England, and Germany affect the marketing of banking services to young adults aged sixteen to twenty-two?

2. You have been asked to attend a meeting with Belgian, Turkish, and Japanese colleagues to develop a global plan for a new aftershave. Using the Hofstede scores for these countries, discuss the challenges you would face in the meeting. Assume your native culture.

3. What effects might the Internet have on cultural differences?

4. Why do you think food is such a culturally sensitive product?

5. When a firm enters a new market, how can managers "learn" the culture?

CASE 3.1

Banning Barbie

The Institute for Intellectual Development of Children and Young Adults has declared Barbie a cultural threat to Iran. The tall, blond, blue-eyed doll represents the American woman who never wants to get old or pregnant. She wears makeup and indecent clothes. She drinks champagne in the company of boyfriend doll Ken. To replace Barbie, the Institute has designed Sara. Sara has darker skin and black hair, and she wears the traditional floor-length chador.

Since its Islamic Revolution over 25 years ago Iran has been particularly wary of Western influences. In the mid-1990s, a Coca-Cola factory was shut down for "promoting American culture." A call to ban Barbie is not popular with all Iranians, however. Toy-store owners think Barbie is about business, not culture, and many moderate Iranians oppose attempts to protect national culture by force and prohibitions.

In the Arab world at large, Barbie remains the most popular doll among affluent consumers, but she is about to face new competition. The proposed Leila doll will attempt to give Arab girls a feeling of pride in belonging to their own culture. Leila will have black eyes and hair and will look about ten years old. Her wardrobe options will include Western outfits as well as traditional dresses from the various Arab regions, such as Egypt, Syria, and the Gulf states.

Both Sara and Leila will have brother dolls, not boyfriend dolls. The idea of having a boyfriend is a concept not acceptable to most Middle Eastern families. Sara's brother, Dara, is dressed in the coat and turban of a Muslim cleric or mullah. Arab children have suggested grandparent dolls for Leila.

The Arab League has sponsored feasibility studies to interest private-sector investors in producing Leila and her family. However, both Leila and Sara will enjoy government subsidies.

Currently, 90 percent of toys in the Middle East are imported. High tariffs on imported raw materials have made it cheaper to import toys than to produce them locally. Sara and Leila will sell at about $10, whereas Barbie commands between $30 and $150 in the capital cities of Cairo and Tehran.

In the United States, competition was also emerging. A manufacturer in Livonia, Michigan, introduced a Razanne doll for Muslim Americans. The doll's creator claimed that the main message of the doll was that what matters is what's inside you, not how you look. Razanne had the body of a preteen and came in three types: fair-skinned blond, olive-skinned with black hair, and black skin with black hair. Her clothing was modest but her aspirations were those of "a modern Muslim woman." For example, there was a Muslim Girl Scout Razanne and the manufacturers were discussing the possibility of an Astronaut Razanne.

Discussion Questions

1. Why is Barbie popular in the Middle East?
2. Should Muslim countries ban Barbie? Why or why not?
3. Should local producers receive subsidies for making Sara and Leila? Why or why not?
4. Where might Razanne be exported? What cultural adaptations might be necessary to market this doll overseas?

Sources: Hasan Mrove, "Arabs to Make Their Own Decently Dressed, Dark Haired, Dark Eyed Barbies," *Deutsche Presse-Agentur*, June 16, 1999; "Toy Shop Owners in Tehran Dismiss Barbie Threat," *Deutsche Presse-Agentur*, October 23, 1996; "Iran's Sara Challenges Barbie Doll," *Toronto Star*, October 28, 1996, p. A2; Tarek El-Tablawy, "Doll Offers Modest Image for Muslim Girls," *Associated Press*, October 8, 2003.

CASE 3.2

Sacred Work, Sacred Leisure

Unlike their counterparts in many countries, employers in the United States are not required by law to provide paid vacations for their employees. In fact, American culture in general appears suspicious of leisure. Some attribute this to the Protestant work ethic. Many Americans fill their free time with intellectually or physically demanding hobbies or *volunteer work*. Even on vacation, Americans stay in touch with the workplace via their cellular phones and laptop computers.

Europeans, on the other hand, hold leisure in high regard. A French law passed in 2000 gave France the shortest workweek in Europe. Companies with more than twenty employees were required to cut work hours from 39 to 35 per week. Besides creating more leisure time for workers, this move was expected to help ease unemployment. In Germany, however, longer workweeks may soon be the norm. To Germans, prosperity once meant less work and more leisure time. However, a low birthrate has resulted in fewer workers supporting more and more retired Germans in the generous state pension system. Germans in the workforce may soon have to work longer hours to support the retirees.

The restful German Sunday is also under attack. Sunday is designated "a day for spiritual reflection" in the German constitution. This custom results in a ban on Sunday shopping. Since the reunification of Germany in 1990, former East Germans who grew up in a largely atheistic society have waged war on Sunday closings. East German cities routinely exploit loopholes in the law to allow stores to stay open; one loophole that is commonly invoked allows sales to tourists. Department stores in Berlin now welcome tens of thousands of Sunday shoppers, using the argument that their products could be of interest to tourists. Union leaders, bent on protecting leisure time for their members, have joined churches in denouncing this trend.

If Germans may soon work longer hours, Japanese may soon work less. Japanese workers take an average of only 9 vacation days a year. However, many have been reconsidering the value of leisure since their prime minister suffered a stroke brought on by overwork. Japan has seen a sharp increase in suicides and *karoshi*, or death caused by overwork. The secretary-general of Japan's ruling party made longer vacations a campaign pledge. Japan has also introduced "Happy Mondays," creating longer weekends by switching certain public holidays from Saturdays to Mondays. The government hopes that more holidays will deliver the added bonus of encouraging Japanese to spend more money in pursuit of leisure and thus boost the economy.

Discussion Questions

1. What cultural factors influence a society's attitudes toward work and leisure?
2. How can different attitudes toward leisure affect the marketing of products?

Sources: William Drozdiak, "German Shoppers Seek to Bring Down Another Wall," *Gazette* (Montreal), p. B3; Andrew McCathie, "A Revolution Takes Hold in German Retailing," *Deutsche Presse-Agentur*, July 20, 1999; and "A Great Time to Work," *The Economist*, August 6, 1999.

NOTES

1. Kathy Chen, "Acquired Taste," *Wall Street Journal*, February 28, 2003, p. A1.
2. "Give Me a Big Mac But Hold the Beef," *Guardian*, December 28, 2000, p. 4.
3. "Cultural Explanations: The Man in the Baghdad Café," *The Economist*, November 9, 1996, pp. 23–26.
4. Francis Fukuyama, *Trust: The Social Virtues and the Creation of Prosperity* (New York: Free Press, 1996), p. 6.
5. David Murphy, "Selling Christmas in China," *Wall Street Journal*, December 24, 2002, p. B1.
6. Hugh Pope, "A New Holiday Hit in Muslim Turkey," *Wall Street Journal*, December 24, 2003, p. A1.
7. Farnaz Fassihi, "As Authorities Frown, Valentine's Day Finds Place in Iran's Heart," *Wall Street Journal*, February 12, 2004, p. A1.
8. Michael Arndt, "Where's the Beef? Everywhere," *Business Week*, June 4, 2001, p. 14.
9. Joel Greenberg, "Who in Israel Loves the Orthodox? Their Grocers," *New York Times*, October 17, 1997, p. 4.
10. Barry Shlachter, "A Matzo Monopoly No More," *Houston Chronicle*, April 8, 2001.
11. Shahidan Shafie and Osman Mohamed, "'Halal'—The Case of the Malaysian Muslim Consumers' Quest for Peace of Mind," *Proceedings of the American Marketing Association* (Winter 2002), p. 118.
12. Kang Siew Li, "Coca-Cola's Global Ramadhan Commercial," *Business Times*, *The New York Straits Times Press*, January 14, 1998, p. 17.
13. Anna Slater, "Indian Monsoon Drenches the Land; Marketers Drench the Consumer," *Wall Street Journal*, July 24, 2003, p. A12.
14. Henry Sender, "Foreign Car Makers Make Mark in India," *Asian Wall Street Journal*, August 22, 2000, p. 1.
15. "U.S. Company Criticized for Misusing Images of Indian Hindu Deities," *BBC Monitoring*, November 18, 2000.
16. John Pomfret, "80-Year-Old Cashes In on Famous Name," *Seattle Times*, August 25, 1998, p. A13.
17. "Trouble Brewing," *Newsweek*, July 19, 1999, p. 40.
18. Karin Esterhammer, "Fall Festivals Fill Japan's Streets with Pageantry," *Los Angeles Times*, June 10, 2001, p. L6.
19. Sheryl Wu Dunn, "Korean Women Still Feel Demands to Bear a Son," *New York Times International*, January 14, 1997, p. A3.
20. Fuq-in Bian, John R. Logan, and Yanjie Bian, "Intergenerational Relations in Urban China," *Demography* 35, no. 1 (February 1998), pp. 119–122.
21. Simon Saulkin, "Chinese Walls," *Management Today* (September 1996), pp. 62–68.
22. Fukuyama, *Trust*, pp. 62, 98.
23. "Teaching Business How to Train," *Business Week/ Reinvesting America*, 1992.
24. Paul Osterman, "Reforming Employment and Training Programs," *USA Today*, January 1, 1999, p. 20.
25. "U.S. Pupils Short on Basics, Study Finds," *International Herald Tribune*, May 6, 1994, p. 3.
26. "Math, Physics Scores in U.S. Come Up Short," *Pittsburgh Post-Gazette*, February 25, 1998, p. A1.
27. "Baffled: Reading Comprehension," *The Economist*, December 9, 1995, p. 27.
28. Joop Hartog, "Behind the Veil of Human Capital," *OECD Observer*, January 1999, p. 38.
29. Scheherazade Daneshkhu, "Poor Communication and Bureaucracy Make Eastern Europe Frustrating," *Financial Times*, September 9, 1996, p. 12.
30. Edward T. Hall, *The Dance of Life* (New York: Anchor Press), p. 12.
31. "Why Is Jack a Dull Boy?" *The Economist*, January 5, 1996, p. 112.
32. "Business: Undue Diligence," *The Economist*, August 24, 1996, pp. 47–48.
33. Christopher Rhoads, "German Labor Talks to Focus on Hours," *Wall Street Journal*, January 20, 2004, p. A10.
34. Jo Johnson and Ralph Atkins, "Workers at French Plant Vote for a Longer Week," *Financial Times*, July 20, 2004, p. 1.
35. K. Sivakumar and Cheryl Nakata, "The Stampede Towards Hofstede's Framework: Avoiding the Sample Design Pit in Cross-Cultural Research," *Journal of International Business Studies* 32, no. 3 (2001), p. 555.
36. Geert Hofstede, *Culture and Organizations: Software of the Mind* (New York: McGraw-Hill, 1991), p. 23.
37. Ibid., p. 50.
38. Ibid., p. 123.
39. K. Sivakumar and Cheryl Nakata, "The Stampede Toward Hofstede's Framework: Avoiding the Sample Design Pit in Cross-Cultural Research," *Journal of International Business Studies* 32, no. 3 (2001), pp. 555–574.
40. Tomasz Lenartowicz, James P. Johnson, and Carolyn T. White, "The Neglect of Intracountry Cultural Variation in International Management Research," *Journal of Business Research* 56, no. 12 (2003), pp. 999–1008.
41. Samuel P. Huntington, *Who Are We?: The Challenges to America's National Identity* (New York: Simon and Schuster, 2004), pp. 365–366.
42. Ronald Inglehart and Wayne E. Baker, "Modernization, Culture Change, and the Persistence of Traditional Values," *American Sociological Review* 65 (February 2000), p. 31.
43. Jean-Claude Usunier, *Marketing Across Cultures* (New York: Prentice-Hall, 2000), pp. 416–420.
44. Harry C. Triandis, "The Many Dimensions of Culture," *Academy of Management Executive* 18, no. 1 (2004), p. 90.
45. Judith Bowman, "Before Going Overseas, Be Ready: Know the Protocol," *Mass High Tech*, April 26, 199, p. 31.
46. Valerie Reitman, "Japanese Workers Take Classes on the Grim Art of Grinning," *Los Angeles Times*, April 8, 1999, p. E4.

47. "Se Habla Ingles," *Wall Street Journal*, December 30, 2004, p. A8.
48. "English and Electronic Commerce: The Default Language," *The Economist*, May 15, 1999, p. 67.
49. "It's Barbara Calling," *The Economist*, April 29, 2000.
50. Kevin Voigt, "Japanese Firms Want English Competency," *Wall Street Journal*, June 11, 2001, p. B7.
51. Kathryn Kranhold, Dan Bilefsky, Matthew Karnitschnig, and Ginny Parker, "Lost in Translation?" *Wall Street Journal*, May 18, 2004, p. B1.
52. Paula Prada and Bruce Orwall, "A Certain 'Je Ne Sais Quoi' at Disney's New Park," *Wall Street Journal*, March 12, 2002, p. B1.
53. "Big Mac's Counter Attack," *The Economist*, November 13, 1993, p. 71.
54. Elizabeth Brent, "Japan's Deep Recession Spells Big Changes for Branches of U.S. Brands," *Nation's Restaurant News*, February 15, 1999, pp. 1–5.
55. Phillip R. Harris and Robert T. Moran, *Managing Cultural Differences*, 2nd ed. (Houston: Gulf, 1987), pp. 212–215.
56. Robert Frank, "Big Boy's Adventures in Thailand," *Wall Street Journal*, April 12, 2000, p. B1.
57. Michael Schuman, "Foreign Flavor," *Wall Street Journal*, July 24, 2000, p. A1.
58. Philip R. Harris and Robert T. Moran, *Managing Cultural Differences*, 4th ed. (Houston, TX: Gulf, 1996), pp. 218–223.

4 POLITICAL AND REGULATORY CLIMATE

OIL-RICH VENEZUELA was once considered an attractive Latin American market. However, when Venezuelans elected Lieutenant Colonel Hugo Chavez president, he threatened to default on Venezuela's foreign debt and to reassert government control over much of the economy. The new president overhauled the country's constitution and judiciary, centralizing more power in the presidency. The response of foreign businesses was immediate. The next year foreign investment fell 40 percent. Eli Lilly and Honda were among the multinational firms that closed operations in Venezuela.[1] Across the globe, Exxon found itself embroiled in a guerrilla war between separatists and the Indonesian government. After sustaining twenty-eight attacks in only 1 month, Exxon shut down a natural gas plant when it came under mortar fire.[2]

This chapter identifies the political forces that influence global marketing operations. These forces include both the host and home governments of international firms. Governments both support and restrict business as they seek to achieve a variety of goals from self-preservation to protecting their nation's cultural identity. International marketers must also be aware of special-interest

LEARNING OBJECTIVES

After studying this chapter, you should be able to

▶ List and explain the political motivations behind government actions that promote or restrict international marketing.

▶ Identify pressure groups that affect international marketing.

▶ Discuss specific government actions salient to international marketing, such as boycotts and takeovers.

▶ List and compare the four basic legal traditions that marketers encounter worldwide.

▶ Cite examples illustrating how national laws can vary and change.

▶ Differentiate between the steps involved in managing political risk and those involved in planning for regulatory change.

groups that exert pressure on governments with respect to an increasing number of issues from environmental concerns to human rights.

Dealing simultaneously with several political and regulatory systems makes the job of the global marketing executive a complex one. These factors often precipitate problems that increase the level of risk in the international marketplace. Global companies have learned to cope with such complexities by developing strategies that address the more predictable regulatory changes and the less predictable political risks. These strategies are explained at the end of the chapter.

HOST COUNTRY POLITICAL CLIMATE

The rapidly changing nature of the international political scene is evident to anyone who regularly reads, listens to, or watches the various news media. Political upheavals and changes in government policy occur daily and can have an enormous impact on international business. For the executive, this means constant adjustments to exploit new opportunities and minimize losses.

Besides the international company, the principal players in the political arena are the host country governments and the home country governments. Sometimes transnational bodies or agencies such as the EU or the WTO can be involved. Within a national market, the interactions of all these groups result in a political climate that may positively or negatively affect the operations of an international business. The difficulty for the global company stems from the firm being subject to all these forces at the same time. The situation is further complicated by the fact that companies maintain operations in many countries and hence must simultaneously manage many sets of political relationships.

In this section of the chapter, we discuss the political climate of host countries. Any country that contains an operational unit (marketing, sales, manufacturing, finance, or research and development) of an international company can be defined as a **host country**. International companies deal with many different host countries, each with its own political climate. These political climates are largely determined by the motivations and actions of host country governments and local interest groups.

Host country a country that contains an operational unit (marketing, sales, manufacturing, finance, or R&D) of an international company

Political Motivations

Businesses operate in a country at the discretion of its government, which can encourage or discourage foreign businesses through a variety of measures. The host government plays the principal role in host countries in initiating and implementing policies regarding the operation, conduct, and ownership of businesses. Today more than 190 nations have been accepted as members of the United Nations, a figure that gives some indication of the large number of independent countries that exist at this time. Although each government may give the impression of acting as a single and homogeneous force, governments in most countries represent a collection of various, and at times conflicting, interests. Governments are sharply influenced by the prevailing political philosophy, local pressure groups, and the government's own self-interest. All of these factors lead to government actions that international companies must recognize and actively incorporate into their marketing strategies. Of prime importance is the marketer's ability to understand the rationale behind government actions.

To understand how government decisions are made, and how business and government are related in a particular country, it is helpful to examine the prevailing political structure. Is it a democracy, a dictatorship, or a monarchy? One way to classify governments is by the degree of representation of the populace in government. Democratic or parliamentary governments hold regular elections so that government policies better reflect the will of the people. Over the past decade, the world has seen a considerable shift toward democratic government. This was most apparent in Eastern Europe, where communist governments were swept away in the 1989 political upheaval. However, changes in

Latin America have been equally significant. In the early 1980s, true democracies existed in only a few countries, Venezuela and Costa Rica among them. Now, most military dictatorships in that region have been supplanted, and democratic governments hold sway in nearly all Latin American countries.

Whether in a democracy or in a dictatorship, governmental behavior makes sense only if there is a rational basis for the leaders' actions and decisions. As many political scientists have pointed out, these actions usually flow from the government's interpretation of its own self-interest. This self-interest, often called national interest, may be expected to differ from nation to nation, but it typically includes the following goals:

▶ *Self-preservation.* This is the primary goal of any entity, including states and governments.

▶ *Security.* To the greatest extent possible, each government seeks to maximize its opportunity for continued existence and to minimize threats from the outside.

▶ *Prosperity.* Improved living conditions for the country's citizens are an important and constant concern for any government. Even dictatorships base their claim to legitimacy in part on their ability to deliver enhanced prosperity.

▶ *Prestige.* Most governments or countries seek this either as an end in itself or as a means of reaching other objectives.

▶ *Ideology.* Governments frequently protect or promote an ideology in combination with other goals.

▶ *Cultural identity.* Governments often intervene to protect the country's cultural identity.[3]

The goals just cited are frequently the source of government actions either encouraging or limiting the business activities of international companies see Table 4.1). Many executives erroneously believe that such limiting actions occur

| | GOAL | | | | | |
Action	Self-Preservation	Security	Prosperity	Prestige	Ideology	Cultural Identity
"Buy local"	X	X	X			
Nontariff barriers	X		X			
Subsidies	X		X	X		
Operating restrictions	X	X				X
Local content			X			
Ownership conditions		X			X	X
Boycotts					X	
Takeovers	X	X	X		X	

TABLE 4.1 Host Government Goals and Policy Actions

X = Likelihood of using given action to accomplish that goal.

largely in developing countries. On the contrary, there are many examples of restrictive government actions in the most developed countries. Such restrictive behavior most often occurs when a government perceives the attainment of its own goals to be threatened by the activities or existence of a body beyond its total control, namely the foreign subsidiary of a multinational company.

National Sovereignty and the Goal of Self-Preservation

A country's self-preservation is most threatened when its national sovereignty is at stake. **Sovereignty** is the complete control exercised within a given geographic area, including the ability to pass laws and regulations and the power to enforce them. Governments or countries frequently view the existence of sovereignty as critical to achieving the goal of self-preservation. Although sovereignty may be threatened by a number of factors, it is the relationship between a government's attempt to protect its sovereignty and a company's efforts to achieve its own goals that are of primary interest to us.

Subsidiaries or branch offices of international companies can be controlled or influenced by decisions made at headquarters, beyond the physical or legal control of the host government. Therefore, foreign companies are frequently viewed as a threat to the host country's national sovereignty. (It is important to recognize in this context that *perceptions* on the part of host countries are typically more important than actual facts.)

Many attempts at restricting foreign firms are now discouraged under agreements established by the World Trade Organization (WTO). Still, these agreements exclude a number of sensitive areas. Countries often limit foreign ownership of newspapers, television, and radio stations for reasons of preserving national sovereignty. They fear that if a foreign company controlled these media, it could influence public opinion and limit national sovereignty. For example, the head of the Mexican entertainment company Grupo Televisa SA had to consider becoming a U.S. citizen in order to increase his company's participation in Univision Communication, the number one Spanish-language television network in the United States.[4]

The Need for National Security

It is natural for a government to try to protect its country's borders from outside forces. The military typically becomes a country's principal tool to prevent outside interference. Consequently, many concerns about national security involve a country's armed forces or related agencies. Other areas sensitive to national security are aspects of a country's infrastructure, its essential resources, utilities, and the supply of crucial raw materials, particularly oil. To ensure their security, some host governments strive for greater control of these sensitive areas and resist any influence that foreign firms may gain over such industries.

The protection of national security interests such as defense and telecommunications through regulations requiring local sourcing is declining. This trend has been influenced by two factors. First, it is not economical for each country to have its own defense and telecommunications industry. The high cost of research and development means that in many cases, the small local

Sovereignty supremacy of authority or rule free from external control

defense supplier will have inferior technologies. Connecticut-based Sikorsky had supplied Marine One, the U.S. president's helicopter fleet, since 1957, but in 2005 lost the contract to Lockheed, which proposed to source key parts from European partners. Some members of Congress criticized the decision, citing security concerns with using non-U.S. suppliers, but the decision was made to buy the most technologically advanced design.[5]

Fostering National Prosperity

Another key goal for governments is to ensure the material prosperity of their citizens. In fact, a major opposition party in Macedonia calls itself the Party for Democratic Prosperity.[6] Prosperity is usually expressed in national income or gross national product (GNP), and comparisons between countries are frequently made in terms of per-capita income or GNP per capita. (Comparisons are also made on the basis of GNP adjusted by purchasing-power parity to reflect comparable standards of living.) However prosperity is measured, most governments strive to provide full employment and an increasing standard of living. Part of this goal is to enact an economic policy that will stimulate the economic output of businesses active within their borders. International companies that set up production facilities in a host country can assume an important role, because they can add to a host country's GNP and thus enhance its income.

Many host governments also try to improve the nation's prosperity by increasing its exports. Particularly in Europe, heads of governments often engage in state visits to encourage major export transactions. Political observers often note that both the French president and the German chancellor spend a substantial amount of their state visits on business and trade affairs, more so than is typically the case for the president of the United States. Attracting international companies with a high export potential to set up operations in their countries is of critical interest to host governments. Frequently, such companies can expect special treatment or subsidies, especially from governments in developing countries. For example, Egypt offered attractive tax holidays to foreign investors who undertook export-oriented projects, and Mexico exempted foreign investors from local-partner requirements if their projects were totally for export.

How does the United States promote exports? Check out the export promotion links on our website (college.hmco.com/business/).

Enhancing Prestige

When Olusegun Obasanjo was elected president of Nigeria, he inherited a decision to host the next All-Africa Games. Nigeria had recently rescheduled its foreign debt. By hosting the games, the Nigerian government had accrued building costs for a new stadium that exceeded $340 million, twice what the government planned to spend on health care for one year.[7]

The pursuit of prestige has many faces. Whereas the governments of some countries choose to support team sports or host international events to enhance national prestige, other governments choose to influence the business climate for the same reason. Having a national airline may give rise to national prestige for a developing country. Other countries may support industries that achieve leadership in certain technologies, such as telecommunications, electronics, robotics, or aerospace.

China's interest in hosting the 2008 Olympics was motivated by a desire to enhance the country's international prestige.

Promoting Ideology

For nearly 50 years North and South Korea have been technically at war. In the 1950s, North Korea was the richer and more industrialized of the two Koreas. North Korea pursued the ideology of *juche,* or self-reliance.[8] Today it is South Korea that is by far the wealthier and more industrialized country.

Governments often attempt to promote ideology. In doing so, they affect business in a variety of ways. Throughout most of the twentieth century, communist governments disallowed private enterprise. Trade with noncommunist Western countries was strongly discouraged. Like North Korea, the Soviet Union paid a high price for its desire to be free of the capitalist world. Rather than taking advantage of licensing technology that was developed in the West, the Soviets followed the more expensive route of attempting to develop their own parallel technologies.

In the 1950s and 1960s, many developing countries adopted the ideology of nonalignment. In practice, this meant strengthening trade and business ties with China and the Soviet Union in order to be less dependent on Europe and the United States. Egypt under President Nasser was a leader in this movement. When President Sadat succeeded Nasser, he sought to diminish his country's growing dependence on the Soviet Union. He sought to establish a closer relationship with the United States and personally met with CEOs from Fortune 500 companies to ask them to invest in Egypt.

For seven decades the Institutional Revolutionary Party (PRI) ruled Mexico, until Vicente Fox of the National Action Party (PAN) took office as president. The PRI had instituted many restrictions on multinational firms. President Fox, a former CEO of Coca-Cola in Mexico, aligned himself with a more liberal and outward-looking economic ideology that encouraged free trade. His party proved especially popular among younger and more urban Mexicans.

The role that ideology plays in communist China seems ambiguous from the point of view of foreign firms doing business there today. China reopened trade and investment relations with the West in the early 1970s. In the past 30 years, the country has undergone significant market liberalization. General Motors and Starbucks operate with and alongside China's traditional state-owned industries. Some state-owned enterprises have been privatized. In other words, they have been sold, wholly or in part, to private owners. Chinese firms must now generate profits or face the specter of new bankruptcy laws. Still the Chinese government insists that these changes do not compromise communist ideology.

Protecting Cultural Identity

With the global village becoming a reality, one of the major effects on countries is in the area of culture. Governments can sometimes resist what they believe to be a foreign assault on their culture. For example, both Iran and Venezuela have at one time attempted to outlaw foreign brand names, requiring international marketers to establish names for their products in Persian and Spanish, respectively.

Whereas most countries once were able to determine broadcast policy on their own, control over broadcasting, and therefore culture, is now perceived to be in the hands of a few large, mostly U.S. firms. These firms are most visible in entertainment, the production and distribution of movies, TV programs, videos, and music recordings. Even more important have been the roles of TV companies through the use of satellite transmission. As we saw in Chapter 3, this massive invasion of foreign cultural products has prompted a negative reaction among certain European governments. Led by the French, they have resisted an effort to open up European markets to more foreign movies and TV programs. Recently, the Internet has become an even greater challenge. China bans access to a number of websites, ranging from those carrying foreign news reports to those displaying sexually explicit pictures. Cuba and Iran also restrict access to certain foreign websites.[9]

Host Country Pressure Groups

When the Chinese government prepared to sell stock in a newly formed subsidiary of its mammoth state-owned oil company, it targeted large investors and public pension funds in the United States. However, it met with opposition from several quarters. The AFL-CIO, a major labor interest group, persuaded many key investors to issue statements that they would not participate in the sale. Religious and conservative groups complained that the Chinese parent firm was involved in the Sudan, a country condemned by the United Nations for allowing slavery and alleged to be supporting terrorists. Environmental groups feared that U.S. investment dollars would support environmentally damaging oil projects in Tibet.[10]

As this case illustrates, host country governments are not the only forces able to influence the political climate and affect the operations of foreign companies. Other groups have a stake in the treatment of companies and in political and economic decisions that indirectly affect foreign businesses. In most instances, they cannot act unilaterally. Thus they try to pressure either the host government or the foreign businesses to conform to their views. Such pressure groups exist in most countries and may be made up of either ad hoc groups or established associations. Political parties are common pressure groups, although they frequently cannot exert much influence outside the government. Parties generally associated with a nationalist point of view frequently advocate the adoption of policies restricting foreign companies.

Some of the most potent pressure groups are found within the local business community itself. These include local industry associations and occasionally local unions. When local companies are threatened by foreign competition, they frequently petition the government to help by placing restrictions on the foreign competitors. In China, local newsprint factories were being hurt by cheap newsprint from the United States, Canada, and South Korea. In response, the Chinese government assessed a 55–78 percent tax on U.S., Canadian, and South Korean newsprint.[11] In the wake of the terrorist attacks of September 11, 2001, Pakistan became a potentially critical U.S. ally in the Afghan war. The Pakistani government consequently asked the United States to reduce tariffs on textiles from Pakistan. However, officials at the American Textile Manufacturing Institute moved immediately to stop any possible cuts in tariffs that could hurt U.S. textile firms.[12]

HOST GOVERNMENT ACTIONS

Governments promulgate laws and take actions in a variety of ways to advance their agendas. In Chapter 2 we reviewed a number of government actions that affect a firm's ability to transfer products across borders. Many government actions, such as those affecting exchange rates, can indirectly affect international markets. Other actions can have a more direct impact on a firm's ability to access a foreign market and operate successfully. Some of these actions are discussed next.

Government Subsidies

Government subsidies represent free gifts that host governments dispense in the hope that the overall benefits to the economy will far exceed such grants. They are popular instruments used to attract foreign investment. Governments are especially inclined to use direct or indirect subsidies to encourage firms that will be major exporters. Exporters bring multiple benefits, providing employment and increasing national revenue through export sales.

An example of a direct subsidy is a government's paying $1 for each pair of shoes to help a local producer compete more effectively in foreign markets. An indirect subsidy is the result of a subsidy on a component of the exported product. For example, a government may provide a subsidy on the electricity used to manufacture tents that are then exported. Or it might subsidize research in the pharmaceutical industry. WTO agreements outlaw direct export subsidies as well as local-content subsidies that are contingent on the use of domestic over imported goods. Indirect subsidies are usually not prohibited. However, they remain a contentious issue between trading nations.

Ownership Restrictions

Host governments sometimes pursue the policy of requiring that local nationals become part owners of foreign subsidiaries operating within their borders. These governments believe that this guarantees that multinationals will contribute to the local economy. Restrictions can range from an outright prohibition of full foreign ownership to selective policies aimed at key industries.

India has used ownership conditions extensively. India's Foreign Exchange Regulation Act of 1973 stipulated that foreign ownership could not exceed 40 percent. International Business Machines Corporation (IBM) decided to leave rather than give up majority control over its subsidiary. Coca-Cola also decided to leave rather than share its secret formula with Indian partners. However, when changes in the government brought a softening of India's stance, the country tentatively began to court firms. Coke negotiated a return to India without revealing its cola formula.

In many ways, the Indian case reflects the patterns of many countries. The 1960s and 1970s saw a tightening of the control over foreign ownership. More recently, the trend has been toward investment liberalization. Most countries now recognize that foreign investment provides significant benefits to the nation, such as employment, technology, and marketing know-how. This new trend has brought the elimination of many prior restrictions, such as those related to ownership. Nonetheless, ownership restriction persists in some markets. In the wake of U.S. occupation, many Iraqi businesses feared that large corporate investors from abroad would take over whole sectors of the economy and crowd out local competition. Consequently, they called for investment rules similar to those in the United Arab Emirates, which require that domestic ventures be at least 51 percent locally owned.[13]

Operating Conditions

Governments establish and enforce many regulations that affect the environment in which businesses operate. Host countries control firms in the areas of product design and packaging, pricing, advertising, sales promotion, and distribution. Some of these restrictions, and strategies to deal with them, are included in later chapters that deal directly with the marketing mix. Where such operating restrictions apply to all firms, domestic and international, the competitive threat is lessened. However, companies may still find restrictions a problem when the way they have to operate varies from that to which they are accustomed.

Where operating restrictions apply to foreign or international firms only, the result will be a lessening of competitiveness, and companies should seriously consider these constraints before entering a market. One such restriction involves work permits or visas for foreign managers or technicians whom multinational firms may wish to employ in their various national subsidiaries. Any citizen of an EU country is free to work in any other EU country, but visa constraints remain an operational hindrance in most of the world.

Some host governments impose local content requirements on products or services sold in their countries. For product-based companies, local-content laws mean that some part of the manufacturing must be done in the host country. Such restrictions are often applied to encourage the use of local suppliers. Local-content requirements also appear in regional agreements such as NAFTA and MERCOSUR to ensure that products granted exemption from tariffs are indeed primarily produced in the region.

Sometimes operating conditions are affected by what governments fail to do. Kidnappings for ransom have risen in Latin America. Mexico City has become particularly notorious for kidnappings, and foreign companies can find it difficult to recruit expatriate managers for their Mexico City operations. In any case, operating costs may increase in these countries as a result of the need to provide employees with heightened security.

What countries are the most dangerous and why? Check out *Current Travel Warnings* on our website (college.hmco.com/business/).

Boycotts of Firms

Government boycotts can be directed at companies of certain origin or companies that have engaged in transactions with political enemies. Boycotts tend to shut some companies completely out of a given market. For example, the United States imposed a two-year ban on imports from Norinco, a major Chinese defense and industrial manufacturer, because of the company's alleged sale of ballistic-missile technology to Iran. The Norinco boycott made it illegal for U.S. companies to purchase products from the company or any of its many subsidiaries.[14]

One of the most publicized boycott campaigns was the 50-year boycott waged by Arab countries against firms that engaged in business activity with Israel. The boycott was administered by the Arab League. Ford Motor Company was one U.S. company placed on the Arab boycott list when it supplied an Israeli car assembler with flat-packed cars for local assembly. Xerox was placed on the list after financing a documentary on Israel, and the Coca-Cola Company was added to the boycott list for having licensed an Israeli bottler.

The Arab boycott became less relevant with the changing political situation in the Middle East. The last major fighting between Israel and the Arab states took place in 1973, and since then Egypt has signed a peace treaty with Israel. By the 1990s, many Arab countries only selectively enforced the boycott. After the Iraq conflict and Desert Storm, many more countries abandoned it. Coca-Cola returned to the Arab soft-drinks market and Coca-Cola attained a 33 percent share of the Arab Gulf's $1.2 billion market.[15]

Takeover a host-government-initiated action that results in a loss of ownership or direct control by a foreign company

Expropriation the formal seizure of a business operation, with or without the payment of compensation

Takeovers

Though relatively rare, no action a host government can take is more dramatic than a takeover. Broadly defined, **takeovers** are any host-government-initiated actions that result in a loss of ownership or direct control by the foreign company. There are several types of takeovers. **Expropriation** is a formal, or legal,

WORLD BEAT 4.1

Is the Arab Boycott Dead?

EVEN IF ARAB GOVERNMENTS fail to enforce the formal boycott of Israel and firms sympathetic to Israel, this doesn't stop Arab consumers from organizing grassroots boycotts. American firms are often targets because of perceived U.S. support of Israel. These impromptu consumer boycotts have been a way for Arab consumers, many living under nondemocratic regimes, to vent their frustration with the slow progress of peace negotiations between Israel and the Palestinians.

In the United Arab Emirates, supporters of a boycott distributed a list of American brands and firms to avoid. In Egypt, boycott victims included the perennial targets McDonald's and Coca-Cola. But even Pepsi—a longtime favorite in the Arab World from the days of the Arab boycott against Coke—failed to escape unscathed. A chain message circulated among Egyptian high school students claimed that Pepsi stood for Pay Every Penny to Support Israel and called for a ban on the soft drink. Fliers were distributed asking consumers to stop eating at Pizza Hut and to reject American products such as Gillette razors, Nike shoes, and Marlboro cigarettes.

Americana Foods—an Egyptian company that owns franchises for Pizza Hut, KFC, Baskin-Robbins, Hardee's, TGI Friday's, and Subway—saw its sales plunge 30 percent. Procter & Gamble's top-selling detergent, Ariel, saw sales collapse, partly because the brand shared its name with Ariel Sharon, the leader of Israel's Likud Party. Even U.K.-based Sainsbury's saw its supermarkets in Cairo subject to violent attacks as a consequence of the firm's alleged connections with Israel.

McDonald's responded to the situation with leaflets stressing its local Egyptian ownership of outlets and its employment of 2,000 Egyptians. Sales soon recovered. Outlets of A&W, Chili's, and Radio Shack displayed Palestinian flags. Coca-Cola sponsored Egypt's most popular soccer team as well as the Palestinian national soccer team. Sainsbury's took to playing Koranic music in its supermarket aisles and published an advertisement signed by 4,800 Egyptian employees stating that the company did not support Israel.

Sources: "Cairene Shoppers' Intifada," *The Economist*, November 4, 2000; Simon Bowers, "Protests Force Sainsbury Out of Egypt," *Guardian*, April 10, 2001; and James Cox, "Firms Say Arab Boycott Sinking," *USA Today*, June 4, 2001, p. B05.

---

seizure of an operation with or without the payment of compensation. Even when compensation is paid, there are often concerns about the adequacy of the amount, the timeliness of the payment, and the form of payment. **Confiscation** is expropriation without any compensation. The term **domestication** is used to describe the limiting of certain economic activities to local citizens. This can involve a takeover by compensated expropriation, confiscation, or forced sale. Governments may also domesticate an industry by merely requiring the transfer of partial ownership to nationals or by requiring that nationals be promoted to higher levels of management. If an international company cannot or will not meet these requirements, however, it may be forced to sell its operations in that country.

Today expropriations have virtually ceased. In fact, since the mid-1970s a reverse trend has emerged. In renewed attempts to encourage foreign investment,

Confiscation expropriation without compensation

Domestication the limitation of certain economic activities to local citizens

countries such as Algeria, Egypt, and Tanzania have considered returning companies to prior foreign owners, or at least allowing these former owners to repurchase them. The British bank Barclays International returned to Egypt, where it had been expropriated 15 years earlier. Like many oil-exporting countries, Saudi Arabia nationalized its energy sector in the 1970s, but it began to reopen the sector in 1999. In 2001 Saudi Arabia named Exxon, the world's largest publicly owned oil company, as operator of a major natural-gas project requiring an investment of $15 billion.[16]

HOME COUNTRY POLITICAL FORCES

Managers of international companies need to be concerned not only about political developments abroad; many developments that take place at home also have a great impact on what a company can do internationally. Political developments in a company's home country tend to affect either the role of the company in general or, more often, some particular aspects of its operations abroad. Consequently, restrictions can be placed on companies not only by host countries but by home countries as well. Therefore, an astute international marketer must be able to monitor political developments both at home and abroad. This section of the chapter explores home country policies and actions directed at international companies.

Home Country Actions

Home countries are essentially guided by the same six interests described earlier in this chapter: self-preservation, national security, prosperity, prestige, ideology, and cultural identity. For example, subsidies, offered by host governments to foreign investors, may also be offered by home governments as well. In general, a home government wishes to have its country's international companies accept its national priorities. As a result, home governments at times look toward international companies to help them achieve political goals.

In the past, home country governments have tried to prevent companies from doing business overseas on ideological, political, or national security grounds. In the extreme, this can result in an embargo on trade with a certain country. The U.S. embargo on trade with Cuba dates back to 1962, following the assumption of power of Fidel Castro. For nearly 40 years, U.S. businesses could not trade with Cuba, and many restrictions still apply today. Another long-running trade embargo imposed by the U.S. government involved Vietnam. Imposed in 1975, this embargo was lifted in 1994. On the other hand, the United States, an ally of Israel, passed legislation forbidding U.S. firms from complying with the Arab boycott. The U.S. government did not want U.S.-based multinational firms to comply with someone else's embargo.

Stolt-Nielsen SA disclosed in its annual report that it paid a $95,000 fine to settle a U.S. investigation concerning its dealings with embargoed Sudan. The firm is one of the world's largest chemical-shipping companies. Although it is registered in Luxembourg, its top shipping executives are based in Greenwich, Connecticut. U.S. sanction laws apply to any foreigner living in the United States as well as the U.S.-based units of foreign companies. Rival companies, such as

Norwegian Odfjell ASA, that don't have executives in the United States can trade freely with countries embargoed by the United States.[17] Other organizations fined for allegedly breaking a U.S. embargo are Chevron Texaco, for trading with Iraq (fined $14,071); Wal-Mart and the New York Yankees, for trading with Cuba (fined $50,000 and $75,000, respectively); Exxon Mobil, for trading with Sudan (fined $50,000); and Fleet Bank, for trading with Iran (fined $41,000).[18]

Unilateral restrictions, those imposed by one country only, put businesses from that country at a competitive disadvantage and are often fought by business interests. Because of this risk to the competitiveness of their businesses, governments prefer to take multilateral actions together with many other countries. Such actions may arise from a group of nations or, increasingly, from the United Nations. The trade embargo by the international community against South Africa was one of the first such actions. As a result of consumer group pressures, many companies had already left South Africa to protest its apartheid regime. However, the embargo affected a wider group of firms in the late 1980s when it was imposed by most countries. When the political situation in South Africa changed and apartheid was abolished, the United States, together with other nations, lifted the embargo. The United States has since been the largest foreign investor in South Africa, some of the largest firms being Dow Chemical, Ford, General Motors, Coca-Cola, and Hyatt.

Other multilateral actions by the international community are the trade sanctions enforced by the United Nations against Iraq as a result of the Gulf War. Another multinational embargo was imposed against Serbia. Although this embargo was partially lifted in 2000, Serbia's access to international funds is still contingent on its continued transition to democracy.

For the latest information on unilateral U.S. actions, check out *U.S. Trade Sanctions and Embargoes* on our website (college.hmco.com/business/).

Home Country Pressure Groups

The kinds of pressures that international companies are subject to in their home countries are frequently different from the types of pressures brought to bear on them abroad. International companies have had to deal with special-interest groups abroad for a long time. The types of special-interest groups found domestically have come into existence only recently. Such groups are usually well organized and tend to get extensive media coverage. They have succeeded in catching many companies unprepared. These groups aim to garner support in order to pressure home governments to sponsor regulations favorable to their point of view. They also have managed to place companies directly in the line of fire.

International companies come under attack for two major reasons: (1) for their choice of markets and (2) for their methods of doing business. A constant source of controversy involves international companies' business practices in three areas: product strategies, promotion practices, and pricing policies. Product strategies include, for example, the decision to market potentially unsafe products such as pesticides. Promotional practices include the way products are advertised or pushed through distribution channels. Pricing policies include the possible charging of higher prices in one market than in another.

The infant formula controversy of the early 1980s involved participants from many countries and serves as a good example of the type of pressure that international companies sometimes face. Infant formula was being sold all over the world as a substitute for or supplement to breast-feeding. Although even the producers of infant formula agreed that breast-feeding was superior to bottle-feeding, changes that had started to take place in Western society decades before had caused infant breast-feeding to decline. Following World War II, several companies had expanded their infant formula production into developing countries, where birthrates were much higher than in the West. Companies that had intended their products to be helpful found themselves embroiled in controversy. Critics blasted the product as unsafe under Third World conditions. Because the formula had to be mixed with water, they maintained, poor sanitary conditions and contaminated water in developing countries led to many infant deaths. Poor mothers could also water down the formula to such an extent that babies were malnourished. As a result, these critics urged an immediate stop to all promotional activities related to infant formula, such as the distribution of free samples.

The Nestlé Company, as one of the leading infant formula manufacturers, became the target of a boycott by consumer action groups in the United States and elsewhere. Under the leadership of INFACT, the Infant Formula Action Coalition, a consumer boycott of all Nestlé products was organized to force the company to change its marketing practices. Constant public pressure resulted in the development of a code sponsored by the World Health Organization (WHO) that primarily covers the methods used to market infant formula. Under the code, producers and distributors may not give away any free samples. They must avoid contact with consumers and are forbidden to do any promotion geared toward the general public. The code is subject to voluntary participation by WHO member governments.

Boycotts have even been attempted at the state level in the United States. Massachusetts passed a state law denying state contracts to companies that did business in Myanmar (formerly Burma) because of that country's brutal dictatorship. Apple, Motorola, and Hewlett-Packard all cited the Massachusetts law when pulling out of Myanmar. A U.S. District Court judge subsequently ruled that the Massachusetts law interferes with the federal government's right to set foreign policy.[19] Despite this setback, global firms must contend with the growing influence of home country pressure groups.

What causes are global rights activists pursuing now? Check out the *Public Citizen: Global Trade Watch* home page on our website (college.hmco.com/business/).

LEGAL ENVIRONMENTS

In many ways, the legal framework of a nation reflects a particular political philosophy or ideology. Just as each country has its own political climate, so the legal system changes from country to country. Internationally active companies must understand and operate within these various legal systems. Most legal systems of the world are based on one of four traditions: common law, civil law, Islamic law, or socialist law.

Common Law

Common law is derived from English law found in the United Kingdom, the United States, Canada, and other countries previously part of the British Commonwealth. Common law acknowledges the preeminence of social norms.

Law arises from what society acknowledges as right and from what has commonly been done and accepted. Laws passed in such countries are frequently interpreted in the courtroom, where a jury consisting of citizens often determines the outcome of a case. Lawyers in these countries are as likely to look to prior case decisions as to the law itself in order to argue their own cases.

Civil Law

Civil, or code, law is based on the Roman tradition of the preeminence of written laws. It is found in most European countries and in countries influenced by European colonialism, such as countries in Latin America. In these countries, laws may be more encompassing as well as precise. Judges play a far more important role in the civil-law system than under common law, whereas juries usually play a lesser role. A traditional difference between civil-law countries and common-law countries has been the way they have viewed trademark protection. The first to officially register a trademark in civil-law countries owned the trademark. However, in common-law countries, someone who actually used the trademark before another registered it could successfully challenge the registration.

Islamic Law

Islamic law is derived from the Koran as well as from other Islamic traditions. Islamic law dominates family law in most Muslim countries, but its application to business situations varies greatly from country to country. To begin with, there are four major schools of Islamic law, and countries differ as to which they follow. Furthermore, not all Muslim countries apply Islamic law to commercial transactions. Some do, of course. Saudi Arabia forbids the collection of interest on loans. An importer cannot go to a bank and pay interest to borrow money to import automobiles from overseas. However, an importer can borrow money and pay interest in many Muslim countries. In fact, during the nineteenth and twentieth centuries, most Muslim countries adopted their commercial laws from one or more European countries. Because of this, business law in the Middle East often falls under the civil-law tradition.

Socialist Law

Socialist law arose from the Marxist ideological system established in China, Russia, and other former Eastern bloc countries during the twentieth century. Under Marxist rule, economic power was often centralized, and market economies were virtually unknown. Business laws as we know them were absent or underdeveloped. For example, Chinese citizens have only recently been allowed to bring lawsuits against foreign companies or Chinese government ministries. This has inspired activists in China to consider suing tobacco companies for targeting young people.[20]

As many socialist countries liberalize their economies, they are often forced to look outside for quick fixes for their lack of legal sophistication. For example, Russia turned to the United States and law professors in Houston to help develop laws pertaining to petroleum. When Russia joined the WTO, it agreed to adopt new laws concerning trademarks and patents. Unfortunately, many observers note that Russia today has difficulty enforcing these laws effectively. Even the judges have little experience with the new legislation.

China faces similar problems. The Chinese legal system has inspired little confidence from foreign investors. However, when China joined the WTO, the government began training judges to administer the new trade regulations. Legal teams were organized to ensure that city and provincial governments adhered to the new policies.[21]

NATIONAL REGULATORY ENVIRONMENTS

Regulatory environments also vary among countries. Businesses face greater regulatory burdens in developing countries than they do in developed countries. It can take 153 days to establish a business in Mozambique compared with 3 days in Canada. It takes twenty-one steps to register a commercial property in Nigeria compared with only three steps in Finland. The World Bank estimates that the least regulated countries from a business point of view are New Zealand, the United States, and Singapore.[22]

Japan has had the most regulated business environment among the developed countries. Twenty years after Temple University established its Tokyo campus, it is the only U.S. university offering full-degree courses. Forty other U.S. universities pulled out of Japan due to a plethora of regulations. For example, to qualify as an official university, universities must own their own buildings, have their own sports field and gym, operate on less than a 25 percent debt-equity ratio, and get government approval for new programs. Even Temple doesn't meet all these criteria. Without official status, Temple operates at a competitive disadvantage when trying to recruit students.[23]

In recent years, however, Japan has experienced a trend toward deregulation and market liberalization. As a result of this shift, conflict has increased and corporate lawsuits are becoming more common. Japan now needs more lawyers as Japanese increasingly shun mediation and the number of court cases soars. Japan estimates that it will need to more than double its number of lawyers by 2018. In 2004 alone, nearly seventy new law schools opened within Japanese universities.[24]

Japan is not the only country where international marketers face ambiguous or evolving regulatory environment. In addition to dealing with many different legal systems' national laws, managers must constantly contend with changes. As the global marketplace becomes ever more interconnected, regulatory changes appear all the more regularly.

Legal Evolution

One area of law that has seen considerable evolution worldwide is product liability law. Regulations concerning product liability were first introduced in the United States. If a product is sold in a defective condition such that it becomes unreasonably dangerous to use, then both the manufacturer and the distributor can be held accountable under U.S. law. For a long time, product liability laws in Europe were lax by U.S. standards, but they have been expanded in the past 20 years. Still there are differences that result from the different legal and social systems. In the EU, trials are decided by judges, not common jurors, and the extensive welfare system automatically absorbs many of the medical costs that are subject to litigation in the United States. Traditionally, product liability suits seldom posed problems for international marketers in developing countries. However, when accidents attributable to Firestone tires on Ford Explorers occurred, plaintiffs appeared in Saudi Arabia and Venezuela as well as in the United States. Today, global publicity surrounding product crises no doubt prompts more consumers in more countries to seek redress for problems.

A second area of law that varies from country to country involves bankruptcy. In the United Kingdom, Canada, and France, the laws governing bankruptcy favor creditors. When a firm enters bankruptcy, an administrator is appointed. The administrator's job is to recover the creditors' money. In Germany and Japan, on the other hand, bankruptcies are often handled by banks behind closed doors. The emphasis is on protecting the company and helping it reestablish itself. In the United States, bankruptcy law also tends to protect the company. Management prepares a reorganization plan that is voted on by the creditors. Creditor preference varies by country as well. For example, Swiss law gives preference to Swiss creditors.

As with product liability, attitudes toward bankruptcy and regulations pertaining to it have not remained static. In China, bankruptcies were unheard of under the communist system until China drafted its first bankruptcy code in 1988. One proponent of the new law noted that nobody understood it and everybody was scared of it. A major case involving a trust and investment corporation revealed that many vagaries in the law still existed. Creditors settled out of court and experienced huge losses. Nonetheless, the number of bankruptcies in China has soared since 2000.[25]

Today the regulation of transactions in cyberspace is critical to the future of electronic commerce. WTO members have made a political commitment to maintain a duty-free cyberspace.[26] However, many other issues concerning the governance of the Internet have not been resolved, and it even remains unclear which country can claim territorial jurisdiction in this inherently international medium. What will be the future of Internet taxation, privacy safeguards, and censorship? The complexity of the technology, as well as its rapid change, challenge traditional ideas of regulation.[27]

In the following chapters, we will be discussing other national and international laws that affect the management of products, pricing, distribution, and promotion. In many cases these laws are also evolving. Regional associations, especially the European Union (EU), are increasingly setting supranational laws that affect marketing within their member states. Attempts are also under way to set global standards of legal protection, such as in the area of patents and trademarks. In the future, this may help simplify the job of the international marketer.

Some moves to internationalize laws, however, are opposed by multinational firms. The Hague Conference on International Private Law has considered a global treaty for enforcement of legal judgments. This agreement would require U.S. courts to enforce judgments by foreign courts in exchange for similar treatment abroad for U.S. judgments. Internet providers were among the many U.S. firms that opposed the treaty. E-commerce businesses were especially concerned that the treaty would subject them to a plethora of lawsuits by allowing consumers to sue businesses under local law wherever their websites were accessible.[28] For the time being, however, national laws still prevail in the vast majority of cases, and even global standards, when established, will be administered through local legal systems.

Attitudes Toward Rules

Egypt experiences 44 traffic deaths per 100 million kilometers of driving. This compares with 20 deaths in Turkey and only 1.1 in the United States. To try to decrease traffic fatalities, the Egyptian government began the new millennium by instituting tough new speeding and seat belt laws, complete with hefty fines. Seat belt sales soared at first and then precipitously declined. One auto parts dealer who once sold 250 seat belts a day saw his sales fall to only 2 or 3 a day. A year later, Egypt's fatality statistics remained the same. Many Egyptians had chosen to buy cheap seat belts that could fool the police but didn't really work. Furthermore, the police were deluged with complaints when they gave out tickets. Because the seat belts didn't work, why should the driver be fined for not buckling up? One Egyptian summed up the public's skepticism, "I think those laws are just so the government can make our lives more miserable than they already are. They want to imitate the West in everything."[29]

Jean-Claude Usunier notes that rules and laws can be established that are respected and implemented quite explicitly. On the other hand, there may be a discrepancy between rules and what people actually do. He suggests that attitudes toward rules are affected by two basic criteria—the level of power distance in a society and whether a society has a positive or a negative human nature orientation (HNO). **HNO-positive societies** assume people can be trusted to obey the rules, whereas **HNO-negative societies** assume just the opposite. The United States is an HNO-positive society with low power distance. This results in pragmatic rules that most people respect and obey. In countries such as Italy and France, HNO is also positive but power distance is high. Ordinary people view themselves as being better than their rulers. As a result, many feel that laws can be challenged to a certain degree. In Germany and Switzerland, power distance is low but HNO is negative. Laws are made democratically, but society still does not trust people to obey them. To ensure compliance, rules must be applied strictly and with very explicit sanctions. In many developing countries, power distance is high and HNO is negative. Rules may often be strict, formal, and even unrealistic. In this atmosphere there is often a high discrepancy between the law and what people actually do or what is even enforced by the authorities.[30] Societies such as these can be especially confusing to international marketers who come from countries such as the United States.

Harry Triandis explains differences in attitudes toward rules by categorizing cultures as either tight or loose. In **tight cultures**, there are many rules, norms, and standards for correct behavior. In **loose cultures**, such rules are few. Tight cultures criticize and punish rule breakers more severely. Triandis proposes that tight cultures are likely to be more isolated and less influenced by other cultures, since agreement on norms is important. Afghanistan under the

HNO (human nature orientation)-positive societies societies that assume people can be trusted to obey the rules

HNO (human nature orientation)-negative societies societies that assume people cannot be trusted to obey the rules

Tight cultures societies with many rules, norms, and standards for correct behavior

Loose cultures societies with few rules, norms, or standards for correct behavior

Taliban would be an extreme example of a tight culture. High population density may also contribute to tight cultures, since people might need tightness to interact more smoothly under close conditions.[31]

REGULATORY CHANGE

International marketers must understand the different political and regulatory climates in which they operate. This is a challenging job in itself because of the many national markets involved. They must also be prepared to deal with changes in those environments. These changes can be moderate or drastic, and they can be more or less predictable. The more moderate and predictable changes we call **regulatory change**. The more drastic and unpredictable changes we call political risk, which we discuss in the next section. Regulatory change encompasses many government actions, such as changes in tax rates, the introduction of price controls, and the revision of labeling requirements. Although less dramatic than the upheavals associated with political risk, regulatory changes are very common. International marketers lose far more money to regulatory change than to political risk.

Regulatory change moderate and relatively predictable change in laws and regulations

Predicting Regulatory Change

Whatever strategy a firm chooses to employ in the face of regulatory change, it is useful to be able to predict whether and when such change will occur. Nothing is certain, but most regulatory change affecting international marketers should not come as a total surprise. Many government actions have economic bases. By understanding the issues covered in Chapter 2, an international marketer can identify probable government responses to prevailing conditions. For example, if export earnings are depressed in a developing country and if foreign investment is low, the government may be forced to devalue the currency. No one may be able to predict what day this will occur, but contingency plans should be in place for when it does occur.

It is also very important that the international marketer listen for signals from the government or influential parties. For months before Egypt disallowed additional foreign investment in packaged foods, local business leaders could be heard in the local media calling for such restrictions. When foreign investors first returned to China, the Chinese government warned them concerning repatriation of profits. They were told that their ability to remove profits from China would be somehow contingent on their export sales. Many firms paid no attention to this warning and later discovered that they did not qualify to repatriate profits. Some even admitted that they thought China had been joking about the possible restriction.

Firms can find themselves caught in embarrassing situations if they fail to heed signals. On the other hand, if they take signals seriously, they can formulate plans for different contingencies. How should the firm respond to a currency devaluation, an increased tax, or new restrictions on advertising? Contingency planning enables marketing managers to avoid crises and to make deliberate and careful decisions about what strategy it will be appropriate to employ in the face of regulatory change.

Managing Regulatory Change

James Austin suggests four strategic options for a company to consider when faced with regulatory change:

▶ *Alter.* The company can bargain to get the government to alter its policy or actions.

▶ *Avoid.* The company can make strategic moves that bypass the impact of a government's action.

▶ *Accede.* The company can adjust its operations to comply with a government requirement.

▶ *Ally.* The company can attempt to avoid some risks of government actions by seeking strategic alliances.[32]

Before deciding to try to alter a new regulation, the company should assess its bargaining power vis-à-vis the government. As depicted in Figure 4.1, a company is more likely to try to alter a new regulation when the regulation significantly affects its operations and the firm's bargaining power is high. If the firm's bargaining power is low, it will be more successful by seeking an appropriate ally or allies. If a policy is not very threatening and the firm's power is relatively low, the firm may be best served by acceding. After all, the firm should pick its battles with a government. It is too expensive and exhausting to fight every new regulation.

A firm's bargaining power is enhanced by its ability to pay taxes, employ citizens, and deliver exports to assist the national trade balance. During diplo-

FIGURE 4.1
Strategic Approaches to Regulatory Change

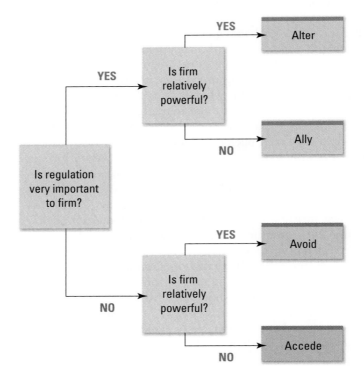

matic tensions between the United States and France prior to the Iraq War, the South Carolina state legislature took up a resolution calling for a boycott of French products. The resolution passed the state House, 90–9. But suddenly the bill died and wasn't taken up by the state Senate. As it turned out, most of the tires sold in the United States by the French group Michelin were made in factories located in South Carolina.[33]

To bargain more successfully, a company should utilize political mapping of a government.[34] **Political mapping** consists of identifying all individuals involved in a regulatory decision—politicians, bureaucrats, pressure groups—and understanding their various points of view. This allows the firm to better address their concerns. However, it is not always easy to do this. Chinese companies estimated that billions of dollars in Chinese-Iraqi contracts were left in limbo after the United States invaded Iraq. They were particularly concerned because China did not support the U.S. invasion. Even more daunting was identifying who in Iraq could make a decision about the many contracts.[35] Similarly, multinational firms have noted that shifting power among bureaucrats in China makes it difficult to do political mapping in that country.[36]

> **Political mapping** the process of identifying all individuals involved in a regulatory decision—politicians, bureaucrats, key members of pressure groups—and understanding their various points of view

Ravi Ramamurti argues that increasingly a company's bargaining power lies not in itself alone but in the motivation and power of its home government to influence the firm's host government.[37] For example, Motorola discovered after it had designed and test-marketed a new pager in Japan that the pager did not meet new industry standards. These standards were developed by Motorola's Japanese competitors and enforced by the Japanese government. Instead of redesigning its pager, Motorola first attempted to convince the Japanese government to alter its policy and allow the Motorola design to go to market. Redesigning the pager would prove costly, and Motorola believed its bargaining power was high, especially if the U.S. government would back it in its appeal.[38]

If a firm believes its bargaining power is relatively weak, an ally strategy may be employed. During the Firestone tires/Ford Explorer product-harm crisis, the government of Saudi Arabia impounded the affected vehicles as they arrived on the shipping dock. However, Saudi Ford dealers were able to help rescind this order by convincing the government that they were the ones being hurt and not the multinational companies.[39] Pepsi tried unsuccessfully for several years to enter the Indian market as a wholly owned subsidiary. Finally, the company found a powerful local partner in the Indian beverage industry with whom to enter into a joint venture. The joint venture was quickly approved.

Pepsi also employed the other strategy associated with low bargaining power—accede—when negotiating to enter the Indian market. At the time, India had strict foreign exchange regulations that would stop Pepsi from taking profits out of the country. Pepsi believed that any attempt to convince the Indian government to alter this policy on its behalf would prove futile. The firm also expected to reinvest all Indian profits in the local market for the foreseeable future. Therefore, Pepsi acceded to the government policy. This accession allowed the firm to save time on lengthy negotiations and enter a potentially lucrative market sooner.

Other companies find that they can avoid regulations by making relatively minor changes in their marketing mix. For example, Clearasil could sell its product in Japanese supermarkets if it did not explicitly promote the product as an acne medicine. Otherwise, it was restricted to selling through pharmacies.

For years Brazil's price control board allowed firms to set any price they wanted on newly introduced products. Current products or improved versions of current products, however, were subjected to a tedious and unpredictable appeal process before any increase in price was authorized. As a result, companies such as Gillette were inclined to introduce an improved product, such as a better razor blade, as a totally new product rather than as an improved version of an existing line.

POLITICAL RISK

Recently, the U.S. Securities and Exchange Commission (SEC) announced new disclosure rules for firms seeking to sell securities in the United States. Firms must now report their activities in countries subject to American government sanctions, such as Cuba, Iraq, and the Sudan. The SEC requires firms to disclose anything that could make their offering risky or speculative. In the past, this included environmental risks and impending lawsuits. Now it includes political risks as well.[40]

The presence of political risk means that a foreign company can lose part or all of its investment, market, or earnings in another country as a result of political actions on the part of a host government, the firm's home government, or pressure groups. As we have noted, the political climate of a country is hardly ever static. Sometimes, a firm is faced with sudden and radical changes in the political climate of a host country.

WORLD BEAT 4.2

Staying Put in Indonesia

AFTER PRESIDENT SUHARTO WAS OUSTED in 1998, Indonesia sank into race riots, bombings, religious massacres, secessionist revolts, labor strikes, and a 90 percent depreciation of the rupiah. Years later, the Economist Intelligence Unit still gives Indonesia very high scores on political risk. Yet management consultants estimate that fewer than 300 of the 3,000 foreign companies in Indonesia fled the chaos. Manufacturers of everything from Energizer batteries to L'Oreal cosmetics seem determined to stay put. Why? Indonesia possesses among the lowest costs in the world, a big domestic market, and proximity to the rest of Asia.

Of course, not all companies proved immune to Indonesia's increased political unrest. British Petroleum faced a legal battle with the state of East Kalimantan over ownership of an $800 million coal mine. And Freeport McMoRan Cooper & Gold saw its stock price plunge over 10 percent after gunmen ambushed one of its convoys.

Sources: Michael Shari, "Staying Put," *Business Week*, September 17, 2001, p.18; Carl Mortished, "BP in Battle over Coalmine in Indonesia," *The Times*, July 13, 2002, p. 52; Timothy Mapes and Cynthia Schreiber, "Security Concerns Hit Freeport," *Asian Wall Street Journal*, September 5, 2002, p. A3; and "Indonesia: Country Risk Summary," *Economist Intelligence Unit*, January 25, 2005.

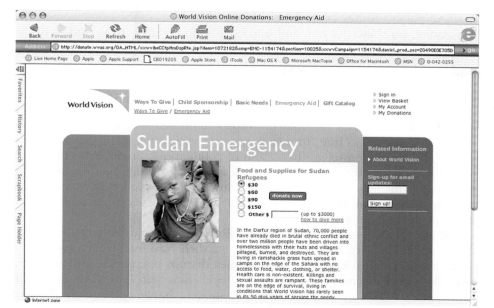

Political unrest discourages foreign investment. This is one reason why African markets have received relatively low attention from many global marketers.

Political risk is the possibility that an unexpected and drastic change due to political forces will result in adverse circumstances for business operations. Sudden changes of power, especially when the new leadership is committed to a leftist economic and political philosophy, have led to hostile political climates and takeovers. Such changes in government can happen as a result of unexpected coup d'états or revolutions. However, as occurred in Venezuela, it can sometimes result from a democratic election.

All political instability may not pose the possibility of negative consequences to every firm. Many businesses in the tiny emirate of Kuwait viewed the Iraq war and the toppling of the regime of Saddam Hussein as presenting potential business opportunities in the neighboring country of 20 million people.[41] The security industry is booming in Central America where gang-related crime is a serious problem. Guatemala's business community alone pays $335 million for protection from 250 licensed security firms. Who has the biggest market share in the region? Wackenhut, a Miami-based security firm, acquired by Denmark's Group 4 Flack.[42]

The fall of the Iranian shah in 1979 is a vivid example of a sudden change that caught many companies by surprise and did adversely impact their business interests. Unlike communist revolutions earlier in the century, Iran's revolution was centered on Islam. Still, anti-American sentiment resulted in the taking hostage of U.S. citizens at the American Embassy in Tehran. President Jimmy Carter retaliated by seizing Iranian assets under U.S. jurisdiction and ordered all U.S. companies to cease doing business with Iran. The impact on U.S. business alone involved around 4,000 firms whose claims against Iran were eventually settled by the International Tribunal at the Hague. One of the largest settlements outside the petroleum industry was $49.8 million paid to the tobacco company R.J. Reynolds.[43] And not only U.S. companies sustained damage. Many companies operating from Europe and Japan were forced, as a

Political risk the possibility that an unexpected and drastic change due to political forces will result in adverse circumstances for business operations

result of the revolution, to shut down either all or parts of their operations. The subsequent war between Iran and Iraq further limited the attractiveness of the Iranian market and inflicted additional losses on remaining foreign investors.

The Iranian experience taught international marketers an important lesson pertaining to political risk. For many years, firms believed political risk applied only to capital investments in foreign countries. After all, expensive manufacturing plants could be seized. Surprisingly, the Reynolds case involved damage not to brick-and-mortar facilities but rather to unpaid accounts receivable for cigarettes exported to Iran. In fact, many companies that were simply exporting to Iran found themselves the victims of political risk. So did firms that were licensing their technology or brand names to local Iranian manufacturers. In many cases, the new government forbade importers and licensees from making payments to foreign businesses. However a firm chooses to enter a market, political risk may be a concern.

What can companies do? Internationally active companies have reacted on two fronts. First, they have started to perfect their own intelligence systems to avoid being caught unaware when changes disrupt operations. Second, they have developed several risk-reducing strategies that help limit their exposure, or the losses they would sustain, should a sudden change occur. The following sections will concentrate on these two solutions.

Political Risk Assessment

The business disruption in Iran inspired many companies to establish systems to systematically analyze political risk. To establish an effective political risk assessment (PRA) system, a company has to decide first on the objectives of the system. Another aspect concerns the internal organization, or the assignment of responsibility within the company. Finally, some agreement has to be reached on how the analysis is to be done.

Objectives of Political Risk Assessment. Companies everywhere would like to know about impending government instabilities in order to avoid making new investments in those countries. Even more important is the monitoring of existing operations and their political environment. Particularly with existing operations, knowing in advance about potential changes in the political climate is of little value unless such advance knowledge can also be used for future action. As a result, PRA is slowly moving from predicting events to developing strategies that help companies cope with changes. But first, PRA has to deal with the potential political changes. Many questions must be answered: Should we enter a particular country? Should we stay in a particular country? What can we do with our operations in market X, given that development Y can occur? In undertaking PRA, companies are well advised to look for answers to six key questions:

► How stable is the host country's political system?
► How strong is the host government's commitment to specific rules of the game, such as ownership or contractual rights, given its ideology and power position?
► How long is the government likely to remain in power?

▶ If the present government is succeeded by another, how will the specific rules of the game change?

▶ What would be the effects on our business of any expected changes in the specific rules of the game?

▶ In light of those effects, what decisions and actions should we take now?

Organization and Analysis. One survey of large U.S.-based international firms found that over half the firms had internal groups reviewing the political climate of both newly proposed and current operations. In companies that did not have formalized systems for PRA, top executives tended to obtain firsthand information through foreign travel and talking with other businesspeople.[44]

Rather than rely on a centralized corporate staff, some companies prefer to delegate PRA responsibility to executives or analysts located in a particular geographic region. Some use their subsidiary and regional managers as a major source of information. Other firms employ distinguished foreign-policy advisers or maintain outside advisory panels.

Several public or semipublic sources exist that regularly monitor political risk. The Economist Intelligence Unit (EIU), a sister company of the *Economist*, monitors some eighty countries on the basis of a variety of economic and political factors. These factors include debt, current account position, economic policy, and political stability. *Euromoney* publishes country risk ratings, including political risk evaluations (see Table 4.2).

Usually firms use several approaches and sources to assess political risk. What companies do with their assessment depends on the data they collect. Political risk assessment can help the firms stay out of risky countries.

TABLE 4.2 SAFEST COUNTRIES: POLITICAL RISK RATINGS

RANKING	COUNTRY	RANKING	COUNTRY
1	Norway	16	France
2	Switzerland	17	Australia
3	Luxembourg	18	Singapore
4	United States	19	Iceland
5	Denmark	20	Spain
6	Sweden	21	New Zealand
7	United Kingdom	22	Italy
8	Finland	23	Bermuda
9	Austria	24	Taiwan
10	Ireland	25	Portugal
11	Netherlands	26	Hong Kong
12	Canada	27	Greece
13	Japan	28	Slovenia
14	Belgium	29	Malta
15	Germany		*(continued)*

TABLE 4.2 (CONTINUED)

Ranking	Country	Ranking	Country
30	Qatar	71	Philippines
31	United Arab Emirates	72	El Salvador
32	Cyprus	73	Turkey
33	Kuwait	74	Iran
34	Bahamas	75	Vietnam
35	Czech Republic	76	Peru
36	Bahrain	77	Colombia
37	Korea South	78	Macau
38	Hungary	79	Algeria
39	Brunei	80	Jordan
40	Estonia	81	Fiji
41	Israel	82	Guatemala
42	Saudi Arabia	83	Ukraine
43	Chile	84	Bhutan
44	Barbados	85	Indonesia
45	Poland	86	St. Lucia
46	Slovak Republic	87	Azerbaijan
47	Malaysia	88	Sri Lanka
48	Lithuania	89	Pakistan
49	Mexico	90	Samoa
50	Croatia	91	Vanuatu
51	China	92	Macedonia (FYR)
52	Oman	93	Jamaica
53	Latvia	94	Maldives
54	Botswana	95	St. Vincent and the Grenadines
55	Trinidad & Tobago		
56	Thailand	96	Grenada
57	South Africa	97	Bangladesh
58	Tunisia	98	Bolivia
59	Mauritius	99	Honduras
60	India	100	Armenia
61	Russia	101	Tonga
62	Kazakhstan	102	Belize
63	Bulgaria	103	Albania
64	Morocco	104	Venezuela
65	Romania	105	Ghana
66	Egypt	106	Dominica
67	Costa Rica	107	Ecuador
68	Brazil	108	Cape Verde
69	Panama	109	Lebanon
70	Antigua and Barbuda		

(continued)

TABLE 4.2 (CONTINUED)

RANKING	COUNTRY	RANKING	COUNTRY
110	Senegal	149	Georgia
111	Mongolia	150	Madagascar
112	Niger	151	New Caledonia
113	Seychelles	152	Ethiopia
114	Lesotho	153	Nepal
115	Papua New Guinea	154	Togo
116	Paraguay	155	Angola
117	Guyana	156	Myanmar
118	Dominican Republic	157	Central African Republic
119	Moldova	158	Serbia and Montenegro
120	Tanzania	159	Zambia
121	Swaziland	160	Malawi
122	Kenya	161	Sierra Leone
123	Bosnia-Herzegovina	162	Guinea
124	Gabon	163	Congo
125	Cameroon	164	Sao Tome & Principe
126	Burkina Faso	165	Haiti
127	Gambia	166	Mauritania
128	Syria	167	Suriname
129	Mozambique	168	Côte d'Ivoire
130	Laos	169	Tajikistan
131	Yemen	170	Sudan
132	Belarus	171	Libya
133	Turkmenistan	172	Rwanda
134	Mali	173	Zimbabwe
135	Uzbekistan	174	Eritrea
136	Benin	175	Micronesia (Fed. States)
137	Djibouti	176	Namibia
138	Uganda	177	Burundi
139	Uruguay	178	Somalia
140	Nigeria	179	Liberia
141	Argentina	180	Dem. Rep. of the Congo (Zaire)
142	Cambodia		
143	Equatorial Guinea	181	Cuba
144	Kyrgyz Republic	182	Marshall Islands
145	Solomon Islands	183	Afghanistan
146	Nicaragua	184	Korea North
147	Chad	185	Iraq
148	Guinea-Bissau		

SOURCE: Rankings from "Country Risk Survey Results," *Euromoney*, March 2005. Reprinted with permission.

However, go/no-go decisions can be difficult to make. Risk analysis is not fortunetelling. No one can predict with certainty when the next revolution or war will take place. Like Iran in the late 1970s, some politically risky countries possess very attractive markets. Therefore, political risk analysis is only one of the activities that must be undertaken in the course of deciding whether or not to enter or stay in a foreign market. Many companies integrate their political assessments into their overall financial assessments of projects. In cases where the firm expects higher political risk, the company may add anywhere from 1 to 5 percent to its required return on investment. In this manner the company balances political risk against market attractiveness.

Risk Reduction Strategies

Political risk assessment not only aids firms in market entry and exit decisions but can also alert them to the necessity of risk-reducing strategies. Such strategies can enable companies to enter or stay in riskier markets. A classic way to deal with politically risky countries is to seek higher and faster returns on investment. The average return on foreign direct investment in Africa is often higher than that for any other region of the world, according to an UNCTAD study. This is partially because firms invested in projects that promised quick returns.[45] Many companies have also experimented with different ownership and financing arrangements. Others utilize political risk insurance to reduce potential losses.

Local Partners. Relying on local partners who have excellent contacts among the host country's governing elite is a strategy that has been used effectively by many companies. This may range from placing local nationals on the boards of foreign subsidiaries to accepting a substantial capital participation from local investors. For example, General Motors joined forces with Shanghai Automotive Industry Corporation, a state-owned firm, in a 50-50 joint venture to make Buicks, minivans, and compact cars in China.

However, the use of local partners may not decrease the chance of expropriation, and such partners can become liabilities if governments change. General Motors entered into a joint venture in Iran with a partner closely connected with the shah. After the revolution ousted the shah, GM's partner's shares were expropriated. GM then found itself in partnership with the new Islamic government.

Minimizing Assets at Risk. If a market is politically risky, international marketers may try to minimize assets that are at risk. For example, R.J. Reynolds could have refused to extend credit to its cigarette importer in Iran. Instead of accumulating accounts receivable that were at risk, the firm could have demanded payment before shipment. However, as we have mentioned before, some politically risky countries can be attractive markets. This was the case in Iran in the mid-1970s, when many foreign firms were vying for Iranian markets. In light of such intense competition, few companies could afford to be heavy-handed with their Iranian customers.

Another way to minimize assets at risk is to borrow locally. Financing local operations from indigenous banks and maintaining a high level of local accounts payable minimize assets at risk. These actions also maximize the neg-

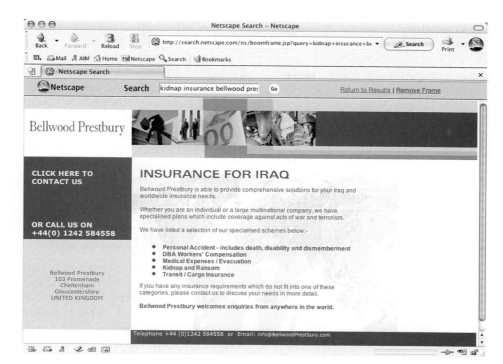

Private insurers, such as Bellwood Prestbury, now offer kidnap and ransom insurance to firms involved in politically risky markets.

ative effect on the local economy if adverse political actions are taken. Typically, host governments are reluctant to cause problems for their local financial institutions. Local borrowing is not always possible because restrictions may be imposed on foreign companies that might otherwise crowd local companies out of the credit markets. However, projects located in developing countries can sometimes qualify for loans from the World Bank. Pioneer, a major global firm in hybrid seeds, was offered such financing when it considered investing in Ethiopia. These arrangements not only reduce the capital at risk but also lend multilateral support for the venture.

Finally, larger multinational firms may attempt to diversify their assets and markets across many countries as a way to manage political risk. If losses are realized in one market, their impact does not prove devastating to the company as a whole. Of course, this is more difficult to do if a company is small. Several smaller U.S. firms faced bankruptcy as a result of losses ensuing from the Iranian Revolution.

Political Risk Insurance. As a final recourse, international companies can often purchase insurance to cover their political risk. With the political developments in Iran and Nicaragua occurring in rapid succession and the assassinations of President Park of Korea and President Sadat of Egypt all taking place between 1979 and 1981, many companies began to change their attitudes on risk insurance. Political risk insurance can be costly but can offset large potential losses. For example, as a result of the UN Security Council's worldwide embargo on Iraq, companies stood to collect $100–$200 million from private insurers and billions from government-owned insurers.[46]

Companies based in the United States can utilize the Overseas Private Investment Corporation (OPIC). OPIC was formed by the U.S. government to facilitate the participation of private U.S. firms in the development of less developed countries. Since the Islamic Revolution in Iran OPIC has covered exporters as well as foreign investors. OPIC offers project financing and political risk insurance in one hundred developing countries. The agency covers losses caused by currency inconvertibility, expropriation, and bellicose actions such as war and revolution. Selected projects utilizing OPIC are listed in Table 4.3. But even OPIC faces challenges from special-interest groups. A lawsuit was brought against OPIC by Friends of the Earth, Greenpeace, and others. They accused the agency of failing to conduct environmental reviews before financing projects that contributed to global warming.[47]

For more information on OPIC, check out its home page on our website (college.hmco.com/business/).

GLOBAL MARKETING AND TERRORISM

The Overseas Security Advisory Council is a public-private partnership that seeks to provide early warning of bombings or other attacks to corporate offices worldwide as terrorists look increasingly toward "soft targets." The council is overseen by the U.S. State Department and advises international companies such as Citigroup, Boeing, Dupont, and McDonald's. Its site gets about 1.8 million visits a month, and the council distributes about 10,000 e-mails daily. Jennifer Harris, twenty-three, handled a call from a company whose chief executive officer was planning to meet with a regional governor in India. Ms. Harris's research revealed that there had been seven attempts on the governor's life in the past year. The CEO decided to telephone instead.[48]

The rise of international terrorism has affected global marketers in different ways. Faced with the possibility of terrorist attack, Starbucks pulled out of Israel.[49] General Electric was one of several companies that chose to stop seeking contracts in Iran when it was criticized by a U.S. senator for taking "blood money" from a state that supported terrorists.[50]

Whole industries have also been affected by the rise in terrorism. One of the immediate industries to feel the impact of global terrorism was tourism. With a high risk of terrorism, Americans spent more tourism dollars in Mexico instead of taking trans-Atlantic flights to Europe.[51] Tourists from the Middle East began to shun the United States where they faced new border checks and suspicion, favoring a new destination—Malaysia. In 2003, Middle East tourists to the United States dropped 36 percent from three years earlier.[52]

Another industry directly affected by global terrorism is international education. Tightened security in the United States has made acquiring student visas more difficult for foreign students planning to study there. Consequently, a battle for global market share of international students has emerged. Among the most aggressive countries are Malaysia, India, China, Sweden, and the Netherlands. Two other proactive competitors are the Middle East kingdom of Dubai and Singapore. Dubai particularly targets students from the Middle East who face difficulties in obtaining U.S. visas. Both Dubai and Singapore follow the model of partnering with high-quality foreign universities to set up local programs. Among such universities participating in Dubai are the University of Southern Queensland, India's Mahatma Gandhi University, and Dublin Business School. Singapore has attracted Stanford and Cornell from the United

TABLE 4.3 SELECTED OPIC PROJECTS

COUNTRY	COMPANY	PROJECT DESCRIPTION	AMOUNT IN U.S. DOLLARS
Afghanistan	American Wool-Cashmere, Inc.	Cashmere wool brokerage business	3,000,000 Finance
	Shelter for Life International, Inc.	Heavy equipment	4,500,000 Insurance
	Tarsian & Blinkley, LLC	Manufacture and sale of traditional Afghani women's wear	150,000 Finance
Angola	Seaboard Overseas, Ltd.	Flour mill and commodity trading operations	5,990,962 Insurance
	American Commodity Associates, LLC	Food production facility	40,000,000 Insurance 22,600,000 Finance
Bolivia	Western Wireless International Corporation	Wireless communications	50,000,000 Finance
Brazil	Bank Boston NA	Branch banking	44,100,000 Insurance
	El Paso Corporation	895 MW natural gas-fired power plant	200,000,000 Finance
	GE Energy Rentals, Inc.	Power generation	12,103,321 Insurance
El Salvador	Mercury Mortgage Finance, Ltd.	Home mortgage loans	10,000,000 Insurance
Estonia	FOODPRO International, Inc.	Flour milling and prepared dough products operation	9,385,000 Finance
Ghana	George K. Amoah & Chicken George Farms, LLC	Poultry production and distribution	16,977,600 Insurance
Guatemala	RiceX Company	Manufacture rice-based nutritional drink	6,000,000 Finance
Hungary	Jim Barna	Log home manufacturing facility	1,050,000 Finance
Jamaica	Citibank Jamaica Framework Agreement	Telecommunications expansion	10,000,000 Finance
Kazakhstan	Pride International, Inc.	Oil and gas wells	150,000,000 Insurance
Mozambique	David F. Herbert	Resort	3,668,850 Insurance
Kyrgyz Republic	Hyatt International Corporation	Hotel	9,700,000 Insurance
Nigeria	AES Nigeria Holdings, Ltd.	Emergency power barges	200,000,000 Insurance
Nicaragua	CRISF, Inc.	Mango plantation	5,250,000 Insurance
Peru	Alliance Holding Group, Inc.	Small regional air carrier and charter aviation business	1,900,000 Finance
Philippines	U.S. Bank National Association	Privatization of power company	250,000,000 Insurance
South Africa	John R. Young	Game park and guest lodge resort	742,500 Insurance
Russia	HBK Investment L.P.	Construction and operation of a crude oil and petroleum product export terminal	130,000,000 Finance
	Nypro, Inc.	Injection molding facility	2,700,000 Finance
Thailand	Deep Sea Adventure Tours, Inc.	Underwater submarine reef tours	2,430,000 Insurance
Turkey	James E. Carter	Health and fitness club	750,000 Insurance
Vietnam	GE Energy Rentals Inc.	Power generation	12,314,398 Insurance

SOURCE: www.opic.gov.

States, French business school INSEAD, and the German Institute of Science and Technology. Singapore's target is 150,000 foreign students by 2012, resulting in a contribution of 5 percent to the national economy.[53]

Global terrorists may particularly target infrastructure such as ports, airlines, and other transportation and communication systems.[54] Such attacks threaten to wreak havoc as companies try to supply international buyers. Dow Corning makes over 10,000 deliveries a month to 20,000 customers in fifty countries. Its products are used in the manufacture of products from shampoos to textiles. September 11 and other terrorist attacks can disrupt the firm's ability to deliver products to customers. For example, Dow Cornings's team of planners met for months to discuss backup plans if the war in Iraq were to upset their global logistics. During the Persian Gulf War in 1991, one product destined for a cosmetics company in France ended up in Saudi Arabia. This held up production for two weeks and upset the French customer.

Similar to Dow, a number of large companies already had systems in place to respond to disruptions caused by situations other than terrorism. For example, DaimlerChrysler had control centers to deal with disruptions from hurricanes to industrial disputes.[55] However, Dow Corning's chief logistics officer for China estimates that most big companies could be better prepared with scenario planning. They would probably only have to invest $1.5 million in contingency plans.[56]

Corporate security has been heightened in a number of companies. PepsiCo, with over $500 billion in sales and over 143,000 employees worldwide, responded to the terrorist threat by creating a new position—vice president of global security. At Oracle, a corporate steering committee coordinates a number of departments, including security, information technology, product development, and human resources. At Marriott, crisis management has been centralized to ensure consistency across its different businesses. Seventy percent of respondents to a survey administered by the U.S. Chamber of Commerce reported that that their firms had reviewed their security policies in light of a terrorist threat, and 53 percent had acted on recommendations arising from those reviews.[57]

The U.S. government has made certain precautions mandatory by law. Companies that export agricultural products or processed foods to the United States must register with the U.S. Department of Agriculture and submit to increased scrutiny. The Treasury Department maintains a list of individuals and organizations believed to be linked with terrorism. To do business with anyone or any company on that list is a criminal offense for U.S. citizens or companies. Needless to say, these new regulations have vastly increased demand by companies for preemployment screening as well as background checks on clients, vendors, distributors, and business partners.[58]

Nonetheless, 90 percent of the respondents in the Chamber of Commerce survey reported that they did not believe their company would be a target of terrorists.[59] As the immediate threat fades, many midsize companies, in particular, may regard the expense of planning for terrorist attacks as too costly. In another survey, conducted by the Conference Board, 40 percent of top executives of midsize companies agreed that "security is an expense that ought to be minimized."[60]

CONCLUSION

In this chapter, we have outlined major political and regulatory issues facing international companies. Our approach was not to identify and list all possible government actions that may have an impact on international marketing. Instead, we have provided a background to make it easier to understand these actions and the motivations behind them. It is up to executives with international responsibility to devise strategies and systems for dealing with these challenges posed by governments.

What is important is to recognize that companies can—to a degree—forecast and manage regulatory change. They can also adopt risk reduction strategies to compensate for some of the more unpredictable political risks. For effective global marketing management, executives must be forward looking, must anticipate potentially adverse or even positive changes in the environment, and must not merely wait until changes occur. To accomplish this, systematic monitoring procedures that encompass both political and regulatory developments must be implemented.

The past several years have brought enormous political changes to the world, changes that are affecting global marketing operations of international firms. On the one hand, these changes have resulted in the opening of many previously closed markets. On the other hand, global terrorism has emerged, presenting its own challenges. Regulatory change and political risk will continue to play a large role in global marketing. Firms must learn how to avoid disasters as well as how to identify and take advantage of opportunities.

How do political issues affect your marketing plans? Continue with your *Country Market Report* on our website (college .hmco.com/business/).

QUESTIONS FOR DISCUSSION

1. The construction industry in Japan has traditionally been dominated by the domestic suppliers. Few foreign construction companies have won projects in Japan. What aspects of Japan's political forces may have influenced this local control over the Japanese construction market? What political or regulatory forces may lead to the opening of this market for foreign firms?

2. Do ownership restrictions such as local-partner requirements always ensure that multinational firms will contribute more to the local economy than they would otherwise?

3. What are the different methods a company can use to obtain and/or develop political risk assessment information? What do you think are the strengths and weaknesses of each?

4. John Deere has decided to enter the tractor market in Central America. What strategies could it use to reduce the possible effects of political risk?

5. Choose a cause promoted by Public Citizen's Global Trade Watch. Do you agree with the cause? Why or why not? What firms are or could be involved in the controversy?

6. How is global terrorism similar to and different from prior political risk faced by global marketers?

CASE 4.1
Cuba: Reentering the World

In the 1950s, the economy of Cuba was dominated by Spanish landowning families and U.S. corporations. A communist revolution led by Fidel Castro resulted in thousands of confiscations of foreign and local properties. These confiscations included factories, plantations, mines, and real estate. The U.S. government responded to the confiscations by placing an embargo on Cuba in 1962. The embargo disallowed U.S. exports to or imports from Cuba. In addition, U.S. foreign investment in Cuba was forbidden. Castro originally offered to pay claimants with money from sugar sales to the United States, but the U.S. government refused to negotiate with the dictator. Today the United States recognizes nearly 6,000 claims against Cuba, totaling nearly $7 billion in today's prices.

For years Cuba remained a satellite of the Soviet Union. Virtually all its trade was with Russia or the Soviet bloc. With the dissolution of the Soviet Union, Cuba was left one of the few remaining communist states in the world. It lost its traditional trading partners and found itself financially destitute. Though wary of capitalism, the island nation began tentatively to encourage foreign investment in the mid-1990s. Investments, primarily from Canada and the EU, quickly grew to several hundred in number.

The United States, never having lifted its embargo on Cuba, was quick to respond. The Helms-Burton law was passed allowing U.S. citizens to sue foreign companies that used property that had been previously confiscated by the Cuban government. In addition, the U.S. government would deny visas to corporate officers of such companies. Some foreign companies quickly complied by checking for claims against their new Cuban investments. Many more ignored the U.S. threat. President Clinton eventually waived the right to sue under the Helms-Burton law in response to an EU initiative to ask for a WTO ruling against the American law.

Then, after nearly 40 years, the United States partially lifted its embargo against Cuba.

Supported by a politically powerful farm lobby, the embargo was amended to allow sales of agricultural products and medicine to Cuba. Still the Cuban government remains wary of closer economic ties with the United States. Although the Cuban economy has improved somewhat, the country remains a tightly controlled society with eleven million people living at subsistence level.

Cuba has once again suggested that it is ready to meet its claims obligations under international law, but it is unclear where Cuba would find the money. Cuba has stated that it plans to seek redress from the United States for the economic cost inflicted by the U.S. embargo, a cost estimated at $60 billion. Another option could be the sale of government-owned properties. Some suggest that after the death of Castro, who is now approaching 80, the U.S. government should offer Cuba a bailout plan to welcome the nation back into the fold. In the meantime, a Miami financier proposes pooling corporate and personal claims against Cuba into a fund that would issue shares to claim holders. These shares would then be speculatively bought and sold.

Discussion Questions

1. List the various issues covered in Chapter 4 that are illustrated by this case.
2. Should claim holders be compensated? If so, *who* should pay? Why?
3. If you were considering investing in the proposed claims fund, what discount rate would you apply? In other words, how many cents on the dollar do you think these claims are worth? Why?

Sources: Christopher Marquis, "Helms-Burton Puts Squeeze on Cuba's Sugar," *Record,* November 28, 1996, p. A10; James Cox and Christina Pino-Marino, "Awaiting a Return to the Good Life in Cuba," *Financial Post,* March 30, 1999, p. C16; and Christopher Marquis, "Despite U.S. Restrictions Against Cuba, Door Opens Wider for Visits by Americans," *New York Times,* June 19, 2000, p. A10.

CASE 4.2

Coke Under Fire

For over two years, Coca-Cola struggled to acquire the soda brands of Cadbury Schweppes, which included Dr Pepper and 7-Up. The proposed purchase originally encompassed all of Cadbury Schweppes's international markets except those in the United States, France, and South Africa. A successful purchase would increase Coca-Cola's market share in soda in over 150 countries. For example, Coca-Cola's share in Canada was expected to rise from 39.4 percent to 49.1 percent. In Mexico, its share would rise from 68.4 percent to 72.6 percent.

Not everyone was pleased with the proposed purchase. Pepsi, Coke's major rival, sent letters to legislators in Canada asking the Canadian government to disallow the purchase of the Canadian operations, maintaining that it would result in weaker competition, higher prices, and the loss of three hundred jobs in Pepsi's Canadian operations. Smaller independent bottlers joined Pepsi in opposition. Canada's Federal Competition Bureau agreed to undertake a costly investigation that resulted in Coke canceling its plans in Canada. In the meantime, Australia, Belgium, and Mexico rejected the purchase. A number of European countries and the Chilean government also put it under review. As a result, Coke scaled back on its attempts to buy the brands in Europe. Instead, South Africa was added to the deal.

The Cadbury Schweppes purchase is not the only encounter Coke has had with competition regulators in Europe and elsewhere. In May 2000, the offices of Coca-Cola Enterprises were raided in London and Brussels. EU regulators were seeking incriminating documents related to Coke's allegedly having given German, Austrian, and Danish supermarkets illegal incentives to stock fewer rival products. A similar investigation the year before in Italy had resulted in a $16 million fine being levied on the company. If found guilty in the broader EU case, the company could be fined as much as $14.4 billion.

Doug Daft, the new head of Coca-Cola, visited Europe and personally met with top antitrust officials at the EU and various European countries. He wanted to present Coke's case personally and to achieve a better understanding of the concerns of the officials. He stated that Coke was committed to playing by the house rules wherever they did business. However, what Coke called aggressive yet honest competition, Europe viewed as abrasive, domineering, and unacceptable American behavior.

Meanwhile, problems were cropping up back in the home market as well. A jury in Daingerfield, Texas, found the company guilty of breaking Texas antitrust laws and assessed a $15.6 million fine. Coke was accused of demanding exclusive advertising, displays, and vending machines from retailers. In addition, a U.S. Federal Trade Commission report concluded that acquisitions of other soft-drink brands by industry leaders resulted in higher prices to American consumers.

Discussion Questions

1. Why do you think some countries disallowed the Cadbury Schweppes acquisition whereas others did not?
2. Given Mr. Daft's statement that Coca-Cola was committed to playing by the rules, why was the firm in trouble in so many countries?
3. What advice would you give Coca-Cola concerning its handling of government relations?

Sources: Betsy McKay, "New Formula," *Wall Street Journal*, June 23, 2000, p. A1; Eric Beauchesne, "Pepsi Challenge Builds Against Coke Merger," *Ottawa Citizen*, July 13, 2000; Betty Liu, "Coke Abandons Cadbury Plans," *Financial Times*, July 27, p. 21; and Constance L. Hays, "How Coke Pushed Rivals Off the Shelf," *New York Times*, August 6, 2000, Section 3, p. 1.

NOTES

1. Kerry A. Dolan, "Dancing with Chavez," *Forbes*, November 13, 2000, p. 72.

2. Carl Mortished, "Ethnic Violence Threatens World Energy Security," *Times of London*, April 2, 2001, p. 4M20.

3. Vern Terpstra and Kenneth David, *The Cultural Environment of International Business*, 3rd ed. (Cincinnati: Southwestern, 1992), p. 203.

4. Michael Allen and Eduardo Porter, "Grupo Televisa Chief Weighs U.S. Citizenship to Pursue Bid," *Wall Street Journal*, July 1, 2003, p. B8.

5. Lolita C. Baldor, "Lockheed Martin Wins Presidential Helicopter Contract," *Associate Press Newswires*, January 28, 2005.

6. "Macedonia to Form a Unity Government," *New York Times*, May 11, 2001, p. 14.

7. "Bill, Borrow, and Embezzle," *The Economist*, February 17, 2001.

8. "About Face," *The Economist*, December 9, 2000.

9. "U.S. Hackers to Release Software to Bypass Government Block," *AFX News Limited*, December 6, 2000.

10. Aaron Berstein, "Pouring Oil on the Flames," *Business Week*, April 3, 2000, p. 108.

11. "China Starts New Antidumping Tax on Newsprint," *Dow Jones News Service*, June 3, 1999.

12. Helene Cooper, "Looming Battle," *Wall Street Journal*, October 29, 2001, p. A1.

13. Neil King Jr., Iraq's Business Elite Gropes in Dark," *Wall Street Journal*, June 25, 2003, p. A4.

14. "Chinese Defense Firm Banned for Selling Tech to Iran," *Dow Jones Business News*, May 22, 2003.

15. "Coke Opens Saudi Plant in Cola War," *Agence France-Presse*, May 5, 1999, p.1.

16. Bhushan Bahree, "Exxon, Shell Poised to Win Saudi Deals," *Wall Street Journal*, June 1, 2001, p. A11.

17. James Bandler, "Ports in a Storm," *Wall Street Journal*, May 20, 2003, p. A1.

18. "Wal-Mart, NY Yankees, Others Settle Charges of Illegal Trading," CNN.com, April 14, 2003.

19. "U.S. Court Hears Appeal of Massachusetts' Burma Law," *Dow Jones News Service*, May 4, 1999.

20. Leslie Chang, "Chinese Lawyers Plan to Take On Big Tobacco," *Wall Street Journal*, May 16, 2001, p. A17.

21. Peter Wonacott, "As WTO Entry Looms, China Rushes to Adjust Legal System," *Wall Street Journal*, November 9, 2001, p. A13.

22. Michael Schroeder, "Regulatory Rules Stifle Business in Poor Countries," *Wall Street Journal*, September 8, 2004, p. A17.

23. Sebastian Moffett, "Taking on Japan's Red Tape," *Wall Street Journal*, September 8, 2004, p. A17.

24. Ichiko Fuyuno, "Japan Grooms New Lawyers," *Wall Street Journal*, April 3, 2004, p. A18.

25. "Of Laws and Men," *The Economist*, April 7, 2001.

26. Charlene Barshefsky, "Trade Policy for a Networked World," *Foreign Affairs*, March/April 2001, p. 141.

27. Stephen J. Kobrin, "Territoriality and the Governance of Cyberspace," *Journal of International Business Studies* 32, no. 4 (2001), pp. 687–704.

28. "Telecom, Web Firms Want Cautious Moves on Global Legal Pact," *Wall Street Journal*, June 6, 2001, p. A28.

29. Susan Postlewaite, "A Crackdown on Madcap Drivers," *Business Week International Editions*, April 30, 2001, p. 5.

30. Jean-Claude Usunier, *Marketing Across Cultures* (New York: Prentice-Hall, 2000), pp. 83–85.

31. Harry C. Triandis, "The Many Dimensions of Culture," *Academy of Management Executive* 18, no. 1 (2004), p. 92.

32. James E. Austin, *Managing in Developing Countries* (New York: The Free Press, 1990), p. 166.

33. Glenn R. Simpson, "Multinational Firms Take Steps to Avert Boycotts Over War," *Wall Street Journal*, April 4, 2003, p. A1.

34. Austin, *Managing in Developing Countries*, pp.148–153.

35. Peter Wonacott, "Chinese Firms Find Their Iraq Projects in Limbo," *Wall Street Journal*, July 10, 2003, p. A8.

36. Usha C. V. Haley, "Assessing and Controlling Business Risks in China," *Journal of International Mangement* 9 (2003), p. 243.

37. Ravi Ramamurti, "The Obsolescing 'Bargaining Model' ? MNC-Host Developing Country Relations Revisited," *Journal of International Business Studies* 21, no. 1 (2001), pp. 23–39.

38. David B. Yoffie and John J. Coleman, "Motorola and Japan," Harvard Business School Case # 9-388-056.

39. Orit Gadiesh and Jean-Marie Pean, "Manager's Journal: Think Globally, Market Locally," *Wall Street Journal*, September 9, 2003, p. B2.

40. "A Long Arm for Securities Law," *The Economist*, May 19, 2001.

41. Chip Cummins, "Business Mobilizes for Iraq," *Wall Street Journal*, March 24, 2003, p. B1.

42. Joel Millman, "Gangs Plague Central America," *Wall Street Journal*, December 11, 2003, p. A14.

43. "Slow Progress on Iran Claims," *New York Times*, November 14, 1984, pp. D1, D5.

44. Stephen J. Kobrin et al., "The Assessment and Evaluation of Noneconomic Environments by American Firms: A Preliminary Report," *Journal of International Business Studies* 11 (Spring–Summer 1980), pp. 32–47.

45. "Business in Difficult Places," *The Economist*, May 20, 2000.

46. "Political Risk Insurers Fear Crisis Escalation," *Business Insurance* 24, no. 33a (1990), p. 1.

47. Vanessa Houlder, "Climate Change Could Be Next Legal Battlefield," *Financial Times*, July 14, 2003, p. 10.

48. Gary Fields, "Protecting 'Soft Targets'," *Wall Street Journal*, November 26, 2003, p. A4.

49. "Starbucks Plots Global Conquests," *Kitchener-Waterloo Record*, April 16, 2003, p. E4.
50. Kathryn Kranhold and Carla Anne Robbins, "GE to Stop Seeking Business in Iran," *Wall Street Journal*, February 3, 2005, p. A3.
51. John Lyons, "Mexico's Safety Wins Tourists," *Wall Street Journal*, April 28, 2004, p. A15.
52. John Krich, "Malaysia Draws New Tourists," *Wall Street Journal*, April 23, 2004, p. A13.
53. "Fight for Global Education Pie Get Fiercer," *Straits Times*, February 14, 2005.
54. Thomas Mucha, "10 Ways to Protect Your Business from Terror," *Business* 3, no. 1 (January 2002), pp. 50–51.
55. Michael Czinkota and Gary Knight, "Managing the Terrorism Threat," *European Business Forum*, no. 20 (Winter 2005), p. 45.
56. Gabriel Kahn, "A Case Study of How One Company Prepared for War," *Wall Street Journal*, March 25, 2003, p. A14.
57. Sherry L. Harowitz, "The New Centurions," *Security Management*, January 1, 2003, p. 50.
58. Howard Winn, "Risk Management: The Quest for Quality," *Far Eastern Economic Review*, October 21, 2004, p. 46.
59. Ibid.
60. Paul Magnusson, "What Companies Need to Do," *Business Week*, August 16, 2004, p. 26.

Maps

MAP I.   THE WORLD

ALASKA (U.S.)

CANADA

UNITED STATES

MEXICO

GUATEMALA
EL SALVADOR

COSTA RICA

PANAMA

Hawaiian Is.

PACIFIC OCEAN

Equator

Galapagos Is.

ECUADOR

PERU

COLOMBIA

VENEZUELA

BRAZIL

BOLIVIA

PARAGUAY

CHILE

Easter Is.

URUGUAY

ARGENTINA

Bermuda

ATLANTIC OCEAN

BAHAMAS

CUBA
JAMAICA   HAITI
BELIZE
HONDURAS   Puerto Rico
NICARAGUA

DOMINICAN REP.
Virgin Is.
ST. KITTS AND NEVIS
ANTIGUA AND BARBUDA
DOMINICA
BARBADOS
ST. LUCIA
GRENADA   ST. VINCENT AND
THE GRENADINES
TRINIDAD AND TOBAGO
GUYANA
FR. GUIANA

SURINAM

Falkland Is.

GREENLAND
(DENMARK)

80°N

ICELAND

NORWAY   FINL
SWEDEN   ESTO

60°N

UNITED
KINGDOM   DEN.
NETH.
IRELAND
GERMANY   POLAND
BEL.
LUX.   CZ
AUS   HUNG
FRANCE   SLN
SWITZ.   B. H.
ITALY   S. M.
ALBANIA
SPAIN   GREE

40°N   PORTUGAL

Azores

MALTA
TUNISIA

MOROCCO

WESTERN
SAHARA
(MOROCCO)

ALGERIA   LIBYA

MAURITANIA   MALI   NIGER   CHA

20°N

CAPE
VERDE

SENEGAL   BURKINA
FASO   BENIN
GAMBIA
GUINEA-BISSAU   GUINEA   NIGERIA

SIERRA   IVORY   CAMEROON   AFRIC
LEONE   COAST
LIBERIA   TOGO
GHANA
EQUATORIAL GUINEA   CE

SÃO TOMÉ AND PRINCIPE   GABON   DE
OF
REP. OF CONGO

ANGOL

ANGOL

NAMIBIA

BO

S
A

0°

20°S

40°S

60°S

80°S

160°W   140°W   120°W   100°W   80°W   60°W   40°W   20°W   0°   20°E

ABBREVIATIONS

AUS.	AUSTRIA
BEL.	BELGIUM
B. H.	BOSNIA AND HERZEGOVINA
CR.	CROATIA
CZ.	CZECH REPUBLIC
DEN.	DENMARK
HUNG.	HUNGARY
LUX.	LUXEMBOURG
MAC.	FORMER YUGOSLAV REPUBLIC OF MACEDONIA
NETH.	NETHERLANDS
S. M.	SERBIA AND MONTENEGRO
SLK.	SLOVAKIA
SLN.	SLOVENIA
SWITZ.	SWITZERLAND

MAP 2. CONTEMPORARY EUROPE

No longer divided by ideological competition and the cold war, today's Europe features a large number of independent states.

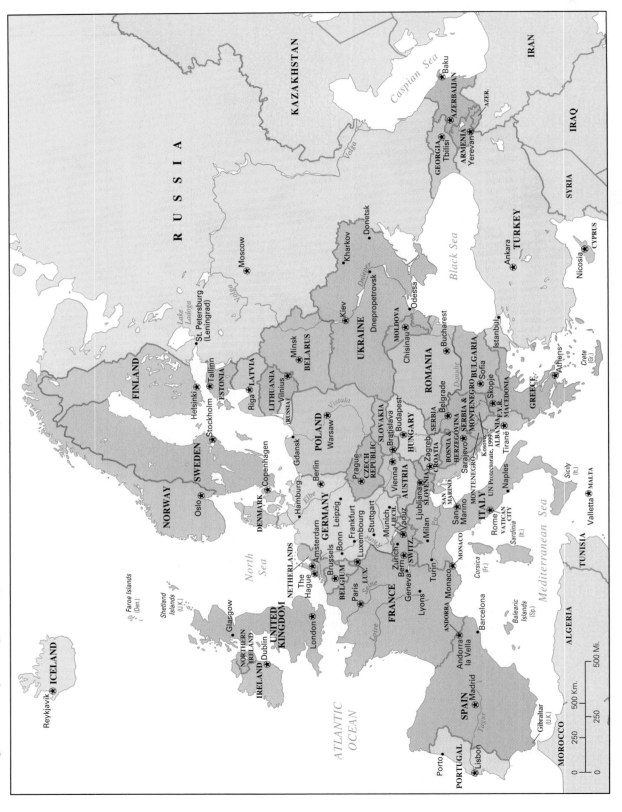

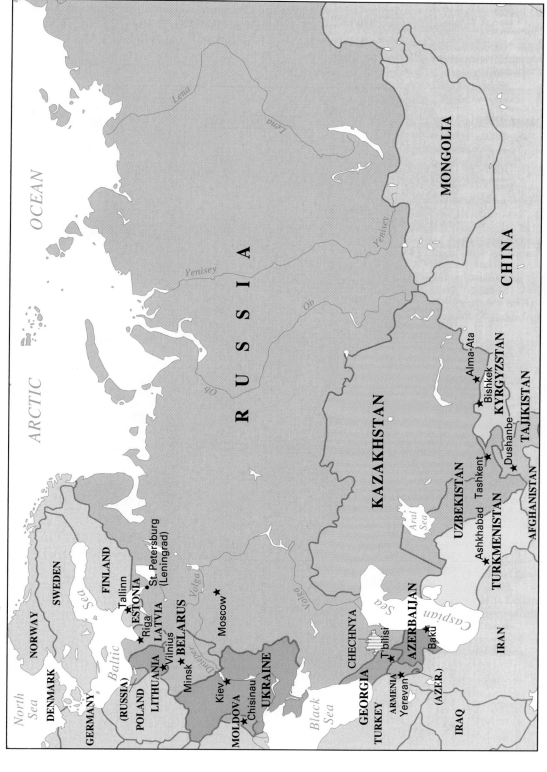

MAP 3. THE END OF THE SOVIET UNION

When Communist hardliners failed to overthrow Gorbachev in 1991, popular anti-Communist sentiment swept the Soviet Union. Following Boris Yeltsin's lead in Russia, the republics that constituted the Soviet Union declared their independence.

MAP 4. THE END OF SOVIET DOMINATION IN EASTERN EUROPE

The creation of new countries out of Yugoslavia and Czechoslovakia and the reunification of Germany marked the most complicated change of national borders since World War I. The Czech Republic and Slovakia separated peacefully, but Slovenia, Croatia, Macedonia, and Bosnia and Herzegovina achieved independence only after bitter fighting.

MAP 5.   CENTRAL AMERICA AND THE CARIBBEAN

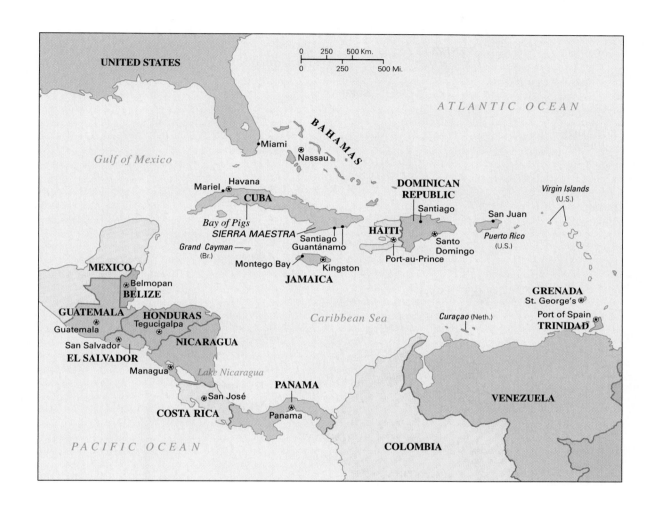

MAP 6. MODERN SOUTH AMERICA

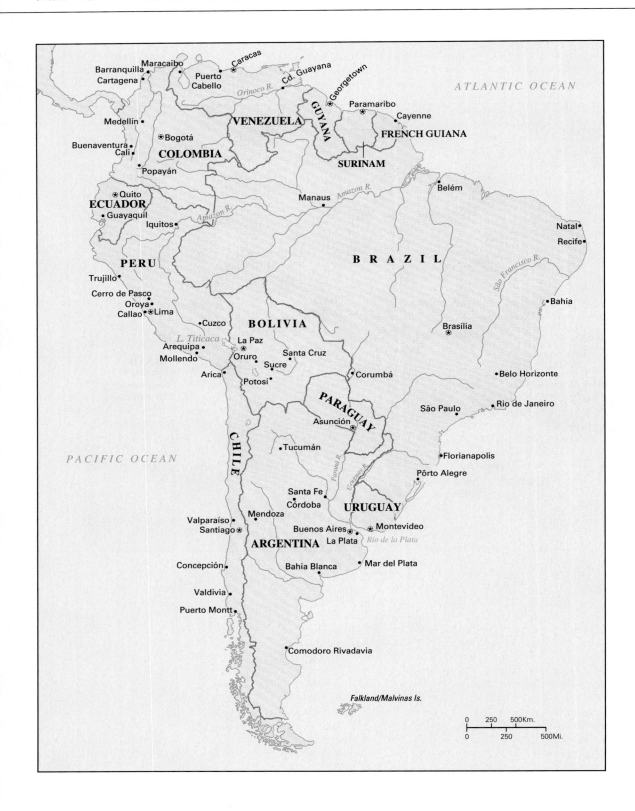

MAP 7. NEW STATES IN AFRICA AND ASIA

Divided primarily along religious lines into two states, British India led the way to political independence in 1947. Most African territories achieved statehood by the mid-1960s, as European empires passed away, unlamented.

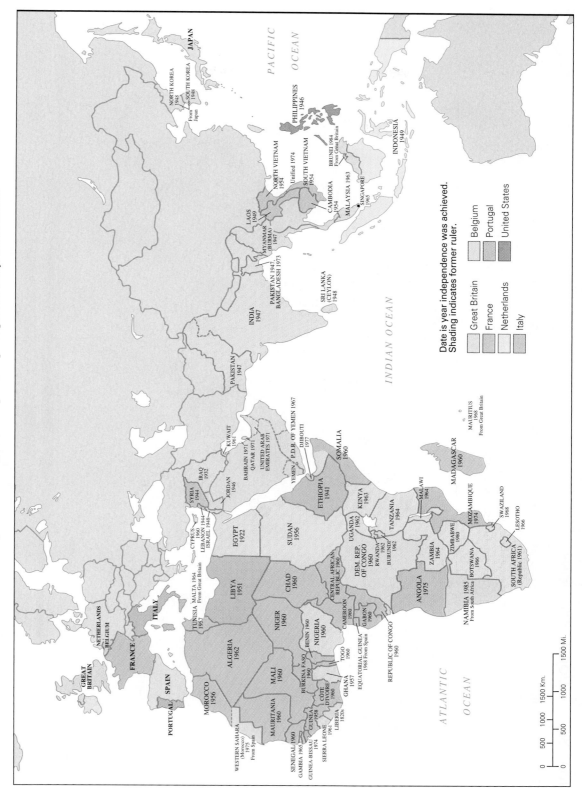

Date is year independence was achieved.
Shading indicates former ruler.

Great Britain
France
Netherlands
Italy

Belgium
Portugal
United States

MAP 8. WORLD RELIGIONS

Believers in Islam, Christianity, and Buddhism make up large percentages of the population in many countries. Differing forms of these religions seldom coincide with national boundaries. As religion revives as a source of social identity or a rationale for political assertion or mass mobilization, the possibility of religious activism spreading across broad geographic regions becomes greater, as does the likelihood of domestic discord in multireligious states.

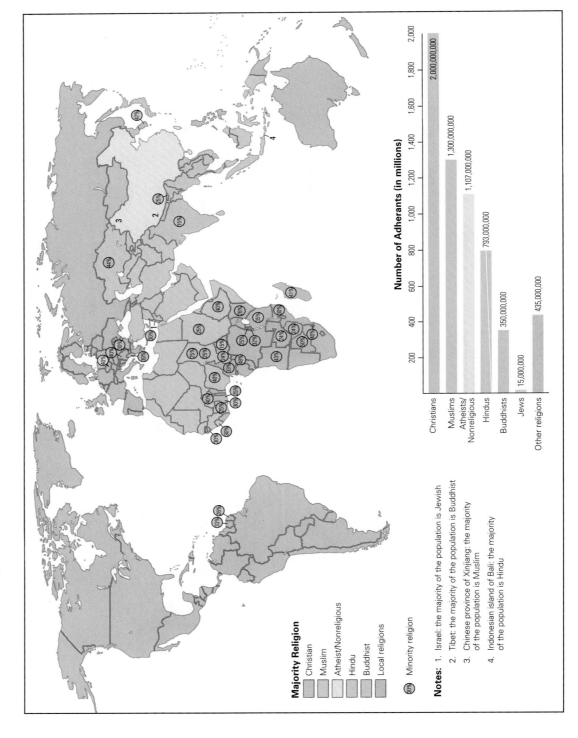

Majority Religion

- Christian
- Muslim
- Atheist/Nonreligious
- Hindu
- Buddhist
- Local religions

60% Minority religion

Notes: 1. Israel: the majority of the population is Jewish
2. Tibet: the majority of the population is Buddhist
3. Chinese province of Xinjiang: the majority of the population is Muslim
4. Indonesian island of Bali: the majority of the population is Hindu

Number of Adherants (in millions)

Religion	Adherents
Christians	2,000,000,000
Muslims	1,300,000,000
Atheists/Nonreligious	1,107,000,000
Hindus	793,000,000
Buddhists	350,000,000
Jews	15,000,000
Other religions	435,000,000

Map 9.   Modern Islam

Although the Islamic heartland remains the Middle East and North Africa, Islam is growing steadily in Africa south of the Sahara and is the faith of heavily populated Indonesia.

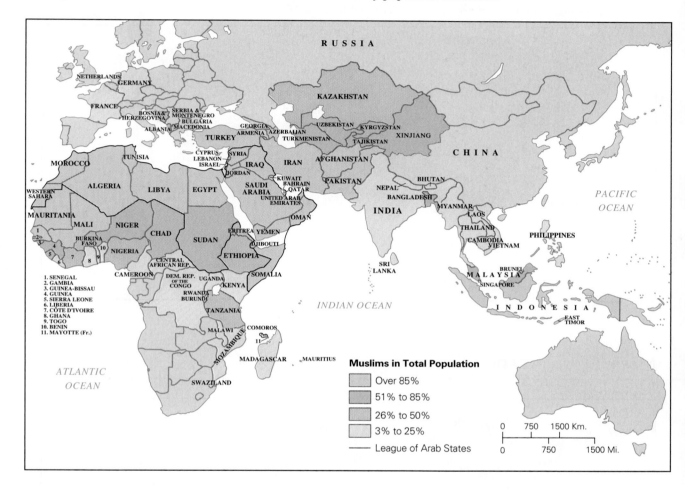

Muslims in Total Population

- Over 85%
- 51% to 85%
- 26% to 50%
- 3% to 25%
- —— League of Arab States

1. SENEGAL
2. GAMBIA
3. GUINEA-BISSAU
4. GUINEA
5. SIERRA LEONE
6. LIBERIA
7. CÔTE D'IVOIRE
8. GHANA
9. TOGO
10. BENIN
11. MAYOTTE (Fr.)

Map 10.   Water Supply Coverage

Environmental experts estimate that the current global population has about 80 percent of the water it needs and about 60 percent of sanitary water supplies. These maps show the differences between raw water supplies and sanitary water supplies, by national boundaries.

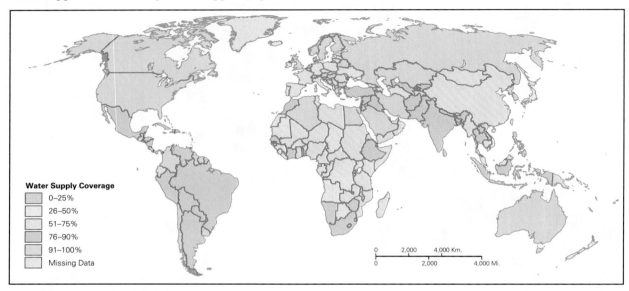

Water Supply Coverage
- 0–25%
- 26–50%
- 51–75%
- 76–90%
- 91–100%
- Missing Data

Map 11.   Sanitation Coverage

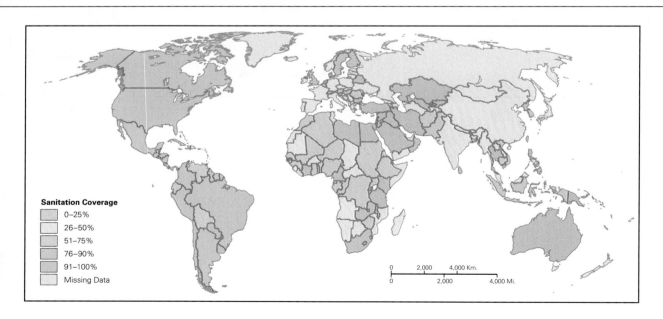

Sanitation Coverage
- 0–25%
- 26–50%
- 51–75%
- 76–90%
- 91–100%
- Missing Data

Map 12. World Population Growth

At current rates of growth, every three years, the world's population will increase by the equivalent of a nation the size of the United States. Most of this population increase will be in some of the world's poorest nations. (NG Maps/National Geographic Society Image Collection. Reprinted with permission.)

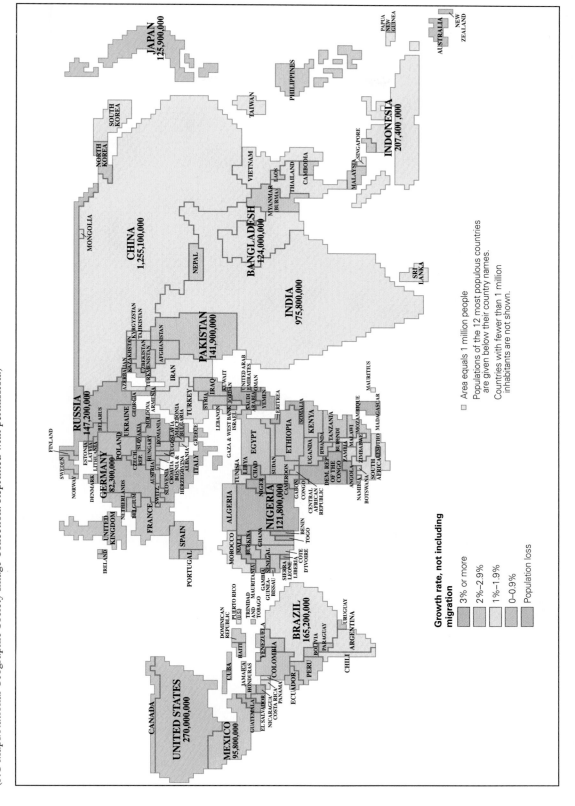

ANALYZING GLOBAL OPPORTUNITIES

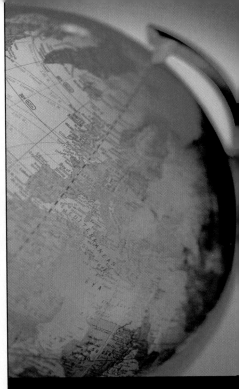

PART 2

147

5 GLOBAL MARKETS

SINCE THE SIGNING OF NAFTA many U.S.-based companies have eyed Mexico's market with great interest. Thanks in part to the rising purchasing power of women, Mary Kay, a Dallas-based manufacturer of cosmetics, has watched Mexico become one of its top foreign markets. Wal-Mart has become Mexico's number one retailer. But for latecomer Starbucks, Mexico presented an enigma. Mexico was the fifth-largest producer of coffee in the world, yet Mexicans rarely drank coffee. The average Mexican consumed less than 2 pounds of coffee a year, compared with the 10 pounds consumed by the average American and the 26 pounds consumed by the average Swede. Could Starbucks create a greater demand for coffee among Mexican consumers? Could its upscale coffee shop format offer a product that was attractive to customers in a developing country?[1]

To begin to develop an effective strategy for global markets, a firm must first consider the type of market in which it competes. Markets can comprise consumers, businesses, or governments.

In this chapter we explore issues that arise when targeting these different categories of markets in global markets. We address factors

LEARNING OBJECTIVES

After studying this chapter, you should be able to

▶ List the factors that influence consumers' abilities to buy and explain how these affect various national markets.

▶ Describe Maslow's hierarchy-of-needs model and apply it to consumers in different cultures.

▶ Give examples of how consumer behavior is similar across cultures and examples of how it may differ from one culture to another.

▶ Explain why business-to-business markets vary in buyer needs and behavior from one country to another.

▶ List the special qualities of national and multinational global buyers.

▶ Describe the five "screens" a foreign firm must pass through to win a government contract.

▶ Explain the role of bribery in international contracts.

that make each category similar—and yet different—across cultures. Consumer markets may exhibit global segments whose needs and behaviors are relatively uniform across cultures. Business-to-business markets can produce global buyers with unique demands. Government buyers often have multiple agendas. Still, national differences affect all these markets, making the job of addressing their wants and needs all the more challenging for the global marketer.

UNDERSTANDING MARKETS AND BUYERS

In every marketing situation, it is important to understand potential buyers and the process they use to select one product over another. Most elements of a marketing program are designed to influence the buyer to choose one's product over competitors' products. In the case of each type of buyer—consumer, business, and government—the marketer must be able to identify who the buyers are and how they make a purchase decision.

Furthermore, to assume that buyers in different countries engage in exactly the same buying processes and apply exactly the same selection criteria can be disastrous. Buyers can differ in terms of who decides to buy, what they buy, why they buy, how they buy, when they buy, and where they buy. When launching disposable diapers worldwide, Procter & Gamble established a global marketing team in Cincinnati, believing that babies' diaper needs would be the same around the globe. They later found out that whereas mothers in most countries are concerned about keeping their babies' bottoms dry, Japanese mothers are not. In Japan, babies are changed so frequently that thick, ultra-absorbent diapers were not necessary and could be replaced by thin diapers that take up less space in the small Japanese home.[2] Similarly, many business supply firms have discovered that CEOs in developing countries make purchase decisions that are usually delegated to purchasing managers in developed countries.

THE CONSUMER MARKET

Consumers around the world have many similar needs. There is even some evidence that global consumption patterns are converging. The traditionally wine-drinking French are drinking more beer, and beer-drinking Germans are drinking more wine. Japan, traditionally a fish-eating country, is consuming more beef. One study even suggested that the Swiss prefer French cheese to their traditional Swiss varieties.[3]

All people must eat, drink, and be sheltered from the elements. Once these basic needs are met, consumers then seek to improve their standard of living with a more comfortable environment, more leisure time, and increased social status. Still, consumption patterns vary greatly from one country to another, because consumers vary widely in their ability and motivation to buy. For example, consumption patterns for wine still vary tremendously from country to country. In France, the average annual consumption is 73 liters (19 gallons) per person, compared with 1.6 liters in Japan and 8 liters in the United States. The high consumption of wine in Europe relative to that in the United States is offset by the high U.S. consumption of soft drinks. The average American drinks five times as many soft drinks as a French consumer, three times as many as an Italian, and two and one-half times as many as a German.[4]

Basic needs and the desire for an improved standard of living are universal throughout the world, but unfortunately, not everyone can achieve these objectives. The economic, political, and social structure of the country in which consumers live affects their ability to fulfill their needs and the methods they use to do so. To understand a consumer market, we must examine the following three aspects:

A veiled Moroccan woman sits by an advertisement for a foreign film. Many motion picture firms rely on international consumer markets to cover the costs of producing films.

▶ The consumer's ability to buy
▶ Consumer needs
▶ Consumer behavior

Ability to Buy

To purchase a product, a consumer must have the ability to buy. The medium of exchange in most societies is currency. The ability to buy a product is affected by the amount of wealth a country possesses. A country accumulates wealth by the production and sale of goods within the country and the sale of goods to other countries (exports). The inflows of money from the latter are offset by the outflows of money to pay for necessary imports.

A very important indicator of total consumer potential is **gross national product (GNP)** because it reflects the generation of wealth in a country, which is an indicator of market size. The GNP per capita expresses this value per person, so it is a crude indicator of potential per consumer. GNP and **per-capita income (PCI)** can vary significantly from country to country. With a PCI of $36,486 in Japan and $38,451 in Sweden, one can expect the demand for automobiles to be greater in those countries than in Kenya or Vietnam, each with a PCI below $530. One of the main reasons why Starbucks was attracted to Mexico was its increasing income per capita. Despite some cultural differences among markets, Starbucks noticed a strong correlation between PCI and coffee consumption.

It is important to note, however, that PCI statistics have an inherent flaw that can undermine their comparability across all markets. The International Monetary Fund (IMF) recognizes that converting income denominated in local currencies into dollars at market rates can underestimate the true purchasing power of consumers in poor countries relative to those in rich countries.

Gross domestic product the total market value of all goods and services produced within the borders of a country during a specific period

Per-capita income (PCI) a country's average income per person for a specific period

Purchasing-power parity
a theory that prices of internationally traded commodities should be the same in every country and therefore that the true exchange rate is the ratio of these prices in any two countries

Because of this, the IMF suggests using statistics pertaining to **purchasing-power parity**, which take into account national differences in product prices. For example, assessed in terms of purchasing-power parity, India's buying power increases from $651 (PCI) to $3,018. Table 5.1 shows purchasing-power parity for selected developed and developing countries.

Distribution of wealth also has implications for market potential. The government has a major influence on the distribution of wealth in a national market. A government may take a large share of the wealth through taxes or ownership of industries. The government also sets policies and laws to regulate the distribution of wealth. For example, a graduated income tax with a 60 to 90 percent tax on high levels of income and no taxes on low levels of income will

TABLE 5.1 PER-CAPITA INCOME AT MARKET EXCHANGE RATES AND PURCHASING-POWER PARITY IN SELECTED COUNTRIES, 2005		
	MARKET EXCHANGE RATES	PURCHASING POWER PARITY
Argentina	$4,132	$11,981
Brazil	3,310	8,594
Chile	5,741	10,981
Egypt	1,117	4,048
Ethiopia	120	749
Germany	33,099	29,204
Hungary	10,896	16,338
India	651	3,018
Indonesia	1,093	3,660
Iran, Islamic Republic of	2,607	7,630
Japan	36,486	29,164
Kazakhstan	3,185	7,858
Kenya	489	1,084
Korea	14,649	19,515
Mexico	6,566	9,726
Paraguay	1,170	4,222
Philippines	1,084	4,651
Poland	6,372	12,263
Romania	3,277	7,957
Russia	4,749	10,300
Sweden	38,451	29,544
Switzerland	49,246	30,365
Turkey	4,636	7,301
United Arab Emirates	20,960	19,598
Vietnam	528	2,684

SOURCE: Data selected from "World Economic Outlook Database," *International Monetary Fund,* http://www.imf.org.

help to distribute the income more evenly. The revenue that remains in the private sector will be distributed among workers, managers, and owners of the industries. Low wages and unemployment will tend to increase the size of the lower-income class. Concentration of business ownership in a few families will decrease the size of the upper class.

Income distribution across the population of a country can distort the market potential in a country. For example, if a few people possess nearly all the wealth and the remainder are poor, there will be few people in the middle. As a result, many products that depend on a middle-class market may fare poorly. For example, in Belgium the top 10 percent of the population accounts for about 20 percent of the nation's income and consumption. In Armenia, this same group garners over 35 percent of income. In Bolivia, Colombia, and Guatemala, the top 10 percent accounts for about 46 percent of the nation's income.[5]

Surprisingly, lower-income segments of the population can be attractive markets for consumer goods. In many developing countries, the buying power of the poor may be underrepresented in official statistics. Much of the income earned by the poor in these countries is never reported to the authorities. Thus they are said to participate in the **informal economy**. Informal economies can be very large. The World Bank estimates that the informal economy generates 40 percent of the gross national product (GNP) in low-income countries.[6] In addition, the relatively high cost of real estate in urban centers keeps many of the poor locked in slums. Any increase in their disposable income is spent not on relocating but on purchasing more upscale consumer products. For example, mothers in poor neighborhoods of Calcutta, India, often buy the most expensive brand of milk for their children.

> **Informal economy** the totality of economic activity of individuals and businesses that operate without licenses, permits, or reporting procedures required by law

Consumer Needs

Money is spent to fulfill basic human needs. Abraham **Maslow's hierarchy of needs** divides human needs into four levels and proposes that humans will satisfy lower-level needs before seeking to satisfy higher-level needs. The lowest level of needs is physiological needs. These include the need for safety, food, and shelter. The second level encompasses the social needs of friendship and love. The third level consists of the need to receive respect from others, and the highest level of needs is related to self-actualization or developing one's personality. The structure of consumption for each country varies depending on the income per capita. A developing country, such as China, spends over 50 percent of the national income on food, whereas consumers in developed countries, such as France and the United States, spend less than 20 percent on food.

> **Maslow's hierarchy of needs** a theory stating that human needs are divided into four levels and that humans satisfy lower-level needs before seeking to satisfy higher-level needs

Although it is possible to generalize about the order of consumer purchases on the basis of Maslow's hierarchy of needs, there is some debate about its cross-cultural applicability. Hindu cultures emphasize self-actualization before materialism. In developing countries, consumers may deprive themselves of food in order to buy refrigerators to establish their social status and fulfill their need for esteem.[7] Consumers from more individualistic countries such as the United States may attach less importance to purchases related to belonging to a group and more importance to hobby-related products that may enhance self-actualization.

In Japan, on the other hand, great attention and expense are devoted to ritual gift giving even among business associates, and Japanese children are

WORLD BEAT 5.1

Japan: The Future of Luxury?

JAPANESE CONSUMERS like things just right, as Otis, the world leader in elevators, discovered. To satisfy the Japanese, the company would need to develop an elevator with absolutely no jostling. European and U.S. consumers are willing to accept a slight jostling in return for a faster ride—but not the Japanese.

Besides being demanding consumers, the Japanese are big buyers of luxury goods, and brand image is everything in Japan where there is little difference between rich and poor. Shopping bags—with the proper name displayed—are prized by customers who may carry the bag around for hours and even "wear" the bag five or ten times later. Young women sometimes pay the equivalent of $50 to $100 for Chanel makeup just to get the prestigious bag. The demand for designer shopping bags has even created a secondhand market for them on the Internet.

After a decade of poor economic performance, some believe that luxury brands still sell in Japan, but maybe not as well. Luxury retailers such as Ferragamo, Louis Vuitton, and Coach are opening their own retail outlets in a bid to capture a great share of the possibly contracting market. On the other hand, a major segment fueling Japan's continued interest in luxury goods is single, working women—an increasing part of the population. Some suggest that splurging on luxuries, such as a handbag that costs $1,300, gives Japanese women an illusion of wealth and decreases anxiety over jobs and the future.

Sources: J. Lynn Lunsford, "Going Up," *Wall Street Journal*, July 2, 2003, p. A1. Sebastian Moffett, "The Japanese Paradox," *Wall Street Journal*, September 23, 2003, p. B1; Valerie Reitman, "In the Grip of Status," *Los Angeles Times*, June 12, 2001, p. E1; and Sheridan Prasso, "A Yen for Luxury—Still," *Business Week*, July 7, 2003, p. 14.

socially obliged to hold lavish funerals for their parents. Signs of status continue to be important to Japanese consumers. Despite nearly a decade of poor economic performance in Japan, Japanese shoppers are still attracted to European luxury goods. They purchase about 40 percent of the world's high-quality leather goods and account for over half of all sales of such companies as Gucci and Louis Vuitton.[8]

Consumer Behavior

The ability to buy is influenced by a variety of economic elements, which are much easier to identify and quantify than elements related to consumers' motivations to buy. As we noted earlier, all consumers exhibit some similarities as members of the human race. However, buyer behavior is not uniform among all humans. Buyer behavior is learned, primarily from the culture, and so it differs from one culture to another. Throughout this book many cultural differences in consumer behavior will be addressed.

One example of similarities and differences in consumer behavior across cultures is attitudes toward color. A study of consumers in eight countries revealed that some universal color preferences do exist. Blue was either the first or the second favorite color in every country, and there was no difference in liking in respect to black, green, red, or white. However, there were differences in preferences for brown, gold, orange, purple, and yellow. Black and red signify happiness to the Chinese and are commonly chosen for wedding invitations. In India, Hindus consider orange the most sacred color. The color purple is associated with expensive products in Japan, China, and South Korea but with inexpensive products in the United States.[9] This last finding has possible implications for product design and packaging of luxury products that are marketed cross-culturally.

As we discussed in Chapter 3, culture consists of widely shared norms or patterns of behavior within a large group of people. These norms can directly affect product usage. For example, it may prove difficult to sell insurance in some Muslim countries because religious leaders consider buying insurance gambling, which is prohibited under Islam.[10] Mothers in Brazil believe that only they can properly prepare foods for their babies and therefore are reluctant to buy processed foods. This cultural norm in Brazil caused difficulty for Gerber, despite the fact that its products sold well in other Latin American countries.[11]

The structure of the family and the roles assigned to each member also play an important part in determining what products are purchased and how the decision to purchase is made. Table 5.2 shows the results of a study that

TABLE 5.2 MEAN NUMBER OF PURCHASE DECISIONS BY PRODUCT TYPE

PRODUCT	UNITED STATES	VENEZUELA	PRODUCT	UNITED STATES	VENEZUELA
GROCERIES			**VACATIONS**		
Husband	.23	.23	Husband	1.00	1.51
Joint	.60	.69	Joint	3.68	3.18
Wife	3.20	3.08	Wife	.40	.41
FURNITURE			**SAVINGS**		
Husband	.41	1.16	Husband	1.00	1.07
Joint	3.41	2.71	Joint	1.61	1.60
Wife	2.23	2.16	Wife	.44	.34
MAJOR APPLIANCES			**HOUSING**		
Husband	.98	1.97	Husband	.34	.87
Joint	3.21	2.10	Joint	2.47	1.82
Wife	.85	.93	Wife	.34	.39
LIFE INSURANCE			**DOCTOR**		
Husband	2.65	3.38	Husband	.03	.10
Joint	1.23	.55	Joint	.35	.42
Wife	.15	.05	Wife	.62	.49
AUTOMOBILES					
Husband	2.59	4.16			
Joint	3.06	1.42			
Wife	.41	.40			

SOURCE: Adapted from Robert T. Green and Isabella Cunningham, "Family Purchasing Roles in Two Countries," *Journal of International Business Studies* 11 (Spring–Summer 1980), p. 95. Reprinted by permission.

examined and compared decision-making roles in families from the United States and Venezuela. Nine products and services were picked, and each family surveyed was asked to identify which member made the decision to purchase the product. The overriding contrast between the two samples involved the role of the husband. More joint decisions regarding major purchases were made in the United States than in Venezuela. In all purchase decisions except those involving groceries and savings, the Venezuelan husband made more decisions than the U.S. husband.

International marketers should be aware that variations in family purchasing roles exist in foreign markets as a result of social and cultural differences. Marketing strategy may need to change to take into account the respective roles of family members. For example, a U.S. manufacturer of appliances or furniture may find it advisable to incorporate the husband into a Venezuelan marketing strategy to a larger extent than in the United States.

Segmenting Markets

Global marketers must remember that proper market segmentation is important for two reasons:

▶ You do not need every consumer in a country to buy your product in order to be successful in that market—you just need a large enough segment of the market to be willing and able to buy your product.

▶ How—and how much—you adapt your marketing mix (product, price, distribution, promotion) in a national market will depend on the segment you target in that market.

Most segmentation is done at the local level. Should we target French housewives or French working women? Should we develop a different marketing mix for Brazilian teens than the one we developed for Brazilian adults?

Within any country there may be segments that are more open to the idea of buying foreign products as well as possessing the means to do so. Certain segments within a national market may be inclined to purchase global brands because they enhance their self-image of being cosmopolitan, sophisticated, and modern.[12] Such **cosmopolitans** arguably make easier targets for global marketers. Cosmopolitans have often been associated with younger, more urban consumers. Urban populations in emerging markets have long been thought to be more accessible (physically and psychologically) than rural populations. Furthermore, they tend to be richer. Economists at the World Bank were startled to discover that the average family of four living in Hanoi spent the equivalent of $20,000 when calculated as purchasing-power parity—even though Vietnam is considered one of the poorest countries in the world.[13] Table 5.3 depicts the urban-rural distribution of population across selected countries.

The cosmopolitan phenomenon has motivated some global marketers to think in terms of **global segments**, transnational consumer segments based on age, social class, and lifestyle rather than on national culture. For example, social class is a grouping of consumers based on income, education, and occupation. Within a culture, consumers in the same social class tend to have similar purchase patterns. Even across cultures this may be the case, especially among young, affluent professionals. A study of MBA students representing

Cosmopolitans consumers who purchase global brands to enhance their self-image of being sophisticated and modern

Global segments transnational consumer segments based on lifestyle or demographics such as age and social class rather than on nationality

TABLE 5.3 URBAN/RURAL POPULATION DISTRIBUTION (%)		
COUNTRY	URBAN	RURAL
Afghanistan	23	77
Bermuda	100	0
Bolivia	63	37
Brazil	83	17
Burundi	10	90
Chile	87	13
China	39	61
Egypt	42	58
France	76	24
Germany	88	12
Greece	61	39
India	28	72
Japan	65	35
South Korea	80	20
Mexico	75	25
Nigeria	47	53
Poland	62	38
Russian Federation	73	27
Saudi Arabia	88	12
Singapore	100	0
Turkey	66	34
United States	80	20

SOURCE: Adapted from *Indicator of Human Settlements,* 2003 (updated 2004), Population Division of the United Nations Secretariat.

thirty-eight nationalities revealed cross-cultural similarities in how these students evaluated product quality. The students were young, affluent, mobile, well educated, and fluent in English. Across nationalities and cultural groups, all rated brand names the highest as a cue to product quality. Similarly, all rated retailer reputation the lowest and placed price between the other two cues. The importance of physical appearance of the product did vary some among cultures, however.[14] As this study shows, some—but not all—aspects of buyer behavior may converge across cultures when examining a transnational segment. However, for most products and segmentation schemes, persistent national differences appear to limit the usefulness of global segmentation.

Of course, some marketers simply decide that they will only target segments in international markets that resemble their domestic buyers. Such a strategy appears easy. Marketers simply sell their product to anyone overseas who wants to buy it as is. This strategy has sometimes been employed by producers of high-end luxury goods under the assumption that luxury buyers are relatively similar across national markets. However, regional differences can arise even among luxury buyers. Lexus sedans went from zero to luxury-class market leader in the United States in a 10-year period, but sales remained stymied in Europe. Europeans associated luxury with brand heritage and attention to detail, while Americans focused on comfort, size, and dependability. The biggest selling point of the Lexus in the U.S. market was its reliability; it didn't break down. For Europeans, that just wasn't enough from a luxury car.[15]

Just-like-us segments market segments in foreign countries that closely resemble marketers' domestic buyers

Targeting the **just-like-us segment** overseas is likely to result in sales to few consumers worldwide and limits a firm's global profit potential. In addition, such a strategy blinds marketers to unique national opportunities. For example, toy stores in China discovered that some of their biggest buyers were adults shopping for themselves. The same proved true for comic books. For some adults it was an excuse to enjoy a childhood they missed first time around when China was much poorer and consumer products practically were nonexistent in the marketplace. For others, it was a way to escape and relax in the very competitive climate of reform-era China.[16] If toy manufacturers simply targeted children like they would in most countries, they could miss the adult-market opportunity in China.

BUSINESS MARKETS

It is commonly said that business buyers around the world are much more predictable and similar than consumers in their purchasing behavior. They are thought to be more influenced by the economic considerations of cost and product performance and less affected by social and cultural factors. After all, purchasing agents in Japan who are buying specialty steel for their companies will attempt to get the best possible products at the lowest cost, which is similar to how purchasing agents in the United States or Germany would act.

In fact, business-to-business marketing in the global arena is considerably influenced by variations across cultures. Take, for instance, the offer of a personal gift to a prospective buyer. Small gifts are often given at first meetings in Japan. Similarly, such gifts are customarily exchanged with Chinese buyers as a way of saying, "I hope this friendship will last." In Latin America, Europe, and the Arab world, however, offering a gift at first meeting is usually considered inappropriate and may even be construed as a bribe.[17]

A number of cross-cultural differences can be observed in buyer motivation and behavior. Because business markets often encompass longer-term relationships between customer and supplier, cultural attitudes toward social relationships are especially important. Sales are often subject to negotiations, and negotiating encompasses many aspects of culture. In addition to dealing with cross-cultural differences, international marketers increasingly find themselves selling to multinational firms, whose buyer behavior presents its own set of challenges.

The Business Buyer's Needs

Industrial products, such as machinery, intermediate goods, and raw materials, are sold to businesses for use in a manufacturing process to produce other goods. If the objective of the manufacturer is to maximize profit, the critical buying criterion will reflect the performance of the product purchased relative

Headquartered in St. Louis, Missouri, Emerson is active in 150 countries. It is one of many business-to-business marketers with a global presence.

to its cost. This **cost–performance criterion** is a key consideration for industrial buyers, along with such other buying criteria as the service and dependability of the selling company.

Similar considerations arise in other business-to-business sales transactions. A study of how international companies chose foreign exchange suppliers revealed that price was an important factor in both the selection of a supplier and the volume of business allotted to a supplier. Also, large suppliers were generally preferred over smaller suppliers. Nonetheless, account management and service quality could outweigh price, and customers favored suppliers from their home markets.[18]

Because the cost–performance criterion is often critical, the economic situation in the purchasing country affects the decision process. This is particularly true for the purchase of new machinery. When buying machinery, a firm must weigh the advantages of adopting a capital-intensive technology against those of adopting a labor-intensive technology. Labor costs play a key role in this decision. Countries with a surplus of labor normally have lower labor costs because

Cost-performance criterion the expected performance of industrial products or capital equipment relative to the costs to purchase and use such products or equipment

supply exceeds demand. These lower pay rates weigh heavily in favor of a labor-intensive method of manufacture. Therefore, these countries will be less apt to purchase sophisticated automatic machinery; the same job can be done with the cheaper labor.

As Figure 5.1 shows, wage levels vary from country to country. Selling an industrial robot that replaces three workers in the manufacture of a product can be more easily justified in Norway or Germany, where average labor costs are 20 percent more than in the United States, than in Britain, where labor costs are less than 80 percent of the U.S. labor rate. Developed countries with a high labor rate are prime targets for automated manufacturing equipment. Companies that want to export to developing countries where labor is cheaper must be aware that labor-saving measures may not be appreciated or readily applied. For example, the Chinese government encourages the import of labor-intensive technology that can effectively utilize its vast population.

Of course, there are exceptions to this rule. When international banks expanded into the Arab Gulf, they were faced with a decision concerning the level of technology for teller services. In other developing countries, the banks employed older, labor- and paper-intensive technology. However, labor in the Gulf was scarce and expensive as a consequence of the region's sudden oil wealth and its small population. In light of this, many banks chose to purchase the latest technology available from the United States.

FIGURE 5.1

Index of Manufacturing Labor Cost per Worker-Hour for Selected Countries

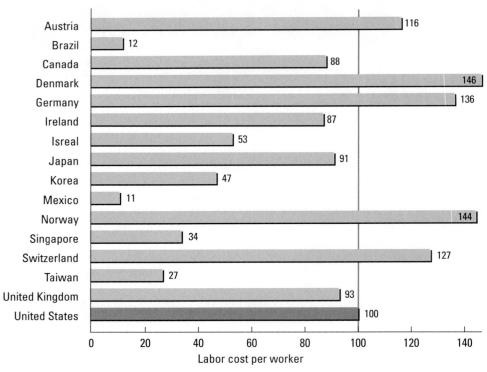

NOTE: United States = 100.

SOURCE: Based on figures from the United States Department of Labor, Bureau of Labor and Statistics, 2004.

The newly industrialized countries of Asia, such as South Korea, Taiwan, and Singapore, are becoming increasingly important markets for industrial products. For example, during the 1990s, Asia-Pacific overtook both North America and Europe as the major market for new elevator sales. Still, some differences can be observed in buyer needs and wants in these markets. Business buyers look for long-term commitment from their suppliers. They expect to see foreign firms adapt products to local needs and commit themselves to frequent contact with the buyer. A global competitor should expect to keep a well-stocked warehouse and to locate a technical staff and sales office in the local market. Because many of the industrial buyers in this region are medium-sized firms, they might expect more regular training to be provided over the life of the business relationship. Price can be a critical factor in the sales as well, because many of these businesses work on tight margins. Similarly, special product features that might appeal to buyers in more industrially developed markets are less important in these markets.[19]

Developing Business Relationships

Business-to-business sales usually involve ongoing relationships. The seller and buyer communicate more directly and establish a relationship that continues over time. For example, sales may involve the design and delivery of customized products, or after-sale service may be an important component of the product. These business relationships are based on mutual understanding, past experiences, and expectations for the future.

Building such a relationship involves a social exchange process. One firm (usually, but not always, the supplier) takes the initiative and suggests that the two firms do business. If the other firm responds, commitments gradually are made. The parties determine how to coordinate their activities, trust is established, and a commitment to a continued relationship arises. The firms may become increasingly interdependent, such as by agreeing to develop a new product together.[20] Because of this close working relationship, cultural sensitivity will be necessary in cases in which seller and buyer come from different cultures.

Although these business relationships have an overall informal character, specific transactions, many of which can be unique to the relationship, will need to be formalized. Because of this, negotiations are often involved in business-to-business sales. Negotiations encompass not only specifics concerning price and financing terms but also such issues as product design, training, and after-sale service.

Cross-cultural negotiations are a particular challenge to global marketers. To begin with, marketers may face the translation problems that we discussed in Chapter 3. Furthermore, whereas some cultures enter negotiations with a win-win attitude, other cultures envisage negotiations as a zero-sum game wherein one side is pitted against the other. Americans can be especially nonplused when they find themselves negotiating with Russians. Russian negotiators often begin with unreasonable requests in order to test their American counterparts and see how tough they really are. Russian negotiators can surprise Americans with emotional outbursts and anti-Western tirades. Russians also take advantage of Americans' sense of urgency and desire to use time effectively. They may ask the same question repeatedly, feign boredom, and even appear to fall asleep during negotiations![21]

Perhaps some of the toughest cross-cultural negotiations took place after China reopened to world trade. Many foreign firms were interested in the potential of the Chinese market. Americans wanted to negotiate clear, legal contracts with Chinese clients and partners. The Chinese, on the other hand, interpreted this approach as betraying a lack of trust on the part of Americans. They sought to establish close relationships with foreign firms based on mutual loyalty. To them a contract was far less important than these relationships. For their part, Americans found the Chinese as irreverent of time as the Russians. Unlike the Russians, the Chinese appeared passive in their demeanor. Any display of anger, frustration, or aggression on the part of American negotiators was likely to backfire, and mock tantrums were definitely taboo.[22] Furthermore, many Chinese would appear at the negotiating table, and American negotiators found it difficult to figure out who had real authority to agree to terms. Cross-cultural negotiations frustrated many Americans and discouraged, or at least delayed, their entry into this huge market. In the meantime, competitors from Japan and Asia's overseas Chinese community found the negotiations less culturally harrowing. As a result, many entered the Chinese market more rapidly.

Because negotiations involve many aspects of culture—social relationships, attitudes toward power, perceptions of time, and of course language—they must be undertaken with the greatest cultural sensitivity. In most business-to-business sales, negotiations do not end with the first purchase decision. They permeate the continuing relationship between global marketer and buyer. For this reason, global marketers must never assume that marketing industrial products or services remains the same worldwide.

Marketing to Global Buyers

Global buyers present marketers with new challenges. There are two kinds of global buyers: national global buyers and multinational global buyers.[23] **National global buyers** search the world for products that are used in a single country or market. Their job has been far easier since the introduction of the Internet. **Multinational global buyers** similarly search the world for products but use those products throughout their global operations. Such buyers are commonly multinational firms, but they also include organizations such as the World Health Organization. Because both national and multinational global buyers are relatively sophisticated about suppliers and prices, competition for their business tends to be intense.

Multinational global buyers in particular may represent large accounts. They use their market power to command better service and even lower prices. Finding cost-effective inputs is increasingly crucial for most multinational firms, because they too are often under pressure to deliver good products at a low price. Centralized purchasing is one way in which multinational corporations attempt to keep costs down. For example, General Motors and three Japanese automakers—Fuji Heavy Industries, Isuzu Motors, and Suzuki Motor—announced that they had unified their purchasing organizations for selected parts, components, and services in order to reduce costs. GM holds equity stakes in the three Japanese firms.[24]

National global buyers firms that search the world for products that are used in a single country or market

Multinational global buyers firms that search the world for products to be used throughout their global operations

Many Fortune 500 companies have recognized this strategic importance of purchasing and have elevated purchasing managers to the vice-president level within their organizations. Firms that sell to multinational global buyers often give them special attention. Practicing what is called **global account management**, they assign special account executives and service teams to these valuable but demanding global buyers. We will discuss this further in Chapter 14.

Global account management the assignment of special account executives and service teams to handle the needs of valuable but demanding global buyers

GOVERNMENT MARKETS

A large number of international business transactions involve governments. For example, 80 percent of all international trade in agricultural products is handled by governments. The U.S. government buys more goods and services than any other government, business, industry, or organization in the world.[25] Selling to governments can be both time-consuming and frustrating. However, governments are large purchasers, and selling to them can yield enormous returns.

The size of government purchases depends on the economic or political orientation of the country. In highly developed, free-market countries, the government plays less of a role than in other markets. The amount of government purchases is also a function of state-owned operations. For example, in the United States the only government-owned operation is the postal system, whereas in India the government owns not only the postal system but also much of the telecommunications, electric, gas, oil, coal, railway, airline, and shipbuilding industries.

The Buying Process

Governmental buying processes tend to be highly bureaucratic. To sell to the U.S. Department of Defense, for example, a firm has to get on a bidding list for each branch of the armed forces. These bidding lists are issued on an annual basis. A firm that is unable to get on the list must wait a full year to try again. Similarly, negotiating with foreign governments can be a very long and formal process.

As we saw in Chapter 4, governments pursue several different agendas, which often complicate government purchasing. For example, a government might wish to promote its local industry as well as decrease its trade deficit. For these reasons, governments often discriminate against foreign suppliers and give preference to local suppliers. In some sophisticated industries such as aerospace, there may be no viable local competitor in many countries. Then the government might ask potential foreign suppliers to subcontract simpler project inputs to local firms. Alternatively, Saudi Arabia asks major foreign government contractors to invest some of their profits in local Saudi industries.

Global marketers pursuing government sales in high-tech fields may also run afoul of the national agendas of their home countries. The threat of compromising national security has prompted governments, especially that of the United States, to institute restrictions on the overseas sale of certain technologies, such as nuclear plants, computers, telecommunications, and military weapons.

Fluor Corporation is one of the world's largest engineering, procurement, and construction organizations. It maintains offices in twenty-five countries across six continents. Fluor markets to governments as well as to businesses.

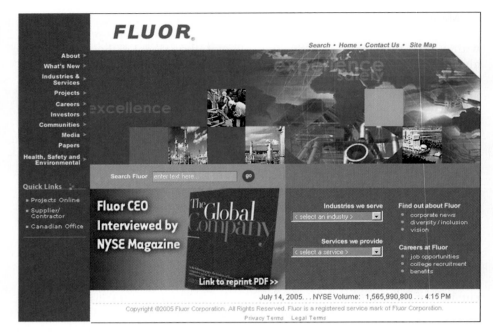

Government procurement processes vary from country to country. In Belgium, 90 percent of all public contracts are awarded to the lowest bidder. The remaining 10 percent are granted through "invitation to tender," with factors other than price coming into play. These other factors may include the company's financial viability, technical competence, and after-sale service. Central government supplies, excluding data processing and telecommunications, must be bought through the Central Supplies Office. Regional, local, and quasi-governmental bodies, such as Sabena Airlines, purchase supplies independently.

Here are several recommendations to companies that wish to sell to the Belgian government:

▶ *Manufacture in Belgium.* Preference is given to a local supplier if other things are equal.

▶ *Develop a European image.* A strong EU image has given an advantage to companies such as Siemens and Philips.

▶ *Use the appropriate language.* Although both Flemish and French are officially accepted, ask which is preferred in the department that is receiving the bid.

▶ *Emphasize the recruitment of labor following the winning of a contract.* Companies are favored if they will employ Belgian citizens.

▶ *When new technology is involved, get in at the beginning.* It is often difficult and expensive for the government to change to a different technology at a later date.

▶ *Whenever possible, use local contractors.* The Belgian government likes a bidder to use as many local contractors as possible.[26]

Government Contracts in Developing Countries

Figure 5.2 depicts the various "screens" that global marketers must pass through to secure large government contracts in developing countries. [27] A foreign firm must first address the **eligibility screen**. To make the bidding process efficient and manageable, governments seek to weed out firms that are not serious or are too small to handle the contract. For example, Saudi Arabia may ask bidders on a contract to submit a $100,000 fee with their bid or to provide a bond for 1 percent of the tender value. Alternatively, governments may simply restrict the bidding to several well-known international firms that are invited to

Eligibility screen the initial requirement placed by governments on firms seeking to bid on government contracts in developing countries. Firms must be judged to be serious in their intent and large enough to handle the contracts.

FIGURE 5.2
Marketing to Governments in Developing Countries

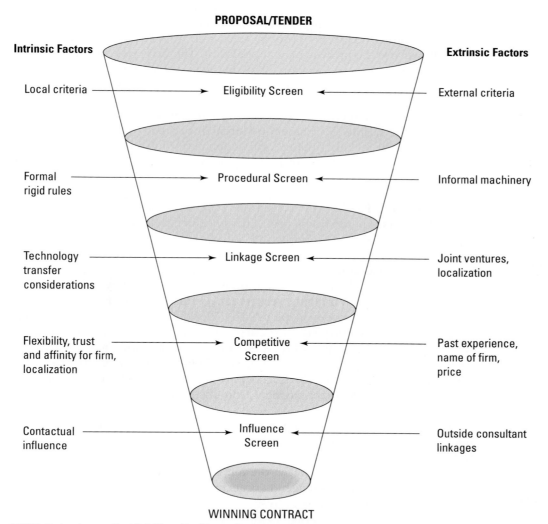

SOURCE: Mushtaq Luqman, Ghazi M. Habib, and Sami Kassem, "Marketing to LDC Governments," International Marketing Review 5, no. 1 (Spring 1988), p. 59.

bid on a particular project. This approach is common in the defense and civil aviation industries.

If the project is complicated or represents a new task for the purchasing government, outside consultants may be employed to design the project and oversee its implementation. For example, Bechtel, a large U.S. engineering firm, could be hired as a consultant for complex construction projects. As a result, Bechtel's designs are more likely to follow U.S. industry standards, and this gives U.S. firms a competitive advantage when bidding on the contract.

Political considerations can play a role at this stage as well. For example, China is now the world's largest arms importer, ahead of India, Turkey, Taiwan, and Saudi Arabia. Ninety percent of Chinese arms imports are from Russia.[28] Russian armament firms are considered to be more reliable than American ones. U.S. firms could at any time be forbidden by the U.S. government to enter into or fulfill a contract with China.

Procedural screen a requirement that firms bidding on government contracts in developing countries follow numerous bureaucratic procedures

After passing the eligibility screen, the foreign firm encounters the **procedural screen**. At this point, numerous bureaucratic procedures must be followed and numerous forms properly filled out. And this can be all the more difficult because the process may not be overt. The firm may need to take special care to discover who is actually in charge and to understand exactly what needs to be done. Hiring local consultants who have had experience with the process is often a good idea.

Linkage screen a common requirement that international firms bidding on government contracts in developing countries identify ways in which specific local businesses will participate in or otherwise benefit by the proposed contracts

The firm must then negotiate the **linkage screen**. It must address and implement the various government requirements related to assisting local businesses. This can include finding local suppliers to outsource a portion of the contract. Alternatively, it might involve finding a local partner with whom to establish a joint venture.

Competitive screen a requirement that firms bidding on government contracts in developing countries be competitive in experience, reputation, and cultural sensitivity as well as in price

After passing through these three screens, the firm must still face the **competitive screen**. Passing this screen not only involves bidding a competitive price; the firm's reputation, its past experience in developing countries, and its cultural sensitivity are also important. Because large projects can take several years to negotiate and many years to implement, the firm must exhibit an ability to be flexible as situations evolve and change.

Firms may even be asked to help finance the project they bid on. A good example of how governments seek creative financing from firms involves India's highway improvement plans. The World Bank estimates that India's annual highway spending will soon quadruple to $4 billion a year, making India very attractive to international road-building firms. But how India will finance road construction remains uncertain. One Indian state sought builders that would agree to operate the roads as private concerns before turning them over to the state. In lieu of direct payment from the government, the builders could collect tolls for 10 years [29]

Influence screen a requirement that firms bidding on government contracts in developing countries identify key decision makers and assure their proposals meet the needs of all parties

The final hurdle, the **influence screen**, requires a firm to identify the ultimate decision makers and to be sure it meets their needs. For example, selling radar to the Taiwanese may involve high officers in the air force who are pursuing a defense agenda. However, the ministry of industry may be involved as well. It may be pursuing an agenda of technology transfer and local outsourcing. The firm must be sure to address all these concerns. Managing this process is challenging for global marketers, but winning a large and attractive contract can make it all worthwhile.

For current examples of available government contracts, check out the *Government Tenders* links on our website (college.hmco.com/business/).

Bribery and Government Markets

Bribery is the giving of something of value to an individual in a position of trust to influence their judgment or behavior. Bribes can be offered to purchasing agents or other decision makers within companies to induce them to favor one supplier over another. Most bribery scandals in international marketing, however, involve government contracts. Government employees are in a particular position of trust because they are hired to work for the public good. If a government is awarding an aerospace contract, the government employees responsible for choosing the supplier should consider the value of the supplier to the country as a whole. If a key decision maker influences the decision for his or her personal gain, then public trust is betrayed. Bribes offered to win contracts are most common in industries where contracts are large and where few public employees are involved in the award decision.

Bribery is more endemic in less developed countries. A recent study confirmed that a country's GNP per capita is the best barometer of the level of government bribery (corruption) in that country. The same study also showed that bribery is more prevalent in countries that score higher on the Hofstede power-distance dimension.[30] Table 5.4 lists ratings by country on an index of perceived corruption.

Although most developing countries seek foreign investment for economic growth, several studies have found that governmental corruption is a serious obstacle to foreign investment in a country. The difference in corruption levels between host and home countries affects investment as well: Corruption significantly reduces investment from less corrupt countries.[31] Another study found that foreign entrants into national markets chose joint ventures more often than wholly owned subsidiaries as the level of corruption increased.[32]

U.S. Foreign Corrupt Practices Act.

Virtually all countries outlaw the bribing of their own government officials. In the late 1970s, the United States went a step further and outlawed the bribing of foreign officials. Until then, American firms that bribed foreign officials were not prosecuted under U.S. law, even though U.S. law disallowed claiming foreign bribes as tax deductions. This resulted in many multinationals keeping records of these bribes for their tax accountants. When government investigators were searching for illegal contributions to President Nixon's reelection fund, they discovered many such entries in company books.

The American public was dismayed. Despite heavy business lobbying against its passage, the U.S. Foreign Corrupt Practices Act (FCPA) was passed in 1977. This law forbids U.S. citizens to bribe foreign government employees and politicians. U.S. citizens are also forbidden to pay money to agents or other individuals who in turn pass money on to government employees. They are required to report any bribery occurring within their organizations and must not cover it up. The firm itself is required to keep good records. If audited, it must be able to account for all payments overseas. Fines are assessed for noncompliance.

Most important, perhaps, managers involved face jail sentences. In one case prosecuted under the law, Lockheed Martin Corporation was accused of paying $1 million to an Egyptian parliamentarian. The company was fined $25 million, and two company executives were jailed.[33] Although originally envisaged as a deterrent to U.S. citizens, the U.S. FCPA has been increasingly interpreted in such a way as to prosecute non-U.S. citizens as well. For example, a Swiss

Bribery giving something of value to an individual in a position of trust to influence his or her judgment or behavior

TABLE 5.4 CORRUPTION PERCEPTIONS INDEX

Country Rank	Country	2004 CPI Score[a]	Country Rank	Country	2004 CPI Score[a]
1	Finland	9.7	39	Malaysia	5.0
2	New Zealand	9.6		Tunisia	5.0
3	Denmark	9.5	41	Costa Rica	4.9
4	Iceland	9.5	42	Hungary	4.8
5	Singapore	9.3		Italy	4.8
6	Sweden	9.2	44	Kuwait	4.6
7	Switzerland	9.1		Lithuania	4.6
8	Norway	8.9		South Africa	4.6
9	Australia	8.8	47	South Korea	4.5
10	Netherlands	8.7	48	Seychelles	4.4
11	United Kingdom	8.6	49	Greece	4.3
12	Canada	8.5		Suriname	4.3
13	Austria	8.4	51	Czech Republic	4.2
14	Luxembourg	8.4		El Salvador	4.2
15	Germany	8.2		Trinidad and Tobago	4.2
16	Hong Kong	8.0	54	Bulgaria	4.1
17	Belgium	7.5		Mauritius	4.1
	Ireland	7.5		Namibia	4.1
	USA	7.5	57	Latvia	4.0
20	Chile	7.4		Slovakia	4.0
21	Barbados	7.3	59	Brazil	3.9
22	France	7.1	60	Belize	3.8
	Spain	7.1		Colombia	3.8
24	Japan	6.9	62	Cuba	3.7
25	Malta	6.8		Panama	3.7
26	Israel	6.4	64	Ghana	3.6
27	Portugal	6.3		Mexico	3.6
28	Uruguay	6.2		Thailand	3.6
29	Oman	6.1	67	Croatia	3.5
	United Arab Emirates	6.1		Peru	3.5
31	Botswana	6.0		Poland	3.5
	Estonia	6.0		Sri Lanka	3.5
	Slovenia	6.0	71	China	3.4
34	Bahrain	5.8		Saudi Arabia	3.4
35	Taiwan	5.6		Syria	3.4
36	Cyprus	5.4	74	Belarus	3.3
37	Jordan	5.3		Gabon	3.3
38	Qatar	5.2		Jamaica	3.3

(continued)

TABLE 5.4 (CONTINUED)

Country Rank	Country	2004 CPI Score[a]	Country Rank	Country	2004 CPI Score[a]
77	Benin	3.2	114	Congo, Republic	2.3
	Egypt	3.2		Ethiopia	2.3
	Mali	3.2		Honduras	2.3
	Morocco	3.2		Moldova	2.3
	Turkey	3.2		Sierra Leone	2.3
82	Armenia	3.1		Uzbekistan	2.3
	Bosnia and Herzegovina	3.1		Venezuela	2.3
	Madagascar	3.1		Zimbabwe	2.3
85	Mongolia	3.0	122	Bolivia	2.2
	Senegal	3.0		Guatemala	2.2
87	Dominican Republic	2.9		Kazakhstan	2.2
	Iran	2.9		Kyrgyzstan	2.2
	Romania	2.9		Niger	2.2
90	Gambia	2.8		Sudan	2.2
	India	2.8		Ukraine	2.2
	Malawi	2.8	129	Cameroon	2.1
	Mozambique	2.8		Iraq	2.1
	Nepal	2.8		Kenya	2.1
	Russia	2.8		Pakistan	2.1
	Tanzania	2.8	133	Angola	2.0
97	Algeria	2.7		Congo, Democratic Republic	2.0
	Lebanon	2.7		Côte d'Ivoire	2.0
	Macedonia	2.7		Georgia	2.0
	Nicaragua	2.7		Indonesia	2.0
	Serbia and Montenegro	2.7		Tajikistan	2.0
102	Eritrea	2.6		Turkmenistan	2.0
	Papua New Guinea	2.6	140	Azerbaijan	1.9
	Philippines	2.6		Paraguay	1.9
	Uganda	2.6	142	Chad	1.7
	Vietnam	2.6		Myanmar	1.7
	Zambia	2.6	144	Nigeria	1.6
108	Albania	2.5	145	Bangladesh	1.5
	Argentina	2.5		Haiti	1.5
	Libya	2.5			
	Palestine	2.5			
112	Ecuador	2.4			
	Yemen	2.4			

[a]10 = highly clean and 0 = highly corrupt.
SOURCE: 2004 Transparency International, www.transparency.org.

WORLD BEAT 5.2

Cleaning Up Russia

DESPITE ITS SIZE, RUSSIA attracts far less capital than smaller countries such as Poland and the Czech Republic. Russia received less foreign direct investment in 10 years than China received on average in a single year. And that's not all: Indigenous Russian capital is moving out fast! Government corruption presents a major impediment to investment—both foreign and local. An estimated US$30 billion a year is collected by corrupt officials.

President Vladimir Putin has spearheaded reforms such as increasing judges' low salaries fivefold to counter courtroom bribes. A new law also bans the intervention of state prosecutors in private litigation between contending business parties, and new rules sharply restrict the discounts that railroad regulators can offer shippers.

These discounts often rewarded customers who paid the biggest bribes. Another law reduced the number of business activities that required a license from 2,000 to 100. Fewer licenses reduce the opportunity for a bureaucrat to receive a bribe. The need to receive—and pay for—official signatures has stifled the creation of new businesses. President Putin reportedly remarked that an entrepreneur should receive a medal for personal bravery at the moment of business registration.

Sources: Vladimir Kvint, "The Scary Business of Russia," *Forbes*, May 23, 2005, p. 42; Guy Chazan, Gregory L. White, and Betsy McKay, "Coke Expands Russian Presence," *Wall Street Journal Europe*, April 1, 2005, p. A1; and Paul Starobin and Catherine Belton, "Cleanup Time," *Business Week*, January 14, 2002, pp. 46–47.

Expediting payments small bribes paid to civil servants to perform their duties in a timely manner

lawyer was indicted in the United States for conspiring to bribe foreign officials in connection with a failed $450 million Caspian Sea oil deal. The lawyer was charged with one count of conspiracy to violate the U.S. FCPA.[34]

U.S. firms are allowed to make expediting payments, however. **Expediting payments** are small sums paid to civil servants to do their jobs. For example, if office computers were sitting at customs and not being processed, an expediting payment might speed up the paperwork. Two multinational companies, Unilever and BP Amoco, admitted in parliamentary hearings in London that their managers did make facilitating payments in developing countries. The counsel for Unilever said that although these payments were not encouraged, they were tolerated as long as they were small and were used to expedite something that would have happened eventually anyway. The general auditor of BP Amoco said the payments were made to avoid delays and not to gain an unfair advantage over competitors.[35] However, some firms have refused to participate in facilitating payments. Procter & Gamble refused to do so when entering Brazil, despite the prevalence of such payments there. One P&G manager recalls that government employees soon learned not even to ask the firm for such payments.

Many U.S. businesses feared that the U.S. FCPA would put them at a competitive disadvantage overseas, especially in emerging markets, because other competitor nations had not adopted a similar law. The law no doubt has been a handicap in some cases, but overall it does not appear to have undermined U.S. exports to bribe-prone countries. The law may have helped U.S. managers in one respect: It has kept them out of jail overseas. A study of bribery scandals in the Middle East over a period of nearly 20 years revealed no American having been imprisoned for bribing a government official. This was in contrast to the experiences of Asians and Europeans.[36]

Other Antibribery Conventions. In 1997, thirty-four nations signed an antibribery pact. These included the twenty-nine members of the Organization for Economic Cooperation and Development (OECD), as well as Argentina, Brazil, Chile, Bulgaria, and Slovakia. Under the agreement, the member countries agreed to propose to their parliaments national laws designed to combat overseas bribery.[37] Similarly, the United Nations Convention Against Corruption was signed in December 2003. Signatories include the United States, Russia, China, Japan, and much of Europe. National governments must still ratify the law and put in place regulations to support it. The convention aims at encouraging the recovery of funds moved overseas by corrupt officials and was prompted by developing countries anxious to recover such funds.[38]

Table 5.5 ranks twenty-one leading exporting countries in terms of perceptions of the propensity of their firms to bribe in developing countries. Watchdog organization Transparency International noted that domestic companies in developing countries would receive lower ratings than the multinational firms—1.9 on average.

Check out our website for the latest country corruption scores (college.hmco.com/business/).

TABLE 5.5 BRIBE PAYERS INDEX		
RANK	COUNTRY	SCORE[a]
1	Australia	8.5
2	Sweden	8.4
2	Switzerland	8.4
4	Austria	8.2
5	Canada	8.1
6	Netherlands	7.8
	Belgium	7.8
8	United Kingdom	6.9
9	Singapore	6.3
	Germany	6.3
11	Spain	5.8
12	France	5.5
13	USA	5.3
	Japan	5.3
15	Hong Kong	4.3
	Malaysia	4.3
17	Italy	4.1
18	South Korea	3.9
19	Taiwan	3.8
20	China (PRC)	3.5
21	Russia	3.2

[a]0 = very high level of bribery; 10 = negligible bribery.
SOURCE: Transparency International, *Bribe Payers Index 2002.*

CONCLUSION

Which buyers will you target? Continue with your *Country Market Report* on our website (college.hmco.com/business/).

In this chapter we introduced some basic issues of buyer behavior across cultures. We showed that buyers in various national markets can exhibit similar needs, wants, and even behaviors. In many ways, however, buyers differ from one culture to another. This is true whether the buyer is a consumer, a business, or a government. The challenge to the global marketer is to understand when it is possible to exploit similar needs and behaviors and when it is important to adapt to different buyer conditions. In addition, we observed that many buyers increasingly search the world for products. This intensifies competition and makes it all the more imperative that global marketers understand their markets and address the needs of their buyers.

QUESTIONS FOR DISCUSSION

1. What critical factors influence a consumer's ability to purchase a product such as a stereo system?

2. Given the data on family decision making in the United States and Venezuela that appears in Table 5.2, how will the marketing of automobiles be different in the two countries?

3. Will the buying process be more similar from country to country for deodorant or delivery vans? Why?

4. If you were selling a product that is purchased mostly by governments, such as a nuclear power plant, how would you prepare to sell to Belgium, Egypt, and Mexico? What means would you use to understand the government buying process in each of these countries?

5. Why do you think that the U.S. Foreign Corrupt Practices Act allows expediting payments? Why are these payments seen as less reprehensible than other forms of bribery?

CASE 5.1

What Teens Want

Increasingly, consumer product companies and retailers are targeting teens. In the United States, the teen and preteen market comprises about sixty million consumers. Their online purchases alone total $1.5 billion each year. Some teen-specific sites, such as Delias.com, have proved successful. Delias sells clothes that appeal to teens while providing chatrooms and links to other teen sites. Two of the most popular teen sites are Amazon.com and Gap.com. Wal-Mart .com is also popular, despite the fact that it does nothing in particular to attract teens to its site. Teens like it for its good prices.

Marketers in Europe also are trying to understand the teen market better. European teens were once seen as being closer to their parents and more irreverent than American teens. They also watched television less and were more influenced by European music trends. However, a recent study of German teens—thought to be indicative of most Europeans—showed the teens spending their leisure time watching television, talking on the phone, and listening to music, in that order. At the top of the shopping list for buyers ten to seventeen years old was a computer, preferably one connected to the Internet. Other favored products were video recorders, televisions, and mobile phones. Already, 62 percent of this age group owned a television, and 32 percent owned a video recorder.

But does a global teen segment exist? Clinique, a division of the cosmetics company Estée Lauder, has begun a multinational survey to determine what teens find "cool." The results so far from the United States and the United Kingdom have revealed no clearly targetable differences. Mothers and daughters appeared surprisingly similar in what they wanted in cosmetics and fragrances, although teens seemed to appreciate advertising geared to them. Teens also shopped for upscale fragrances at mass markets where prices were cheaper.

Whether it is possible to extrapolate teen consumer behavior from the developed to the developing world is even more problematic. A study comparing Asian teens to their parents discovered that the teens ranked values such as individualism, freedom, and ambition significantly higher than their parents did. However, at a United Nations convention on youth, one girl from Bangladesh described her 15-year-old sister as pregnant and working in a textile factory all day. To her, luxury products and the Internet had little

meaning. However, a study of homeless street kids in Brazil revealed that the desire to own global brands was a major impetus for their leaving home for life on the streets. Those who were able to find work would usually spend their first earnings on a pair of Reebok or Nike shoes.

Discussion Questions

1. Would it be useful for global marketers to think of teens as a global segment? Why or why not?
2. Suggest ways in which teen consumer behavior is likely to differ between developed and developing countries.
3. Why do you think street kids in Brazil are attracted to global brand names?

Sources: Arundhati Parmar, "Global Youth United," *Marketing News,* October 28, 2002, p. 49; "Television and Telephoning Among Top Ten Adolescent Leisure Pursuits," *Deutsche Presse-Agentur,* May 11, 2000; Anne-Beatrice Clasmann, "Young People in Developing Nations Seek More Responsibility," *Deutsche Presse-Agentur,* February 26, 2000; Mario Osava, "Children—Brazil: Street Kids Are Caught Up by Consumer Fever," Inter Press Service, December 9, 1999; and Nicole Grasse, "For Teens Dubbed Generation Y, Online Shopping Is as Common as a Can of Coke," Responsive Database Services, May 2000, p. 52.

CASE 5.2
Questionable Payments

Scenario 1: Thomas Karel is a Swiss national who works as the export manager for a major U.S. producer of machinery and software systems for petroleum exploration. His company is bidding on a $25 million contract that could produce $5 million in profit for his firm. The potential customer is the state-owned oil company in a Latin American country. Thomas has recently heard from his company's agent in that country. The agent suggests that he can "nail down" the contract if Thomas will give him $1 million to pass on to an influential cabinet member in charge of awarding the contract. The competition, a French

multinational firm, is also bidding on the contract. *What should Thomas do?*

Scenario 2: David Yang has been sent to a country in Southeast Asia to negotiate the possible sale of a large-scale traffic control system to be adopted across the country. The contract involves not only traffic lights but also their installation and servicing, as well as computer software to monitor traffic flows. Another American in the country has suggested to David that he retain the public relations firm owned by the wife of the country's prime minister. The prime minister is not directly involved with the negotiations for the traffic control system. *What should David do?*

Scenario 3: Michael Avila is the general manager of a subsidiary in the Middle East of an American shipping company. His company specializes in moving the household belongings of expatriates working for multinational companies. Michael is about to authorize the monthly slush fund for payments to customs officials to expedite the movement of his clients' goods through customs when he catches sight of an article in the local newspaper. The government has announced a crackdown on corruption. *What should Michael do?*

Scenario 4: Ana Weiss is the new general manager of DeluxDye in Taiwan. DeluxDye produces high-quality industrial paints and dyes that are used in the manufacture of such products as toys and housewares. Compared to competitors' products, DeluxDye products are relatively expensive to purchase. However, they save costs over the long run. Their higher quality ensures more consistent color and performance and less manufacturing downtime. The money customers save can more than make up for the higher initial price of the product.

Corporate guidelines, established in the United States, forbid the paying of any bribes, however small. In Taiwan, Ana's sales force is complaining that their inability to offer "tea money" is discouraging sales growth in the market. Tea money consists of small cash payments or gifts, such as tickets to rock concerts or sports events. These payments are often given to lower-level employees who act as gatekeepers to the higher-level manager—often the head of one of Taiwan's many family-owned manufacturing firms—who in turn makes the buying decision. DeluxDye believes its products are superior to those of its competitors and insists that its sales forces around the world promote the product on its merits alone. Bribery is immoral, and it casts doubts on the integrity of the briber. *What should Ana do?*

Discussion Questions

1. Explain and defend a course of action for each of the managers above.
2. When considering questionable payments, should marketers emphasize ethical concerns, legal considerations, or making the sale? Explain your answer.

Notes

1. Brendan M. Case, "Latin Flavor Brewing," *Dallas Morning News*, March 26, 2002, p.1D.
2. Brian Dumaine, "P&G Rewrites the Rules of Marketing," *Fortune*, November 6, 1989, p. 48.
3. Sara Calian, "Swiss Cheese Now a Mature Market in Switzerland," *Wall Street Journal*, March 3, 1996, p. A1.
4. *Beverage Industry Annual Manual* (Cleveland: Harcourt, 1987), p. 16.
5. "Distribution of Income or Consumption," *2001 World Development Indicators* (Washington, DC: World Bank), p. 70.
6. Diana Farrell, "The Hidden Dangers of the Informal Economy," *McKinsey Quarterly* no. 3 (2004), pp. 26–38.
7. Jean-Claude Usunier, *Marketing Across Cultures* (New York: Prentice-Hall, 2000), p. 104.
8. Deborah Ball, "Despite Downturn, Japanese Are Still Having Fits for Luxury Goods," *Wall Street Journal*, April 24, 2001, p. B1.
9. Thomas J. Madden, Kelly Hewlett, and Martin S. Roth, "Managing Images in Different Cultures: A Cross-National Study of Color Meaning and Preferences," *Journal of International Marketing* 8, no. 4 (2000), pp. 90–107.
10. D. E. Allen, "Anthropological Insights into Consumer Behavior," *European Journal of Marketing* 5 (Summer 1971), p. 54.
11. Ann Helmings, "Culture Shocks," *Advertising Age*, May 17, 1982, p. M-9.
12. Jan-Benedict E.M. Steenkamp, Rajeev Batra, and Dana L. Alden, "How Perceived Brand Globalness Creates Brand Value," *Journal of International Business Studies* 34, no. 1 (2003), pp. 53–65.
13. Margot Cohen, "Urban Vietnamese Get Rich Quick," *Wall Street Journal*, October 26, 2004, p. A22.
14. Niraj Dawar and Philip Parker, "Marketing Universals: Consumers' Use of Brand Name, Price, Physical Appearance, and Retailer Reputation as Signals of Product Quality," *Journal of Marketing* 58, 2 (April 1994), pp. 81–95.

15. Gail Edmondson, Paulo Prada, and Karen Nickel Anhalt, "Lexus: Still Looking for Traction in Europe," *Business Week*, November 17, 2003, p. 122.

16. Leslie Chang, "In China, Adults Find Comfort as Toys Become More Available," *Wall Street Journal,* September 12, 2002, p. A13.

17. The Parker Pen Company, *Do's and Taboos Around the World* (Elmsford, NY: The Benjamin Company, 1985).

18. Douglas Bowman, John U. Farley, and David C. Schmittlein, "Cross-National Empirical Generalization in Business Services Buyer Behavior," *Journal of International Business Studies* 31, 4 (2000), pp. 667–685.

19. Lawrence H. Wortzel, "Marketing to Firms in Developing Asian Countries," *Industrial Marketing Management* 12 (1983), pp. 113–123.

20. Desirée Blankenburg Holm, Kent Eriksson, and Jan Johanson, "Business Networks and Cooperation in International Business Relationships," *Journal of International Business Studies* 27 (1996), pp. 1033–1053.

21. James K. Sebenius, Rebecca Green, and Randall Fine, "Doing Business in Russia: Negotiating in the Wild East," Harvard Business School, Note #9-899-048 1999, pp. 6–7.

22. John L. Graham and N. Mark Lam, "The Chinese Negotiation," *Harvard Business Review*, October 2003, pp. 82–91.

23. George S. Yip, *Total Global Strategy* (Englewood Cliffs, NJ: Prentice-Hall, 1995), pp. 32–33.

24. "GM Network Unifies Auto Parts Buys," Dow Jones Newswire, June 11, 2002.

25. *Selling to the Government Markets*: *Local*, *State*, *Federal* (Cleveland: Government Product News, 1975), p. 2.

26. The information in this section has been drawn from *Business International*, "How to Sell to Belgium's Public Sector," *Business Europe*, October 2, 1981, pp. 314–315.

27. Mushtaq Luqmani, Ghazi M. Habib, and Sami Kassem, "Marketing to LDC Governments," *International Marketing Review* 5, no.1 (Spring 1988), pp. 56–67.

28. David Lague and Susan V. Lawrence, "China's Russian-Arms Spree," *Wall Street Journal*, December 10, 2002, p. A15.

29. Daniel Pearl, "In India, Roads Become All the Rage," *Wall Street Journal*, January 3, 2001, p. A10.

30. Bryan W. Husted, "Wealth, Culture, and Corruption," *Journal of International Business Studies* 30, no. 2 (1999), pp. 339–359.

31. Mohsin Habib and Leon Zurawicki, "Corruption and Foreign Direct Investment," *Journal of International Business Studies* 33, no. 2 (2002), pp. 291–307.

32. Jonathan P. Doh, Peter Rodriguez, Klaus Uhlenbruck, Jamie Collins, and Lorraine Eden, "Coping with Corruption in Foreign Markets," *Academy of Management Executive* 17, no. 3 (2003), pp. 114–127.

33. Kate Gillespie, "Middle East Response to the U.S. Foreign Corrupt Practices Act," *California Management Review* 29, 4 (1987), pp. 9–30.

34. Kara Scannell, "Swiss Lawyer Faces Charges in Bribery Case," *Wall Street Journal*, September 15, 2003, p. A16.

35. "Two Companies Admit Payments to Officials," *New York Times*, January 11, 2001, p. CP 10.

36. Kate Gillespie, "Middle East Response to the U.S. Foreign Corrupt Practices Act," *California Management Review* 29, 4 (1987), pp. 9–30.

37. "Thirty-four Nations Sign Anti-Bribery Agreement at OECD," Dow Jones Newswire, December 17, 1997.

38. Associated Press, "U.N. Anticorruption Treaty Aims to Ease Retrieval of Dirty Money," *Wall Street Journal*, December 9, 2003, p. A10.

6 GLOBAL COMPETITORS

PROCTER & GAMBLE largely created the market for shampoo in China. Previously, most Chinese washed their hair with bar soap. Slick Western-style commercials launched P&G's Head and Shoulders brand, and its success encouraged other multinationals to develop the Chinese market further. These multinationals included Japan's Kao Corporation, France's L'Oreal, and Anglo-Dutch Unilever, as well as U.S.-based Colgate-Palmolive and Bristol-Myers Squibb. For 10 years, big global brands such as Coke and Head and Shoulders killed local brands in China. Then things changed. Chinese brands recaptured two-thirds of the shampoo market and strongly reasserted themselves in other consumer nondurables such as soap, laundry detergent, and skin moisturizer. A state-owned company even pro-

duced one of China's largest-selling brands of toothpaste.

Local brands competed mainly on price but were learning to develop other selling points as well. One Chinese shampoo, Olive, successfully advertised that it made black hair glossier, an attribute that appealed to local consumers. Procter & Gamble took note and introduced a new shampoo that included traditional medicinal elements to add sheen to black hair. The general manager of P&G's shampoo business summed up the new environment: "These days new local brands are always coming at you. And we take them very seriously, whereas five years ago all eyes were on the other multinationals."[1]

To begin to develop an effective strategy for global markets, a firm must consider not only buyers but competitors as well. Understanding

LEARNING OBJECTIVES

After studying this chapter, you should be able to

▶ Describe ways in which one global competitor can address another.

▶ List and explain four basic strategic options that local firms can employ in the face of competition from multinational firms.

▶ Explain how attitudes toward competition have evolved differently in different cultures, and cite examples from both developed and developing countries.

▶ Note examples of how home governments can still support the global competitiveness of their firms despite the trend toward trade liberalization.

▶ Discuss the major competitors from developing countries—state-owned enterprises and business groups—and explain how they differ from multinational companies.

▶ Describe how a firm's country of origin can help or hurt it in the global marketplace.

global buyers is only half the job. Global marketers must compete for those buyers. Potential competitors include both global competitors and local competitors. Each presents unique challenges. Furthermore, the national origin and cultural heritage of firms can determine their organization, their sources of competitive advantage, and the tactics they employ to compete.

In this chapter we address issues of global competition. We begin by noting ways in which competitors can engage each other globally— global firm versus global firm, and local firm versus global firm. We explore why cultures developed different attitudes toward competition and look at differences among competitors from different parts of the world. The chapter concludes by examining how buyers respond to firms from different countries.

177

THE GLOBALIZATION OF COMPETITION

To be successful in global markets, firms must not only understand their potential buyers but also learn to compete effectively against other firms from many different countries. International firms have both advantages and disadvantages when they encounter local competition in foreign markets. Multinational corporations may be larger than local firms and may have better access to sources of finance. They may enjoy greater experience worldwide in product development and marketing. This experience can be brought to play in the new market. However, local competitors may better understand the local culture and hence operate more effectively not only in addressing consumer needs but in dealing with local distributors and governments as well. Today many local competitors, even those in less developed markets, have built up popular brands that a foreign newcomer can find difficult to dislodge.

Global Firm versus Global Firm

Some industries are becoming increasingly global. In these industries, the same global competitors hold significant global market share and face each other in virtually every key market. Major global competitors such as Kodak and Fuji Film consider each other carefully on a worldwide basis. They watch each other's moves in various markets around the world in order to respond to, or even preempt, any actions that will give the competitor a market advantage. Unilever, a European-based firm, and Procter & Gamble of the United States clash in many markets, particularly in laundry products. The two firms compete with each other in most world markets, and action in one market easily spills over into others. Observers have described this competitive action as "The Great Soap Wars."

George Yip suggests several ways in which one global competitor can address another.[2]

Cross-country subsidization
the utilization of profits from one country in which a business operates to subsidize competitive actions in another country

▶ **Cross-country subsidization.** Using profits from one country in which a business operates to subsidize competitive actions in another country. Bic was one of the first companies to do this effectively. Bic used profits made in France to attack competitor Scripto's pen business in Britain. Then Bic used profits made in Europe to attack Scripto in its U.S. home market. Because Scripto's national subsidiaries were largely independent of each other, the firm didn't see Bic coming.

Counterparry a counterattack against a competitor in one country in response to a prior attack by that competitor in another country

▶ **Counterparry.** Defending against a competitive attack in one country by counterattacking in another country. Fuji successfully entered the United States and gained 25 percent of the film market. Kodak counterattacked in Japan, exerting great efforts to strike back at Fuji in its home market.

Globally coordinated move the employing of simultaneous actions across countries to gain competitive advantage over global or local rivals

▶ **Globally coordinated moves.** Mounting a coordinated assault in which competitive moves are made in different countries. For example, some multinational firms now choose global rollouts for products. By introducing new products in all major national markets simultaneously, a firm ensures that its global competitors have no time to learn from one market in order to respond in another.

An Egyptian girl drinks a bottle of Coke in downtown Cairo. Coca-Cola was once banned by the Arab boycott, giving rival Pepsi an advantage in the Middle East. Now both global competitors contend for the Arab market.

▶ **Targeting of global competitors.** Identifying actual and potential global competitors and selecting an overall posture—attack, avoidance, cooperation, or acquisition. We will have more to say about cooperating with potential competitors in Chapter 9.

Targeting of global competitors the process of identifying actual and potential global competitors, planning how to compete against each of them, and implementing those plans

One of the longest-running battles in global competition has been the fight for market dominance between Coca-Cola and PepsiCo, the world's largest soft-drink companies. Traditionally, the two firms have been relatively close in the U.S. market, but Coca-Cola has long been the leader in international markets. In terms of worldwide market share, Coke leads Pepsi by better than a two-to-one margin. However, the battle for global market share is an ongoing one that erupts simultaneously on several fronts.

Some of the most dramatic action has taken place in Latin America. Coke struck at Pepsi in Venezuela, the only market in Latin America where Pepsi led Coke by a substantial margin (76 percent share versus 13 percent), thanks to long-standing ties with a local bottler. In a bold play for share, Coke negotiated with Pepsi's Venezuelan bottler to acquire a controlling interest in that company. The day after the deal was announced, the Venezuelan bottler switched to bottling Coke, and Pepsi lost its distribution literally overnight. It took Pepsi 30 months and a combined investment of more than $500 million to reestablish itself in the country.[3]

Another arena, and potentially the largest prize, is Asia. Because the mature U.S. market is growing slowly, Coke and Pepsi have set their sights on major growth markets, such as China, India, and Indonesia, that are home to almost half the world's population. In India, Pepsi attempted to preempt Coke. Coca-Cola had previously relinquished its position in the Indian market when the Indian government passed a law that would require the company to share its secret cola formula with local partners. Although the law was later repealed, Coke delayed returning to India while rival Pepsi made India a priority market. When Coke finally returned, it found Pepsi well established in the market. Coke, at an estimated market share of 16.5 percent, was trailing Pepsi's 23.5 percent share, when Pepsi accused Coke of hoarding over five million returnable Pepsi bottles collected from recyclers in order to disrupt Pepsi production. Pepsi called the police, and a court ordered Coke to return the bottles. The two companies subsequently agreed to a regular exchange of bottles.[4]

As can be expected in true global competition, Coke and Pepsi square off in all important markets. Both firms coordinate their strategies across markets, leverage knowledge and experience gained in many national markets, and employ vast global resources as they battle for global market share.

Global Firm versus Local Firm

Local firms can compete effectively against much larger international companies if they act wisely. Ramlösa, the leading Swedish bottler of mineral water, competed effectively against Perrier of France, probably the most successful marketer of mineral water worldwide. Ramlösa sold its mineral water primarily in Sweden, with some minor export business to Norway and Finland. Ramlösa executives had watched Perrier invade market after market in Europe and finally dominate the premium segment for mineral water worldwide.[5]

When Perrier attacked in Denmark, Ramlösa executives realized that it would not be long before Perrier would invade their market also. In Sweden, Ramlösa enjoyed a market share of close to 100 percent, and it was feared that an aggressive new entrant like Perrier might lower Ramlösa's share considerably. Having studied Perrier's strategy in other European markets, the firm searched for a solution. Because Perrier entered markets by creating a premium positioning for their product, Ramlösa decided to preempt Perrier by launching its own premium brand of mineral water. The company invested in expensive packaging and bottles, advertised to obtain a premium image, and increased the price by almost 50 percent, even though the mineral water of the premium brand was identical to that sold under its regular label.

When Perrier finally entered the Swedish market, it followed its proven strategy of aiming to capture the premium segment. However, with Ramlösa already strong in the premium segment, Perrier was forced to enter with an ultrapremium positioning. This resulted in such a high price that Perrier gained very little market share. By anticipating Perrier's arrival and correctly predicting its competitor's strategy, Ramlösa was able to prevent Perrier from cashing in on the approach that had been so successful elsewhere.

Strategies for Local Firms

Although global firms may have superior resources, they often become inflexible after several successful market entries and tend to stay with standard

A billboard in Moscow advertises American cosmetics. When Russia opened to the West, foreign products became all the rage. Later, local firms benefited from a consumer backlash against foreign brands.

approaches when flexibility is needed. In general, the global firm's strongest local competitors are those who watch global firms carefully and learn from their moves in other countries. With some global firms, it is several years before a product is introduced in all markets, and local competitors in some markets can take advantage of such advance notice by building defenses or launching a preemptive attack on the same segment.

Niraj Dawar and Tony Frost suggest four successful strategies for smaller local firms that suddenly find themselves competing with more powerful multinationals. Depending on the type of industry they are in, local firms can choose to be defenders, extenders, contenders, or dodgers. In industries where customization to local markets remains a competitive asset, defender and extender strategies can be successful. Other industries, such as telecommunications and automobiles, are by nature more global—buyer needs vary relatively little from one market to another, and both economies of scale in production and high R&D costs favor enterprises with global reach and vast resources. In such global industries, local firms must consider contender or dodger strategies.[6]

Defender Strategy. A defender strategy focuses on leveraging local assets in market segments where multinational firms may be weak. Local assets often include knowledge of local tastes and customs, as well as good relationships with local distributors and suppliers. A good example of a defender strategy is the trend in Turkey for restaurants to bring back regional cuisines to compete with multinational fast-food chains. Ibrahim Tatlises, a Turkish pop music and television star, successfully created a fast-food chain based on lahmacun, a thin pizzalike dough with meat and spices.[7] Despite their local assets, local firms may need to seek out new efficiencies to defend their home markets. Chilean banks chose to outsource check processing to a single service supplier in order for all to achieve the necessary economies of scale to compete with the multinationals.[8]

Extender Strategy. Sometimes local firms find that the assets that worked well for a defender strategy can also work in certain foreign markets. Extenders focus on expanding into foreign markets similar to their own, using successful practices and competencies that they have already developed in their home market. SAB's (South African Breweries, now SABMiller PLC) earlier experience in African countries with primitive distribution channels and antiquated production facilities proved useful when the company entered Eastern Europe.[9] Televisa, Mexico's largest media company, has extended to become one of the world's largest producers of Spanish-language soap operas.[10] Its impact is felt in the United States as well as in Latin America. In some local markets, such as Los Angeles and Houston, Spanish-language Univision is the most-watched network.[11] However, when Mexican packaged-foods giant Bimbo moved into the United States, it faced more difficulties. Like Televisa, Bimbo knew the Mexican consumer and was well poised to target the Mexican market in the United States. However, like SAB, one of Bimbo's key competencies—the ability to deal with small mom-and-pop stores—did not extend well into the U.S. market.[12]

Contender Strategy. Competing in more global industries can be difficult for smaller local firms faced with established global competitors. Yet some have succeeded by upgrading their capabilities to take on the multinational companies. This usually means expanding their resources to invest in the necessary R&D expenditures and larger-scale production that these industries can demand. Many privately held local companies find that they need to go public to raise more money through a stock offering. Because their resources may still be limited compared to those of entrenched multinational firms, contenders may seek out niches—at least at first—that are underserved by their competitors. Arçelik is a top competitor in the Turkish market for appliances such as refrigerators, washing machines, and dishwashers. At home Arçelik enjoys a renowned brand name and vast distribution. It first entered the British market by targeting consumers who wanted small, tabletop refrigerators, a segment that U.S. and European competitors ignored. However, Arçelik moved beyond its initial niche by investing heavily in R&D. The Japan Institute of Product Maintenance chose Arçelik's washing-machine factory in Turkey for the first award for excellence given any such plant outside Japan.[13]

Dodger Strategy. If local firms in more global industries lack the resources or managerial vision to become contenders, they can find themselves edged out even in their home market by multinational firms offering better and cheaper products. To survive, a local firm can avoid, or dodge, competition by finding a way to cooperate with its more powerful competitors. It can focus on being a locally oriented link in the value chain, becoming, for instance, a contract manufacturer or local distributor for a multinational firm. Many dodgers just sell out to a multinational firm that wishes to acquire them. Many such acquisitions have occurred in Europe and the United States, and they have in developing countries, as well.

Car manufacturer Daewoo held about 12 percent of the South Korean automobile market and aspired to become a global competitor, investing in emerging markets such as India, Romania, and Iran. However, the firm soon ran up $47 billion in liabilities. When the company was on the verge of collapse, its chairman fled the country. General Motors reached an agreement with Daewoo's creditors to purchase the firm's automotive assets, giving GM a greater participation in the attractive Korean car market, as well as a production base for serving the rest of Asia. Subsequently, GM began to phase out the Daewoo brand name outside Korea.[14]

CULTURAL ATTITUDES TOWARD COMPETITION

Table 6.1 lists the top one hundred companies in the world and their nations of origin. Not surprisingly, understanding and responding appropriately to competitors is much more difficult if competitors come from different countries and cultures. Cultures vary in their attitudes toward competition and in their histories of industrial development. These attitudes affect the rules of the competitive game—both written and unwritten—in societies. Understanding these attitudes and histories can help marketers better understand both local competitors in host markets and global competitors that come from different home markets.

Is competition good or bad? Most Americans would agree that competition is good. It encourages new ideas and keeps prices down. However, this is not a universal attitude. In the late nineteenth and early twentieth centuries, the United States established antitrust laws to discourage monopolies and encourage competition. Shortly before, Americans watched powerful firms cut prices to drive competitors out of the market. Afterward, these firms or trusts took advantage of their monopolist positions to raise prices to consumers. Newspapers roused citizens across the country, and the U.S. government received a mandate to trust-bust. Even years later, General Motors was forced to operate divisions as separate firms to help dissipate its strong market power in the United States. Other countries have experienced different histories relating to competition and have therefore developed different attitudes toward it.

Competition in Europe

Europe, like the United States, is a major source of multinational corporations. However, industry structure and attitudes toward competition have traditionally differed between these two regions. In most European countries, family-owned

TABLE 6.1　TOP 100 GLOBAL FIRMS

RANK	COMPANY	COUNTRY	RANK	COMPANY	COUNTRY
1	General Electric	USA	42	AstraZeneca	Britain
2	Microsoft	USA	43	Time Warner	USA
3	Exxon Mobil	USA	44	J.P. Morgan Chase	USA
4	Pfizer	USA	45	Telefonica	Spain
5	Wal-Mart Stores	USA	46	Samsung Electronics	Korea
6	Citigroup	USA	47	Gazprom	Russia
7	BP	Britain	48	Deutsche Telecom	Germany
8	American International Group	USA	49	Amgen	USA
9	Intel	USA	50	Nokia	Finland
10	Royal Dutch/Shell Group	Neth./Britain	51	3M	USA
11	Bank of America	USA	52	Fannie Mae	USA
12	Johnson & Johnson	USA	53	American Express	USA
13	HSBC Holdings	Britain	54	Unilever	Neth./Britain
14	Vodafone Group	Britain			
15	Cisco Systems	USA	55	Hewlett Packard	USA
16	International Business Machines	USA	56	Comcast	USA
17	Procter & Gamble	USA	57	Viacom	USA
18	Berkshire Hathaway	USA	58	Abbott Laboratories	USA
19	Toyota Motor	Japan	59	Aventis	France
20	Coca-Cola	USA	60	Siemens	Germany
21	Novartis	Switzerland	61	Genentech	USA
22	GlaxoSmithKline	USA	62	Wachovia	USA
23	Total	USA	63	Tyco International	USA
24	Merck	USA	64	France Telecom	France
25	Nestlé	Switzerland	65	Oracle	USA
26	Wells Fargo	USA	66	eBay	USA
27	Atria Group	USA	67	Medtronic	USA
28	Chevron Texaco	USA	68	Morgan Stanley	USA
29	Roche Holding	Switzerland	69	Barclays	Britain
30	Verizon Communications	USA	70	China Mobile (Hong Kong)	China
31	Royal Bank of Scotland Group	Britain	71	BNP Paribas	France
32	NTT DoCoMo	Japan	72	Mitsubishi Tokyo Financial	Japan
33	PepsiCo	USA	73	Merrill Lynch	USA
34	Dell	USA	74	Banc One	USA
35	UBS	Switzerland	75	Qualcomm	USA
36	Eli Lilly	USA	76	U.S. Bancorp	USA
37	ENI	Italy	77	BHP Billiton	Australia/Brit.
38	Home Depot	USA			
39	United Parcel Service	USA	78	L'Oreal	France
40	Nippon Telegraph & Telephone	Japan	79	News Corp.	Australia
41	SBC Communications	USA	80	Kraft Foods	USA

(continued)

TABLE 6.1 (CONTINUED)

Rank	Company	Country	Rank	Company	Country
81	SAP	Germany	91	Walt Disney	USA
82	Banco Santander Centarl Hispano	Spain	92	ING Groep	Netherlands
83	HBOS	Britain	93	TIM	Italy
84	ConocoPhillips	USA	94	Motorola	USA
85	Mizuho Financial	Japan	95	Deutsche Bank	Germany
86	Enel	Italy	96	BellSouth	USA
87	Bristol-Myers Squibb	USA	97	Nissan Motor	Japan
88	Sanofi-Synthelabo	France	98	Goldman Sachs Group	USA
89	E.ON	Germany	99	DaimlerChrysler	Germany
90	Wyeth	USA	100	Texas Instruments	USA

Source: Data from "The *Business Week* Global 1000 Scoreboard," *Business Week*, July 26, 2004, p. 69. Reprinted with permission. Rank based on market value.

businesses play a greater role in the economy than they do in the United States. In Germany, family-owned businesses employing fewer than five hundred persons account for 79 percent of all employment. Even among publicly traded companies, it is not uncommon to find the board dominated by the founding family and their friends. Many Europeans remain suspicious of the pressures caused by stock markets, believing they force management toward short-term goals to the detriment of longer-term goals. Some also believe that the corporate governance associated with publicly traded companies is a burden that is more about policing than adding value.[15]

Despite European Union (EU) integration, emotional ties to national champions still persist in Europe. In fact, a recent survey suggests that barriers to integration within the EU may be emotional rather than regulatory. A corporate-reputation survey undertaken in the largest EU countries revealed a significant bias toward national heritage companies. Thirteen of the fifteen "most visible" companies cited by respondents in Germany and France were based in the respondents' home countries. Among British respondents, eleven of fifteen were U.K.-based companies.[16]

For many years, European governments allowed their firms to engage in cartel behavior that was outlawed in the United States. Even as late as the 1970s, European airlines met openly to discuss and later establish the mutual dropping of first-class services on trans-European flights. In fact, Europe rarely enforced antitrust laws until the 1980s. However, the EU has surprised many with a new vigilance in enforcing antitrust laws.

Although Europe imported much of its antitrust law from the United States, it has evolved differently. In the United States, the laws aim to protect consumers from monopolists. In the EU, they exist to guarantee fairness among competitors in the unified market. For example, under U.S. law, if a merger helps enable two companies to offer a broad portfolio of related products, this is seen as creating efficiencies that could in turn benefit consumers. In the EU, however, this would be seen as having the potential of blocking competitors out of the market. Consequently, the EU objected to a merger between two EU firms, Grand Metropolitan and Guinness, that would have created the world's largest liquor company. The EU feared that the new firm, by combining their portfolios of products from champagne to whiskey, could pressure distributors to shut out competitors. The EU also blocked a merger under their jurisdiction of General Electric and Honeywell International, two U.S.-based multinationals in the aerospace industry, despite the fact that the United States had approved the merger. This decision prompted allegations that European takeover rulings were biased against U.S. firms. However, an independent inquiry found no evidence of systematic bias.[17]

Historically, European governments have intervened more than the U.S. government to save their failing companies. Recently this may be changing. After September 11 devastated the airlines industry, the U.S. government offered its airlines a $5 billion bailout with an additional $10 billion in loan guarantees. But European antitrust legislation refused to allow European governments to bail out airlines. European carriers had to respond immediately— cutting costs and reducing debts. This has left them leaner and meaner than U.S. rivals.[18]

Competition in Japan

In the last three decades, Japanese markets have experienced more intense competition than markets in the United States and Europe. Whereas IBM enjoyed dominance in the computer mainframe market in the United States, four major competitors—Fujitsu, Hitachi, NEC, and IBM Japan—fought for market share in Japan. In fact, four to eight strong contenders can be found in virtually every industry. Japanese firms are rarely seen to leave mature industries through acquisition, bankruptcy, or voluntary exit.[19]

Horizontal keiretsus large and diverse industrial groups in Japan

Largely contributing to this phenomenon are the **horizontal keiretsus**. *Keiretsu* means "order or system." In Japan, six large industrial groups, or keiretsus, have evolved, and each keiretsu is involved in nearly all major industries. Group companies are technically independent and publicly owned. However, they are loosely coordinated by minority cross-shareholdings and personal relationships. A major player in these groups is the keiretsu bank. Group companies and especially the group bank will help members out in times of trouble. When Mazda faced bankruptcy, the Sumitomo Bank provided the car company with generous financing and encouraged employees of group companies to buy Mazdas. Banks retain shares of group companies despite low returns and have been effective in preventing takeovers by competitors.[20]

For decades Japanese managers never worried about stock prices, and postwar Japan never experienced a hostile takeover of a major business. Despite increased competition, weak companies were not forced out of the Japanese market. However, the poor economic environment in Japan during the late 1990s began to show cracks in the system. The Japanese government made it clear that it would allow banks to fail, which caused Japanese banks to be more wary about propping up group companies. In fact, Japan is experiencing one of the biggest transfers of corporate ownership in 50 years, with many U.S. companies now buying into Japanese firms. Despite these recent trends, a study of Japanese keiretsus revealed that the system appeared to be very much intact.[21]

Competition in Emerging Markets

Developing countries have traditionally been wary of competition. In the mid-twentieth century, many of these countries were still dependent on commodities and were attempting to industrialize rapidly. However, the moneyed segments of society preferred to keep to the businesses they knew best—agriculture, commerce, and the military. The few who ventured into industry and were successful discovered that others quickly followed them into the same business. Soon there were far too many competitors vying for market share in a small market. New ventures failed. As a consequence, potential industrialists became even harder to find. To encourage local investment in industry and the building of factories, governments often limited foreign competition by raising tariffs or imposing quotas on imports. In addition, many governments licensed local production. For example, the Iranian government refused to issue further licenses for new factories once producers could establish that they were capable of supplying the entire Iranian market.

More recently, most developing countries, as well as the transitional economies of the former Soviet bloc, have embraced market liberalization. **Market liberalization** is the encouraging of competition where prior monopolies or strict entry controls previously existed. It takes a variety of forms. Production licensing is often relinquished and import controls relaxed. Host governments may further competition by encouraging multinational corporations to invest in their markets. India liberalized its market and encouraged foreign investment by granting multinational firms freer access to foreign exchange, the right to hold majority equity stakes in their Indian investments, and permission to use foreign brand names where these were previously not permitted. Other countries, such as Egypt, courted foreign investors with tax holidays for up to 10 years.

Market liberalization the encouragement of competition where monopolies or strict entry controls previously existed

There are several reasons for this change in attitude toward competition in the emerging world. Some of the pressure to liberalize markets is external. Many countries in the emerging world have joined the WTO and needed to remove barriers to imports in order to comply with WTO regulations. For example, India dismantled the last of its major import quotas in response to a ruling from the WTO. Until then, manufacturers of consumer goods faced virtually no import competition in India. Other countries are under pressure to liberalize from bilateral partners such as the United States.

Much of the pressure to liberalize is internal, however. After 50 years of protection, local competitors have often failed to delivery quality products for reasonable prices. Part of this failure is due to conditions outside their control, such as limited financing available for businesses in developing countries. Still, consumers in the emerging world, along with their governments, have begun to think that protecting infant industries contributes to their failure ever to grow up. A study of 3,000 Indian firms revealed that productivity grew more slowly in the 1990s than in the 1980s.[22] Furthermore, many governments are setting their sights on competing in export markets. Allowing more competition in the national market forces local companies to be more globally competitive. Multinational corporations in particular, with their higher technology, more extensive financial resources, and global market know-how, are expected to help fuel export expansion.

As developing countries liberalize their markets, governments are also cracking down on what they deem to be improper competitive behavior. Many actions that have been accepted for many years are now outlawed. In Mexico, a new antitrust commission acts as both judge and jury on complaints of anticompetitive behavior brought against firms. The commission has the authority to investigate allegations and impose fines. It can block any corporate acquisition in Mexico and can prevent the creation of a private monopoly in cases where the government decides to sell prior state-owned monopolies to the private sector.

Mexico's antitrust commission found Coca-Cola and its bottlers guilty of abusing their dominant position in Coke's largest market outside the United States. Needless to say, Pepsi initiated the investigation. Coke had a 72 percent share of the Mexican carbonated soft-drinks market and most of its sales came from small mom-and-pop stores located across the country. Coke was ordered by the commission to stop using its exclusivity agreements that forbade the small retailers from carrying competitors' products. Pepsi has similar agreements with its retailers in Mexico. But the ruling doesn't apply to Pepsi, because Pepsi doesn't occupy the dominant position in the market.[23]

HOME COUNTRY ACTIONS AND GLOBAL COMPETITIVENESS

In Chapter 4, we discussed how the home governments of firms can affect these firms' international marketing—in particular, how home governments might possibly harm their firms and in so doing create political risk. However, most home governments are eager for their firms to prove competitive in the global marketplace, and many seek out specific ways to improve the competitiveness of their firms. The WTO discourages direct government subsidies to firms and restricts, in most cases, the ability of member states to protect home markets with quotas and high tariffs. Still, many other government policies exist that can affect global competitiveness. Governments can offer export assistance in the form of export promotion organizations that help educate local firms about foreign markets. Home governments may also assist in negotiations for major contracts with foreign governments. And governments can pursue economic and competition policies at home that enhance the ability of their firms to compete in foreign markets. These policies can include tax rates, labor laws, and the extent to which home governments tolerate monopolistic or oligopolistic behavior in the home market.

The heads of state of the EU met in Barcelona and determined that Europe should try to become the world's most competitive economy. The Barcelona summit resolved to liberalize labor markets by lowering labor taxes and reducing benefits to the unemployed. It also took steps to deregulate energy markets, giving businesses the freedom to choose their gas and electricity suppliers. It

WORLD BEAT 6.1

Unfriendly Skies: Airbus versus Boeing

AEROSPACE is a truly global industry. Buyers are global, and research and development (R&D) costs are high. Competitors are few, and they keep close tabs on one another. In fact, the industry is increasingly defined by just two firms—Airbus and Boeing. The competition between Airbus and Boeing involves governments as well—subsidies being the bone of contention. A top executive at Boeing called for more ambitious funding from the U.S. government to support American aerospace companies and help them over the next technology hurdle. But at the same time, the U.S. government was scolding Europe for subsidizing Airbus. Both sides have filed complaints at the World Trade Organization (WTO), each arguing that government subsidies give the other's national champion an unfair advantage.

Some economists assert that the cutthroat competition between Airbus and Boeing is to be expected of two dominant giants in an industry where contracts are blockbuster sized. Invariably governments will be drawn into the fray. What the industry could use is more players and less concentration of competitive power in the hands of two global firms. But what would it take to attract a new entrant into this market? A firm thinking about entering aerospace would need to possess key qualities. It would have to have access to substantial funding to cover development costs—on average $37 million for each aircraft manufactured. And management would also have to love a challenge to take on this tough duopoly. According to one analyst, to take on Airbus and Boeing, a firm's management would need to be ambivalent toward profits, be a glutton for punishment, and, of course, be clueless about what they were getting into.

Sources: "Airbus, Boeing Feud Not Surprising," *Inside FAA*, January 18, 2005; Rebecca Christie, "Boeing's Albaugh Calls for More Government-Funded Big Research," Dow Jones News Service, January 19, 2005; and Associated Press, "Boeing Executive Hopes for Progress in European Subsidy Talks," January 27, 2005.

was hoped that these measures would decrease the costs of European-based businesses, allowing them to compete more effectively internationally.[24]

One ongoing controversy concerning home government policy and competitiveness involves the cement industry. Mexico's Cemex grew from a regional player to the world's third-largest cement supplier and the leading brand in the United States. U.S. rivals accused Cemex of using its dominance in Mexico to finance its expansion overseas unfairly and to cut prices in the U.S. market. Cemex's position in the Mexican market, where it held a 60 percent share of the market, allowed it to charge unusually high prices. Profits in Mexico were an extraordinary 46 percent before taxes—nearly double what they were in the more competitive U.S. market. Such profits at home enabled Cemex to buy competitors abroad as well as to decrease prices in foreign markets. An investigation by Mexico's competition commission found Cemex innocent of monopolistic behavior. Unsatisfied with the commission's decision, the U.S. government decided to impose antidumping duties on cement imported from

Mexico. In some years, these have amounted to more than 100 percent for Cemex.[25]

COMPETITORS FROM EMERGING MARKETS

Until recently, most global strategists focused on the multinational companies from the United States, Europe, and Japan. But as we saw in the cases of Procter & Gamble in China and Arçelik in Britain, multinational companies increasingly find themselves competing with firms from developing countries. Table 6.2 lists the largest global firms from key emerging markets. Major firms in developing countries are usually quite different from those in the United States. Large firms that have evolved locally in emerging markets are usually one of two types—state-owned enterprises and business groups. With the trend toward market liberalization, both face strong challenges at home from foreign multinationals. Nonetheless, these local firms can still prove quite competitive both in their own national markets and, increasingly, in global markets. Furthermore, new entrepreneurial ventures from developing countries are evolving and targeting overseas markets.

State-Owned Enterprises

State-owned enterprises (SOEs) sometimes appear in the developed world, especially Europe, but their scope and impact have been significantly greater in developing countries. In the second half of the twentieth century, many governments in developing countries were trying to end their dependence on commodity exports by rapidly industrializing their economies. Often the private sector failed to meet government expectations in this regard. Most shied away from investing in factories and production, areas they knew little about. To meet their goals, governments increasingly fell back on doing the job themselves and established SOEs that operated not only in the manufacturing sector but sometimes in wholesaling and retailing as well. For example, SOEs in Egypt came to account for 25 percent of nonagricultural employment in the country.

Being state owned gave firms certain competitive advantages over firms in the private sector, but some disadvantages were also involved. State-owned firms received priority access to financing that was scarce in the developing world. They were protected from bankruptcy, and they often were granted monopoly positions in their home markets. These advantages were offset by the many ancillary agendas they were forced to accept. Sri Lanka's state-owned timber company was expected to sell timber below market prices to subsidize housing in the country. Egyptian college graduates were guaranteed jobs in SOEs, and the Venezuelan government could commandeer the earnings of its state-owned oil company to help with a fiscal shortfall.

In the 1980s and 1990s, many SOEs in developing countries, as well as those in the former Soviet Union and Eastern Europe, underwent privatization. **Privatization** occurs when SOEs or their assets are sold to private firms or individuals. Rather than investing the money necessary to revamp these enterprises, governments choose to sell them. Part of the impetus to do so involves a

Privatization the practice of selling state-owned enterprises or their assets to private firms or individuals

TABLE 6.2 TOP EMERGING MARKET COMPANIES FROM SELECTED COUNTRIES

COUNTRY AND COMPANY	GLOBAL RANK	COUNTRY AND COMPANY	GLOBAL RANK
BRAZIL		**CHINA**	
Petrobras	9	China Mobil	1
Vale do Rio Doce	24	Petrochina	3
Banco Itau	35	China Telecom	11
AMBEV	38	CNOOC	21
Banco Bradesco	55	Huaneng Power	26
Electrobras	71	China Unicom	34
Banco do Brasil	83	Jiangsu Expressway	48
INDIA		**KOREA**	
Oil & Natural Gas	13	Samsung Electronics	2
Reliance Industries	31	SK Telecom	16
Hindustan Lever	37	KT	23
Indian Oil	52	Kookmin Bank	30
Wipro	78	Posco	39
State Bank of India	79	Hyundai Motor	49
Infosys Technologies	85	LG Electronics	64
ITC (89)	89	Woori Finance	91
MALAYSIA		**MEXICO**	
Malayan Banking	32	TELMEX	10
Tenaga Nasional	40	Walmart de Mexico	17
Telekom Malaysia	45	Bancomer	18
Malaysian Int'l Shipping	86	America Movil	21
Maxis Communications	88	CEMEX	36
Petronas Gas	90	Grupo Televisa	53
Plus Exressways	102	FEMSA	74
Public Bank	104	Coca-Cola FEMSA	84
TAIWAN		**SOUTH AFRICA**	
Taiwan Semiconductor	6	Anglo American	8
Chunghwa Telecom	14	Sasol	33
United Microelectronics	28	Anglo American Platinum	41
Cathay Financial Holdings	29	Anglogold	46
Hon Hai Precision	42	Old Mutual	57
Fubon Financial	43	Standard Bank	59
Nan Ya Plastic	44	Gold Fields	60
Formosa Plastics	50	Firstrand	66

SOURCE: Adapted from "Top 200 Emerging Market Companies," *Business Week*, July 14, 2003, p. 67. Reprinted with permission.

change in ideology. Many governments have lost faith in continued government-led industrialization. Privatizations have swept through more than a hundred countries and have involved over 75,000 SOEs. In many cases, multinational corporations have purchased these firms. For example, Philip Morris, the U.S.-based food and tobacco company, was able to acquire a stake in Czechia's Tabak, previously the Czech monopolist in tobacco.

In a number of cases, however, privatizations have not proceeded smoothly. The privatization of India's 240 SOEs has been repeatedly sidetracked. All major bidders for Air India withdrew from its first privatization attempt, afraid that the Indian government would not allow the painful employment cuts that would be necessary to make the airline profitable. Singapore Airline, a potential buyer, allegedly withdrew because of political opposition to the privatization. However, India's stalled privatization campaign was given added impetus by the sale of two of the country's most promising SOEs—a gasoline retailer and India's only international phone service.[26]

The global impact of SOEs in the oil industry continues despite the trend toward privatization. The state-owned oil companies of Kuwait and Venezuela have ventured out of their countries and have invested in Europe and the United States. The Kuwaiti company purchased refinery capacity in Europe as well as an extensive network of retail outlets from former Gulf Oil. Both of these SOEs are considered serious global competitors. In Russia, a major source of future oil supplies, the state has moved to increase its ownership in the previously privatized sectors of oil and natural gas.

Although the era of SOEs is waning, their importance in the Chinese market is still largely intact. For example, private express shipping companies, including U.S.-based FedEx, UPS, and DHL, were directed not to deliver letters or packages under 1.1 pounds and not to charge prices below those of the China Post. In addition, they could not deliver any mail to private homes or to offices of the Chinese government. The industry estimated that the new restrictions could amount to a loss of 60 percent of the Chinese market just as business was soaring. Industry executives claimed that the order violated commitments China made when it entered the WTO. However, the Chinese government maintained the action was legal and noted that China Post had to deliver mail to all locations in China, including places where it could not make a profit. Private companies were under no such obligation. China also invoked an antiterrorism rationale for the move. The government needed to ensure that all deliveries were subjected to screening for anthrax and other poisons.[27]

Hybrid a firm in which a government holds a partial, though usually significant, equity position

Chinese SOEs or hybrids dominate many sectors of the Chinese economy. (**Hybrids** are firms in which governments hold a partial, though usually significant, equity position.) Incidents such as the one involving the express shipping carriers have led to concerns that China's new antitrust laws—based on European laws—may target foreign multinationals while sidestepping reforms to China's powerful SOEs. While Chinese SOEs are proving worthy adversaries to foreign firms, they are increasingly open to hiring foreign managers, particularly in middle management positions. In response to growing foreign competition in the Chinese hotel industry, the Jinjiang Group even hired an American to be the new president of its core business unit, Jinjiang International Hotel Management.[28]

Business Groups

In the private sector of developing countries, business groups have emerged as the major competitors. **Business groups** differ from large corporations in developed countries in several key ways. Business groups have been exclusively or almost exclusively concentrated in their home markets. Most striking is their diversity. Business groups participate in many industries. It would not be uncommon to find a business group involved in steel, insurance, packaged goods, automobile distribution, and textiles. For example, Arçelik is part of the larger Koç Group in Turkey. This group participates in industries as diverse as consumer goods, energy, mining, finance, and construction. Group businesses are often interlinked, with group companies owning partial shares of each other. The true bond, however, is not one of equity ownership but is a fiduciary bond or bond of trust. It is the culture of businesses in the group to work for the good of the whole. Managers often move between these companies, and personal bonds are forged. In the difficult business environments of developing countries, all eventually benefit from mutual aid.[29]

Similar to Japanese keiretsus, most groups have a financial core—a business with access to cash to finance the other businesses. This is commonly a bank or an insurance company. In the case of Arab Contractors in Egypt, it was the parent company's own extensive retirement fund. This financial core proved a key competitive advantage in an environment where financing was scarce. Because these groups evolved in highly controlled economies, another competitive advantage was their adroit handling of government relations. For example, the Tata Group established India's first steel mill and attempted to address seriously the industrial policy goals of India. Dynastic marriages between business group families and politically connected families were not uncommon. For example, the son of the head of Arab Contractors married the daughter of Egyptian president Anwar Sadat.

Like virtually all firms in developing countries, business groups began as family-owned enterprises, and today the original families still play an important role in most cases. However, as these firms expanded, more professional management was introduced. Other changes have swept through business groups as well. Perhaps the most important of these has been the new competition that business groups face from multinational corporations. Many more multinational corporations have entered emerging markets in the wake of trade and investment liberalization. With the lifting of protectionist policies that once protected local firms by excluding imports and even discouraging foreign investment, multinationals now threaten business groups with new technology, quality products at competitive prices, global brands, and strong financial resources. They also compete for the best management talent in the country, something that was once the domain of the business groups. Also, as governments loosen their hold over their economies, the groups' competitive advantage in managing government relations has become less important.

In response to these new threats, many business groups are rethinking the strategies that have served them well in the past. Some argue that the diversity of the past should be abandoned. Instead, the firm should restructure itself around its strongest business or businesses and expand these into foreign

Business groups large business organizations consisting of firms in diverse industries interlinked by both formal and informal ties

markets. In other words, business groups are considering becoming more like multinational firms. Tata, India's largest business group, refocused itself at home by cutting back participation in low-margin businesses. Still the group remained in such varied industries as tea, cars, power, and phone networks. With global ambitions, it purchased Britain's Tetley Tea to gain an immediate international brand.[30]

Anticipating an alignment with Europe and a subsequent loss of protection for local industries, Turkey's business groups have also been adapting to changing times. One of the largest of these groups, Haci Omer Sabanci Holding, is streamlining its activities by focusing on core areas such as energy, the Internet, and telecommunications, while planning to sell its interest in areas such as textiles and plastics. The Turkish group, like many groups in Latin America, is also actively seeking out foreign multinational firms as joint venture partners.[31]

Even so, some still argue that it is premature to expect that business groups will disband in developing countries. The political and economic environments in these countries remain tumultuous, and the strategic value of rendering mutual assistance and forming strong government ties is as real today as before. Whatever their future, business groups currently represent the strongest local competition in many developing countries.

New Global Players

Recently, firms from developing countries have appeared as major regional and even global competitors in a number of industries. These firms increasingly challenge the established positions of multinationals from the United States, Europe, and Japan. Some, like Arçelik, are outstanding units of older, restructuring business groups. Others are firms that have been established more recently. Acer, the Taiwanese computer giant rose to a strong position in the Asian consumer PC market.[32] Hikma Pharmaceuticals was established in Jordan and carved out a niche for itself as a respected producer of generic drugs with operations in the United States, Europe, and several developing countries. A number of firms, such as Mexico's Cemex and South African Breweries, have used a strong cash flow from their dominant position in one of the larger emerging markets to fund the purchase of established companies abroad. This has helped catapult such companies into positions among the top-ranked global competitors of their industries. Outward foreign direct investment (FDI) from developing countries now accounts for over 10 percent of global FDI, according to the United Nations Conference on Trade and Development (UNCTAD).[33] The success of companies from newly emerging markets requires a rethinking of the impact that competitors from the emerging world may have on global markets in the future.

THE COUNTRY-OF-ORIGIN ADVANTAGE

Does an international company enjoy a market advantage—or disadvantage—because of the reputation of its home market? When Arçelik entered the European market, the firm was concerned that its home country, Turkey, would diminish its brand in the eyes of European consumers. Consumer response to the country of origin of products has been studied for 30 years. The findings are

WORLD BEAT 6.2

Dracula: Made in Romania?

IT'S A CREEPY MORNING high in the Transylvanian mountains. Mist hovers over the long grass. Giant limbs of ancient oaks creak in the wind. Crows circle overhead. Werewolves, blood-sucking vampires, and legions of the undead have all emerged from the fog of these Transylvanian forests. But this latest creature, emerging from the haze of Transylvania's modern-day industrial pollution, may be the spookiest yet: Dracula Park.

"We'll have Draculas who will walk, speak, fly, land," says Dan Matei-Agathon, Romania's tourism minister. He offers a set of fangs, along with his business card, to a visitor in his Bucharest office. "But don't get the wrong idea," he adds. "This won't be Disneyland."

Certainly not; a German firm that runs a cowboys and Indians theme park in Bavaria is in on construction. "We know the border between interesting and ridiculous," assures the ministry's man in charge of the project.

Thus, there will be an interesting Dracula golf course. There will be an interesting Dracula food court that serves fare from the Middle Ages. There will be a bizarre bazaar, where all Draculabilia from around the world will be on sale, from Dracula chess pieces and Dracula salt and pepper shakers to Dracula vodka (clear, not red) and Dracula baseball bats. There will be interesting amusements: One would-be vendor has proposed drawing visitors' portraits using the subjects' own blood.

Getting a bite out of the Dracula action has become a national obsession for Romania. "There's big money in Dracula all over the world—except in Romania," says Mr.

Agathon. He shows off a Dracula watch. It's made in Switzerland. "See," he says, "I'm still wondering what Switzerland's connection to Dracula is."

For ages, Romania refused to acknowledge officially the vampire Dracula of novelist Bram Stoker and Hollywood's Bela Lugosi. Instead, they venerated the historical Dracula, Vlad Tepes, as a heroic count who fought off hordes of foreign invaders and brought law and order to this realm of southeastern Europe. Yes, "Vlad the Impaler" accomplished this by skewering his foes on stakes, "but he never sucked blood," the local mayor hastens to add. "That's silly."

Still, the mayor says, "This myth, his legend, we must use." He envisions 3,000 new jobs and a million visitors coming to this walled medieval fortress, home of Dracula. "If people believe this vampire comes from Transylvania, and this is his home, then why shouldn't we profit?"

But no sooner had they settled on a name than a letter arrived from Universal Studios in California. It informed the Romanians that Universal holds worldwide rights to the character Count Dracula as portrayed in seven films, including the legendary 1930s film with Bela Lugosi. This was news to Mr. Agathon.

mixed, but certain trends can be observed. Although certain biases persist, consumers seem to change their minds over time, reflecting a dynamic environment for global competition.

Country of origin denotes the country with which a firm is associated—typically its home country. For example, IBM is associated with the United States and Sony with Japan. Several studies have concluded that consumers usually favor products from developed countries over those from less developed

Country of origin the country with which a firm is associated—typically its home country

countries. The reputation of some countries appears to enhance the credibility of competitors in product groups for which the country is well known, such as wines and perfumes for France, video recorders for South Korea, and Persian carpets for Iran. A positive or negative effect of country of origin can sometimes be product-specific. Russian automobiles may evoke a negative image in the minds of consumers, but Russian vodka may evoke a positive response.[34] In a few cases, country of origin can connote more general product attributes. Germany is known for engineering quality and Italy for design quality.

A country-of-origin bias is not limited to products or to consumer markets. Country-of-origin biases toward services appear to be similar to those toward products.[35] They have been observed among industrial buyers as well. Buyers of industrial products in South Korea rated Japanese, German, and American suppliers higher than suppliers from their own country.[36] Another study revealed that U.S. buyers were more willing to purchase from established industrialized countries than from newly industrialized ones, with the exception of Mexico.[37]

The issue of country of origin is increasingly complicated by the fact that multinational companies produce products in various countries. Which matters most to consumers—the home country associated with the brand or the country where the product is actually manufactured or assembled? Research on this question is inconclusive. A strong global brand may sometimes offset a negative **country of manufacture**. However, this is not always the case. For example, a study of Nigerian consumers of high-technology products revealed that where a product was produced was considered more important than the company name or brand of the product.[38] Globalization has also resulted in products whose inputs come from a number of countries. One study confirmed that

Country of manufacture the country in which a product is manufactured or assembled

In spite of estranged relations between Iran and the United States, the appeal of American products persists in Iran. On a billboard in Tehran, a local candy manufacturer mimics American soft drink Coca-Cola.

country of parts affected perceptions of both manufacturing quality and over-all quality of products.[39]

Country of parts the country in which an input to a final product is produced

Managing Country-of-Origin Perceptions

Buyer attitudes toward certain countries can change, and this has important implications for global competitors. Both Japan and South Korea saw their products rise in esteem over a relatively short period of time.[40] Now Japanese products score higher than U.S. or German products in some countries, including China and Saudi Arabia.[41] In recent years, a number of countries, including Portugal, Estonia, and Poland, have employed branding experts to help them project a better image. Finland even undertook a campaign to enhance its image as a center of high-tech innovation, hoping that a better national image would help its high-tech companies in the U.S. market. But countries must realize branding is more than hype, it must be backed by reality. Consequently, major changes in country brand image can take 20 years to achieve.[42]

Firms that suffer from a negative country of origin commonly settle for lower prices to offset perceptions of lower quality. However, there are a number of strategies that can improve buyer perception of the quality of products that suffer from a negative country-of-origin effect:

▶ Production may be moved to a country with a positive country-of-origin effect. If this is too difficult, key parts can be sourced from such countries. Kia's Sorento is assembled in Korea but relies on high-profile brand-name components from European and the U.S. suppliers to boost its image overseas.[43]

▶ A negative country-of-origin bias may be offset by using a channel that distributes already accepted complimentary products. A study determined that consumers dining in a Mexican theme restaurant were significantly more likely to buy Mexican wine than were consumers in other restaurants.[44]

▶ Communication and persistence can eventually pay off. When Arçelik attempted to introduce its Beko brand washing machines to the French furniture chain Conforama, the French sales staff objected to displaying the Turkish product. Then Valerie Lubineau, Beko's head of marketing in France, revealed that the firm had been manufacturing Conforama's respected in-house brand for years. Eight months later, the new Beko machines were outselling their European rivals.[45] Firms that consistently provide good products and service can even change buyers' attitudes toward their country of origin. A study showed industrial buyers who were experienced with suppliers from Latin America rated these countries higher than buyers who had had no such business dealings.[46]

Beyond Quality

Up until now we have been discussing how country of origin can affect perceptions of quality. However, country of origin can affect purchase behavior in other ways. Some consumers are disinclined to purchase foreign products

Consumer ethnocentrism the belief that purchasing imported products results in job loss and consequently hardship for a buyer's home country

Consumer animosity political objection to purchasing products from a specific foreign country

altogether. They believe that buying imported products results in job loss, and consequently hardship, at home. This phenomenon is called **consumer ethno-centrism**. Within a national population, some segments will exhibit higher levels of consumer ethnocentrism than others. Research has not revealed consistent results as to who is more likely to be ethnocentric. However, several studies suggest that women and older consumers may be more ethnocentric.

Other buyers harbor political objections to purchasing products from a specific foreign country. This phenomenon is called **consumer animosity**. For example, Chinese rate Japanese products high in quality. However, many Chinese harbor animosity toward the Japanese because of Japan's occupation of China during World War II. This animosity can negatively affect purchase of Japanese products independent of judgments concerning product quality.[47]

Consumer animosity surfaced in response to the Iraq War, particularly pitting Britain and the United States against Canada, France, and Germany. Activist websites in Germany urged consumers not to purchase 250 British and American products and suggested local alternatives.[48] But it was the U.S. consumer population that exhibited the greatest consumer animosity.

French officials and businesses became very concerned about an American backlash against French products when France objected to America's invasion of Iraq. Exports of French wine to the United States dropped nearly 18 percent, and overall French exports decreased by over 17 percent, suggesting that Americans responded to calls to boycott French products. The president of France's principal employer's association called upon U.S. consumers not to take out their antagonism out on French businesses, but to send telegrams to the French embassy.[49] Similarly, the president of Canada's Automotive Parts Manufacturers Association reported that members had noticed a chilly response from purchasing agents for U.S. automakers. Although most Canadians agreed with their government's refusal to join the U.S.-led war in Iraq, Canadian business leaders also worried that deteriorating relations with the United States could imperil the $1 billion in daily trade between the neighboring countries.[50]

CONCLUSION

This chapter has introduced some basic issues of global competition. We have explored ways by which global competitors engage each other and strategies that local firms employ to survive in an increasingly global marketplace.

We also saw that the cultural challenge in the global marketplace is not limited to buyers. The rules of the competitive game will vary from country to country. Both local and global competitors may possess strengths and weaknesses that reflect to some extent the environment and history of their home countries. Strategic global marketers must not only target appropriate buyers worldwide but also understand and successfully engage the competition that exists for those buyers.

What competitive environment will you encounter? Continue with your *Country Market Report* on our website (college.hmco.com/business/).

QUESTIONS FOR DISCUSSION

1. What advantages might a Japanese competitor have in the Japanese market over an American firm attempting to enter that market?
2. What do you think governments should be allowed to do to help their home firms be more globally competitive? What do you think constitutes unfair assistance?
3. Are business groups doomed?
4. Nearly all studies of the country-of-origin effect focus on how buyers evaluate products and on their intention to purchase products. How might the country-of-origin effect manifest itself in other situations?

CASE 6.1

Buzzing Around McDonald's

Jollibee is the dominant fast-food restaurant chain in the Philippines, with over 60 percent share of the market. A survey revealed that 69 percent of Filipino respondents visited Jollibee most often, compared with only 16 percent for McDonald's. Jollibee's founder, Tony Tan, is ethnically Chinese. His family immigrated from China, and his father worked as a cook in a Chinese temple. Mr. Tan was just getting started with Jollibee when McDonald's entered the market in 1981. His friends suggested that he apply for a McDonald's franchise. Mr. Tan declined.

Instead, Mr. Tan went on to develop his own chain that offers unique Filipino food, such as spaghetti with meat sauce topped with smoked fish, deep-fried pork skin, bean curd, sliced boiled eggs, and spring onions. In keeping with local tastes that appreciate food with lots of sugar and salt, Jollibee hamburgers are especially sweet. Beef is served with honey and rice, and of course there are mango shakes. Jollibee is recognized by its bee icon, which symbolizes the Filipino spirit of lightheartedness and happiness as well as representing a busy worker. Besides its flagship Jollibee restaurants, Jollibee Foods Corporation (JFC) also owns a chain of Chinese restaurants, Chowking, in the Philippines. But the importance of this chain is relatively low compared to JFC.

Only 2 percent of Filipino respondents in a poll replied that Chowking was their most visited restaurant.

A poll of Asian business leaders conducted by *Asian Business Magazine* rated Jollibee number one in Asia in terms of growth potential and contribution to society, number two in honesty and ethics, number three in long-term vision, and number four in financial soundness. In total, Jollibee received the highest ranking of all firms in the consumer category—ahead of major multinationals such as Coca-Cola, Nestlé, and Procter & Gamble. Another poll, this one conducted by *Far Eastern Economic Review*, ranked Jollibee the highest on its leading-companies indicator, ahead of Toyota Motor of Japan and Singapore Airlines.

Like most other fast-food chains in the Philippines, Jollibee buys most of its food inputs from overseas. Imports tend to be cheaper and of better quality than food products available locally. The company decided that it would build a $32 million food-processing plant and logistics and distribution center in the Philippines with the incentive of a 4-year tax holiday from the government of the Philippines. The center would serve both local and international operations. Keeping costs low is essential to a company already working on low margins. With the country in recession, Jollibee refused to raise prices in the Philippines, opting instead to try to increase revenues through expansion. Mr. Tan announced that he would like to see JFC open at least fifteen stores in every major market around the world. To finance expansion, the company has gone public, raising money by selling shares on the stock market.

Jollibee had already begun its overseas expansion in 1987 with a restaurant in Brunei, a small, oil-rich country with a relatively large Filipino migrant worker population. JFC moved on to enter other Asian and Middle East markets such as Indonesia, Kuwait, Malaysia, Guam, and New Guinea. In 1998, the company opened its first restaurant in the United States in a location near San Francisco. Soon five more locations were opened in California, in areas with high Filipino populations where brand awareness of Jollibee was already high. For example, the clientele at the restaurant in the San Francisco Bay area is about evenly split between ethnic Filipinos and others. All the U.S. restaurants exceeded expectations. However, an attempt to open a Jollibee restaurant in China proved less successful. The restaurant was eventually closed.

Discussion Questions

1. What strategies did Jollibee follow—or consider following—during its evolution: dodger, defender, extender, and/or contender? Explain your answer.
2. Which strategy do you think is most appropriate for Jollibee? Why?
3. Why do you think Jollibee was successful in the United States but not in China?

Sources: "Jolly News for Jollibee," *Borneo Bulletin*, January 11, 2002; Rosemarie Francisco, "Jollibee Food Stays Cheap," Reuters English News Service, May 5, 2002; "Philippines' Jollibee Foods to Build $31.9 MLN Processing Plant," *Asia Pulse*, May 1, 2002; "Jollibee's Sweet Filipino Burger Chain Seeking Fast-Food Niche," *Houston Chronicle*, July 14, 2000; Doris C. Dumlao, "Jollibee Eyes Foreign Markets," *Philippine Daily Inquirer*, July 2, 2001, p. 1; and "Face Value," *The Economist*, March 2, 2002, p. 62.

CASE 6.2

Arming the Gulf

At the beginning of the twenty-first century, U.S. defense companies held about 44 percent of the world armaments market. Nonetheless, the market was shrinking and becoming more competitive. U.S. defense purchases were down as a result of the dissolution of the Soviet Union. Low oil prices had reduced the ability of major Middle Eastern clients to purchase arms, and the Asian economic crisis had caused other major clients such as Taiwan to cut back orders. There had been few large deals in the industry for several years. U.S.-based Lockheed Martin Corporation could boast of a major contract with the United Arab Emirates (UAE), but negotiations had been tortuous.

The UAE first considered major defense purchases shortly after its neighbor Kuwait was invaded by Iraq. It proceeded to buy Mirage jets from France and invited companies from France, Sweden, Russia, and the United States to bid on an order of expensive advanced fighter planes. Six years later, the competitors were narrowed down to Lockheed and France's Dassault Aviation S.A. In an attempt to remain in the bidding, another U.S. firm, McDonnell Douglas, had offered steep price cuts but to no avail. Two years later, the UAE announced its final decision in favor of Lockheed. Still, details of the contract remained unresolved, and negotiations began that lasted two more years. At one time, Lockheed became so discouraged that its negotiators were called home. The U.S. government intervened and brought the two sides back together.

Like virtually all defense firms worldwide, Lockheed needed permission from its home government to make sales to foreign governments. Accordingly, the U.S. government closely monitored and even joined in the sales negotiations. U.S. firms could not sell to embargoed countries. Certain technologies could not even be sold to friendly countries. Yet the U.S. government under the Clinton administration played the most proactive role in assisting U.S. defense firms of any administration in 20 years. Both President Clinton and Vice President Gore became personally involved in promoting the Lockheed sale.

The UAE finally agreed to purchase Lockheed's Desert Falcon planes. To clinch the deal, Lockheed made concessions that would have seemed outlandish 20 years earlier. The company agreed to supply state-of-the-art technology and to put up a $2 billion bond to safeguard against technological failure. It also signed on to an "offset" agreement of $160 million to help the UAE expand its state-owned petroleum sector. Offset agreements had become increasingly a part of arms deals. Defense contractors found themselves agreeing to reinvest part of their earnings in the client country, participating in projects such as building hotels and factories, or, in the case of Korea, helping to upgrade the electronics industry.

As Lockheed relaxed with the Desert Falcon contract in hand, across the globe the Russian government was hosting Ural Expo Arms. Fifty foreign delegations were in attendance to view its eight hundred exhibits. The Expo was designed to highlight Russian defense suppliers and to help increase overseas sales. Russia's world market share was fluctuating between 2 and 4 percent, and the Russian government was eager to increase exports to generate foreign exchange. Longtime clients such as India and China appeared to show some preference for the Russians. Potential clients agreed that Russian products possessed certain advantages, such as simplicity of use, reliability, and low cost. However, Russian servicing was unreliable, and spare parts could be hard to get. The Russian bureaucracy moved very slowly in approving export licenses, and Russian firms rarely became involved in offset agreements. Furthermore, there were so many intermediaries involved in Russian defense sales that the Russian companies themselves saw only a fraction of the profits. Still, Russian President Putin vowed to increase armament purchases at home and to support Russia's defense industry abroad.

Discussion Questions

1. How is the global arms market similar to other government markets? How does it differ?

2. How can home governments help and hurt firms competing in this market?

3. What qualities are necessary for a firm to compete in this market? Why are Russian companies relatively weak competitors?

Sources: Tim Weiner, "Russia and France Gain on U.S. Lead in Arms Sales, Report Says," *New York Times*, August 4, 1998, p. 5; Anne Marie Squeo and Daniel Pearl, "The Big Sell," *Wall Street Journal*, April 20, 2000, p. A1; and Guy Chazan, "Russia's Defense Industry Launches Bid to Boost Sales," *Wall Street Journal*, July 14, 2000, p. A10.

CASE 6.3
The New Cola Wars

For many years, the battle between Coke and Pepsi dominated the world stage. Private labels began to make inroads supported by powerful retailers, but no national or global brands arose to threaten the cola duopoly. More recently, however, newcomers with unique histories and international ambitions have emerged to challenge the status quo.

Europe and the Middle East

Mecca Cola was launched in France and the Middle East in late 2002 by a Tunisian-born businessman who had moved to France over 20 years earlier. His goal was to make the new product the cola of choice for Muslims worldwide and to combat America's imperialism by providing a substitute for American products. The company pledged 20 percent of its profits to Palestinian and Muslim charities. Despite its desire to distance itself from competitors such as Coca-Cola, Mecca Cola's packaging was surprisingly similar to that of Coke's—white script on red cans.

In February 2003, the company dubbed itself the sponsor of the one-million-strong peace march in London that demonstrated against U.S. involvement in Iraq. The company handed out 36,000 bottles of cola and 10,000 T-shirts bearing the messages "Stop the war" and "Not in my name." On the heels of this publicity, Mecca Cola entered the U.K. market with the stated goal of capturing 5 percent of the world's tenth-largest cola market. Distribution of Mecca Cola in Britain was primarily through small shops in communities where Britain's 1.5 million Muslims were concentrated. But succeeding in the U.K. market would not be easy. Sales of carbonated drinks had stabilized. The market was saturated with soda brands, and mineral waters and fruit juices were attacking cola's traditional position.

Qibla Cola was launched in Britain in late 2002, and by early 2004 it had plans to enter the U.S. market. Its slogan: Qibla Cola, liberate your taste.

(Qibla means "direction" in Arabic.) The Qibla Cola Company also called for a boycott of all American brands to protest the U.S.-led war in Iraq and proclaimed that people should switch to brands that were independent of governments and their unjust policies. Management was planning to target students and young people and claimed that through its branding and distribution it would position itself as a global rather than a Middle Eastern or ethnic brand. Qibla's early distribution was through an informal network of independent retailers, but it aspired to enter supermarkets. The company vowed to give 10 percent of profits to humanitarian causes around the world.

In the Middle East itself, Coca-Cola had already encountered a competitor that positioned itself as an Islamic alternative to Coke: Zam Zam cola from Iran. But as Zam Zam was expanding into Middle Eastern markets such as Saudi Arabia, Coke was returning to shelves in Iran. The United States still imposed trade sanctions on Iran but had exempted foodstuffs. Elsewhere in the Middle East, the Coca-Cola Company signed a franchise with the National Beverage Company (NBC) to bottle and distribute Coke products throughout the West Bank and Gaza Strip. Arguably, the benefits of direct and indirect jobs created for Palestinians by this project far outweighed the charitable contributions that Palestinians would receive from Mecca Cola.

Latin America

Half a world away, Coca-Cola faced a different kind of challenge in Latin America, where Kola Real was emerging as a multinational threat. Kola Real had been established by a family who had seen its farm in southern Peru destroyed by the Shining Path terrorist group. Eduardo and Mirtha Aranos decided to turn disaster into opportunity. Rebels routinely hijacked Coca-Cola trucks, so the couple, along with their five sons, decided to make their own cola and sell it locally. By cutting costs such as advertising, the Ajegroup's new cola sold at an extremely low price compared to Pepsi and Coke. Kola Real captured 22 percent of the Peruvian market. Kola Real then moved into neighboring Ecuador and Venezuela. The new cola captured 16 percent of the market in Ecuador and 17 percent of the market in Venezuela and forced Coke to cut prices in those markets.

But it was the subsequent entry into Mexico by the Ajegroup that truly threatened the global market leader. Eleven percent of Coca-Cola's global profits came from Mexico, where Mexicans drank more Coke per capita than any other nation. A former head of Coca-Cola's Mexican operations, Vincente Fox, had even become president of Mexico. When the Ajegroup entered the market with cola prices set at 20 to 50 percent below those of competition, Pepsi experienced a rapid 5 percent drop in sales and Coca-Cola saw sales growth disappear. Still Coke was reluctant to lower prices. Regional newcomers had previously entered the soft-drink market in Brazil and eventually captured 30 percent of the market. As a result, Brazilian profit margins decreased for Coke and Pepsi. The possibility of the same thing happening in Mexico was a real threat.

Furthermore, most newcomers in Latin America had distributed through supermarkets, which were growing in strength but still held smaller market shares of the retail market than did the many small mom-and-pop stores throughout Latin America. Newcomers did price lower than the multinational brands but did not compete aggressively on price. The Ajegroup, however, introduced big bottles at very low prices (the brand was even called Big Cola in Mexico) and relied on hundreds of salespeople to reach the smaller stores that in Mexico accounted for 75 percent of cola sales. In a short time, they succeeded in gaining distribution in 25 percent of such outlets in Mexico City.

Some distributors declined the new cola, citing threats from the Coca-Cola Company to pull Coke products in retaliation (an allegation Coke denied). An earlier ruling by Mexico's antitrust board had ordered Coke to stop abusing its market power over distributors. As a result of this ruling, many distributors first became aware that they had a choice about what they sold. Still, Coke could buy loyalty by offering free refrigerators to chill Cokes and buying its small retailers life-insurance policies. Coca-Cola also offered free cases of Coke, and Coke employees were constantly visiting stores to help with stocking and display. The Ajegroup, on the other hand, kept an eye on costs. Even distribution was outsourced to third parties who often delivered in rundown trucks.

Just three years after entering the Mexican market, Big Cola had grabbed 7 percent market share with a stated goal of increasing market share to 10 percent. Long the largest international market for Coke and Pepsi, Mexico had come to represent 45 percent of Ajegroup's consolidated sales. Consequently, the company was opening a plant in Monterrey in order to increase its presence in the north of the country and had even decided to move its international headquarters to Mexico. In the meantime, the Ajegroup was moving quickly into Costa Rica, Panama, and Nicaragua.

Discussion Questions

1. Which do you think is the bigger threat to Coca-Cola—brands like Qibla and Mecca Cola or the Ajegroup? Why?

2. What are the strengths and weaknesses of Qibla and Mecca Cola compared to Coca-Cola?

3. Why has the new cola launched by the Ajegroup been so successful? Do you think this cola could successfully expand outside Latin America? Why or why not?

4. Evaluate Coca-Cola's response to Ajegroup. What suggestions would you give Coca-Cola?

Sources: Grant F. Smith, "Georgia Exports to Saudi Arabia: Coke, Innovation and Islam," Saudi-American Forum Essay #33, November 9, 2004; Meg Carter, "New Colas Wage Battle for Hearts and Minds," *Financial Times*, January 8, 2004, p. 13; Bill Britt, "Mecca Cola Mimics Coke," AdAge.com, February 24, 2003; Hillary Chura, "Qibla Calls for Boycott of U.S. Brands," AdAge.com, April 3, 2003; David Luhnow and Chad Terhune, "Latin Pop," *Wall Street Journal*, October 27, 2003, p. A1; Amy Guthrie, "Peru's Kola Real Sets Up Headquarters in Mexico City," Dow Jones Newswires, July 7, 2004; "Peruvian Ajegroup Holds 17 Pct Market Share in Venezuela," *Spanish News Digest*, August 30, 2004; and Reuters, "Peru Bottler Ajegroup Grows in Mexico, Centam," January 20, 2005.

NOTES

1. Michael Flagg, "Enjoy Shinier Hair! Chinese Brands Arrive," *Wall Street Journal*, May 24, 2001, p. A17.
2. George S. Yip, *Total Global Strategy* (New York: Prentice-Hall, 2002), pp. 171–175.
3. "PepsiCo's Venezuelan Joint Venture Inaugurates $32 Million Plant," *Financial Times*, May 27, 1999, p. 19.
4. Manjeet Kripalani and Mark L. Clifford, "Finally Coke Gets It Right," *Business Week*, February 10, 2003, p. 18.
5. Jean-Pierre Jeannet, *Competitive Marketing Strategies in a European Context*, Lausanne: IMD, 1987.
6. Niraj Dawar and Tony Frost, "Competing with Giants," *Harvard Business Review* 77 (March-April 1999), pp. 119–129.
7. Guliz Ger, "Localizing in the Global Village: Local Firms Competing in Global Markets," *California Management Review* 41, no. 4 (Summer 1999), pp. 64–83.
8. Tomas Elewaut, Patricia Lindenboim, and Damian L. Scokin, "Chile's Lesson in Lean Banking," *McKinsey Quarterly*, no. 3 (2003).
9. Jack Ewing and Joseph Weber, "The Beer Wars Come to a Head," *Business Week*, May 24, 2004, p. 68.
10. Dawar and Frost, "Competing with Giants," p. 124.
11. Jaime Mejia and Gabriel Sama, "Media Players Say 'Si' to Latino Magazines," *Wall Street Journal*, May 15, 2002, p. B4.
12. David C. Gregorcyk, *Internationalization of Conglomerates from Emerging Markets: Success Stories from Mexico.* Unpublished honors thesis, Teresa Lozano Long Institute of Latin American Studies, The University of Texas at Austin, 2005.
13. Hugh Pope, "Turkish Surprise," *Wall Street Journal*, September 7, 2004, p. A1.
14. Moon Ihlwan, "Daewoo: GM's Hot New Engine," *Business Week*, November 29, 2004, pp. 52–53.
15. Marcus Walker and Martin Gelnar, "Europe's Dysfunctional Family Businesses," *Wall Street Journal*, December 22, 2003, p. A13.
16. Hannah Karp and Andrew Wallmeyer, "Europe Firms Enjoy Homegrown Edge," *Wall Street Journal*, November 17, 2004.
17. Nikki Tait, "European Takeover Rulings Have Not Been 'Biased'," *Financial Times*, July 14, 2003, p. 10.
18. Carol Matlack, Joseph Weber, and Wendy Zellner, "In Fighting Trim," *Business Week*, April 28, 2003, p. 26.
19. Hiroyuki Tezuka, "Success as the Source of Failure? Competition and Cooperation in the Japanese Economy." *Sloan Management Review* 38 (Winter 1997), pp. 83–93.
20. Ibid.
21. J. McGuire and S. Dow, "The Persistence and Implications of Japanese Keiretsus," *Journal of International Business Studies* 34 (2003), pp. 374–388.
22. Ibid.
23. Betsy McKay and David Luhnow, "Mexico Finds Coke and Its Bottlers Guilty of Abusing Dominant Position in Market," *Wall Street Journal*, March 8, 2002, p. B3.
24. Gary S. Becker, "Is Europe Starting to Play by U.S. Rules?" *Business Week*, April 22, 2002, p. 24.
25. Peter Fritsch, "Hard Profits," *Wall Street Journal*, April 22, 2002, p. A1.
26. Eric Bellman, "After Delays, India Sells Stakes in Two Big Firms," *Wall Street Journal*, February 6, 2002, p. A12.
27. Josh Gerstein, "Chinese Law Delivers Shipping Controversy," *USA Today*, April 5, 2002, p. B8.
28. Ben Dolven, "China Recruits Foreign Talent," *Wall Street Journal*, April 15, 2004, p. A13.
29. James E. Austin, *Managing in Developing Countries* (New York: The Free Press, 1990), pp. 127–129.
30. Manjeet Kripalani, "Ratan Tata," *Business Week*, July 26, 2004, pp. 50–51.
31. James M. Dorsey, "Turkish Conglomerate Prepares to Slim Down," *Wall Street Journal*, August 14, 2000, p. A14.
32. Bruce Einhorn, Stuart Young, and David Rocks, "Another About-Face for Acer," *Business Week*, April 24, 2000, p.146.
33. Oxford Analytica Ltd., August 26, 2004.
34. Eugene D. Jaffe and Israel D. Nebenzahl, *National Image and Competitive Advantage* (Copenhagen: Copenhagen Business School Press, 2001), p. 53.
35. Rajshekhar G. Javalgi, Bob D. Cutler, and William A. Winans, "At Your Service! Does Country of Origin Research Apply to Services?" *Journal of Services Marketing* 15, no. 6/7 (2001), pp. 565–582.
36. Dae Ryun Chang and Ik-Tae Rim, "A Study on the Rating of Import Sources for Industrial Products in a Newly Industrialized Country: The Case of South Korea," *Journal of Business Research* 32 (1995), pp. 31–39.
37. Hans B. Thorelli and Aleksandra Glowaka, "Willingness of American Industrial Buyers to Source Internationally," *Journal of Business Research* 32 (1995), pp. 21–30.
38. Chike Okechuku and Vincent Oneyemah, "Nigerian Consumer Attitudes Toward Foreign and Domestic Products," *Journal of International Business Studies* 30, 3 (1999), pp. 611–622.
39. Gary S. Inch and J. Brad McBride, "The Impact of Country-of-Origin Cues on Consumer Perceptions of Product Quality: A Binational Test of the Decomposed Country-of-Origin Construct," *Journal of Business Research* 57 (2004), pp. 256–265.
40. Michael A. Kamins and Akira Nagashima, "Perceptions of Products Made in Japan versus Those Made in the United States Among Japanese and American Executives: A Longitudinal Perspective," *Asia Pacific Journal of Management* 12, no. 1 (1995), pp. 49–68; and Inder Khera, "A Broadening Base of U.S. Consumer Acceptance of Korean Products" in Kenneth D. Bahn and M. Joseph Sirsy (eds.), *World Marketing Congress* (Blacksburg, VA: Academy of Marketing Science, 1986), pp. 136–141.
41. Owen Brown, "China Consumers Rate Japan Cars, Electronics Tops," *Wall Street Journal*, June 7, 2004, p. A17.

42. Jim Rendon, "When Nations Need a Little Marketing," *New York Times*, November 23, 2003, p. 5.
43. Sarah McBride, "Kia's Audacious Sorento Plan," *Wall Street Journal*, April 8, 2002, p. A12.
44. Janeen E. Olsen, Linda Nowak, and T. K. Clarke, "Country of Origin Effects and Complimentary Marketing Channels: Is Mexican Wine More Enjoyable When Served with Mexican Food?" *International Journal of Wine Marketing* 14, no. 1 (2002), pp. 23–34.
45. Hugh Pope, "Turkish Delight," *Wall Street Journal*, September 7, 2004, p. A1.
46. Massoud M. Saghafi, Fanis Varvoglis, and Tomas Vega, "Why U.S. Firms Don't Buy from Latin American Companies," *Industrial Marketing Management* 20 (1991), pp. 207–213.
47. Jill G. Klein, Richard Ettenson, and Marlene D. Morris, "The Animosity Model of Foreign Product Purchase: An Empirical Test in the People's Republic of China," *Journal of Marketing* 62 (1998), pp. 89–100.
48. John Quelch, "The Return of the Global Brand," *Harvard Business Review* 81 (August 2003), pp. 22–23.
49. John Carreyrou and Jenny E. Heller, "U.S.Rift Hits Bottom Line," *Wall Street Journal*, June 16, 2003, p. A13.
50. Tamsin Carlisle and Joel Baglole, "Canadian Businesses Fear Fallout of Iraq Stance," *Wall Street Journal*, March 28, 2003, p. A11.

7 GLOBAL MARKETING RESEARCH

SPANISH RETAILER ZARA takes only 4 or 5 weeks to design a new fashion collection, compared with the 6 months it takes its major competitors. Zara's designers frequent fashion shows and talk to customers. One designer remarks, "We're like sponges. We soak up information about fashion trends from all over the world." The firm sent out new khaki skirts during the night to some of its 449 stores worldwide. From their desks at headquarters, Zara managers can check real-time sales on computers to see where the skirts are selling. They keep in constant contact with store managers in order to spot and react to trends quickly. After selling well in Asia earlier in the year, camouflage motifs are now popular in France and Lebanon. But stripes outsell camouflage in Spain. Long plaid skirts are big in Kuwait.[1]

Our purpose in Chapter 7 is to explore methods for collecting appropriate data to better understand potential markets. Our emphasis is managerial rather than technical. Throughout

LEARNING OBJECTIVES

After studying this chapter, you should be able to

- ▶ List and describe the four steps involved in the research process.

- ▶ Differentiate between the challenges posed by secondary data collection and those posed by primary data collection.

- ▶ Note cultural differences in marketing research, and explain ways in which market researchers can adjust to them.

- ▶ Describe problems related to comparability of studies undertaken in different national markets.

- ▶ Explain the value of analysis by inference to global marketers.

- ▶ Note ways to monitor global competitors.

- ▶ Explain the requirements for a global marketing information system.

CHAPTER OUTLINE

the chapter, we focus on how companies can obtain useful and accurate information that will help them make more informed strategic decisions, such as decisions related to market choice and to the marketing mix that will be discussed in later chapters. This chapter begins by examining the scope and challenges of international research. We then describe the research process, with particular emphasis on data collection. The chapter concludes with a discussion of global information systems.

THE SCOPE OF GLOBAL MARKETING RESEARCH

Global marketing research is meant to provide adequate data and cogent analysis for effective decision making on a global scale. The analytic research techniques practiced by domestic businesses can be applied to international marketing projects. The key difference is in the complexity of assignments because of the additional variables that international researchers must take into account. Global marketers have to judge the comparability of their data across a number of markets and are frequently faced with making decisions based on the basis of limited data. Because of this, the researcher must approach the research task with flexibility, resourcefulness, and ingenuity.

Traditionally, marketing research has been charged with the following three broad areas of responsibility:

▶ *Environmental studies.* Given the added environmental complexity of global marketing, managers need timely input on various national environments.

▶ *Market studies.* One of the tasks that researchers most frequently face is to determine the size of a market and the needs of potential customers.

▶ *Competitive studies.* Another important task for the international marketing researcher is to provide insights about competitors, both domestic and foreign.

In earlier chapters we have covered many issues involved in an environmental study. Of particular interest are the economic, physical, sociocultural, and political environments of a market. Studies focusing on a national market are frequently undertaken when a major decision regarding that market has to be made. This could include a move to enter the country or an effort to increase significantly the firm's presence in that market through large new investments. As a company gains experience in any given country, its staff and local organization accumulate considerable data on the social and cultural situation, and this store of information can be tapped whenever needed. Therefore, a full study of these environmental variables is most useful when the company does not already have a base in that country and its relevant experience is limited.

Nonetheless, managers should carefully monitor changes in their markets. They may also find it useful to keep informed about the latest regulations governing their industry in other countries, even if they do not conduct any business there. Policies in one country often spread to others. This is particularly true within regional blocs. And on an even larger scale, the trade and investment policies of a country have been shown to be influenced by the country's trading partners.[2]

Global marketing research also is used to make both strategic and tactical decisions. Strategic decisions include deciding what markets to enter, how to enter them (exporting, licensing, joint venture), where to locate production facilities, and how to position products vis-à-vis competitors. Tactical decisions are decisions about the specific marketing mix to be used in a country and are made on an ongoing basis. Decisions about advertising, sales promotions, and sales forces all require data derived from testing in the local market. The type of information required is often the same as that required in domestic marketing research, but the process is made more complex by the variety of cultures and environments. Table 7.1 shows the various types of tactical marketing decisions needed and the kinds of research used to collect the necessary data.

The complexity of the international marketplace, the extreme differences that exist from country to country, and the company's frequent lack of familiarity with foreign markets accentuate the importance of international marketing research. Before making market entry, product positioning, or marketing mix decisions, a marketer must have accurate information about the market size, customer needs, competition, and relevant government regulations. Marketing research provides the information the firm needs to avoid the costly mistakes of poor strategies or lost opportunities.

The lack of proper marketing research can sabotage product development for a foreign market. On the strength of a research study conducted in the United States, one U.S. firm introduced a new cake mix in England. Believing that homemakers wanted to feel that they participated in the preparation of the cake, the U.S. marketers devised a mix that required homemakers to add an egg. Given its success in the U.S. market, the marketers confidently introduced the product in England. The product failed, however, because the British did not like fancy American cakes. They preferred cakes that were tough and spongy and could accompany afternoon tea. The ploy of having homemakers add an egg to the mix did not eliminate basic differences in taste and style.[3]

TABLE 7.1 INTERNATIONAL MARKETING DECISIONS REQUIRING MARKETING RESEARCH	
MARKETING MIX DECISION	TYPE OF RESEARCH
Product policy	Focus groups and qualitative research to generate ideas for new products
	Survey research to evaluate new product ideas
	Concept testing, test marketing
	Product benefit and attitude research
	Product formulation and feature testing
	Price sensitivity studies
Pricing	Survey of shopping patterns and behavior
Distribution	Consumer attitudes toward different store types
	Survey of distributor attitudes and policies
Advertising	Advertising pretesting
Advertising post-testing, recall scores	Surveys of media habits
Sales promotion	Surveys of response to alternative types of promotion
Sales force	Tests of alternative sales presentations

SOURCE: Susan P. Douglas and C. Samuel Craig, *International Marketing Research,* © 1983, p. 32. Reprinted by permission of Prentice-Hall, Inc., Englewood Cliffs, New Jersey.

On the other hand, well-conceived market research can provide insights that promote success. Whirlpool's market research helped speed its entry into the European microwave market. Although less than one-third of European households owned microwave ovens, research suggested that European consumers would buy a microwave that performed like a conventional oven. Whirlpool introduced a model that incorporated a broiler coil for top browning and a unique dish that sizzled the underside of the food. This new product, the Crisp, became Europe's best-selling microwave.[4]

Companies also use research to position a product better in foreign markets. PepsiCo's research found that the youth market in Europe was ready for a new cola that did not contain sugar. However, Pepsi also found that the youth market, especially males, was adverse to a diet soda. Therefore, the soft-drink giant launched Pepsi Max not as a diet soda but as a trendy, cool, sugar-free cola. The TV campaign showed Pepsi Max drinkers "Living Life to the Max," performing death-defying stunts.[5]

CHALLENGES IN PLANNING INTERNATIONAL RESEARCH

After determining what key variables to investigate, international marketers still face a number of challenges. Whereas domestic research is limited to one country, international research includes many. The research design is more complex because the researcher defining the possible target market must choose which countries or segments to research. For many countries, secondary information may be limited or expensive. Primary research can prove culturally challenging. In addition, the comparison of research results from one national study to another is hindered by the general difficulty of establishing comparability and equivalence among various research data. Definitions of socioeconomic status, income, and education can vary widely among countries, which makes even the simplest demographic comparisons between markets challenging.

THE RESEARCH PROCESS

Although conducting marketing research internationally adds to the complexity of the research task, the basic approach remains the same for domestic and international assignments. Either type of research is a four-step process:

1. Problem definition and development of research objectives
2. Determination of the sources of information
3. Collection and analysis of the data from primary and secondary sources
4. Analysis of the data

These four steps may be the same for both international and domestic research, but problems in implementation may occur because of cultural and economic differences from country to country.

WORLD BEAT 7.1

Middle East Research

MARKETING RESEARCH PROFESSIONALS working in Middle Eastern nations with predominantly Muslim populations say that the area's already limited acceptance of Western marketing research methods was not undermined by the terrorist attacks in September 2001 and their military aftermath—but neither is there any reason to expect tremendous growth in the region.

According to an industry newsletter, the international marketing research industry's total research revenues derived from studies done in Muslim nations amount to no more than about $25 million annually, a tiny slice of the $4.3 billion in non-U.S. research revenues posted by the twenty-five largest international marketing research firms alone. The most significant new trend in the research industry—the Internet interview—is not even an option in the Middle East because of the small number of consumers with home Internet service.

In the Middle East, one distinct social boundary exists between men and women in nearly all endeavors, including, for example, most research focus groups. In conservative Saudi Arabia, where strict interpretation of Islam demands segregation of the sexes, mixed-gender groups are flatly prohibited. But even in more liberal Muslim nations such as Egypt, mixed-gender groups are usually not recommended. Muslim women often defer to men, letting males dominate the conversation, which skews the results of a focus group. Segregation still is the best way to get Muslim women to open up. Yet the idea

of females caught on tape and possibly observed by strangers also conflicts with cultural norms.

In rural areas of Saudi Arabia, mail is delivered not to homes or P.O. boxes, but only to businesses, so researchers can't use the postal system for consumer recruitment. Mall intercept is not common or widely understood by consumers, and this makes it difficult to approach strangers in Middle Eastern shopping malls. Western researchers are left to recruit via word of mouth (so-called *snowballing*). Typically, they partner with a local research company or use other local contacts willing to inquire among their own social circles for participants. But although a native can better explain the project's concept and more effectively recruit fellow citizens, each "seed contact" can be allowed to generate only a small number of referrals, lest the information be collected from within too narrow a circle of acquaintances. A few weeks of recruitment fieldwork in the United Kingdom could translate into many more weeks for the same study in a Muslim country. As a result, research projects typically take much longer to complete in Muslim countries.

Source: From Steve Jarvis, "Western-Style Research in the Middle East," *Marketing News*, April 29, 2002, pp. 37–38. Copyright ©2002 American Marketing Association (Chic.). Reproduced with permission of American Marketing Association (Chic.) via Copyright Clearance Center.

Problem Definition and Development of Research Objectives

In any market research project, the most important tasks are to define the problem and, subsequently, to determine what information is needed. This process can take weeks or months. It eventually determines the choice of methodologies, the types of people to survey, and the appropriate time frame in which to conduct the research.

Marketing problems may differ between countries or cultures. This may reflect differences in socioeconomic conditions, levels of economic development, cultural forces, or the competitive market structure. For example, bicycles in a developed country may be competing with other recreational goods, such as skis, baseball gloves, and exercise equipment. In a developing country, however, they provide basic transportation and hence compete with small cars, mopeds, and scooters. A global firm could fail to understand why growth in bicycles was declining in Malaysia if it asked questions only about the consumer's purchase and use of other recreational products.

Data Collection

Primary data data collected for a specific research purpose and obtained by direct observation or by direct contact with sources of information

Secondary data data already in existence that was collected for some purpose other than the current study

For each assignment, researchers may choose to base their analyses on **primary data** (data collected specifically for this assignment), **secondary data** (previously collected and available data), or a combination of both secondary and primary sources. Because costs tend to be higher for research based on primary data, researchers usually exhaust secondary data first. Often called desk research or library research, this approach depends on the availability and reliability of material. Secondary sources may include government publications, trade journals, and data from international agencies or service establishments such as banks, ad agencies, and marketing research companies.

UTILIZING SECONDARY DATA

For any marketing research problem, the location and analysis of secondary data should be a first step. Although secondary data are not available for all variables, data can often be obtained from public and private sources at a fraction of the cost of obtaining primary data. Increasingly, these sources are disseminating or selling their data over the Internet.

Sources of Secondary Data

A good approach to locating secondary sources is to ask yourself who would know about most sources of information on a specific market. For example, if you wanted to locate secondary information on fibers used for tires in Europe, you might consider asking the editor of a trade magazine on the tire industry or the executive director of the tire manufacturing association or the company librarian for Akzo Nobel, a Dutch company that manufactures fibers.

Sources of secondary data for international markets include Web search engines, banks, consulates, embassies, foreign chambers of commerce, libraries with foreign information sections, foreign magazines, public accounting firms, security brokers, and state development offices in foreign countries. Marketers can also "eavesdrop" on the Internet. Every day customers comment online concerning products and services. By monitoring chatrooms, newsgroups, and listservs, marketers can analyze comments to learn what their customers and their competitors are thinking.[6] For-pay subscription sources for secondary research, such a Factiva or Euromonitor, can often be accessed via a university or corporate library.

Check out our website (college.hmco.com/business/) for ideas and links to online sources of secondary data.

A census taker collects information in Delhi, India.

Many governments collect and disseminate information concerning foreign markets to encourage their national firms to export. To make access to information easier and more streamlined, the U.S. government combined the foreign market research of its various embassies, departments, and bureaus into a single export portal located at www.export.gov. Although designed for exporters, the site is useful to foreign investors as well.

Problems with Secondary Data

There are problems associated with the use of secondary data. They include (1) the fact that not all the necessary data may be available, (2) uncertainty about the accuracy of the data, (3) the lack of comparability of the data, and (4) the questionable timeliness of some data. In some cases, no data have been collected. For example, many countries have little data on the number of retailers, wholesalers, and distributors. In Ethiopia and Chad, population statistics were unavailable for many years.

The quality of government statistics is definitely variable. For example, Germany reported that industrial production was up by 0.5 percent in one month but later revised this figure, reporting that production actually declined by 0.5 percent, an error of 100 percent in the opposite direction. An *Economist* survey of twenty international statisticians rated the quality of statistics from thirteen developed countries on the criteria of objectivity, reliability, methodology, and timeliness. The leading countries were Canada, Australia, Holland, and France; the worst were Belgium, Spain, and Italy.[7]

Although a substantial body of data exists from the most advanced industrial nations, secondary data are less likely to be available for developing countries. Not every country publishes a census, and some published data are not considered reliable. In Nigeria, for example, population size is of such political sensitivity that published census data are generally believed to be highly suspect. A study by the International Labor Organization found actual unemployment to be 10.4 million people in Russia, compared with the official figure of 1.7 million people unemployed![8] However, income remains the most problematic demographic category of all state statistics in developing countries. For example, in Central Asia a significant share of family income comes from the informal economy such as black markets, street vending, and bribery. Since respondents won't admit these sources of income, Central Asian governments estimate incomes based on questions relating to household expenditures.[9]

According to a report by the U.S. Foreign Commercial Service in Beijing, Chinese government statistics are often riddled with *shuifen* or "water content." China has begun to crack down on fraudulent statistics, however, using new laws to discipline local officials who exaggerate their successes. Still, data reliability remains a problem in many developing countries. For this reason, companies sometimes have to proceed with the collection of primary data in developing countries at a much earlier stage than in the most industrialized nations.

The entry of private-sector data collectors into major emerging markets may help ameliorate the shortcomings of government statistics. Since the late 1990s the Gallup Organization has collected data on the Chinese. Gallup interviewers poll 4,000 randomly selected respondents from both rural and urban China. Questions cover a wide range of topics: How much money do you make? What do you buy? What are your dreams? The results of these surveys are compiled in Gallup publications of consumer attitudes and lifestyles in modern China.[10]

Another problem is that secondary data may not be directly comparable from country to country. The population statistics in the United States are collected every 10 years, whereas population statistics in Bolivia are collected every 25 years. Also, countries may calculate the same statistic but do so in different ways. Gross domestic product (GDP) is the value of all goods and services produced in a country and is often used in place of GNP. GDP per capita is a common measure of market size, suggesting the economic wealth of a country per person. As we noted in Chapter 5, the International Monetary Fund (IMF) has decided that the normal practice of converting expressions of GDP in local currencies into dollars at market exchange rates understates the true size of developing economies relative to rich ones. Therefore, the IMF has decided to use purchasing-power parity, which takes into account differences in prices among nations.

Finally, age of the data is a constant problem. Population statistics are usually between 2 and 5 years old at best. Industrial production statistics can be from 1 to 2 years old. With different markets exhibiting different growth rates, it may be unwise to use older data to make decisions among markets. Market surveys previously undertaken by governments or private research firms are seldom as timely as a marketing manager truly needs.

ANALYSIS BY INFERENCE

Data available from secondary sources are frequently of an aggregate nature and fail to satisfy the specific information needs of a firm. A company must often assess market size on the basis of very limited data on foreign markets. In such cases, market assessment by inference is a possibility. This technique uses available facts about related products or other foreign markets as a basis for inferring the necessary information for the market under analysis. Market assessment by inference is a low-cost activity that should take place before a company engages in the collection of any primary data, which can be quite costly. Inferences can be made on the basis of related products, relative market size, and analysis of demand patterns.

Related Products

Few products are consumed or used "in a vacuum"—that is, without any ties to prior purchases or to products in use. If actual consumption statistics are not available for a product category, proxies can prove useful. A **proxy** is a related product that indicates demand for the product under study. Relationships exist, for example, between replacement tires and automobiles on the road and between electricity consumption and the use of appliances. In some situations, it may be possible to obtain data on related products and their uses as a basis for inferring usage of the product to be marketed. From experience in other, similar markets, the analyst is able to apply usage ratios that can provide for low-cost estimates. For example, the analyst can determine the number of replacement tires needed by looking at the number of automobiles on the road. Radio audiences also tend to increase with the number of automobiles in a country. This was observed in China, prompting more interest in radio advertising among firms operating there.[11]

Proxy a product the demand for which varies in relationship with the demand for another product being investigated

Relative Market Size

Quite frequently, if data on market size are available for other countries, this information can be used to derive estimates for the particular country under investigation. For example, say that market size is known for the United States and that estimates are required for Canada, a country with a reasonably comparable economic system and consumption patterns. Statistics for the United States can be scaled down, by the relative size of GNP, population, or other factors, to about one-tenth of U.S. figures. Similar relationships exist in Europe, where the known market size of one country can provide a basis for inferences about a related country. Of course, the results are not exact, but they provide a basis for further analysis.

Analysis of Demand Patterns

By analyzing industrial growth patterns for various countries, researchers can gain insights into the relationship of consumption patterns to industrial growth. Relationships can be plotted between GDP per capita and the percentage of total manufacturing production accounted for by major industries.

Electricity consumption can be used as an indicator of demand for electrical appliances in developing countries.

During earlier growth stages with corresponding low per-capita incomes, manufacturing tends to center on necessities such as food, beverages, textiles, and light manufacturing. With growing incomes, the role of these industries tends to decline, and heavy industry assumes greater importance. By analyzing such manufacturing patterns, it is possible to make forecasts for various product groups for countries at lower income levels, because they often repeat the growth patterns of more developed economies.

Similar trends can be observed for a country's import composition. With increasing industrialization, countries develop similar patterns modified only by each country's natural resources. Energy-poor countries must import increasing quantities of energy as industrialization proceeds, whereas energy-rich countries can embark on an industrialization path without significant energy imports. Industrialized countries import relatively more food products and industrial materials than manufactured goods, which are more important for the less industrialized countries. Understanding these relationships can help the analyst determine future trends for a country's economy and may help determine future market potential and sales prospects.

COLLECTING PRIMARY DATA

Often, in addition to secondary data or when secondary data are not available or usable, the marketer will need to collect primary data. Researchers can design studies to collect primary data that will meet the information requirements for making a specific marketing decision. Primary sources frequently reveal data that are simply not available from secondary sources. For example, Siar Research International undertook a survey on shaving habits in Central Asia and discovered that over 50 percent of Kazakhstan men shave every day, whereas most Azerbaijan men shave only once a week.[12]

For the global marketer, collecting primary data involves developing a research instrument, selecting a sample, collecting the data, and (often) comparing results across cultures.

Developing a Research Instrument

The process of developing a research instrument such as a survey questionnaire or a focus group protocol must often be done with multiple markets in mind, and every effort should be made to capture the appropriate environmental variables. Even research aimed at a single market might be compared, at a later date, with the results of research in another country. Nonetheless translation of a questionnaire is prone to difficulties. For instance, a surprising problem arises when translating questionnaires from English (an alphabetic-based language) into Japanese (a character-based language): They become longer! Since most respondents around the world prefer shorter questionnaires to longer ones, this presents market researchers yet another cross-cultural obstacle.[13]

Indeed, a major challenge of instrument design involves translation from one language to another. Accurate translation equivalence is important, first to ensure that the respondents understand the question and second to ensure that the researcher understands the response. **Back translation** is commonly used. That is, first the questionnaire is translated from the home language into the language of the country where it will be used; this is done by a bilingual speaker who is a native speaker of the foreign country. Next a bilingual person who is a native speaker of the home language translates this version back into the home language. This translation is then compared to the original wording. Another translation technique is **parallel translation**, in which two or more translators translate the questionnaire. The results are compared, and any differences are discussed and resolved.

Idiomatic expressions and colloquialisms are often translated incorrectly. One international market research firm discovered this when working with a camera manufacturer. The client proposed to use in an advertisement a direct translation into Spanish of the English sentence "I get a good shot every time I use it." Unfortunately, this translated into "I get a good *gunshot* every time."[14] To avoid these translation errors, experts suggest the technique of back translation be used even in the local dialect, so that *ji xuan ji*, which means "computers" to Chinese speakers in China and Taiwan, does not become "calculators" to Chinese speakers in Singapore.[15] Even within the same city, differences in social class can result in different idioms. In one study of the adoption of new products, interviewers in Mexico City were selected from among the same social class as respondents.[16]

Translation problems also arise with measurement scales. U.S. respondents may readily recognize and understand the "school-grade" scale of A–F. However, such a scale would be meaningless elsewhere.[17] Similarly, researchers who employ scales with concepts such as "satisfied," "happy," and "delighted" may discover that some cultures fail to determine sufficient differences between such terms. In general, unless a researcher is very familiar with a culture, it is best to employ a numeric, or Likert, scale.

Finally, even with the best of translations, research can suffer if a concept is not readily understood. For example, Western researchers discovered that the Vietnamese tend to be very literal in their understanding of ideas. If a company

Back translation a technique in which a questionnaire is translated from one language into a second language, translated back from the second language into the first language, and then compared with the original text

Parallel translation a technique in which two or more translators translate a questionnaire, compare their translations, and resolve any differences between the translations

asks for an opinion on a new package design concept, Vietnamese consumers may say they never saw it before, so it can't be done. Researchers must instead explain that the new packaging is available in other countries and then ask what consumers think of it.[18]

Selecting a Sample

After developing the instrument and translating it into the appropriate language, the researcher must determine the appropriate sample design. What population is under investigation? Is it housewives between twenty and forty years old or manufacturing directors at textile plants? When investigating buyer behavior, researchers must remember that the purchase decision maker can vary by country. For example, the key decision maker for purchasing diagnostic equipment in the United States is often a laboratory director. In Europe, where medical testing is more decentralized, the decision maker could be a department director or nurse manager.[19] The international market researcher must adjust the target population accordingly.

Researchers prefer using a probability sample in order to have greater assurance that sample results can be extrapolated to the population under investigation. To have a probability sample, potential respondents must be randomly selected from frames, or lists, of the population. In many countries, such lists are difficult to find.[20] In many developing countries, the existing infrastructure and the lack of available data or information substantially interfere with attempts to use probability samples. Sampling of larger populations requires the availability of detailed census data, called census tracts, or neighborhood maps from which probability samples can be drawn. Even where such data are available, they are often out of date. Some market researchers use telephone directories. However, in Mexico, for example, the telephone directory may not correspond with those who currently possess the phone numbers. Further difficulties arise from inadequate transportation, which may prevent fieldworkers from reaching selected census tracts in some areas of the country. Sampling is particularly difficult in countries where several languages are spoken. Carrying out a nationwide survey under such conditions may be impractical.

Collecting Data

The next task of the international market researcher is to collect the data. An immediate problem may involve finding the right people to undertake the data collection. Finding the proper personnel in developing countries can be particularly challenging since most people may not even understand the concept of marketing research. To overcome this problem in South Africa, the managing director of one research firm guest lectures at tecknicons (schools where students who do not attend universities go to earn diplomas) in order to generate interest in marketing research. She reports that interest in this new profession is high, and she encourages students to volunteer at market research firms in order to gain experience.[21]

Another problem in developing countries can be the fact that many data collectors are poorly paid and are often paid by the response. This can lead to collectors simply filling out questionnaires themselves. Some of the safeguards against this in developed countries cannot be easily replicated in developing ones. To ensure quality, supervisors can call back respondents on a random basis to confirm their responses. Alternatively, supervisors can randomly listen in on telephone interviews. However, phone interviews are rare in developing countries, and collectors must often intercept respondents on the streets. This can make it more difficult for supervisors to check responses.

Collection Methods. Data can be collected by mail, by telephone, electronically, or face-to-face. In developed countries, telephone interviews have often been the method of choice. However, as noted, interviews by telephone are more difficult in developing countries where landline phones have less penetration and (as also noted earlier) telephone directories may be nonexistent or woefully out-of-date. For example, in the Central Asian nation of Kazakhstan, only 70–80 percent of households in large cities have telephones. In smaller cities, telephone connection is extremely low.[22]

Face-to-face interviews may be necessary in developing countries, but researchers may encounter challenges in approaching respondents in these traditional collectivist societies. Face-to-face interviews are decreasing in some developed countries, such as Holland, and being replaced by more Internet-based research. In Scandinavia, where Internet access is high, Internet research has become increasingly popular. Even so, market researchers suggest supplementing such research with telephone or face-to-face interviews in order to ensure a representative sample from the population. While developing countries lag behind developed ones in Internet access, market researchers are planning for the future. The number of consumers with Internet connection is rising in developing countries, where access is increasingly possible via mobile phones as well as via computers.

Participation and Response. A major issue in primary research, of course, is the willingness of the potential respondent to participate in the study. For example, in many cultures a man will consider it inappropriate to discuss his shaving habits with anyone, especially with a female interviewer. Respondents in the Netherlands or Germany are notoriously reluctant to divulge information about their personal financial habits. The Dutch are more willing to discuss sex than money.[23]

In Japan, consumers will generally not respond to telephone interviews. Only 5 percent of interviews are done by telephone, compared with 30 percent in business offices, 20 percent by mail, 19 percent in the surveyor's office, 14 percent in focus groups, and the rest in other ways.[24] Although personal interviews are expensive and time-consuming, the Japanese preference for face-to-face contact suggests that personal interviews yield better information than data collected by mail or telephone. In fact, Japanese managers are skeptical about Western-style marketing research. Senior and middle managers often go into the field and speak directly with consumers and distributors. This technique of collecting "soft data," though less rigorous than large-scale consumer studies, gives the manager a real feel for the market and the consumers.[25]

Developing countries can present additional problems to market researchers, including poor infrastructure, lower literacy levels, and disinclination to share information with strangers. In Mexico, respondents prefer shorter question-naires and may be less forthcoming if interviewed at home than they would be if intercepted on the street. This is particularly true regarding information about personal income, because respondents may believe that the researchers are the tax authorities in disguise.[26] Convincing business buyers to participate in research studies is also difficult in many developing countries. Potential respondents are often concerned that the information they provide will be released to competitors or to the authorities.

Government Regulation of Data Collection

Survey design, sampling, and data collection can all be affected by national leg-islation. For example, market researchers in the United States, where telephone interviews are common, now face state and national no-call lists that restrict their access to potential respondents. In Germany, street and mall interviews have become less common because researchers must have a license from local authorities to approach respondents.[27] Opinion polls in China are subject to government screening; in addition, questions about politics and sex are often disallowed.[28]

Data collection and privacy concerns being raised in the European Union (EU) may affect marketing research globally. The EU Data Privacy Directive requires unambiguous consent from a person for each use of his or her per-sonal data.[29] This limits both the use of telephone interviews and how data over the Internet is collected and used. All fifteen EU nations have data privacy leg-islation and a government privacy commission to enforce the EU policy. This legislation stipulates that data cannot be sent to a country that is not a member of the EU unless that country has an adequate level of privacy protection. The U.S. Department of Commerce has worked with EU officials to develop the Safe Harbor framework. This framework provides a streamlined way for individual U.S. firms to comply with the European standards and thus continue to receive data from Europe. More recently, Japan has exhibited concerns about privacy similar to those in the EU and passed legislation forbidding market research companies from using secondhand lists to contact individuals without first acquiring the consent of those individuals.[30]

For more on Safe Harbor, including how to apply and who has applied, check out the *Safe Harbor* link on our website (college.hmco.com/business/).

Comparing Studies Across Cultures

A researcher must deal with problems of comparability when survey research is undertaken in more than one country to compare buyer attitudes or behav-ior in different markets. Were the samples similar in all markets? A study com-paring software adoption among small-business owners in Brazil with that among managers in large U.S. corporations may identify differences based more on firm size than on nationality. Are measures comparable cross-culturally? For example, measures of affluence such as size of residence or number of vacations may prove problematic because Europeans live in smaller homes and receive more vacation days than Americans do.[31] Needless to say, issues of comparability should be addressed at the beginning—not the end—of the research process.

Another issue of comparability that arises concerns the response to scales. Some cultures express themselves comfortably in extremes, whereas responses in other cultures hover more centrally, making it difficult to determine whether consumers in that country are indeed more neutral about products or whether these tepid responses are an artifact of culture. When interpreting surveys in particular, researchers should be concerned with **scalar equivalence**. What does it mean to rate a product "7" or "8" on a 10-point scale? In Latin America, an "8" would indicate lack of enthusiasm, whereas in Asia it would be a very good score.[32] One study of respondents in Australia, France, Singapore, and the United States suggests that the use of a 5- or 7-point scale (as opposed to a 10-point scale) minimizes such cross-cultural differences without sacrificing much research insight.[33]

Scalar equivalence the similarity among respondents in their interpretation of calibrations along a continuum

Another issue that affects comparability is **courtesy bias**. Courtesy bias arises when respondents attempt to guess what answer the interviewer wants to hear and reply accordingly. For example, a taste test could result in respondents saying they liked the product even if they didn't. The level of courtesy bias varies among cultures. It can be a particular problem in Mexico as well as in many Middle Eastern and Asian countries.

Courtesy bias a phenomenon in which respondents fail to reply honestly but instead supply the answer they believe an interviewer wishes to hear

WORLD BEAT 7.2

Researching Russia

DESPITE CONCERNS about political and economic risk, the Russian consumer market is expected to grow rapidly due to a rise in personal incomes. As the economy recovers, more Russians are buying foreign goods. Major multinational companies have already reported growth rates of 15–30 percent. But Russia has proven a tumultuous market. To better understand the Russian consumer, global marketers are increasingly turning to market research.

Ford Motor Company discovered via market research that the Russian consumer was surprisingly biased against the Russian worker. As a result, when the company began production in Russia, it started slowly. Clothing producer Benetton's market research revealed that when Russian women shopped for clothes they prized quality first, followed by product assortment, brand name, and country of origin. Other market research revealed that the average Russian woman spent a relatively large proportion of her salary on cosmetics. Even when grocery shopping, Russian women care what they look like! Increasingly, foreign firms are careful to better understand this emerging but unique market.

Sources: Douglas Birch, "Ford Changed Russian Market," *Baltimore Sun*, June 25, 2004, p. D15; Susan B. Glasser, "Cosmetics Are White Hot in Russia," *Washington Post*, May 1, 2004, p. A2, "Russia: Consumer Goods and Retail Forecast, *Economist Intelligence Unit-Executive Briefing*, January 19, 2005.

Focus Groups

When surveys prove difficult to administer, another technique that can be used for collecting marketing research data is focus groups. The focus group can also be used at an early stage in the development of a new product concept to gain valuable insights from potential consumers. The researcher assembles a set of six to twelve carefully selected respondents to discuss a product. The research company assembles the participants and leads the discussion; this avoids the bias that the active presence of a company representative might introduce. Of course, the discussion leader must speak in the mother tongue of the participants. Representatives of the company can observe the focus group via video- or audiotaping, through a one-way mirror, or by sitting in the room.

As with surveys, focus groups may face government regulation in certain countries. Communist Vietnam has only recently opened to Western businesses, yet marketing researchers find that the Vietnamese are enthusiastic about joining focus groups. Participation rates can range between 35 and 50 percent. But similar to China, the government of Vietnam restricts what can be asked in these groups and bans topics it considers too sensitive.[34]

Focus groups are also subject to a number of cross-cultural challenges:

▶ In certain Central Asian countries such as Kazakhstan, Turkmenistan, and Uzbekistan, men and women should be not be present in the same focus group.[35] In some Muslim countries, it can even be difficult to find women who will agree to participate at all.

▶ In other countries, such as Japan, it may be difficult to get participants to criticize a potential product due to courtesy bias.

▶ Expect participants in polychronic cultures such as Thailand, Malaysia, and Indonesia to show up late—or not at all—for the focus group. Plan on inviting a few extra participants to be sure you have enough for your group to continue.[36]

▶ In high-power-distance countries (most developing countries) young participants may not contradict older ones.

▶ A focus group in Brazil consisting of eight women can take an hour longer than a similar focus group in the United States due to the considerable time participants invest up front getting to know one another.[37] After all, introductory chats are the norm in high-context cultures.

Given these many cultural challenges, focus group leaders must be resourceful at using a questioning technique—and even interpreting body language—to get full value from this research approach.

Observation

Finally, observation can be a powerful research tool, especially in developing countries where other techniques may be taboo or difficult to administer. In Cuba, where administering questionnaires on the street is strictly forbidden, foreign marketers can explore how Cubans behave by unobtrusively watching them shop. However, this approach should be used with caution. Unless a researcher is very familiar with the culture, observations can prove difficult to interpret and can lead to wrong research conclusions.[38]

Carefully crafted observational studies designed to understand subtle nuances in consumer behavior are sometimes referred to as **consumer ethnographies** and can prove useful in an increasingly complex global marketplace. Often these studies are administered by trained anthropologists. Visual cues are used to supplement field notes. Such cues are collected via photographs or videotape (when culturally acceptable) and capture elements of décor, design aesthetics, color, fashion, architecture, and icons.[39]

Observation is particularly useful for revealing new ideas about consumer behavior that are free from the biases that researchers may bring to a study. For example, 98 percent of U.S. households use products made by Procter & Gamble. However, outside the United States this number is far lower. To better understand consumers overseas, P&G has introduced videotape to learn about the lifestyles and local habits of consumers in other countries. Participant households include young couples, families with children, and empty nesters. Videotaping one household in Thailand revealed that a mother engaged in multiple tasks, from watching television to cooking a meal, while feeding her baby. Procter & Gamble believes that the behaviors that consumers don't talk about—such as multitasking while feeding a baby—could inspire product and package design in ways that could give the company a competitive edge over its rivals.[40]

Consumer ethnographies carefully crafted observational studies designed to capture nuances in consumer behavior

STUDYING THE COMPETITION

Results in the marketplace do not depend solely on researching buyer characteristics and meeting buyer needs. To a considerable extent, success in the marketplace is influenced by a firm's understanding of and response to its competition. Firms may investigate competitors in order to **benchmark**. Benchmarking involves identifying best practices in an industry in order to copy those practices and achieve greater efficiency. For example, when the pharmaceutical firm Merck decided to rejuvenate its subsidiary (Merck Banyu) in the important Japanese market, it looked into what competitors, including world leader Pfizer, were doing. As a result, Banyu salespersons were told to focus on a smaller number of drugs in order to achieve increased efficiencies.[41]

Benchmarking the act of identifying best practices in an industry in order to adopt those practices and achieve greater efficiency

Keeping track of a firm's competitors is also an important strategic function. Kodak learned through competitive intelligence that Fuji was planning a new camera for the U.S. market. Kodak launched a competing model just one day before Fuji. Motorola discovered through one of its intelligence staff who was fluent in Japanese that the Japanese electronics firms planned to build new semiconductor plants in Europe. Motorola changed its strategy to build market share in Europe before the new capacity was built. This type of strategic intelligence can be critical to a firm.[42]

To undertake effective research about its competition, a company must first determine who its competitors are. The domestic market will certainly provide some input here. However, it is important to include any foreign company that either currently is a competitor or may become one in the future. The monitoring should not be restricted to activity in the competitors' domestic market but, rather, should include competitors' moves anywhere in the world. Many foreign firms first innovate in their home markets, expanding abroad only when

The major player in its Mexican home market, Bimbo now competes in the United States. One reason for Bimbo's entering the U.S. market was to better understand its potential American competition.

the initial debugging of the product has been completed. Therefore, a U.S. firm would lose valuable time if it began monitoring a Japanese competitor's activities only upon that competitor's entry into the U.S. market. Any monitoring system needs to be structured in such a way as to ensure that competitors' actions will be spotted wherever they occur first. Komatsu, Caterpillar's major competitor worldwide in the earth-moving industry, subscribed to the *Journal Star*, the major daily newspaper in Caterpillar's hometown, Peoria, Illinois. Also important are the actions taken by competitors in their foreign subsidiaries. These actions may signal future moves elsewhere in a company's global network of subsidiaries.

Table 7.2 lists the types of information a company may wish to collect on its competitors. Aside from general business statistics, a competitor's profitability may shed some light on its capacity to pursue new business in the future. Learning about others' marketing operations may enable a company to assess, among other things, the market share to be gained in any given market. Whenever major actions are planned, it is extremely helpful to anticipate the reactions of competitive firms and include them in the company's contingency planning. Of course, monitoring a competitor's new products or expansion programs may give early hints of future competitive threats.

Analysis that focuses solely on studying the products of key competitors can often miss the real strength of the competitor. To understand an industry and where it is headed over the next 5 years, it is important to study the core competencies in the industry. For example, Chaparral Steel, a profitable U.S. steel maker, sends its managers and engineers to visit competitors, customers, and suppliers' factories to identify the trends and skills that will lead steel making in the future. Chaparral also visits university research departments to spot new competencies that may offer an opportunity or pose a threat.[43]

TABLE 7.2 MONITORING COMPETITION: FACTS TO BE COLLECTED

OVERALL COMPANY STATISTICS
Sales, market share, and profits
Balance sheet
Capital expenditures
Number of employees
Production capacity
Research and development capability

MARKETING OPERATIONS
Types of products (quality, performance, features)
Service and/or warranty granted
Prices and pricing strategy
Advertising strategy and budgets
Size and type of sales force
Distribution system (includes entry strategy)
Delivery schedules (also spare parts)
Sales territory (geographic)

FUTURE INTENTIONS
New product developments
Current test markets
Scheduled plant capacity expansions
Planned capital expenditures
Planned entry into new markets/countries

COMPETITIVE BEHAVIOR
Pricing behavior
Reaction to competitive moves, past and expected

There are numerous ways to monitor competitors' activities. Thorough study of trade or industry journals is a starting point. Also, frequent visits can be made to major trade fairs where competitors exhibit their products. At one such fair in Texas, Caterpillar engineers were seen measuring Komatsu equipment.[44] In fact, the high level of competitive espionage that goes on at trade fairs can sometimes discourage participation. When one manufacturer exhibited a new toy at the famous Hong Kong Toy Fair, within three days retailers were being offered a duplicate toy. Some toy makers like Mattel stopped exhibiting at the show. Instead, they decided to invite perspective buyers to their own in-house presentations.[45]

Important information can also be gathered from foreign subsidiaries located in the home markets of major competitors. The Italian office equipment manufacturer Olivetti assigned a major intelligence function to its U.S. subsidiary because of that unit's direct access to competitive products in the U.S. marketplace. A different approach was adopted by the Japanese pharmaceutical company Esei, which opened a liaison office in Switzerland, home base to several of the world's leading pharmaceutical companies.

Governments may also develop market reports (see, for example, the U.S. Export Portal). Some of these reports are free and others are provided for a fee. Private research organizations, such as PriceWaterhouseCoopers Industry Reports and Hoover's Online, also provide reports on particular companies or industries. These reports are easier to find on developed countries but are increasingly available for developing countries as well. In some cases, however, there may be no research report covering a specific country or product category. And be aware that reports from private sources can sell for hundreds or even thousands of dollars.

Check out our *International Trade Fairs* link on our website (college.hmco.com/business/).

OUTSOURCING RESEARCH

The global firm can either attempt to collect and analyze all data itself or outsource some of its marketing research by utilizing marketing research companies. Today all major national markets have local marketing research firms that can assist the international marketer. The early marketing research industry in China was strongly supported by Procter & Gamble—in fact, some believe that it wouldn't have survived without P&G.[46]

Furthermore, the demand for quality multicountry research has spurred the marketing research industry to expand beyond traditional national boundaries and become increasingly global. The top twenty-five marketing/advertising/public opinion research conglomerates going into 2003 accounted for 66 percent of world spending. In 2002 alone, the top twenty-five acquired thirty-six research firms around the world.[47] Table 7.3 lists the world's top research companies.

Harris Interactive recognizes the cultural and methodological differences affecting market research in different national markets. In addition to establishing its own international subsidiaries, Harris Interactive collaborates with local market research companies in North and South America, Europe, Africa, and the Asia-Pacific Region.

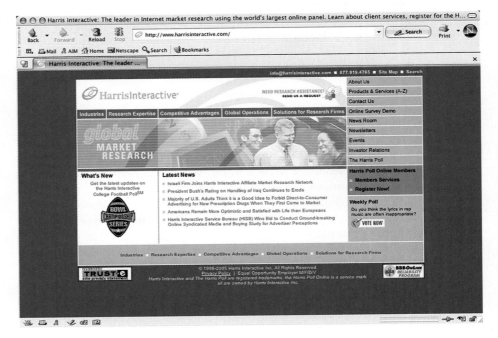

TABLE 7.3 TOP 25 GLOBAL RESEARCH ORGANIZATIONS

RANK	ORGANIZATION	PARENT COUNTRY	WEBSITE	NO. OF COUNTRIES WITH SUBSIDIARIES/ BRANCH OFFICES[a]	GLOBAL RESEARCH REVENUES (US$ IN MILLIONS)	PERCENT OF GLOBAL REVENUES FROM OUTSIDE HOME COUNTRY
1	VNU NV	Netherlands	www.vnu.com	81	$3,048.3	99.0%
2	Taylor Nelson Sofres plc	U.K.	www.tns-global.com	70	1,565.1	83.5
–	Taylor Nelson Sofres	U.K.	www.tns-global.com	54	1,050.5	78.6
–	NFO WorldGroup Inc.	U.K.	www.nfow.com	40	514.6	93.5
3	IMS Health Inc.	U.S.	imshealth.com	75	1,381.8	61.1
4	The Kantar Group	U.K.	www.kantargroup.com	61	1,002.1	66.1
5	GfK Group	Germany	www.gfk.com	48	673.6	62.8
6	Ipsos Group SA	France	www.ipsos.com	36	644.6	84.1
7	Information Resources Inc.	U.S.	www.infores.com	18	554.3	30.0
8	Westat Inc.	U.S.	www.westat.com	1	381.6	NA
9	Synovate	U.K.	www.synovate.com	46	357.7	91.3
10	NOP World	U.K.	www.nopworld.com	6	335.6	80.5
11	Arbitron Inc.	U.S.	arbitron.com	3	273.6	2.9
12	Maritz Research	U.S.	maritzresearch.com	4	188.8	34.9
13	Video Research Ltd.	Japan	www.videor.co.jp	4	166.7	1.1
14	J.D. Power and Associates	U.S.	jdpower.com	6	144.8	17.8
15	Harris Interactive	U.S.	harrisinteractive.com	4	137.0	19.0
16	Opinion Research Corp.	U.S.	opinionresearch.com	6	131.2	35.4
17	INTAGE Inc.	Japan	www.intage.co.jp	2	122.3	1.0
18	The NPD Group Inc.	U.S.	npd.com	11	117.6	17.7
19	AGB Group	Italy	agb.com	19	81.6	79.0
20	Market & Opinion Research Int'l	U.K.	www.mori.com	2	64.4	2.8
21	Lieberman Research Worldwide	U.S.	lrwonline.com	1	63.2	8.7
22	Dentsu Research Inc.	Japan	www.dentsuresearch.co.jp	1	57.0	1.1
23	ABT Associates Inc.	U.S.	abtassociates.com	3	54.0	4.3
24	Nikkei Research Inc.	Japan	nikkeiresearch.com	4	52.1	3.5
25	Wirthlin Worldwide	U.S.	wirthlin.com	4	52.0	22.9
	TOTAL				$11,651.0	67.3%

[a]Includes countries that have subsidiaries with an equity interest or branch offices or both.
SOURCE: Adapted from "Top 25 Global Research Organizations," *Marketing News*, August 15, 2004, p. 44.

DEVELOPING A GLOBAL INFORMATION SYSTEM

Companies that already have become global marketers, as well as those that plan to do so, must look at the world marketplace to identify global opportunities. The forces that affect an industry must also be analyzed to determine the firm's competitiveness. To evaluate the full range of opportunities requires a global perspective for market research. Researchers must provide more than data on strictly local factors within each country. All firms that market their products in overseas markets require information that makes it possible to perform analysis across several countries or markets. However, leaving each local subsidiary or market to develop its own database will not result in an integrated marketing information system (MIS). Instead, authority to develop a centrally managed MIS must be assigned to a central location, and market reports need to be sent directly to the firm's chief international marketing officer.

For example, Coca-Cola has joined forces with its bottling partners around the world to share information and best practices. In a planned 7-year rollout, Coca-Cola plans to boost revenue by sharing sales information and communicating more effectively with partners. The new system will upgrade and expand data warehouses, decision support systems, and a worldwide Intranet to improve communications.[48]   Similarly, Wal-Mart has pioneered an MIS that opens its computer system to its suppliers across the globe. Suppliers can track how well their products are selling worldwide or at one particular store.[49]

A principal requirement for a worldwide MIS is a standardized set of data collected from each market or country. The actual data collection can be left to a firm's local units, but they must proceed according to central and uniform specifications. By assessing buyer needs on a worldwide basis, the company ensures that products and services are designed with the global marketplace in mind.

CONCLUSION

In this chapter, we discussed some major challenges and difficulties that companies encounter in securing data necessary for international marketing. Major difficulties include the lack of basic data on many markets and the likelihood that research methods will have to be adapted to local environments. A final goal of global marketing research is to provide managers with a uniform database covering all the firm's present and potential markets. This will allow for cross-country comparisons and analysis, as well as the incorporation of worldwide consumer needs into the initial product design process. Given the difficulties in data collection, achieving this international comparability of data is indeed a challenge for even the most experienced professionals.

Still, the world has changed greatly in the past 25 years. At that time, market information around the world was sparse and unreliable, especially in developing and undeveloped countries. Now, through the efforts of governments, transnational organizations, and global marketing research companies, information is available for virtually every market in the world from Canada and Mexico to Uzbekistan and Mongolia. As a revolutionary communications tool, the Internet is also pushing research horizons. Today global marketers can use more widely available information to make better market decisions and devise more effective marketing strategies.

It's time to consider the sources for your own research. What are their strengths and weaknesses? What are some possible sources and costs for some customized primary research? Continue with *Country Market Report* on our website (college.hmco.com/ business/).

QUESTIONS FOR DISCUSSION

1. Why is it so difficult to do marketing research in multicountry settings?
2. What are the challenges of using a marketing research questionnaire that is developed in the United States but will be used in Japan and Mexico as well?
3. If you were estimating the demand for vacuum cleaners, what type of inference analysis would you use? Give a specific example.

4. Note various ways in which the Internet could assist international marketing researchers.
5. List ways in which Kodak might monitor Fuji Film. Why is such surveillance important?

CASE 7.1

Surveying the Turkish Clothing Industry

Gretchen Renner had escaped to the serenity of a small tea garden overlooking the Bosporus Sea, which separates the European and Asian sides of Istanbul. As she sipped a glass of strong tea, she fought the urge to abandon her thesis research project and return to the United States.

Before arriving in Istanbul, Gretchen had been excited about the project. She had designed a survey to measure Turkish clothing firm owners' use and satisfaction with the services offered by the Textile Association of Istanbul (TAI). This association offers marketing, export counseling, and educational services designed to encourage producers to pursue export opportunities.

Two months before Gretchen had come to Turkey, a Turkish friend had told her that she must apply for a research visa from the Turkish government. Foreigners planning to conduct research projects in Turkey must possess a government-approved research visa to display to government officials and potential research participants. Foreigners conducting research projects without a research visa in Turkey risk arrest and deportation. Gretchen was surprised that the research visa application had to be completed prior to her arrival in Turkey. She waited four months to receive the visa, inconveniently postponing her trip.

Once in Turkey, Gretchen sought a list of Turkish clothing firm owners from which she could draw a representative sample for her survey. Although TAI was supportive of Gretchen's project, it hesitated to share its membership list. Gretchen spent months developing relationships with key officials at TAI, conducting interviews, and collecting information. TAI officials readily shared information about the organization's history, structure, and services. Yet each time she asked about the list, she was denied access. Some of Gretchen's contacts claimed that releasing such information compromised the firms' privacy. Others maintained that no precedent existed for releasing the list to a non-TAI employee. Additionally, several of her close contacts explained to her that she could not have the list because she was not Turkish. Finally, with no explanation, TAI supplied the list of names.

Problems then emerged during survey pretesting. The questionnaire was administered via the telephone by interviewers employed by *İtimat*, a well-known Istanbul market research firm. During this pretesting, Gretchen and her interviewers discovered that it was difficult to circumvent gatekeepers, such as secretaries and receptionists, to interview Turkish clothing firm owners.

Hoping to increase response rates, Gretchen sent potential respondents a presurvey fax introducing herself, explaining the survey's objectives, and noting the involvement of *İtimat*. But respondents voiced concerns about the fax. Most complained that no high-level *İtimat* executive had signed the fax; it had been signed only by Gretchen and an *İtimat* interview supervisor. Others were suspicious of Gretchen's authenticity. They remembered Turkish media reports that several Europeans recently had posed as academic researchers to expose child labor practices in Turkish clothing factories. Because of Gretchen's German name and the unfamiliar name of her university, many suspected that Gretchen was actually an industrial spy.

Even when Gretchen or the interviewers gained access to firm owners, few agreed to participate in the survey. One scoffed, "If you really valued my opinion, you would make an appointment and discuss this with me in person. I am a very busy person. I don't have time to talk on the phone about such things."

Face-to-face interviews, however, would be more time-consuming than telephone interviews. First, it would take time to get past the gatekeepers to make appointments with potential respondents. Second, because the firms were widely dispersed and Istanbul is a very large and traffic-congested city, Gretchen and her team of four

İtimat interviewers could complete only ten surveys a day. Gretchen needed to complete three hundred surveys. Gretchen's research funding was dwindling, and she had to return home in 6 weeks.

Looking toward the Asian side of Istanbul, Gretchen wondered how she could successfully complete her research project in the remaining time.

Discussion Questions

1. What cultural factors might contribute to the obstacles Gretchen encountered while attempting to execute the survey? How might Hofstede's dimensions of culture explain Gretchen's difficulties?

2. Why do you think Gretchen finally received the list of Turkish clothing exporters from TAI? If TAI had not supplied the list, where else could Gretchen have looked to find a suitable list?

3. How should Gretchen proceed with the survey? Do you think the benefits of the face-to-face option outweigh the costs? Or could changes be made to the telephone survey to increase response rates? Are there other research options that Gretchen should consider instead?

Source: Prepared by Liesl Riddle. Used by permission.

CASE 7.2
Selector's European Dilemma

Ken Barbarino, CEO of Selector Inc., was ecstatic. The president of Big Burger, one of Selector's largest clients, had arranged for Ken to meet with the vice president of Big Burger's European operations. "Selector is going global," Ken smiled to himself.

Selector was a market research firm that provided market analyses to restaurant and retail chains. Selector's products helped clients select optimal geographic locations for successful chain expansion.

Although Big Burger was an international restaurant chain, currently Big Burger utilized Selector's services only for its U.S. operations. Specifically, Selector provided Big Burger's real estate team with trade-area profiles for prospective Big Burger locations. Because Big Burger was a quick-service hamburger restaurant, most of its customers were drawn from the homes and businesses within a 2-mile radius around each location. Selector's trade-area profiles provided Big Burger with an overview of the individuals, households, and businesses within a potential location's trade area.

By purchasing and amalgamating databases from a large number of data vendors, Selector had amassed a broad warehouse of U.S. demographic, business, and consumer behavior data, and the reports were extremely detailed. For example, Selector's trade-area profile described proximal households according to their composition, annual income, type of residence, and commute time to work. It also reported the number of area households that dined at a quick-serve hamburger restaurant last year as well as the total dollars these households spent at quick-serve hamburger restaurants during that year. Selector's trade-area profiles also included a count of the total number of businesses and employees in the 2-mile radius, as well as the percentage of businesses and employees within each 2-digit standard industry code (SIC) and a list of all quick-serve hamburger restaurants within a 5-mile radius and their gross unit sales. These trade-area profiles enabled Big Burger's real estate team to determine whether there was enough demand in the trade area to support a successful Big Burger location.

Ken waltzed into the office of Selector's research director, Katrina Walsh. "Guess what? Big Burger is sending us overseas!" he exclaimed. Ken told Katrina that the president of Big Burger had asked Selector to provide trade-area profiles for their prospective European locations. The president had arranged for Ken to meet with Big Burger's vice president of European operations in 2 weeks to demonstrate the trade-area profiles that could be used to assess potential European

Big Burger locations. Big Burger had provided Ken with the addresses of seven potential sites (two in London, one in Madrid, and four in Berlin) so that Selector could create examples of their trade-area profiles for these sites. Katrina was excited about the international project and assured Ken she would acquire the European data that was needed to generate the trade-area profiles.

Katrina contacted Selector's data vendors—the companies that sold the various databases that Selector had compiled in its broad data warehouse—and inquired about purchasing European demographic, business, and consumer behavior data. She quickly learned that acquiring the data at a small, precise level of geography would be a greater challenge than she had anticipated.

In the United States, the U.S. Census Bureau aggregates the data it collects into a set of standard hierarchical geographic units (see Table 1). To protect individual privacy, data are released at the Zip+4 level and higher. The standardization of the Census Bureau's geographic order and the degree of detail within the Zip+4 level enable companies like Selector to extract precise data for a geographic area, such as a 2-mile radius around a particular location, because the Census Bureau units are typically small enough to fit within that area.

However, as Katrina learned from her data vendors, European countries were geographically organized in a different way. All members of the European Union were organized according to the Nomenclature of Territorial Units for Statistics (NUTS) devised by the Statistical Office of the European Communities (Eurostat) in 1988. There

TABLE 1	U.S. STATISTICAL TERRITORIAL UNITS: LOWEST FIVE GEOGRAPHIES AVAILABLE FROM THE U.S. CENSUS	
STATISTICAL UNIT	TOTAL NUMBER	APPROXIMATE NUMBER OF HOUSEHOLDS
Metropolitan standard unit	316	30,245
Zip code	41,940	3,167
Census tract	62,276	1,551
Block group	229,466	420
Zip+4	28,000,000	10

were several design challenges associated with the NUTS program because the countries possessed divergent geographic organizational systems and were reluctant to abandon their existing geographic hierarchies. Five NUTS levels were created. The geographic data of most EU countries are divided into NUTS Levels 1–3. Some countries further divide their geographic data into NUTS Levels 4 and 5.

Ideally, Eurostat would have liked to standardize units by either territorial size or population size. It proved difficult to do either. For example, the largest geographic unit, NUTS Level 1, includes British government office regions, German *länder*, and Finish *ahvenanmaa*. But the southeast government office region of England possesses over 17 million inhabitants, whereas the Finish *ahvenanmaa*, Åhland, includes only 25,000 people. These disparities also exist at lower levels of geography. Greater London, Berlin, and the Spanish provinces of Madrid and Barcelona—all NUTS Level 3 geographies—comprise populations exceeding 3 million people, whereas several NUTS Level 3 regions in Germany, Belgium, Austria, Finland, and Greece include fewer than 50,000 people. The NUTS levels also differed greatly in territorial size. For example, some Level 5 geographies could be as small as 50 square meters, and others could comprise an entire town.

Katrina also discovered that it would be challenging to acquire data for a 2-mile radius around a specific address in Europe. NUTS data—even those at Levels 4 and 5—were for areas much larger than the 2-mile radius that Big Burger was interested in. Even a simple analysis of the NUTS level that a prospective site

resided in would not be comparable across national boundaries within the EU. Furthermore, although she could identify data vendors that could provide demographic and "firmographic" data, such as the total population, the number of households, household composition, marital status, the sex and age distribution of the population, and the number of businesses and employees, she could not locate a data vendor that offered the more important consumer behavior data. Estimating quick-serve hamburger dollar demand would be extremely difficult—if not impossible—without a measure of the total dollars spent on quick-serve hamburger restaurants and the number of households dining at quick-serve hamburger restaurants last year. It was also unclear whether Katrina would be able to acquire a reliable database of quick-serve restaurant competitors and their unit sales, because most of the existing European restaurant databases were old and out-of-date.

With 10 days left to go before Ken's meeting with Big Burger, Katrina wondered how she would generate trade-area profiles for Big Burger's seven European prospective locations.

Discussion Questions

1. What assumptions have Ken and Katrina made in their response to Big Burger's request for European trade-area data?
2. How—if at all—can Katrina utilize the available European data?
3. What should be included on the trade-area profiles for Big Burger's seven European locations?

Source: Prepared by Liesl Riddle. Used with permission.

NOTES

1. Carlta Vitzthum, "Just-in-Time Fashion," *Wall Street Journal*, May 23, 2001, p. B1.
2. Balaji R. Koka, John E. Prescott, and Ravindranath Madhavan, "Contagion Influence on Trade and Investment Policy: A Network Perspective," *Journal of International Business Studies* 30, no. 1 (1999), pp. 127–148.
3. David A. Ricks, *Blunders in International Business*, 3rd ed. (New York: Blackwell, 1999), pp.130–136.
4. "How to Listen to Consumers," *Fortune*, January 11, 1993, p. 77.
5. Juliana Koranteng, "Tracking What's Trendy, Hot Before It's Old News," *Advertising Age International*, May 1996, p. 130.

6. Pierre Berthon, Leyland Pitt, Constantine S. Katsikeas, and Jean Paul Berthon, "Virtual Services Go International," *Journal of International Marketing* 7, no. 3 (1999), p. 98.

7. C. Samuel Craig and Susan P. Douglas, *International Marketing Research: Concepts and Methods* (New York: Wiley, 1999), pp.16–19.

8. "Russia's Unemployment Rate Rises Year-on-Year," *Interfax News Agency*, June 21, 1999, p. 1.

9. Leonard Gurevich, "Focus on Central Asia: Conducting Research in the Post-Soviet Era, *Quirk's Marketing Research Review*, no. 1048 (November 2002).

10. Brian Palmer, "What the Chinese Want," *Fortune*, October 11, 1999.

11. Geoffrey A. Fowler, "China Radio Is Wave of Future for Advertising," *Wall Street Journal*, April 28, 2004, p. A6.

12. "Sharp as a Razor in Central Asia," *The Economist*, June 5, 1993, p. 36.

13. Lyn Montgomery, "Simplifying Research in Japan," *Quirk's Marketing Research Review*, no. 729 (November 2001).

14. Eileen Moran, "Managing the Minefields of Global Product Development," *Quirk's Marketing Research Review*, no. 625 (November 2000).

15. Kevin Reagan, "In Asia, Think Globally, Communicate Locally," *Marketing News*, July 19, 1999, pp. 12–14.

16. J. Brad McBride and Kate Gillespie, "Consumer Innovativeness Among Street Vendors in Mexico City," *Latin American Business Review* 1, no. 3 (2000), pp. 71–94.

17. Moran, "Managing the Minefields."

18. Dana James, "Back to Vietnam," *Marketing News*, May 13, 2002, pp. 1, 13–14.

19. Moran, "Managing the Minefields."

20. See, for example, N. L. Reynolds, A. C. Simintiras, and A. Diamantopoulos, "Sampling Choices in International Marketing: Key Issues and Guidelines for Research," *Journal of International Business Studies* 34 (2003), p. 81.

21. Arundhati Parmar, "South African Research," *Marketing News*, September 15, 2003, p. 19.

22. Gurevich, "Focus on Central Asia."

23. Robin Cobb, "Marketing Shares," *Marketing*, February 22, 1990, p. 44.

24. H. Lee Murphy, "Japanese Keeping Fewer Secrets from U.S. Firms," *Marketing News*, June 21, 1999, p. 4.

25. Johny K. Johansson and Ikujiro Nonaka, "Market Research the Japanese Way," *Harvard Business Review* 65 (May–June 1987), pp. 16–22.

26. McBride and Gillespie, "Consumer Innovativeness," p. 80.

27. "Research in Denmark, Germany and the Netherlands," *Quirk's Marketing Research Review*, no. 731 (November 2001).

28. Gabriel Kahn, "Chinese Puzzle: Spotty Consumer Data," *Wall Street Journal*, October 15, 2003, p. B1.

29. James Heckman, "Marketers Waiting, Will See on EU Privacy," *Marketing News*, June 7, 1999, p. 4.

30. "Japan-Market Research-Competitive Landscape," *Datamonitor Market Research Profiles*, November 1, 2004.

31. J. M. Batista-Foguet, J. Fortiana, C. Currie, and J. R. Villalba, "Socio-Economic Indexes in Surveys for Comparisons Between Countries," *Social Indicators Research* 67 (2004), p.328.

32. Jennifer Mitchell, "Reaching Across Borders," *Marketing News*, May 10, 1999, p. 19.

33. Irvine Clarke III, "Global Marketing Research: Is Extreme Response Style Influencing Your Results?" *Journal of International Consumer Marketing* 12, no. 4 (2000), pp. 91–111.

34. Dana James, "Back to Vietnam," *Marketing News*, May 13, 2002, p. 1.

35. Gurevich, "Focus on Central Asia."

36. Rod Davies, "Focus Groups in Asia." Posted on *Orient Pacific Century*, 2005, www.orientpacific.com (accessed June 1, 2005).

37. Sharon Seidler, "Qualitatively Speaking: Conducting Qualitative Research on a Global Scale," *Quirk's Marketing Research Review*, no. 1182 (December 2003).

38. Elizabeth Robles, "In Cuba, the Usual MR Methods Don't Work," *Marketing News*, June 10, 2002, p. 12.

39. Tim Plowman, Adrien Lanusse, and Astrid Cruz, "Observing the World," *Quirk's Marketing Research Review*, no. 1171 (November 2003).

40. Emily Nelson, "P&G Checks Out Real Life," *Wall Street Journal*, May 17, 2001, p. B1.

41. Peter Landers, "Merck, Pfizer in Japan," *Wall Street Journal*, October 2, 2003, p. B4.

42. "High Price of Industrial Espionage," *Times of London*, June 5, 1999, p. 31.

43. C. K. Prahalad and Gary Hamel, "The Core Competence of the Corporation," *Harvard Business Review* 68 (May–June 1990), pp. 79–91.

44. Ibid.

45. Geoffrey A. Fowler, "Copies 'R' Us," *Wall Street Journal*, January 31, 2003, p. B1.

46. Barton Lee, Soumya Saklini, and David Tatterson, "Research: Growing in Guangzhou," *Marketing News*, June 10, 2002, pp. 12–13.

47. Jack Honomichl, "Acquisitions Help Firms' Global Share Increase," *Marketing News*, August 18, 2003, p. H3.

48. Bob Violino, "Extended Enterprise: Coca-Cola Is Linking Its IT System with Those of Worldwide Bottling Partners As It Strives to Stay One Step Ahead of the Competition," *Information Week*, March 22, 1999, pp. 46–54.

49. Gabriel Kahn, "Made to Measure," *Wall Street Journal*, September 11, 2003, p. A1.

DEVELOPING GLOBAL PARTICIPATION STRATEGIES

PART 3

235

8 GLOBAL MARKET PARTICIPATION

KRAFT IS THE LARGEST packaged-foods company in North America. In the United States, it has dominated grocery store shelves for years, with such famous brands as Jell-O, Kool-Aid, Life Savers, Oreo cookies, and Philadelphia Cream Cheese. However, Kraft is stuck in a slow-growth industry in the United States. Despite careful cost cutting and imaginative marketing, sales dropped 16 percent over a seven-year period. These numbers are all the more worrisome because U.S. sales account for 73 percent of total firm sales. This percentage stands in striking contrast to Heinz, where U.S. sales account for only 56 percent of total sales. Furthermore, Kraft's strongest overseas market is Western Europe, a market that is nearly saturated as well. Kraft now plans to expand into emerging markets. Unfortunately, major global competitors such as Unilever and Nestlé entered these markets much earlier. Also, Kraft's strongest products— convenience foods—don't sell as well in developing countries where consumers have less disposable income. In contrast, Unilever offers such basics as fortified rice in India.[1]

In this chapter, we introduce key issues that companies face as they pursue global market participation. Historically, internationalization

LEARNING OBJECTIVES

After studying this chapter, you should be able to

▶ List and describe five reasons for which firms internationalize.

▶ Differentiate between born-global firms and other companies.

▶ Explain the difference between a standalone attractive market and a globally strategic one.

▶ Cite the advantages and disadvantages of targeting developed countries, developing countries, or transitional economies.

▶ List and describe the filters used for screening national markets.

▶ Explain the pros and cons of choosing markets on the basis of market similarity.

CHAPTER OUTLINE

patterns of firms range from opportunistic, or unplanned, responses to overseas opportunities to carefully constructed expansion. Increasingly, firms must determine whether going international is merely an option or a necessity for survival in the global marketplace. Firms must be more proactive in selecting an appropriate course for market expansion. Entering new foreign markets can be expensive and can place heavy demands on management time. Firms must decide which regions and specifically which foreign markets will receive priority.

237

INTERNATIONALIZING MARKETING OPERATIONS

Internationalization the expansion of a firm beyond its domestic market into foreign markets

Internationalization is the term we use for a firm's expansion from its domestic market into foreign markets. Whether to internationalize is a strategic decision that will fundamentally affect any firm, including its operations and its management. Today, most large companies operate outside their home markets. Nonetheless, it is still useful for these companies to consider their motivations for continued international expansion. For many smaller or newer companies, the decision to internationalize remains an important and difficult one. There can be several possible motives behind a company's decision to begin to compete in foreign markets. These motives range from the opportunistic to the strategic.

Opportunistic Expansion

Many companies, particularly those in the United States, promote their products in trade journals or on the Internet to their U.S. customers. These media are also read by foreign business executives or distributors, who place orders that are initially unsolicited. Such foreign transactions are usually more complicated and more involved than a routine shipment to a domestic customer. Therefore, the firm must decide whether to respond to these unsolicited orders. Some companies adopt an aggressive policy and begin to pursue these foreign customers actively. Many have built sizable foreign businesses by first responding to orders and then adopting a more proactive approach later. Most large, internationally active companies began their internationalization in this opportunistic manner.

Pursuing Potential Abroad

Some firms maximize their domestic market and then deliberately reach out for more potential abroad. This is particularly true of firms, such as Anheuser-Busch, that began internationalizing more recently. With a 45 percent market share in the United States, Anheuser-Busch dominates its home beer market. A latecomer to international expansion, the company remained domestic until 1982. Now Anheuser-Busch has become active in a number of major international markets, including Japan and China, and is trying to build a global brand for Budweiser. Still, international sales are only a small percentage of total corporate sales as the firm continues to pursue its potential abroad.[2]

A need to spread risk by diversifying beyond a single country can also motivate a firm to internationalize. This is less of a factor for U.S.-based companies than for firms in smaller home markets. For example, Saint-Gobain, a large French company founded by King Louis XIV some 330 years ago, has a long-standing tradition in glass and building materials. For years it followed a strategy designed to help the firm break out of its France-only position. Acquiring large companies in the same field in Germany and the United Kingdom, the company was able to expand international sales until French sales were only 25 percent of corporate sales. The acquisition of Norton Company and Carborundum significantly strengthened Saint-Gobain's position in the U.S.

market. The company now ranks as the number one worldwide producer for several business lines, including flat glass, insulation, ductile iron pipes, major industrial ceramics, and abrasives. About two-thirds of its 120,000 employees currently work outside France.[3]

Following Customers Abroad

For a company whose business is concentrated on a few large customers, the decision to internationalize is usually made when one of its key customers moves abroad to pursue international opportunities. Many of the major U.S. automobile component suppliers have established operating plants abroad to supply their customers in foreign locations. PPG Industries, a major supplier of car body paints to automobile manufacturers, originally did little overseas business other than licensing its technology to other foreign paint makers. However, the company followed its major customers abroad and began to service them directly in Europe and elsewhere. The company then began to sell to non-U.S. car companies as well and achieved the leading position in supplying paints to car manufacturers worldwide.[4]

The service sector has seen similar expansions triggered by client moves overseas. The establishment of international networks of major U.S. professional accounting and consulting firms, such as Deloitte Touche Tohmatsu, was motivated by a desire to service key domestic clients overseas. Now Deloitte has 28,000 employees and professionals in its U.S. operation and another 54,000 spread over some 130 countries' operations.[5] Similarly, express shipper DHL probably became the first Western firm to reenter war-torn Afghanistan in 2002. Its rationale: The U.S. military was one of its biggest customers.[6]

DHL follows customers abroad—even to the gates of China's Forbidden City.

Exploiting Different Market Growth Rates

Market growth rates are subject to wide variations among countries. A company based in a low-growth country may suffer a competitive disadvantage and may want to expand into faster-growing countries to take advantage of growth opportunities. The area of the Pacific Rim (which includes Japan, South Korea, Taiwan, China, Hong Kong, Thailand, Singapore, Malaysia, and Indonesia) experienced above-average economic growth rates in the 1990s. This prompted many international firms to invest heavily in that region. For example, the chemicals industry in Asia experienced above-average growth rates, ranging between 12 percent for China and 7–9 percent for several other Asian Pacific Rim markets. This enormous growth soon made the non-Japanese Asian chemicals market the largest in the world, surpassing those in the United States, Europe, and Japan.[7] Although the region suffered from a substantial economic recession in 1998, many of its economies have rebounded and are rapidly making up the lost ground.

On the other hand, the U.S. market is currently the target market of many Japanese pharmaceutical companies that have been late in moving out of their home market. For years these firms concentrated solely on Japan, the world's second-largest pharmaceutical market. Recent growth in the Japanese market has been relatively flat, partly because of a crackdown on high pharmaceutical prices by the Japanese government's national health insurance company. However, the U.S. market continues to climb and is now nearly four times the size of the Japanese market.[8]

When the market for a firm's product becomes mature, a company can open new opportunities by entering foreign markets where the product may not be very well known. Among U.S. firms following this strategy are many packaged-goods marketers, such as Philip Morris, Coca-Cola, and PepsiCo. They often target markets where the per-capita consumption of their products is still relatively low. With economic expansion and the resulting improvement in personal incomes in these new markets, these companies can experience substantial growth over time—even though operations in the United States show little growth.

For example, one report showed Coca-Cola selling 189 twelve-ounce servings per person annually in the United States, whereas its international average was only 37 servings. This number varied widely: 215 in Iceland, 173 in Mexico, 111 in West Germany, 61 in the United Kingdom, 35 in Japan, and 26 in France. China trailed with 0.3 serving per capita. When consumption in China reaches the levels of other Asian countries, such as Australia, Coca-Cola of China will become as large as the entire Coca-Cola Company is today.[9]

Globalizing for Defensive Reasons

Sometimes companies are not particularly interested in pursuing new growth or potential abroad but decide to enter the international business arena for purely defensive reasons. When a domestic company sees its markets invaded by foreign firms, that company may react by entering the foreign competitor's home market in return. As a result, the company can learn valuable information about the competitor that will help in its operations at home. The company

Our passion for change has built the most
innovative global cement company around.

As global building needs evolve, a passion for change enables CEMEX to thrive in developing
countries and mature markets alike. It's a passion that allows us to capitalize on strategic
opportunities for growth in over 30 countries on five continents, and develop new technologies
to better serve our customers. And it's a passion that fuels our growth as a global leader and
positions us as the largest cement manufacturer in North America. When you're passionate
about something, you can effect change—and improve the quality
of service for customers worldwide.
To learn more about us, visit **www.cemex.com**.

Mexican firm CEMEX entered international markets when foreign firms began entering the Mexican market. CEMEX has since evolved into a global leader in the cement industry.

can also slow down a competitor by denying it some of the cash flow from its profitable domestic operation—cash that could otherwise be invested in expansion abroad.

Many U.S. companies opened operations in Japan to be closer to their most important competitors. Major companies such as Xerox and IBM use their local subsidiaries in Japan to learn new ways to compete with the major Japanese firms in their field. Similarly, Kao, the Japanese packaged-goods giant, opened an office in Cincinnati to be close to the headquarters of Procter & Gamble.

Cemex is the largest cement producer in the Western Hemisphere and the third-largest producer worldwide. The Mexican company began its drive to internationalize by expanding across its border into the United States. Cemex then acquired two large cement plants in Spain, taking the company into Europe. Cemex's entry into international markets occurred partly in response to the invasion of its market by Holderbank, a Swiss-based company and the world's largest cement producer. Cemex has since expanded its international operations into about twenty countries and now generates half of its income abroad.[10]

Check out the Japanese links on our website (college.hmco.com/business/).

Born Globals

Most large global corporations have followed a similar sequence of internationalization. Typically, these companies develop their domestic markets and then tentatively enter international markets, usually by exporting. As their international sales grow, these companies gradually establish marketing and production operations in many foreign markets. This traditional pattern seems to be followed by most firms. However, some newer firms are jumping into global markets without going through the various stages of development. Such firms are termed **born global**.

Born-global firms recognize from the beginning that their customers and competition are international. This is particularly true of many high-tech start-up companies. Logitech, the maker of computer input devices, is one such company. Logitech's market coverage and its marketing strategy were global virtually from its inception. The company not only opened sales offices rapidly throughout the world but also established factories in China, Taiwan, the United States, Switzerland, and Ireland.[11] As a result Logitech has become the world's leading PC mouse maker, having attained a global market share of 50 percent.[12]

Even when a new company isn't technically born global, most firms today begin internationalizing earlier and faster than they did in the past. This is due in part to the advantages of internationalization discussed earlier in this chapter. However, a fast move overseas can be taxing even for the most successful domestic companies, since developing each new national market can entail significant start-up costs. Starbucks is a case in point. Starbucks began its overseas expansion in 1996, but only projected to see its first profit for its international business in 2004. In 2003, its 1,650 overseas stores contributed a mere 7 percent of the company's revenue.[13]

Born global term referring to a firm that establishes marketing and other business operations abroad upon formation of the firm or immediately thereafter

Evaluating National Markets

Whether a domestic firm is first internationalizing or an established multinational is looking to extend its global reach, deciding which markets to enter, and prioritizing those markets, is a major requirement for successful global marketing strategy. The most common way to assess a national market is to evaluate its standalone attractiveness. However, George Yip suggests that global marketers should further assess national markets on global strategic importance as well.[14] (See Table 8.1.)

Standalone Attractive Markets

A national market can appear attractive in a number of ways. First, the potential primary market needs to be assessed. Two key considerations are the size of market and its growth rate. Then the firm must consider its possible competitive position. What share of market could it reasonably attain? The less competitive a national market, the better chance to attain a larger market share. A government may also increase the standalone attractiveness of its national market by offering potential market entrants a variety of incentives. A low level

TABLE 8.1 EVALUATING NATIONAL MARKETS	
STANDALONE ATTRACTIVE MARKETS	GLOBALLY STRATEGIC MARKETS
Large markets	Potential source of major profits
Significant potential for growth	Important foreign market for key competitors
Less competitive market	Home market of major customers
Government incentives	Lead market

of taxation and regulation will increase market attractiveness. In addition, governments can grant individual firms that choose to invest in their country tax or other incentives.

Globally Strategic Markets

Some standalone attractive markets are also globally strategic markets. However, certain standalone *unattractive* markets might also be judged to be globally strategic. Globally strategic markets are the current and future battlegrounds where global competitors engage one another.

As global marketers eye the array of countries available, they soon become aware that not all countries are of equal importance on the path to global leadership. Markets that are defined as crucial to global market leadership, markets that can determine the global winners among all competitors, markets that companies can ill afford to avoid or neglect—such markets are **must-win markets**. Typically, these markets show potential for major profits. A market that delivers large profits can subsidize competitive battles elsewhere in the world. In the past, the United States has been the largest single market for many industries, making it globally strategic to many firms. Similarly, the larger developed countries often qualify as must-win markets because of their relative wealth and purchasing power. More recently, China has emerged as another country that many global firms consider to be a must-win market. China is a very competitive market, and for many foreign companies, current profits in this market are dismal. However, many firms are afraid to leave this potentially large market for their competitors to exploit unchallenged.

Must-win markets markets crucial to a firm's global market leadership

Other globally strategic markets are the home countries of global customers. As multinational business buyers become more centralized in their purchasing decision making, having a presence close to their headquarters can give a global supplier an advantage. Many multinationals also have major sales in their home markets and consequently want global suppliers to understand—and supply—their needs in those markets.

The home markets and important foreign markets of global competitors are also globally strategic markets. This is where innovations are likely to first appear. As noted in Chapter 6, a presence in such markets allows a firm to undertake counterparries against its global competitors in markets where such

WORLD BEAT 8.1

Say Goodbye to the World's Best Market

IN 2005, THE NEW PRESIDENT of Japanese car manufacturer Mitsubishi Motors traveled to Detroit to begin talks with potential buyers of Mitsubishi's U.S. operations. Weak sales by the U.S. subsidiary were compounded by losses due to extending credit to young car buyers, many of whom had poor credit ratings and later defaulted on their loans.

For most global competitors, a presence in the U.S. market would seem like a no-brainer. But all companies do not agree. For example, European car manufacturer Peugot chose to bypass the U. S. market for a faster-growing developing market—China. Peugot left the U.S. market in 1991 when its sales there were dwindling. While Peugot's CEO recognizes that the firm must some day reenter the United States, it had no plans to do so in the immediate future.

Carlsberg agrees. The U.S. beer market is the largest in the world, but the Danish brewer puts Serbia higher than the United States on its list of new markets to investigate. Carlsberg is the world's fifth-largest brewer, and its chief executive thinks the company can be successful without the U.S. market. Instead he wants the company to focus on faster-growing markets in Eastern Europe, Russia, and Asia.

But is America phobia a good idea? One beer analyst in Amsterdam estimates that Carlsberg's shares trade in Denmark at about 10 percent lower than rival global brands that are active in the U.S. market.

Sources: Neal E. Boudette, "Road Less Travelled," *Wall Street Journal,* August 4, 2003, p. A1; Dan Bilefsky, "Not on Tap," *Wall Street Journal,* October 7, 2003, p. B1; and Norihiko Shirouzu and Jathon Sapsford, "An Ailing Mitsubishi Motors Seeks Buyer for U.S. Operations," *Wall Street Journal,* February 18, 2005, p. B1.

---

actions will deliver the most harm. The home markets of major global competitors in an industry are usually lead markets as well.

Lead markets countries or regions possessing major research and development sites for an industry

Lead markets are major research and development sites and vary by industry. Such markets are characterized as having demanding customers who push for quality and innovation. For example, Japan is a lead country for many industries, but Toray Industries, a major Japanese company in a number of plastic and textile industries, runs its artificial-leather affiliate, Alcantara, from Italy. Alcantara's success can be attributed largely to the design of its leather products. Toray's management considers Italy the world leader in design, and Italy is a recognized lead market for high-end textiles and clothing.[15]

GEOGRAPHIC MARKET CHOICES

While evaluating national markets one by one has its advantages, at any one time, a company may decide to target the developed nations of Europe, Japan, and North America. Alternatively, it may prefer to pursue less developed countries in Latin America, Africa, Asia, or the former Soviet bloc. Each of these options presents its own challenges and opportunities as depicted in Table 8.2.

TABLE 8.2 Marketing Attractiveness by Country Category		
Developed Countries	**Developing Countries**	**Transitional Economies**
Richest markets	Poorer markets	Many close to Western Europe
Potential sources of major profits	Great variation in size of national markets	Some members of EU
Lead markets	Generally higher growth potential	Educated population
Major markets of key competitors	Poorer markets are usually less competitive	Cultural distance from West varies across countries
Home markets of many global customers	Cultural distance is higher for triad firms but lower for regional competitors	High growth potential, especially for Russian Federation
Lower political risk	Government incentives may be available for less attractive markets	Less developed legal infrastructure relating to business and marketing
	Higher political risk	Higher political risk
	Some developing countries emerging as lead markets and home markets of global competitors	

Targeting Developed Economies

Developed economies account for a disproportionately large share of world gross national product (GNP) and thus tend to attract many companies. Ten developed countries (the United States, Canada, the United Kingdom, Germany, France, the Netherlands, Sweden, Switzerland, Japan, and Australia) account for 50 percent of the world's international trade, 70 percent of its inward investment, and 90 percent of its foreign direct investment. As a result, companies that see themselves as world-class marketers cannot afford to neglect these pivotal markets.[16] Firms with technology-intensive products have especially concentrated their activities in the developed world. Although competition from both international firms and local companies is usually more intense in these markets, developed countries are often deemed to be more standalone attractive than are most developing countries. This is primarily because the business environment is more predictable and the trade and investment climate is more favorable. Also, developed countries are usually more globally strategic as they are most often the home countries or major markets of global competitors as well as lead research markets.

Developed countries are located in North America (the United States and Canada), Western Europe, and Asia (Japan, Australia, and New Zealand). Although some global firms such as IBM operate in all of these countries, many others may be represented in only one or two areas. U.S. multinational companies established strong business bases in Europe very early in their development but only more recently in Japan. Japanese firms tend to start their overseas operations in the United States and Canada and then move to Europe.

Kenichi Ohmae first articulated the importance of developing a competitive position in the major developed markets. Ohmae maintained that for most

Triad the United States, Europe, and Japan

industries, it was important to compete effectively in all three parts of the **triad** of the United States, Europe, and Japan. The three areas of this strategic triad account for about 80 percent of sales for many industries. In these cases, the position of competitors in triad markets can determine the outcome of the global competitive battle. Companies need to be strong in at least two areas and at least to be represented in the third. Real global competitors are advised to have strong positions in all three areas.[17]

Because of the importance of the triad countries in international trade, global companies go to great lengths to balance their presence such that their sales begin to mirror the relative size of the three regions. A company underrepresented in one area or another will undertake considerable investment, often in the form of acquisitions, to balance its triad portfolio. Alcatel, a leading European manufacturer of telecommunications equipment, realized that 50 percent of the global opportunity for its market was located in the United States. In response, the company began a major investment drive into the LAN (local area network) switching business, acquiring Xylan Corporation and Assured Access Technology, two California-based firms.[18]

Though the more mature markets of developed countries are arguably more difficult to enter, these markets may still hold potential for a late entrant who is determined and creative—as Toyota discovered. While the European auto market shrank in 2003, Toyota's European sales soared. What contributed to this surge in sales? A design studio in France that turned out models that looked distinctively Mediterranean. Products were well received and deemed to match the avant-garde styling of the Europeans while ranking first in quality surveys across Europe.[19]

Targeting Developing Countries

Developing countries differ substantially from developed countries in terms of both geographic region and level of economic development. Markets in Latin America, Africa, the Middle East, and some parts of Asia are characterized by a higher degree of risk than markets in developed countries. The past experience of international firms doing business in developing countries has not always been positive. Trade restrictions often forced companies to build local factories in order to access the local market. Many firms believed that such an investment was not justified, given the market size and the perceived risk of the venture. However, with the present trend toward global trade liberalization, many formerly closed countries have opened their borders to imports. This has encouraged many more firms to consider emerging markets. However, political and economic risks are still higher in developing countries than in the triad.

Because of the less stable economic climates in those areas, a company's operation can be expected to be subject to greater uncertainty and fluctuation. Furthermore, the frequently changing political situations in developing countries often affect operating results negatively. As a result, some markets that have experienced high growth for some years may suddenly experience drastic reductions in growth. For example, Whirlpool's sales in Brazil, measured in U.S. dollars, declined by $200 million as a result of a devaluation of the Brazilian currency.[20] Despite the difficulties associated with operating in these emerging markets, the average market value of multinational firms with operations in developing countries has been shown to be significantly higher than that of multinationals that are not present in such countries.[21]

Developing countries may appear to be attractive markets for several reasons. Market growth in developing countries can sometimes be higher than in the triad, often as a result of higher population growth. Middle-class consumers are appearing in markets once seen as consisting of a small elite and a large impoverished underclass. India now boasts the world's largest middle-class market in absolute numbers. In very poor developing countries, governments may still offer multinational companies government incentives such as tax breaks for bringing manufacturing jobs to the country.

With a substantial increase in global migration, remittances sent home from emigrant workers overseas has significantly increased the buying power in many developing countries—including Turkey, Pakistan, and the Philippines. In Latin America, Mexico receives over $10 billion annually in remittances, and Brazil receives over $4.5 billion. Even smaller countries like Colombia, El Salvador, and the Dominican Republic each receive over $2 billion in remittances. While many of the overseas workers who send remittances home work in the United States, this is in no way the sole destination of workers. At least 500,000 Latin Americans work in Spain, and Brazil receives half its remittances from Brazilians of Japanese descent who work in Japan.[22]

In many situations, the higher risks in these markets are compensated for by higher returns, because competition can be less intense in developing markets. Hyundai, the largest of Korea's major car manufacturers, has expanded by acquiring or building car plants in Turkey, India, Egypt, Botswana, and Eastern Europe. Hyundai was particularly attracted to these markets by the lack of intense competition there.[23]

When evaluating developing countries, most firms focus on standalone attractiveness. However, some developing countries are becoming increasingly globally strategic. The growth potential of markets in China and India put them into this category. As the second-largest beer market in the world, China has attracted as many as sixty foreign brewers. Carlsberg of Denmark, a brewer with a large international business, predicts that China will be the world's largest beer market in the near future, usurping that distinction from the United States. Carlsbad plans to invest as much as $1 billion in the country.[24] Coke considered India a problematic market and had withdrawn from India, but as soon as Pepsi invested there, Coke committed itself to reentering India. At the time, Coke still considered India to be unattractive on a standalone basis but was afraid it could lose its permanent global position to Pepsi if Pepsi captured the Indian market unopposed.

Thus firms should watch for rapidly changing competitive situations in major emerging markets and adapt accordingly. Citibank had long been a favorite bank among the Brazilian elite. However, it became distracted by a merger with Travelers Group and failed to pursue the Brazilian market aggressively just as other foreign banks were rapidly making headway through acquisitions. Because of this, Citibank dropped to fourteenth place in the market.[25]

In addition, as we saw in Chapter 6, competitors from certain emerging markets such as China, India, Mexico, and South Korea are now global contenders. Multinationals may need to establish a presence in the home countries of key competitors from the emerging markets just as they have done in the home markets of their more traditional triad competition. For example, Taiwanese electronics companies have become world leaders in several important product categories. Elitegroup and First International are the world's largest independent manufacturers of printed circuit boards. GVC, another Taiwanese company, has risen to the leading position as modem producer, surpassing Hayes of the United States.[26] In certain industries, international firms must be present in Taiwan if they intend to keep abreast of product development changes.

Targeting Transitional Economies

Table 8.3 lists the top twenty emerging markets. While most of these are traditional developing countries, three—Russia, Poland, and the Czech Republic—are transitional economies from the former Soviet bloc. The economic liberalization of such countries opened a large new market for many international firms. This market typically represents about 15 percent of the worldwide demand in a given industry. Unlike most other less developed countries, these transitional economies lack a recent history of free enterprise or commercial law. Because of this, even new laws to protect companies—such as laws pertaining to patent and trademark protection as well as minority shareholder rights—have proven difficult to enforce. Most of these markets still suffer under poorly performing economies. Nonetheless, the transitional economies of Eastern Europe enjoy the location advantage of being next to the triad region of Western Europe, and the sheer size of the potential Russian market makes it of interest to many global marketers. While many companies consider these countries as offering more long-term rather than immediate potential, many have moved to take advantage of opportunities in areas where they once were prohibited from doing business.

TABLE 8.3 LARGEST EMERGING MARKETS					
COUNTRY	RANK		COUNTRY	RANK	
	SIZE	GROWTH RATE		SIZE	GROWTH RATE
China	1	7	Philippines	11	9
India	2	2	Argentina	12	4
Russia	3	15	Egypt	13	3
Brazil	4	18	Thailand	14	8
Mexico	5	17	Venezuela	15	24
South Korea	6	11	Colombia	16	19
Indonesia	7	6	Malaysia	17	1
South Africa	8	20	Chile	18	12
Turkey	9	13	Peru	19	16
Poland	10	23	Czech Republic	20	21

SOURCE: Adapted from *Market Potential Indicators 2004*, Global Edge, Michigan State University (www.globaledge.msu.edu).

IKEA is one of many multinational firms that are betting on the future of the Russian market despite its problematic past.

The first wave of investments into Eastern Europe was led by companies marketing industrial and construction equipment, such as Otis Elevator. Otis was attracted to the Polish market because most of Poland's 60,000 operating elevators were old, and the replacement and service markets looked promising.[27] Companies marketing consumer goods tended to enter the region later. Procter & Gamble has set up regional centers for each of its product lines, making the Czech Republic its center for detergents and Hungary its center for personal-care products.

Because of its size and its abundant natural resources, Russia has the most potential to become a globally strategic market among the transitional economies. However, the Russian market has proved to be more problematic than most markets in Eastern Europe and is often viewed by firms as less attractive on a standalone basis. Liberalization has been slower, and markets have often been plagued by a greater lack of regulation and by the presence of organized crime. Procter & Gamble entered Russia by slowly introducing a line of products while expanding its geographic reach. Still the company estimates that only 10 to 15 percent of the Russian population can afford Western consumer goods.[28] The year after Cadbury opened its first chocolate plant in Russia, the Russian ruble underwent a significant devaluation. Cadbury's Russian operation took years to recover from that shock.[29] Although the Russian market may present auto manufactures with one of their best potential growth markets, bureaucratic impediments and political uncertainties have made most global automotive companies cautious of the Russian market.[30]

COUNTRY SELECTION

After determining what type of foreign markets it wishes to pursue, the firm must choose which countries in particular to target. There are more than two hundred countries and territories, but very few firms compete in all of these. Adding another country to a company's portfolio requires additional investment in management time and effort, as well as in capital. Each additional country also represents a new business risk. It takes time to build up business in a country where the firm has not previously been represented, and profits may not be realized until much later on. Consequently, companies need to perform a careful analysis before they decide to move ahead.

The Screening Process

The assessment of country markets usually begins with gathering relevant information on each country and screening out the less desirable countries. A model for selecting foreign markets is shown in Figure 8.1.

The model includes a series of filters to screen out countries. The overwhelming number of market opportunities makes it necessary to break the selection process down into a series of steps. Although a firm does not want to miss a potential opportunity, it cannot conduct extensive marketing research studies in every country of the world. The screening process is used to identify good prospects. Two common errors that companies make in screening countries are (1) ignoring countries that offer good potential for the company's products and (2) spending too much time investigating countries that are poor prospects.

The first stage of the selection process is to use macroindicators to discriminate between countries that represent basic opportunities and those that either offer little or no opportunity or involve excessive risk. **Macroindicators** describe the total market in terms of economic, social, geographic, and political information. The variables that are included reflect the potential market size and the market's acceptance of the product or similar products. The second stage of the screening process focuses on microlevel considerations such as competitors, ease of entry, cost of entry, and profit potential. The focus of the screening process switches from total market size to profitability. The final stage of the screening process is an evaluation and rank-ordering of the potential target countries on the basis of corporate resources, objectives, and strategies. Lead markets and must-win markets receive extra consideration.

Macroindicators data useful in estimating the total market size of a country or region

Criteria for Selecting Target Countries

The process of selecting target countries through the screening process requires that the companies decide what criteria to use to differentiate desirable countries from less desirable countries. In this section, we explain several key factors and their uses in the market selection process.

Market Size and Growth. The greater the potential demand for a product in a country, the more attractive that market will be to a company. Measures of

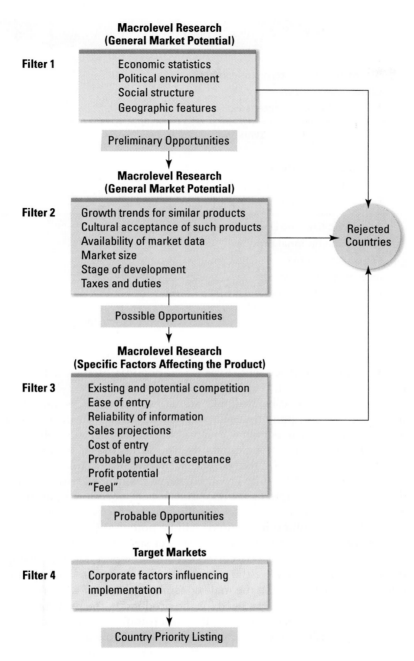

FIGURE 8.1
A Model for Selecting Foreign Markets
SOURCE: R. Wayne Walvoord, "Export Market Research," Global Trade Magazine, May 1980, p. 83. Reprinted by permission.

market size and growth can be made on both a macro and a micro basis. On a macro basis, it may be determined that the country needs a minimum set of potential resources to be worth further consideration. The macroindicators of market potential and growth are generally used in the first stage of the screening process, because the data are readily available and can be used to eliminate

TABLE 8.4 MACROINDICATORS OF MARKET SIZE
GEOGRAPHIC INDICATORS Size of country, in terms of geographic area Climatic conditions Topographical characteristics
DEMOGRAPHIC CHARACTERISTICS Total population Population growth rate Age distribution of the population Degree of population density
ECONOMIC CHARACTERISTICS Total gross national product Per-capita income Income growth rate Personal or household disposable income Income distribution

quickly those countries with little or no potential demand. Table 8.4 summarizes the potential macroindicators of market size.

A variety of readily available statistics can serve as macroindicators of market size. A company that sells microwave ovens may decide not to consider any country with a personal disposable income per household of less than $10,000 a year. The rationale for this criterion is that if the average household has less than $10,000, the potential market for a luxury item such as a microwave oven will not be great. However, a single statistic can sometimes be deceptive. For example, a country may have an average household income of $8,000, but there may still be a million households with an income of over $10,000. These million households will be potential buyers of microwaves.

Because the macroindicators of market size are general and crude, they do not necessarily indicate a perceived need for the product. For example, a country such as Iran may have the population and income to suggest a large potential market for razors, but the male consumers, many of whom are Muslims and wear beards, may not feel a need for the product. In the next stage of the screening process, it is recommended that microindicators of market potential be used. **Microindicators** usually indicate actual consumption of a company's product or a similar product, therefore signaling a perceived need. Table 8.5 lists several examples of microindicators of market size.

These microindicators can be used to estimate market size further. The number of households with televisions indicates the potential market size for televisions if every household purchased a new television. Depending on the life of the average television in use, one can estimate the annual demand. As we noted in Chapter 7, consumption figures for similar or substitute products can be used as proxies if actual consumption statistics are not available for a cer-

Microindicators data useful in estimating the consumption of a certain product in a country or region

TABLE 8.5 MICROINDICATORS OF MARKET SIZE

Radios	Hotel beds
Televisions	Telephones
Cinema seats	Tourist arrivals
Scientists and engineers	Passenger cars
Hospitals	Civil airline passengers
Hospital beds	Steel production
Physicians	Rice production
Alcohol consumption	Number of farms
Coffee consumption	Land under cultivation
Gasoline consumption	Electricity consumption

tain product category. For example, if a firm is trying to measure the potential market size and receptivity for a palm-held communicator, it might choose as a proxy the number of telephone lines per person, the number of personal computers per person, or cellular telephone usage. Similarly, in determining the market size for surgical sutures, marketers might use the number of hospital beds or the number of doctors as a proxy. The number of farms might indicate the potential demand for tractors, just as the number of cars is likely to indicate the number of tires needed.

Political Conditions. The influence of the host country's political environment was described in detail in Chapter 4. Although political risk tends to be more subjective than the quantitative indicators of market size, it is equally important. Any company can be hurt by political risk, which can result in anything from limitations on the number of foreign company officials and on the amount of profits paid to the parent company, to refusal to issue a business license. Though less radical than invasions, industrial disputes such as strikes can be a major disruption to business. The incidence of such events varies greatly from country to country. The most "strike-prone" among the developed countries are Greece, Norway, and Canada.[31] Table 8.6 shows some indicators of political risk that may be used in country selection.

TABLE 8.6 INDICATORS OF POLITICAL RISK

Probability of nationalization	Percentage of voters who are Communist
Bureaucratic delays	Restrictions on capital movement
Number of expropriations	Government intervention
Number of riots or assassinations	Limits on foreign ownership
Political executions	Soldier/civilian ratio
Number of Socialist seats in the legislature	

WORLD BEAT 8.2

The Lure of Rural Markets

WHEN MULTINATIONAL FIRMS enter developing countries, they usually target urban markets. In some developing countries, this can be just one or two major cities, such as Tehran in Iran or Santiago in Chile. Urban markets have the most sophisticated and richest consumers as well as the most developed distribution systems. For these reasons, many multinational firms, such as Nestlé in India, still focus on the urban market. However, some global marketers are awakening to the potential of long overlooked rural markets in developing countries and transition economies. But the decision to expand to the rural market may be as complex as a decision to enter a different national market, and new marketing strategies involving adaptations to products, price, distribution channels, and promotion may be needed to succeed in the rural markets.

Coca Cola actively pursues rural consumers in two of the developing world's largest markets—China and India. Its strategy is to provide extremely cheap sodas to populations once considered too poor or difficult to reach. This decision came as Coke watched a considerable decline in its growth rate in the major Chinese and Indian cities. But rural markets are not free from competition. Local Chinese soda companies have already achieved a first mover advantage in China's countryside. Ironically, they targeted rural China to avoid competing head-on with Coca-Cola!

Sources: "Coca-Cola to Focus on Indian Rural Areas for Growth," *Asia Pulse*, May 13, 2004; "Why Nestle India Does Not Want a Revolution," *Financial Express*, May 18, 2003; and Dexter Roberts, "China's Power Brands," *Business Week*, November 8, 2004, p. 50.

Competition. In general, it is more difficult to determine the competitive structure of foreign countries than to determine the market size or political risk. Because of the difficulty of obtaining information, competitive analysis is usually done in the last stages of the screening process, when a small number of countries are being considered. However, when firms seek to identify globally strategic markets (as opposed to simply standalone attractive markets) competitive analysis will be undertaken earlier in the screening process.

As noted in Chapter 7, there are various sources of information on competition, though availability varies widely, depending on the size of the country and the product. Many of the larger countries have chambers of commerce or other in-country organizations that may be able to assist potential investors. For example, if a firm is investigating the Japanese market for electronic measuring devices, the following groups could help it determine the competitive structure of the market in Japan:

▶ U.S. Chamber of Commerce in Japan
▶ Japan External Trade Organization (JETRO)
▶ American Electronics Association in Japan
▶ Japan Electronic Industry Development Association
▶ Electronic Industries Association of Japan
▶ Japan Electronic Measuring Instrument Manufacturers Association

Market Similarity. Strong evidence exists that market similarity can be used for country selection. A study of 954 product introductions by 57 U.S. firms found a significant correlation between market selection and market similarity.[32] As shown in Table 8.7, the selection of foreign markets follows market similarity very closely. Even born-global firms show a propensity to first enter national markets that are more similar to their home markets.[33]

The concept of market similarity is simple. Managers believe that their success in the home market is more easily transferable to markets similar to the one in which they already compete. This idea is sometimes called **psychic distance**. Therefore, when a company decides to enter foreign markets, it will first tend to enter markets that are psychically close or most similar to its home market. For example, a U.S. firm usually enters Canada, Australia, and the United Kingdom before entering less similar markets such as Spain, South Korea, and India. The premise behind the selection of similar markets is the desire of a company to minimize risk in the face of uncertainty. Entering a market that has the same language, a similar distribution system, and similar customers is less difficult than entering a market in which all these variables are different.

Psychic distance the perceived degree of similarity between markets

TABLE 8.7 CORRELATION OF SIMILARITY AND POSITION IN THE ENTRY SEQUENCE

COUNTRY	SIMILARITY TO THE UNITED STATES	POSITION IN INVESTMENT SEQUENCE
Canada	1	2
Australia	2	3
United Kingdom	3	1
West Germany	4	6
France	5	4
Belgium	6	10
Italy	7	9
Japan	8	5
Netherlands	9	12
Argentina	10	15
Mexico	11	8
Spain	12	13
India	13	16
Brazil	14	7
South Africa	15	14
Philippines	16	17
South Korea	17	18
Colombia	18	11

SOURCE: Reprinted from *Journal of Business Research* 11, no. 4, William H. Davidson, "Market Similarity and Market Selection: Implications for International Market Strategy," p. 446. Copyright © 1983, with permission from Elsevier.

There are two dangers of choosing markets on the basis of similarity. First, the benefits of similarity need to be balanced against the market size. Australia may be similar to the United States but may have relatively little demand compared with China or Indonesia. Air France flies to more African cities than any non-African airline. France's colonial history arguably gives Air France (and other French companies) a competitive advantage in its old African empire, which includes Cameroon, Chad, Gabon, Guinea, Ivory Coast, Mali, Senegal, and other countries, due to linguistic, economic, and cultural ties.[34] However, some have argued that French firms have sometimes lost out on bigger growth markets in the Pacific Rim because of their emphasis on markets in Africa.

A second problem associated with selecting national markets based on perceived cultural similarity is the fact that firms can overestimate the degree of similarity between markets. When Starbucks internationalized, it discovered that just because foreign consumers spoke English didn't mean that the markets operated the same. For example, in the United States, the firm's strategy was to find the best corners in the best markets to locate its stores. That approach proved too expensive in Britain where real estate prices were higher.[35] When Canadian retail chains entered the United States, managers assumed that the United States was just like Canada only bigger. They believed that the retail concepts that worked in Canada would work in the United States. Instead, U.S. consumers proved very different from Canadian consumers. They demanded more service, shopped harder for bargains, and were far less loyal to national chains than were their Canadian counterparts. In addition, competition proved far more intense in the United States. As a result, familiarity bred carelessness, and the chains struggled to survive in what proved to be a very alien market.[36]

Psychic-distance paradox a phenomenon in which a market thought to be similar to another market turns out to be dissimilar

This culture shock experienced by managers entering foreign markets that they had perceived to be similar to their own is sometimes called the **psychic-distance paradox**. A study of firms from Denmark, Sweden, and New Zealand suggests that this shock effect may be more common among producers of customized products than among producers of more standardized products.[37]

Listing Selection Criteria

A good way to screen countries is to develop a set of criteria that serve as minimum standards that a country must meet in order to move through the stages of the screening process. The minimum cutoff number for each criterion will be established by management. As one moves through the screening process, the selection criteria become more specific. The screening process that could be used by a manufacturer of kidney dialysis equipment is depicted in Table 8.8.

The analysis begins by looking at gross national products. Introduction of dialysis equipment in a new market requires a significant support function, including salespeople, service people, replacement parts inventory, and an ensured continuous supply of dialysate fluid, needles, tubing, and so on. Some countries lack the technical infrastructure to support such high-level technology. Therefore, management may decide to consider only countries that have a minimum size of $15 billion GNP, a criterion that excludes many of the developing economies of the world from consideration.

The selection process continues by examining the concentration of medical services in the remaining countries. Hemodialysis is a sophisticated procedure

TABLE 8.8	SCREENING PROCESS EXAMPLE: TARGETING COUNTRIES FOR KIDNEY DIALYSIS EQUIPMENT	
FILTER NUMBER	TYPE OF SCREENING	SPECIFIC CRITERIA
1	Macrolevel research	GDP over $15 billion GDP per capita over $1,500
2	General market factors related to the product	Fewer than 200 people per hospital bed Fewer than 1,000 people per doctor Government expenditures over $100 million for health care Government expenditures over $20 per capita for health care
3	Microlevel factors specific to the product	Kidney-related deaths over 1,000 Patient use of dialysis equipment—over 40 percent annual growth in treated population
4	Final screening of target markets	Numbers of competitors Political stability

that requires medical personnel with advanced training. For a country to support advanced medical equipment, it requires a high level of medical specialization. Higher levels of medical concentration allow doctors the luxury of specializing in a field such as nephrology (the study of kidneys). Management may determine that a population of less than 1,000 per doctor and a population of less than 200 per hospital bed indicate that medical personnel will be able to achieve the level of specialization needed to support a hemodialysis program.

Public health expenditures reflect the government's contribution to the medical care of its citizens—a factor of obvious importance with respect to hemodialysis. Management may believe that countries that do not invest substantially in the health care of their populations generally are not interested in making an even more substantial investment in a hemodialysis program. Thus, countries that do not have a minimum of $20 in public health expenditure per capita or $100 million in total expenditures for health care would be eliminated from consideration.

Then management may decide that there are two microlevel factors to consider: the number of kidney-related deaths and the growth rate of the treated patient population. The number of deaths due to kidney failure is a good indicator of the number of people in each country who could have used dialysis equipment. The company will be interested only in countries with a minimum of 1,000 deaths per year due to kidney-related causes. Analysis of the growth rate of the population requiring kidney treatment demonstrates a growth in potential demand.

Finally, management must consider political risk and competition. Newly opened markets with the greatest growth potential may be the best targets for a new supplier of dialysis equipment, because competition is not so entrenched as it would be in a mature market. Alternatively, management may decide to enter a lead market where a major competitor is strong in order to monitor technology development and possibly block that competitor. The weighting of these microlevel factors will determine the primary target market.

Grouping International Markets

A final consideration in selecting national markets is the option of entering a group of countries in a single geographic region, be they the developed countries of Western Europe or the less developed countries in South America or the Middle East. It is often necessary to group countries together so that they can be considered as a single market or as a group of similar markets. Two principles that often drive the need for larger market groupings are critical mass and economies of scale. **Critical mass**, a term used in physics and military strategy, embodies the idea that a certain minimum amount of effort is necessary before any impact will be achieved. **Economies of scale** is a term used in production situations; it means that greater levels of production result in lower costs per unit, which obviously increases profitability.

The costs of marketing products within a group of countries are lower than the costs of marketing products to the same number of disparate countries for four reasons. First, the potential volume to be sold in a group of countries is sufficient to support a full marketing effort. Second, geographic proximity makes it easy to travel from one country to another, often in 2 hours or less. Third, the barriers to entry are frequently the same in countries within an economic group—for example, the European Union (EU). Finally, in pursuing countries with similar markets, a company gains leverage with marketing programs.

There is some debate over the long-term role of market groups. The EU has become a strong group with a single currency, but many economic groups may become subordinate to the role of the World Trade Organization (WTO). Also, given the broad membership of the WTO and its strong enforcement powers, the regional market group will generally need to conform to the rules and practices of the WTO when dealing with all other WTO countries.

It is also important to remember that just being neighbors isn't enough to make countries into a viable market group. Take, for example, the countries in the Caucasus region. Armenia and Azerbaijan are technically at war. Turkey blockades Armenia in sympathy with Azerbaijan. Relations between Georgia and Armenia remain strained, as do relations between Iran and Azerbaijan. Travel and shipping among the countries are poor as well. Roads are bad, and the easiest flight connections in the region are all via Moscow or Istanbul.[38] Clearly these countries do not present themselves as a likely group to the global marketer.

> **Critical mass** the minimal effort and investment needed to compete effectively in a market
>
> **Economies of scale** profitability gained through the phenomenon that as the size of a production run increases, per-unit costs decrease

Which countries belong to which regional groups? Check out *Regional Groups* on our website (college.hmco.com/business/).

CONCLUSION

Any company that wishes to engage in global marketing must make a number of very important strategic decisions concerning global market participation. At the outset, the company must commit itself to some level of internationalization. Increasingly, firms are finding that an international presence must be pursued for competitive reasons. It is a necessity, not simply an option. Once committed, the company needs to decide where to go, both in terms of geographic regions and specific countries. Standalone attractiveness of markets must be balanced with their global strategic importance. Firms must determine what participation they want and need in developed, developing, and transitional economies. Being in the right international markets establishes the groundwork for the firm's global marketing strategy.

How standalone attractive or strategically important is your market choice? Continue with your *Country Market Report* on our website (college.hmco.com/business/).

QUESTIONS FOR DISCUSSION

1. Why might a firm in packaged goods choose to enter a globally strategic market rather than a market that is more standalone attractive? In what way would your answer differ for a firm manufacturing and marketing medical diagnostic equipment?

2. What advantages might a Korean-based company such as Hyundai have entering markets in developing countries?

3. Discuss the pros and cons of packaged-goods manufacturers' targeting Eastern Europe and Russia.

4. What could be the advantages and disadvantages of being a born-global firm?

5. Unlike firms early in their internationalization, MNCs (multinational corporations) do not appear to favor entering new markets that are similar to their home markets over entering those that are dissimilar. Why do you think that is?

CASE 8.1

Indian Food Goes Global

Mr. R. Krishnan, president of South Indian Foods Limited (SIFL), was deep in thought in his office at corporate headquarters in Coimbatore, India. Eleven years earlier he had founded SIFL with the help of his wife, Maya. Now, after returning from a weeklong business trip to the United States, Mr. Krishnan was pondering the future of his company. Should SIFL enter foreign markets? If so, which ones?

SIFL began as a company selling only three items but had quickly expanded to a dozen products. It produced and marketed batters, pastes, and flours that formed the ingredients of traditional South Indian cooking. For example, its Maami's Tamarind Mix consisted of mustard,

ground nuts, asafetida, curry leaves, coriander powder, and dried chilies fried in oil and then combined with tamarind extract, salt, turmeric, and vinegar. The mix was next bottled and vacuum-sealed to preserve the traditional home-made flavor and aroma of tamarind mix.

The company began to market its products in and around Coimbatore. Soon, however, new production units were established in Bangalore and Madras to serve the whole South Indian market. Then three more manufacturing units were established in the states of Maharashtra, Andhra Pradesh, and West Bengal. SIFL estimated that its share of market varied between 19 and 27 percent across its product categories in the territories where it competed. Recently, new competitors had entered the market. Their market shares were slightly lower than those of SIFL. In response to increased competition, however, SIFL attempted to avoid adding new product lines that might have to compete head-on with aggressive competitors.

SIFL attributed part of its success to its promotional efforts. It used advertising campaigns in local radio and newspapers. Handbills, printed in the local language of the different Indian states, were distributed in newspapers in selected cities. The company also offered sample packets of its batter products. All these efforts had helped make Maami's a household name in South India.

When Mr. Krishnan raised the question of international expansion at an emergency board meeting, there was great enthusiasm but little agreement. Some of the managers' comments were as follows:

KRISHNAN: Why can't we think of going international? Our strategy did very well in the Indian market. With our state-of-the-art production facilities and marketing expertise, I believe we could easily create a niche overseas.

SUNDER: We have to be optimistic about the U.S. market. As you know, the Indian population there is large enough to absorb our product. Our market research also reveals that our dishes are even favored by native Americans.

SHANKAR: I accept your views, but we are forgetting the fact that in the U.S. market we have to compete with powerful packaged-food companies.

KRISHNAN: What about Asia? In South Asia, the raw materials necessary for making our products are readily available.

MAYA: I do not think targeting all of Asia is a viable option. Although the Chinese and Japanese are accustomed to rice, most of these Asian countries are culturally different from India. Why not the United Kingdom? It has a considerable South Indian population.

DINAKAR: Why not set up production facilities in the United States or the United Kingdom? I believe production overseas would be a better choice than exporting to these markets.

Discussion Questions

1. What are SIFL's motivations for expanding abroad?
2. What are the advantages of targeting Indian populations residing in foreign countries? What problems might arise?
3. What are the pros and cons of entering the United States first? The United Kingdom? Neighboring Asian markets?
4. Is there any advantage or disadvantage to this product being "Made in India"?
5. SIFL will face competitors such as Kraft in the United States. What overall posture should SIFL adopt in relation to these strong competitors—attack, avoid, or cooperate? How might U.S. competitors respond to SIFL's entry into the market?
6. To investigate the competitive environment for these products in your country, visit a local grocery store or supermarket. What Indian foods or food products are sold there? Do they appear to be targeted at ethnic communities or at a wider segment? What firms make these products? What insights could your visit give SIFL?

Source: This case is based on *South Indian Foods Limited (A)* by K. B. Saji. Used by permission.

CASE 8.2
Gillette Targets Emerging Markets

As it entered the twenty-first century, Gillette faced a difficult choice. Should it continue targeting emerging markets or not? Its strategy to move aggressively into markets in the developing world and the former Soviet bloc had been hailed as a success only a few years before. Recent poor earnings, however, had management considering whether this choice had been a wise one.

The Boston-based firm was founded in 1895 and is still best known for its original products, razors and razor blades. By the end of the twentieth century, Gillette had grown into a global corporation that marketed its products in 200 countries and employed 44,000 people worldwide. About 1.2 billion people use Gillette products every day. Its sales are about equally distributed among the United States (30 percent), Western Europe (35 percent), and the rest of the world (35 percent).

As markets matured in developing countries, Gillette sought growth through product diversification, moving into lines such as home permanents, disposable lighters, ballpoint pens, and batteries. In the mid-1990s, Gillette targeted several key emerging markets for growth. Among them were Russia, China, India, and Poland. Russia was already a success story. Gillette had formed a Russian joint venture in St. Petersburg, and within 3 years Russia had become Gillette's third-largest blade market.

Gillette's move into the Czech Republic had prospered as well, and in 1995 Gillette bought Astra, a local, privately owned razor blade company. Astra gave Gillette expanded brand presence in the Czech market. Astra's relatively strong position in export markets in East Europe, Africa, and Southeast Asia proved a boon to Gillette in those markets as well. Just as in other markets in the developing world, 70 percent of East European blade consumers used the older, lower-tech double-edge blade. (In more developed markets, consumers appreciated product innovation,

and the shaving market had moved to more high-tech systems such as Gillette's Sensor.)

Then disaster struck. A financial crisis that began in Thailand quickly spread across Asia. Many wary investors responded by pulling money out of other emerging markets as well, depressing economies across the globe. Bad economies meant slower sales for Gillette, especially in Asia, Russia, and Latin America. In Russia, wholesalers could not afford to buy Gillette products. Consequently, these products disappeared from retail stores, and Gillette's Russian sales plummeted 80 percent in a single month. Gillette found it could not meet its projected annual profit growth of 15–20 percent. The price of Gillette shares tumbled 36 percent in 6 months. To save money, Gillette planned to close 14 factories and lay off 10 percent of its workforce.

Despite its recent bad experience in developing countries and in the former Soviet bloc, Gillette was still moving ahead with plant expansion plans in Russia and Argentina that would total $64 million. Some even suggested that this was a good time to expand in the emerging markets by buying up smaller competitors that had been hurt even worse by the crises. Meanwhile, back in the developed world, another large global consumer-products firm, Unilever, announced that it would be entering the razor market.

Discussion Questions

1. Why do companies such as Gillette target emerging markets? Do you agree with this strategy?
2. What are the dangers to Gillette of targeting emerging markets?
3. Why would local, privately owned companies like Astra want to sell out to companies like Gillette? Why are such companies attractive acquisitions to multinational firms?

4. What global strategy would you suggest for a company such as Gillette? Explain your choice.

Sources: Claire Oldfield, "Unilever Goes for a Cut of Razor Market," *Sunday Times*, September 10, 2000; Mark Maremont, "Gillette Won't Meet Profit-Growth Goal While Emerging Markets Face Turmoil," *Wall Street Journal*, September 30, 1998; Mary Kelleher, "Latin America's Pain Starts to Hurt Banks, Consumer Product Firms," *Toronto Star*, September 19, 1998, p. C4; "Gillette Acquires Leading Czech Blade and Razor Company," *Business Wire*, October 16, 1996; and Alex Pham, "Russian Mayor Seeks to Lure Business," *Boston Globe*, February 21, 1995, p. 53.

CASE 8.3
The Global Baby Bust

Most people think that the world faces an over-population problem. But Phillip Longman argues otherwise in his book *The Empty Cradle*. He warns instead of a global baby bust. World population growth has fallen 40 percent since the late 1960s. The human population is expected to peak at nine billion by 2070, and many countries will see their population shrink long before that. Japan will have 49 retirees per 100 workers as early as 2025.

Falling birthrates mainly account for these declines (see Table 1). Several factors contribute to the falling birthrates. Around the world, more women are entering the workforce, and young people delay raising a family in order to attain the higher levels of education needed to compete in a global marketplace. However, a major reason for falling birthrates is the high cost of raising a middle-class child in an industrialized country—a cost estimated at more than $200,000 (exclusive of college) in the United States.

As developing countries become more industrialized and urban, they too face a high cost of raising children. In Mexico, where fertility rates have declined precipitously, the population is aging five times faster than it is in the United States. By 2050, Algeria could well see its average age increase from 21.7 to 40. One of the greatest declines in population growth is occurring in China, where government policy has long supported one child per family. It is predicted that 60 percent of China's population could be over 60 by midcentury.

A nation may experience a "demographic dividend" when birthrates first fall. More working-age citizens support fewer children, freeing up money for consumption and investment. Many attribute the recent boom markets in Asia, such as China and South Korea, to this demographic dividend. However, as population growth continues to slow, the nation faces the problem of supporting older populations. For example, by 2040, Germany's public spending on pensions will exceed 15 percent of GNP, and Italy's working population is expected to plunge to 41 percent by 2050. Even China will have 30 retirees for every 100 persons in the workforce by 2025. The level of entrepreneurship in a nation also declines as its population ages. Japan and France, with their high ratios of retirees to workers, rate among the lowest countries for entrepreneurship. On a more positive note, a decline in terrorism is associated with an aging population. Longman points to the fact that Europe's Red Guard, a terrorist organization active in the 1970s, is now defunct.

Is immigration the answer for industrialized countries? To sustain its current ratio of workers to retirees over time, the United States would need to absorb almost eleven million immigrants a year. Such an influx would require building the equivalent of another New York City every 10 months. By 2050, 73 percent of the U.S. population would be immigrants or descendants of immigrants who arrived since 1995. However, before this occurs, a potential political backlash against immigrants could materialize. Supply is a

TABLE 1	BIRTHRATES FOR SELECTED COUNTRIES, 2000 AND 2025			
COUNTRY	BIRTHS PER 1000 POPULATION, 2000	ANNUAL RATE OF GROWTH (%) 2000	BIRTHS PER 1000 POPULATION 2025	ANNUAL RATE OF GROWTH (%) 2025
Algeria	20	1.5	13	0.8
Argentina	18	1.1	13	0.5
Brazil	19	1.3	13	0.5
China	14	0.7	11	0.2
Czech Republic	9	-0.1	7	-0.4
Egypt	26	2.0	17	1.1
Ethiopia	42	2.5	27	1.5
Ghana	29	1.7	18	0.8
France	13	0.5	10	0.1
Greece	10	0.2	8	-0.2
Hungary	10	-0.3	8	-0.4
India	25	1.6	17	0.9
Indonesia	23	1.6	15	0.8
Iran	18	1.2	13	0.7
Italy	9	0.3	7	-0.3
Japan	10	0.2	8	-0.6
Kenya	37	2.1	19	1.2
Mexico	23	1.4	16	0.8
Poland	10	0.0	9	-0.3
Russia	9	-0.4	8	-0.6
Saudi Arabia	30	2.9	22	1.3
South Korea	13	0.8	9	-0.1
Spain	10	0.2	7	-0.3
Sweden	10	0.0	10	-0.1
Thailand	17	1.1	12	0.3
Turkey	19	1.3	12	0.6
Ukraine	9	-0.7	9	-0.5
United Kingdom	11	0.4	10	0.2
United States	14	1.0	14	0.8
Switzerland	11	0.5	9	0.0
South Africa	22	0.6	15	-0.7

SOURCE: Adapted from U.S. Census Bureau (www.census.gov).

problem also. Puerto Rico—once a major source of immigration to the United States—no longer provides a net flow of immigrants to the United States despite its lower standard of living and free access to the United States. In addition, the United States would have to compete with Europe for immigrants from the developing world. In fact, to sustain its current age structure, even South Korea would have to bring in six billion immigrants by 2050.

Discussion Questions

1. What are the implications of the global baby bust for marketers of consumer goods?

2. What are the implications of the global baby bust for marketers who sell to governments?
3. Why do you think entrepreneurship in a nation declines as its population ages? How could this impact global marketing?
4. How does the global baby bust affect the relative attractiveness of different national markets?

Sources: Phillip Longman, "The Global Baby Bust," *Foreign Affairs*, May/June 2004, pp. 64–79; Erika Kinetz, "As the World Comes of (Older) Age," *International Herald Tribune*, December 4, 2004, p. 14; and Pete Engardio and Carol Matlack, "Global Aging," *Business Week*, January 31, 2005, pp. 44–47.

Notes

1. Julie Forster and Becky Gaylord, "Can Kraft Be a Big Cheese Abroad as Well?" *Business Week,* June 4, 2001, pp. 63–67.
2. "This Bud's for Them: Anheuser-Busch Takes Closer Aim at Foreign Markets," *New York Times*, June 23, 1999, p. C1.
3. "Compagnie de St.-Gobain," *Industry Week*, June 7, 1999, p. 38.
4. Jean-Pierre Jeannet, "The World Paint Industry" (Lausanne: IMD International, 1993).
5. "Deloitte & Touche Secure E-Business Practice to Globalize" PR Newswire, July 2, 1999.
6. Michael Zielenziger, "DHL Worldwide Express Starts Service in Kabul, Afghanistan," *San Jose Mercury News*, April 6, 2002.
7. "Bayer Plans Investments in Asia Through 2010," *Chemical Market Reporter*, February 22, 1999, p. 28.
8. Peter Landers, "U.S. Is Tonic for Japan's Top Pharmaceuticals," *Wall Street Journal*, May 21, 2002, p. B6.
9. Richard Seet and David Yoffie, "Internationalizing the Cola Wars (A): The Battle for China and Asian Markets," Harvard Business School, Case 9-795-186, 1995.
10. "Mexico's Cemex Wins Bet on Acquisitions," *Wall Street Journal*, April 30, 1998, p. A14.
11. Vijay Jolly, "Logitech International (A)," (Lausanne: IMD International, 1991).
12. "PC Mouse Maker Logitech Still No. 1," *Taiwan Economic News*, June 8, 1999.
13. "Boss Talk: It's a Grande-Latte World," *Wall Street Journal*, December 15, 2003, p. B1.
14. George S. Yip, *Total Global Strategy II* (Upper Saddle River, NJ: Prentice-Hall, 2003), p.76.
15. "Manager's Hands-Off Tactics Right Touch for Italian Unit," *Nikkei Weekly*, February 3, 1997, p. 17.
16. "Subramanian Rangan: Seven Myths to Ponder Before Going Global," *Financial Times*, Mastering Strategy, Part 10, November 29, 1999, p. 2.
17. Kenichi Ohmae, *Triad Power: The Coming Shape of Global Competition* (New York: Free Press, 1985).
18. "Alcatel Open to More Acquisitions," *Business World*, March 25, 1999.
19. Gail Edmondson and Adeline Bonnet, "Toyota's New Traction in Europe," *Business Week*, June 7, 2004, p. 64.
20. "Whirlpool Says Net Fell by 65 Percent on Impact of Brazil Devaluation," *Wall Street Journal*, April 16, 1999, p. B2.
21. Christos Pantzalis, "Does Location Matter? An Empirical Analysis of Geographic Scope and MNC Market Valuation," *Journal of International Business Studies* 32, no. 1 (2001), pp. 133–155.
22. Joel Millman, "Latin Americans Boost Home Coffers," *Wall Street Journal*, March 17, 2003, p. A2.
23. "Fast Drive Out of the Shadows," *Financial Times*, June 17, 1996, p. 17.
24. "Carlsberg A/S," *Food and Drink Weekly*, October 26, 1998.
25. Pamela Druckerman, "As Brazil Booms, Citibank Is Racing to Catch Up," *Wall Street Journal*, September 11, 2000, p. A30.
26. "Acer's Semiconductor Unit Weighs Market Listing as Picture Brightens," *Dow Jones Business News*, January 20, 1999.
27. "Otis Signs $5 Million Contract with TPSA," *Polish Press Agency*, June 9, 1999.
28. "The Frugal Felicia Proves to Be a Firm Favourite," *Western Morning News* (Devon, U.K.), July 7, 1999.
29. Sarah Ellison, "Cadbury Schweppes Works to Tempt More Sweet Tooths," *Wall Street Journal*, April 24, 2001, p. B4.

30. "Russia's Vast Potential Drawing U.S. Auto Makers," *Tribune Business News* (*Detroit Free Press*), August 18, 1998.

31. "Greece Is OECD's Most Strike Prone Nation," *Financial Times*, April 9, 1998, p. 7.

32. William H. Davidson, "Market Similarity and Market Selection: Implications for International Market Strategy," *Journal of Business Research* 11, no. 4 (1983), p. 446.

33. Sylvie Chetty and Colin Campbell-Hunt, "A Strategic Approach to Internationalization: A Traditional Versus a 'Born-Global' Approach," *Journal of International Marketing* 12, no. 1 (2004), pp. 57–81.

34. Daniel Michaels, "Landing Rights," *Wall Street Journal*, April 30, 2002, p. A1.

35. "Boss Talk: It's a Grande-Latte World," *Wall Street Journal*, December 15, 2003, p. B1.

36. Shawna O'Grady and Henry L. Lane, "The Psychic Distance Paradox," *Journal of International Business Studies* 27, no. 2 (1996), pp. 319, 324–325.

37. Torben Pedersen and Bent Petersen, "Learning about Foreign Markets: Are Entrant Firms Exposed to a 'Shock Effect'?" *Journal of International Marketing*, 12, no. 1 (2004), pp. 103–123.

38. "The Caucasus, a Region Where Worlds Collide," *The Economist*, August 19, 2000.

9 GLOBAL MARKET ENTRY STRATEGIES

EVEN THE ARTS are going global. Russia's Bolshoi Ballet has actively sought overseas expansion since the collapse of the Soviet Union left the world-famous dance troupe strapped for funds. The Guggenheim art museum in New York, concerned with its limited endowment, has also expanded into foreign markets. But what is the best way for ballet companies and art museums to enter foreign markets? Traditionally, they exported their product by taking their dancers or art exhibits on tour. Today other market entry options are being employed. The Bolshoi has licensed its name to schools in Brazil and Tokyo and recently announced a similar move into Australia. The Guggenheim has established subsidiary branches in Bilbao, Venice, and Berlin and plans to open another in Rio de Janeiro.[1] Even the Vatican is considering ways to enter world markets by licensing the images from its repository of manuscripts, prints, coins, and artwork to interested companies in the fields of collectibles, giftware, apparel, and décor.[2]

Any enterprise, whether a for-profit company or a not-for-profit museum, that pursues a global strategy must determine the type of presence it expects to maintain in every market where it competes. A company may choose to export to the new market, or it may decide to

After studying this chapter, you should be able to

▶ Differentiate among market entry options—indirect exporting, direct exporting, licensing, franchising, contract manufacturing, assembly, and full-scale integrated manufacturing—and note the conditions under which each is an appropriate strategy.

▶ Explain the role of export management companies, export agents, and export consortiums.

▶ Note the ways in which the Internet has affected the international entry strategies employed by firms.

▶ List the pros and cons of establishing wholly owned subsidiaries and the pros and cons of establishing joint ventures.

▶ Compare and contrast technology-based, production-based, and distribution-based strategic alliances.

▶ Explain when entering a market by acquisition is desirable.

▶ Define entry strategy configuration, bundling, and unbundling, and explain their significance to market entry strategies.

▶ Explain why market exit—and possibly reentry—strategies might be necessary.

produce locally. It may prefer full ownership of a local operation, or it may seek partners. Once a commitment has been made, changes can be difficult and costly. Therefore, it is important to approach these decisions with the utmost care. Not only is the financial return to the company at stake, but the extent to which the company can implement its global marketing strategy also depends on these decisions. In this chapter, we concentrate on the major entry strategies by explaining each alternative in detail and citing relevant company experiences. An overview of possible entry strategies appears in Figure 9.1.

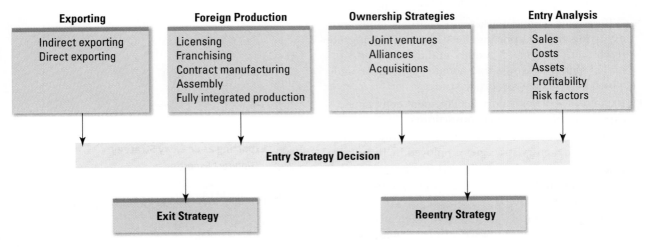

FIGURE 9.1
Market Entry Strategies

EXPORTING AS AN ENTRY STRATEGY

Exporting to a foreign market is a strategy that many companies follow for at least some of their markets. Few countries offer a large enough market to justify local production. Exporting allows a company to manufacture its products for several markets centrally and thus achieve economies of scale. When this occurs, a firm can realize more profits, lower its prices, or sometimes do both. In addition, both transportation costs and government tariffs have fallen considerably in the past 25 years. These conditions make exporting all the more cost-effective.

Many firms use exporting as a way to grow their business while limiting risk and avoiding large investments. For example, Invensys Energy Systems, a New Zealand manufacturer of standby power equipment, sells 90 percent of their $35 million to more than thirty countries through export arrangements with other companies to market and service their equipment.[3]

Home governments often assist firms by providing information on export markets. As a result there is a great deal of information available on export markets. A study that included 992 export decision makers from the United Kingdom, Austria, Germany, New Zealand, and the United States found that firms serving a few countries used less information than firms serving many countries. The study also identified that the sheer volume of export information could be a problem for both large and small exporters without sufficient staff to understand and interpret the available information.[4]

A firm has two basic options for carrying out its export operations. Markets can be contacted through an intermediary located in the exporter's home country—an approach called **indirect exporting**. Alternatively, markets can be reached directly or through an intermediary located in the foreign market—an approach termed **direct exporting**.

Indirect exporting exporting through an intermediary located in the exporter's home country

Direct exporting exporting through an intermediary located in a foreign market

Indirect Exporting

Several types of intermediaries located in the home market are ready to assist a manufacturer in contacting international markets or buyers. A major advantage of using a domestic intermediary lies in its knowledge of foreign market conditions. Particularly for companies with little or no experience in exporting, the use of a domestic intermediary provides the exporter with readily available expertise.

Export Management Company. An export management company (EMC) is a firm that handles all aspects of export operations under a contractual agreement. The EMC normally takes responsibility for the marketing research, patent protection, channel credit, and shipping and logistics, as well as for the actual marketing of products in a foreign market or markets. An EMC can operate either as a merchant that takes title to the products or as an agent that does not take title but provides services for a fee or commission. Arrangements between an EMC and a manufacturer will vary, depending on the services offered and the volume expected. The advantages of an EMC include the following: (1) little or no investment is required to enter the international marketplace, (2) no in-house personnel are required, and (3) the EMC offers an established network of sales offices as well as international marketing and distribution knowledge. The main disadvantage is that the manufacturer gives up direct control of the international sales and marketing effort.

Export Agents. Export agents are individuals or firms that also assist manufacturers in exporting goods. They are similar to EMCs, except that they tend to provide more limited services and to focus on one country or one part of the world. Export agents understand all the requirements for moving goods through international channels, but they do not provide all the services that an EMC provides. These agents focus more on the sale and handling of goods. The advantage of using an export agent is that the manufacturer does not need to have an export manager to handle all the documentation and shipping tasks. The main disadvantage is the export agent's limited market coverage. To cover different parts of the world, a firm would need the services of numerous export agents.

Direct Exporting

A company engages in direct exporting when it exports directly to customers or solely through intermediaries located in foreign markets. In other words, no domestic intermediary is involved. In direct exporting, an exporter must deal with a large number of foreign contacts, possibly one or more for each country the company enters. A direct exporting operation requires more expertise, management time, and financial resources than does indirect exporting, but it gives the company a greater degree of control over its distribution channels.

Independent Distributor versus Marketing Subsidiary. To handle the marketing of its products within its target market, the company must choose between relying solely on local independent distributors and establishing its own marketing

WORLD BEAT 9.1

Small Firms in Global Markets

DOMESTIC MARKETS often only offer a small portion of the total global market opportunity. Pacific World Corporation is a small, California-based private company with only thirty-five employees. A successful manufacturer of artificial fingernails and nail care products, the company began exporting its products in 1992. In 1995, the company conducted an evaluation of the world market for nail care products and developed a detailed strategic export plan. The company's Nailene brand is one of the most widely distributed artificial nail care brands in the world.

With exports representing 25 percent of its sales, Pacific World has grown its sales and profits through the development of a clear export strategy. The key element of the strategy is the selection of high-quality distributors or agents in the targeted export countries. For example, in 2004, Pacific World introduced Eyelene Long Wearing Eyelashes, with a self-adhesive technology, in Canada. The new lashes were introduced to the market through Trilogy Brand Management, Pacific World's distributor in Canada.

According to Joel Carden, senior vice president of sales and category management, Pacific World has been successful because the company focuses on end consumer needs as well as differentiation for its retail customers. Distributors and agents in export markets are able to communicate the points of differentiation for their retailers. The company believes that the continued growth of global exports depends on the maintenance of the long-term partnerships it has with the distributors and agents. Although the use of distributors and agents as export partners saves considerable investment costs, management needs a clear strategy and must attend to these important relationships.

Sources: "Turning the Corner on Export Profits," *World Trade*, April 1999, pp. 36–40; "Key to Access Is Value," *Drug Store News*, February 2004, p. 10.; Don Mills, "New Nail Art Launches in Canada," *Cosmetics*, May 2004, p. 34.

---

subsidiary. In making this choice, the company must consider costs, control, and legal restrictions.

An independent distributor earns a margin on the selling price of the products. Although using an independent distributor entails no direct cost to the exporter, the margin the distributor earns represents an opportunity that is lost to the exporter. By switching to a sales subsidiary to carry out the distributor's tasks, the exporter can keep the margin previously paid to the distributor. For example, say a manufacturer of electronic machinery exports products priced at $7,500 each (at the factory in Boston). With airfreight, tariffs, and taxes added, the product's landed costs amount to $9,000. An independent distributor will have to price the products at $13,500 to earn a desired gross margin of 33⅓ percent, or $4,500 per machine.

Alternatively, the exporter can set up a wholly owned marketing subsidiary, in this case consisting of a manager, a sales manager, several sales agents, clerical staff, a warehousing operation, and the rental of both an office and a warehouse location. If the total estimated cost of these arrangements is $450,000 annually, the firm can break even at sales of one hundred machines.

With increasing volume, the incentive to start a marketing subsidiary grows. On the other hand, if the anticipated sales volume is small, using the independent distributor will be more efficient because sales are channeled through a distributor who is maintaining the necessary staff for several product lines.

Firms marketing products that require the development of special skills or special working relationships with customers tend to have their own marketing subsidiaries. This way the company may better control the delivery of after-sale service. If the firm has definite ideas about the correct way to price and promote its products, it may wish to establish a marketing subsidiary as well. The subsidiary could then implement the full strategy for the marketing mix, such as setting prices, developing advertising programs, and choosing media.

Still, a commitment to a marketing subsidiary should not be made without careful evaluation of all the costs involved. The operation of a subsidiary adds a new dimension to a company's international marketing operation. It requires a financial commitment in a foreign country, primarily for the financing of accounts receivable and inventory. Also, the operation of a marketing subsidiary entails a number of general administrative expenses that are essentially fixed in nature. The size of the available market in a country will often determine the appropriate market entry strategy. For example, Duckworth and Kent, the world's leading manufacturer of titanium ophthalmic surgery instruments, located in the United Kingdom, has a marketing subsidiary in the United States, its largest market, but uses distributors in most other markets.[5]

Firms may also face government restrictions on the use of wholly owned marketing subsidiaries. Although these constraints are declining with trade liberalization, they persist in some developing countries such as Saudi Arabia. Exporters to Saudi Arabia have traditionally been required to use Saudi agents or establish a marketing subsidiary with a Saudi partner.

Cooperating for Export. Companies that compete against each other in their domestic market may sometimes unite to address export markets. Brazil's Ministry of Development, Industry and Foreign Trade promotes such **export consortiums** wherein companies unite to share the logistical and promotion costs of entering foreign markets. Brazil's two largest frozen meat processors have formed a consortium to target Russia and selected countries in Africa, the Middle East, and the Caribbean. These markets currently account for less than 3 percent of the exports of either firm. However, they expect their consortium, BRF Trading Company, to sell about $150 million in these markets in the first year of operation. It is very unlikely that Brazilian antitrust law would allow such cooperation in the domestic market, but governments often encourage it in export markets.[6]

Export cooperation can also occur among small and medium-sized enterprises (SMEs). One study of exporter SMEs in the Jutland peninsula of Denmark revealed that 83 percent cooperated with other firms in the same industrial sector. For example, a manufacturer of windmills exported to California purchased the motors from another local SME. Firms in the textile and clothing sector mounted mutual exhibits at trade fairs. Manufacturers of wooden furniture might contribute different products—a desk, chair, or bookshelf—to a commonly marketed export suite. The success of these smaller ventures in competitive export markets can be attributed in part to this sort of cooperation.[7]

> **Export consortium** a group of companies that agrees to share the logistical and promotional costs of exporting to foreign markets

Exporting and the Internet. The Internet has greatly increased the ability of firms to export directly. The impact has been felt by SMEs as well as larger multinationals. In 1987, SMEs accounted for about one-quarter of total U.S. exports. By 2001, this figure had risen to about one-third. The Internet can be credited with supporting this trend. SMEs can take advantage of virtual trade missions, videoconferencing, and online ordering. They can reach markets with daily communication and advertising without the need to send full-time sales-people into the field or to employ traditional export management companies.[8] For example, EBags, an online seller of luggage, handbags, and shoes located in Denver, Colorado, has opened a U.K. website (www.ebags.co.uk), and plans a French website in 2006, to capitalize on the untapped international market.[9]

Exporters using the Internet as an entry option can face language problems, as well as a number of fulfillment challenges. These challenges include cross-border issues involved with completing a sale, such as shipping the product, collecting funds, and providing after-sale service to customers all over the world. New export management consultants have arisen to help with a number of these problems. One such company, Next Linx, was founded by Rajiv Uppal, an Indian-born engineer working in the United States. Uppal realized that new e-exporters still needed to know that their product would be hit with an education tax in Pakistan or that the same product would be subject to state tariffs as well as a national tariff in Brazil. Exporters of wine to the European Union would face the EU's 132 different categories of wine, each with its own tariff schedule. The Next Linx system was designed to calculate import duties, taxes, and shipping costs. It determines whether a customer's product needs an export license and whether the importer is located in an embargoed country.[10] It then prints all relevant shipment documentation at a cost of as little as $10 per order. A number of competitors have entered this market as well. A key to competitiveness is the ability of any online export consultant to stay alert to the constant regulatory and logistics changes that affect its customers.

FOREIGN PRODUCTION AS AN ENTRY STRATEGY

Licensing

With licensing, a company assigns the right to a copyright or patent (which protects a product, technology, or process) and/or a trademark (which protects a product name) to another company for a fee or royalty. Proprietary information, or trade secrets not protected by patents, can also be licensed. The foreign company, or licensee, gains the right to exploit the patent or trademark commercially on either an exclusive (the sole right to sell in a certain geographic region) or a nonexclusive basis.

Sometimes the licensee initiates the contract. Infopro, the largest information-technology media group in Taiwan, specializes in publishing Chinese-language editions of American publications under license. It recently entered a licensing agreement with the Harvard Business School to produce a Chinese version of the prestigious management journal *Harvard Business Review*. The new *Infopro Harvard Business Review* is designed to have about 70 percent of its content translated from the original American text, supplemented with locally researched articles on business and management techniques.[11]

Licenses are signed for a variety of time periods. Depending on the investment needed to enter the market, the foreign licensee may insist on a longer licensing period to recover the initial investment. Typically, the licensee makes all the necessary capital investments (machinery, inventory, etc.) and markets the products in the assigned sales territories, which may consist of one or several countries. Licensing agreements are subject to negotiation and tend to vary considerably from company to company and from industry to industry.

Reasons for Licensing. Licensing can be very attractive for some companies; an example is Everlast Worldwide Inc. Since 1910 Everlast has been the preeminent brand in the world of boxing equipment. Its products have been used for training and professional fights by leading figures in the sport. Everlast's licensed products generate over $200 million in retail sales each year, which prompted the company to create a new management position: senior vice president of global licensing.[12]

Companies use licensing for many reasons. A company may not have the knowledge or the time to engage more actively in international marketing. If so, it can still realize income from foreign markets by using licensees. Licensing may also be employed for less attractive foreign markets, allowing the firm's scarce managerial resources to be concentrated on more lucrative markets. The market potential of the target country may be too small to support a new manufacturing or marketing operation. A licensee may have the option of adding the licensed product to an ongoing operation, thereby reducing the need for a large investment in new fixed assets. Finally, a company may not have sufficient capital to be able to expand into multiple markets. Using licensing as a method of market entry, a company can gain market presence without making an equity investment.

In some countries where the political or economic situation appears uncertain, a licensing agreement may avoid the potential risk associated with investing in fixed facilities. Both commercial and political risks are absorbed by the licensee. In other countries, governments favor the granting of licenses to independent local manufacturers as a means of building up a local industry. In such cases, a foreign manufacturer may prefer to team up with a capable licensee despite a large market size, because other forms of entry may not be possible.

Licensing can also help global firms enter difficult markets. Roche continues to expand in the Japanese pharmaceutical market through licensing its products with Chugai Pharmaceuticals. The Japanese market is difficult to penetrate without knowledge of the drug approval process and access to the distribution channels. Chugai Pharmaceuticals has licensed two cancer drugs and a hepatitis drug from Roche. The licensing approach for Roche also speeds up the market entry process for Roche, giving them fast access to the second-largest pharmaceutical market in the world.[13]

Disadvantages of Licensing. A major disadvantage of licensing is the company's substantial dependence on the local licensee to produce revenues and thus royalties. **Royalties** are usually paid based on a percentage of sales volume. Once a license is granted, royalties are paid only if the licensee is capable of performing an effective marketing job. Because the local company's marketing skills may be less developed, revenues from licensing may suffer accordingly. Although there is a great variation from one industry to another, licensing fees

Royalties payments by a licensee to a licensor in exchange for the right to produce and market the licensor's product or service within a certain region

in general are substantially lower than the profits that can be made through exporting or local manufacturing. Depending on the product, licensing fees may range anywhere between 1 percent and 20 percent of sales, 3 to 5 percent being more typical for industrial products.

Ironically, if a local licensee is too successful, an international firm may reconsider the wisdom of licensing. More direct participation in a successful market can reap higher rewards in profits than mere licensing fees. Such a situation arose between Mexico's Televisa and Los Angeles–based Univision. Televisa is the world's largest producer of Spanish-language television programming. Univision is the leader in the rapidly growing U.S. Hispanic media market. Hispanics account for 12 percent of the U.S. population, and Univision has captured 80 percent of Hispanic television viewers. Under a licensing agreement dating from the early 1990s, Univision received the right of first refusal on Televisa's programming. Most of Univision's programming is from Televisa, but the Mexican company receives only 9 percent of Univision's advertising revenue. In 2001, Televisa proposed a partial merger with its U.S. licensee, because U.S. law forbids foreign entities to own more than 25 percent of a U.S. broadcaster. Although Univision was not enthusiastic about the idea, Televisa threatened to look for new partners if its offer was not considered.[14]

Some licensing contracts include provisions for the licenser to increase its participation if it eventually wishes to do so. Hutchinson Whampoa Ltd. of Hong Kong announced that it was forming a new company that would license Priceline's patented bidding system to allow consumers to purchase tickets online. The service would be targeted at Hong Kong, Singapore, and Taiwan, with a later rollout to other Asian countries. As part of the arrangement, Priceline would be given the option of eventually buying up to 50 percent of the new company.[15]

Another potential disadvantage of licensing is the uncertainty of product quality. A foreign company's image may suffer if a local licensee markets a product of substandard quality. For this reason, firms often seek licensees based on their production knowledge and reputation for quality. For example, U.S.-based Miller Brewing Company recently decided to expand into the French and Dutch markets using a Dutch licensee. The licensee is responsible for the production and marketing of Miller's largest international brand, Miller's Genuine Draft. It is essential that the licensee maintain Miller's quality standards in these important markets. Therefore, Miller selected a licensee well known as a quality brewer.[16] Even when a quality licensee is located, however, ensuring uniform quality requires the licenser to provide additional resources that may reduce the profitability of the licensing activity.

Licensing will also require a certain commitment of management time and resources. Licensees may need to be trained. Appropriate records must be kept, and licenser audits must be conducted. Serious consideration must be given to problems that could arise. In case of disagreements between licenser and licensee, there must be provisions for dispute resolution. In the context of which national law will the contract be interpreted? How and in which country will arbitration take place? What are the conditions for termination of the licensing contract?

The possibility of nurturing a potential competitor is viewed by many companies as a final disadvantage of licensing. Licenses are usually limited to a specific time period. Licensees can use similar technology independently after the license has expired and can, therefore, turn into a competitor. This is less of a concern if the licensed technology changes quickly or if a valuable brand name is involved. Of course, firms must be careful that they—and not their licensee— hold the trademark to their brand in each national market.

Franchising

Franchising is a special form of licensing in which the franchiser makes a total marketing program available, including the brand name, logo, products, and method of operation. Usually, the franchise agreement is more comprehensive than a regular licensing agreement, inasmuch as the total operation of the franchisee is prescribed.

According to the International Franchise Association, there are about 15,000 franchising companies worldwide. The Internet has had a profound impact on the industry and has helped fuel its recent growth. Franchisers use websites to communicate with current franchisees as well as to recruit new ones. Dot-com companies have also joined the ranks of franchisers.[17]

Numerous companies that successfully exploited franchising in their home market are exploiting opportunities abroad. Among these companies are McDonald's, Kentucky Fried Chicken (KFC), Burger King, and other U.S. fast-food chains with operations in Latin America, Asia, Europe, and the Middle East. About 80 percent of all McDonald's restaurants are franchised, and the firm operates in more than 30,000 restaurants in 119 countries serving 47 million customers each day.[18] Service companies such as Holiday Inn, Hertz, and Manpower have also successfully used franchising to enter foreign markets.

The United States is home to the greatest number of franchisers. As of 2001, there were 2,200 franchise systems in operation in the United States, compared to 890 in Japan, 450 in Australia, and 268 in Malaysia. Franchising accounts for about 40 percent of retail sales in the United States, compared to about 5 percent in Malaysia.[19] In China, the percentage drops to only 2 percent.[20]

However, growth rates for franchising are higher in many non-U.S. markets. In recent years, the market in the United States has only grown 5 to 10 percent, compared to about 15 percent in Europe and 20 to 25 percent in Latin America.[21]

In 1997, there were only 30 franchising operations in Venezuela and 300 retail outlets. These figures grew to 1,900 franchising operations and 18,000 retail outlets by 2001, making Venezuela the third-largest franchise country in Latin America, after Brazil and Mexico. Poor economic conditions in the country probably contributed to the industry's growth as many laid-off professionals became franchisees. Many even became franchisers themselves, including an economics professor who began a franchise chain of coconut drink kiosks. Such local chains have begun to challenge the dominance of the multinational franchisers. In 1997, 70 percent of franchisers operating in Venezuela were foreign. By 2001, only 45 percent were foreign.[22]

In fact, franchisers of many national origins have entered international markets. Singapore-based Informatics Holdings Inc. franchises computer training schools in Asia. Interbrew franchises its Belgium Beer Café. The Japanese company Yohinoy D&C has opened ninety-one stores in California that sell *gydun,*

Master franchises franchises that include exclusive rights to market within a whole city or country

The International Franchise Association gives tips on how to avoid franchising pitfalls. The U.S. Federal Trade Commission's website lists complaints against franchisers. Check out these and other franchise links on our website (college.hmco.com/business/).

a seasoned beef and rice dish. Even an Egyptian college student who began exporting hookahs, Egypt's traditional water pipes, to the United States has recently branched into franchising. He supplies fifty accounts with a complete hookah system for a water pipe café, including equipment, staff training, and management advice.[23]

Many franchisees worldwide are individual entrepreneurs. In some countries, companies or wealthy individuals buy **master franchises** that give them exclusive rights to a whole city or even a whole country. Master franchisees have traditionally been sophisticated partners of established multinational franchise chains. With its rapid global growth, however, the franchising industry has been hit with numerous complaints and has even been plagued by fraud in the past few years. One individual on the Internet actually claimed his government had privatized its Consumer Protection Agency, for which he was selling local franchises.[24] As a result of the surge in complaints, many countries are tightening their franchising laws to help protect franchisees.

Local Manufacturing

Another widely practiced form of market entry is the local manufacturing of a company's products. Many companies find it advantageous to manufacture in the host market instead of supplying that market with products made elsewhere. Sometimes local production represents a greater commitment to a market. Numerous factors, such as local costs, market size, tariffs, labor laws, and political considerations, may affect a choice to manufacture locally. The actual type of local production depends on the arrangements made. It may be contract manufacturing, assembly, or fully integrated production.

Contract Manufacturing. Under contract manufacturing, a company arranges to have its products manufactured by an independent local company on a contractual basis. The local manufacturer's responsibility is restricted to production. The local producer manufactures in accordance with orders from the international firm. The products are then turned over to the international company, which assumes the marketing responsibility for sales, promotion, and distribution. In a way, the international company "rents" the production capacity of the local firm to avoid establishing its own plant and to circumvent barriers that prevent the import of its products.

Typically, contract manufacturing is chosen for countries with a low-volume market potential combined with high tariff protection. In such situations, local production appears advantageous to avoid high tariffs, but the local market does not support the volume necessary to justify the building of a single plant. These conditions tend to exist in the smaller countries of Central America, Africa, and Asia. Contract manufacturing is also employed where the production technology involved is widely available. Otherwise, contract manufacturers would not have the necessary know-how. If research and development and/or marketing are of crucial importance in the success of the product, then contract manufacturing can be an attractive option, especially when excess capacity in an industry makes manufacturing the least profitable part of the product's value chain. However, contract manufacturing is viable only when an appropriate local manufacturer can be located. For example, Finnish tire manufacturer

Nokian Tyres contracted with Matador AS of Slovakia to produce up to 500,000 tires in 2005, to serve the European car market.[25]

Assembly. By moving to an assembly operation, the international firm locates a portion of the manufacturing process in the foreign country. Typically, assembly consists only of the last stages of manufacturing and depends on a ready supply of components or manufactured parts to be shipped in from another country. (In the chemical and pharmaceutical industry, this latter stage is referred to as **compounding**.) Assembly usually involves the heavy use of labor rather than extensive investment in capital outlays or equipment. Sometimes host governments force firms to establish assembly operations either by banning the import of fully assembled products or by charging excessive tariffs on them.

Compounding a term referring to the last stages of manufacturing in the chemical and pharmaceutical industries

Motor vehicle manufacturers have made extensive use of assembly operations in numerous countries. General Motors has maintained major integrated production units only in the United States, Germany, the United Kingdom, Brazil, and Australia. In many other countries, disassembled vehicles arrive at assembly operations that produce the final product on the spot. BMW operates assembly plants in Indonesia, Malaysia, Thailand, the Philippines, and Vietnam. BMW reports that a demand of 1,500 cars per year can justify the cost of a local assembly plant. Local assembly plants let BMW test the waters and expand into markets where tariffs and other local hurdles cannot be overcome with an export strategy of shipping completed cars to these markets.[26]

Full-Scale Integrated Production. Establishing a fully integrated local production unit is the greatest commitment a company can make for a foreign market. Building a plant involves a substantial capital outlay. Companies do so only where demand appears ensured. International companies can have any number of reasons for establishing factories in foreign countries. These reasons are related primarily to market demand or cost considerations. Often, the main reason is to take advantage of lower costs in a country, thus providing a better basis for competing with local firms or other foreign companies already present. Also, high transportation costs and tariffs may make imported goods noncompetitive.

Although most manufacturing tends to shift from developed to developing countries, Mexican firms are moving production to the United States. The DuPont Company sold three plants to Alfa SA. Alfa is refitting the former textile plants to produce plastics used in beverage containers and frozen-food trays. Since 1994 Mexico has moved from number thirty-three to the sixth-largest investor in the United States (in 2004). The Alfa case illustrates reasons why U.S. manufacturing looks good to Mexican firms:

▶ Though production costs are higher in the United States, production in Mexico would result in longer delivery times to the U.S. market.

▶ The plants were available relatively cheap as U.S. firms withdraw from older, lower technology industries.

▶ Local governments offered tax and job-creation credits—in this case, $1 million.

▶ Alfa was able to renegotiate contracts with the workforce, decreasing wages by up to 25 percent in some cases.[27]

▶ *Establishing Local Operations to Gain or Defend Market Position.* Some companies build a plant to gain new business and customers. Local production can represent a strong commitment to a market and is often the only way to convince clients to switch suppliers. This is of particular importance in industrial markets, where service and reliability of supply are main factors in the choice of product or supplier. In some developing countries, establishing local operations may be the only way to enter a local market, although this requirement is becoming more rare with the spread of trade liberalization and the impact of the World Trade Organization.

At other times, companies establish production abroad to protect markets already built through exporting. Such markets can be threatened by protectionist government policies or by relative changes in currency exchange rates. In the late 1980s, the surge in market share of imported Japanese cars prompted the United States to threaten Japan with import quotas if it didn't place voluntary restrictions on car exports to the United States. Also, the Japanese yen had begun to appreciate against the dollar, making Japanese imports more expensive. In response to these threats, Japanese car manufacturers began to build factories in the United States to protect their market share. In 1982, Honda became the first Japanese car manufacturer to set up production in the United States. By 1993, Japanese car manufacturers produced more cars in the United States than they exported there from Japan. Japan's major producers are Toyota, Honda, Nissan, Mitsubishi, Mazda, and Suzuki.

Following an established customer can also be a reason for setting up plants abroad. In many industries, important suppliers want to nurture a relationship by establishing new offices near customer locations. When customers move into new markets elsewhere, suppliers move, too. Deutsch Advertising, a North America advertising firm, had worked with Novartis since 2002 on the antifungal drug Lamisil. Now Deutsch is following Novatis into Italy, Germany, the United Kingdom, and Switzerland.[28]

▶ *Shifting Production Abroad to Save Costs.* Firms can shift production abroad to save costs in order to be competitive in the host market. When Mercedes-Benz was looking at new opportunities in the automotive market, the company targeted the luxury sports utility vehicle segment. In the United States, its major market, the company was suffering a 30 percent cost disadvantage against major Japanese and U.S. competitors in this segment. Despite the fact that the company had never before produced cars outside Germany, Mercedes-Benz decided to locate a new factory to produce such vehicles in the United States, where total labor, components, and shipping costs were among the lowest in the developed world.[29]

Some products may be too costly to transport long distances, and this makes them poor candidates for export. Fresh orange juice is one such product. Brazil is currently the top producer of orange juice in the world, whereas the United States consumes 40 percent of all orange juice. The U.S. market has a strong demand for fresh, not-from-concentrate orange juice that sells for higher prices. This fresh product is particularly costly to ship because it consists mainly of water.[30] During the 1990s, Brazilian orange juice firms bought land to develop orange groves in Florida. By 2001, multinationals with Brazilian ties accounted for about half of Florida's orange juice industry.[31]

Sometimes, international firms with plants in Taiwan, Malaysia, Thailand, and other foreign countries may have little intention of penetrating these markets with the help of their new factories. Instead, they locate abroad to take advantage of favorable conditions that reduce the manufacturing costs of products that are sold elsewhere. This strategy has been employed by many U.S. companies in the electronics industry and has more recently been adopted by Japanese and European firms as well. Morinaga, Japan's leading dairy company, built a new powdered-milk plant in China not so much to enter the Chinese market as to establish a low-cost base from which to capture share in other Asian markets. Such decisions of a sourcing or production nature are not necessarily tied to a company's market entry strategy but may have important implications for its global competitiveness.

Manufacturing and Intrafirm Licensing. Although international licensing arrangements were originally designed as an alternative for firms manufacturing abroad, today they are sometimes used in conjunction with a firm's own manufacturing operations. A firm may license its trademark or technology to its own manufacturing subsidiary if taxes on royalties are less than taxes on repatriated profits. Such an arrangement might also be employed when a subsidiary is not wholly owned but, rather, shared with a local partner. A licensing contract with its own joint venture can give an international firm a greater and more guaranteed payback on its contribution to the venture.

OWNERSHIP STRATEGIES

As we have noted, companies investing in foreign markets also face ownership decisions. Do they want to establish a wholly owned subsidiary or a joint venture? Alternatively, they may decide to explore longer-term contractual relationships, or alliances.

Wholly Owned Subsidiaries

Wholly owned subsidiaries are operations in a host country that are fully owned by a foreign parent firm. They can involve marketing, assembly, or full-scale integrated production operations. Firms must have the necessary capital investment and must be committed to devoting the management time necessary to establish and run an overseas operation on their own. There are, of course, advantages to this entry option. The firm has a free hand to establish the strategy for the subsidiary. It is also able to keep all the profits of the subsidiary and need not share them with partners. For these reasons, national markets that are more strategically important may be good candidates for a wholly owned subsidiary. Such a subsidiary can also be more easily integrated into a global network. For example, a parent can allot the U.S. export market to its wholly owned subsidiary in Taiwan. If relative production and transportation costs change, however, the firm can take the U.S. market away from the Taiwanese subsidiary and give that market to its wholly owned Mexican subsidiary. There would be no local Taiwanese partner to oppose this move.

If firms do not have the resources to invest in a wholly owned subsidiary, or if host government restrictions disallow them, companies can consider entering a market with a joint venture or other alliance partner.

Joint Ventures

Under a joint venture arrangement, the foreign company invites an outside partner to share stock ownership in the new unit. Traditionally, the other partner has been a local firm or individual located in the host market. The particular equity participation of the partners may vary, with some companies accepting either a minority or a majority position. In most cases, international firms prefer wholly owned subsidiaries for reasons of control; once a joint venture partner secures part of the operation, the international firm can no longer function independently. This sometimes leads to inefficiencies and disputes over responsibility for the venture. If an international firm has strictly defined operating procedures for budgeting, planning, manufacturing, and marketing, getting the joint venture to accept the same methods of operation may be difficult. Problems may also arise when the partner wants to maximize dividend payout instead of reinvestment, or when the capital of the venture has to be increased and one side is unable to raise the required funds. Experience has shown that joint ventures can be successful if the partners share the same goals and if one partner accepts primary responsibility for operational matters.

Reasons for Entering into Joint Ventures. Despite the potential for problems, joint ventures are common because they offer important advantages to the foreign firm. Sometimes the partner is an important customer who is willing

Wal-Mart internationalized by using different ownership strategies in different countries. Market entry by acquisition has increasingly become the most common mode of entry, however.

to contract for a portion of the new unit's output in return for an equity participation. In markets where host governments disallow wholly owned investments, joint ventures with a local partner may be the only alternative. For example, the Vietnamese government has steered a number of multi-national companies into joint ventures with local partners, many of whom do not provide capital contributions equal to their equity shares in these ventures.[32]

If a firm is trying to enter many foreign markets quickly, joint ventures may help leverage scarce capital and managerial resources. By bringing in a partner, the company can share the business and political risks for a new venture. Furthermore, the partner may have important skills or contacts of value to the international firm. In some cases, the partner may provide local manufacturing or excellent government or distribution contacts. Even in e-marketing, an international joint venture partner can sometimes be advisable. German-based e-financialdepot.com Inc. signed a joint venture with EqTechnologies Inc. (EQTI) to launch its financial services—such as marketing and trading technologies and online mortgage and insurance services—in the Middle East and Africa. EQTI, a management consulting firm, focuses on taking successful U.S. and European high-tech and Internet companies into Africa and the Middle East. It was chosen for its excellent connections in the region.[33]

Many international firms have entered Japan via joint ventures. During the 1960s and 1970s, the Japanese market was viewed as a difficult environment, much different from other industrialized markets. Government regulations tightly controlled equity participation in ventures. When McDonald's entered Japan in 1971, it did so in a joint venture with Fujita & Company, a trading company owned by private Japanese businessman Den Fujita. Fujita was adept at locating real estate and obtaining government permits for new outlets. He also insisted on some practices that differed from the typical U.S. approach of McDonald's, such as opening the first store in the fashionable Ginza shopping district rather than going to a suburban location.[34] The chain grew enormously; just 27 years after its entry into the market, McDonald's has 2,400 restaurants operating in Japan, with sales of more than $3 billion. Each year the chain adds 400 to 500 new restaurants.[35]

Gillette, the U.S. razor blade manufacturer, has extensive experience with joint ventures in China. In the early 1980s, the company formed its first, small joint venture, called Shenmei Daily Use Products, with Chinese authorities in a province northeast of Beijing. Then a second joint venture was formed with the Shanghai Razor Blade Factory, and Gillette obtained 70 percent ownership and management control.[36] The Shanghai plant evolved into Asia's largest blade plant. Gillette's joint venture now controls 80 percent of China's $51 million razor blade market.[37]

With the liberalization of industry and trade in Eastern Europe and Russia over the past few years, many international firms have pursued joint ventures in those countries. Originally, Western firms were not allowed to own any stock, capital, or real estate. Restrictions on foreign investments have now been lifted in many countries, and foreign firms are allowed to start new companies with full ownership. However, because of the difficulties of operating in these markets, many foreign firms continue to prefer joint ventures with local partners. For example, Scottish & Newcastle, a U.K. brewing company, established a joint venture with the Baltic Beverages to serve Russia, Kazakhstan, and the other Baltic countries. Sales rose 18 percent in 2004.[38]

Of course, to enter into a joint venture, an international firm must find an available partner. Table 9.1 gives some indication why local partners seek to establish joint ventures with international firms. A survey of Mexican companies identified access to technology and association with recognized international brands as the two most often cited reasons why local firms sought U.S. partners. In liberalizing markets such as Mexico, some firms seek international ties to become more competitive and thus block new competitors from entering their previously protected markets. Others go so far as to try to co-opt potential competitors by directly partnering with them.

Joint Venture Divorce: A Constant Danger. Not all joint ventures are successful or fulfill their partners' expectations. Various studies have placed the instability rates of joint ventures at between 25 and 75 percent.[39] There are a number of reasons for ending a joint venture. Sometimes the regulations that force foreign firms to take local partners are rescinded. When China first opened to foreign investment, foreign firms were required to partner with Chinese enterprises. Later, China began considering wholly owned foreign investments. As a result,

TABLE 9.1 WHAT MOTIVATES MEXICAN FIRMS TO SEEK U.S. PARTNERS?

MOTIVATION	PERCENTAGE OF RESPONDENTS
Access to technology	71
Access to recognized brand	56
Product/service knowledge of partner	47
Access to products and services	40
Supplier access	33
Access to new products/market areas	27
Short-term credit	24
Access to raw materials	22
Customer access	22
Reduce costs	22
Block competitors	20
Capital access	18
Access to marketing infrastructure	16
Geographic market access	16
Reduce risks	13
Co-opt competitor	13
Geographic market knowledge of partner	13
Access to long-term credit	11

SOURCE: Reprinted from *The Columbia Journal of World Business,* Winter 1995, Kate Gillespie and Hildy J. Teegen, "Market Liberalization and International Alliance Formation: The Mexican Paradigm," p. 63. Copyright © 1995, with permission from Elsevier.

joint ventures are no longer the most common mode of entry into China,[40] and many foreign partners who entered China early now seek exclusive ownership of their Chinese joint ventures. When joint ventures are used to enter many international markets relatively cheaply and quickly, a parent firm may wish later to increase its stake in the venture or even reclaim full control when financial resources are more readily available. Starbucks began its international expansion in 1996 and established 1,500 coffeehouses in countries outside North America within 10 years.[41] In some markets, Starbucks stores operate under joint venture agreements in which the company holds about 20 percent. The company plans eventually to increase this stake to at least 50 percent.[42]

Sometimes the choice of partner turns out to be less than ideal. Cristal, a U.K.-based food hygiene consultancy, advises hotels, food processing plants, and restaurants around the world. Joint ventures have played an important part in the firm's international expansion. In Egypt, however, Cristal chose a well-established partner with expertise in engineering rather than in tourism. Trying to learn the tourism industry and the food hygiene industry in a short time proved overwhelming. Cristal had to buy back shares from the partner and take over management of the venture.[43]

At times, problems can arise between parents over the strategic direction of the joint venture. Brasil Telecom is a joint venture between Telecom Italia and Opportunity, a local Brazilian investment company. Despite being one of Brazil's largest fixed-line telecommunications companies, Brasil Telecom found itself headed for arbitration in London when its two parents became deadlocked over expansion options. The Italian parent wanted to move quickly into mobile telephone operations. Opportunity wanted the joint venture to pursue what it thought were more profitable businesses, such as acting as an Internet service provider. The relationship between the parent companies became increasingly hostile, and both wished to take full control of the joint venture.[44]

In some cases, however, joint venture divorce can be amiable. Teijin of Japan dissolved its joint venture with U.S.-based Molecular Simulations (MSI), a major global player in computerized chemistry. The negotiated settlement specified that Teijin would receive $10 million from Pharmacopeia, the company that had since acquired MSI. Teijin was willing to sell its share in the joint venture because it had already accomplished its objective—gaining adequate expertise in computerized chemistry through the venture.[45]

Even when one parent agrees to sell its stake in the venture, buying out partners can be expensive. Glaxo, the large U.K.-based pharmaceutical company, entered Japan via a joint venture in 1994. Until recently, a local partner in Japan was considered necessary for an international company in the medical field, because Japan's health culture is unique. (Among other things, Japanese doctors both prescribe and sell drugs.) However, Glaxo was dissatisfied with its performance in Japan, the world's second-largest pharmaceuticals market. Its market share amounted to only 2 percent, compared to 5 percent worldwide. Glaxo decided to assume full control and bought back the other half of its joint venture for almost $600 million.[46]

It is always wise to have a "prenuptial agreement." Yet a surprising number of joint venture agreements fail to acknowledge the possibility of joint venture dissolution. In 1999, AT&T and British Telecom formed a joint venture, Concert,

WORLD BEAT 9.2

Going It Alone in Overseas Markets

COMPANIES WANTING TO ENTER NEW MARKETS can form a joint venture with a local partner who has knowledge and access to the target country. However, the number of joint ventures for overseas affiliates of U.S. firms decreased from 29 percent in 1982 to 20 percent in 1997, which is the last year that these statistics were available. During the same time period, the number of wholly owned subsidiaries for U.S. firms increased from 72 to 80 percent.

In the past, a number of factors contributed to the use of joint ventures by U.S. firms. First, many developing countries required joint ventures with significant local ownership. Second, information about international opportunities and operating conditions was less accessible; therefore, companies used local joint venture partners to reduce the perceived risk of entering an unknown country. Third, in many markets there were limited numbers of locals who had the education or expertise to work for a foreign company, and joint venture partners served as good sources for managerial talent. Today, none of these factors pose the problems they did in the past.

In addition, conflicts are common between U.S. firms and their local joint venture partners. Local partners tend to be focused on their local markets and therefore prefer investments in the local economy, whereas U.S. firms increasingly want to move manufacturing to whichever country offers the most attractive cost structure. Furthermore, joint ventures require sharing the profits of a venture, and many U.S. firms prefer to go it alone rather than share potential profits. For example, rather than form joint ventures with existing auction websites, eBay would rather purchase the largest domestic auction website in the target country or start a new site from scratch. eBay buys the leading auction website, when there is one, to get immediate access to the active customers as well as to eliminate a local competitor.

Sources: Mihir A. Desai, C. Fritz Foley, and James R. Hines, Jr., "The Cost of Shared Ownership: Evidence from International Joint Ventures," *Journal of Financial Economics* 73, no. 2 (August 2004), pp. 323–374; Margaret Popper, "Flying Solo Overseas," *Business Week*, May 20, 2002, p. 28; and Erick Schonfeld, "The World According to Ebay," *Business 2.0* (January/February 2005), pp. 765–782.

to serve large multinational business customers. A former AT&T executive involved in the negotiations claims that the absence of an exit agreement was deliberate. It was intended to make sure both companies remained committed to the partnership. Two years later, however, the venture was losing $210 million a quarter and was judged a failure by both parents. Without an exit agreement, there was no simple way to determine how Concert's assets—including 75,000 kilometers of fiber optic cable—would be divided.[47]

Strategic Alliances

A more recent phenomenon is the development of a range of strategic alliances. Alliances encompass any relationship between firms that exceeds a simple sales transaction but stops short of a full-scale merger. Thus, the traditional joint venture between a multinational corporation (MNC) and a local company is a form of alliance. So is a contract manufacturing or licensing agreement.

However, the term **strategic alliance** is commonly used to denote an alliance involving two or more firms in which each partner brings a particular skill or resource—usually, they are complementary. By joining forces, each firm expects to profit from the other's experience. Typically, strategic alliances involve technology development, production, or distribution. The number of strategic alliances has been driven by the increased globalization of firms. As firms expand into multiple countries, they often use strategic alliances to speed up entry into multiple markets as well as to gain access to assets and technologies that may be specific to certain countries.[48]

Technology-based Alliances. Many alliances are focused on technology and the sharing of research and development expertise and findings. The most commonly cited reasons for entering these technology-based alliances are access to markets, exploitation of complementary technology, and a need to reduce the time it takes to bring an innovation to market.

One of the companies most experienced with technological alliances is Toshiba, a major Japanese electronics company. The company's first technological tie-ups go back to the beginning of this century, when it contracted to make lightbulb filaments for U.S.-based General Electric. The company has since engaged in alliances with many leading international companies, many of whom are competitors. For example, IBM, Sony, and Toshiba joined forces to create the Cell Alliance, which created the Cell chip that was launched in February 2005 to compete with chips by Intel. Sony will use the chip in PlayStation 3, Toshiba will use it in digital television sets, and IBM will use it in computer servers and workstations.[49]

French carmaker Peugot has bucked the industrywide trend toward global mergers and has become one of the most profitable carmakers outside Japan. Management contends that the key to its success has been producing innovative cars in quick succession and that mergers can slow down innovation if managers are struggling to integrate two companies. Instead, Peugot has relied on alliance partners to cut costs of developing new components—such as an alliance with Ford to develop diesel engines.[50]

Production-based Alliances. A large number of production-based alliances have been formed, particularly in the automobile industry. These alliances fall into two groups. First, there is the search for efficiency through component linkages that may include engines or other key components of a car. Second, companies have begun to share entire car models, either by developing them together or by producing them jointly. With development costs of a new-car-model generation now surpassing $2 billion, U.S. automobile manufacturers have been very active in creating global alliances with partners, primarily in Japan. Ford's major Japanese partner is Mazda, of which Ford owns a 25 percent equity share. The two firms have collaborated intensively, creating more than ten projects over the years.

Alliances have also been known to run into trouble when their respective partners changed strategic direction. Volvo of Sweden and Renault of France entered a far-reaching production alliance in 1990. The two companies agreed to a series of interlocking deals linking each other's truck and bus divisions. Separately, Renault bought 25 percent of Volvo's car operation and another 10

Strategic alliance an alliance involving two or more firms in which each partner contributes a particular skill or resource—usually complementary—to a venture

percent of Volvo Corporation. In return, Volvo acquired 20 percent of Renault with an option to purchase another 5 percent later on.

In 1993, both Volvo and Renault came to the conclusion that a full-scale merger was necessary. In the end, the deal did not go through because of resistance by Volvo shareholders and senior managers who saw increased profitability in Volvo's business with a decline in Renault's profitability. Following abandonment of the full merger, the two companies decided to unravel their existing cross-shareholdings, and many of the anticipated joint projects were shelved. The Volvo car business was acquired by Ford in 1998.[51] This shows that even two originally willing partners can have difficulties sustaining an alliance.

Distribution-based Alliances. Alliances with a special emphasis on distribution are becoming increasingly common. General Mills, a U.S.-based company marketing breakfast cereals, had long been number two in the United States, with some 27 percent market share, compared to Kellogg's 40 to 45 percent share. With no effective position outside the United States, the company entered into a global alliance with Nestlé of Switzerland. Forming Cereal Partners Worldwide (CPW), owned equally by the two companies, General Mills gained access to the local distribution and marketing skills of Nestlé in Europe, the Far East, and Latin America. In return, General Mills provided product technology and the experience it had acquired competing against Kellogg's. CPW was formed as a full business unit with responsibility for the entire world except the United States. In 2004, CPW reached sales of $1 billion and a market share outside the United States of 25 percent.[52]

The Future of Alliances. Although many older alliances were spawned by technology exchange and were contracted among manufacturing companies, some of the most innovative arrangements are signed by service firms. Many of these, however, have proved to be short-lived in a never-ending rearrangement between the world's leading players. This is particularly true of large telecommunications carriers. One alliance was WorldPartner, which included AT&T, the Japanese KDD, Singapore Telecom, and Unisource of Europe, itself a combination of several European firms. The alliance served about seven hundred international clients, in thirty-five countries. However, the alliance was effectively dissolved as a result of AT&T's move to link up with British Telecommunications.

No less active in forming and breaking international alliances are airlines. Some two hundred international airlines are or have been members of at least one alliance. These alliances allow airlines to offer fuller services and more extensive routes, as well as providing cost savings to the participating firms. For example, the Star Alliance of thirteen airlines has agreed to a standard set of specifications for either the Airbus A350 or the Boeing 7E7, which will result in a significant reduction in the inventory costs for replacement engines, brakes, avionics, and other replacement parts, which the Star Alliance member will share.[53]

Strategic alliances have typically been the domain of large companies, but SMEs are increasingly being encouraged to look for partnering opportunities. For example, the Productivity and Standards Board of Singapore united with the U.S. Chamber of Commerce to launch UspartnerSingapore, a business-matching initiative to bring together Singapore and U.S. SMEs. The project focuses on firms in the information technology, telecommunications, life sciences, franchise, and business services industries. Besides employing the Internet to match companies, the program offers market research and potential funding. The program aims at establishing at least forty successful alliances.[54]

Although many alliances have been forged in a large number of industries worldwide, it is not yet clear whether these alliances will actually become successful business ventures. Experience suggests that alliances with two equal partners are more difficult to manage than those with a dominant partner. Furthermore, many observers question the value of entering alliances with technological competitors. The challenge in making an alliance work lies in the creation of multiple layers of connections, or webs, that reach across the partner organizations.

Many strategic alliances fail. Perhaps more surprisingly, recent research shows that strategic alliances may continue in effect for years even after they have proven unviable. For example Global One, a three-way alliance between Deutsche Telekom, France Telecom, and Sprint was formed in 1994. Only in 2000, after 6 years of higher than expected losses, internal conflicts, and expert assessment that the alliance was a failure, did the partners dissolve the partnership. Research indicates that the high cost of terminating an alliance, high sunk costs, and high alliance visibility all contribute to a delay in dissolving failing alliances.[55]

ENTERING MARKETS THROUGH MERGERS AND ACQUISITIONS

International firms have always made acquisitions. However, the need to enter markets more quickly has made the acquisition route extremely attractive. This trend has probably been aided by the opening of many financial markets, making the acquisition of publicly traded companies much easier. Even unfriendly takeovers in foreign markets are now becoming increasingly common. The result: During the 1990s alone, cross-border mergers and acquisitions increased fivefold.[56]

By purchasing an established business, the firm eliminates the need to build manufacturing and distribution capabilities from scratch. Buying an established brand gives the firm immediate market presence and market share. South Africa Breweries (SAB) purchased Miller Beer from Philip Morris in 2002 for $3.4 billion., which gave them instant access to the U.S. market as well as the well-known brands of Miller Lite, Miller High Life, Miller Genuine Draft, and Milwaukee's Best. The acquisition also gave SAB a strong foothold as the second-largest brewer in the world to battle Anheuser Bush. SAB continued its expansion strategy with acquisitions in Italy, China, and Colombia.[57]

Acquisition is also an attractive strategy when a market is already dominated by established brands and saturated with competitors. New entrants would find such a market difficult to break into, and the addition of a totally new player might make the market even more competitive and unprofitable for all. eBay has translated its online auction business into thirty-one countries and expects revenue from international operations to exceed domestic revenues in 2005.[58] It also spent more than $1.6 billion on acquisitions, including $150 million to take full control of Eachnet in China.[59] In some extreme cases, the government might allow entry only by acquisition in order to protect a depressed industry from new entrants. Such was the case with the Egyptian banking industry in 2001, when the government would allow international banks only to buy existing Egyptian banks and refused to grant them licenses to start new businesses. [60]

Because they are often late movers into international markets, firms from developing countries frequently opt for acquisitions as a route to enter markets, including more mature markets such as the United States. Mexico's Bimbo is a bakery with a virtual monopoly at home. It expanded into the United States with the purchase of Texas-based Mrs. Baird's Bakeries for $300 million. Later purchases of several other bakeries in Canada and the United States elevated Bimbo to third-largest bakery in the world. A number of Indian companies—in industries as diverse as telecommunications, auto parts, and pharmaceuticals—are also entering developed countries via acquisition.[61]

Sometimes an international firm may choose—or settle for—a partial acquisition. In many ways, such an acquisition can resemble an alliance with equity ownership involved. For example, General Motors currently owns 49 percent of Japanese truck maker Isuzu Motors Ltd. GM had largely abandoned trying to sell cars on its own in Japan and instead bought stakes in three domestic automakers, including 20 percent stakes in Suzuki Motor Corporation and Fuji Heavy Industries Ltd., the maker of Subaru vehicles. Isuzu is particularly hoping that the new owners will help the firm reduce costs by tapping into GM's global purchasing network for cheaper parts. Also, Isuzu plans to sell its trucks in GM dealerships and to offer more GM vehicles in Isuzu showrooms.[62]

PORTAL OR e-BUSINESS ENTRY STRATEGIES

The technological revolution of the Internet, with its wide range of connected and networked computers, has given rise to the virtual entry strategy. Employing electronic means, primarily through the use of webpages, e-mail, file transfer, and related communications tools, firms have begun to enter markets without establishing a physical presence in the host country. A company that establishes a server on the Internet and opens up a webpage can be contacted from anywhere in the world. Table 9.2 rates the websites of the top twenty-five global brands. Consumers and industrial buyers who use modern Internet browsers can search for products, services, or companies and, in many instances, can make purchases online.

The number of global Internet users in 2005 was 817 million, which is 13 percent of the world population. Internet usage in the United States and Canada reached 66 percent of the population.[63] Whatever the forecasts, most experts agree that the opportunities for Internet-based commerce are huge.

Although it is difficult to guess how much actual trading is done with international customers at all Internet sites, the trend is clear when one looks at some major Internet companies. Forrester Research estimated that in the United States in 2004 online sales were $144 billion, and this figure is expected to grow to $316 billion by 2010.[64] Amazon.com, the leading Internet retailer, early established a presence overseas. After establishing a website in the United States, it then opened a second one in Britain (Amazon.co.uk) by acquiring

TABLE 9.2 THE TOP TWENTY-FIVE GLOBAL BRANDS' WEBSITES		
BRAND	WEBSITE	SCORE
IBM	www.ibm.com	81.8
Intel	www.intel.com	80.3
Microsoft	www.microsoft.com	76.5
Nokia	www.nokia.com	75.9
Disney	www.disneygo.com	75.0
Mercedes	www.mercedes.com	71.2
Kodak	www.kodak.com	70.8
Compaq	www.compaq.com	70.5
Sony	www.sony.com	70.0
McDonald's	www.mcdonalds.com	68.0
Heinz	www.heinz.com	67.8
Coca-Cola	www.coca-cola.com	67.7
BMW	www.bmw.com	66.9
Hewlett-Packard	www.hp.com	65.7
Cisco Systems	www.cisco.com	65.6
American Express	www.americanexpress.com	65.4
Ford	www.ford.com	62.2
General Electric	www.ge.com	61.6
AT&T	www.att.com	61.6
Nescafé	www.nescafe.com	59.5
Toyota	www.toyota.com	58.8
Honda	www.honda.com	54.6
Gillette	www.gillette.com	53.0
Citibank	www.citibank.com	51.3
Marlboro	No site found	—

NOTE: BrandNet tested websites for the top twenty-five global brands on the basis of the Intesbrand/Citibank top sixty international brand league table (July 2000). The overall evaluation is based on how local websites translate the core global online proposition, content, and services. This is the first survey of global brands. Sites will be reevaluated on a regular basis.
SOURCE: "The Top 25 Global Brand Websites," *Marketing Week,* November 2, 2000, p. 40. Reprinted with permission.

Bookpages, an existing U.K. Internet book retailer. In Germany, the company purchased Telebuch to establish Amazon.de. Both international websites are patterned after the U.S. one. The German site is entirely in German, and the merchandise inventory is specific to the different markets.[65] Each of these operations has its own fulfillment operation that packages and ships from local stocks. A customer can always order from the United States, but international customers who do so must pay the extra charges for shipment and delivery.

U.S. portal sites, such as AOL, are also engaged in expanding internationally. AOL has tended to engage in joint ventures in overseas markets. In Europe, AOL established a venture in 1995 with Bertelsmann, a leading German media company. Its Japan operation was established in 1997 with Mitsui, a Japanese

Amazon's German website is patterned after its U.S. site.

trading house, and Nhihon Keizai Shimbun, a publisher. Although clearly dominant in the United States, AOL has encountered stiff local competition. For example, Brazil, with its eighteen million Internet users, is one of the world's most important markets. AOL has had to battle established local providers in Brazil, some supported by foreign venture capital.

E-commerce is expanding rapidly through Asia. China, Australia, South Korea, Taiwan, and Hong Kong are the main user markets. Chinese Internet users grew to ninety-four million in 2004.[66] In India, where the creation of commercial software has become a major export industry, the leading portal service, Satyam Infoway, has acquired a smaller company, with a search engine that provides access to Indian sports, culture, and food recipes, something of great value to the many Indians living overseas. All the main players in this market are local and provide local content. Currently, India, with its small population of 18.4 million Internet users, is still too small for large players.[67]

A third group of major Internet players with global ambitions is made up of service providers, such as Schwab and Merrill Lynch with their online trading. Financial services firms, however, encounter legal restrictions and need to obtain regulatory approval for offering their services to any given country. On the other hand, it is difficult for governments to police the access. Financial services firms will probably have to provide special access, or qualifying service, to local customers before they can sign on. Given the low cost of the Internet, it is very likely that many more established firms will use the Internet as the first point of contact for countries where they do not yet have a major base.

Would-be Internet-based global marketers still face many challenges. One of the biggest is language. English is the dominant language on the Internet, with 34 percent of users using English, followed by 14 percent using Chinese.[68] One research company estimated that within 3 years, 60 percent of the world's Internet users and 40 percent of its e-commerce revenue would be from outside the United States, mostly from non-English-speaking areas. Although many people are able to surf the Net in English, they still prefer to do transactions in their local language.[69]

ENTRY STRATEGY SELECTION AND CONFIGURATION

This chapter has explained the various entry strategies available to international and global firms. A number of variables influence the choice of entry strategy. A recent meta-analysis of more than six hundred articles found that the mode of entry chosen by a firm was significantly influenced by country risk, cultural distance, company assets, international experience, and advertising intensity in the potential country.[70] In reality, however, most entry strategies consist of a combination of different formats. We refer to the process of deciding on the best possible entry strategy mix as **entry strategy configuration**.

> **Entry strategy configuration** the process by which a firm determines the best possible entry strategy for a country or region

Rarely do companies employ a single entry mode per country. A company may open up a subsidiary that produces some products locally and imports others to round out its product line. The same foreign subsidiary may even export to other foreign subsidiaries. In many cases, companies have bundled such entry forms into a single legal unit, in effect layering several entry strategy options on top of each other.

Bundling of entry strategies is the process of providing just one legal unit in a given country or market. In other words, the foreign company sets up a single company in one country and uses that company as a legal umbrella for all its entry activities. However, such strategies have become less typical—particularly in larger markets—and many firms have begun to unbundle their operations.

> **Bundling** the act in which a firm combines all its operations in a certain country or region into a single legal unit

When a company **unbundles**, it essentially divides its operations in a country into different companies. The local manufacturing plant may be incorporated separately from the sales subsidiary. When this occurs, companies may select different ownership strategies, for instance allowing a joint venture in one operation while retaining full ownership in another part. Such unbundling becomes possible in the larger markets, such as the United States, Germany, and Japan. It also enables the firm to run several companies or product lines in parallel. ICI, the large U.K. chemicals company, operates several subsidiaries in the United States that report to different product line companies back in the United Kingdom and are independently operated. Global firms that grant such independence to their product divisions will find that each division will need to develop its own entry strategy for key markets.

> **Unbundling** the act in which a firm divides its operations in a certain country or region into different legal units

EXIT STRATEGIES

Circumstances may make companies want to leave a country or market. Failure to achieve marketing objectives may be the reason, or there may be political, economic, or legal reasons for a company to want to dissolve or sell an operation. International companies have to be aware of the high costs attached to the liquidation of foreign operations; substantial amounts of severance pay may have to be dispensed to employees, and any loss of credibility in other markets can hurt the company's future prospects.

Consolidation

Sometimes an international firm may need to consolidate its operations. This may mean a consolidation of factories from many to fewer such plants. Production consolidation, when not combined with an actual market withdrawal, is not really what we are concerned with here. Rather, our concern is a company's actual abandonment of its plan to serve a certain market or country.

Market consolidation often occurs when an international firm acquires more debt than it can handle. To service the debt, poorly performing markets must be abandoned. Even successful operations may be sold to raise cash. Avon Products sold 60 percent of its successful Japanese company for about $400 million to reduce Avon's debt in the United States. Dutch retailing giant Ahold had to exit the Latin American market when an accounting scandal back home in Europe prompted creditors to call in the company's 11 billion euro debt.[71]

Consolidation can also be an option if a firm fails to establish itself in a particularly competitive market. In 2002, Yahoo announced that it would suspend its auction sites in five European markets—the United Kingdom, Ireland, France, Germany, and Spain. Yahoo found itself a distant third in these markets. Auctions have proved to be well suited to the Internet, but sellers and buyers tend to gravitate to the largest sites, leading to natural monopolies in online auction markets. eBay, the auction leader in the United States and most of Europe, agreed to pay exiting Yahoo to promote eBay's European auction sites through banner ads and text links.[72]

Political Considerations

Changing government regulations can at times pose problems that induce some companies to leave a country. India is a case in point. There, the government adopted in 1973 its Exchange Regulation Act that required most foreign companies to divest themselves of 60 percent ownership in each of their subsidiaries by the end of 1977. Companies that manufactured substantially for export and those whose operations used advanced technology were exempted. Because IBM's Indian operation did little exporting and sold mostly older computer models, the computer manufacturer was asked to sell 60 percent of its equity to Indian citizens. In light of the new requirements, Coca-Cola eventually chose to leave the Indian market in 1977.

Political risk can also motivate firms to leave a market. Sainsbury is a U.K.-based supermarket chain that employs 100,000 people worldwide. It entered the Egyptian market in 1999 by purchasing 80 percent interest in a state-owned retailer. The subsidiary posted a $15 million operating loss for the first half of 2000, partly as a result of problems with goods clearing customs and difficulty in obtaining building permits. These losses were exacerbated by an organized campaign against the company orchestrated by anti-Israel protesters who generally targeted Western companies operating in Egypt.[73] In 2002, Sainsbury announced that it would pull out of Egypt, selling its stake to its Egyptian partner and incurring a loss of $140–175 million.[74]

Exit strategies can also be the result of negative reactions in a firm's home market. When the policy of apartheid that then existed in South Africa was being widely challenged on moral grounds, many multinational corporations

Private security officers stand guard outside a KFC restaurant in Rawalpindi, Pakistan, after the United States led attacks on neighboring Afghanistan. As icons of American culture, U.S.-based fast-food chains are sometimes targets of politically motivated mobs. One such mob burned a KFC restaurant in Karachi, Pakistan. Mob violence in India encouraged KFC to leave that market.

exited that country by abandoning or selling their local subsidiaries. In 1984, some 325 U.S. companies were maintaining operations in South Africa. Two years later, this number had decreased to 265. Some of the U.S. firms that left were Coca-Cola, General Motors, IBM, Motorola, and General Electric. Many European firms also withdrew from that country, among them Alfa-Romeo of Italy, Barclays Bank of the United Kingdom, and Renault of France.[75]

Reentry Options

Several of the markets left by international firms over the past decades have become attractive again, and some companies have reversed their exit decisions and entered those markets a second time. For example, since July 1991, when the ban on investing in South Africa was lifted, a number of firms have returned. Among them is Honeywell, a manufacturer of industrial controls equipment. The company returned by repurchasing the industrial distributor it had sold to local interests in 1985.[76]

In India, the government relaxed earlier restrictive ownership legislation as part of its overall policy of economic liberalization in August 1991. Coca-Cola reentered India in 1993 to counter the first-time entry of rival PepsiCo. General Motors returned to India after a much longer absence. After producing cars in India from 1928 to 1953, GM left because of poor economic prospects. After a time, however, it developed licensing agreements with Hindustan Motors. This later evolved into the announcement of a full-scale 50:50 venture to produce GM models jointly in India again.[77] More recently, DHL Worldwide Express returned to Afghanistan after exiting 15 years earlier when market prospects looked bleak.[78]

CONCLUSION

Market entry strategies can have a profound impact on a firm's global strategy. They determine the number of foreign markets a firm can enter and the speed at which a firm can internationalize. They affect the profits the firm will make in each national market and the risk it will assume. They can even obligate a firm to local partners, thus constraining its power to act solely in its global self-interest.

Given the implications of the market entry decision, surprisingly few multinationals appear to recognize its strategic importance. A study of 228 U.S. manufacturing firms revealed that only 34 percent approached market entry options using any strategic rules.[79] Another study of 105 firms in four European countries found that only 36 percent of managers even reviewed alternative entry options.[80] Franklin Root suggests that managers often employ the "naïve rule" for entry mode selection—they simply utilize the same strategy worldwide, ignoring differences among national markets.[81]

Choosing the best entry strategy is complex and involves many considerations. The relative importance of these considerations varies by industry and by the strategic goals of each firm. It also varies according to the strategic importance of each national market. Table 9.3 presents some key considerations and their impact on the potential appropriateness of different entry options. Clearly, no one option is ideal under all conditions.

For example, speed of market entry may be an important consideration in some cases. If a firm is in an industry where products face high development costs, it will want to sell in many countries. If it is not already present in many markets, it will need to expand rapidly to keep up with global competitors. This is all the more true if products have a short life cycle, as is the case with many high-technology products. Often the need to be in many markets quickly requires a firm to take partners, because it simply doesn't have enough money or managerial talent to take on the task itself. Licensing, joint venturing, or entering distribution alliances becomes attractive.

In all cases, managers must decide how many resources they can and want to commit to a market. Resources include investments necessary for increasing or relocating manufacturing, as well as investments related to product research and development and to the implementation of marketing strategy. Exporting or licensing might require no new capital investment or very little incremental investment to increase current production. Wholly owned manufacturing facil-

TABLE 9.3	APPROPRIATENESS OF MARKET ENTRY STRATEGIES					
			MODE OF ENTRY			
STRATEGIC CONSIDERATION	INDIRECT EXPORTING	DIRECT EXPORTING-MARKETING SUBSIDIARY	LICENSING	WHOLLY OWNED PRODUCTION	JOINT VENTURE	ACQUISITION
Speed of entry	High	High	High	Low	Low	High
Ease of exit	High	Moderate	Moderate	Low	Low	Low
Rapidly changing technologies	Low	High	High	Moderate	Moderate	Moderate
Resource demands	Low	Moderate	Moderate	High	High	High
Profit potential	Low	High	Low	High	Moderate	Moderate
Competitive intensity of market	Low	Moderate	Moderate	Moderate	Moderate	High
Integration into global network	Low	High	Low	High	Low	Moderate
Strategically important country	Low	High	Low	High	Moderate	Moderate
Unimportant market	High	Low	Moderate	Low	Low	Low
Cultural distance	High	Low	Moderate	Low	Moderate	Low
Congruence with host government's goals	Low	Low	Moderate	High	High	Moderate

ities require significant capital investments. Joint ventures and other alliances can cut capital costs in research and development, manufacturing, and distribution. Another important resource is management time. Direct exporting may not require additional capital investment but will require a greater commitment of management time than indirect exporting. Joint ventures and alliances can help ease the demands on this critical resource.

Other concerns include profitability and flexibility. Will exporting to a market produce higher returns than producing there? Economies of scale in global or regional production may or may not offset the costs of transportation and tariffs. Licensing and joint ventures require that profits be shared. If the political environment or the business prospects of a country are uncertain, the flexibility involved with an entry strategy becomes a consideration. How quickly and at what cost can the firm expand in the market or retreat from it? Redirecting exports is easier than closing a plant. Partnership or licensing agreements can limit future actions both within the market and globally.

Firms must also consider different entry strategies for different countries. Establishing a sales subsidiary may be the best alternative for entering some countries, whereas joint ventures may be necessary to enter others. Firms should allot their greatest efforts and resources to the most strategic global markets. They should always consider how an entry strategy will later affect their ability to integrate operations in that country into the global whole.

What could be an appropriate entry strategy for your target market? Continue with your *Country Market Report* on our website (college.hmco.com/business/).

Firms must balance the advantages and disadvantages of different entry strategies. Even when a firm is clear about its strategic goals, rarely does an entry option present no drawbacks whatsoever. Also, governments may disallow the ideal market entry choice, forcing a company to fall back on a less desirable option or to avoid the market altogether. Compromises must often be made. Marketers should expect to manage a variety of entry strategies, and still other types of entry strategies may be devised in the future, presenting international marketers with new opportunities and challenges.

QUESTIONS FOR DISCUSSION

1. Why might entry strategies differ for companies entering the United States, those entering China, and those entering Costa Rica?

2. How might the entry strategy of a born-global firm (see Chapter 8) differ from that of a mature multinational company?

3. Why would licensing sometimes be appropriate—and sometimes inappropriate—for a strategically important country?

4. Is there such a thing as a "no-fault" joint venture divorce? Or is joint venture dissolution always the result of some sort of failure?

5. If a company exits a market and then wishes to return 10 years later, what peculiar challenges might it face?

CASE 9.1

Unhappy Marriage

In 1993, Anheuser-Busch purchased 17.7 percent of Grupo Modelo for $477 million, with an option of increasing its shares to 50.2 percent. At the time of the purchase, Anheuser held 45 percent of the U.S. beer market. Modelo was the world's tenth-largest beer producer. It held 50 percent of the Mexican beer market and exported to 124 countries in every continent of the world. However, with the passing of NAFTA (North American Free Trade Agreement), Mexico's 20 percent tariffs on imported beer were to be phased out. Modelo feared that U.S. breweries would invade its market. Anheuser viewed its stake in Modelo as a profitable acquisition of brands such as Corona, as well as a way to increase Anheuser's distribution network in Mexico quickly.

Anheuser told its U.S. distributors that they would soon have access to a major imported beer.

Distributors assumed this meant Corona, which was fast growing in popularity in the United States. However, in late 1996, management at Modelo renewed the firm's 10-year contract with its existing U.S. distributors, dashing Anheuser's hopes of gaining Modelo brands for its own U.S. distribution system. In December 1996, Anheuser announced that it would exercise its option to increase its stake in Modelo.

A 6-month dispute over price ensued, and the parties settled for $605 million. In June 1997, Anheuser opted to increase its stake to the full 50.2 percent. Discussions became so contentious that the two parties went into international arbitration, and the price was eventually set at $556 million. By 1998, the price of Anheuser's stake in Modelo, as valued on the Mexican stock exchange, was twice what it had paid for the stock. However, its 50.2 percent stake in Modelo did not give Anheuser a controlling share of board votes. It held only ten of the twenty-one seats on the board of directors.

Despite trade liberalization, Modelo's brands increased their share of the Mexican market to 55 percent by 1998. In the United States, where beer imports accounted for 14 percent of the market, Corona had pulled ahead of Heineken to become the best-selling import. Corona was enjoying 40 percent growth per year in the United States and had already become the tenth-best-selling beer in that market. It was particularly successful among college students and consumers in their twenties. Anheuser's major brand, Budweiser, found itself competing against Corona. Anheuser began a campaign to disparage the freshness of Corona. It distributed display cards to thousands of bars and restaurants, noting that Corona didn't put the manufacturing date on its bottles. Anheuser also introduced three Corona clones—Azteca, Tequiza,

and Rio Cristal—all produced in the United States.

Discussion Questions

1. Why did Anheuser purchase its stake in Grupo Modelo?
2. Why was Grupo Modelo willing to sell the stake?
3. What went wrong? Why?
4. What lessons about choosing international partners can be learned from this case?

Sources: "U.S. Brewers Forge Partnerships with Two Largest Mexican Beer Producers," *SourceMex*, March 31, 1993; Rekha Balu and Jonathan Friedland, "Anheuser-Busch Paying $556 Million, Raises Stake in Brewer Grupo Modelo," *Wall Street Journal*, September 11, 1998, p. B8; and Jonathan Friedland and Rekha Balu, "Head to Head," *Wall Street Journal*, October 22, 1998, p. A1.

CASE 9.2

Déjà Vu?

In 1990, Coca-Cola, the world's largest soft-drinks company, and Nestlé, the world's largest packaged-foods company, announced that they were forming a joint venture to develop and market ready-to-drink coffee and tea products. Each would contribute $50 million to the new venture. Nestlé possessed well-known trademarks in coffee and tea. It sold iced coffee in Europe and had recently test-marketed a mocha cooler in the United States. Still, it was not very active in the ready-to-drink category overall. For its part, Coke offered a global distribution system for soft drinks.

The newly formed company, Coca-Cola Nestlé Refreshment, had its headquarters in Tampa, Florida. (Coca-Cola was headquartered in Atlanta, Georgia, and Nestlé in Vevey, Switzerland.) The only market excluded from the venture was Japan, where Coke already had a position in ready-to-drink coffee. Nestlé came to the venture

with prior experience with an alliance partner; it distributed General Mills cereals through its international distribution system. Coke, on the other hand, had no such alliance experience. In 1992, the venture launched its first product, Nestea Iced Tea, a single-serve tea drink. In the following two and a half years, more than a dozen tea and coffee drinks were developed.

In 1994, the two companies announced that they were dissolving the equity joint venture and were closing the Tampa office. Some believed the venture had moved too slowly and had been beaten to the market by an alliance between Pepsi and Lipton. Under new terms, Coke received a 100-year license to use the Nestea trademark anywhere in the world and would pay Nestlé an undisclosed royalty for Nestea sales. Nestlé would continue to try to sell Nescafé products through the Coke distribution system.

During the 1990s, Nestlé embarked on an aggressive acquisition strategy. By 2001, it slowed down this activity to concentrate more on the 7,000 brands it already had. Coca-Cola continued in the 1990s to dominate in worldwide soda sales but saw Pepsi dramatically expand its noncarbonated lines. To help its ailing juice business, Coca-Cola entered a joint venture in 1996 with France's Groupe Danon to expand the distribution of Minute Maid refrigerated orange juice in supermarkets throughout Europe and Latin America.

In 2001, Coke and Nestlé announced that they were resurrecting their earlier alliance and renaming the venture Beverage Partners Worldwide. The new headquarters were to be located in Zurich, Switzerland, and the revived venture would operate in forty countries. Nestlé would develop the products, and Coke would distribute them. However, Coke would contribute the teas it developed for the Chinese market, along with its line of Planet Java coffees. Nestlé would add its Belte tea line. This time around, the parents envisioned that the venture would operate with the "speed and culture of a start-up company."

Discussion Questions

1. Why were Coca-Cola and Nestlé interested in forming a joint venture in 1990?
2. What do you think went wrong the first time?
3. What might be different in 2001? Do you think this resurrected venture may work better? Why or why not?

Sources: Michael J. McCarthy, "Coke, Nestle Get Together Over Coffee," *Wall Street Journal*, November 30, 1990, p. B1; Laurie M. Grossman, "Coca-Cola, Nestle Are Ending Venture in Tea and Coffee But Plan Other Ties," *Wall Street Journal*, August 30, 1994, p. B3; and Marcel Michelson, "Nestle, Coca-Cola Boost Health Drinks Venture," Reuters English News Service, January 30, 2001.

NOTES

1. Carolyn Webb, "The Fine Art of Franchising," *The Age*, May 8, 2001, p. 1.
2. "1451 International Launches the Vatican Library Collection Licensing Program," *Businesswire*, February 12, 2001.
3. "DHL Major Exporter of the Year Award," *NZ Business*, December–January 2001, p. N6.
4. Anne L. Souchon, Adamantios Diamantopoulos, Hartman H. Holzmuller, Catherine N. Axinn, James M. Sinkula, Heike Simmet, and Geoffrey R. Durden, "Export Information Use: A Five-Country Investigation of key Determinants," *Journal of International Marketing* 11, no.3 (2003), pp. 106–127.
5. "Eye Surgery the Material Difference," *Metalworking Production*, March 15, 2004, p. 13.
6. Amy Guthrie, "Brazil's Top Poultry Producers Target Export Markets," Dow Jones Newswires, May 9, 2001.
7. Niles Hansen, Kate Gillespie, and Esra Gencturk, "SMEs and Export Involvement: Market Responsiveness, Technology and Alliances," *Journal of Global Marketing* 7, 4 (1994), pp. 7–27.
8. S. Mitra Kalita, "Going Global," *Newsday*, March 19, 2001, p. C18.
9. "As American Markets Become Saturated, Internet Retailers Are Looking Abroad," *New York Times*, January 10, 2005, p. 36.
10. Chandrani Ghosh, "E-Trade Routes Planning to Do Global Business on the Web? Next Linx Will Ease the Way," *Forbes*, August 7, 2000, p. 108.
11. "Harvard Business School Publishing and New York Times Syndicate Announce Harvard Business Review to Be Published in Mandarin Chinese," *Businesswire*, July 17, 2001.
12. "Everlast Worldwide Inc. Announces New Head of Global Licensing," *PR Newswire*, October 25, 2000.
13. "Roche Grows Position in Japan," *Chemical Market Reporter*, December 22–29, 2003, p. 10.
14. David Luhnow, "Mexico's Televisa Wants New Univision Deal," *Wall Street Journal*, February 21, 2001, p. A18.
15. Nick Wingfield, "Priceline.com Plans Asia Partnership with Hutchinson," *Wall Street Journal*, January 26, 2000, p. A19.
16. Tom Daykin, "Miller Gets Deal with Dutch Firm," *Milwaukee Journal Sentinel*, July 11, 2001, p. 3D.
17. Judith Rehak, "Franchising the World: Services and Internet Fuel of Global Boom," *International Herald Tribune*, October 14, 2000, p. 20.
18. McDonald's Corporation, www.mcdonalds.com/corp/about.html (accessed February 20, 2005).
19. Vasantha Ganesan, "Malaysia Has Potential to Be Franchise Hub in Next Ten Years," *Business Times (Malaysia)*, June 8, 2001.
20. Dai Yan, "Bright Future for Franchising," *China Daily*, November 18, 2000.
21. Rehak, "Franchising the World."
22. Christina Hoag, "Franchise Fever Hits Venezuela," *Houston Chronicle*, July 10, 2001, p. 1.
23. "Happy Hookahs," *The Economist*, May 5, 2001.

24. Rehak, "Franchising the World."

25. "Nokian Tyres Expands Contract Manufacturing in Slovakia," *Nordic Business Report*, November 8, 2004, p.1.

26. "BMW Testing the Water for Local Facilities," *Businessline* (Islamabad), May 17, 2002.

27. Joel Millman, "Go North," *Wall Street Journal*, May 10, 2004, p. A1.

28. "Europe First Stop? Novartis Win Kindles Deutsch Global Plan," *Advertising Age*, November 1, 2004, p. 3.

29. "Why Mercedes Is Alabama Bound," *Business Week*, October 11, 1993, p. 138.

30. Doreen Hemlock, "Florida, Brazil Compete in Citrus Industry," Knight Ridder Tribune Business News, July 11, 2001.

31. Andrew Meadows, "Florida Citrus Processors Concentrate on Brazilian Juice Invasion," Knight Ridder Tribune Business News, June 9, 2001.

32. Dana James, "Back to Vietnam," *Marketing News*, May 13, 2002, p. 13.

33. "e-financialdepot.com Signs New International Joint Venture for Entry into Africa and Middle East," News Wire, April 4, 2001.

34. "Den Fujita, Japan's Mr. Joint-Venture," *New York Times*, March 22, 1992, Sect. 3, p. 1.

35. "McDonald's Co. Japan Ltd," *Nation's Restaurant News*, January 1, 1998, p. 112.

36. "Many Chinese Make Light Work of Razor Sales Targets," *Financial Times*, June 14, 1993.

37. "The Next CEO's Key Asset: A Worn Passport," *Business Week*, January 19, 1998, p. 76.

38. "Baltic Boost for Brewer," *Daily Post* (Liverpool, England), Februrary 16, 2005, p.10

39. Aimin Yan and Yadong Luo, *International Joint Ventures* (Armonk, NY: M.E. Sharpe, 2001), p. 223.

40. Usha C.V. Haley, "Assessing and Controlling Business Risks in China," *Journal of International Management* 9 (2003), pp. 237–252.

41. www.starbucks.com (accessed June 9, 2005).

42. Jennifer Ordonez, "Starbucks to Start Major Expansion Overseas," *Wall Street Journal*, October 27, 2000, p. B10.

43. "The Advantages of Marrying Local," *Financial Times*, December 21, 2000, p. 16.

44. Janine Brewis, "Brasil Telecom Fears Takeover Bid," *Financial Times*, November 16, 2003, p.1.

45. Yan and Luo, *International Joint Ventures*, p. 281.

46. "Glaxo to Buy Out Partner in Japan for $594 Million," *Financial Times*, November 22, 1996, p. 15.

47. "Alliance Tips for a Beautiful Relationship," *Financial Times-FT.com* (accessed July 11, 2001).

48. Rajneesh Narula, "Globalisation and Trends in International R&D Alliances," MERIT-Infonomics Research Memorandum Series, 2003, pp. 2–7.

49. Dean Takahashi, "New Chip called a Threat to Intel," Knight Ridder Tribune Business News (Washington), February 8, 2005, p. 1.

50. Neal E. Boudette, "Road Less Travelled," *Wall Street Journal*, August 4, 2003, p. A1.

51. "AB Volvo," *CEO Wire*, CNN Financial News, December 7, 2004.

52. http://www.cerealpartners.co.uk/about.aspx (accessed February 22, 2005).

53. Justin Wastnage, Star Alliance in Defining Moment, *Flight International* 166, no. 4965 (January 3, 2005), p. 15.

54. Eugene Low, "S'pore, US in Business Matching Initiative," *Business Times* (Singapore), November 15, 2000.

55. Andrew Delios, Andrew C. Inkpen, and Jerry Ross, "Escalation in International Strategic Alliances," *Management International Review* 44, no. 4 (2004), p. 457.

56. David Wessel, "Cross-Border Mergers Soared Last Year," *Wall Street Journal*, September 19, 2000, p. A18.

57. "SABMiller to Buy Stake in Italian Brewer," *International Hearld Tribune*, May 15, 2003, p. 3.

58. Erick Schonfeld, "The World According to Ebay," *Business 2.0*, January/February 2005, pp. 765–782.

59. Chris Nuttall, "EBay Backs Its $100 million Outlay in China," *Financial Times*, February 11, 2005, p. 19.

60. Mahmoud Kassem, "Banks Seek Takeover Targets in Egypt," *Wall Street Journal Europe*, July 11, 2001.

61. Joanna Slater, "India Looks Beyond Borders," *Wall Street Journal*, December 31, 2003, p. A7.

62. Todd Zaun, "Japan's Isuzu Will Cut Jobs, Close Factory," *Wall Street Journal*, May 29, 2001, p. A14.

63. http://www.internetworldstats.com/ (accessed February 22, 2005).

64. Ibid.

65. "Internet Retailing: A New Leaf," *The Economist*, October 23, 1999, p. 72.

66. "94 million Chinese Can't Be Wrong," *Internet Week*, January 20, 2005, p. 2.

67. http://www.internetworldstats.com/stats3.htm#asia (accessed February 22, 2005).

68. Ibid.

69. "Idiom App Speaks Your Language," *Computer World*, May 31, 1999, p. 66.

70. Hongxin Zhao, Yadong Luo, and Taewon Suh, "Transaction Cost Determinants and Ownership-Based Entry Mode Choice: A Meta-Analytical Review," *Journal of International Business Studies* 35, no. 6 (2004), pp. 524–544.

71. Andrea Welsh and Ann Zimmerman, "Wal-Mart Snaps Up Brazilian Chain," *Wall Street Journal*, March 2, 2004, p. B3.

72. Nick Wingfield and Mylene Mangalindan, "Yahoo Agrees to Cede Most Auction in Europe to eBay," *Wall Street Journal Europe*, May 24, 2002, p. A5.

73. William A. Orme, "A Grocer Amid Mideast Outrage," *New York Times*, January 25, 2001, p. C1.

74. "Sainsbury's to Pull Out of Egypt," *Jerusalem Post Daily*, April 10, 2001, p. 10.

75. "South Africa: Time to Stay—or Go?" *Fortune*, August 4, 1986, p. 45; "If Coke Has Its Way, Blacks Will Soon Own 'The Real Thing,'" *Business Week*, March 27, 1987, p. 56; "High Risks and Low Returns," *Financial Times*, November 25, 1986, p. 10.

76. "Honeywell's Route Back to South Africa Market," *New York Times*, January 31, 1994, p. D1.

77. "Indian Venture for 20,000 Cars a Year," *Financial Times*, May 12, 1994, p. 15.

78. "DHL Resumes Afghanistan Service," *Jakarta Post*, March 20, 2002, p. 12.

79. Kwon, Yung-Chul and Michael Y. Hu, "Comparative Analysis of Export-Oriented and Foreign Production-Oriented Firms' Foreign Market Entry Decisions," *Management International Review* 35, no. 4 (1995), pp. 325–336.

80. Frank Bradley and Michael Gannon, "Does the Firm's Technology and Marketing Profile Affect Foreign Market Entry?" *Journal of International Marketing* 8, no. 4 (2000), pp. 12–36.

81. Franklin Root, *Entry Strategies for International Markets* (Lexington, MA: Lexington Books, D.C. Heath, 1994).

Designing Global Marketing Programs

PART 4

301

10 GLOBAL PRODUCT STRATEGIES

EVEN INTERNET FIRMS that only virtually enter international markets must consider the possible need to alter their products for many new environments. Simply translating the text of a website may not be enough. Do people read from right to left or from left to right, from top to bottom or from bottom to top? What colors and shapes do they like? The answers to these questions will strongly influence the graphical layouts of the site and its use of icons.[1] What standards—governmental or societal—could affect the content of the site? U.S. Internet firms routinely alter the content of their sites in Asia, self-censoring to avoid offending local governments, especially those in China, Singapore, and Malaysia, which have clamped down on Internet access. Yahoo carried a story of doctors harvesting organs from executed prisoners in China. The story appeared in the "world news" section of Yahoo's website in the United States and other parts of the world—but not in China.[2]

LEARNING OBJECTIVES

After studying this chapter, you should be able to

▶ List the advantages of product standardization and product adaptation.

▶ Differentiate between mandatory and discretionary product adaptations.

▶ Explain the concepts of global product standards and generic management system standards.

▶ Explain why product lines can vary from country to country.

▶ Define modularity and explain its impact on global product development.

▶ Compare and contrast the product development roles played by a multinational firm's headquarters and the roles played by its subsidiaries.

▶ Explain the importance of lead markets and note their importance to product development.

▶ Describe how companies may access new products by purchasing research and development or by importing products from other firms.

▶ Discuss the use of acquisitions, joint ventures, and alliances for the purpose of product development.

▶ Explain the process of introducing new products to global markets, including concept testing, test marketing, and the timing of new product introduction.

This chapter examines issues pertaining to the adaptation of products to global markets. In this chapter we begin by exploring the many environmental factors that can prevent the marketing of uniform or standardized products across a multitude of markets. Subsequent sections focus on packaging and labeling, product warranties, and product-line management across countries. The chapter concludes with a discussion of global product development.

PRODUCT DESIGN IN A GLOBAL ENVIRONMENT

One of the principal questions in global marketing is whether a firm's products can be sold in their present form or whether they need to be adapted to foreign market requirements. Standardizing products across markets has certain advantages. Economies of scale in manufacturing may be realized. If products have high development costs and short life cycles, as is the case for many high-technology products, they may need to enter global markets very rapidly. In other words, firms must sell high volumes in many markets to recoup their investment before the product becomes obsolete. Adapting such a product to different national markets may simply take too long. Furthermore, if buyers themselves are international firms, they may prefer a standardized product that is available worldwide.

Nonetheless, in many cases products do need to be adapted for different national markets. The benefits of adaptation are compared with those of standardization in Table 10.1. Many adaptations are **discretionary;** that is, firms may choose to make certain adaptations or not to do so. In some cases, however, adaptations are **mandatory**. They are necessary for the product to be sold in a local market. Some mandatory adaptations are responses to differing physical realities. For example, consumer electronics must be adapted to work with different voltages, alternating currents, and electric plug designs, each of which varies from country to country.

Discretionary adaptation a product adaptation that is optional but possibly desirable for a certain market

Mandatory adaptation a product adaptation that a firm must make to sell a product in a certain country or region

TABLE 10.1 BENEFITS OF PRODUCT STANDARDIZATION AND OF PRODUCT ADAPTATION
BENEFITS OF STANDARDIZATION
Lower costs of manufacturing may be achieved through economies of scale.
Lower input costs may be achieved through volume purchasing.
Cost savings may be achieved by eliminating efforts—market research, design, and engineering—to adapt products.
Fast global product rollouts are possible because no time is needed to make product adaptations.
International customers may prefer the same product to be available worldwide.
Standardized products may enhance consumer perceptions of a global brand.
BENEFITS OF ADAPTATION
Mandatory adaptations allow products to be sold in otherwise closed markets.
Products can be sold for use in different climates and with different infrastructures.
Modified products may perform better under different use conditions.
Product costs may be decreased by varying local inputs.
Product costs may be decreased by eliminating unnecessary product features.
Greater sales may be attained by better meeting industry norms or cultural preferences.

Most mandatory adaptations are made to adhere to national legal requirements. For example, a French court required Yahoo to block French users from accessing Nazi memorabilia on its U.S.-based website, thereby setting a precedent and suggesting that Web companies operating on the global Internet could be required to conform to standards of individual countries. The judge gave Yahoo 3 months to comply with the ruling by installing a key-word-based filtering system to block French citizens from viewing Yahoo sites where Nazi items were being sold—or else be subject to fines of more than 1,000,000 francs ($12,940) a day.[3]

Sometimes discretionary adaptations can become mandatory. Originally, Microsoft declined to translate its software into Icelandic, a language spoken by only 270,000 people. Customers in Iceland were apparently able to manage without it. However, when Iceland's government demanded that Microsoft translate its program, the firm agreed rather than face leaving the market.[4]

Selecting the most desirable product features for each market is an involved decision for global marketers. The approach taken should include a thorough review of a number of factors that could determine both discretionary and mandatory adaptations. These include climatic, infrastructure, and use conditions; performance and quality standards; and cultural preferences.

Climatic, Infrastructure, and Use Conditions

International marketers often adapt products to conform to physical realities such as regional variations in climate and infrastructure. Air conditioners in Saudi Arabia must be able to operate under conditions that are hotter and dustier than those in most U.S. locations. Paint must be adapted to various climatic conditions, such as heat, cold, moisture, and wind. Automobile manufacturers must consider which side of the street cars are driven on—the left or the right—and adjust the steering wheel accordingly. For instance, drivers in Britain and Japan drive on the left. Marketers of packaged foods must consider the distribution infrastructure of the country. How long will the product be in the distribution channels? Are warehouses air-conditioned and trucks refrigerated? Most chocolate is easily damaged if not kept cool. One worldwide manufacturer of industrial abrasives even had to adjust products to differing availability of raw materials. The firm responded by varying the raw-materials input from one country to another, while maintaining exacting performance standards.

Products may also need to be adapted to different use conditions in various markets. Procter & Gamble was forced to adapt the formulation of its Cheer laundry detergent to accommodate different use conditions in the Japanese market. Cheer was initially promoted as an all-temperature detergent. However, many Japanese consumers washed their clothes in cold tap water or used leftover bath water. The Japanese also liked to add fabric softeners that decreased the suds produced by detergent. Procter & Gamble reformulated Cheer to work more effectively in cold water with fabric softeners added and changed its positioning to superior cleaning in cold water.

In some local markets, customers may even expect a product to perform a function different from the one for which it was originally intended. One U.S.

The typical Japanese home is smaller than its U.S. counterpart, creating a demand for smaller appliances.

exporter of gardening tools found that its battery-operated trimmers were used by the Japanese as lawn mowers on their small lawns. As a result, the batteries and motors did not last as long as they would have under the intended use. Because of the different function desired by Japanese customers, a design change was eventually required.

Adapting to Performance and Quality Standards

Manufacturers typically design products to meet domestic performance standards. Such standards do not always apply in other countries, and product changes are required in some circumstances. Some companies go to great lengths to meet different quality standards in foreign markets. The experience of BMW, the German automaker exporting to Japan, serves as an excellent example of the extra efforts frequently involved. BMW found that its customers in Japan expected the very finest quality. Typically, cars shipped to Japan had to be completely repainted. Even very small mistakes were not tolerated by customers. When service was required, the car was picked up at the customer's home and returned when the work was completed.

The necessity to increase product quality or performance for a foreign market tends, if the need exists, to be readily apparent. Opportunities for product simplification are frequently less obvious to the firm. Products designed in highly developed countries often exceed the performance needed in developing countries. Customers in these markets may prefer products of greater simplicity, not only to save costs but also to ensure better service over the products' lifetime. Companies have been criticized for selling excess performance where simpler products will do. Some multinational firms are addressing this issue. For example, when Philips created a product line for consumers in rural India, it focused on scaling back features in order to deliver inexpensive products such as a wind-up radio and a back-to-basics television set.[5] Also ready to fill this market gap are companies from less developed countries whose present levels of technology are more in line with consumer needs. For example, local Egyptian firms that produce consumer products invest very little in elaborate features or attractive packaging in order to deliver products at very low prices.

Of course, manufacturers from developing countries can face the opposite challenge when attempting to sell overseas. They must increase the performance of their products to meet the standards of industrialized countries. Producing quality products that are competitive on export markets has become something of a national obsession in Mexico. Major companies such as the Alfa business group and Cemex have joined forces with universities to establish programs to supply Mexican industry with top-flight engineers. And the effort has paid off. Fifteen years after the country joined NAFTA, Mexico's exports had more than doubled.[6]

Global Standards. A lack of international standards is readily apparent in the movie industry. The ultragrisly movie *Hannibal* grossed more than $230 million worldwide, but its scenes of cannibalism and dismemberment caused an outcry in Italy, where its rating suggested it was appropriate for all audiences. In the United States, no one under 17 was supposed to be admitted without an adult, but children as young as 8 were seen entering with their parents. In Western Europe, viewers had to be at least 15—with or without accompanying adults. But in Portugal and Uruguay, they only had to be 12 years old.[7]

Many countries have organizations that set voluntary standards for products and business practices. Groups such as the Canadian Standards Association and the British Standards Institute (BSI) formulate standards for product design and testing. If producers adhere to these standards, buyers are assured of the stated level of product quality.

The unification of Europe has forced Europeans to recognize the need for multicountry standards. In areas where a European standard has been developed, manufacturers who meet the standard are allowed to include the European Union (EU) Certification Symbol, CE. Firms both in and out of the EU are eligible to use the CE symbol, but they must be able to demonstrate their compliance with the standards.

The U.S. standard-setting process is much more fragmented than Europe's. In the United States, there are over 450 different standard-setting groups, loosely coordinated by the American National Standards Institute (ANSI). After a standard is set by one of the 450 groups, ANSI certifies that it is an "American National Standard," of which there are over 11,000 on the books.

Incompatible national standards both help and hinder global competitors. Incompatible technologies in the mobile phone industry mean that it is very difficult for a single make of handset to compete worldwide. As of 2001, the United States used four cellular technologies, which made it expensive for firms to make cell phones for every network operator. Japan had its own mobile network technology that was different from the U.S. technologies. This protected Japanese competitors at home by making it difficult for foreign firms to enter

WORLD BEAT 10.1

Rolling Over

WHEREAS THE EUROPEANS build car roofs to withstand being dropped upside down or flipped off a moving dolly, their U.S. counterparts employ a less rigorous safety test that hasn't been changed in 30 years. U.S. automakers say their roofs match the Europeans' in safety. However, the National Highway Traffic Safety Administration (NHTSA) test, developed by General Motors in the late 1960s, calls for vehicles to be tested with their windshields. Vehicle roofs lose between 10 percent and 40 percent of their structural strength without the windshield. In a rollover, the windshield frequently breaks when the roof first hits the ground. Some of the most popular SUVs in the United States have a significant chance of rolling over in a one-vehicle accident, and a quarter of the 42,000 road deaths in the United States are caused by rollovers.

Europe has no roof-strength standards, but all three of the U.S. automakers' affiliates—GM's Saab, Ford's Volvo, and DaimlerChrysler's Mercedes-Benz—choose to subject their vehicles to tougher roof tests. Saab tests vehicles by ramming them into a bundle of electrical cable to simulate hitting a moose. In the past 20 years, the number of German traffic deaths has dropped 70 percent while in the United States it has only dropped 20 percent. Increasingly competing on price, U.S. automakers claim to have trouble pricing in safety innovations.

Sources: Milo Geyelin and Jeffrey Ball, "How Rugged Is Your Car's Roof?" *Wall Street Journal*, March 4, 2002, p. B1; Christine Tierney, "American Drivers: Stiffed on Safety?" *Business Week*, April 28, 2003, p. 96; and David Welch, "Stability Shouldn't Be Optional," *Business Week*, August 30, 2004, p. 50.

the Japanese market. On the other hand, the lack of technologies overseas that were compatible with Japanese standards handicapped Japanese competitors abroad.[8]

Given the growth in international commerce, there are benefits to having international standards for items such as credit cards, screw threads, car tires, paper sizes, and speed codes for 35 mm film. And country-to-country differences become immediately obvious when you try to plug in your hair dryer in various countries. Although national standards institutes ensure consistency within countries, an international agency is necessary to coordinate across countries.

The International Standards Organization (ISO), located in Geneva, was founded in 1947 to coordinate the setting of global standards. The ISO is a non-governmental organization, a federation of national standards bodies from some 140 countries. Each member of the ISO is the firm "most representative of standardization in its country"; only one such member is allowed per country. Most standards set by the ISO are highly specific, such as standards for film speed codes or formats for telephone and banking cards. ISO standards for components of freight containers have made it possible for shipping costs around the world to be lowered substantially.[9]

To set an international standard, representatives from various countries meet and attempt to agree on a common standard. Sometimes they adopt the standard set by a particular country. For example, the British standard for quality assurance (BS5750) was adopted internationally as ISO 9000 in 1987. This standard was revolutionary in that it was a **generic management system standard**. As the first such international standard, ISO 9000 ensured that an organization could consistently deliver a product or service that satisfied the customer's requirements because the company followed a state-of-the art management system. In other words, the company possessed quality management. ISO 9000 can be applied to any organization, large or small, whatever its product or service. ISO 14000 is a similar generic management system standard that is primarily concerned with environmental management. Companies that meet this standard must show that they do minimal damage to the environment.

Mandatory Standards. Sometimes product standards are not voluntary but regulated by law. In these cases of mandatory standard, adaptation is mandatory, not discretionary, for market entry. Most often these mandatory standards involve product quality and safety, hygiene, and environmental concerns. Meeting these standards can add costs to the product, but failing to comply may keep a firm out of an important markets. For example, Kinder eggs, made by Italian candy giant Ferrero SpA, are popular in one hundred countries and are ranked on the ACNielsen list of top global brands. But they are illegal in the United States. Wrapped in orange and white foil, the hollow chocolate eggs contain intricate plastic or wooden toy prizes. These represent a choking hazard according to the U.S. Consumer Product Safety Commission.[10]

Many believe that Europe has come to dominate the creation of international standards through its influence at the ISO and its proactive stance toward setting mandatory standards. Already the standards established by the European Commission have become effective standards for firms in Asia and Latin America that aspire to export to Europe. EU standards concerning consumer safety are generally tougher than their U.S. counterparts—forcing U.S. companies to take note and conform. In 2002, the Illinois Department of Agriculture asked local farmers not to plant a corn developed by the Monsanto Company because it wasn't approved in the EU. California-based Mattel has reformulated the plastic it uses in its Barbie dolls and other toys to adhere to recently established EU standards.[11]

The EU also has greater authority to recall products and impose emergency bans when products are thought to be unsafe. The EU's precautionary principle allows regulators to ban products based on a lower burden of proof of their danger than can regulators in the United States. For example, the EU banned cheap Chinese cigarette lighters that were also deemed unsafe in Canada and Mexico. The same lighters remained available in the U.S. market despite 3 years of government testing.[12]

Adapting Products to Cultural Preferences

Cultural adaptations are usually discretionary adaptations. Yet understanding cultural preferences and adapting products accordingly can be extremely important to success in local markets. To the extent that fashion and tastes differ by country, companies often change their styling. Color, for example,

> **Generic management system standard** an international standard covering a particular set of corporate behaviors to which companies can choose to comply and consequently become certified as to their compliance

Visit the ISO and the ANSI links on our website (college.hmco.com/business/).

should reflect the aesthetic values of each country. For Japan, red and white have happy associations, whereas black and white indicate mourning. Green is an unpopular color in Malaysia, where it is associated with the jungle and illness. Textile manufacturers in the United States who have started to expand their export businesses have consciously used color to suit local needs. For example, the Lowenstein Corporation has successfully used brighter colors for fabrics exported to Africa.

The scent and sounds of a product may also have to be changed from one country to another. Strawberry-scented shampoo failed to sell in China, where consumers shun nonedible items that smell like foods.[13] Word processing engineers had to change programs destined for Japan that "pinged" when users tried to do something that was not possible. Japanese office workers complained that they were mortified that co-workers could hear when they made mistakes. The "ping" was deleted.[14]

As we noted in Chapter 3, food is one of the most culturally distinct product areas. Nestlé's popular instant coffee, Nescafe, is produced in more than two hundred variations—more variations than the number of countries where it is sold. Product adaptations are even necessary within some national markets. In Switzerland, the French-speaking Swiss like strong, black coffee. The German-speaking Swiss prefer light coffee with milk.[15]

Cultural differences relating to food can extend beyond mere taste. As we discussed in Chapter 3, religion can dictate what people will and will not eat, and other traditional beliefs may require product adaptations. Frito-Lay wondered why its potato chips didn't sell in China in the summertime. Research revealed that Chinese consumers associated fried foods like potato chips with *yang*, which according to Chinese traditional medicine generates body heat and should be avoided in hot weather. The company then introduced a "cool lemon" variety packaged in pastel shades. The new lemon chips became Frito-Lay's best-selling item in China.[16] In general, a branded food product in the United States is likely to be considerably higher in fat, sodium, and added sweeteners than the same branded product sold in the Chinese, Japanese, and European markets.[17]

Even factual knowledge is not immune to a little cultural tweaking. Microsoft's online encyclopedia, *Encarta*, lists the height of Europe's highest mountain, Mont Blanc, as 4,808 meters (15,770 feet) in its French version. In the Dutch version, this height is listed as 4,807 meters. The Italians believe the correct height to be 4,810 meters, so that's what the Italian version says.[18]

Product Size and Dimensions

Within 3 years of entering the U.S. market, IKEA, the Swedish furniture and household products company, decided to abandon its smaller European sizes in furniture and bed linens and developed bigger sizes for the new market. American homes are 1,800 square feet on average—twice the size of the average European home. Larger furniture just looked better in American homes. Even drinking glasses had to be made bigger to accommodate ice, which is rarely used in Europe.[19]

When other design features require no modification, product size and dimensions may need adaptation. Product size can be affected by physical surroundings and available space. In many countries, limited living space necessitates home appliances that are substantially smaller than those found in a country such as the United States, where people live in larger dwellings. Recently, U.S.-made major appliances have been imported into Japan by discount chains. Although the volume is still small by international standards, certain wealthier Japanese consumers favor these large appliances. However, some customers have had to return them after purchase because they could not get the refrigerators through their apartment doors.

The different physical characteristics of consumers can also influence product design. Swiss watch manufacturers learned over the years to adapt their watchbands to different wrist sizes. For example, Japanese have smaller wrists than Americans. A leading Italian shoe manufacturer had a similar experience exporting shoes to the United States. The company learned that Americans have thicker ankles and narrower, flatter feet. To produce a properly fitting shoe, the Italian company decided to make appropriate changes in its design to achieve the necessary comfort for U.S. customers.

In markets where many potential consumers have little disposable income, packaged-goods manufacturers often determine that smaller sizes are necessary to offer the customer an accessible product. In India, Hindustan Lever Ltd., a subsidiary of Unilever, sells Sunsilk shampoo in bottles for the upper classes and in sachets, good for one use, to consumers who cannot afford to buy a bottle.[20] Similarly, Coca-Cola launched its powdered soft drink concentrate Sunfill in single-serving packets in India to attract consumers who could not afford to buy larger sizes.[21]

One important factor, particularly for U.S. firms, is whether to select a metric or a nonmetric scale for the sale of their products abroad. With Europe and Japan operating on the metric standard, the United States is one of the few remaining major nonmetric markets. The firm must often go beyond a single translation of nonmetric into metric sizes (or vice versa) to help consumers understand the design of its products. In some cases, companies may be required to change the physical sizes of their products to conform to legal standards based on the metric scale.

PACKAGING AND LABELING FOR GLOBAL MARKETS

Differences in the marketing environment may require special adaptations in product packaging. Different climatic conditions often demand a change in the package to ensure sufficient protection or shelf life. The role a package assumes in promotion also depends on the market retailing structure. In countries with a substantial degree of self-service merchandising, firms should choose a package with strong promotional appeal for consumer products. In addition, distribution handling requirements are not identical the world over. In the high-wage countries of the developed world, products tend to be packaged in such a way as to reduce further handling by retail employees. For consumer products, all mass merchandisers have to do is place products on shelves. In countries with lower wages and less elaborate retailing structures, individual orders may be filled from larger packaged units, a process that entails extra labor on the part of the retailer.

Specific packaging decisions that may be affected include size, shape, materials, color, and text. Size may differ by custom or in terms of existing standards, such as metric and nonmetric requirements. Higher-income countries tend to require larger unit sizes; these populations shop less frequently and can afford to buy larger quantities each time. In countries with lower income levels, consumers buy in smaller quantities and more often. Gillette sells razor blades in packages of five or ten in the United States and Europe, whereas singles are sold in some emerging markets.

Packages can assume almost any shape, largely depending on the customs and traditions prevailing in each market. Materials used for packaging can also differ widely. Whereas Americans prefer to buy mayonnaise and mustard in clear plastic containers, consumers in Germany and Switzerland buy these same products in tubes. Cans are the customary material in which to package beer in the United States, whereas most European consumers prefer glass bottles.

The package color and text have to be integrated into a company's promotional strategy and therefore may be subject to specific tailoring that differs from one country to another. The promotional effect is of great importance for consumer goods and has led some companies to attempt to standardize their packaging in color and layout. In areas such as Europe and Latin America, where consumers frequently travel to other countries, standardized colors help them identify a product quickly. This strategy depends on devising a set of colors or a layout with an appeal beyond one single culture or market. An example of a product with a standardized package color is Procter & Gamble's leading detergent, Tide. The orange and white box familiar to millions of U.S. consumers can be found in many foreign markets, even though the package text may appear in the language of the given country.

Cultural implications of packaging and labeling can sometimes create problems in unexpected ways. One exporter of software to Saudi Arabia identified its CD-ROMs for the Saudi market by putting the Saudi flag on the box. The flag bears the word *Allah*, the Arabic word for "God." For many devout Muslims, to discard the box would imply disrespect for God. As a result, the local distributor was left with lots of boxes that both customers and employees declined to throw away.[22]

In 1998, a new British law cut the number of pills that could be sold in packages of aspirin and acetaminophen to reduce overdoses leading to death and liver failure caused by impulsive self-poisoning. Tablets were also required to be blister-wrapped to make swallowing large quantities impulsively even more difficult. Three years later, in 2001, deaths by overdoses of these pills had decreased dramatically in the United Kingdom.[23]

Labeling is another concern for international marketers. Labeling helps consumers understand better the products they are buying and can convey rudimentary instructions for their use. What languages must the labels be in? What government requirements are involved?

Increasingly, packaged-foods companies must adhere to government requirements concerning labeling, but many other products are affected as well. China is home to two-thirds of the world's cashmere goats. When the country began exporting cashmere sweaters and other garments, many manufacturers exaggerated the amount of cashmere in their products. This brought them into collision with the United States' 60-year-old Wool Products Labeling Act, which requires that fabrics and garments made out of wool and other fine animal hairs be accurately labeled to reflect their true content. The Federal Trade Commission can seek penalties in federal court as high as $11,000 for each violation.[24]

GLOBAL WARRANTY AND SERVICE POLICIES

Buyers around the world purchase products with certain performance expectations and consider company policies for backing promises. As a result, warranties and service policies can become an integral aspect of a company's international product strategy. Companies interested in doing business abroad frequently find themselves at a disadvantage, relative to local competitors, in the area of warranties and service. With the supplier's plant often thousands of miles away, foreign buyers sometimes want extra assurance that the supplier will back the product. Thus, a comprehensive warranty and service policy can become a very important marketing tool for international companies.

Product Warranties

A company must address its warranty policy for international markets either by declaring its domestic warranty valid worldwide or by tailoring warranties to specific countries or markets. Although declaring a worldwide warranty with uniform performance standards would be administratively simple, local market conditions often dictate a differentiated approach. In the United States, most computer manufacturers sell their equipment with a 30- or 60-day warranty, whereas 12 months is more typical in Europe and Japan.

Companies are well advised to consider actual product use. If buyers in a foreign market subject the product to more stress or abuse, some shortening of the warranty period may become necessary. In developing countries, where technical sophistication is below North American and European standards, maintenance may not be adequate, causing more frequent equipment breakdowns. Another important factor is local competition. Because an attractive warranty policy can be helpful in obtaining sales, a firm's warranty policy should be in line with those of other firms competing in the local market.

Still, failure to maintain quality, service, or performance in one country can rapidly have a negative impact in other countries. Perrier, the French bottled-water company, had to withdraw its Perrier water from U.S. retail stores after the product was found to contain benzene in concentrations above the legal limit. This U.S. test result triggered similar tests by health authorities in other countries. Soon Perrier had to withdraw its products in other countries, eventually resulting in a worldwide brand recall. Nearly 10 years later, Coca-Cola experienced a similar problem with bottling plants in Belgium, leading to a recall of many products not only in Belgium but also in France and

Poland. Some two hundred consumers complained of illness after drinking Coca-Cola products. This prompted the largest product recall in the firm's history.[25]

Global Product Service

For some products, no warranty will be believable unless backed with an effective service organization. Although service is important to the consumer, it is even more crucial to the industrial buyer, because any breakdown of equipment or product is apt to cause substantial economic loss. This risk has led industrial buyers to be conservative in their choice of products, always carefully analyzing the supplier's ability to provide service in the event of need.

To provide the required level of service outside the company's home base poses special problems for global marketers. The selection of an organization to perform the service is an important decision. Ideally, company personnel are preferable because they tend to be better trained. However, this approach can be organized economically only if the installed base of the market is large enough to justify such an investment. In cases where a company does not maintain its own sales subsidiary, it is generally more efficient to turn to an independent service company or a local distributor. To provide adequate service via independent distributors requires extra training for the service technicians, usually at the manufacturer's expense. In any case, the selection of an appropriate service organization should be made in such a way that fully trained service personnel are readily available within the customary time frame for the particular market.

Closely related to any satisfactory service policy is an adequate inventory for spare parts. Because service often means replacing some parts, the company must store sufficient inventory of spare parts within reach of its markets. Whether this inventory is maintained in regional warehouses or through sales subsidiaries and distributors depends on the volume and the required reaction time for service calls. Industrial buyers will generally want to know, before placing substantial orders, how the manufacturer plans to organize service.

Firms that demonstrate serious interest in a market by committing themselves to setting up their own sales subsidiaries are often at an advantage over firms that use distributors. One German truck manufacturer that entered the U.S. market advertised the fact that "97 percent of all spare parts are kept in local inventory," thus assuring prospective buyers that they could get spares readily. Difficulty in establishing service outlets may even influence a company's market entry strategy. This was the case with Fujitsu, a Japanese manufacturer of electronic office equipment. By combining forces with TRW, a U.S.-based company, Fujitsu was able to sell its office equipment in the U.S. market backed by the extensive service organization of TRW.

Because the guarantee of reliable and efficient service can be such an important aspect of a firm's entire product strategy, investment in service centers sometimes must be made before any sales can take place. In this case, service costs must be viewed as an investment in future volume rather than merely as a recurring expense.

MANAGING A GLOBAL PRODUCT LINE

In early sections of this chapter, we discussed issues concerning individual products. Most companies, however, manufacture or sell a multitude of products. Starbucks doesn't vary its product formulations from country to country, but the product line can vary. For example, green tea Frappuccino was the largest-selling Frappuccino in Taiwan and Japan before the product was offered elsewhere. Also, food makes up a larger portion of sales in China, Japan, and the United Kingdom than it does in the United States.[26] A Starbucks outlet in the Japanese city of Kobe quietly began selling beer and wine. Pronto Cafes, one of Starbucks's competitor chains in Japan, sold coffee by day and liquor at night. Selling alcohol in Starbucks USA would be far more difficult because of the stricter alcohol licensing laws in the United States.[27]

As with each individual product decision, the firm can either offer exactly the same line in its home market and abroad or, if circumstances demand, make appropriate changes. In some cases, product lines abroad may be broader than those at home. About 90 percent of Coca-Cola's global sales are in traditional brands such as Coke and Sprite. In Japan, however, these account

A McDonald's employee in Hong Kong points to a picture of the fast-food chain's rice-based products. Adapting to cultural preferences can pay off for global marketers. When McDonald's introduced rice meals in Japan, sales jumped 30 percent in one year.

for only one-third of sales as a consequence of 25 years of successful product innovation in the Japanese subsidiary.[28] However, the product lines abroad are frequently characterized by a narrower width than those found in a company's domestic market.

The circumstances that can lead to deletions from product lines vary, but some reasons dominate. Lack of sufficient market size is a frequently mentioned reason. Companies with their home base in large markets such as the United States, Japan, or Germany will find sufficient demand in their home markets for even the smallest market segments, justifying additional product variations and greater depth in their lines. Abroad, opportunities for such segmentation strategies may not exist, because the individual segments may be too small to warrant commercial exploitation. Lack of market sophistication is another factor in product-line variation. Aside from the top twenty developed markets, many markets are less sophisticated and their stage of development may not demand some of the most advanced items in a product line. Finally, new-product introduction strategies can affect product lines abroad. For most companies, new products are first introduced in their home markets and are introduced abroad only after the product has been successful at home. As a result, the lag in extending new products to foreign markets also contributes to a product-line configuration that differs from that of the firm's domestic market.

Firms confronted with deletions in their product lines sometimes add specialized offerings to fill the gap in the line, either by producing a more suitable product or by developing an entirely new product that may not have any application outside a specific market. However, such a strategy can be pursued only by a firm with adequate research and development (R&D) strength in its foreign subsidiaries.

Exploiting Product Life Cycles

Experience has shown that products do not always occupy the same position on the product life cycle curve in different countries. As Figure 10.1 shows, it is possible for a product to be in different stages of the product life cycle in dif-

FIGURE 10.1
Possible Product Life Cycle for a Product in Different Countries

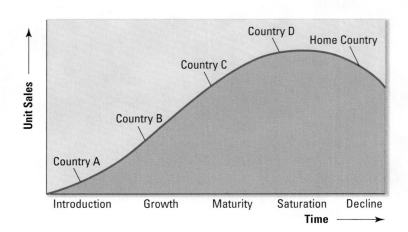

ferent countries. A firm can extend product growth by expanding into new markets to compensate for declining growth rates in mature markets. On the other hand, a company can enter new national markets too rapidly, before the local market is ready to absorb the new product. To avoid such pitfalls and to take advantage of long-term opportunities, international companies may pursue the following strategies.

During the introductory phase in a product's life cycle, the product may have to be debugged and refined. This job can best be handled in the original market or in a country close to company R&D centers. Also, the marketing approach will have to be refined. At this stage, the market in even the more advanced countries is relatively small, and demand in countries with lower levels of economic development will hardly be commercially exploitable. Therefore, the introductory stage is usually limited to the advanced markets, often the company's domestic market.

When a product faces life cycle maturity or decline in one market, it may still be marketed successfully in others. Volkswagen originally introduced its famous Beetle car in the 1930s but later withdrew it from production everywhere except Mexico. It should be remembered, however, that for some high-technology products, life cycles are very short. In these cases, products are likely to be sold worldwide—or at least in all viable markets—soon after their introduction in the domestic market.

DEVELOPING A GLOBAL PRODUCT

Firms increasingly experience pressure for cost reduction in order to remain competitive. Yet there are relatively few opportunities for producing completely standardized products. As a result, many firms now employ a new strategy, global product development. In **global products**, a portion of the final design is standardized. However, the design retains some flexibility so that the end product can be tailored to the needs of individual markets. This represents a move to standardize as much as possible those areas involving common components or parts.

> **Global product** a product for which a portion of the final design is standardized and a portion can be adapted to individual markets

One of the most significant changes in product development strategy is the move toward **modularity**. This process involves the development of standard components that can easily be connected with other standard components to increase the variety of products. By doing this, global firms can realize significant cost savings from standardization while providing some customization for different markets.

> **Modularity** a process involving the development of standard components that can easily be connected with other standard components to increase the variety of final products

This modularized approach has come to be especially important in the automobile industry, in which both U.S. and European manufacturers are increasingly creating world components to combat growing Japanese competitiveness. For example, General Motors has established a modular product architecture for all its global automobile projects. Future GM cars will be designed using combinations of components from seventy different body modules and about a hundred major mechanical components such as engines, power trains, and suspension systems. GM aims to save 40 percent in radio costs by reducing the 270 types of car radios it uses worldwide to only 50.[29]

The challenge faced by GM and other automobile manufacturers is similar to that faced by manufacturers and marketers of both industrial and consumer products all over the world. Cost pressures force them to standardize, while market pressures require more customization of products. Conceptually, these companies can gain from increasing the standardized components in their products while maintaining the ability to customize the product "at the end" for each market segment.

Most international firms must take advantage of economies of scale on the standardized portion, or core, of their products. Different firms achieve different levels of standardization, but rarely is a firm able to standardize its product 100 percent. For one company, even moving from a global core representing 15 percent of the total product to 20 percent of the total product may result in a considerable cost improvement and represent the maximum level of standardization desirable. For another firm, the core may have to represent 80 percent of the total product to achieve the same effect. These levels depend on the characteristics of the market that the company or industry faces.

NEW PRODUCT DEVELOPMENT PROCESSES FOR GLOBAL MARKETS

Many firms now develop new products with global markets in mind. These global products are based on cores and derivatives. The product core might be the same for all products in all regions. An extended core might apply for each region but differ across regions. Each region might launch product derivatives specific to the regional conditions. This core strategy allows for maximizing the appeal of different configurations, while maintaining a stable product base and thus reducing basic development costs.

The shift from local to global development requires that the company consider the unique or special concerns for major markets from the outset, rather than later attempting to make various adaptations to the initial model or prototype. The early introduction of global considerations not only ensures that the product will achieve wide acceptance but also makes it possible to maximize the commonality of models to achieve economies in component manufacturing. A global product, then, is not identical in all countries. Instead, a global product is engineered from the outset with the goal of maximizing the percentage of identical components, design, and parts to the point where local needs can be met with a minimum of additional costs in tooling, engineering, and development.

Developing new products or services for global markets poses unique challenges to a firm. In contrast to the strictly domestic company, international firms can assign development responsibilities to any one of their often numerous international subsidiaries. Aside from the question of who should perform development work, there are organizational problems to overcome that pertain to participation by experts in many subsidiaries. No doubt, the future success of international firms will depend to a substantial degree on how well they marshal their resources on a global scale to develop new products for foreign markets.

WORLD BEAT 10.2

The Global Picture

TECHNOLOGICAL CHANGE and the need to cut costs have pushed the motion picture industry toward global products and global launches. Once a blockbuster movie at Columbia Pictures could take 7 months to arrive in some countries. Now this time is cut to 60 days. The Internet is one reason for this new speed. Foreign consumers are using Web retailers such as Amazon.com to buy films on DVD as soon as they are available in the United States. In many cases, these films have not yet opened in all national markets. Furthermore, movie fans around the world can access movie promotions on the Web. These promotions appear even before the domestic launch. Waiting months to see these movies frustrates foreign consumers.

But creating a global motion picture for a global launch isn't easy. When Universal developed the film *Dr. Seuss' How the Grinch Stole Christmas*, it realized prior to production that the movie would be translated into thirty languages. However, Dr. Seuss presents peculiar problems because of the tricky language that makes it difficult to translate. Local writers were given leeway to adjust the translated verse if they thought it didn't make sense. In some cases, the translators were able to preserve rhymes partly by making up their own words to go with Dr. Seuss' made-up words. In Spanish, the "Pontoos" mountains where the Grinch lives were replaced by the "Pontienes" range—a word concocted to rhyme with "los quienes," meaning "the Whos" in Spanish. Furthermore, the translation problem was avoided somewhat in the film by a decision to modify the original English-speaking version of the movie. The Seussian metered narration was left out of long stretches of the movie and replaced by new dialogue.

Motion picture producers are also looking for ways to cut costs on new product development by avoiding developing a new film from scratch. To do so, they are looking overseas for ideas. DreamWorks has led the Hollywood movement to remake Asian films. It spent $1 million for the rights to the Japanese horror flick *Ringu*, which was selling to packed theaters in Asia. Hollywood's version *The Ring* netted $200 million worldwide and $129 million in the United States.

Sources: Bruce Orwall, "Can Grinch Steal Christmas Abroad?" *Wall Street Journal*, November 16, 2000, p. B1; Bruce Orwall and Evan Ramstad, "Fast Forward," *Wall Street Journal*, June 12, 2000, p. A1; and Karen Mazurkewich, "Hollywood Sees Starry Remakes in Asian Films," *Wall Street Journal*, July 11, 2003, p. B1.

The Organization of Head-Office-Sponsored Research and Development

Most companies that currently engage in R&D on a global scale originally conducted their development efforts strictly in centralized facilities in the firm's domestic market. Even today, the largest portion of R&D monies spent by international firms goes to support efforts in domestically located facilities. As a result, most new product ideas are first developed in the context of the domestic market. Initial introduction at home is followed by a phase-in introduction to the company's foreign markets.

There are several reasons for this traditional approach. First, R&D must be integrated into a firm's overall marketing strategy. This requires frequent contacts and interfacing between R&D facilities and the company's main offices.

Such contacts are maintained more easily with close proximity. Many companies centralize R&D because they are concerned that duplication of efforts will result if this responsibility is spread over several subsidiaries. Centralized R&D is thought to maximize results from scarce research funds. A final important reason for centralization is the company's experience in its domestic market. Typically, the domestic market is very important to the company, and in the case of international companies based in the United States, Germany, and Japan, it is often the largest market as well. As a result, new products are developed with special emphasis on the domestic market, and R&D facilities, therefore, should be close by. Traditionally, the level of R&D in a company or country has been considered one of the best indicators of long-term growth.

There are many good reasons for centralizing product development at the company's head office, but it remains a challenge for a centralized engineering and development staff of the firm to keep all relevant product modifications in mind before the design is frozen. Experience shows that later changes or modifications can be expensive. To keep a product acceptable in many or all relevant markets from the outset requires the product development staff to become globalized early in the creation process. Only a "globally thinking" product development staff will ensure the global acceptability of a product by incorporating the maximum possible number of variations in the original product.

International Lead Markets and Research and Development

As we noted in Chapter 8, participation in lead markets can be an important part of global strategy. In general, a **lead market** is a market whose level of development exceeds that of the markets in other countries worldwide and whose developments tend to set a pattern for other countries. Lead markets are not restricted to technological developments as embodied in product hardware. The concept covers developments in design, production processes, patterns in consumer demand, and methods of marketing. Therefore, virtually every phase of a company's operation is subject to lead market influences, although those focusing on technological developments are of special importance.

In the middle of the twentieth century, the United States achieved a position of virtual dominance as a lead market. Not only were U.S. products the most advanced with respect to features, function, and quality, but they also tended to be marketed to the most sophisticated and advanced consumers and industrial buyers. This U.S. advantage was partially based on superior production methods, especially the pioneering of mass production in the form of the assembly line. The U.S. advantage extended to management methods in general, and particularly to access to new consumers. The rapid development of U.S.-based multinational firms was to a considerable degree based on the exploitation of these advantages in applying new U.S. developments abroad and in creating extensive networks of subsidiaries across a large number of countries. But the overwhelming lead of the United States over other countries did not last. Foreign competitors from Europe and Japan eroded the U.S. firms' advantages. As a result, no single country or market now unilaterally dominates the world economy.

The fragmentation of lead markets has led to a proliferation of product development centers, substantially complicating the task of keeping abreast of the latest developments in market demands, product design, and production techniques. Even formerly developing countries, such as South Korea, have achieved lead-market status in some categories. Samsung Electronics tied for third place in *Business Week's* Industrial Design Excellence Awards for 2003.[30]

To prosper in today's increasingly internationalized business climate, corporations must keep track of evolving lead markets as major sources for new product ideas and production techniques. New product ideas can stem from influences in buyer demand, manufacturing processes, and scientific discoveries. No single country may play a lead role in all facets of a firm's business. This means that any corporate R&D effort must look for new developments abroad rather than solely in the domestic market.

The Role of Foreign Subsidiaries in Research and Development

Each year General Motors gives what it calls Kettering Awards to employees whose ideas help GM retain technology leadership, improve customer service, or save production time and costs. Kettering Awards have recognized researchers and engineers not only from the United States, Canada, and Germany but from Brazil and India as well.[31]

Subsidiaries may assume certain R&D functions if products require some adaptation to the local market. They may assume a more global role when they are located in a lead market. A subsidiary located in a lead market is usually in a better position to observe developments and to accommodate new demands. Consequently, international firms with subsidiaries in lead markets have an opportunity to turn such units into effective "listening posts." Global firms may also take a more proactive stance toward subsidiary research in lead markets. Kodak's Pocket Camera was conceived and developed in the company's Japanese subsidiary before it was launched in the United States. And Swiss pharmaceutical giant Novartis AG announced in 2002 that it would move its worldwide research headquarters to Cambridge, Massachusetts.[32]

Increasingly, multinational firms are investing in research facilities abroad in order to obtain input from key markets. To globalize their own research, Japanese companies have made heavy investments in U.S.-based research facilities. Hundreds of Japanese scientists already work side by side with Americans in research laboratories on exchange programs. This investment aims at accessing scientific talent in other countries. Companies chasing such talent around the world are opening development centers wherever talent can be found. In China, many Western firms have opened development facilities to obtain access to Chinese scientific talent and to understand the Chinese market better. Among those firms are Intel and Microsoft, which have opened research centers near Beijing, where many of China's leading universities are clustered.[33]

To develop a global product also requires a different organizational setup. Changes instituted by General Motors are indicative of actions taken by other international firms. With the advent of world cars, GM realized that the company needed closer coordination between its domestic units and its overseas subsidiaries. Therefore, GM moved its international staff from New York to Detroit in order to speed up communication between domestic and international staffs, and it adopted the "project center" concept to manage its engineering effort. Each division or foreign subsidiary involved in a new car design lends engineers to a centrally organized project center, which designs, develops, and introduces the new model. Upon introduction of the model, the project center is disbanded. Of course, not every firm will find a project center approach feasible. Other alternatives include assigning primary responsibility to a subsidiary that has special capability in the new product field.

In the future, international companies will have to make better use of the talents of local subsidiaries in the development of new products. Increasingly, the role of the subsidiary as simply a selling or production arm of the company will have to be abandoned, and companies will have to find innovative ways to involve their foreign affiliates in the product development process. This involvement can be patterned after several role models. The **strategic leader** role, with responsibility for developing a new range of products to be used by the entire company, may be assigned to a highly competent subsidiary in a market of strategic importance. Another subsidiary with competence in a distinct area may be assigned the role of **contributor**, adapting some products in smaller but still important markets. Most subsidiaries, being smaller and located in less strategic markets, will be expected to be **implementers** of the overall strategy, without making a major contribution either technologically or strategically.[34]

Strategic leader the home base or major subsidiary of a multinational firm, responsible for developing products used by the entire company

Contributor a subsidiary responsible for adapting some products for smaller markets

Implementer a subsidiary the primary role of which is to implement a firm's global strategy

Purchasing Research and Development from Foreign Countries

Instead of developing new products through its own R&D personnel, a company may acquire such material or information from independent outside sources. These sources are usually located in countries that have acquired lead-market status. Managers commonly read literature published in lead markets. Also, through regular visits to foreign countries and trade fairs, managers maintain close contact with lead markets. Increasingly, however, these ad hoc measures are becoming insufficient for maintaining the necessary flow of information in rapidly changing markets.

For companies without immediate access to new technology embodied in new products, the licensing avenue has been the traditional approach to gaining access to new developments from lead markets. U.S. technology has been tapped through many independent licensing arrangements. Japanese companies have made extensive use of the licensing alternative to acquire technologies developed in countries that were lead markets from Japan's point of view.

Licensing can be a boon to entrepreneurs who have few funds for R&D. One Spanish entrepreneur who originally organized study-abroad programs for Spanish university students decided to bring U.S. universities to Spain via the Internet. Building on his relationships with three prestigious American universities—Columbia University, the University of Chicago, and the University of California at Berkeley—he secured the Spanish-language rights to their online courses. The company translates courses and contracts with banks and with small and medium-sized businesses interested in outsourcing corporate education. The company is investigating expansion in Mexico, Chile, and Argentina as well.[35]

Importing as a Source of New Products

Some corporations decide to forgo internally sponsored R&D, instead importing finished products directly from a foreign firm to supplement their product lines. For example, Dutch brewing giant Heineken NV formed an alliance with Mexico's Fomento Economico Mexicano SA (Femsa) to become the sole U.S. importer for 3 years of two popular Mexican beer brands. The alliance is expected to help the company break into the Hispanic market and boost Heineken's volume by 28 percent in the competitive U.S. beer market.[36] Such a strategy should be pursued with great care, because firms may establish or expand a market position for competitors who may choose to pursue the market on their own in the future. This strategy may best apply in areas that do not represent the core of the firm's business and technology.

Acquisitions as a Route to New Products

Acquiring a company for its new technology or products is a strategy many firms have followed in domestic markets. To make international acquisitions in order to gain a window on emerging technologies or products is becoming an acceptable strategy for many firms. Robert Bosch, a German firm, acquired an interest in American Microsystems, and Philips of Holland purchased Signetics. In both cases, the foreign firms had to pay substantial premiums over the market value of the stock as a price for an inside look at new product development. Even companies from developing countries are beginning to follow this route. Recently, Indian software companies have been acquiring software companies in the United States. These acquisitions are partially motivated by a desire to access more value-added products.

Alliances for New Product Development

Many companies are finding alliances an effective way to share technology and R&D for competitive advantage. To share the huge cost of developing new products, some companies have established joint ventures or joined consortia to share in new product development. Under the **consortium approach**, member firms join in a working relationship without forming a new entity. On completion of the assigned task, member firms are free to seek other relationships with different firms. There is a shift toward such nonequity forms of R&D agreements occurring more or less uniformly across countries. This is most likely due to improved protection for contracts and intellectual property.[37]

Consortium approach an approach involving firms united in a working relationship without the formation of a new legal entity

Because the development of new aircraft is particularly expensive, the aircraft industry offers several examples of the consortium approach to product development. The high development costs require that large passenger aircraft be built and sold in series of two hundred or three hundred units to break even. Under these circumstances, several companies form a consortium to share the risk. One of the first highly successful efforts was the European Airbus, developed and produced by French, British, and German manufacturers.

The consortium approach can be employed by global buyers as well as manufacturers. Several global airlines that have alliances to sell tickets and buy fuel together are considering joint purchases of jetliners. One such group comprises Air Canada, Austrian Airlines, Lufthansa, and SAS. Joint purchases will require an alignment of normally diverse tastes for options such as cabin interiors, seating configurations, and flight kitchens. In return for agreeing to standard features, manufacturers have agreed to pass some of the cost savings from standardization on to the customers.[38]

INTRODUCING NEW PRODUCTS TO GLOBAL MARKETS

Once a product has been developed for commercial introduction, a number of complex decisions still need to be made. Aside from the question of whether to introduce the product abroad, the firm has to decide on a desirable test-marketing procedure, select target countries for product introduction, and determine the timing or sequence of the introduction. Given the large number of possible markets, decisions surrounding new product introduction often have strategic significance.

Determining which product to introduce abroad depends, of course, on sales potential. Following a careful analysis, a marketer develops a list of target countries. The company then can choose from among several paths leading to actual introduction in the target countries.

Concept Tests

Once a prototype or sample product has been developed, a company may decide to subject its new creation to a series of tests to determine its commercial feasibility. It is particularly important to subject a new product to actual use conditions. When the development process takes place outside the country of actual use, a practical field test can be crucial. The test must include all necessary usage steps to provide complete information. In a classic case, CPC International tested the U.S. market for dehydrated soups made by its newly acquired Knorr subsidiary. The company concentrated primarily on taste tests to ensure that the final product suited U.S. consumers. Extensive testing led to different soup formulations from those sold in Europe. CPC, however, had neglected to have consumers actually try out the product at home as part of their regular cooking activities. Such a test would have revealed consumers' discontent with the Knorr dehydrated soups' relatively long cooking time—up to 20 minutes, compared with 3 minutes for comparable canned soups. The company recognized these difficulties only after a national introduction had been completed and sales fell short of expectations.

The concept-testing stage would be incomplete if the products were tested only in the company's domestic market. A full test in several major markets is essential so that any shortcomings can be addressed at an early stage before costly adaptations for individual countries are made. Such an approach is particularly important in cases where product development occurs on a multinational basis with simultaneous inputs from several foreign subsidiaries. When Volkswagen tested its original Rabbit models, test vehicles were made available

Fifteen hundred multinational firms operate in Ontario, Canada. Canada has also proven to be a good test market for products later launched in the United States.

to all principal subsidiaries to ensure that each market's requirements were met by the otherwise standardized car.

Test Marketing

Just as there are good reasons to test-market a product in a domestic market, an international test can give the firm valuable insights. A key question is where the market test should be held. Companies in the United States have largely pioneered test-marketing procedures, because it has been reasonably simple to isolate a given market in terms of media and distribution. This may not always be possible in smaller countries and even less so in countries where most of the media are national rather than local. As a result, the opportunities for small local market tests are substantially reduced outside the United States.

To overcome the shortage of test-market possibilities, international firms often substitute the experience in one country for a market test in another. Special attention should be given to the lead market as a potential test market. Any new product that succeeds in its lead market may be judged to have good potential elsewhere as other markets mature. Although market tests are commonly conducted by U.S.-based firms before full-scale introduction in the U.S. market, subsidiaries tend to use these early U.S. results as a basis for analysis. However, use of the U.S. market as a test market depends on the market situation and on the degree to which results can be extrapolated to other countries. Circumstances are never exactly the same, and early U.S. results must be regarded with caution.

Another approach to test marketing is to use a foreign country as a proving ground before other markets are entered. In Europe, smaller markets such as the Netherlands, Belgium, Austria, and Switzerland may be used to launch a new product. Because of these countries' small size, a test would include national introduction, and the results would be assumed to be applicable in other countries. Sometimes the test market may not even be the place of initial launch. IBM tested a new branding campaign for its Global Services line in Canada but launched it in the United States. Testing overseas prior to U.S. launch may even be cheaper, but it requires a better understanding of how to translate foreign results into probable outcomes in the U.S. market.

The selection of countries for new product launches is increasingly based on test marketing in perhaps one or two countries, with a rapid move toward a global rollout. Heinz tested its new teenager-oriented ketchup campaign in Canada and then rolled it out worldwide with minor modifications. Clearly, global marketing is moving rapidly toward the time when testing and test interpretation will be done on the basis of data from different—and sometimes distant—markets, and the time when each local market was tested locally before launch is rapidly passing.[39]

Timing of New Product Introductions

Eventually, a company will be faced with establishing the sequence and the timing of its introduction of a new product in its home market and foreign markets. When should the product be introduced in each market? Should the firm use a phased-entry or a simultaneous-entry approach? As we have noted, firms usually introduce new products first in their domestic markets to gain experience in production, marketing, and service.

Foreign market introductions are usually attempted only after a product has proved itself in the domestic market. However, another market may prove the better choice. DaimlerChrysler of Germany, the largest truck company in the world, traditionally launches new innovations in its home market of Germany because of its large size and sophisticated buyers. However, German buyers are relatively slow to adopt service innovations. Analysis undertaken when the company was considering a launch of a remote diagnosis system (RDS) revealed that Japan would be a better market for an initial product launch.[40]

Although international firms have subsidiaries in numerous countries, initial product introductions were traditionally limited to the industrialized nations, and new product introductions in overseas markets lagged considerably behind introductions in home markets. Today, the average time lag between domestic introduction and foreign introductions has diminished considerably. One year after being introduced in the United States, Vanilla Coke was expanded to more than thirty countries.[41]

Increasingly, companies have to invest ever larger amounts for developing new technologies or products. As these investments rise, the time required to bring new generations of products to the market has increased, leaving less time for the commercialization of products before patents expire or new competitors come out with similar products. As a result, companies have been forced to introduce new products rapidly to virtually all markets, including those in major developing countries.

Technological advances sometimes aid in promoting global launches. Madonna's children's book *The English Roses* hit bookstores in one hundred countries in thirty languages simultaneously. An alliance of copublishers in different countries worked together utilizing new digital printing technology that allowed plants to switch quickly among languages. The alliance was also able to garner cost advantages from their greater bargaining power with paper suppliers as well as the ability to save costs on illustrations. The simultaneous launch also took advantage of the ability to create global buzz via Internet discussion sites.[42]

Global launches are not without their challenges. When DHL Worldwide Express rolled out a new supply-chain solution for its high-tech customers, thirty staff members from around the world engaged in what was described as a grueling process.[43] When Avon planned a worldwide launch of a new lipstick on a single day, the plan was later abandoned for fear that the product would not be available in all the markets by the appointed day.[44]

CONCLUSION

To be successful in global markets, companies often need to be flexible in product and service offerings. Although a given product may be very successful in a firm's home market, environmental differences between markets can often force a company to make unexpected or costly changes. A small group of products may be marketed worldwide without significant changes, but most companies will find that global success depends on a willingness to adapt to local market requirements. For companies that successfully master these additional international difficulties while showing a commitment to foreign customers, global success can lead to increased profits and to more secure market positions both domestically and globally.

When companies search for new markets for their products, they face the difficult task of adapting those products to new environments. Such adaptations are frequently expensive when done after the fact. In the future, companies will increasingly consider international opportunities early in the development cycle of a new product. Incorporating international requirements and standards early will enable new products to be usable immediately in many markets. Such a move toward global integration of the product development cycle will result in the development of more world products. These products will be produced in modular forms to include as many world components as possible, and they will incorporate a set of unique components to fit the product needs of individual markets. The challenge for international marketers is to find the best tradeoffs between the standardized world components of a product and the tailor-made components designed for specific markets.

Another increasingly influential factor in new product development is speed. For competitive reasons, companies want to be among the first to enter with a new product or service, because early entrants tend to obtain the biggest

Do you need to adapt your product for your target country? Continue with your *Country Market Report* on our website (college.hmco.com/business/).

market share. To increase speed to market, companies may work on collaborative development processes. They can opt to reduce the time between first domestic introduction and worldwide launch. In the end, many firms will undertake multicountry launches or simultaneous global product rollouts. Still, the risk increases with such global launches, because less time is available to test the product, ensure that it meets the market performance needs, and sufficiently tailor it to a given country.

QUESTIONS FOR DISCUSSION

1. Compare probable product adaptations for consumer products versus high-technology industrial products. What differences exist? Why?

2. American fast food, music, and movies have become popular around the world with little product adaptation, whereas U.S. retailers, banks, and beer companies have had to adapt their products more to global markets. Why?

3. What, in your opinion, will be the future for global products?

4. What is the impact of a loss of lead-market position in several industries for U.S.-based corporations?

5. If you were to test-market a new consumer product today for worldwide introduction, how would you select test countries for Europe, for Asia, and for Latin America?

CASE 10.1

"Ethical" Products

As global competition increases, consumers demand quality products at cheap prices. To lower costs, many international firms have moved production to developing countries. Much of this manufacturing is outsourced to local contractors. Increasingly, however, many consumers are factoring ethical, as well as economic, concerns into their buying decisions. To meet these new concerns of consumers, firms must now ensure that no products are produced in sweatshops where workers are underage, overworked, or beaten.

Consumer concern over products made in sweatshops exploded in the late 1990s. Activists embarrassed famous brands with exposés of working conditions abroad. Key targets were Wal-Mart stores and Nike shoes. Student

protests ensued, and consumer boycotts proved costly to the firms. Subsequently a White House task force was established, including consumer activists and industry representatives, to suggest codes of conduct for overseas production. The task force even considered allowing complying firms to label their products "not made in sweatshops."

Mattel and Disney are two companies that have adopted codes of conduct and attempt to enforce them. Mattel hired an independent panel to monitor its factories and is considered by many to be a model for others. Social auditors visit Mattel factories three times a year. Disney had completed 10,000 overseas inspections by 2001 and had cut off subcontractors that failed to make improvements.

In fact, a new industry of social auditing appears to have emerged overnight. Companies have hurried to become certified under the new global standard in ethical production—Social Accountability 8000. Both nongovernmental agencies operating in developing countries and major international auditing firms have become involved in overseeing firm compliance to the new standard. During 2000, PricewaterhouseCoopers conducted 15,000 inspections related to SA 8000 in the Chinese province of Guangdong alone.

Nike has formed a labor practices department and has supplied Global Alliance, a Baltimore-based activist group, with a $7.9 million grant to study social problems in its contracted factories. Still, a report released in 2001 identified widespread problems among Nike's Indonesian subcontractors. Major concerns dealt with limited medical care and forced overtime. Sexual molestation was widespread in a workplace environment where female workers accounted for over 84 percent of the workforce. Nearly 14 percent of interviewed workers reported witnessing physical abuse, especially when managers were under pressure to meet production goals. Nike, with six full-time staff in Indonesia for labor practices alone, was poised to respond to the findings. However, the company noted that it had far more leverage over its shoe subcontractors, who often worked exclusively for Nike. Its clothing subcontractors were a different story. Those local firms often worked for a dozen different companies.

Gap released a report admitting problems with working conditions in many of the 3,000 factories that produce Gap clothing. Ten to 25 percent of factories in China and Taiwan were found to use psychological coercion or verbal abuse. More than 50 percent of factories in sub-Saharan Africa violated safety procedures. Ninety percent of factories applying for contracts failed the retailer's initial evaluation. Labor-rights groups applauded this new openness on the part of the company.

In the meantime, Italian apparel manufacturers were taking advantage of sweatshop concerns. The Italian Trade Commission spent $25 million on a 5-year promotional campaign to convince U.S. consumers to buy Italian. The advertisements presented Italy as a country where skilled artisans produced high-quality garments. The campaign was deemed a success, and the Italian share of the U.S. apparel-import market climbed over 20 percent.

Discussion Questions

1. What can global firms do to make their products more socially acceptable?
2. What do you think they should do? Why?
3. What are the costs to global firms of keeping their products sweatshop-free?
4. What are the possible costs of not complying with SA 8000?

Sources: Shu Shin Luh, "Report Claims Abuses by Nike Contractors," *Wall Street Journal*, February 22, 2001, p. A16; "Business Ethics: Sweatshop Wars," *The Economist*, February 27, 1999, p. 62; Wendy Bounds and Deborah Ball, "Italy Knits Promotional Support in U.S.," *Wall Street Journal*, December 15, 1997, p. B2; and Amy Merrick, "Gap Offers Unusual Look at Factory Conditions," *Wall Street Journal*, May 12, 2004, p. A1.

CASE 10.2
Rethinking World Cars

With automobile markets maturing in the triad, both Ford and General Motors must look for growth elsewhere. Two large emerging markets, India and Russia, promise sales growth but present challenges as well.

India is the world's second most populous country and one of its poorest, with a per-capita income of only $425 a year. For 40 years the Indian car market was protected from foreign competition and was dominated by only two models of cars. When the government liberalized the automobile market, global competitors flocked to India. Soon there were fifteen automobile firms with production in India, a phenomenon that led to considerable overcapacity in the market.

Ford was among the firms that had been attracted to India. However, the Ford Escort fared poorly in this market. The company found out firsthand that the Indian consumer wanted the best but would not spend much money for it. Ford responded by designing the Ikon, their first car built for consumers in the developing world. More than four hundred engineers and development personnel were assigned the task, at a cost of $500 million.

Essentially, Ford remade its Fiesta model. More headroom was added to accommodate men who wore turbans. Doors opened wider for women who wore saris. The air conditioning was adjusted to India's heat, and air-intake valves were fitted in such a way as not to be vulnerable to the flooding that accompanied India's monsoon season. Shock absorbers were toughened to withstand potholed streets. Ford even convinced certain of its suppliers to set up plants near the Ford plant in India in order to meet India's local-content requirements. Extensive product testing was done under India's harsh driving conditions. The Ikon was priced between $9,500 and $16,000, and its sales in India quickly surpassed those of the Escort. In addition, over 50 percent of pro-duction of the Ford Ikon was exported to South America and South Africa.

About the time the Ikon was enjoying its first sales in India, General Motors decided to take quite a different route to the market in Russia. GM identified Russia as one of eight countries that would account for two-thirds of global growth in car sales in the coming decade. Unfortunately, Russia continued to be plagued with both political and economic risk. Furthermore, GM was concerned that a stripped-down model of a Western car—GM's traditional approach to markets in developing countries—would not be cheap enough for the Russian market. Although such a car could be assembled inexpensively in Russia, the engineering to create the adapted model would be extremely expensive. Also, market research showed that Russians thought little of cars assembled in Russia, even if they included foreign-made parts and bore a prestigious brand name. If a car were assembled in Russia, it would be attractive only if it sold at an extremely low price.

GM decided, therefore, to put its Chevrolet brand on a product developed by Avtovaz, a struggling automobile producer from the Soviet era. As the Soviet car producer, Avtovaz had dominated not only the Russian market but also the Soviet bloc market until the fall of communism, when it lost its captive export markets and the Russian market became deluged with imported cars. Avtovaz's cheapest car, priced at $3,000, was the boxy four-door "classic." Most of its models included no automatic transmission, no emission controls, and no power steering. The company developed only one new model in the 1990s. With Russia's political uncertainty and collapsed economy, Avtovaz lacked the funds to bring the model to production.

After considerable negotiations, GM and Avtovaz agreed to enter a $333 million joint venture to produce the Niva. GM would contribute much-needed cash, as well as designing and supervising the production facilities. Avtovaz would contribute the Niva design and would also save GM the costs of developing a parts and distribution system, because the car would be sold and serviced through the Avtovaz system. Still concerned about political risk in Russia, GM convinced the European Bank for Reconstruction and Development to lend the venture $93 million and to invest another $40 million in exchange for a 17 percent equity stake.

The new Niva was noisy, delivered a rough ride, and had a low-power engine, but it passed basic safety testing, carried a GM logo, and could be sold for $7,500. The premium model would get Opel transmissions. Surveyed consumers liked the Niva better than other Russian models. In addition, GM identified, among its international oper-

ations, potential export markets for up to 25,000 of the 75,000 cars to be produced each year.

Discussion Questions

1. What are the similarities and differences between the car markets in India and Russia?
2. Which market do you think is the most difficult? Why?
3. Compare the pros and cons of Ford's model invention strategy and GM's joint venture strategy.

Sources: Gregory L. White, "Off Road," *Wall Street Journal*, February 20, 20001, p. A1; Jon E. Hilsenath, "A Car to Suit India's Taste," *Wall Street Journal*, August 8, 2000, p. A17; and "Ford India Upbeat on SUV Market," *Business Line*, February 28, 2004, p. 3.

CASE 10.3
Launching Intuition

In the first year of the new millennium, Estee Lauder launched Intuition, its biggest new fragrance in 5 years. The new fragrance was allotted a record-breaking $30 million advertising budget. Lauder aimed for $100 million in sales in the first year, more than double the sales of most other new fragrances.

A typical launch of a Lauder fragrance began with its introduction in the United States. The product would then be introduced to overseas markets in 6 months to a year. In an unprecedented move, the launch of Intuition bypassed the United States. Instead, it was introduced in France and Britain in September, with a rollout to the rest of Europe, Asia, and Latin America in October. Approximately 40 percent of sales of prestige fragrances take place in November and December.

Estee Lauder owned five of the top ten women's fragrances sold at department stores across the United States. However, only one Lauder perfume,

Pleasures, made the top ten in Europe. The U.S. fragrance market, especially for the premier lines sold in department stores, remained in a slump. For the past 5 years, sales had been flat or down each year. In Europe, the market had grown about 8 percent the previous year.

Recently Lauder's overseas sales had reached 50 percent, and creative divisions had been established in Paris and Tokyo to develop products for local consumer needs. Intuition was the first collaborative effort between Lauder's U.S. and European development centers. Intuition's formula was lighter than the traditionally heavy European fragrances and was targeted at the younger woman (starting in her midtwenties). It was marketed as Lauder's first fragrance with a European sensibility, although the company wanted Intuition eventually to be seen as a global fragrance. At an unspecified date, Intuition was to be introduced in the United States. Some managers believed that U.S. sales might even be improved if Intuition could be billed as previously "available only in Europe."

Discussion Questions

1. What are possible reasons for the unconventional development and launch of Intuition?

2. What difficulties might the company face with such a launch?

Sources: "Estee Lauder Follows Its Intuition with European Fragrance Debut," *The Rose Sheet,* September 3, 2000; Emily Nelson, "Nosing Abroad," *Wall Street Journal,* September 30, 2000, p. B1; and "Will Europe Take to Intuition?" *Straits Times,* November 1, 2000.

NOTES

1. Pierre Berthon, Leyland Pitt, Constantine S. Katsikeas, and Jean Paul Berthon, "Virtual Services Go International: International Services in the Marketspace," *Journal of International Marketing* 7, no. 3 (1999), p. 96.
2. Chen May Yee, "E-Business in Asia, It's Not a Wide-Open Web," *Wall Street Journal,* July 9, 2001, p. B1.
3. Mylene Mangalindan and Kevin Delaney, "Yahoo! Ordered to Bar the French from Nazi Items," *Wall Street Journal,* November 21, 2000, p. B1.
4. Peter Ford, "Need Software in, Say, Icelandic? Call the Irish," *Christian Science Monitor,* February 6, 2001, p.1.
5. Cris Prystay, "Companies Market to India's Have-Littles," *Wall Street Journal,* June 5, 2003, p. B1.
6. Elisabeth Malkin, "Mexico Goes Top-Flight," *Business Week,* June 26, 2000.
7. Claudia Puig, "'Hannibal' Ignites Worldwide Controversy," *USA Today,* March 7, 2001, p. D06.
8. Robert A. Guth and Almar Latour, "Japanese Makers Hope to Export Web-Ready Cellphones Worldwide," *Wall Street Journal,* April 19, 2001, p. B1.
9. International Standards Organization website, www.iso.ch.
10 Barbara Carton, "No Yolk," *Wall Street Journal,* June 24, 2002, p. A1.
11. Brandon Mitchener, "Increasingly, Rules of Global Economy Are Set in Brussels," *Wall Street Journal Europe,* April 23, 2002. p. A1.
12. Alexei Barrionuevo, "Worlds Apart on Product Safety," *Wall Street Journal,* September 15, 2004, p. A19.
13. Geoffrey A. Fowler and Ramin Setoodeh, "Outsiders Get Smarter About China's Tastes," *Wall Street Journal,* August 5, 2004, p. B1.
14. Ford, "Need Software in, Say, Icelandic?"
15. Arundhati Parmar, "Dependent Variable," *Marketing News,* September 16, 2002, p. 4.
16. Fowler and Setoodeh, "Outsiders Get Smarter About China's Tastes."
17. Deborah Ball, Sarah Ellison, Janet Adamy, and Geoffrey A. Fowler, "Recipes Without Borders?" *Wall Street Journal,* August 19, 2004, p. A6.
18. Ford, "Need Software in, Say, Icelandic?"
19. Catherine Arnold, "Foreign Exchange," *Marketing News,* May 15, 2004, p. 13.
20. Arundhati Parmar, "Dependent Variable," *Marketing News,* September 16, 2002, p. 4.
21. "Coke Sells Water by the Cup in India," *Daily News,* available at AdAge Global, www.adageglobal.com (accessed May 14, 2002).
22. Ford, "Need Software in, Say, Icelandic?"
23. John O'Neil, "Reducing Drug Overdoses, by Packaging," *New York Times,* May 29, 2001, p. 8.
24. Kathy Chen, "Cashmere Clothes to Undergo More FTC Monitoring," *Wall Street Journal,* May 4, 2001, p. B1.
25. "Coca-Cola Poland Details Scope of Product Recalls," *Wall Street Journal,* July 14, 1999, p. A17.
26. "Boss Talk: It's a Grande-Latte World," *Wall Street Journal,* December 15, 2003, p. B1.
27. Jason Singer and Martin Fackler, "In Japan, Adding Beer, Wine to Latte List," *Wall Street Journal,* July 14, 2003, p. B1.
28. Michael Flagg, "Coca-Cola Adopts Local-Drinks Strategy in Asia," *Wall Street Journal,* July 30, 2001.
29. Lee Hawkins, Jr., "New Driver," *Wall Street Journal,* October 6, 2004, p. A1.
30. "Winners for 2003" *Business Week,* July 7, 2003, p. 70.
31. "GM Innovations Recognized," PR Newswire, April 25, 2001.
32. Jeffrey Krasner, "Drug Research Giant Heads to Cambridge," *Boston Globe,* May 7, 2002, p. A1.
33. Charles Bickers and Trish Saywell, "China: Back to the Future," *Far Eastern Economic Review,* March 11, 1999, p. 10.
34. Kasra Ferdows, "Making the Most of Foreign Factories," *Harvard Business Review* 75 (March–April 1997), pp. 73–88.
35. Keith Johnson, "The Business-Spanish Lessons: An Entrepreneur Wants to Bring U.S. Universities to Spaniards," *Wall Street Journal,* March 12, 2001, p. R18.
36. "Heineken Signs Deal with Femsa to Import Beers," *Wall Street Journal,* June 22, 2004, p. B3.
37. Rajneesh Narula and Geert Duysters, "Globalisation and Trends in International R&D Alliances," *Journal of International Management* 10 (2004), p. 213.
38. "Airlines Move Toward Buying Planes in Alliances," *Dow Jones Business News,* May 19, 2003.
39. "Test It in Paris, France, Launch It in Paris, Texas," *Advertising Age,* May 31, 1999, p. 28.

40. Marian Beise and Thomas Cleff, "Assessing the Lead Market Potential of Countries for Innovation Projects," *Journal of International Management* 10 (2004), pp. 453–477.

41. Chad Terhune, "Coca-Cola Posts 11% Increase in Profit," *Wall Street Journal*, July 18, 2003, p. B2.

42. Charles Goldsmith, "Latest Madonna Release," *Wall Street Journal*, September 4, 2003, p. B1.

43. "DHL and EXE Begin Global Roll-Out," Business Wire, February 13, 2002.

44. Nanette Byrnes, "Panning for Gold in Local Markets," *Business Week*, September 18, 2000, p. 54.

11 GLOBAL STRATEGIES FOR SERVICES, BRANDS, AND SOCIAL MARKETING

HEWLETT-PACKARD CORPORATION wins a US$3 billion contact to manage Procter & Gamble's global information technology services.[1] The head of Microsoft's Russian operations lectures her employees on the value of intellectual property and exhorts them not to buy counterfeit products.[2] In Kenya, a local office of Care International promotes behavioral changes that will decrease diarrheal diseases.[3]

In Chapter 10 we discussed the global implications of product development. In this chapter we examine issues related specifically to service marketing, global brands, and brand protection. In addition, we explore the role of social marketing in the international arena. Although many of the issues covered in Chapter 10 apply to services as well, we begin this chapter by discussing what makes services different from physical products. We then

LEARNING OBJECTIVES

After studying this chapter, you should be able to

▶ Describe ways in which marketing services differs from the international marketing of physical products.

▶ Explain how culture can affect key aspects of services marketing.

▶ Compare the advantages and disadvantages of using global brand names and using single-country brand names.

▶ Differentiate between a global brand name and a global brand strategy.

▶ Identify the strengths and weaknesses of global brands versus local brands.

▶ Define *private branding* and explain why it is used by some international firms.

▶ Differentiate among trademark preemption, counterfeiting, and product piracy, and suggest ways in which firms can seek to minimize each of these.

▶ Explain how global social marketing is similar to—and different from—the international marketing of products and services.

illustrate how culture can affect a number of issues associated with services marketing. We continue with a discussion of the various implications of selecting brand names for international markets and present the pros and cons associated with global branding. The following section focuses on brand protection. We conclude by examining how global marketing can be extended to many aspects of social marketing.

MARKETING SERVICES GLOBALLY

More than half of Fortune 500 companies are primarily service providers.[4] The value of services produced in the world today now exceeds that of manufactured physical products,[5] and international trade in services represents about 25 percent of total world trade.

One of the largest categories of service exports is business services. These services are provided to firms, governments, or other organizations and include communication services, financial services, software development, database management, construction, computer support, accounting, advertising, consulting, and legal services. Many services are now aimed at multinational companies themselves. IBM's Global Services is its most rapidly growing division and is currently driving company growth while the hardware divisions struggle. Global Services supplies multinational firms with a variety of information technology services, from running a customer's information technology department to consulting on system upgrades and building global supply-chain management applications.[6]

Services aimed at business buyers that are most likely to be exported are those that have already met with success domestically. The experience of U.S.-based service companies can be used as an example. Some of the services that have been most successfully marketed abroad are financial services. Commercial banks such as Citibank, Chase, and BankAmerica have built such extensive branch networks around the world that foreign deposits and profits make up nearly half of business volume. Advertising agencies have also expanded overseas either by building branch networks or by merging with local agencies. More recently, many U.S.-based marketing research firms have expanded into foreign countries.

International accounting services have experienced tremendous growth as well. Overseas expansion is important to U.S.-based accounting firms for several reasons. Among the leading accounting firms, international revenue typically exceeds domestic revenue. Revenue is growing more rapidly abroad, and margins are also better for international operations. Many of the firms' accounting clients have gone through globalization themselves and demand that their accountants have a global presence as well. Also, the liberalization of trade in Europe and elsewhere has boosted cross-national business, increasing demand for international accountants.

The legal profession is also finding numerous opportunities overseas. Many U.S. law firms have opened up overseas branch locations, primarily in London, to capture business from investment banks and other financial services firms that must have a presence in both New York and London, major capital market centers. U.S. and British law firms have recently targeted the Japanese market. In 2005, Japan first allowed foreign law firms to hire Japanese lawyers, merge with Japanese firms, and practice Japanese law.[7]

Trade in business services has traditionally taken place primarily among developed economies such as the United States, the Netherlands, France, Japan, the United Kingdom, Germany, and Italy. However, service providers from developing countries are increasingly visible on the global stage. For example 43 of the top 225 international construction companies are now Chinese. These firms operate projects in 180 countries and account for 17.5 percent of construction projects in Asia, 9.5 percent in the Middle East, and 7.4 percent in Africa. China's largest construction company, China State, has even entered developed markets, winning a contract to build a Marriott Hotel in New York and three schools in South Carolina.[8]

Marketing services to consumers abroad—such as gyms, cleaning services, restaurant chains, and insurance policies—has also expanded. However, marketing services to consumers may turn out to be more difficult than selling to businesses. Because consumer behavior and usage patterns usually differ more between countries than business usage patterns do, many services have to be adapted even more to local conditions to make them successful.

Services differ from physical products in four key ways. They are *intangible*. They cannot be stored or readily displayed or communicated. Production and consumption of services are *simultaneous*. Services cannot be inventoried, and production lines do not exist to deliver standardized products of consistent quality. Therefore, delivered services are *heterogeneous* in nature. Finally, because services cannot be stored, they assume a *perishable* nature.[9]

The Mexican affiliate of Ernst & Young places an advertisement in English. Many service providers in fields such as accounting and consulting have followed multinational clients abroad.

These unique qualities of services affect their international marketing. Guaranteeing service quality worldwide is more difficult, and there are fewer opportunities to realize economies of scale with services than with physical products. **Back-stage elements of services** (planning and implementation aspects of services invisible to the customer) are easier to standardize cross-culturally than **front-stage elements of services** (aspects of service encounters visible to the customer).[10] For example, a fast-food provider such as McDonald's might standardize purchasing and inventory procedures, but its counter personnel in Saudi Arabia would still need to speak Arabic, and its seating design would need to accommodate separate areas for men and women.

Culture and the Service Experience

Culture affects a number of aspects of the service experience, including customer expectations, customer satisfaction and loyalty, the waiting experience, and the recruitment and behavior of service personnel.

Customer Expectations. Customers may exhibit different expectations concerning service levels. Department stores in Japan still employ women in kimonos to bow and greet customers as they arrive at the store. Service personnel are available and solicitous. In the United States, consumers tend to be willing to forgo high levels of service in favor of low prices. They are more accustomed to self-service and may even feel nervous in the presence of hovering salespeople. Consumers in Switzerland are delighted when their local grocer chooses the best produce for them. As regular customers from the neighborhood, they deserve the best. Of course, this means that new customers are given the poorer produce. This would seem discriminatory and unfair to American customers. If residing in Switzerland, they would prefer to drive to a hypermarket where produce is prepackaged and the service encounter can be avoided altogether.

Asian cultures traditionally expect and deliver high levels of service. While an American saying purports that "the consumer is always right," a similar saying in Japan states that "the customer is God."[11] Despite higher expectations of service, Asian business customers complain less when they receive poor service than do customers in the West.[12] One possible explanation is that customers in more collectivist cultures may tend to self-sacrifice and maintain self-discipline in order not to harm the relationship with the service provider. Alternatively, lack of complaining may be attributed to an attempt not to embarrass the service provider or cause a loss of face. However, dissatisfied customers are likely to voice dissatisfaction to other members in their reference group.[13] Customers in collectivist cultures may exhibit more loyalty and stay with a poor service provider longer than customers in a more individualistic culture, but their loyalty is not absolute. Given a lack of complaints, service providers can be caught unaware when these dissatisfied customers eventually leave.

The Waiting Experience. Time is always an aspect of services, and attitudes toward the time it takes to be served vary across cultures. For example, waiters in European restaurants take care not to hurry patrons. Eating a meal is supposed to be an enjoyable experience most often shared with friends. Servers also wait to be asked to deliver the bill for the meal; diners may wish to sit for hours. Americans would wonder what had happened to their waiter. Americans expect fast service at restaurants and like the bill to be dropped promptly on the table. What would be a good service experience for a European diner would be a bad one for an American.

Attitudes toward waiting in line vary as well. The English are famous for their orderly and patient waits in lines, or queues. In the French-speaking part of Switzerland, members of this otherwise polite population are likely to become a jostling mob when caused to wait at an entrance. Americans introduced the idea of establishing a single line leading to multiple service points instead of having separate lines for each point. This invention addressed the common American complaint that one inevitably ended up standing in the slowest-moving line. Americans have difficulty understanding why the rest of the world hasn't adopted this idea.

In certain parts of the world, social norms may require that men and women stand in different lines. This can be observed at metro stops in Mexico City during rush hours. In Egypt the imported design of having an "in" line leading to a service point and an exit leading away from it was reinterpreted as one line for men and one for women, with each line alternately taking its turn at the service point.

Service Personnel. When the local manager of a U.S.-based hotel chain was preparing to open a new hotel in Egypt, he was faced with a dilemma. American tourists would expect waitresses who could take their order in English. Egyptian women who spoke English almost invariably came from the upper classes. No young lady from those classes would be caught in public serving food to strangers. In a panic, the manager called friends and family and finally borrowed enough sisters, daughters, and nieces to staff the restaurant in time for opening day. Within a week, one waitress met and married a Saudi multimillionaire who came to eat at the restaurant. Whether apocryphal or not, the story spread like wildfire, and the manager never again had trouble recruiting waitresses!

In many cultures, such as the Middle East, working in a service occupation is often considered akin to being a servant. This social stigma can make it hard to recruit qualified personnel for some positions, especially those that require higher levels of education as well as technical and interpersonal skills. Until relatively recently, stewardesses for many airlines from the Middle East had to be imported from Europe, and nursing has never achieved the status in the Middle East as it has in the West. Men as well as women feel the stigma. It is not uncommon for well-paid technical repairmen, such as those who work in the air-conditioning industry, to dress in a suit and tie and carry their tools in a briefcase.

Service personnel are also critical for the delivery of professional services. Properly trained professionals may be difficult to find in some countries. However, many multinational service firms gain a recruiting advantage by offering salaries in excess of local competition.

BRANDING DECISIONS

Whether marketing products or services, global firms must manage and defend the value of their brands. Brands provide a name or symbol that gives a product (or service) credibility and helps the consumer identify the product. A brand that consumers know and trust helps them make choices faster and more easily.[14] A globally recognized brand name can be a huge asset even when a firm enters new markets. For example, when McDonald's opened its doors in Johannesburg, South Africa, thousands of people stood in line. When Coke entered Poland, its red and white delivery trucks drew applause at traffic lights.[15]

Business Week ranks the top global brands using a methodology developed by Interbrand Corporation. This methodology estimates the net present value of future sales of the brand taking into consideration factors such as market leadership, stability, and global reach—the brand's ability to cross geographical and cultural borders. Furthermore, all brands must be global in nature—at least a third of brand revenues must be derived outside the firm's domestic market. As Table 11.1 shows, the top global brands are dominated by U.S. brands, fol-

TABLE 11.1 TOP 30 GLOBAL BRANDS		
RANK	BRAND	HOME COUNTRY
1	Coca-Cola	U.S.
2	Microsoft	U.S.
3	IBM	U.S.
4	GE	U.S.
5	Intel	U.S.
6	Nokia	Finland
7	Disney	U.S.
8	McDonald's	U.S.
9	Toyota	Japan
10	Marlboro	U.S.
11	Mercedes-Benz	Germany
12	Citi	U.S.
13	Hewlett-Packard	U.S.
14	American Express	U.S.
15	Gillette	U.S.
16	BMW	Germany
17	Cisco	U.S.
18	Louis Vuitton	France
19	Honda	Japan
20	Samsung	S. Korea
21	Dell	U.S.
22	Ford	U.S.
23	Pepsi	U.S.
24	Nescafé	Switzerland
25	Merrill Lynch	U.S.
26	Budweiser	U.S.
27	Oracle	U.S.
28	Sony	Japan
29	HSBC	Britain
30	Nike	U.S.

SOURCE: Adapted from "The 100 Top Brands," *Business Week*, August 1, 2005. Reprinted with permission.

lowed by European brands, although a number of Asian companies such as Toyota, Honda, and Samsung have built strong global brands.

Selecting Brand Names

Selecting appropriate brand names on an international basis is substantially more complex than deciding on a brand name for just one country. Typically, a brand name is rooted in a given language and, if used elsewhere, may have either a different meaning or none at all. Ideally, marketers look for brand names that evoke similar emotions or images around the world.

Brand name and symbol selection is critical. International marketers must carefully evaluate the meanings and word references in the languages of their target audiences. Can the name be pronounced easily, or will it be distorted in the local language? A good example of brand adaptation is the name choice for Coca-Cola, which means "tasty and happy" in Chinese. Mercedes-Benz's Chinese name means "striving forward fast," and Sharp's means "the treasure of sound." However, branding in Asia, and especially in China, may rely even more on the visual appeal of logos than on brand names. The simple graphical logos of Volkswagen, Mercedes-Benz, and Lexus are rated high, whereas the icons of Cadillac, General Motors, and Fiat are less appealing.[16]

Single-Country versus Global Brand Names. Global marketers are constantly confronted with the decision of whether the brand name needs to be universal. Brands such as Coca-Cola and Kodak have universal use and lend themselves to an integrated international marketing strategy. With worldwide travel so common, many companies do not think they should accept a brand name unless it can be used universally.

Of course, using the same name elsewhere is not always possible. In such instances, different names have to be found. Procter & Gamble had successfully marketed its household cleaner, Mr. Clean, in the United States for some time. This name, however, had no meaning except in countries using the English language. This prompted the company to arrive at several adaptations abroad, such as *Monsieur Propre* in France and *Meister Proper* in Germany. In all cases, however, the symbol of the genie with gleaming eyes was retained because it evoked similar responses abroad and in the United States.

Selecting a Global Name

Given the almost unlimited possibilities for names and the restricted opportunities to find and register a desirable one, international companies devote considerable effort to the selection procedure. One consulting company specializes in finding brand names with worldwide application. The company brings citizens of many countries together in Paris where, under the guidance of a specialist, they are asked to state names in their particular language that would combine well with the product to be named.[17] Speakers of other languages can immediately react if a name comes up that sounds unpleasant or has distasteful connotations in their language. After a few such sessions, the company may accumulate as many as a thousand names that will later be reduced to five hundred by a company linguist. The client company then is asked to select fifty to one hundred names for further consideration. At this point, the names are subjected to a search procedure to determine which have not been registered in any of the countries under consideration. In the end, only about ten names may survive this process. From these, the company will have to make the final selection. Although this process may be expensive, the cost is generally considered negligible compared with the advertising expenditures invested in the brand name over many years.

When confronted with the need to search for a brand name with global applications, a company can consider the following:

▶ An arbitrary or invented word not to be found in any dictionary of standard English (or other language), such as Toyota's Lexus.

▶ A recognizable English (or other-language) word, but one totally unrelated to the product in question, such as the detergent Cheer.

▶ An English (or other-language) word that merely suggests some characteristic or purpose of the product, such as Mr. Clean.

▶ A word that is evidently descriptive of the product, although the word may have no meaning to persons unacquainted with English (or the other language), such as the diaper brand Pampers.

▶ A geographic place or a common surname, such as Kentucky Fried Chicken.

▶ A device, design, number, or some other element that is not a word or a combination of words, such as the 3M Company.[18]

Changing Brand Names

At times, firms may choose to change the name of a brand in local markets or even worldwide. This is not an easy choice. If a product has substantial market share in one or more markets, changing its name can confuse or even alienate consumers. Colgate-Palmolive, the large U.S.-based toiletries manufacturer, purchased the leading toothpaste brand in Southeast Asia, "Darkie." With a minstrel in blackface as its logo, the product had been marketed by a local company since 1920. After the acquisition in 1985, Colgate-Palmolive came under pressure from many groups in the United States to use a less offensive brand name. The company sponsored a large amount of research to find both a brand name and a logo that were racially inoffensive and yet close enough to the original to be recognized quickly by consumers. The company changed the name to "Darlie" after an exhaustive search. Still, in some markets where the "Darkie" brand had as much as 50 percent market share, it was a substantial marketing challenge to convert brand loyalty, intact, from the old to the new name.[19]

Today some multinational companies are reconsidering earlier decisions concerning brand names. Unilever launched Jif household cleaner in the United Kingdom in 1974. Twenty-five years later, the product held a 74 percent share of the market. Despite Jif's market dominance and name recognition, Unilever decided to change its name to correspond to the name under which it was sold in other major markets. When the product was first rolled out, it received different names based in part on ease of pronunciation in each local language. This resulted in Jif becoming Cif in France and thirty-nine other countries. It was Viss in Germany and Vim in Canada. The product wasn't introduced in the United States, where the name was already associated with a peanut butter marketed by competitor Procter & Gamble. Unilever undertook extensive market research to ensure that consumers would not be upset by the change and also supported the new name with substantial promotion to reassure the customer that Cif was actually Jif.[20]

Federal Express launched its courier business in the United States in the 1970s. The Federal Express name reflected the U.S. overnight delivery service. As Federal Express opened its international operations, however, the name was a problem. In Latin America *federal* connoted corrupt police, and in Europe the name was linked to the former Federal Republic of Germany. In 1994, Federal Express changed its name to FedEx, which in some cases is used as a verb meaning "to ship overnight."[21] Because FedEx dealt with many multinational companies as clients, it wanted a single name to use globally.

Global Brand Strategies

The concept of global branding goes beyond simply establishing a global brand name. Yet experts disagree on what exactly makes a global brand. Is it global presence or global name recognition? There are certainly brand names such as Coca-Cola that are well known in most countries of the world. Does the name connote similar attributes worldwide? Is the product the same? Is the brand a powerful player in all major markets? Heineken qualifies on the first two conditions, but not on the third. It has positioned itself as a quality imported beer in its many export markets. The beer and the bottle remain the same across markets. However, its lack of adaptation has kept it a well-known but minor player in the various national markets.

As we have noted, *Business Week* defines a global brand as one with at least a third of sales outside the firm's domestic market. Other definitions are less encompassing, describing global brands as brands whose positioning, advertising strategy, personality, look, and feel are in most respects the same in all countries.[22] Firms that develop global brands with these characteristics are said to follow a **global brand strategy**.

Several steps are involved in developing and administering a global brand strategy:

1. A firm must identify common customer needs worldwide and determine how the global brand can deliver both functional and emotional benefits to these customers.
2. A process must be established to communicate the brand's identity to consumers, channels, and the firm's own employees.
3. There should be a way to track the success of the global identity of the brand, such as the customer opinion surveys employed by Pepsi.
4. The firm must determine whether it will follow a more centralized, top-down approach to global branding or a more gradual, bottom-up approach. Sony and Mobil take **top-down approaches** wherein a global management team determines the global brand strategy and then country strategies are derived from it. In a **bottom-up approach**, country strategies are grouped by similarities in such variables as the level of economic development and the competitive situation (whether or not the brand is dominant in the market). Common elements are first identified within these groupings.

Global brand strategy a strategy in which the positioning, advertising, look, and personality of a brand remain constant across markets

Top-down approach an approach to global branding in which a global team determines the global brand strategy and country strategies are derived from this strategy

Bottom-up approach an approach to global branding in which brand strategy emerges from shared experiences and best practices among the firm's subsidiaries

WORLD BEAT 11.1
Repositioning Beer

BELGIAN BREWER INTERBREW NV decided that its financial future lay in snob appeal. So it decided to sell its Stella Artois brand—a beer known in Belgium as "fit for an old peasant"—as a premium label elsewhere. The strategy began in London where the beer, now the top import in the United Kingdom, was advertised as "reassuringly expensive." Then Interbrew chose the New York market to put its strategy seriously to the test. The company hired a team of young partygoers to identify the twenty most exclusive bars in the city. Stella, priced at a premium $100 a keg, was supplied to those twenty bars. Sales doubled from the year before.

SABMiller PLC also announced its plans to introduce plebian Miller Genuine Draft as a sophisticated interna-tional premium brew in Hungary, Slovakia, Romania, the Czech Republic, Poland, and Italy. The firm hopes that the new European branding will create a "global buzz" for the struggling U.S. icon. The beer will be priced similar to other export beers such as Heineken and will be targeted at hip bars. The only problem: Europeans tend to think U.S. beers are too light and watery.

Sources: Dan Bilefsky, "How Belgium's 'Peasant' Beer Became 'Premium' in U.S." *Wall Street Journal,* April 12, 2002, p. A13; Dan Bilefsy, "Miller Beer Aims to be Icon in Europe," *Wall Street Journal,* June 13, 2003, p. B7; and Dan Bilefsky, "U.S. Beer Has Euro-Puzzle," *Wall Street Journal Europe,* July 21, 2004, p. A5.

Over time, a more global strategy emerges as subsidiaries share experiences and best practices.[23]

Brand champion a manager or group within a firm charged with the responsibility for building and managing a global brand

In any case, a **brand champion** should be given the responsibility for building and managing a global brand. This should include monitoring the brand across markets, as well as authorizing the use of the brand on other products and businesses (brand extensions). The brand champion can be a senior manager at corporate headquarters, a product development group, or the manager of a lead country or one with major market share for the brand. For example, Unilever at one time gave its French subsidiary custody over its Lipton brand.[24]

For multinational firms, global branding offered a way to cut costs and present a consistent customer communication about the brand. Global branding became popular as a strategy among transnational companies as early as the mid-1980s. Today Unilever claims that three-fourths of its business comes from twenty global brands.[25] Some of the original enthusiasm with global branding has abated, however, as consumers in different countries reject brands they judge as resulting from least-common-denominator thinking. Multinational firms have responded with more hybrid **global strategies**, through which they attempt to combine the quality improvements and cost savings of backstage activities such as technology, production, and organization with elements more tailored to local tastes such as adapting product features, distribution, and promotion.[26]

Global strategy a strategy that captures the quality improvements and cost savings of standardized backstage activities but adapts key elements of the marketing mix, such as product features, distribution, and promotion to local tastes

International brand a brand that follows a global strategy but does not maintain a strict standardized marketing strategy and mix across all national markets

Some propose that the term **international brands** be used to differentiate brands that follow such a global strategy from other global brands that maintain a more standardized marketing strategy and mix across national markets.[27] However, the term *global brand* continues to be commonly used for both.

Consumer Response to Global Brands. It is interesting to note that when Interbrand polled consumers about the global impact of global brands, the ranking of brands varied from that of *Business Week* (see Table 11.2). To better understand what consumers worldwide thought of global brands, Douglas Holt, John Quelch, and Earl Taylor conducted the Global Brands Study. This study utilized both qualitative and quantitative research design and incorporated responses from 3,300 consumers in forty-one countries.[28] The researchers concluded that consumers evaluate global brands on three key dimensions:

▶ *Quality signal.* Consumers observe the fierce competitive battles among global brands over quality. Global brands become a cue for quality. Forty-four percent of brand preference is explained by this dimension.

▶ *Global myth.* Global brands are symbols of cultural ideals relating to modernity and a cosmopolitan identity. A focus-group participant in the Global Brands Study opined, "Local brands show what we are; global brands show what we want to be." Another participant remarked, "Global brands make us feel like citizens of the world."[29] Twelve percent of brand preference is explained by this dimension.

▶ *Social responsibility.* Because the firms behind global brands are perceived to have extraordinary power and influence, consumers expect these companies to address social problems—a demand that local firms can more easily dodge. For example, local companies would not be asked to address global warming, but multinational energy companies such as BP and Shell would be. Eight percent of brand preference is explained by this dimension.

TABLE 11.2 Brands with Most Global Impact			
Rank	**2004**	**2003**	**2002**
1	Apple	Google	Google
2	Google	Apple	Apple
3	Ikea	Mini	Coca-Cola
4	Starbucks	Coca-Cola	Starbucks
5	Al Jazeera	Samsung	Ikea
6	Mini	Ikea	Nike
7	Coca-Cola	Nokia	Nokia
8	Virgin	Nike	BMW
9	eBay	Sony	Volkswagen
10	Nokia	Starbucks	Absolut

Source: Adapted from Readers' Choice 2002 Global Top Votes, 2003 Global Top Votes, and 2004 Global Top Votes, Interbrand, brandchannel.com.

The research team goes on to identify four global segments based on these three dimensions of global brands:

Global citizens consumers who associate global brands with quality and innovation and expect transnational firms to behave responsibly regarding workers' rights and the environment

▶ **Global citizens.** These consumers rely on the success of a global brand to identify products of quality and innovation. However, they also expect transnational firms to behave responsibly on issues such as workers' rights and the environment. This segment was the largest in the study and accounted for 55 percent of consumers. Global citizens were relatively rare in Britain and the United States but more common in Brazil, China, and Indonesia.

Global dreamers consumers who equate global brands with quality and are attracted by the lifestyle they portray

▶ **Global dreamers.** This segment was the second-largest in the study—23 percent of consumers. These consumers both equate global brands with quality and are attractive by the lifestyle they portray. However, these consumers are less concerned with social issues relating to transnational firms.

Antiglobals consumers who are skeptical of the quality of global brands and of the transnational companies who own them

▶ **Antiglobals.** This segment—about 13 percent of consumers—is skeptical of the quality of global brands as well as the transnational companies who own them. They prefer to buy local and avoid global brands. This segment is relatively more common in Britain and China and relatively less common in Egypt and South Africa.

Global agnostics consumers who judge global brands and local brands by the same criteria and are neither impressed nor alienated by the fact that a brand is global

▶ **Global agnostics.** This segment judges global brands and local brands by the same criteria and is neither impressed nor alienated by the fact that a brand is global. Estimated at about 8 percent of consumers, global agnostics' numbers are relatively high in the United States and South Africa and low in Japan, Indonesia, China, and Turkey.

Pan-regional Branding

Although there are few genuinely global brands, pan-regional branding is increasing in importance. For example, the Shangri-La Hotel chain, with thirty-four hotels, has built a strong regional brand across Asia. Shangri-La offers all the amenities of a luxury hotel, along with Asian hospitality. The staff uniforms reflect the local costumes. Shangri-La uses its advertising to appeal to executives in Asia, who are often judged by the hotels they choose. The tag line on Shangri-La ads is "It must be Shangri-La."[30] In Latin America, Brazil's Varig Airlines has undertaken a design and logo change to broaden its regional appeal. The revamped Varig logo is modern and warm-looking, which supports an advertising program that features well-rested passengers getting off their flights.[31]

Eurobrands regional brands in Europe

In the case of Europe, regional brands are called **Eurobrands**. In a survey of more than two hundred European brand managers in thirteen countries, 81 percent indicated that they were aiming for standardization and homogenization of brands, whereas only 13 percent said they were leaving each country free to decide its own strategy.[32] The survey clearly indicates a strong preference for a Eurobrand strategy for most companies. Two European firms that adopted Eurobrand strategies early are Electrolux and Danone.

Electrolux, the Swedish white-goods (household appliances) company, made over a hundred acquisitions in about 10 years, which left the company with over twenty brands sold in forty countries. Large markets such as the United Kingdom and Germany had as many as six major Electrolux brands. A

An advertisement for Shangri-la Hotels, a well-known regional brand in Asia.

study by Electrolux found a convergence of market segments across Europe, with the consumers' need for "localness" being primarily in terms of distribution channels, promotion in local media, and use of local names instead of product design and features. From this analysis, Electrolux developed a strategy with two pan-European brands and one or two local brands in each market. The Electrolux brand was targeted to the high-prestige, conservative consumers, and the Zanussi brand was targeted to the innovative, trendsetter consumers. The local brands were targeted to the young, aggressive urban professionals and to the warm and friendly, value-oriented consumers.[33]

As BSN, the third-largest food group in Europe, has grown beyond its base in France to become a pan-European company with global aspirations, it has found its name to be a weakness. BSN, which stands for the two former companies Boussois and Souchon-Neuvesel that merged in 1966, was recognized by 93 percent of people in France, but only by 7 percent in Italy and 5 percent in Spain. To support its global image, BSN changed its name to Danone after its dairy and yogurt brand.[34] Danone developed into one of the world's top brand names.[35]

Other cases of Eurobrands—products marketed across Europe with the same brand name, formula, and packaging, as well as the same positioning and advertising strategy—include Procter & Gamble's Pampers and Head & Shoulders, Michelin tires, and Rolex watches. Purely national brands in Europe are expected to decline in share from more than 50 percent today to about thirty percent in the next decade.

Global Brands versus Local Brands

When Procter & Gamble tried to replace in Belgium its leading local and very profitable detergent Dash with its European-wide brand Ariel, it discontinued advertising for Dash. However, P&G soon saw its sales in detergents plummet and it was forced to renew its support for Dash.[36] The findings from the Global Brands Study raise questions as to the intrinsic value of global brands compared with local brands. A study of consumers in France, Germany, Italy, and the United Kingdom further highlights what might well be the countervailing power of local brands. Consumers reported that local brands possessed the same quality as that of global brands. Furthermore, local brands were deemed more reliable and thought to deliver more value for money.[37]

Although evidence indicates that local brands remain powerful in the United States and Europe, there is also evidence that local brands can be competitive in developing countries as well. Global brands were especially attractive to consumers in Russia and former Soviet satellite states during the late 1990s. More recently there appears to be a backlash against global brands, as consumers possibly become disenchanted with their higher prices and the sometimes monopolization of markets by such brands. Nostalgia for local brands has motivated multinational firms to resurrect local brands. Kraft bought the traditional Hungarian candy bar, Sport Szelet, and markets it complete with its 50-year-old package design. Unilever followed suit with the traditional Baba personal-care brand.[38]

When asked whether they preferred a local or a global brand for products of identical price and quality, Chinese consumers overwhelmingly preferred local brands for food, toiletries, and household items, although they preferred global brands for home electronics. Consumers were evenly split between local and global brands when it came to clothes. Therefore, it is understandable that when France's packaged-foods company Danone buys Chinese companies, it continues to sell products under the Chinese brands. Overall, 80 percent of Danone's sales in China are credited to these Chinese brands. The company was even asked by the Chinese government to create a Chinese cola to compete with Coke and Pepsi. Future Cola holds the number three spot in China and is known as "the Chinese people's own cola."[39]

Private Branding

The practice of private branding, or supplying products to another party for sale under that party's brand name, has become quite common in many markets. Some Japanese companies, such as Ricoh (now a global leader in small personal copiers and fax machines), used private branding to gain market access in Europe and the United States. Today many Chinese companies employ this strategy as a means to enter export markets.[40]

Private branding offers particular advantages to a company with strong manufacturing skills but little access to or experience with foreign markets. Arranging for distribution of the firm's product through local distributors or companies with existing distribution networks reduces the risk of failure and provides for rapid volume growth via instant market access.

Private-branding contracts are not without drawbacks for the manufacturer. With control over marketing in the hands of another manufacturer or distributor, the firm remains dependent and can only indirectly influence marketing. For long-term profitability, companies often find that they need to spend the money to create brand equity, which requires promoting and selling products under their own brands. Changing from a supplier to a global brand powerhouse is not easy, however. In the 40 years since Asia emerged as a major manufacturing center, only a few companies have been successful in establishing world-class brands—among them Sony and Canon from Japan and Samsung from South Korea. Many Asian manufacturers still lack marketing departments and suffer from a lack of experience in direct selling to overseas retailers.[41]

Trademarks and Brand Protection

Violations of **trademarks**—the names, words, and symbols that enable customers to distinguish among brands—have been an inescapable problem for global marketers. These violations can involve the legal hijacking or local **preemption** of a brand name. For example, someone could register the Gucci brand name in a country where Gucci had yet to register its brands. If Gucci wanted to enter that market, it would have to buy back its brand name or sell under another. Trademark preemption is especially easy in countries that do not require that the brand be sold in the market after registration.

International treaties to protect well-known international brands from being preempted in local markets go back to the Paris Convention of 1883. However, problems can arise even in signatory countries. Claiming its rights under the Paris Convention, Gucci fought two cases in Mexico against infringing firms. It won one case but lost the other. In the latter case, the Mexican judge was not convinced that the Mexican government had even ratified the Paris Convention more than 100 years before.

Today, the Paris Convention has been superseded by trademark protection rules under the World Trade Organization. Countries that join the WTO must establish national laws that protect global brands. These laws must encompass a procedure by which the owners of famous international brands can successfully oppose the registration of their brands by local preemptors. Local laws must be adequate to deter counterfeiters, and countries must not discriminate between local and foreign firms who apply for trademark protection. Depending on a country's level of economic development, it may be allowed up to 11 years to bring its local laws into compliance.

Holding countries to these requirements is somewhat ambitious, however, given the fact that the signatory countries of the WTO exhibited very different levels of trademark protection at the time they joined. A study of national trademark protection in the years prior to establishment of the WTO shows distinct patterns across country categories. Developed countries provided the best

Trademarks the names, words, and symbols that enable customers to distinguish among brands

Preemption the legal hijacking or registration of a brand name when the brand is not yet registered

WORLD BEAT 11.2

Brand Preemption in Indonesia

BRITAIN'S IMPERIAL TOBACCO GROUP PLC, the world's fourth-largest cigarette maker, was planning to build a $70 million factory in Indonesia to produce its premier Davidoff cigarettes. But a local company, Sumatra Tobacco, that specialized in claiming famous trademarks, already owned the Davidoff name in Indonesia. In total, this local company had registered 201 famous trademarks in Indonesia, including Chanel and Remy Martin. Sumatra Tobacco not only made products associated with the famous brands but applied the brands to product extensions as well—such as their Rolex cigarettes, which Sumatra Tobacco sold in China.

Imperial Tobacco is not the only firm that has faced brand preemption in Indonesia. Intel, the world's largest manufacturer of microprocessors, has lost battles against the Indonesian maker of Intel jeans and the Indonesian maker of Intel home electronics. Originally the problem was Indonesia's trademark law dating from 1961, which stated that the first party to register a trademark in Indonesia was the owner of that trademark

in the country. Indonesia's new (2001) trademark law was supposed to stop such preemption of famous international brands, but the courts don't always appear to be enforcing the law.

Imperial appealed its case to Indonesia's Supreme Court. In the meantime, the company began looking for other sites for a Southeast Asian manufacturing center. Eventually the Supreme Court ruled in favor of Imperial Tobacco. Still, Sumatra Tobacco contested the decision, causing Imperial to further delay its planned investment in Indonesia. Some observers expect that other investment in Indonesia will be hampered until Indonesian judges are given adequate training in intellectual property rights.

Sources: Tom Wright, "Indonesia Turns to Trademark Piracy," *Wall Street Journal*, September 9, 2003, p. A20; Timothy Mapes, "Big Cigarette Firm Fumes at Jakarta Over a Trademark," *Wall Street Journal*, May 22, 2003, p. A12; and Gunawan Suryomurcito, "Intellectual Property Laws Still Weak," *Jakarta Post*, January 31, 2005, p. 6.

---

overall protection. Less developed countries and the transition economies of Russia and Eastern Europe exhibited much weaker local laws, and processing times for foreign trademark applications were exceptionally slow in the transition economies. Many newly industrialized countries, including Taiwan and South Korea, had already established local laws on a par with those of developed countries. However, a lack of resources undermined the ability of such countries to enforce these laws adequately.[42]

The norms established by the WTO are no doubt a step in the right direction, but problems still persist. Although the countries of the former Soviet bloc have adopted trademark protection laws in accordance with WTO guidelines, the enforcement of these laws remains problematic. There have been concerns that Russian judges and prosecutors don't understand the nature of Russia's newly adopted trademark laws—although the laws look good on paper. The U.S.-based tobacco company Philip Morris lost a case it brought in an effort to stop a Russian company from producing cigarettes whose packaging closely resembled that of two of Philip Morris's best-selling brands. Grupo Modelo, the Mexican beer company that makes Corona, also lost a trademark dispute with a Russian brewery that Modelo accused of stealing its brand name.[43]

Counterfeits and Piracy

Today, the biggest problem international marketers face in trying to protect their brands is counterfeiting. **Counterfeiting** is the illegal use of a registered trademark. A counterfeiter copies a branded product, cashing in on its brand equity. Thus counterfeiters injure legitimate businesses by stealing their brand equity. The World Customs Organization estimates that counterfeits account for 5 to 7 percent of global merchandise trade or more than $510 billion a year.[44]

However, consumers can be injured as well when they unwittingly buy counterfeits believing that they are buying the real product. Since counterfeits usually do not mimic the quality or safety of the original product, they can fail to perform as expected. Counterfeit AC Delco brake pads last only half as long as the real thing. Mitsubishi Elevator Company received a complaint from a customer whose new elevator kept stopping between floors. The elevator turned out to be a counterfeit. One of the greatest consumer threats posed by global counterfeiting is the growth in counterfeit pharmaceuticals. The World Health Organization notes that up to 10 percent of medicines worldwide are counterfeits.[45]

The term **piracy** is often applied to the counterfeit production of copyrighted material such as books and computer software. Because illegal production—or more aptly, reproduction—of these products is relatively simple and inexpensive, they become easy targets. Recorded music has long suffered from piracy, and counterfeit music is believed to outsell legitimate music in many countries.

DVDs are also a major target of pirates. Just a few years ago, pirating DVDs required a factory with disc-pressing equipment costing $1 million. As a result, the major players were Asian crime syndicates that could afford such an investment. Now the same technology that allows home-video buffs to "burn" their own DVDs is reshaping the competitive landscape of piracy—and threatening to make it even more costly to the motion picture industry. Piracy has now gone small and mobile, making counterfeiters harder for authorities to locate and crack down on. Hong Kong's authorities have shifted from looking for producers of counterfeits to shutting down the retailers that sell them. In a 5-year period, such stores were cut from 1,000 to only 80.[46]

Counterfeiting of trademark-protected products flourishes in countries where legal protection of such trademarks is weak. China accounts for the production of about two-thirds of all counterfeits. Other problem countries include the Philippines, Russia, Ukraine, Brazil, Pakistan, Paraguay, and Vietnam.[47] In Vietnam, counterfeits thrive because the government has few resources to enforce existing laws effectively or control the borders. Some international consumer goods companies doing business in Vietnam claim their sales are reduced by as much as 50 percent by the ready availability of illegal, and cheaper, products. Procter & Gamble is believed to have lost sales of up to 25 percent as illegal operators collected its containers and refilled them with counterfeit products. The same happened to brand-name cognac and whiskies. Reused bottles were filled with sugar rum.[48]

The emergence of e-business has contributed to the further growth of counterfeit global trade. Total online counterfeit business volume is estimated at $25 billion, a tenth of the total counterfeit volume. Internet counterfeiters are scattered across an estimated 5,000 websites. They include both international

Counterfeiting the illegal use of a registered trademark

Piracy the counterfeit production of copyrighted material

Mickey Mouse is popular in China—maybe too popular. Disney is one of many companies that contend with counterfeit products in the Chinese market.

operators and local teenagers operating out of a basement. Rolex, the Swiss-based producer of luxury watches, regularly checks eBay auctions where, on any given day, hundreds of counterfeit Rolex watches may be up for bids. The manufacturers of many other luxury items do the same. Louis Vuitton regularly checks eBay and acts on counterfeit products.[49] By early 2001, eBay, concerned that it could be held liable for frauds or other illegal sales, began screening and removing from its site items that clearly infringed on copyrights.[50]

Fighting Counterfeits

Multinational companies can try to stop the counterfeiting of their products in a number of ways.[51]

▶ *Do Nothing.* Firms may ignore counterfeits if they are not significantly threatening their brand. Stopping counterfeiters can become an expensive and time-consuming project for a firm. Unfortunately, most firms now realize that doing nothing is no longer an option.

▶ *Co-opt the Offenders.* One manufacturer of hardware products discovered that a counterfeiter from Asia was producing an excellent copy of its product. The counterfeiter was asked to become the firm's legitimate contract manufacturer. Distributors of counterfeits may also be recruited to be legitimate distributors of the brand. However, this option has a downside: Many legitimate contract manufacturers, licensees, and distributors participate in the counterfeit market as well. Their legitimate status can help hide their more nefarious operations. Unilever discovered that one of its suppliers in Shanghai was making excess cases of soap and selling them directly to retailers. Procter & Gamble discovered that a Chinese supplier was selling empty P&G shampoo bottles to another company, which filled them with counterfeit shampoo.[52]

▶ ***Educate Governments.*** Firms can take steps to educate governments about the social and political implications of counterfeits and solicit their assistance in shutting down counterfeiters. Some governments, particularly those in developing countries, have long been unsympathetic to multinational pleas to address counterfeits. Counterfeits often provide employment opportunities in developing countries, and some governments believe that the price consumers in poor countries pay for global brand equity is unnecessary and extreme. However, there are signs that even governments in developing countries are changing their minds about the value of counterfeits due to several factors:

▶ As already noted, counterfeits can sometimes hurt consumers. In Africa, counterfeit drugs account for as much as 40 percent of the market.[53]

▶ Many governments are increasingly concerned about the downside of their large informal economies (including counterfeiters and their distributors) because participants in the informal economy do not pay taxes or adhere to labor codes.[54] One exception to this rule is North Korea, whose government is purported to earn $100 million a year in fees from pirates producing there.[55]

▶ Counterfeits increasingly harm firms from developing countries, not just foreign multinationals. Countries such as Brazil, Korea, and Taiwan now

For Microsoft, fighting piracy is a global effort.

realize that their own domestic brands are being counterfeited. Even Chinese brands such as Tsingtao beer and Li-Ning shoes have become targets of counterfeiters.[56] This has motivated local governments to become more serious about addressing the problem.

▶ Counterfeiting is increasing the domain of organized crime and even terrorists, the latter of which use proceeds from counterfeits to finance their terrorist activities. Both groups threaten the sovereignty of legitimate governments.

▶ *Advertise.* Multinationals can attempt to communicate the advantages of buying the authentic product rather than counterfeits. Additionally, campaigns may be devised to educate consumers about the ethical issues relating to counterfeits. When the Harry Potter series was launched in China, the publisher arranged for the books to be printed on a light green paper and planned a media blitz to explain to consumers how to tell the real thing from the counterfeit.[57]

▶ *Participate Directly in Investigation and Surveillance.* Governments cannot always be relied on to shut down counterfeiting. Increasingly, firms have begun to take over investigatory roles usually played by police. The Motion Picture Association hires its own private police to establish spy networks in Asia, track down pirates of DVDs, and assist customs agents to raid illegal operations.[58] Louis Vuitton is reported to employ twenty full-time staff to work with teams of investigators and lawyers to protect its brand from counterfeiters. However, such activities are not without peril. One executive of a major European alcoholic beverage company was shot at twice and wounded once while trying to help curtail counterfeiters in Thailand.[59]

▶ *Change Aspects of the Product.* Firms can continuously change aspects of their products and employ high-tech labeling and packaging. For instance, Polaproof by Polaroid provides a tamper-proof label. Other approaches include holograms and invisible marking devices or inks. Glaxo Wellcome, a leading U.K. pharmaceutical company, worked on making products and packaging unique so that they could not be copied by counterfeiters. Zantac, its leading ulcer drug, was designed as a five-sided, peach-colored pill. Prescribing doctors could look the drug up in the *Physician's Desk Reference* to verify its design.[60] However, many counterfeiters are very adept at countering these changes and employ state-of-the-art manufacturing facilities.

▶ *Push for Better Legislation Against Counterfeits.* The United States passed the Trademark Counterfeiting Act of 1984, which makes counterfeiting punishable by fines of up to $250,000 and prison terms of up to 5 years. China lowered its threshold for criminal prosecution of counterfeiters in 2004. Now an individual need only be caught with $6,000 worth of counterfeit goods to face prosecution versus $12,000 previously.[61] Many other countries are strengthening their laws and increasing penalties for counterfeiting. This is even true of many newly industrialized countries that were once major offenders. Still, new legislation is only the beginning. The enforcement of new legislation may remain weak in most developing countries for many years in the future.

▶ *Employ Coalitions.* Global firms may achieve better results if they work together to lobby governments for improvements in laws and enforcement. This can be true for home governments as well. The Chinese government appears to have begun to respond to complaints about counterfeiting more seriously since the United States, Europe, and Japan have appeared to speak with a single voice.

▶ *Reconsider More Aggressive Pricing.* In some cases, brand owners may choose to forgo some brand equity and lower prices to address counterfeits. Yamaha decided to lower prices in order to fight counterfeits in China. Its cheapest bike was reduced to $725 from $1,800. Counterfeiters who previously charged $1,000 had to respond by charging only $500.[62]

Similarly, Mexican film and video distributors Videomax and Quality Films, in cooperation with the Motion Picture Association of America, decided to drop prices in the Mexican market and sell legitimate movies through the same street vendors who traditionally sold pirated copies of films. The distributors slashed prices enough that they matched or fell below those of pirated copies.[63]

▶ *Exit or Avoid a Market.* When Microsoft entered the Russian market, it faced a piracy rate for its software of 99 percent. The firm decided that targeting the consumer market was futile. Instead it focused solely on the business market, offering after-sales technology support as an inducement to purchase software legally.[64]

Although international firms continue to devise methods to stop counterfeits, they will remain a problem that global marketers will have to deal with for the foreseeable future. And the longer governments fail to address the problem, the stronger organized crime becomes as a result of its participation in this lucrative industry.

Check out our website (college.hmco.com/business/) for anticounterfeiting links.

SOCIAL MARKETING IN THE GLOBAL CONTEXT

Social marketing is the adaptation of marketing practices to programs designed to influence the voluntary behavior of target groups in order to improve their personal welfare and that of the society to which they belong.[65] The targets of social marketing might not believe—at least in the beginning—that they suffer from or are contributing to a problem. Such might be the case with teenagers who abuse alcohol or drugs or fathers in Bangladesh who do not believe that their daughters should receive an education.[66]

Similar to marketing in the commercial sphere, social marketing has gone global. The global reach of nongovernmental organizations (NGOs) undertaking philanthropic and educational projects has never been greater. And whether they are local or transnational, public or private, organizations involved in social marketing are increasingly interested in exploring best practices from other countries.

As is the case with global products, social marketing programs utilized across countries may exhibit standardized features as well as features adapted to various local conditions and cultures. For example, research demonstrates that high-risk behavior relating to the spread of AIDS can be reduced when popular opinion leaders (POLs) within a community are trained to introduce AIDS prevention endorsements into conversations with their peers. A team of social marketers from Wisconsin chose the POL model for international dissemination. The team identified leading AIDS prevention NGOs in seventy-eight countries in Africa, Eastern Europe/Russia, Central Asia, Latin America, and the Caribbean. Each NGO was paired with a behavioral science consultant who was very familiar with the culture of region the NGO served. Consequently, the NGO received assistance in adapting the POL model to best fit local cultural demands. Fifty-five percent of the NGOs incorporated the POL model into their programs. In addition, these NGOs networked with other organizations in their countries to promote the model. In 26 percent of targeted countries, the government also adopted the model into its official AIDS prevention programs.[67]

As noted earlier, marketing practices developed for commercial enterprises are often readily applicable to social marketing. When the global consulting firm McKinsey developed a program to improve the welfare of coffee growers in developing countries, it first segmented its market. Some growers could reasonably switch to growing specialty coffees in order to realize greater profits. However, others would need to abandon coffee growing altogether in order to survive. Social marketing recommendations were then developed for two different segments.[68] Similarly, social marketers associated with international NGO Care targeted farming and fishing communities in rural Kenya in a campaign to improve water cleanliness and storage and decrease diarrheal diseases. Careful attention was paid to market research that utilized both focus-group and survey methodologies.[69]

Still, certain aspects of social marketing differentiate it from commercial marketing:

▶ Social marketing is not concerned with the profitability of a project the way commercial marketing is. Nonetheless, when people buy into a behavioral change being promoted by a social marketer, they must pay some kind of price. That price may involve a monetary payment or it may involve extra effort or the forgoing of something pleasurable. In some cases it may require a difficult decision to abandon long-held cultural beliefs. To make this price more acceptable, social marketers may be called upon to offer incentives. The Care project in Kenya offered chemical tablets and water storage pots at subsidized prices to households willing to adopt new water quality procedures. The McKinsey report on coffee farming in developing countries suggested that NGOs and governments provide interim loans for farmers transitioning to new crops.

▶ Despite a lack of profit focus, social marketers must still seek monetary compensation to cover expenses and consequently stay in business. However, their funding comes from sources other than their target markets. These sources comprise governments as well as private donors. Additional marketing aimed at these sources of funds is also necessary. Social marketers must understand the motivations and values of these donors, and they must often compete with other social marketers for funding.

▶ Although NGOs may compete for funding, they often work together—formally or informally—to accomplish a common goal. Such **lateral partner-**

Lateral partnerships formal or informal agreements between NGOs to work toward a common goal and to facilitate efficiency

ships help facilitate efficiency savings.[70] They can also assist in the development of better, more effective practices. In the international context they can be especially useful. Multinational social marketers can offer additional funding and experience to local social marketers who provide cultural understanding and community access.

▶ Social marketers, especially in the international context, must consider how governments—both host and home—view the product they are marketing. Sometimes social marketers undertake jobs that fall under the usual auspices of governments. Some governments welcome the help. Others may be embarrassed by it. Also, what constitutes the public good—and the actions needed to accomplish it—can be politically charged subjects.

CONCLUSION

In this chapter we see that social marketing and the marketing of services internationally have much in common with the global marketing of products. However, they each present unique challenges. Whether marketing products or services, additional efforts are required if a company wishes to develop global brands and to police counterfeits. For companies that successfully master these additional international difficulties while showing a commitment to foreign customers, global success can lead to increased profits and to more secure market positions both domestically and globally.

Do you need to adapt your service or social marketing for your target country? How would you register and protect your brand? Continue with your *Country Market Report* on our website (college.hmco.com/business/).

QUESTIONS FOR DISCUSSION

1. Why is it more difficult to pursue product standardization when marketing services?

2. Why do you think Poles already recognized the Coke name and logo when the product was first introduced in Poland?

3. Why is it difficult to decide whether to change a local brand name to a global brand name?

4. Why do you think that Interbrand's Readers' Choice ranking of global brands differs from that of *Business Week*'s?

5. What are the pros and cons of a top-down approach to global branding? What are the pros and cons of a bottom-up approach?

6. How might a global brand be valuable to a social marketer?

CASE 11.1
Chasing Pirates

Pirated software is a major challenge to Microsoft, which loses hundreds of millions of dollars a year to the practice. Piracy also costs governments in lost tax revenues. Mexico, for instance, is estimated to lose $200 million a year to pirated software. Piracy rates vary by country, the rates in developing countries being significantly higher than those in developed countries:

England	20%	Philippines	92%
India	80%	Thailand	82%
Indonesia	97%	Vietnam	97%
Mexico	40%	United States	30%
Pakistan	90%		

To combat piracy, Microsoft added an edge-to-edge hologram on its CD-ROMs to ensure buyers of the product's authenticity. Still, an estimated two million websites sell pirated software. As a result, the company aggressively monitors the Internet to uncover sites for illegal downloading.

Closing down pirates overseas has taken several forms. In Bulgaria, Microsoft launched a campaign to eradicate pirated software by offering full packages discounted 60 percent off their previous price. Buyers were also entitled to the next version at no extra charge. In Pakistan, Microsoft offered to provide a training program for software instructors and to install laboratories in the top fifty universities and colleges in the country. This $150 million package would be in exchange for better government enforcement of antipiracy laws. In Malaysia, Microsoft installed a toll-free phone number and offered substantial rewards for evidence against companies using pirated software.

Bill Gates, chairman and CEO of Microsoft, himself traveled to China to sign an agreement with the government there to promote the authentic use of software. Under the agreement, several key government entities pledged to buy Microsoft and to avoid pirated products. In exchange, Microsoft agreed to provide technical training and consulting. Later the same year, Microsoft brought its first piracy case to the Chinese courts. Engineers were found to be using pirated Microsoft products in the office building of the Yadu Group. The Yadu Group argued that they were innocent because the engineers worked not directly for them but for a sister company. The Chinese court found in favor of Yadu and ordered Microsoft to pay $60 in court costs.

In Singapore, a country of four million people, Microsoft loses over $3 million a year to pirates. Microsoft began a campaign in the Singapore schools to educate students concerning the illegality of piracy. Despite Singapore's excellent reputation for law enforcement in general, U.S. officials put it on their list of thirty-two countries to watch for poor enforcement of copyrights. Under similar pressure from the United States, Taiwan has been cracking down more on piracy. A firm caught exporting pirated software was fined $7.9 million, and its owner was sentenced to 2 years in jail.

After pursuing all the preceding policies, Microsoft decided to introduce a version of Windows software especially for consumers in developing countries. A multicountry launch included Malaysia, Indonesia, India, and Russia. The new software offered fewer features for a lower price. It was installed in low-cost personal computers and not sold separately. The price Microsoft charged computer manufacturers for the product was not made public, but the low-end PCs were expected to retail for about US$300.

Discussion Questions

1. What do you think accounts for the different piracy rates across countries?
2. Identify the different strategies Microsoft uses to combat counterfeits.
3. Why does Microsoft expect each of these efforts to be useful? What is your opinion?

Sources: Dow Jones Business News, May 5, 2000, March 6, 2000, August 24, 1999, and March 28, 1999; "Mexico," Reuters English News Service, May 19, 2000; Ridzuan A. Ghani, "Microsoft in New Campaign to Curb Software Piracy," *New Straits Times*, May 1, 2000, p. 6; "Microsoft Incorporates New Anti-Piracy Technologies," PR Newswires, February 10, 2000; "Microsoft Loses Piracy Suit," *Asian Wall Street Journal*, December 20, 1999, p. 3; and *BBC Worldwide Monitoring*, March 10, 1999; and Cassell Bryan-Low, "Microsoft Battles Piracy in Developing Markets," *Wall Street Journal*, December 23, 2004, p. B4.

CASE 11.2

Fighting AIDS in Asia

Mary Foster had just resigned from her job as a global product manager at a major multinational packaged foods company to head AIDS Prevention International (API), an NGO based in Washington, D.C., dedicated to slowing the spread of HIV/AIDS in developing countries. Mary had been an active volunteer as an MBA student, raising money for AIDS awareness programs in the United States. She welcomed the opportunity to return to this early interest.

API had been recently formed by a very generous U.S. philanthropist. The investment return of API's current endowment would cover annual expenses for operating a headquarters located in the United States as well as small offices in up to four developing countries. In addition, funds would remain to support modest educational programs in these countries as well as further fundraising efforts.

Mary believed that the NGO's resources could best be deployed by focusing on a few countries in Asia. She was currently in the process of prioritizing target countries and deciding which population segments within those countries to target. Other key questions involved the extent to which API should ally with local NGOs and governments and whether API should apply for funding from the U.S. government.

The Global AIDS Epidemic

HIV was first identified in the 1970s. (HIV is the virus that triggers AIDS.) The disease spread first among homosexuals, intravenous drug users, and workers in the sex industry but inevitably entered the general population. AIDS was now the world's fourth-largest infectious killer. The disease first appeared in West Africa. After remaining relatively contained in the Congo's sparsely populated jungles, it began to spread rapidly via rebel armies and truck drivers who frequented brothels. AIDS was already devastating the African continent when it first appeared in the United States in the early 1980s. Africa still remained the hardest hit area of the world. South Africa was host to one in ten new infections.

There were substantial differences in HIV prevalence rates by region (see Table 1). Intraregional differences at the country level could be substantial as well. The highest estimates for new HIV/AIDS infections were in sub-Saharan Africa, Eastern Europe, Central Asia, South Asia, and Southeast Asia. Who was most at risk could also vary by region. In Eastern Europe and Russia, 80 percent of HIV-positive people were less than 30 years of age compared with only 30 percent in Western Europe and North America. In Ukraine, drug injection was the principal mode of transmission while it accounted for only 10 percent of the newly diagnosed HIV cases in Western Europe.

Besides the personal tragedy associated with the disease, the economic impact could be tremendous. For example, loss of productivity combined with increased expenditures to combat the disease contributed to a GNP decrease of 8 percent in Namibia. Kenya—where the government once hesitated in broadcasting the danger of AIDS in its sex industry for fear of scaring away tourists—saw its per-capita income drop 10 percent. In recognition of this economic impact on developing countries, the World Bank joined other transnational institutions such as the United Nations in supporting programs to halt the spread of the disease.

Prioritizing Markets

Mary had narrowed the potential countries to four: Thailand, China, India, and Indonesia.

Thailand

HIV was first detected in Thailand in the mid-1980s among male homosexuals. The government immediately began to monitor high-risk groups, including drug users and prostitutes. Accurate

TABLE 1 ADULT (15–49) HIV PREVALENCE RATE BY REGION	
Sub-Saharan Africa	7.5%
Caribbean	2.3
Eastern Europe/Central Asia	.6
Latin America	.6
North America	.6
South/Southeast Asia	.6
North Africa/Middle East	.3
Western Europe	.3
East Asia	.1

SOURCE: Adapted from UNAIDS, 2004 Report on the Global AIDS Epidemic (www.unaids.org).

information alerted the authorities to rapidly soaring infection rates. The government responded quickly with a survey of sexual behavior among Thais. This survey revealed that Thai men frequently indulged in unprotected commercial sex. These results were highly publicized, and a campaign was launched to persuade prostitutes to insist on condom use. Safe sex was promoted via billboards, leaflets, and television commercials. The results were impressive. In just a few years, adult men reporting nonmarital sex dropped from 28 percent to 15 percent. Men reporting seeing a prostitute fell from 22 percent to 10 percent. The proportion claiming to have used a condom during sex with a prostitute rose to 93 percent. The number of sexually transmitted diseases in government clinics fell from over 400,000 to 50,000.

However, Virginia-based NGO International Social Justice (ISJ) claimed that many if not most of the women employed in Thailand's sex trade (estimated at 200,000) are sold or kidnapped into prostitution and asserted that these women needed liberation, not condoms. Influenced by organizations such as ISJ, the U.S. Leadership Against HIV/AIDS, Tuberculosis and Malarias Act forbade funding for any organization that advocated the legalization of prostitution or did not have a policy explicitly opposing prostitution.

Furthermore, in the wake of the 1997 Asian financial crisis, Thailand cut its expenditures for AIDS prevention. By the mid-2000s, expenditures were still only about half of what they once were.

New infection rates remained high among drug users and homosexual men. Some believed that Thailand's war on drugs, which resulted in the killing of 3,000 alleged drug dealers, had driven drug users underground and away from AIDS preventative services such as needle exchange programs. New HIV infection rates were also up from 11 percent to 17 percent among urban youth. Because earlier campaigns had associated condoms with commercial sex, safe sex may have become stigmatized. Condom usage by young men with steady girlfriends was only 12 percent, and unprotected sex with multiple partners was on the rise among Thai teens. Local NGOs were calling for improved and expanded sex education in Thai schools.

China

HIV first entered China in the late 1980s via infected drug users. In the 1990s, a major epidemic arose in the province of Henan when villagers were recruited to donate blood. In order to donate up to four times a day, villagers were reinfused with their own blood after the plasma had been extracted. Activists estimate that one million became infected with HIV. In one village alone a third of the adult population contracted the disease. No one was ever held accountable. In fact, China's communist government was at first less than enthusiastic about raising AIDS awareness, and many AIDS prevention volunteers reported being harassed by government authorities. Statistics concerning the disease were treated as a state secret.

The government attributed most AIDS cases to intravenous drug use. However, international agencies estimated that only about 60 percent of Chinese infected with HIV/AIDS contracted the disease through use of illicit drugs. Infection from unprotected sex was rising. China's younger generation was reaching puberty earlier and marrying later. Consequently, premarital sex was on the rise. Hundreds of millions of Chinese were on the move as well, as rural Chinese poured into urban areas in search of jobs. Many of these migrants were males who left wives behind in the country. However, many migrants were women in search of jobs that often failed to materialize. The result was a booming commercial sex industry in Chinese cities.

The government announced that it would redouble efforts to educate students regarding AIDS and launched AIDS prevention websites aimed at youth. Despite the new push by the central government, many believed provincial governments were ignoring—even covering up— the problem, and a surprising number of Chinese remained unaware of the disease. Only in 2004 did the Chinese government announce that AIDS prevention would be added to the country's educational curriculum. Yao Ming of the Houston Rockets basketball team had even made a video for AIDS prevention to be aired in his homeland. Still, there was concern about how much television airtime the Chinese government would give to the video. In the past, similar celebrity videos were granted little airtime by the government who controlled the television media.

India

India, with an estimated five million persons infected with HIV, ranked second only to South Africa for the highest number of infected persons. In recognition of this crisis, the government organized a Parliamentary Forum on HIV/AIDS, which brought together more than 1,200 elected political figures from across the country. As in many developing countries, controversy surrounded AIDS statistics collected by the government. To address this problem, the Indian government hired a prestigious (and independent) private company to estimate the level of HIV/AIDS in India.

Nonetheless, a government survey showed that prevention programs were only reaching about 30 percent of the population. Women who were infected by their husbands were often blamed by their in-laws. NGOs that operated homes for AIDS patients or AIDS orphans were often evicted if their landlords discovered the nature of their operations. Police were even known to harass health workers who were trying to disseminate the government's own AIDS prevention information.

Health workers in India believed that the disease was spreading fastest in rural areas where prevention programs were the weakest and record-keeping the worst. Hope Foundation was disseminating AIDS information and condoms at truck stops. India's five million truckers covered 5,000 miles of highways and reported three to five sexual partners a week. In 6 years, the HIV infection rate among truckers fell from 10 percent to 4 percent.

To address the threat of AIDS to young people, the government had established two national prizes to award colleges or youth groups who acted as agents of change by implementing their own AIDS awareness initiatives. Still AIDS carried a social stigma in India. When the disease first entered the country, many Indian officials declared that India's moral character and conservative sexual mores would prevent the spread of AIDS. Sex was rarely a subject of public discourse. It was largely absent from Indian films, and schools offered little or no sex education.

Indonesia

Indonesia historically enjoyed a low rate of HIV infection, but that was changing fast, particularly among drug users and throughout the nation's expanding commercial sex industry, where only one man in ten used a condom. The World Health Organization had given Indonesia even a higher priority for AIDS attention than China or Thailand.

However, Indonesia was Islam's most populous country, and AIDS prevention endeavors were proving controversial with conservative Muslims. Islam forbade extramarital sex. One Muslim politician remarked that AIDS prevention should focus on improving people's morality and not urge them to protect themselves by using condoms. The Indonesian Ulemas' Council, the country's highest Islamic authority, proclaimed that Muslims should fight AIDS by being more religious and closer to family.

DKT Indonesia, a Washington-based NGO, produced a line of condoms that it sold at discount rates in Indonesia to truck drivers, sailors, and prostitutes. The NGO also placed a few condom advertisements with Indonesia's MTV affiliate but used dancing strawberry cartoons rather than images of real people. Attempts to get other AIDS prevention advertisements aired met with less success. Another U.S.-based NGO, Family Health International, aired a commercial briefly that depicted men visiting prostitutes. But stations immediately pulled the ad when fundamentalist Muslim clerics complained.

The Indonesian government officially proposed new education programs in schools along with better training for health-care workers and voluntary HIV testing and counseling. However, some within the government questioned spending on AIDS prevention when the country needed basic education and health care. Also, much of the country's health-care budget fell under the auspices of provincial governments sympathetic to views of Islamic fundamentalist groups. As one local AIDS activist noted: Many considered AIDS a punishment from God for wrongdoing. Others viewed it as a Western phenomenon—and nothing to do with them.

As Mary contemplated the challenges of each of these four potential Asian markets, she wondered whether any of her experience as a global product manager could be put to use in this new context of international social marketing.

Discussion Questions

1. Given that there are many multinational and local "competitors" participating in the social marketing of AIDS prevention, what role should API play? What products/services could it deliver?
2. What elements of these services might be standardized across developing countries? What elements might need to be adapted? Why?
3. What suggestions would you give Mary for prioritizing the four Asian markets?
4. Should API partner with local governments? Local NGOs? Should it pursue funding from the U.S. government?
5. How might Mary's experience as a global product manager be useful in this new setting?

Sources: "Global Disaster," *Economist*, January 2, 1999; Geoffrey Cowly and Sudip Mazumdar, "A Deadly Passage to India," *Newsweek*, November 25, 2002, p. 38; Sabin Russell, "AIDS in India," *San Francisco Chronicle*, July 6, 2004, p. A1; Amy Kazmin, "Deliver Them from Evil," *Financial Times*, July 9, 2004; Shawn W. Crispin, "Dangerous Liaisons," *Far Eastern Economic Review*, July 15, 2004, p. 48; Cris Prystay and Timothy Mapes, "Risky Business," *Wall Street Journal*, March 25, 2004, p. A1; "Tall Order," *ABC News: World News Sunday*, October 17, 2004.

NOTES

1. Pui-Wing Tam, "H-P Lands $3Billion Contract to Manage P&G Tech Services," *Wall Street Journal*, April 14, 2003, p. B4.
2. Cassell Bryan-Low, "Microsoft Battles Piracy in Developing Markets," *Wall Street Journal*, December 25, 2004, p. B4.
3. Philip Makutsa, Kilungu Nzaku, Paul Ogutu, Peter Barasa, Sam Ombeki, Alex Mwaki, and Robert E. Quick, "Challenges in Implementing a Point-of-Use Water Quality Intervention in Rural Kenya," *American Journal of Public Health* 91, no. 10 (October 2001), pp. 1571–1573.
4. Mary Anne Raymond and John D. Mittelstaedt, "Perceptions of Factors Driving Success for Multinational Professional Services Firms in Korea," *Journal of Consumer Marketing* 14, no. 1 (2001), p. 24.
5. Peggy Cloninger, "The Effect of Service Intangibility on Revenue from Foreign Markets," *Journal of International Management* 10 (2004), p. 126.
6. Suzanne Koudsi, "Sam's Big Blue Challenge," *Fortune*, August 13, 2001, p. 144.
7. Martin Fackler and Ichiko Fuyuno, "Japan Lawyers See Seismic Shift," *Wall Street Journal*, September 16, 2004, p. A15.
8. David Murphy, "Chinese Builders Go Global," *Far Eastern Economic Review*, May 13, 2004, p. 30.
9. Pierre Berthon., Leyland Pitt, Constantine S. Katsikeas, and Jean-Paul Berthon, "Virtual Services Go International: Services in the Marketspace," *Journal of International Marketing* 7, no. 3 (1999), pp. 85–86.
10. Raymond and Mittelstaedt, "Perceptions of Factors," p. 26.
11. Michael Laroche, Linda C. Ueltschy, Shuzo Abe, Mark Cleveland, and Peter P. Yannopoulos, "Service Quality Perceptions and Customer Satisfaction: Evaluating the Role of Culture," *Journal of International Marketing* 12, no. 3 (2004), pp. 58–85.
12. Ibid.; and Raymond and Mittelstaedt, "Perceptions of Factors," p. 39.
13. Laroche et al., "Service Quality Perceptions," p. 77.
14. Betsy Morris, "The Brand's the Thing," *Fortune*, March 4, 1996, p. 75.
15. Ibid.
16. Bernd Schmitt, "Language and Visual Imagery: Issues of Corporate Identity in East Asia," *Columbia Journal of World Business* 30 (Winter 1995), pp. 2–36.
17. "Trademarks Are a Global Business These Days, But Finding Registrable Ones Is a Big Problem," *Wall Street Journal*, September 4, 1975, p. 28.
18. George W. Cooper, "On Your 'Mark,'" *Columbia Journal of World Business* 5 (March–April 1970), pp. 67–76.
19. "Darkie No, Darlie Yes," *South China Morning Post*, May 16, 1999, p. 2.

20. Ernest Beck, "Unilever Renames Cleanser," *Wall Street Journal*, December 27, 2000, p. B8.
21. Alice Z. Cuneo, "Landor: Experts on Identity Crisis," *Ad Age International*, March 1997, p. I-44.
22. David A. Aaker and Erich Joachimsthaler, "The Lure of Global Branding," *Harvard Business Review* 77 (November–December 1999), pp. 137–144.
23. Ibid.
24. Susan P. Douglas, C. Samuel Craig, and Edwin J. Nijssen, "Integrating Branding Strategy Across Markets: Building International Brand Architecture," *Journal of International Marketing* 9, 2 (2001), p. 110.
25. Johnny Johansson and Ilkka A. Ronkainen, "Consider Implications of Local Brands," *Marketing News*, May 15, 2004, p. 46.
26. Douglas B. Holt, John A. Quelch, and Earl L. Taylor, "How Global Brands Compete," *Harvard Business Review* 82 (September 2004), pp. 68–75.
27. Isabelle Schuiling and Jean-Noel Kapferer, "Real Differences Between Local and International Brands: Strategic Implications for International Marketers," *Journal of International Marketing* 12, no. 4 (2004), pp. 97–112.
28. Ibid., p. 69.
29. Ibid., p. 71.
30. Jane Blennerhassett, "Shangri-La on Earth," *Advertising Age International*, March 1997, p. I-24.
31. Claudia Penteado, "Regional Brands: Varig Eyes the Skies Outside of Brazil," *Advertising Age International*, March 1997, p. I-19.
32. "Who Favors Branding with Euro Approach?" *Advertising Age International*, May 25, 1992, p. I-16.
33. Christopher A. Bartlett and Sumantra Ghoshal, "What Is a Global Manager?" *Harvard Business Review* (September–October 1992), p. 125.
34. "BSN Puts New Name on the Table," *Financial Times*, May 11, 1994, p. 18.
35. "Danone Hits Its Stride," *Business Week International*, February 1, 1999, p. 18.
36. Schuiling and Kapferer, "Local and International Brands."
37. Ibid.
38. Marta Karenova, "Nostalgia Revives Soviet-Era Brands," *Wall Street Journal*, November 19, 2004, p. A12.
39. Leslie Chang and Peter Wonacott, "Cracking China's Market," *Wall Street Journal*, January 9, 2003, p. B1.
40. Paul Gao, Jonathan R. Woetzel, and Yibing Wu, "Can Chinese Brands Make It Abroad?" in "Global Directions," special edition issue four, *McKinsey Quarterly* (2003), pp. 52-65.
41. Geoffrey A. Fowler, "A Starck Vision of Asia's Future as Elite Producer of Brands," *Wall Street Journal*, April 7, 2004, p. B1.
42. Kate Gillespie, Kishore Krishma, and Susan Jarvis, "Protecting Global Brands: Toward a Global Norm," *Journal of International Marketing* 10, 2 (2002), pp. 99–112.
43. Guy Chazan, "Philip Morris Suffers a Setback in Russian Suit on Trademarks," *Wall Street Journal*, October 13, 1999, p. A26.
44. Frederik Balfour, "Fakes," *Business Week*, February 7, 2005, pp. 54–64.
45. Ibid., p. 62.
46. Geoffrey A. Fowler, "Hollywood's Burning Issue," *Wall Street Journal*, September 18, 2003, p. B1.
47. Balfour, "Fakes," p. 56.
48. "Vietnam's Prolific Counterfeiters Take a Walk on 'LaVile' Side," *Asian Wall Street Journal*, June 4, 1998, p. 1.
49. "Sleaze E-Commerce," *Wall Street Journal*, May 14, 1999, p. W1.
50. Glenn R. Simpson, "E-Bay to Police Site for Sales of Pirated Items," *Wall Street Journal*, February 28, 2000, p. A3.
51. The first eight suggestions listed here are forwarded by Robert T. Green and Tasman Smith, "Countering Brand Counterfeiters," *Journal of International Marketing* 10, no. 4 (2002), pp. 89–106.
52. Gabriel Kahn, "Factory Fight," *Wall Street Journal*, December 19, 2002, p. A1.
53. Balfour, "Fakes," p. 62.
54. Diana Farrell, "The Hidden Dangers of the Informal Economy," *McKinsey Quarterly*, no. 3 (2004), pp. 26–38.
55. Ibid.
56. Dexter Roberts, Frederik Balfour, Bruce Einhorn, and Michael Arndt, "China's Power Brands," *Business Week*, November 8, 2004, p. 50.
57. Matt Forney, "Harry Potter, Meet 'Ha-li Bo-te,'" *Wall Street Journal*, September 21, 2000, p. B1.
58. Geoffrey A. Fowler, "Hollywood's Burning Issue," *Wall Street Journal*, September 18, 2003, p. B1.
59. Green and Smith, "Countering Brand Counterfeiters," pp. 91, 101.
60. "Businesses Battle Bogus Products," *AP Online*, January 26, 1999.
61. Balfour, "Fakes," p. 62.
62. Ibid., p. 60.
63. Ken Bensinger, "Film Companies Take to Mexico's Streets to Fight Piracy," *Wall Street Journal*, December 17, 2003, p. B1.
64. Cassell Bryan-Low, "Microsoft Battles Piracy in Developing Markets," *Wall Street Journal*, December 23, 2004, p. B4.
65. Alan R. Andreasen, "Social Marketing: Its Definition and Domain," *Journal of Public Policy and Marketing* 13, no. 1 (Spring 1994), pp. 110–111.
66. George G. Brenkert, "Ethical Challenges of Social Marketing," *Journal of Public Policy and Marketing* 21, no. 1 (Spring 2002), pp. 14–25.
67. "AIDS Prevention Programs Can Be Transferred to Developing Countries," *Ascribe News*, September 23, 2004.
68. Steven G. Friedenberg, Charles Jordan, and Vivek Mohindra, "Easing Coffee Farmers' Woes," *McKinsey Quarterly*, no. 2 (2004), pp. 8-11.
69. Makutsa et al., "Water Quality Intervention in Rural Kenya."
70. Gerald Hastings, "Relational Paradigms in Social Marketing," *Journal of Macromarketing* 23, no. 1 (2003), pp. 6–15.

PRICING FOR INTERNATIONAL AND GLOBAL MARKETS

12

IN RECENT YEARS the U.S. Justice Department has brought some of America's largest criminal cases to trial. The defendants are global managers from Belgium, Britain, Canada, France, Germany, Italy, Japan, Mexico, the Netherlands, South Korea, and Switzerland as well as from the United States. The charge is collusion with competitors to fix global prices. The penalty is a hefty fine for the company and a jail sentence for the manager. One price-fixing case involved vitamins. Multinational pharmaceutical firms reached production and price agreements that raised prices to packaged-foods companies such as General Mills, Kellogg's, Coca-Cola, and Procter & Gamble. These higher prices were of course passed on to consumers who took vitamins, drank milk, or ate cereal. Similarly, investigators uncovered a 17-year price-fixing conspiracy among American, German, and

Japanese producers of sorbates, a food preservative. This cartel is estimated to have affected over a billion dollars in sales in the United States alone. Global cartels have raised prices on such diverse products as soft drinks, dynamite, and offshore oil and gas drilling platforms. Increasingly, governments in Europe and Asia are joining the United States in investigating the pricing policies of global firms.[1]

What would make a manager risk a jail sentence to fix a global price? The globalization of markets offers several possible explanations. Competition has intensified. Firms not only compete in foreign markets but also face foreign competition in their home markets. Consolidation in many industries has created fewer but bigger competitors. Demanding consumers want better products at lower prices. Pressures to lower prices abound. But pricing is

After studying this chapter, you should be able to

▶ Differentiate between full-cost pricing and marginal-cost pricing and explain the implications of both to global marketers.

▶ Note how international transportation costs, tariffs, taxes, local production costs, and channel costs all affect pricing decisions.

▶ Explain how different income levels, buyer power, and competitive situations in national markets can require different pricing strategies across these markets.

▶ Compare and contrast the ways in which exchange rate fluctuations and inflation rates complicate global pricing.

▶ List various examples of government price controls that global marketers might encounter.

▶ Define dumping and describe how it can constrain pricing strategies.

▶ Describe how global marketers can manage export price escalation, determine transfer prices, and effectively quote prices in foreign currencies.

▶ Define parallel imports, explain their causes, and list ways in which they may be controlled.

▶ Differentiate among various forms of countertrade and balance the risk and opportunities of dealing with noncash exchanges.

CHAPTER OUTLINE

the part of the marketing mix that delivers potential profits to the firm. For some companies, the temptation to bring order and certainty to a global market must seem overwhelming.

Managing global pricing is indeed more complex than establishing national pricing strategies. This chapter provides an overview of the key factors that affect pricing policies in an international environment (see Figure 12.1). We assume that you understand the basic pricing decisions that companies must make in a single-country or domestic environment. In this chapter, we focus on the unique aspects of international pricing. First we look at how cost considerations affect international pricing decisions. We next explore the impact of market and environmental factors. Then we examine managerial pricing issues such as transfer pricing, global pricing, and countertrade.

FIGURE 12.1
Global Pricing Strategies

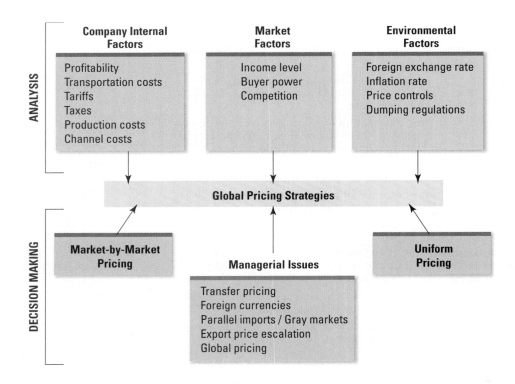

PROFIT AND COST FACTORS THAT AFFECT PRICING

Most companies begin pricing deliberations on the basis of their own internal cost structure and their profit targets. Any effective pricing policy starts with a clear understanding of these cost and profit variables. Therefore, understanding the various cost elements is a prerequisite for a successful international pricing strategy.

According to standard accounting practice, costs are divided into two categories: fixed costs and variable costs. **Fixed costs** do not change over a given range of output, whereas **variable costs** vary directly with output. The relationship of these variables is shown in Table 12.1 for a fictitious company, Western Machine Tool, Inc., a manufacturer of machine tools that sell for $60,000 per unit in the U.S. market.

The total cost of a machine tool is $54,000. Selling it at $60,000, the company will make a profit of $6,000 before taxes from the sale of each unit. However, if one additional unit is sold (or not sold), the marginal impact amounts to more than an additional profit (or loss) of $6,000, because the extra cost of an additional unit will be limited to its variable costs only, or $26,000, as shown in Table 12.2. For any additional units sold, the **marginal profit** is $34,000, the amount in excess of the variable costs.

Let's say Western Machine Tool has a chance to export a unit to a foreign country, but the maximum price the foreign buyer is willing to pay is $50,000. Machine Tool, using full-cost pricing, argues that the company will incur a loss

Fixed costs costs that do not vary with changes in production levels

Variable costs costs that vary with changes in production levels

Marginal profit the change in total profit resulting from the sale of one additional unit of a product

TABLE 12.1 PROFIT AND COST CALCULATION FOR WESTERN MACHINE TOOL, INC.

Selling price (per unit)		$60,000
Direct manufacturing costs		
Labor	$10,000	
Materials	15,000	
Energy	1,000	$26,000
Indirect manufacturing costs		
Supervision	5,000	
Research and development	3,000	
Factory overhead	5,000	13,000
General administrative cost		
Sales and marketing overhead	10,000	
Full costs	5,000	54,000
Net profit before tax	15,000	$ 6,000

of $4,000 if the deal is accepted. However, only $26,000 of additional variable cost will be incurred for a new machine, because all fixed costs are incurred anyway and are covered by all prior units sold. The company can in fact go ahead with the sale and claim a marginal profit of $24,000. In such a situation, a profitable sale may easily be turned down unless a company is fully informed about its cost composition.

Cost components are subject to change. For example, if growing export volume adds new output to a plant, a company may achieve economies of scale that result in overall reductions in unit cost.[2] This consideration further supports the use of a marginal-pricing strategy. Marketers should beware, however, if marginal pricing significantly hurts domestic competition in the export markets. As we will see later in the chapter, this can lead to charges of dumping and consequent legal action against the exporters.

TABLE 12.2 MARGINAL PROFIT CALCULATION FOR WESTERN MACHINE TOOL, INC.

Selling price (per unit)		$60,000
Variable costs		
Direct manufacturing costs		
Labor	$10,000	
Materials	15,000	
Energy	1,000	$26,000
Total variable costs		26,000
Contribution margin (selling price minus variable costs)		$34,000

Transportation Costs

International marketing often requires the shipment of products over long distances. The cost of shipping can become an important part of the international pricing policy of some firms. A study of how U.S. and Korean companies set overseas prices suggests that companies that charge higher prices in foreign markets than in domestic markets do so because of transportation costs. In other words, these companies, both American and Korean, appear to use a cost-plus model for setting prices overseas, consciously adding in transportation costs to establish the price they eventually charge in foreign markets.[3]

For commodities in particular, low transportation costs can determine who gets an order. For more expensive and differentiated products, such as computers or sophisticated electronic instruments, transportation costs usually represent only a small fraction of total costs and have less influence on pricing decisions. For products between the two extremes, companies can substantially affect unit transportation costs by selecting appropriate transportation methods. For example, the introduction of container ocean vessels has made cost-effective shipment of many products possible. Roll-on, roll-off ships (ro-ro carriers) have reduced ocean freight costs for cars and trucks to very low levels, making exporters more competitive vis-à-vis local manufacturers. Still, because all modes of transportation, including rail, truck, air, and ocean, depend on a considerable amount of energy, the total cost is of growing concern to international companies and can be sensitive to the world price of oil.

On the website for 1-800-FLOWERS you can arrange to send roses to friends in a number of different countries, but the price will vary for each market. Florists in the 1-800 network have different labor and rent costs in different regions. The average distance for a floral delivery varies across regions as well, resulting in different fuel costs.

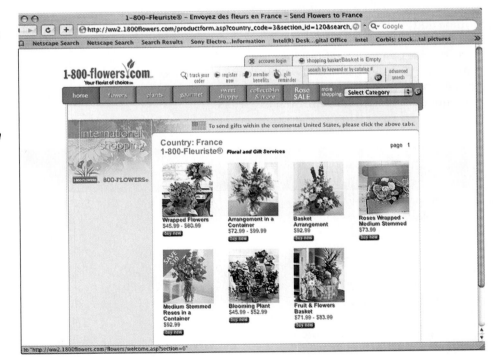

Tariffs

When products are transported across national borders, tariffs may have to be paid. Tariffs are usually levied on the landed costs of a product, which include shipping costs to the importing country. Tariffs are normally assessed as a percentage of the landed value. The World Trade Organization (WTO), like its predecessor, the General Agreement on Tariffs and Trade (GATT), has gone a long way in reducing tariffs. However, they can still prove significant for certain products in certain markets. Tariff costs can have a ripple effect and increase prices considerably for the end user. Intermediaries, whether they are sales subsidiaries or independent distributors, tend to include any tariff costs in their costs of goods sold and to calculate operating margins on the basis of this amount. As a result, the impact on the final end-user price can be substantial whenever tariff rates are high.

Sometimes international firms attempt to avoid or lessen the cost effects of tariffs by having their products reclassified. When the U.S. tariffs for trucks were temporarily increased from 2.5 to 25 percent in an effort to stem imports, Land Rover of the United Kingdom complained that its $40,000 four-wheel-drive vehicle should not be classified as a truck, pointing out that the utility vehicle had four doors, not just two like the typical light truck. The vehicle was reclassified, and the higher duty was avoided.

Check out our website (college.hmco.com/business/) for links to information on national tariffs.

Taxes

Local taxes also affect the final cost of products. A variety of taxes may be imposed. One of the most common is the **value-added tax (VAT)** used by member countries of the European Union (EU). This tax is similar to the sales tax collected by state governments in the United States but involves more complicated assessment and collection procedures based on the value added to the product at any given stage.

Each EU country sets its own VAT structure. However, common to all is a zero tax rate (or exemption) on exported goods. A company exporting from the Netherlands to Belgium does not have to pay any tax on the value added in the Netherlands. However, Belgian authorities do collect a tax, at the Belgium rate, on products shipped from the Netherlands. Merchandise shipped to any EU member country from a nonmember country, such as the United States or Japan, is assessed the VAT rate on landed costs, in addition to any customs duties that may be applied to those products.

Different countries also assess different **sin taxes**. These are taxes assessed on products that are legal but are discouraged by the society. Cigarettes and alcoholic beverages commonly fall into this category. For example, Sweden countered a history of massive alcohol abuse in the nineteenth century by enacting Europe's highest taxes on alcoholic beverages in the twentieth century. These taxes increased prices to consumers, who in turn reduced their consumption. Sweden's alcohol-related deaths and illnesses fell to among the lowest in the developed world. However, Sweden's having joined the EU threatens to undermine these gains. Swedes in the southern part of the country can now drive across a bridge to buy alcohol in Denmark at a far lower price and bring it back into Sweden. Researchers at Sweden's National Institute of Public

Value-added tax (VAT) a tax that is levied at each stage in the production and distribution of a product or service based on the value added by that stage; the tax is ultimately passed on to the buyer

Sin taxes taxes assessed on products that are legal but discouraged by society

Health predict a 10 percent rise in consumption as a result of the relaxed import allowance.[4]

Local Production Costs

Up to this point, we have assumed that a company has only one producing location, from which it exports to all other markets. However, most international firms manufacture products in several countries. In such cases, operating costs for raw materials, wages, energy, and/or financing may differ widely from country to country, allowing a firm to ship from a particularly advantageous location in order to reduce prices by taking advantage of lower costs. Companies increasingly choose production locations that give them advantages in production costs as well as freight, tariffs, or other transfer costs. Consequently, judicious management of sourcing points may reduce product costs and result in added pricing flexibility.

Recently, Mexico has attracted many U.S. candy manufacturers. Part of the attraction is the youthful Mexican market known for its sweet tooth. However,

WORLD BEAT 12.1

Foreign Patients Can Be a Lucrative Market

WHEN ONE THINKS OF INTERNATIONAL OPPORTUNITIES for Thailand, electronics, auto parts, and agricultural products jump to mind, but Thailand sees a big opportunity in health services. Following September 11, security concerns created an opportunity for Thailand to offer medical treatment to Middle Easterners who would have previously gone to the United States or the United Kingdom. The Thai Trade Center set a target of attracting one million foreign patients per year. The Bumrungrad Hospital, one of the top Thai private hospitals, even has a contract with the Dubai Police to offer medical services for its members.

German hospitals have also entered the global health care market, and they actively market to potential foreign patients. With a surplus of 10,000 to 15,000 unemployed doctors, German hospitals can offer highly specialized treatments at up to 50 percent less than the cost in the United States. With help from the German

government, the Kuratorium, a nonprofit organization, was established to develop a website and marketing literature to distribute around the world to attract potential patients to Germany.

Terry Salo, of Victoria British Columbia, Canada, flew 22 hours to Madras India to receive a hip replacement at the Apollo Hospital. In Canada, he would have had to wait a year for free care from the national health service. In the United States and Europe, the same operation that only cost $4,000 in Madras would cost $30,000.

Sources: Jay Solomon, "From Its Base in India, Private-Hospital Chain Enjoys Global Reach," *Wall Street Journal* (Europe), April 26, 2004, p. A1; Wichit Chantanusornsiri, "Thai Officials Promote Country's Health Care Abilities to Wealthy Arabs," *Knight Ridder Tribune Business News*, January 26, 2004, p. 1; and Meera Louis, "Germans Lure Foreign Patients to Hospitals," *Wall Street Journal*, December 6, 2000, p. B12.

Mexico is also being used as a platform to export candy back to the U.S. market. Mexican workers earn as little as one-tenth the pay of U.S. factory workers. Even more important is the lower cost of sugar in Mexico—about half the federally supported U.S. cost.[5]

Channel Costs

Channel costs are a function of channel length, distribution margins, and logistics. Many countries operate with longer distribution channels than those in the United States, causing higher total costs and end-user prices because of additional layers of intermediaries. Also, gross margins at the retail level tend to be higher outside the United States. Because the logistics system in a large number of countries is also less developed than that in the United States, logistics costs, too, are higher on a per-unit basis. All these factors add extra costs to a product that is marketed internationally.

Campbell Soup Company, a U.S.-based firm, found that its retailers in the United Kingdom purchased soup in small quantities of twenty-four cans per case of assorted soups, requiring each can to be handpicked for shipment. In the United States, the company could sell one variety of soup to retailers in cases of forty-eight cans per case. To handle the smaller purchase lots in England, the company had to add another level of distribution and new facilities. As a result, distribution costs were 30 percent higher in England than in the United States.[6]

MARKET FACTORS THAT AFFECT PRICING

Companies cannot establish pricing policies in a vacuum. Although cost information is essential, prices must also reflect the realities of the marketplace. International markets are particularly challenging because of the large number of local economic situations to be considered. Four factors in particular stand out and must be analyzed in greater detail: income level, buyer power, competition, and culture.

Income Level

As we have discussed in previous chapters, the income level of a country's population determines the amount and type of goods and services bought, especially in consumer markets. When detailed income data are not available, incomes are expressed by gross domestic product (GDP) or gross national product (GNP) divided by the total population. GDP is the total value of goods and services produced in a country. GNP includes this plus any income that residents receive from abroad. The new measures, GNP per capita and GDP per capita, are surrogate measures for personal income and are used to compare income levels among countries. To do so, all GNPs and GDPs have to be converted into the same currency. As we also noted earlier, converting GNP or GDP per capita into dollars on the basis of market exchange rates may understate the true purchasing power of a country's consumers. It is more accurate to look at developing countries' GNP or GDP per capita converted into dollars on the basis of relative purchasing power.

Discretionary income income remaining after the basic necessities of food, shelter, and clothing have been acquired

Furthermore, **discretionary income**—the amount left after the basic necessities of food, shelter, and clothing have been acquired—can vary from country to country. In much of Southeast Asia, children in their twenties still live with their parents. Virtually all the income they earn is discretionary, which makes them an attractive target market. In China, employees of state organizations often receive lucrative housing benefits, a practice that markedly increases their discretionary income.

As a result of widely differing income and price levels, elasticity of demand for any given product can be expected to vary greatly. Countries with high income levels often display lower price elasticities for necessities such as food, shelter, and medical care. These lower elasticities in part reflect a lack of alternatives such as "doing it yourself" that forces buyers in these countries to purchase such goods even at higher prices. By contrast, in many countries with lower income levels, a considerable part of the population has the additional alternatives of providing their own food or building their own shelters should they not have enough money to purchase products or services on a cash basis. The availability of such options increases price elasticity, because these consumers can more easily opt out of the cash economy than can consumers in developed economies.

Of course, in any country there will be a mix of different consumers with different income levels and potentially different price elasticities. In a study of the price elasticities of business-to-business (B2B) buyers of information technology system support, it was determined that in each country studied different

Two Burmese monks walk past a billboard advertising Apple Macintosh computers in Myanmar. The appeal of a low price is appropriate in this Asian country where only about one person in a thousand owns a personal computer.

sets of customers existed, with different price elasticities and different needs. The researchers determined that price elasticities could be used to segment across countries and therefore develop different regional or global offers to appeal to the different segments.[7]

Many multinational firms can realistically target only a select segment of the population in poorer countries, even when they adjust their prices downward. To accommodate a lower income level in China, a Big Mac costs the equivalent of $1.26, which is significantly below the cost of $3.00 for a Big Mac in the United States. McDonald's has typically resorted to introductory pricing that attracts more customers. Still, a McDonald's meal remains expensive in the Chinese context. A Chinese family of three can pay about 100 yuan, or about 10 percent of a typical monthly urban salary, to eat one meal out.[8]

Firms should regularly reassess their pricing policy in developing countries, especially if they are charging relatively high prices and targeting the elite. The growing middle classes in these countries can become a more attractive segment to target than a small upper class. For example, General Motors announced its development of a Farmers Car for China's 800 million rural inhabitants, whose incomes are even lower than those of city dwellers, in an attempt to tap a market segment hitherto ignored by multinational car manufacturers. The proposed price of the car was $7,000, down from the $40,000 charged for Buicks then sold to Chinese city dwellers.[9] Soon cars sold in the city were also becoming more affordable, as many manufacturers began to lower automobile prices. As a result of an increase in the incomes of Chinese consumers, competitively priced cars, and availability of consumer credit, China's middle classes are expected to buy five million cars a year by 2010.[10]

Buyer Power

Just as discretionary income is an important consideration in consumer markets, buyer power is crucial in B2B markets. Large buyers can become important to supplier firms, and in turn these buyers can demand lower prices from suppliers. If there are only a few buyers in a national industry, prices may be lower than in markets where there are many smaller buyers. In some global industries in particular, marketers face the challenge of increasing buyer power at the international level. Aircraft component suppliers are increasingly responding to demands from big aerospace companies such as Boeing, Airbus, and Pratt & Whitney to cut prices, even if it means moving production from the United States to Mexico to realize cost savings that can be passed on to the powerful buyers.[11]

Competition

The intensity and power of competition can also significantly affect price levels in any given market. A firm acting as the sole supplier of a product in a given market enjoys greater pricing flexibility. The opposite is true if that same company has to compete against several other local or international firms. Therefore, the number and type of competitors greatly influence pricing strategy in any market. The public postal, telephone, and telegraph (PTT) services of most countries were until recently public monopolies, which could charge high rates with no threat of competition. As the Japanese telecommunications market liberalized, U.S. and other suppliers have been quick to respond. AT&T World Access offered international calling opportunities at approximately half the standard price. After the German telecom market was liberalized, fifty-one new companies entered the market, and long-distance rates dropped 90 percent.[12]

Cartel a group of companies acting together to control the price of certain goods or services

Occasionally, price levels are manipulated by **cartels**, or pricing agreements among competitors. Cartels in the United States are forbidden by law. Furthermore, U.S. companies may find themselves in violation of U.S. laws if they actively participate in any foreign cartel. Although many other foreign governments allow cartels provided that they do not injure the consumer, the EU is becoming stricter toward cartels. The European Commission charged eighteen chemical companies with fixing the price of hydrogen peroxide, which included Akzo Nobel, Arkema, Degussa, Kemira, and Solvay. The companies can be fined up to 10 percent of their annual revenue if found guilty.[13]

The U.S. government has a very strict approach to cartels, and any cartel such as those just described would clearly be against existing U.S. laws. The U.S. Justice Department found four graphite electrode manufacturers guilty of conspiring to suppress and eliminate competition. As a result, one German, one U.S., and two Japanese companies paid fines totaling $284 million.[14]

Culture

Culture can also affect pricing. In some emerging markets, such as Turkey, bargaining is acceptable—even expected—in the more traditional markets. However, fixed prices are replacing bargaining as more consumers shop at modern retail outlets such as supermarkets. Nonetheless, local traditions still play a role in sometimes surprising ways. In China, the number 8 is associated with prosperity and good luck while the number 4 is associated with death. A research study confirmed that marketers in China avoided prices that ended in 4, whereas prices ending in 8 were advertised four times more often than prices ending in other numerals.[15]

ENVIRONMENTAL FACTORS THAT AFFECT PRICING

We have thus far treated pricing as a matter of cost and market factors. A number of environmental factors also influence pricing at the international level. These external variables, which are not subject to control by any individual company, include foreign exchange rates, inflation, and government price controls. These factors restrict company decision-making authority and can become major concerns for country managers.

Exchange Rate Fluctuations

One of the most unpredictable factors affecting prices is the movement of foreign exchange rates. As the exchange rate moves up and down, it affects all producers. When a company's costs are in its domestic currency, as this currency weakens, the firm's costs appear lower in another currency. For example, when the euro was first launched, each euro was valued at $1.20. Six months later, the euro had dropped to $1.00. As a result, products manufactured in Europe were cheaper in dollar terms and more attractive in the U.S. market, as well as in other national markets where governments pegged their currencies to the U.S. dollar.

Foreign exchange fluctuations can also present difficulties for companies that export from countries with appreciating currencies. These firms are forced to accept decreased margins on sales denominated in foreign currencies or else raise prices to maintain their prior margins. The latter option could, of course, cause a drop in export demand. This was clear when the Russian ruble fell 22 percent over a period of a few months. Exports to Russia fell 50 percent. Faced with the option of buying a tube of locally produced toothpaste for 7 rubles or a tube of imported Colgate for 24 rubles, fewer Russian consumers chose the Colgate.[16]

Check out our website (college.hmco.com/business/) for links to national currency information.

Inflation Rates

The rate of inflation can affect product costs and may force a company to take specific action. Inflation rates have traditionally fluctuated over time and, more important, have differed from country to country. The United States and Europe have successfully managed inflation by raising interest rates whenever the economy starts to heat up, keeping inflation at 0 to 2 percent. Historically, inflation has been a problem in developing countries. In some cases, inflation rates have risen to several hundred percent. Argentina, Bolivia, Brazil, and Nicaragua have all experienced four-digit hyperinflation in the past. A company can usually protect itself from rapid inflation if it maintains constant operating margins and makes constant price adjustments, sometimes on a monthly basis.

Price Controls

Despite the official claim that 96 percent of all prices are set by the market, the Chinese government enforces price controls on such key products as fertilizers, fuel, medicines, and transport services.[17] Price controls are most common in developing countries and may be applied to an entire economy to combat inflation. Alternatively, regulations may be applied selectively to specific industries. As a result of market liberalization, across-the-board price controls are now uncommon. Industry-specific controls are more common. In response to rising prices, the Thai government threatened cement producers with price controls if they failed to cap their prices voluntarily through the end of the year. Furthermore, the cement producers agreed to cut off distributors who attracted complaints of overcharging.[18]

Pharmaceuticals are subject to price controls in many countries, including Canada, Japan, and European states. In the EU, where many aspects of the countries' economies are coordinated, methods of controlling prices for drugs can vary considerably. In the United Kingdom, drug prices are established through the Pharmaceutical Price Regulation Scheme (PPRS). Although companies are allowed to set prices for most individual drugs, the government limits their overall profitability. In India, pharmaceutical manufacturers who apply for patent protection must report the price of similar products available within India as well as the price of the drug in every country in which the drug is sold. The Indian government then assesses the therapeutic advantage of the drug and sets a limit on the premium that can be charged for the drug.[19]

Dumping Regulations

Dumping the practice of exporting a product at an "unfair" price and consequently damaging competition in the export market

The practice of exporting a product at an "unfair" price and consequently damaging local competition is referred to as **dumping**. Because of potential injuries to domestic manufacturers, most governments have adopted regulations against dumping. Antidumping actions are allowed under provisions of the WTO as long as two criteria are met: prices are set at less than "normal value" and this results in "material injury" to a domestic industry. The first criterion is usually interpreted to mean selling abroad at prices below those in the country of origin, although there are some exceptions. Subsequently, a complainant government may be required to establish that prices in its country are indeed set below full costs of manufacture, transport, and marketing. The WTO rules prohibit assessment of retroactive punitive duties and require all procedures to be open.

In the 1980s and early 1990s, 80 percent of antidumping charges were brought by the United States, Canada, the EU, and Australia—often against Asian countries. However, many of the new antidumping cases have been brought to the WTO by developing countries such as South Africa, India, Brazil, Indonesia, and Mexico. The United States, the EU, Canada, and Australia have brought less than one-third of the cases. Forty-three of the cases were brought against the EU and its members.[20] International marketers have to be aware of antidumping legislation that sets a floor under export prices, limiting pricing flexibility even in the event of overcapacity or an industry slowdown. On the other hand, antidumping legislation can work to a company's advantage, protecting it from foreign competition. In South Korea, the Korean Trade Commission found that Japanese industrial robots were sold at unfair prices in Korea, thereby harming the Korean robot industry. The Ministry of Commerce, Industry and Energy has asked that antidumping duties of 9 to 19 percent be put on Japanese products.[21]

MANAGERIAL ISSUES IN GLOBAL PRICING

Now that we have given you a general overview of the context of international pricing, we turn to managerial issues—matters that require constant management attention and are never really resolved. These issues include export price escalation, transfer pricing, quoting prices in foreign currencies, parallel markets, setting global prices, and managing countertrade.

Managing Export Price Escalation

The additional costs described earlier may raise the end-user price of an exported product substantially above its domestic price. This phenomenon, which is called export price escalation, may force a company to adopt either of two strategies. First, a company may accept its price disadvantage and adjust the marketing mix to promote a luxury status. By adopting such a strategy, the company sacrifices volume to keep a high unit price. For example, in Guangzhou, China, Pizza Hut found that its typical price per person for a restaurant meal was 40–50 RMB, whereas a value meal at McDonald's cost 16–25 RMB. Pizza Hut decided it was desirable to position itself as a casual dining restaurant with table service, rather than counter service, to differentiate its offerings from the fast-food restaurants and thereby command a higher price.[22]

Alternatively, a company may reengineer its products to be less costly or grant a discount on the standard domestic price to bring the end-user price more in line with prices paid by domestic customers. Such discounts may be justified under a strategy of marginal-cost pricing. Also, export sales may generate greater economies of scale in production, thus covering the lower export price. Because of reduced marketing costs at the manufacturer's level, particularly when a foreign distributor is used, an export price equal to the domestic price is often not justified. However, legal limits related to antidumping regulations may prevent price reductions below a certain point.

Determining Transfer Prices

A substantial amount of international business takes place between subsidiaries of the same company. It is estimated that in-house trading between subsidiaries accounts for one-third of the volume among the world's eight hundred largest multinationals. An **international transfer price** is the price paid by the importing or buying unit of a firm to the exporting unit of the same firm. For example, the U.S. marketing subsidiary of a Taiwanese manufacturer of personal computers will pay a transfer price for the machines it receives from Taiwan. The actual transfer price may be negotiated by the units involved or may be set centrally by the international firm. How these prices are set continues to be a major issue for international companies and governments alike.

International transfer price the price paid by one unit of a firm to import a product or service supplied by another unit of the same firm

Because negotiations of transfer prices do not represent arm's-length negotiations between independent participants, the resulting prices frequently differ from free-market prices. Companies may deviate from arm's-length prices to maximize profits or to minimize risk and uncertainty. To pursue a strategy of profit maximization, a company may lower transfer prices for products shipped from some subsidiaries, while increasing prices for products shipped to others, in order to accumulate profits in countries where it is advantageous, while keeping profits low elsewhere.

Different tax, tariff, or subsidy structures among countries frequently invite such practices. By accumulating more profits in a low-tax country, a company lowers its overall tax bill and thus increases profit. Likewise, tariff duties can be reduced by quoting low transfer prices to countries with high tariffs. In cases where countries use a different exchange rate for the transfer of goods from that used for the transfer of capital or profits, a firm may attempt to use transfer prices to remove money from the country, rather than transferring profits at less advantageous rates. The same is true for countries with limits on profit repatriation. Furthermore, a company may want to accumulate profits in a wholly owned subsidiary rather than in one in which it has minority ownership. By using the transfer price mechanism, it can avoid sharing profits with local partners.

Companies may also use the transfer price mechanism to minimize risk or uncertainty by moving profits or assets out of a country with chronic balance-of-payment problems and frequent devaluations. Because regular profit remittances may be strictly controlled in such countries, many firms see high transfer prices as the only way to repatriate funds and thereby reduce the amount of assets at risk. The same practice may be employed if a company anticipates political or social disturbances or a direct threat to profits through government intervention.

In actual practice, companies choose a number of approaches to transfer pricing. Market-based prices are equal to those negotiated by independent companies or at arm's length. Of thirty U.S.-based firms, 46 percent were reported to use market-based systems.[23] Another 35 percent used cost-based systems to determine the transfer price. Costs were based on a predetermined formula that could include a standard markup for profits.

Internal Considerations. Rigorous use of the transfer pricing mechanism to reduce a company's income taxes and duties or to maximize profits in strong currency areas can create difficulties for subsidiary managers whose profits are artificially reduced. It may be hard to motivate managers when the direct profit incentive is removed. Furthermore, company resource allocation may become inefficient, because funds are appropriated to units whose profits are artificially increased. Conversely, resources may be denied to subsidiaries whose income statements were subject to transfer-price-induced reductions. It is generally agreed that a transfer pricing mechanism should not be used for resource allocations; the gains incurred through tax savings may easily be lost through other inefficiencies.

External Problems. Governments do not look favorably on transfer pricing mechanisms aimed at reducing their tax revenues. U.S. government policy on transfer pricing is governed by tax law, particularly Section 482 of the Revenue Act of 1962. The act is designed to provide an accurate allocation of costs, income, and capital among related enterprises to protect U.S. tax revenue. Market prices are generally preferred by the Internal Revenue Service (IRS). The IRS will accept cost-plus markups if market prices are not available and economic circumstances warrant such use. Not acceptable, however, are transfer prices that attribute no profit to the U.S. unit. Other methods, such as negotiated prices, are acceptable as long as the transfer price is comparable to a price charged to an unrelated party.

In addition, the IRS requires all companies to maintain detailed explanations of the rationale and analysis supporting their transfer pricing policy. The IRS developed the Advanced Pricing Agreement Program (APA), which became effective on December 31, 1993. Under this program, a company can obtain approval from the IRS for their transfer pricing procedures.

The transfer prices between countries can result in billions of dollars of tax liability. The U.S. IRS issued GlaxoSmithKline a tax bill of $5 billion in 2005 as a result of an IRS audit that began in 1992. The IRS argued that the company transferred costs to the United States from other countries at inflated prices to reduce their U.S. tax burden.[24] A lengthy legal battle is expected. Australia, Japan, and Korea all have formal transfer pricing arrangements, and China,

India, and New Zealand all have informal programs.[25] However, the strengthening of government regulations all around the world makes it necessary for global businesses to document and defend their transfer pricing methods. According to a study of 280 multinational companies operating in Europe, 85 percent had been audited on transfer pricing over a 3-year period.[26]

Quoting Prices in a Foreign Currency

For many international marketing transactions, it is not always feasible to quote in a company's domestic currency when selling or purchasing merchandise. Although the majority of U.S. exporters quote prices in dollars, there are situations in which customers may prefer quotes in their own national currency. In fact, a research study of 671 companies in the United States, Finland, and Sweden found that companies that respond to customers' requests for prices quoted in their local currencies benefit from a larger volume of export business.[27]

When two currencies are involved in a market transaction, there is the risk that a change in exchange rates may occur between the invoicing date and the settlement date for the sale. This **transaction risk** is an inherent factor in international marketing and clearly separates domestic from international business. Fortunately, alternatives are available to protect the seller from transaction risk.

For most major currencies, international foreign exchange dealers located at major banks quote a spot price and a forward price. The **spot price** determines the number of dollars to be paid for a particular foreign currency purchased or sold today. The **forward price** quotes the number of dollars to be paid for a foreign currency bought or sold 30, 90, or 180 days from today. The forward price, however, is not necessarily speculation about what the spot price will be in the future. Instead, the forward price reflects interest rate differentials between two currencies for maturities of 30, 90, or 180 days. Consequently, there are no firm indications of what the spot price will be for any given currency in the future.

A company quoting in foreign currency for purchase or sale can simply leave settlement until the due date and pay whatever spot price prevails at the time. Such an **uncovered position** may be chosen when exchange rates are not expected to shift or when any shift in the near future will result in a gain for the company. With exchange rates fluctuating widely on a daily basis, even among major trading nations such as the United States, Japan, Germany, and the United Kingdom, a company can expose itself to substantial foreign exchange risks. Because many international firms are in business to make a profit from the sale of goods rather than from speculation in the foreign exchange markets, managers generally protect themselves from unexpected fluctuations.

One such protection lies in **hedging**. Instead of accepting whatever spot market rate exists on the settlement in 30 or 90 days, a company can opt to contract through financial intermediaries for future delivery of foreign currency at a set price, regardless of the spot price at that time. This allows the seller to incorporate a firm exchange rate into the price determination. Of course, if a company wishes to predict the spot price in 90 days and is reasonably certain about the accuracy of its prediction, it may attempt to choose the more advantageous of the two: the expected spot or the present forward rate. However, such predictions should only be made under the guidance of experts familiar with foreign exchange rates.

Transaction risk the risk that a change in exchange rate that will prove unfavorable to either the seller or the buyer will occur between invoicing and settlement dates

Spot price/spot rate the rate of exchange between two currencies for delivery, one for the other, within one or two business days

Forward price/forward rate the price agreed upon by two parties for one to deliver to the other a set amount of currency at a fixed future date

Uncovered position a strategy in which a firm chooses not to take any action that would alleviate transaction risk

Hedging the act of contracting through financial intermediaries for the future exchange of one currency for another at a set rate

TABLE 12.3 HEDGING SCENARIOS	A	B	C
Spot rate of March 3	$1.31	$1.31	$1.31
Spot rate as of June 3 (estimate)	1.20	1.45	1.31
U.S. dollar equivalent of €18,320,610 at spot rates on June 3	21,984,735	26,564,884	24,000,000
Exchange gain (loss)	(2,015,265)	2,564,884	0

To illustrate the selection of a hedging procedure, assume that a U.S. exporter of corporate jets sells a jet valued at $24 million to a client in Germany (see Table 12.3). The client will pay in euros quoted at the current (spot) rate on March 3 of $1.31, or €18,320,610. This amount will be paid in 3 months (90 days). As a result, the U.S. exporter will have to determine how to protect such an incoming amount against foreign exchange risk. Although uncertain about the outcome, the exporter's bank indicates that there is equal chance for the euro spot rate to remain at $1.31 (scenario C), to devalue to $1.20 (scenario A), or to appreciate to $1.45 (scenario B). As a result, the exporter has the option of selling the amount forward in the 90-days forward market, at $1.3213.[28]

An alternative available to the exporter is to sell forward the invoice amount to obtain a sure $23,947,980 at a cost of $52,020 on the transaction. In anticipation of a devaluation of the euro, such a hedging strategy would be advisable. Consequently, the $52,020 represents a premium to ensure against any larger loss such as the one predicted under scenario A. However, a company would also forgo any gain as indicated under scenario B.

Sometimes hedging is not an option when a firm is dealing with soft currencies or currencies undergoing upheaval. Prior to an expected devaluation of the ruble, nearly all exporters to Russia were seeking hedging contracts. Hedging contracts for rubles became increasingly hard to find and then disappeared from the market altogether. When the Turkish government allowed the pegged lira to float in 2001, the lira collapsed nearly 40 percent over a few days. In the immediate disarray that ensued, hedging opportunities for the lira were similarly difficult to locate.

An alternative to hedging is covering through the money market. This involves borrowing funds in the currency at risk for the time until settlement. For example, a U.S. exporter that is holding accounts receivable in euros and is unwilling to absorb the related currency risk may borrow euros and exchange them for dollars for working-capital purposes. When the customer eventually pays in euros, the U.S. exporter uses these euros to pay off the loan. Any currency fluctuations will be canceled, resulting in neither loss nor gain.

Dealing with Parallel Imports or Gray Markets

As a result of different market and competitive factors, international marketers often choose to sell the same product at different prices in different national markets. When such price differences become large enough, entrepreneurs may step in and buy products in low-price countries to reexport to high-price countries, profiting from the price differential. This arbitrage behavior creates what is commonly called **parallel imports** or the **gray market**, because these imports take place outside of the official distribution channels established by the trademark owner.

Gray markets have never been more robust. Parallel imports within the EU have been encouraged by the introduction of the euro, which allows easy price comparisons from country to country. Similarly, gray markets have soared in response to the Internet, which enables buyers to compare prices easily across markets. In some cases, intermediaries are not even necessary to fuel parallel imports. Many older Americans buy their prescription drugs through one of many online and mail order Canadian pharmacies where prices are considerably cheaper. Although it is technically illegal for individuals to import pharmaceuticals into the United States, the law is not enforced.

Companies deplore gray markets because they hurt relationships with authorized dealers and especially because they undermine a company's ability to charge different prices in different markets in order to maximize global profits. Parallel imports are even credited with adding to Coca-Cola's public relations difficulties subsequent to a product-harm crisis in Europe. The company began a product recall after hundreds of Coke drinkers complained of getting sick. Unfortunately, tracking down the questionable Belgium-produced Coke was complicated; it began showing up in places it shouldn't have been, such as Spain, Germany, and the United Kingdom. But this should have come as no surprise. The gray market for soft drinks in the United Kingdom is estimated at 20 percent share of market.[29]

Parallel imports/gray market imports that enter a market outside the official distribution channels established by the trademark owner

A pharmacy in Tijuana, Mexico. Medicine sold here can cost much more just across the border in the United States. Such discrepancies in prices encourage gray markets.

Exhaustion principle a legal principle that establishes the conditions under which a trademark owner relinquishes its right to control the resale of its product

National exhaustion an exhaustion principle that states that once a firm has sold a trademarked product in a specific country, it cannot restrict the further distribution of that product in that country

Regional exhaustion an exhaustion principle that states that once a firm has sold a trademarked product anywhere in a region (such as the EU), it cannot restrict the resale of that product within that region

International exhaustion an exhaustion principle that states that once a firm has sold a product anywhere in the world, it cannot restrict its resale into a particular country

Seeking Legal Redress. Global firms would like governments to forbid parallel imports from entering their countries. But legal attempts to stop parallel imports have been stymied by the fact that governments around the world have taken different stands on gray markets. At issue is the right of a trademark owner to manage the sale of a trademarked product versus the ability of consumers to enjoy the lower prices usually provided by parallel imports. Most countries adopt some variation of the **exhaustion principle** that establishes the conditions under which a trademark owner relinquishes its right to control the resale of its product. For example **national exhaustion** provides that once a firm has sold its trademarked product in a specific country, it cannot restrict the further distribution of that product in that country. **Regional exhaustion** provides that once a firm has sold a trademarked product anywhere in a region (such as the EU), it cannot restrict the resale of that product within that region.

Most developing countries as well as Australia have adopted the principle of **international exhaustion**.[30] For example, once a firm sells a product anywhere in the world, it cannot restrict its resale into Australia. These countries welcome parallel imports into their country in order to encourage lower prices. With few local firms holding valuable trademarks, such countries are less concerned with the rights of trademark owners.

Laws concerning gray markets vary among developed countries:

▶ Japan recognizes international exhaustion unless otherwise agreed by contract or if the original sale is subject to price controls.

▶ The EU follows the principle of regional exhaustion. Once a trademarked product is sold in anywhere in the EU, the trademark owner cannot restrict its resale within the EU. However, the EU does allow trademark owners to stop parallel imports from coming into the EU from countries outside the EU. For example, Nintendo, the Japanese video game firm, was found in violation of European antitrust laws for working with distributors to illegally prevent sales from one EU country to another in order to keep prices high.[31] But the European Court of Justice upheld the right of Levi Strauss to stop parallel imports of its jeans coming into the United Kingdom from the United States at lower prices.

▶ U.S. laws concerning parallel imports were originally envisaged to be discouraging to gray markets but have since evolved to be surprisingly conducive to parallel imports.[32] These laws are among the most confusing as well. Essentially, a firm exhausts its rights to restrict the resale of a product into the United States once that product is sold anywhere in the world—with certain exceptions. Some of these exceptions have had little effect on gray markets. The one exception that companies have found useful in stopping parallel imports into the United States allows trademark owners to stop parallel imports from entering the U.S. market when those products are materially different from those being officially sold in the United States. For example, in the case of Perugina chocolate made in Venezuela under license from the Italian trademark owner, the court ruled the parallel imported chocolate made in Venezuela was different from the chocolate produced in Italy. The quality level, fat content, ingredients, and packaging

World Beat 12.2

Just Say "No" to Low Drug Prices?

MOST COUNTRIES IN EUROPE have a national health care system that provides free health care to all citizens. The national health care systems negotiate directly with drug companies to decide what drugs will be bought and at what price. The countries of the United Kingdom, France, Germany, Italy, and Spain make up 80 percent of the European market. Given the buying power of these countries and the availability of information on global drug prices, it is not surprising that these governments are squeezing the pharmaceutical companies for lower drug pricing. If a drug company accepts a lower price for one country, it will often be asked for the same low price by other countries. Furthermore, any significant differences in drug pricing from country to country result in parallel imports. Wholesalers buy drugs in lower-priced countries like Spain and Italy and resell them in higher-priced countries such as Germany or the United Kingdom. Government interference with drug prices also occurs in many developing countries. South Africa has approved laws that will limit drug prices as well as the wholesale and retail markups. The minister of health promised that the new legislation will reduce prescription drug prices by 30 percent.

Can pharmaceutical companies fight back? A final drastic measure is to refuse to sell certain drugs in countries where price controls contribute to parallel markets. Pharmaceutical firms have already hinted that this could happen in Europe. However, such a threat may prove hollow in developing countries. In Brazil, the government spends over $350 million per year for HIV/AIDS drugs to serve the 150,000 affected patients. The health minister has demanded a drastic reduction in price from the three drug companies, Merck, Roche, and Abbott, or he will declare a national emergency and begin manufacturing generic versions of the drugs in Brazil. In 2001, the WTO agreed to allow an exemption to intellectual property laws in developing countries that faced such a health emergency.

Sources: Eric Ladley, "Altana Sues over German Pricing," *Med Ad News* (London) 24, no. 2 (February 2005), p. 12.; "Business: The Trouble with Cheap Drugs," *The Economist*, January 31, 2004, p. 60; Tom Nevin, "Industry Backlash Over Cheaper Drugs," *African Business*, February 1, 2005, p. 28; and Christopher Rowland, "Q&A Bain's Paul Rosenberg on Harm of Europe's Drug Price Controls," *Boston Globe*, February 29, 2004, p. C.2.

varied and were likely to cause confusion to the American consumer.[33] Therefore, the Italian trademark owner could restrict the import of the Venezuelan product into the U.S. market.

Other Corporate Responses to Gray Markets. A number of proactive strategies may be implemented to prevent gray markets from arising in the first place. A company may create product differentiation between markets solely to try to stop gray markets. Strategic pricing may be used to keep prices within a range of each other, thus destroying opportunities for arbitrage. Companies may also use strict legal enforcement of restrictive contracts with wholesalers where these are allowed by law. Once the problem of parallel imports arises, a firm may use a number of strategies in a reactive way. These include cutting prices in higher-priced markets, raising prices in lower-priced markets and even acquiring the diverter involved.

Another somewhat controversial option is to limit supplies to distributors in lower-priced markets. The Bayer Group attempted to stop the parallel import into the United Kingdom of a Bayer cardiovascular medicine, Adalat, from France and Spain, where the price of the drug was 40 percent lower. Bayer limited the amount wholesalers in these two countries could receive to the estimated demand of their own markets. The wholesalers complained, and the European Commission fined Bayer for what it considered anticompetitive agreements to limit parallel imports. However, in 2004, the European Court of Justice reversed the earlier ruling of the European Commission, therefore allowing pharmaceutical manufacturers to limit supply to countries that are involved in parallel trade.[34]

Research involving U.S. exporters identified three factors that significantly discouraged parallel imports. Firms that customized products more for local markets experienced fewer problems, as did firms that maintained greater control over their distribution systems, including by owning them. Parallel imports were also less likely to occur if an international firm maintained greater centralized control than if it allowed national subsidiaries greater autonomy.[35] For example, certain national managers at Bausch and Lomb cooperated with gray marketers in order to raise their own local sales figures, even though the parallel imports they helped fuel in other countries hurt the company overall.[36]

Setting Global Prices

To maximize a company's revenues, it would appear logical to set prices on a market-by-market basis, seeking in each market the best combination of price and expected volume to yield the maximum profit. This strategy was common for many firms in the early part of their international development. For many consumer products, there are still significant price differences across many countries. For example, Table 12.4 illustrates how McDonald's Big Mac prices can vary by country.

With the advent of global branding, international firms have become more concerned about issues of global pricing. They rarely dictate uniform prices in every country but do establish a particular pricing policy across countries—relatively higher prices for premium brands and relatively lower prices for value brands. In a study of global pricing policies among multinational companies from developed countries, the likelihood that a subsidiary would follow a pricing policy similar to that of the parent company in the home market was found to be influenced by market similarity in economic conditions, legal environment, customer characteristics, and stage in the product life cycle.[37]

However, for products that are similar in many markets and for which transportation costs are not significant, substantial price differences quickly result in the emergence of parallel imports. This has led some firms to consider a policy of more uniform pricing worldwide. Employing a **uniform pricing**

Uniform pricing strategy a pricing strategy in which a firm charges the same price everywhere when that price is translated into a base currency

TABLE 12.4 BIG MAC PRICES

	Price	
	IN U.S. DOLLARS	PERCENTAGE DIFFERENCE OF LOCAL vs. U.S. PRICE
United States	$3.00	0%
Argentina	1.60	-46
Australia	2.46	-18
Brazil	1.99	-34
Britain	3.61	+20
Canada	2.60	-13
Chile	2.56	-15
China	1.26	-58
Denmark	4.97	+65
Euro Area	3.75	+25
Hong Kong	1.54	-49
Hungary	2.85	-5
Indonesia	1.57	-48
Japan	2.50	-17
Malaysia	1.33	-56
Mexico	2.12	-29
New Zealand	3.16	+5
Poland	2.06	-31
Russia	1.49	-50
Singapore	2.19	-27
South Africa	2.44	-19
South Korea	2.36	-21
Sweden	4.46	+48
Switzerland	5.46	+82
Taiwan	2.32	-23
Thailand	1.52	-49

SOURCE: Adapted from bar chart: "Big Mac Index," *Economist*, December 18, 2004, p.162. (Percentage difference of local vs. U.S. price calculated by author.)

strategy on a global scale requires that a company charge the same price everywhere when that price is translated into a base currency. For example, in India, LVMH sells the Tag Heuer sports watch at prices of Rs 18,000 to Rs 40,000 which is on a par with the international prices that would be paid for the same watch in Dubai.[38]

Global firms need to be careful about presenting varying prices to business customers with international operations.[39] Oracle Corporation began standardizing prices for its software in response to business customers who questioned why the price in their country was higher than the price in other countries. In fact, global customers usually pressure for lower prices as well as for uniform prices. In a research study done with more than fifty executives responsible for global account management in the Americas, Europe, and Asia, global customers reported that they believed global procurement was a way to receive lower prices.[40]

In reality, a uniform pricing strategy becomes very difficult to achieve whenever different taxes, trade margins, and customs duties are involved. Furthermore, firms that start out with identical prices in various countries soon find that prices have to change to stay in line with often substantial currency fluctuations. Although it is becoming increasingly clear that market-by-market pricing strategies will cause difficulties, many firms have found that changing to a uniform pricing policy is rather like pursuing a moving target. However, a company can employ **modified uniform pricing** by carefully monitoring price levels in each country and avoiding large gaps that encourage gray marketers to move in and take advantage of large price differentials.

> **Modified uniform pricing** a pricing strategy in which a firm monitors price levels in different countries to close large price differentials and discourage gray markets

Noncash Pricing: Countertrade

International marketers are likely to find many situations in which an interested customer will not be able to arrange hard-currency financing. In such circumstances, the customer might offer a product or commodity in return. The supplier must then turn the product offered into hard currency. Such transactions, known as **countertrade**, were estimated at 15 to 25 percent of world trade in the mid-1980s, although with the collapse of the former Soviet Union the volume of countertrade has declined. Still, many countries have some form of countertrade requirement as part of their public procurement program. For example, in the Philippines, the Department of Agriculture requires that half the value of imports of agricultural equipment and machinery be paid with agricultural or fishery products.[41]

> **Countertrade** a transaction in which goods are exchanged for other goods

There are a number of different forms of countertrade, which are explained in the following sections.

Barter. Barter, one of the most basic types of countertrade, consists of a direct exchange of goods between two parties. Barter involves no currency and is concluded without the help of intermediaries. One of the largest barter deals ever, valued at about $3 billion, was signed by PepsiCo and Russia. Since 1974 PepsiCo has engaged in business with Russia, shipping soft-drink syrup, bottling it into Pepsi-Cola, and marketing it within Russia. To gain access to the Russian market so early, PepsiCo entered an agreement to export Stolichnaya vodka to the United States, where it was sold through an independent liquor company.

Compensation Transactions. One usually speaks of a compensation transaction when the value of an export delivery is at least partially offset by an import transaction, or vice versa. Compensation transactions are typical for large government purchases, such as for defense projects, when a country wants to obtain some additional exports in exchange for the awarding of a contract. For the past 20 years, the government of Indonesia has required winners of major government contracts to take part of their payment in Indonesian commodities apart from oil and gas. Compensation transactions fall into several categories, as described in the following.

▶ *Full versus Partial Compensation.* Full compensation is similar to barter in that a 100 percent mutual transfer of goods takes place. By signing the sales agreement, the exporter commits itself to purchasing products or services at an amount equal to that specified in the export contract. Under partial compensation, the exporter receives a portion of the purchase price in hard currency and the remainder in merchandise. In either case, the exporter will not be able to convert such merchandise into cash until a buyer can be found, and even then must usually do so at a discount. An option exists to sell such a commitment to a third party who may take over the commitment from the exporter for a fee.

▶ *Triangular Compensation.* **Triangular compensation** arrangements, also called **switch trades**, involve three or more countries. The exporter delivers merchandise to an importer. As payment, the importer transfers **hard goods** (easily salable merchandise) or **soft goods** (heavily discounted merchandise that may prove more difficult to resell) to a specialist firm, or switch trader. The switch trader then reimburses the exporter for the goods received and arranges to resell the merchandise.

> **Triangular compensation/ switch trades** countertrade arrangements involving three or more countries
>
> **Hard goods** countertraded merchandise that is easy to resell
>
> **Soft goods** countertraded merchandise that is difficult to resell

Marc Rich & Company, a Swiss commodities firm, bought 70,000 tons of raw sugar in Brazil and shipped it to Ukraine to be processed. It paid for the processing with some of the sugar and then shipped 30,000 tons of the refined sugar 6,000 miles to several huge Siberian oil refineries, which needed the sugar for their workforce. Strapped for hard currency, the oil refineries paid with 130,000 tons of low-grade A-76 gasoline, which was shipped to Mongolia. The Mongolians paid for the gasoline with 35,000 tons of copper concentrate, which was shipped across the border to Kazakhstan, where it was refined to copper metal and shipped to a Baltic port. Marc Rich then sold the copper on the world market for hard currency—and a profit![42] Needless to say, triangular compensation negotiations can become complex and time-consuming and are best left to firms that specialize in such trades.

Offset Deals. One of the most rapidly growing types of countertrade is the offset transaction. In an offset transaction, the selling company guarantees to use some products or services from the buying country in the final product. These transactions are particularly common when large government purchases are involved, such as purchases of public utilities or defense-related equipment. The South African government used offset deals very effectively to stimulate local industrial development in exchange for purchasing military equipment. Saab and British Aerospace landed the sale of twenty-eight Gripen fighter planes by agreeing to input sourcing and investment in South Africa valued at 480 percent of the contract value.[43]

Cooperation Agreements. **Cooperation agreements**, or **buybacks**, are special types of countertrade deals extending over longer periods of time. Cooperation

> **Cooperation agreements/buybacks** countertrade arrangements extending over years and usually involving capital equipment in exchange for output of that equipment

agreements usually involve related goods, such as payment for new textile machinery by the output produced by these machines.

Although the sale of large equipment or of a whole factory can sometimes be clinched only by a cooperation agreement involving buyback of plant output, long-term negative effects must be considered before any deal is concluded. In industries such as steel or chemicals, the effect of high-volume buyback arrangements between Western exporters of manufacturing technology and Eastern European importers has sometimes been devastating. Western countries, especially Europe, have been flooded with surplus products, and the EU has established a general policy on cooperation arrangements to avoid further disruption of its domestic industries.

Pros and Cons of Countertrade.   The participants in a survey of 196 firms in Australia found that countertrade was of great importance (71 percent) and that it increased sales potential (67 percent), strengthened the firms' competitive position (61 percent), and fulfilled their buyers' requirements (53 percent).[44] Nonetheless, countertrade agreements can be complex and time-consuming. Thus they can be surprisingly demanding of corporate resources. Another danger of countertrade arrangements is the difficulty in finding a buyer for the merchandise accepted as part of the transaction. Sometimes such transactions are concluded with organizations in countries where industry is protected. The merchandise, not easily salable on its own merits, may be of low quality. As a result, the exporter may have to sell the merchandise at a discount. The size of these discounts can vary considerably and can even run as high as a third of product value.

At the conclusion of the sales agreement, the exporter should obtain a very clear understanding of the merchandise offered for countertrade. The origin, quality, quantity, and delivery schedules for the merchandise should all be spelled out. Given such a detailed description, a specialized trader can provide an estimate of the appropriate discount. The astute exporter will raise the price of the export contract to cover such potential discounts. Therefore, it is paramount that the exporter not agree on any price before this other information is in hand. Maintaining flexibility in negotiation requires skill and patience but can spell the difference between making a profit and incurring a loss on a countertrade transaction.

Organizing for Countertrade.   International companies are moving toward organizing countertrade for higher leverage. Many larger firms have established specialized units whose single purpose is to engage in countertrade. Many independent trading companies offer countertrading services, and several large U.S. banks have formed their own countertrade units. Smaller companies can also take advantage of countertrade by utilizing specialist brokers or joining barter networks. Companies such as the Australia-based International Barter Network appeal to small and medium-sized firms by facilitating cash flow and reducing cash expenses. A member company accumulates barter credit when it transfers products to another company within the network. In turn, this credit can be used to purchase goods from other network members worldwide.[45]

Check out our website (college.hmco.com/business/) for countertrade links.

CONCLUSION

Managing pricing policies for an international firm is an especially challenging task. The international marketer is confronted with a number of uncontrollable factors deriving from the economic, legal, and regulatory environment, all of which have an impact on how prices are established in various countries. Although these influences are usually quite manageable in any given country, pricing across many markets means coping with price differentials that evolve out of environmental factors working in various combinations in different countries. Managing these price differentials and keeping them within tolerable limits are major tasks in international pricing.

One of the most critical factors affecting price levels is foreign exchange fluctuation. Today, managers find currencies moving both up and down, and the swings have assumed magnitudes that may substantially affect the competitiveness of a company. Understanding the factors that influence the foreign exchange market and mastering the technical tools that protect firms against large swings have become required skills for the international marketer. To the extent that a company can make itself less vulnerable to exchange rate movements than its competitors are, it stands to gain additional competitive advantage.

Because the factors that affect price levels on an international scale are always fluctuating, the international pricing task is a never-ending process in which each day may bring new problems to be resolved. Whenever a company is slow to adapt or makes a wrong judgment, the market is very quick to exploit any weaknesses. As long as uncontrollable factors such as currency rates and inflation are subject to considerable fluctuations, the pricing strategies of international companies will have to remain under constant review.

What should you consider when setting prices in your target country? Continue with *Country Market Report* on our website (college.hmco.com/business/).

QUESTIONS FOR DISCUSSION

1. Discuss the difficulties involved in having a standardized price for a company's products across all countries. What advantages does charging a standardized price offer?

2. You are an exporter of industrial installations and have received a $100,000 order from a Japanese customer. The job will take 6 months to complete and will be paid in full at that time. Now your Japanese customer has called you to request a price quote in yen. What will you quote in yen? Why?

3. What factors may influence McDonald's to price their Big Mac differently throughout Latin America?

4. What should be the government's position on the issue of parallel imports? Should the government take any particular actions?

CASE 12.1
The Price of Coffee in China

When Starbucks, the Seattle-based coffee shop chain, first entered China, it faced a country of tea drinkers. Still, Japan too had been a country of tea drinkers but had evolved into a major coffee market. Starbucks itself had recently entered Japan and was already the top-ranked restaurant chain, according to a prestigious industry study. Top management at Starbucks was astounded at the firm's brand recognition across Asia, an awareness that had come about with virtually no investment in advertising.

In considering China, Starbucks noted that coffee consumption in a country is directly related to income. The firm sought to take advantage of growing disposable income in China, where per-capita income had reached $750 a year. In particular, Starbucks believed there would be substantial demand among younger urbanites in China. Confident in their decision, the firm entered the Chinese market with plans to open ten shops in Beijing in 18 months. The first Starbucks in Beijing was located in a shopping center across the street from a five-star hotel.

Nevertheless, some were skeptical about the Starbucks move. In the 1990s, coffee sales had grown between 5 and 8 percent a year in China, but when the economy slumped in the late 1990s, many foreign expatriates left the country. Consequently, coffee sales growth had tapered off. However, Starbucks's stated strategy was to set prices lower than those of comparable coffee shops already opened in China. These other coffee shops targeted expatriates, tourists, and elite Chinese. Starbucks hoped to target a larger segment of Chinese society.

Starbucks imported all its coffee beans into China, despite the fact that China was attempting to improve both the quality and the size of its own coffee harvests. Other nations, such as Vietnam, had expanded coffee production. This had resulted in a world supply of coffee beans that exceeded demand by 10 percent. Furthermore, a devaluation of Brazil's currency provided this major coffee exporter with an increased competitive edge over new entrants into the coffee market.

When Starbucks opened in Beijing, the store offered the same coffee products and other merchandise as was available in its U.S. shops. Prices were similar to those charged in New York City, with a grande latte priced at $4.50. A local coffee shop in the same complex that charged prices even higher than those at Starbucks announced that it would lower prices to below those of the new U.S. competitor.

Discussion Questions

1. What are the possible arguments for pricing a grande latte at $4.50 in Beijing?
2. What are the possible arguments for pricing lower? For pricing higher?
3. Could purchasing Chinese coffee beans in the future affect Starbucks's pricing strategy in China? Explain.

Sources: Associated Press, "Starbucks Tries to Tempt Tea-Loving Chinese," January 12, 1999; Ian Johnson, "Reading the Tea Leaves, China Sees a Future in Coffee," *Wall Street Journal*, February 5, 1999, p. B1; and "Trouble Brewing," *The Economist*, March 10, 2001.

CASE 12.2

The Price of Life

In a surprising announcement, Merck declared that it would cut prices 40 to 55 percent in African markets on two of its recent AIDS-fighting drugs. Merck's powerful three-drug cocktail would be available in Africa for $1,330 a year, compared to approximately $11,000 in the United States. The company noted that it would be realizing no profits at this new price. Merck also pledged to extend these discounts to poor countries elsewhere in the world. Bristol-Myers followed suit, promising to slice the price of its AIDS drug Zerit to only $54 a year in Africa. At this price, Bristol-Myers claimed to be selling below costs. The company called on donor governments in Europe, Japan, and the United States to join in a vigorous international response to the AIDS crisis in Africa, where twenty-five million people are estimated to be infected with the HIV virus that eventually causes AIDS.

Only a week before, thirty-nine major pharmaceutical companies had begun litigation to stop Indian pharmaceutical firms from selling generic versions of their patented drugs, including AIDS drugs, in the South African market. Since the 1970s India had refused to recognize pharmaceutical patents in order to supply its vast poor population with recent pharmaceutical products at much cheaper prices. Indian firms had become adept at reverse-engineering drugs and had become efficient producers of high-quality generics. (When it joined the WTO, India agreed to return to honoring international pharmaceutical patents on January 1, 2005.) Two Indian generic drug firms, Cipla and Hetero, had entered a price war in Africa. The effect of this war on the annual cost in U.S. dollars to users for several AIDS drugs is shown in Table 1.

Shortly after September 11, 2001, the U.S. government led the charge among wealthier countries at WTO trade talks in Doha, Qatar, to loosen patent restrictions in order to ease shortages and reduce prices on pharmaceuticals in less developed countries. However, after all other WTO members agreed on a new plan, the United States blocked the proposal. This turnabout was attributed to heavy lobbying by the U.S. pharmaceutical industry.

While pharmaceutical companies faced decreasing prices in Africa, they were under attack in the United States as well. Drug prices were higher in the United States than in Europe, where governments paid for most prescription drugs. Consequently, European governments negotiated prices with pharmaceutical firms. For

TABLE 1 ANNUAL COST IN U.S. DOLLARS TO USERS FOR AIDS DRUGS				
DRUG	U.S. PRICE	AFRICAN PRICE	CIPLA	HETERO
Crixivan (Merck)	$6,016	$600	N/A	$2,300
Stocrin (Merck)	4,730	500	N/A	1,179
Zerit (Bristol-Myers)	3,589	252	$70	47
3TC (Glaxco)	3,271	232	190	98
Combovir (Glaxco)	7,093	730	635	293

SOURCE: Adapted from "New Regime," *Wall Street Journal*, March 7, 2001. Copyright © 2001 by Dow Jones & Co. Inc. Reproduced with permission of Dow Jones & Co. Inc., via Copyright Clearance Center.

example, the antipsychotic drug Clozaril could cost $51.94 in Spain, $89.55 in Germany, $271.08 in Canada, and $317.03 in the United States. Ironically, over-the-counter drugs and generic versions of prescription drugs whose patents had expired were cheaper in the United States than in Europe because of greater competition in the U.S. market.

Discussion Questions

1. What factors contribute to the large disparities in drug prices found among various countries?
2. What could be the motivations for Merck and Bristol-Myers to discount prices further on their AIDS drugs in Africa?

3. Should U.S. consumers pay higher prices than Europeans for pharmaceuticals? Why or why not?
4. Should U.S. consumers pay higher prices than Africans? Why or why not?

Sources: Mark Schoofs and Michael Waldhoz, "New Regime," *Wall Street Journal*, March 7, 2001, p. A1; Michael Waldholz and Rachel Zimmerman, "Bristol-Myers Offers to Sell Two AIDS Drugs in Africa at Below Cost," *Wall Street Journal*, March 15, 2001, p. B1; Jesse Pesta, "India Braces for Brave New Drug World," *Wall Street Journal*, March 7, 2001, p. A17; and Roger Thurow and Scott Miller, "Empty Shelves," *Wall Street Journal*, June 2, 2003, p. A1.

CASE 12.3
Gamali Air

Jennifer Beaudreau, an account manager at Ameridere, was very excited to learn that Gamali Air was seriously considering purchasing two of her company's L700 Turboprop planes. Ameridere had been invited to bid on the contract and had subsequently offered to deliver the two planes for US$46 million. Gamali Air was to pay $12 million in cash upon delivery, $12 million one year later, and $22 million three years after delivery. Interest charges were already included in the $46 million bid.

Gamali, once a part of French West Africa, was now a multiparty democracy with a population of ten million, 85 percent of whom were Muslim. The GDP per capita in Gamali was only U.S. $1,600, and the illiteracy rate remained at about 60 percent. The main industries of Gamali were tourism, agriculture, fish processing, phosphate mining, fertilizer production, and petroleum refining. The latter required the importation of oil since Gamali had no crude oil reserves itself. The country's exports of $1.1 billion included fish, peanuts, refined petroleum products, phosphates,

and cotton. Tourism was another substantial source of foreign exchange. For the past year, however, rising world oil prices caused Gamali to run a significant balance-of-trade deficit, and inflation had risen to 15 percent from a prior low of 8 percent. Inflation was also fueled by government spending to try and offset unemployment, which was currently estimated at 48 percent. High unemployment in the cities contributed to a number of social problems, including juvenile delinquency and drug addiction. Although rebel groups recently signed a peace treaty with the government, the south of Gamali was still plagued with intermittent armed conflict by separatist groups and bandits.

Gamali Air originated in 1965 when it was established as a state-owned enterprise. As a result of privatization, 30 percent of the company had been sold to a Gamali business group whose other group companies included several hotels, a trading company, and investments in construction and textiles. The Gamali government retained the remaining 70 percent of the airline.

With flights to Paris, Lyons, Marseilles, London, and New York, the stated goal of Gamali Air was to become the leading carrier in Africa. The two additional planes would add to the airline's current fleet of four planes. Gamali Air had purchased Boeing and Airbus aircraft in the past, but it was now in the market for planes appropriate for medium hauls. The airline was expanding its regional service within Gamali primarily to service increased demand from tourists visiting its wildlife parks.

Jennifer had supervised the original bid for the sale. Now the vice president of Gamali Air had formally notified her that Ameridere was one of two finalists for the contract. Their remaining competitor was a Brazilian firm that Ameridere had never before bid against. However, Jennifer knew that the Brazilian firm, which was about half the size of Ameridere, was strong in Latin America and Asian markets and had recently won a substantial contract in Europe. Both firms specialized in making smaller planes for regional markets. For example Ameridere's L700 Turboprop was designed for flights fewer than five hundred miles and carried eighty-six passengers. Ameridere was especially well known for the comfort and quietness of its planes as well as its after-sales service. The Brazilian firm was well known for the creative financing packages it offered customers.

Although the recent communication from Gamali Air was exciting, Jennifer realized that Ameridere would have to respond quickly to three requests forwarded by its potential customer:

▶ Ameridere was now asked to present a bid for after-sales service and training for flight and maintenance crews.

▶ Management at Gamali Air also suggested that payment for the planes be made by countertrade. The airline would arrange through the Gamali government to deliver fertilizer or phosphate valued at $46 million over a period of 3 years. These products would be valued at

their world market price less 5 percent on the day it was received by Ameridere. The 5 percent was supposed to cover the cost of shipping the products to possible markets in France or Spain.

▶ Finally, Ameridere was asked to agree to quote the price in Gamali dinars instead of U.S. dollars. The vice president of Gamali Air reminded Jennifer that the dinar had been pegged 1:1 to the euro three years earlier and the euro had increased 30 percent against the dollar in the past year. He noted that if the sale had been concluded a year ago, Ameridere would have realized 30 percent more dollars on its second payment had it quoted the price in dinars rather than in dollars.

Jennifer knew that her company wanted to expand out of its current markets in North America and Europe where sales growth had slowed, and management at Gamali Air had intimated that, all things being equal, they would prefer to work with an American rather than a Brazilian supplier. However, Ameridere had never become involved in countertrade or pricing in foreign currencies. As she sat down to develop answers to the requests made by Gamali Air, Jennifer remembered what her boss had said that morning: "Let's make them a counteroffer both sides can live with."

Discussion Questions

1. Evaluate Gamali Air's countertrade proposal.
2. Evaluate the proposal to quote the price in dinars rather than in U.S. dollars.
3. How would you address each of Gamali Air's requests? Develop a counterproposal that "both sides can live with." Explain why your proposal would be reasonably attractive to both Ameridere and Gamali Air.

Source: Case prepared by Kate Gillespie and David Hennessey for class discussion.

NOTES

1. Stephen Labaton, "The World Gets Tough on Fixing Prices," *New York Times*, June 3, 2001, p. 1.
2. For a detailed discussion of the experience curve concept, see Derek F. Abell, *Managing with Dual Strategies* (New York: The Free Press, 1993), chap. 9.1.
3. Mary Anne Raymond, John F. Tanner Jr., and Jonghoo Kim, "Cost Complexity in Pricing Decisions for Exporters in Developed and Emerging Markets," *Journal of International Marketing* 9, no. 3 (2001), pp. 19–40.
4. Carol J. Williams, "EU Complicates Sweden's Relationship with Liquor," *Washington Post*, March 11, 2001, p. A17.
5. Joel Millman, "Visions of Sugar Plums South of the Border," *Wall Street Journal*, February 13, 2002, p. A15.
6. Philip R. Cateora and John L. Graham, *International Marketing*, 11th ed. (Boston: Irwin McGraw-Hill, 2004), p. 553.
7. Ruth Bolton and Matthew B. Myers, "Price-Based Global Segmentation for Services, *Journal of Marketing*. 67 (July 2003), pp. 108–128.
8. "Big Mac Index," *The Economist*, December 18, 2004, p. 162.
9. Karby Leggett, "In Rural China, GM Sees a Frugal But Huge Market," *Wall Street Journal*, January 16, 2001, p. A19.
10. Dexter Roberts and Alysha Webb, "Motor Nation," *Business Week*, June 17, 2002, pp. 44–45.
11. Joel Millman, "Aerospace Suppliers Gravitate to Mexico," *Wall Street Journal*, January 23, 2002, p. A17.
12. Gautam Naik and William Boston, "Deregulation Dismays Deutsche Telekom," *Wall Street Journal*, January 14, 1999.
13. Ian Young, "Charges 18 Firms with Hydrogen Peroxide Price-Fixing Cartel," *Chemical Week*, February 9, 2005, p. 12.
14. Bruce Ingersoll, "Germany's SGL to Pay $135 Million Fine," *Wall Street Journal*, May 5, 1999, p. B12.
15. Lee C. Simmons and Robert M. Schindler, "Cultural Superstitions and the Price Endings Used in Chinese Advertising," *Journal of International Marketing* 11, no. 2 (2003), pp. 101–111.
16. Betsy McKay, "Ruble's Decline Energizes Firms Who Manage to Win Back Consumers," *Wall Street Journal*, April 23, 1999, p. B7.
17. James T. Areddy, "China's Inflation Weapon," *Wall Street Journal*, August 20, 2004, p. A10.
18. Phusadee Arunmas, "Cement Producers Agree to Ceiling on Prices," *Bangkok Post*, April 26, 2002, p. P1.
19. Gireesh Chandra Prasad, "Patented Drugs to Cost Same Here as Overseas," *Knight Ridder Tribune Business News*, February 2, 2005, p.1
20. Guy de Jonquières, "World Trade: Poorer Nations Starting More Dumping Cases," *Financial Times*, May 6, 1999, p. 21.
21. "S. Korean Trade Panel Finds Japanese Robot-makers Dumping," *Knight Ridder Tribune Business News*, February 25, 2005, p.1.
22. Stephan A. Butscher, "Maximizing Profits in Euro-Land," *Journal of Commerce* (May 5, 1999), p. A5.
23. For a conceptual treatment, see *Transfer Pricing* (Washington, DC: Tax Management, Inc., 1995).
24. Jeanne Whalen, "GlaxoSmithKline Gets New Tax Bill from U.S. Agency," *Wall Street Journal* (Europe), January 27, 2005, p. A4.
25. Michael Happell, "Asia: An Overview," *International Tax Review* 10 (February 1999), pp. 7–9.
26. Foo Eu Jin, "Transfer Pricing Poses Threat to Firms," *Business Times* (Malaysia), March 10, 1999, p. 3.
27. Saeed Samiee, Patrick Anckar, and Abo Akademi, "Currency Choice in Industrial Pricing: A Cross-National Evaluation," *Journal of Marketing* 62, no. 3 (July 1998), pp. 25–27.
28. "Market Data: Currency Futures," *Financial Times*, March 3, 2005, p. 27.
29. Matthew Rose and Ernest Beck, "Coke's Public-Relations Trouble Was Worsened by Gray Trade," *Wall Street Journal*, July 6, 1999, p. A12.
30. Keith E. Maskus and Yongmin Chen, "Parallel Imports in a Model of Vertical Distribution: Theory, Evidence and Policy," *Pacific Economic Review* 7, no. 2 (2002), pp. 319–334.
31. Philip Shishkin, "Europe Decides to Fine Nintendo," *Wall Street Journal*, October 25, 2002, p. B5.
32. For a description of the evolution of parallel import law in the United States, see Kimberly Reed, "Levi Strauss v. Tesco and E.U. Trademark Exhaustion: A Proposal for Change," *Northwestern Journal of International Business and Law* 23 (2002), pp. 139–186.
33. Mary L. Kevlin, "United States: Parallel Imports," *Mondaq Business Briefing*, June 22, 2001.
34. Sarah Houlton, "Parallel Trade Setback," *Pharmaceutical Executive* 24 (March 2004), p. 46.
35. Mathew B. Myers, "Incidents of Gray Market Activity Among U.S. Exporters: Occurrences, Characteristics, and Consequences," *Journal of International Business Studies* 30, no. 1 (1999), pp. 105–126.
36. Mark Maremont, "Blind Ambition," *Business Week*, October 23, 1995, pp. 78–92.
37. Marios Theodosiou and Constantine S. Katsikeas, "Factors Influencing the Degree of International Pricing Strategy Standardization of Multinational Corporations," *Journal of International Marketing* 9, no. 3 (2001), pp. 1–18.
38. "Christian Dior Watches Now in India," *Businessline* (Chennai), November 22, 2002, p. 1.
39. Carol Hymowitz, "Americans Working in Europe Find Ways to Deal with Politics," *Wall Street Journal*, March 25, 2003, p. B1.

40. Das Narayandas, John Quelch, and Gordon Swartz, "Prepare Your Company for Global Pricing," *Sloan Management Review* 42 (Fall 2000), pp. 61–70.

41. "Countertrade Program for Farm Sector Urged," *BusinessWorld* (Manila), November 29, 2004, p. 1.

42. "Commodity Grant: Marc Rich & Co. Does Big Deals at Big Risk in the Former USSR," *Wall Street Journal,* May 13, 1993, pp. 1, A6.

43. Robert Koch, "Saab-British Aerospace Take a Big Step Ahead of Competitors," *Agence France-Presse*, November 18, 1998, p. 1.

44. Aspy P. Palia and Peter W. Liesch, *"Survey of Counter-trade Practices in Australia,"* http://www.netspeed.com.au/jholmes/default.htm (accessed March 4, 2005).

45. "Bartercard Plans Expansion in Thailand," *Bangkok Post*, October 3, 2000, p. 3.

13 MANAGING GLOBAL DISTRIBUTION CHANNELS

SHOPPERS IN CARACAS habitually patronize the small corner store. Venezuela's retail sector essentially consists of family-owned shops, modest-size supermarkets, and a few specialty chains. Even the modern malls are amalgams of boutiques. In summer 2001, however, the hypermarket Tiendas Exito opened in an eastern suburb of Caracas. The new joint venture of French, Colombian, and Venezuelan partners met with some skepticism in the press. Would Venezuelans really abandon the social ritual of shopping at the small local store?

Undaunted, the new hypermarket presented itself as resolved to help its customers curtail their expenses by undercutting competitors' prices by 8 percent. Volume purchasing, centralized warehousing and shipping, and computerized inventory control—all revolutionary in the local context—would be employed to deliver on this promise. And such a promise could be appealing to the Caracas public. An international study placed Caracas as the world's eighth most expensive city to live in, more expensive than Paris, Los Angeles, or Geneva. Yet for salaries, it rated thirteenth-lowest of the fifty-eight cities studied. One month after Tiendas Exito opened, sales were running 35 percent above expectations.[1]

Distribution systems have traditionally been shaped by a variety of factors—level of economic development, disposable income of consumers, the quality of infrastructure such as roads and telecommunications, as well as

LEARNING OBJECTIVES

After studying this chapter, you should be able to

▶ List and describe the key players within both home-market channels and foreign-market channels.

▶ Explain the impact on national channel strategy of distribution density, channel length, and channel alignment.

▶ Describe how costs, product line, control, coverage, and synergy all influence the proper choice of channel members.

▶ Suggest ways to locate foreign distributors.

▶ List ways to motivate and control foreign distributors.

▶ Suggest alternative entry strategies for markets where competitors already control distribution channels.

▶ List and explain the five key areas of global logistics management.

▶ Explain the growing global importance of large-scale retailers, international retailing, direct marketing, online retailing, information technology, and smuggling.

culture, physical environment, and the legal/political system. Global marketers need to understand how environmental influences may affect distribution policies and options. Using this knowledge, they must establish efficient channels for products on a country-by-country basis. They must also consider how the emergence of regional and global distributors and changes in global logistics can affect their operations at the transnational level.

In this chapter, we discuss the structure of global distribution systems and methods for selecting, locating, and managing channel members. We explore how the international firm gains access to local channels and manages international logistics. We conclude with a look at global trends in distribution.

THE STRUCTURE OF THE GLOBAL DISTRIBUTION SYSTEM

Marketers who develop distribution strategies must decide how to transport products from manufacturing locations to the consumer. Although distribution can be handled completely by the manufacturer, often products are moved through intermediaries, such as agents, wholesalers, distributors, and retailers. An understanding of the structure of available distribution systems is extremely important in the development of a strategy. There are two major categories of potential channel members: (1) those located in the home country and (2) those located abroad. The various channels available to a manufacturer are shown in Figure 13.1.

Home-Market Channel Members

From the home country, a manufacturer can utilize the services of an export management company or an export agent, or it can use company personnel to export products. We discussed these channel members in Chapter 9. What follows is a brief review.

Export Management Company. The export management company (EMC) is a firm that handles all aspects of export operations under a contractual agree-

FIGURE 13.1
International Marketing Channel Alternatives

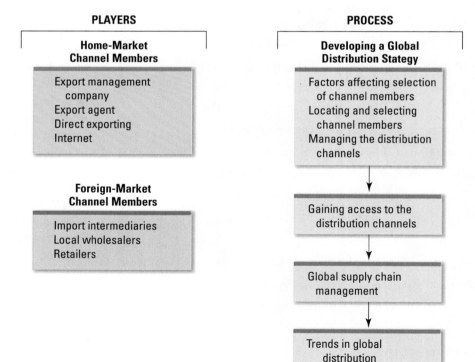

ment. The EMC normally takes responsibility for the promotion of products, marketing research, credit, physical handling or logistics, patents, and licensing. Arrangements between an EMC and a manufacturer will vary, depending on the services offered and the volume expected. The advantages of using an EMC are several: (1) little or no investment is necessary to enter the international marketplace, (2) no company personnel are required, and (3) the EMC has an established network of sales offices, as well as international marketing and distribution knowledge. The main disadvantage of using an EMC is that the manufacturer gives up direct control of the international sales and marketing effort. Also, if the product has a long purchase cycle and requires a large amount of market development and buyer education, the EMC may not expend the effort necessary to penetrate a new market.

Export Agents. Export agents are individuals or firms that assist manufacturers in exporting goods. They are similar to EMCs, except that they tend to provide more limited services and to focus on one country or one part of the world. Export agents understand all the requirements for moving goods through the customs process, but they do not provide the marketing skills that an EMC provides. These agents focus more on the sale and handling of goods. The advantage of using an export agent is that the manufacturer does not need to have an export manager to handle all the documentation and shipping tasks. The main disadvantage is the export agent's limited market coverage. To cover different parts of the world, a firm would need the services of numerous export agents.

Direct Exporting. Instead of using an EMC or export agent, a firm can export its goods directly, through in-house company personnel or an export department. Because of the complexity of trade regulations, customs documentation, insurance requirements, and worldwide transportation alternatives, people with special training and experience must be hired to handle these tasks. Also, the current or expected overseas sales volume must be sufficient to support the in-house staff.

Internet. Many smaller companies have been establishing their own Web presence. This approach gives foreign clients easier access to smaller firms and tends to mitigate the need to use some form of agent. For the Web presence to pay off, the site needs to be constructed in such a way that a foreign buyer can easily access information, obtain forms for ordering, and deliver e-mail questions. Experts also point out that a website needs to be marketed appropriately to the relevant search engines so that it shows up well placed under certain key search names. Often it is necessary to establish a website for each country. eBay has sites in thirty-one countries with 125 million registered users, of which 50 percent are outside the United States.[2] Although the Web presence goes a long way toward reaching and communicating with foreign markets, the manufacturer that sets its sights on exporting still needs to deal with the areas of logistics and credit information. For logistics, companies such as FedEx, UPS, and DHL provide considerable online help, something of great use to smaller companies that have had no opportunity to acquire that particular expertise. Certain types of service companies have found the Internet a useful way to

WORLD BEAT 13.1

Handicrafts Become Big Exports

THE ANCIENT AND MODERN WORLDS are meeting via the Internet. New Internet sites are selling home furnishings, accessories, and toys made by traditional craftspeople. By giving artisans direct access to a global marketplace, the Internet has the potential to improve the lot of poor families from Asia to the Americas.

In the Himalayan Mountains of Nepal, local artisans made a living forming copper into jugs and pots. When plastic and aluminum manufacturers replaced the need for copper jugs and pots, these artisans were forced to seek other work, something that often involved traveling to India. The Internet has created a new opportunity for these villagers to make by hand copper goods for sale on World2Market.com, a website that sells handicrafts made by artisans in developing countries.

Ugandan women are making sparkling bracelets and necklaces, which are marketed through a Colorado company, Bead for Life, founded in 2003 by Torkin Wakefield and Ginny Jordon. More than one hundred Ugandan women make up to $100 per month, which compares favorably with the average family income in Uganda of $25 per month.

In 1997, Tembeka Nkamba-Van Wyk, a South African businesswoman founded the Talking Beads Academy, a cooperative of rural women, who make handicrafts. The company has 30 full-time employees and 4,500 cooperative members on commission. The goods are exported to the United States and France and are available on www.talkingbeats@ananzi.co.za.

In each of these cases, a combination of some outside expertise and help, along with the Internet, has helped spawn and grow these businesses.

Sources: Miriam Jordan, "Web Sites Revive Fading Handicrafts," *Wall Street Journal*, June 12, 2000, p. B1; "In South Africa, Crafts Revival Boosts Exports," *International Trade Forum*, no. 4 (2003), p. 5; and Jenny Deam, "For Life Two Coloradans Discover a Way to Help the Women of Uganda, One Colorful Bead at a Time," *Denver Post*, January 25, 2005, p. F1.

market their services abroad as part or all of the service can be digitized. For example, industries such as software, movies, music, television, newspaper, or spectator sports can all be digitized and marketed on the Internet as an alternative to traditional modes of market entry and distribution.[3]

Foreign-Market Channel Members

As shown in Figure 13.1, once products have left the home market, there are a variety of channel alternatives in the global marketplace: import intermediaries, local wholesalers or agents, and retailers. Even with local manufacturing, the company will still need to get its products from the factory to the consumers.

Import Intermediaries. Import intermediaries identify consumer needs in their local market and search the world to satisfy those needs. They normally purchase goods in their own name and act independently of manufacturers. As independents, these channel members use their own marketing strategies and keep in close contact with the markets they serve. A manufacturer that wants to distribute in an independent intermediary's market area should investigate this channel partner as one way to reach wholesalers and retailers in that area.

Local Wholesalers or Agents. In each country, there will be a series of possible channel members who move manufacturers' products to retailers, to industrial firms, or in some cases to other wholesalers. Local wholesalers will take title to the products, whereas local agents will not take title. Local wholesalers are also called distributors or dealers. In many cases, a local wholesaler receives exclusive distribution rights for a specific geographic area or country.

The functions of wholesalers can also vary by country. In some countries, wholesalers provide a warehousing function, taking orders from retailers and shipping them appropriate quantities of merchandise. Wholesalers in Japan perform basic wholesale functions but also share risk with retailers by providing them with financing, product development, and even occasional managerial and marketing skills.

Retailers. Retailers, the final members of the consumer distribution channel, purchase products for resale to consumers. The size and accessibility of retail channels vary greatly by country. The population per retailer in Europe varies from lows of only 52 people in the Ukraine, 61 in Portugal, 65 in Hungary, and 66 in Spain to highs of to 292 people in Russia, 236 in Germany, and 203 in Austria.[4]

Retailing is exploding in many parts of Asia, where a large portion of the population is crossing the income threshold at which they start to buy entirely new categories of goods, such as packaged foods, televisions, or mopeds. This phenomenon, called **magic moments**, has hit Taiwan, Indonesia, Thailand, Malaysia, and China. When a country crosses the magic-moments threshold, distribution systems start to improve with the emergence of modern stores.[5] Furthermore, China has seen a significant shift from state-owned to private distribution. There has been a 27 percent decline in state-owned retail and wholesale enterprises and a 340 percent increase in privately owned retail and wholesale enterprises.[6] The global marketer must evaluate the available retailers in a country and develop a strategy around the existing—and sometimes evolving—retail structure.

Magic moments a term designating the point at which modern retailing emerges within a country

Business-to-Business Channels. When the firm is selling to businesses instead of consumers, channels may still resemble those we have described. Small businesses in particular may purchase supplies from retail outlets that have been supplied by wholesalers. Many business-to-business sales go through shorter channels, however. Export agents, import intermediaries, or the manufacturer itself often contacts business customers directly without the use of further intermediaries.

ANALYZING NATIONAL CHANNELS

A distribution strategy is one part of the marketing mix, and it needs to be consistent with other aspects of the marketing strategy: product policies, pricing strategy, and communication strategy. Figure 13.2 depicts important factors to consider when developing a distribution strategy. Before deciding on distribution

FIGURE 13.2
Distribution Policies

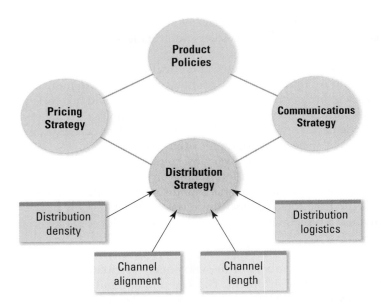

strategies, global marketers must understand the nature of channels in their various markets. Of particular interest are the following variables:

1. *Distribution density.* Density is the amount of exposure or coverage desired for a product, particularly the number of sales outlets necessary to provide for adequate coverage of the entire market.
2. *Channel length.* The concept of channel length involves the number of intermediaries involved in bringing a given product from the firm to the consumer.
3. *Channel alignment and leadership.* Alignment is the structure of the chosen channel members to achieve a unified strategy.
4. *Distribution logistics.* Logistics involves the physical flow of products as they move through the channel.

The decisions involved in the first three of these areas cannot be approached independently. The decisions are interrelated, and they need to be consistent with other aspects of the marketing strategy. Although it is important to evaluate the distribution strategy logically, marketing managers often must work with an international distribution structure established under previous managers. That existing system may limit a company's flexibility to change and grow. Nevertheless, a creative marketer can usually find opportunities for circumventing the current arrangement. For example, Nordica of Italy had been selling in Japan for 25 years when the company decided it wanted more direct control over distribution. Nordica reached a financial agreement with its exclusive distributor, Daiwa Sports, and hired the eighty-five employees who had been handling its line. This allowed Nordica, which was acquired by Tecnica in 2002, to take control without losing the experience and contacts developed by its distributor.[7] The following sections illustrate how company policies must adapt to distribution density, channel length, and channel alignment.

Distribution Density

The number of sales outlets or distribution points required for the efficient marketing of a firm's products is referred to as the **density of distribution**. The density is dependent on the shopping or buying habits of the average customer. Choosing the optimum distribution network requires the marketer to examine how customers select dealers and retail outlets by product category. For many consumer goods, an **extensive**, or wide, distribution is required if the consumer is not likely to exert much shopping effort. Such products, which are called convenience goods, are bought frequently and in nearby outlets. For other products, such as appliances or clothing, consumers may visit two or more stores. These products require a more limited, or **selective**, distribution, with fewer outlets per market area. For specialty goods, products that inspire consumer loyalty to specific brands, a very limited, or **exclusive**, distribution is required. It is assumed that the customer will search for the desired product and will not accept substitutes.

The key to distribution density, then, is the consumer's shopping behavior, in particular the effort expended to locate a desired item. This behavior, however, may vary greatly from country to country. In the United States, for example, where per-capita income is high, consumers shop for many regular-use items in supermarkets and other widely accessible outlets, such as drugstores. In other countries, particularly some with a much lower per-capita income, the purchase of such items is likely to be a less routine affair, and consumers may be willing to exert more effort to locate such items. This makes possible a less extensive distribution of products.

Where consumers buy certain products also varies a great deal from country to country. In Germany, contact lens solution is found only in stores that sell eyeglasses, but in France, it is also found in most drugstores. Whereas many magazines are sold in grocery stores in the United States, in the United Kingdom they are sold mainly through news agents. It is important to find out, early in your distribution analysis, where consumers buy the types of products you plan to market.

In the business-to-business sector as well, differences in buyer behavior or in the use of a particular product may require changes in distribution outlets and density. In the United States, for instance, radiology supply products are sold directly to hospitals and radiology departments through hospital supply distributors. In France, however, patients must pick up radiology supplies by prescription from a pharmacy before visiting the radiology department at the hospital. In this latter case, radiology supplies have to be promoted to physicians and then stocked at pharmacies to be successful. The distribution necessary in France is much more extensive than in the United States, where only hospitals are channel members.[8]

Channel Length

The number of intermediaries directly involved in the physical or ownership path of a product from the manufacturer to the customer is indicative of the **channel length**. Long channels have several intermediaries. Short or direct channels have few or no intermediaries. Channel length is usually influenced by three factors: (1) a product's distribution density, (2) the average order quantity,

Density of distribution the number of sales outlets or distribution points utilized for a given geographic market

Extensive distribution a distribution strategy that employs many sales outlets per market area

Selective distribution a distribution strategy that employs few sales outlets per market area

Exclusive distribution a distribution strategy in which a product is available through only one outlet in a relatively large geographic area

Channel length the number of intermediaries directly involved in the physical or ownership path of a product from the manufacturer to the buyer

Global firms such as Pepsi are increasingly targeting rural markets in developing countries, but establishing distribution to such markets can be challenging.

and (3) the availability of channel members. Products with extensive distribution, or large numbers of final sales points, tend to have longer channels of distribution. Similarly, as the average order quantity decreases, products move through longer channels to enhance the efficiency of distribution.

Because distribution density affects channel length, it is clear that the same factors that influence distribution density influence channel length; foremost among these is the shopping behavior of consumers. The average order quantity often depends on the purchasing power or income level of a given customer group. In countries with lower income levels, people often buy food on a daily basis at nearby small stores. This contrasts sharply with more affluent consumers, who can afford to buy enough food or staples for a week or even a month and who don't mind traveling some distance to do more infrequent shopping.

Wholesale channels in Japan are the longest in the developed world, with most products moving through as many as six intermediaries. This lengthy distribution channel is more reminiscent of distribution systems in developing countries than of those in developed countries. However, the Japanese distribution system is under pressure to change. For example, Seiko Epson bypassed traditional Japanese channel members and began a direct-sales effort to sell its NEC and IBM-compatible PCs. Following the lead of Dell Computer, Seiko Epson chose to attract consumers by offering significant savings through its direct-marketing effort.[9]

Korean automaker Daewoo decided to sell directly to consumers in the United Kingdom rather than go through traditional dealers. It equipped its sales outlets with a multimedia touch-screen kiosk that allows consumers to "build" the car they want on the screen. This approach positioned Daewoo as a manufacturer/dealer offering a hassle-free car-buying experience. In the United

Kingdom, Daewoo sales representatives took cars directly to consumers' homes and completed the entire transaction in the customer's living room on a laptop computer.[10]

Channel Alignment

Channel alignment can be one of the most difficult tasks of marketing. The longer the channel, the more difficult it becomes to ensure that various channel members coordinate their actions so that a unified approach to the marketing of a product or service can be achieved. On an international level, the coordinating task is made all the more difficult because the company organizing the channel may be far away from the distribution system, with little influence over the local scene. The international company will find it much easier to control the distribution channel if a local subsidiary with a strong sales force exists. In countries where the company has no local presence and depends on independent distributors, control is likely to slip to the independent distributor. This loss of control may be further aggravated if the international company's sales volume represents only a small fraction of the local distributor's business. Of course, the opposite will be true when a high percentage of the volume consists of the international corporation's products.

> **Channel alignment** the coordination of various channel members to the end of providing a unified approach to the marketing of a product or service

Often one participant emerges as the **channel captain** or dominant member. The channel captain frequently dictates terms of pricing, delivery, and sometimes even product design that affect other channel members. As a general rule, wholesalers are relatively powerful in developing countries. When countries develop, power shifts from wholesalers to either retailers or manufacturers. This can be seen in the United States where once-strong wholesalers have become less influential, and manufacturers or large retailers (such as Home Depot and Wal-Mart) have become channel captains. There remains one major exception to this rule: Wholesalers continue to dominate channel structure in Japan.

> **Channel captain** the dominant channel participant; dictates terms of pricing, delivery, and sometimes product design

Global marketers must be aware of national differences that can significantly affect a firm's bargaining power in channel negotiations, and they must be prepared to respond to changes that affect bargaining power within national channels. For example, shopping in India has traditionally evoked images of small retail shops and crowded sidewalks. However, shopping centers are now popping up to cater to India's growing middle class, and organized selling outside India's estimated twelve million mom-and-pop outlets is expected to account for 20 percent of Indian retail by 2007 as compared with 2 percent in 2003.[11]

In China, wholesalers currently capture 80 percent of the revenues from distributing consumer products while retailers only realize 20 percent. (In the United States, these numbers are nearly reversed. Wholesales get about 30 percent with the rest going to retailers.) The Chinese government has protected wholesalers, many of whom are government owned. However, joining the World Trade Organization (WTO) is forcing change in China. Three trends are expected to significantly change wholesaling in China in the next 10 years:

▶ Foreign companies will enter wholesaling, originally as joint ventures.

▶ Larger, more modernized retailers may increasingly bypass wholesalers.

▶ Manufacturers will increasingly use third-party logistics providers to cut out traditional wholesalers. This will occur as the consumer goods industry consolidates, making the economics of direct delivery more attractive.[12]

Distribution Logistics

Distribution logistics focuses on the physical movement of goods through the channels. An extremely important part of the distribution system, logistics is discussed in detail later in the chapter.

FACTORS INFLUENCING THE SELECTION OF CHANNEL MEMBERS

A marketer needs to identify and select appropriate distribution partners in various national markets. This selection of distribution partners is an extremely important decision, because the partner often will assume a portion of the marketing responsibility, or even all of it. Also, the distribution partner usually is involved in the physical movement (logistics) of products to the customers. A poor decision can lead to lackluster performance. Changing a distribution partner can be expensive or sometimes impossible because of local laws. Vulcan Chemical was fined $23 million for unfairly terminating the rights of Phillip J. Barker, which had a contract to market and distribute sodium chlorine and chlorine dioxide in Japan, China, South Korea, and Taiwan. Vulcan reported that its sales had fallen to less than $2 million per year, therefore warranting termination of the distribution contract.[13] The very success of a firm's international efforts depends on the partners it selects. Several factors influence the selection of distribution partners. These include costs, the nature of the product and product line, the desired level of control and coverage, and the potential synergy between the international firm and its channels.

Costs

Initial channel costs the costs of locating or establishing a channel

Channel maintenance costs the costs of managing and auditing channel operations

Logistics costs the costs of transporting and storing products and processing those products through customs

Channel costs fall into three categories: initial costs, maintenance costs, and logistics costs. The **initial costs** include all the costs of locating and setting up the channel, such as executive time and travel to locate and select channel members, the costs of negotiating an agreement with channel members, and the capital costs of setting up the channel. Capital costs include the costs for inventories, goods in transit, accounts receivable, and inventories on consignment. The establishment of a direct-sales channel often requires the maximum investment, whereas use of distributors generally reduces the investment required.

The **maintenance costs** of the channel include the costs of the company's salespeople, sales managers, and travel expenses. They also include the costs of auditing and controlling channel operations and the profit margin given to channel intermediaries. The **logistics costs** comprise the transportation expenses, storage costs, the cost of breaking bulk shipments into smaller lot sizes, and the cost for customs paperwork.

Predicting all of these various costs when selecting different channel members is often difficult, but it is necessary in order to estimate the cost of various alternatives. High distribution costs usually result in higher prices at the consumer level, which may hamper entry into a new market. Companies often establish direct channels, hoping to reduce distribution costs. Unfortunately, however, most of the functions of the channel cannot be eliminated, so these costs eventually show up anyway.

Product and Product Line

The nature of a product can affect channel selection. If the product is perishable or has a short shelf life, then the manufacturer is forced to use shorter channels to get the product to the consumer more rapidly. Delta Dairy, a Greek producer of dairy products and chilled fruit juices, was faced with increased transportation costs of shipping from Greece to France when the United Nations banned transit across the former Yugoslavia. In addition, Delta lost 5 days of product shelf life. As a result, the firm set up production in Switzerland to shorten the distance to the French market.[14]

A technical product often requires direct sales or highly technical channel partners. For example, Index Technology of Cambridge, Massachusetts, sold a sophisticated software product to automate the development of software systems called computer-aided systems engineering. The company entered the United Kingdom and Australia with a direct-sales effort, but to limit initial costs, it decided on distributors for France, Germany, and Scandinavia. However, insufficient revenues from these distributors led the company to set up its own sales efforts in France and Germany and to purchase its distributor in Scandinavia. The highly technical nature of the product required Index to invest more time and money in distribution than would be necessary if the firm sold a generic or unsophisticated product.

The size of the product line also affects the selection of channel members. A broader product line is more desirable for channel members. A distributor or dealer is more likely to stock a broad product line than a single item. Similarly, if a manufacturer has a very broad, complete line, it is easier to justify the cost of a more direct channel. With more products to sell, it is easier to generate a high average order on each sales call. With a limited product line, an agent or distributor will group a firm's product together with products from other companies to increase the average order size.

Control, Coverage, and Synergy

Each type of channel arrangement offers the manufacturer a different level of control. With direct sales, a manufacturer can control price, promotion, amount of effort, and type of retail outlet used. If these are important, then the increased level of control may offset the increased cost of a direct-sales force. Longer channels, particularly with distributors who take title to goods, often result in little or no control. In many cases, a company may not know who is ultimately buying the product.

Coverage is reaching the geographic area that a manufacturer wants to cover. Although coverage is usually easy to get in major metropolitan areas, gaining adequate coverage of smaller cities or sparsely populated areas can be difficult. Selection of one channel member over another may be influenced by the market coverage that the respective agents or distributors offer. To assess an agent's or distributor's coverage, the following must be determined: (1) location of sales offices, (2) salespersons' home base, and (3) previous year's sales by geographic location. The location of sales offices indicates where efforts are focused. Salespeople generally have the best penetration near their homes, and past sales clearly indicate the level of the channel member's success in each geographic area.

The choice of channel members or partners can sometimes be influenced by the existence of complementary skills that can increase the total output of the distribution system. This synergy normally occurs when a potential distributor has some skill or expertise that will allow quicker access to the market. For example, when Compaq entered the international personal computer market, it decided to sell only through a network of strong authorized dealers. While Compaq focused on developing market applications such as sales force automation, computer-aided design, and office productivity, it used the dealers to penetrate the marketplace. By the time of its merger with Hewlett-Packard in 2001, Compaq held market shares outside its domestic market of 3.7 percent in Japan, 6 percent in other Asian markets, 17.3 percent in Western Europe, and 14.6 percent in the rest of the world—compared with 13.8 percent in the United States.

LOCATING AND SELECTING CHANNEL PARTNERS

Building an international distribution system normally takes 1 to 3 years. The process involves the series of steps shown in Table 13.1. The critical aspect of developing a successful system is locating and selecting channel partners.

The development of an international distribution strategy in terms of distribution density, channel length, and channel alignment will establish a framework for the "ideal" distribution partners. The company's preference regarding key factors that influence selection of channel partners (costs, products, control, coverage, and synergy) will be used with the distribution strategy to establish criteria for the selection of partners. Selection criteria include geographic coverage, managerial ability, financial stability, annual volume, and reputation. Several sources are useful in locating possible distribution partners. They include:

▶ *U.S. Department of Commerce.* The Agent Distributor Service is a customized service of the Department of Commerce that locates distributors

---

TABLE 13.1 PROCESS OF ESTABLISHING AN INTERNATIONAL DISTRIBUTION SYSTEM

1. Develop a distribution strategy.
2. Establish criteria for selecting distribution partners.
3. Locate potential distribution partners.
4. Solicit the interest of distributors.
5. Screen and select distribution partners.
6. Negotiate agreements.

In developing countries, consumers still shop at traditional markets such as this one in Rajasthan, India. But traditional retailers increasingly face global competition from firms such as Wal-Mart.

and agents interested in a certain product line. Also, the department's Export Marketing Service can be used to locate distribution partners.

▶ *Banks.* If the firm's bank has foreign branches, they may be happy to help locate distributors.

▶ *Directories.* Country directories of distributors or specialized directories, such as those listing computer distributors, can be helpful.

▶ *Trade shows.* Exhibiting at an international trade show, or just attending one, exposes managers to a large number of distributors and their salespeople.

▶ *Competitors' distribution partners.* Sometimes a competitor's distributor may be interested in switching product lines.

▶ *Consultants.* Some international marketing consultants specialize in locating distributors.

▶ *Associations.* There are associations of international intermediaries or country associations of intermediaries; for example, a firm looking for a representative or agent in the United States could contact the following: Manufacturer's Agents National Association, www.manaonline.org; Manufacturer's Agents Association for the Food Service Industry, www.mafsi.org; Representative Location, www.replocate.com; Outsourcing Network, www.outsourcingnetwork.net/mfg-design; or United Association Manufacturers' Representatives, www.rep-search-usa.com.

▶ *Foreign consulates.* Most countries post commercial attachés at their embassies or at separate consulates. These individuals can be helpful in locating agents or distributors in their country.

Check out our website (college .hmco.com/business/) for links to distributor information.

After compiling a list of possible distribution partners, the firm may contact each, providing product literature and distribution requirements. Prospective distributors with an interest in the firm's product line can be asked to supply such information as lines currently carried, annual volume, number of salespeople, geographic territory covered, credit and bank references, physical facilities, relationship with local government, and knowledge of English or other relevant languages. Firms that respond should be checked against the selection criteria. Before making a final decision, a manufacturer's representative should go to the country and talk to retailers or the industrial end users to narrow the field down to the strongest two or three contenders. While in the country, the manufacturer's representative should meet and evaluate the distribution partner candidates.

MANAGING GLOBAL DISTRIBUTION

Selecting the most suitable channel participants and gaining access to the market are extremely important steps in achieving an integrated and responsive distribution channel. However, without proper motivation of and control over that channel, sales may remain unsatisfactory. This section discusses the steps that must be taken to ensure the flow of the firm's products through the channel by gaining the full cooperation of all channel members.

Motivating Channel Participants

Keeping channel participants motivated is an important aspect of international distribution policies. Financial incentives in the form of higher-than-average gross margins can be a very powerful inducement, particularly for the management of independent distributors, wholesalers, and retailers. The expected gross margins are influenced by the cultural history of that channel. For example, if a certain type of retailer usually gets a 50 percent margin and the firm offers 40 percent, the effort the retailer makes may be less than desired. Inviting channel members to annual conferences and introductions of new products is also effective. By extending help to the management of distributorships in areas such as inventory control, accounts collection, and advertising, the international firm can cultivate goodwill that will later stand it in good stead. Special programs may also be instituted to train or motivate the channel members' sales forces.

Programs to motivate foreign independent intermediaries are likely to succeed if monetary incentives are considered along with efforts that help make the channel members more efficient and competitive. To have prosperous intermediaries is, of course, also in the interest of the international firm. These programs or policies are particularly important in the case of independents that distribute products of other manufacturers as well. Often they are beleaguered by the principals of the other products they carry. Each is attempting to get the greatest possible attention and service from the distributor. Therefore, the international firm must find ways to ensure that the channel members devote sufficient effort to its products.

The motivation of channel partners and the amount of effort devoted to the firm's product line can be enhanced by a continuous flow of two-way information between manufacturer and distributor. The amount of effort an international firm needs to expend depends on the marketing strategy for that market. For example, if the firm is using extensive advertising to pull products through a channel, the intermediary may be expected only to take orders and deliver the product; there is no need for it to contribute to the sales effort. If, on the other hand, the marketing strategy depends on the channel members' developing the market or pushing the product through the channel, then a significant sales effort will be required. As much as possible, the manufacturer should send product news and public relations releases to encourage attention to its product line and to support its distributors' efforts in its behalf.

More intense contact between the export manufacturer and the distributor will usually result in better performance by the distributor. Caterpillar found that dealer training could develop a strong competitive advantage that was difficult for Japanese competitor Komatsu to counter in the market for earthmoving equipment. In fact, during the pilot of Caterpillar's training program, participating dealers increased revenue by 102 percent.[15]

Periodic visits to distribution partners can have a positive effect on their motivation and control. Often it is helpful to travel with a channel member salesperson to gain knowledge of the marketplace and to evaluate the skills of the salesperson. The most important benefit of a visit to the channel member is that it gives a clear message that the member's performance is important to the firm. Visits strengthen the personal relationship between the manufacturer and the channel member. A research study on the performance of international distribution partners found that using output controls such as how much volume the partner sold is actually less effective than social controls. Social controls refer to the patterns of interpersonal interactions between the partners, which highlights the need for in-depth relationships with mutual respect and trust.[16]

Changing channel strategies can be costly but necessary, especially as national markets evolve. However, until an international firm decides to eliminate a channel member, it should beware of strategies that cause conflict between manufacturers and channel members. The most common causes of channel conflict are (1) bypassing channels to sell directly to large customers, (2) oversaturating a market with too many distributors, and (3) opening new discount channels that offer the same goods at lower prices.[17]

Controlling Channel Participants

An international company will want to exert enough control over channel members to help guarantee that they accurately interpret and appropriately execute the company's marketing strategies. The firm wants to be sure that the local intermediaries price the products according to the company's policies. The same could be said for sales, advertising, and service policies. Because the company's reputation in a local market can be tarnished when independent intermediaries handle local distribution ineffectively or inefficiently, international companies closely monitor the performance of local channel members. One way to exert influence over the international channel members is to spell out the specific responsibilities of each, such as minimum annual sales, in the distribution agreement. Attainment of the sales goal can be required for renewal of the contract.

Many international companies grant distribution rights only for short time periods, with regular renewal reviews. Caution is advised, however, because cancellation of distribution rights is frequently subject to both social norms and local laws that prohibit sudden termination. Although termination of a distributor or agent for nonperformance is a relatively simple action in the United States, termination of international channel members can be very costly in many parts of the world. In Japan, foreign firms must be especially careful in their selection of a local distributor, because firms are expected to commit themselves to a long-term relationship. When a firm terminates a distributor, it reflects poorly on that firm.[18] Finding another distributor could prove difficult under those circumstances.

In some countries, the international firm may have to pay a multiple of its local agent's annual gross profits in order to terminate the agent. In other countries, termination compensation for agents and distributors can include the value of any goodwill that the agent or distributor has built up for the brand, in addition to expenses incurred in developing the business. The international firm may also be liable for any compensation claimed by discharged employees who worked on the product line. As a result, termination of a channel member can be a costly, painful process governed in nearly all cases by local laws that may tend to protect and compensate the local channel member.

Nonetheless, research suggests that multinational corporations operating in developing countries commonly buy or fire their local distributors or develop their own marketing and sales subsidiaries. These firms complain that distributors in emerging markets often fail to invest in business growth and aren't ambitious enough.[19]

GAINING ACCESS TO DISTRIBUTION CHANNELS

Entry into a market can be accomplished through a variety of channel members. However, the channel member whom it seems most logical to approach may already have a relationship with one of the firm's competitors. This poses some special challenges to international marketers. This section is aimed at illustrating alternatives that companies may employ when they encounter difficulties in convincing channel members to carry their products.

The "Locked-Up" Channel

A channel is considered locked up when a newcomer cannot easily convince any channel member to participate, despite the fact that both market and economic considerations suggest otherwise. Channel members customarily decide on a case-by-case basis what products they should add to or drop from their lines. Retailers typically select products that they expect to sell easily and in volume, and they can be expected to switch sources when better opportunities arise. Similarly, wholesalers and distributors compete for retail accounts or industrial users on economic terms. They can entice a prospective client to switch by buying from a new source that can offer a better deal. Likewise, manufacturers compete for wholesale accounts with the expectation that channel members can be convinced to purchase from any given manufacturer if the offer improves on the offers made by competitors.

Yet there are barriers that limit a wholesaler's flexibility to add or drop a particular line. The distributor may have an agreement not to sell competitive products, or its business may include a significant volume from one manufacturer that it does not want to risk upsetting. In Japan, relationships among manufacturers, wholesalers, and retailers are long-standing in nature and do not allow channel participants to shift their allegiance quickly to another source even when offered a superior product or price. Japanese channel members develop strong personal ties that make it very difficult for any participant to break a long-standing relationship. When Kodak entered the Japanese market, it had difficulty gaining access to the smaller retail outlets because Japan's Fuji Film dominated the four major wholesalers. Kodak worked for years to gain access to these large wholesalers, but it had little success. So when Kodak entered the digital camera market, it decided to acquire Chinon, a Japanese precision instrument company, to ensure better access to the market.[20]

Cultural forces may not be the only impediments blocking access to a channel of distribution. The members of a channel may not be willing to take any risks by pioneering unknown products. Competitors, domestic or foreign, may try to obstruct the entry of a new company. To respond to these challenges, global marketers should think creatively. When American Standard, the world's largest supplier of plumbing fixtures, tried to enter the Korean market, it found itself locked out of the normal plumbing distributors, which were controlled by local manufacturers. American Standard looked for an alternative distribution channel that served the building trade. It found Home Center, one of the largest suppliers of homebuilding materials and appliances, and thus successfully circumvented the locked channels.[21]

Kodak faced a similar challenge in China. When it first entered the market, Kodak was a distant fourth, facing stronger rivals such as Fuji Film and a locked-up distribution channel. Kodak took a gamble, recruiting Chinese entrepreneurs to open Kodak photo stores. The gamble paid off. Ten years later, its market share had soared to 63 percent while Fuji's had shrunk to only 25 percent. With nearly 8,000 photo stores across China, the company succeeded by tapping into the desire of many Chinese to run their own businesses.[22]

Alternative Entry Approaches

International marketers have developed several approaches to the difficult task of gaining access to locked-up distribution channels. These include piggybacking, joint ventures, and acquisitions.

Piggybacking. When a company does not find any channel partners interested in pioneering new products, the practice of piggybacking may offer a way out of the situation. **Piggybacking** is an arrangement whereby another company that sells to the same customer segment takes on the new products. The products retain the name of the true manufacturer, and both partners normally sign a multiyear contract to provide for continuity. The new company is, in essence, "piggybacking" its products on the shoulders of the established company's sales force.

Under a piggyback arrangement, the manufacturer retains control over marketing strategy, particularly pricing, positioning, and advertising. The partner acts as a rented sales force only. Of course, this is quite different from the private-label strategy, whereby the manufacturer supplies a marketer, which then places its own brand name on the product. The piggybacking approach has become quite common in the pharmaceutical industry, where companies involve competitor firms in the launch of a particular new drug. Warner-Lambert, a major pharmaceutical company, launched its leading cholesterol-lowering drug Lipitor in the United States with the help of Pfizer. The drug was one of the most successful introductions ever.[23]

Coca-Cola initiated a new twist on the piggyback arrangement when it offered its extensive distribution system across Africa to assist UNAIDS, a United Nations agency fighting AIDS. Coke's distribution reaches every country in Africa except Sudan and Libya, and its products find their way even to the poorest villages. The company will be contributing warehouse and truck space, as well as logistics assistance, to help charities find the best routes for their literature and testing kits. However, Coca-Cola can't help distribute AIDS drugs that have to be kept cool, because its trucks are not refrigerated.[24]

Joint Ventures. As we noted in Chapter 9, when two companies agree to form a new legal entity, it is called a joint venture. Such operations have been quite common in the area of joint production. Our interest here is restricted to joint ventures in which distribution is the primary objective. Normally, such companies are formed between a local firm with existing market access and a foreign firm that would like to market its products in a country where it has no existing market access. For example, two domestic beer producers had tied up retail outlets in Mexico with exclusivity contracts. As a result, Anheuser-Busch decided to enter Mexico through a joint venture with Mexican beer giant Modelo rather than trying to build a distribution system from scratch. Many distribution joint ventures have been signed between Japanese firms and foreign companies eager to enter the Japanese market. Kodak formed a joint venture with Nagase Sangyo, an Osaka-based trading company specializing in chemicals, to attack global competitor Fuji and Konica in the Japanese market.

Acquisitions. Acquiring an existing company can give a foreign entrant immediate access to a distribution system. For example, to gain access to pharma-

---

Piggyback arrangement an arrangement in which one company agrees to distribute through its established channels the products of another company

ceutical distribution channels in Japan, Merck purchased Japan's Banyu pharmaceutical company. Similarly, Roche Pharmaceutical of Switzerland purchased a controlling stake in Chugai Pharmaceutical.[25] Although it requires a substantial amount of capital, operating results tend to be better than those of new ventures, which usually entail initial losses. It is often less important to find an acquisition candidate with a healthy financial outlook or top products than to find one that has good relationships with wholesale and retail outlets.

Global Logistics

The logistics system, including the physical distribution of manufactured products, is also an important part of international distribution. It involves planning, implementing, and controlling the physical flow of materials and finished products from points of origin to points of use. On a global scale, the task becomes more complex, because so many external variables have an impact on the flow of materials or products. As geographic distances to foreign markets grow, competitive advantages are often derived from a more effective structuring of the logistics system either to save time or costs or to increase a firm's reliability. The emergence of logistics as a means of achieving competitive advantage is leading companies to focus increased attention on this vital area. Many manufacturers and retailers are restructuring their logistics efforts and divesting themselves of their in-house distribution divisions in favor of outside logistics specialists.

A capital- and labor-intensive function outside of the core business of most companies, logistics has become increasingly complex. For many concerns, it represents 16 to 35 percent of total revenues. Marks & Spencer, a U.K. retailer that operates in eight countries, found it could increase its sales per square foot and eliminate the need for most stockrooms by increasing the frequency of delivery. To guarantee delivery reliability, the company used outside contractors. The company spun off its entire logistics system into a partnership with a logistics firm, expecting to save a substantial part of its UK£300 million annual distribution bill.[26]

Logistics Decision Areas

In this section, we describe the objectives of an international logistics system and the various operations that have to be managed and integrated into an efficient system. The total task of logistics management consists of five separate though interrelated jobs: (1) traffic or transportation management, (2) inventory control, (3) order processing, (4) materials handling and warehousing, and (5) fixed-facilities location management. In what follows, we examine each of these decision areas in more detail.

Traffic or Transportation Management. Traffic management deals primarily with the modes of transportation for delivering products. Principal choices are air, sea, rail, and truck, or some combination thereof. Transportation expenses contribute substantially to the costs of marketing products internationally, so special attention must be paid to selecting the transportation mode. Such choices are made by considering three principal factors: lead time, transit time, and cost. Companies operating with long lead times tend to use slower and therefore lower-cost transportation modes such as sea and freight. When a short lead time is called for, faster modes of transportation such as air and truck are used. Long transit times require higher financial costs, because payments arrive later and because higher average inventories are stocked at either the point of origin or the destination. Here again, the modes of transportation appropriate for long transit times are sea and rail, whereas air and truck transportation can result in much shorter transit times. Transportation costs are the third factor to consider when selecting a mode of transport. Typically, air or truck transportation is more expensive than either sea or rail for any given distance.

Local laws and restrictions can have a significant impact on transport costs. For example, there are forty-seven different bans in Europe that restrict transport on holidays, Sundays, and summer holidays. After determining that various European regulations cost haulers over 1.5 billion euros a year, the European Commission proposed that the only driving time restriction should be 7:00 a.m. to 10:00 p.m. on Sundays.[27] Alternatively, market liberalization can have an impact on transport costs. Under the North American Free Trade Agreement (NAFTA), the United States was required to open its borders to Mexican trucking, whose costs are substantially below those of the U.S. trucking industry. The cost of trucking products from Mexico to the United States is expected to fall as a result of this ruling.

Logistics in China continues to be difficult because of poor planning, corruption, and provincial protectionism that often allows only local companies to deliver within many cities. The American Chamber of Commerce in Shanghai estimates that logistics costs 16 percent of product cost versus 4 percent in many developed economies.[28]

Inventory Control. The level of inventory on hand significantly affects the service level of a firm's logistics system. In international operations, adequate inventories are needed as insurance against unexpected breakdowns in the logistics system. However, to avoid the substantial costs of tied-up capital, inventory is ideally reduced to the minimum needed. To reduce inventory levels, a number of companies have adopted the Japanese system of just-in-time (JIT) deliveries of parts and components. For example, many firms kept 30–40 days of buffer stocks of parts and components before instituting JIT. After JIT was implemented, buffer stocks could be lowered to 1–2 days. For companies that are moving manufacturing to China, JIT can become challenging. Shipments from China to the United States take 22–24 days and can sometimes be delayed due to power outages or floods; therefore, instituting JIT with components or parts from China can be problematic.[29]

Order Processing. Because rapid processing of orders shortens the order cycle and allows for lower safety stocks on the part of the client, this area becomes a central concern for logistics management. The available communications technology greatly influences the time it takes to process an order, and the Internet has vastly improved our ability in this regard. It is still true, however, that to offer an efficient order-processing system worldwide represents a considerable challenge to any company today. Doing this can be turned to competitive advantage; customers reap added benefits from such a system, and satisfied customers mean repeat business.

Toshiba Semiconductors, a major chip supplier based in Japan with global operations, revamped its global supply chain network to obtain faster deliveries and to ship its products on the shortest possible notice from any supply point in the world. Its customers required this level of service for JIT delivery. To obtain these benefits, the company is also employing a third-party logistics provider in Europe.[30]

Materials Handling and Warehousing. Throughout the logistics cycle, materials and products will have to be stored and prepared for moving or transportation. How products are stored or moved is the principal concern of materials handling management. For international shipments, the shipping technology or quantities may be different, requiring firms to adjust domestic policies to these new circumstances. Warehousing in foreign countries involves dealing with different climatic conditions. Longer average storage periods may make it necessary to change warehousing practices. In general, international shipments move through different transportation modes than domestic shipments. Substantial logistics costs can be saved if the firm adjusts its shipping arrangements to the prevalent handling procedures abroad.

Automated warehousing is a relatively new concept for the handling, storage, and shipping of goods. Warehouses are often adjacent to the factory, and all goods are stored automatically in bins up to twelve stories high. The delivery and retrieval of all goods are controlled by a computer system. Even though automated warehouses require significant up-front capital and technology, they ultimately reduce warehousing costs significantly.

Radio Frequency Identification Development (RFID) technology involves small identity chips that can be put on pallets, boxes, or individual items. RFID is being used by Wal-Mart, Tesco, Metro, and many other firms to speed up material handling as products move from warehouses to trucks to customers' warehouses. For example, Kimberly-Clark ships cases and pallets from its factory in Germany to Metro, Tesco, and other retailers. It is expected that many suppliers to large retailers will be required to use RFID technology.[31]

Fixed-Facilities Location Management. The facilities crucial to the logistics flow are production facilities and warehouses. To serve customers worldwide and to maximize the efficiency of the total logistics system, production facilities may have to be placed in several countries. This often entails a tradeoff between economies of scale and savings in logistics costs.

The location of warehousing facilities can greatly affect the company's ability to respond to orders once they are received or processed. It can also support the company's warranty policy, particularly its ability to deliver replacement products and parts on a timely basis. A company with warehouses in every country where it does business would have a natural advantage in delivery, but such a system increases the costs of warehousing and, most likely, the required level of inventory systemwide. Therefore, the international firm should seek a balance that satisfies the customer's requirements for timely delivery and also reduces overall logistics costs. Microsoft opened a single warehouse and distribution center in Dublin, Ireland, to serve Europe. The new distribution center both made it possible to serve all European markets effectively and made it unnecessary for Microsoft to keep a warehouse and inventory in each country.[32]

Managing the Global Logistics System

National Semiconductor supplies customers in Asia, Europe, and North America from its plant in Malaysia—all within 2 or 3 days. The company originally used forty-two different freight forwarders and fifteen different airlines. When FedEx took over as exclusive contractor in 1992, distribution costs fell from 3.3 percent to 1.3 percent of total revenues. But National Semiconductor felt that it still took too long for the chips to reach the customers. In 2001, the contract was given to UPS Logistics Group of United Parcel Service Inc. Utilizing custom software, UPS's warehouse in Singapore can process the incoming chips—including bar-coding, repackaging, and putting them on ships and planes—in less than an hour.[33]

The objective of a firm's international logistics system is to meet the company's commitments at the lowest cost. High-quality logistics does pay off. With 50 percent of all customer complaints to manufacturers resulting from poor logistics, there are substantial rewards for well-managed logistics that results in better service. Research by the Strategic Planning Institute revealed that companies with superior service received 7 percent higher prices and grew 8 percent more rapidly than low-service companies. Also, on average they were 12 times more profitable.[34]

With markets becoming more scattered and dispersed over numerous countries, the opportunities to glean competitive advantages in international logistics grow. Firms that are able to coordinate the various logistics areas can achieve both substantial cost savings and enhanced market positions by increasing service levels at minimum costs. As firms expand their global sourcing strategy to support sustainable competitive advantage, they must examine their logistical needs to support multiple locations around the world. These companies are also exploring the outsourcing of activities such as manufacturing, logistics, and in some cases research and development. An analysis of the challenges facing firms with global logistic systems includes the costs of the system, the resources to support the system, exchange rate fluctuations, and the availability of infrastructure and the ease of working with host governments.[35]

GLOBAL TRENDS IN DISTRIBUTION

Distribution systems throughout the world are continually evolving in response to economic and social changes. A manager developing a worldwide distribution strategy must consider not only the state of distribution today but also the expected state of distribution systems in the future. Five major trends are currently prevailing throughout the world: (1) the growth of larger-scale retailers, (2) an increased number of international retailers, (3) the proliferation of direct marketing, (4) the dominant role of information technology to support a distribution strategy, and (5) the emergence of organized smuggling.

Larger-Scale Retailers

The entry of Wal-Mart in the United Kingdom, via its acquisition of Asda's 260 stores, offered consumers decreased prices and a growth in superstores. Wal-Mart has grown faster than any other retailer in the United Kingdom, and it is adding photo centers, jewelry centers, vision centers, and pharmacies.

There is a trend toward fewer but larger-scale retailers. As countries become more economically developed, the retail scene comes to be dominated by fewer, larger stores. Three factors contribute to this trend: an increase in car ownership, an increase in the number of households with refrigerators and freezers, and an increase in the number of working wives. Whereas the European housewife of 20 years ago may have shopped two or three times a day in local stores, the increase in transportation capacity, refrigerator capacity, and family cash flow, along with the reduction in available shopping time, has increased the practice of one-stop shopping in supermarkets.[36]

IKEA, the Scandinavian retailer, has been very successful in Europe, Asia, and the United States in luring customers into its 200,000-square-foot stores. The IKEA strategy of offering a narrow range of low-cost furniture that the customers themselves select, deliver, and assemble results in a lower price to the consumer. Once in the store, customers are given tape measures, catalogs, paper, and pencils. Child-care strollers are available, as well as free diapers. Each store has a restaurant with Scandinavian delicacies such as smoked salmon and Swedish meatballs. Customers can also borrow roof racks to help them bring furniture home. IKEA has created a fun shopping experience that encourages people to enjoy themselves and make purchases. Sales per square foot are three times higher than in traditional furniture stores. IKEA has more than two hundred stores in thirty-two countries and will open its Beijing store in late 2005. IKEA plans to open nine more stores in China by 2011. IKEA believes the growth of profit margin and market potential is greater in China than in any other market.[37]

International Retailers

Many regulatory and cultural factors affect retailing. For example, Greece bans non-Greek store names, and Italian supermarkets cannot have gas pumps.[38] In the Middle East, shopping is a major pastime of many Arab women, most of whom do not work outside the home. Some visit the same store several times a week to look for new merchandise. Dressing rooms are large, and family and friends often shop together. Service demands are high, and Arab women like to be pampered.[39] Understanding these regulatory constraints and cultural demands often gives local retailers an edge over foreign competition.

Despite the challenges of entering foreign markets, the number of international retailers is rising. Most originate in advanced industrial countries and spread to both the developed and the developing countries of the world. Tesco, the U.K. retailer, operates 440 stores in the Czech Republic, Hungary, Poland, Ireland, Slovakia, Turkey, Japan, Malaysia, South Korea, Taiwan, and Thailand.[40] Walgreen's is in Mexico; and Tandy is in Belgium, the Netherlands, Germany, the United Kingdom, and France. The trend was started by a number of large retailers in mature domestic markets that saw limited growth opportunities at home

WORLD BEAT 13.2

Culture Shock in Germany

GERMANS HAVE A SPECIFIC TYPE of shopping behavior, which differs from many other countries. To Germans, a sales clerk meeting them at the door to say hello or helping them pick out a suit is offensive and is interpreted as aggressive sales techniques. Therefore, when Wal-Mart started rolling out its supersized stores with "U.S. hospitality," it ran straight into culture shock. Customers wanted to pack their own purchases and do their shopping without interruptions. So companies like Wal-Mart that built their success partially on service had to change their approach.

In Germany, hard discounters have existed for years. Aldi, founded after World War II by Karl and Theo Albrecht, carries only 700 items in a store versus 150,000 at a Wal-Mart Supercenter. Wal-Mart seems quite luxurious compared to Aldi, where cases of goods are on pallets for the consumer to sort through. According to McKinsey & Co., Aldi's operating margins in Germany are 9.3 percent, making them more efficient than Wal-Mart, which still had not made a profit in Germany as of 2005. Aldi entered the United States in 1976 with Trader Joe's Company, which expects to have 1,000 stores by 2010.

The German market offered Wal-Mart eighty-four million consumers with high average incomes and 99 percent literacy. But adapting to short store hours was a challenge. Until 2003, all stores closed at 6 p.m. on weeknights and 4 p.m. on Saturday. Now stores are open on Monday to Saturday until 8 p.m. but still close on Sunday.

To build store traffic, most of Wal-Mart's ninety-one stores in Germany sponsor a singles night on Friday nights. Single men and women register for a raffle, leave their information on a bulletin board, and receive a small bow for their shopping carriage. The bow signals your availability to others who you may meet at the meat counter or while selecting your fruit.

Sources: Daniel Rubin, "Wal-Mart Runs into Culture Shock in Germany," KRTBN Knight-Ridder Tribune Business News, December 27, 2001; Laura Heller, "Cracking the German Code Not So Easy This Time Around," *DSN Retailing Today*, New York, December 13, 2004, pp. 55–56; Ann Zimmerman and Almut Schoenfeld, "Wal-Mart in Germany Redefines the Term 'Checkout,'" *Wall Street Journal*, November 9, 2004, p. B1; and Jack Ewing and Andrea Zammert, "The Next Wal-Mart?: Like the U.S. Giant, Germany's Aldi Boasts Awesome Margins and Huge Clout," *Business Week*, April 26, 2004, p. 60.

compared to the potential opportunities overseas. Among the most successful have been franchises and discount retailers. The path toward an international presence has been made smoother by a number of facilitating factors, such as enhanced data communications, new forms of international financing, and lower governmental barriers to entry. The single European market has also motivated European retailers to expand abroad as they see a number of new international retailers entering their domestic markets. Retailers are attracted to international markets such as China, which often offer higher growth rates than their home markets. The Chinese Ministry of Commerce reported the combined sales of Carrefour and Wal-Mart in China rose 33 percent in 2004 to $46.6 billion.[41]

Overall, American retailers have entered foreign markets later than European and Japanese retailers. However, Wal-Mart's entry into its first foreign market, Mexico, met with phenomenal success. Ten years after first entering the Mexican market in 1991, Wal-Mart dominated the country's retail sector. The U.S. retailer joint-ventured with Cifra, the leading Mexican retailer and pioneer of discount stores in Mexico. In the early 1990s, the venture faced several problems. Tariffs inflated the prices of products imported from the United States, and Wal-Mart faced considerable red tape in obtaining import permits. Delivery schedules were unreliable because of poor road systems. With the inauguration of NAFTA, tariffs tumbled, paperwork diminished, and road construction and improvement soared. Wal-Mart buys directly from U.S. suppliers and consolidates orders in its own distribution center in Laredo, Texas. Trucks hired from Wal-Mart deliver products to its Mexican stores the next day. As a large-volume buyer, Wal-Mart can require suppliers to label in Spanish. Most important, it can demand lower prices. The company passes these cost savings on to the Mexican customer, offering prices that the traditional small retailers can't match.[42]

Despite its success in Mexico, other markets have proved more difficult. Wal-Mart remains only sixth in Brazil, where it faces stiff local competition as well as French competitor Carrefour. When first entering the market, Wal-Mart failed to note that most target families owned only one car and did all their shopping on weekends. Car parks and store aisles at their superstores were unable to accommodate the weekend rush.[43] However, the company is experimenting with a new concept—smaller outlets in working-class neighborhoods. These outlets have concrete floors, no air conditioning, and less merchandise selection than Wal-Mart's original stores. But they deliver products at prices 5 percent below those charged in the surrounding smaller stores. Credit is even available for qualified customers.[44]

Wal-Mart has also faced problems since it entered the highly regulated German market. German authorities ordered Wal-Mart and two German competitors to raise prices on a number of products. The stores were accused of selling below costs, on a regular basis, products such as milk, sugar, and flour. This endangered small and medium-sized retailers and violated German antitrust law.[45]

JCPenney, a U.S.-based department store chain, is another retailer that discovered the advantages of local partners. After unsuccessful forays into Indonesia, Chile, and the Philippines, Penney bought control of Lojas Renner, a regional Brazilian chain with twenty-one stores. Unlike its earlier attempts at internationalization, here Penney kept the Brazilian management and store name. The joint venture has blended Penney's knowledge of merchandising and its access to capital with Renner's local-market know-how. For example, Renner issues charge cards to customers whose family income may only be $150 a month and offers interest-free installment plans. Customers can ring a bell in the dressing room to call a sales attendant if they want to try a different size— an amenity Penney doesn't offer at home! Two years later, the venture had doubled its number of stores. With sales per square foot in Renner above those in their stores in the United States, Penney is examining how it might learn some lessons from Renner.[46]

Not all attempts to internationalize have been successful for retailers. After a period of internationalization, British retailer Marks & Spencer announced that it would be refocusing operations on the company's core U.K. business, selling and closing stores in the United States and continental Europe. Successful international retailers tend to fall into three distinct categories: replicators, performance managers, and reinventors.[47]

Replicators. Replicators such as Benneton, Zara, and Starbucks develop a simple retail model, identify markets where that model will work, then export the model virtually unchanged. This strategy allows for fast international expansion, and economies of scale can be reaped from standardization even if local variations are accommodated by making minor adaptations to retail format or product offerings. Home and overseas businesses can be globally (or at last regionally) centralized, leading to easier coordination of markets and management of global brands.

Performance Managers. Performance managers such as Ahold and Kingfisher expand globally by acquiring existing retail businesses that they then develop as independent entities. These international retailers add value to these acquisitions in the form of their expertise in corporate finance, postmerger management, and management systems. Acquisitions can be a fast way to enter foreign markets, but transferring expertise and upgrading acquisitions can be time-consuming. Once expertise is transferred, however, performance mangers tend to relinquish autonomy to local management.

Reinventors. Reinventors such as Carrefour and Tesco employ standardized back-end systems and processes while creating a largely tailored retail format for each overseas market. For example, a Tesco supermarket in London will appear vastly different from one in Bangkok or Warsaw. However, a recent study reveals competence in retail logistics to be a major determinant of success for large retailers that move abroad. This competence allows these retailers to contain costs, shorten procurement times, and respond more quickly to customer needs.[48]

Every national market is a potential market for reinventors. But understanding the different markets and adapting to them takes time and can slow the process of internationalization. Finding the proper balance between centralized and local control can also prove challenging.

Direct Marketing

Although the United States is the global leader in direct marketing, the market is also growing elsewhere. The complex, multilayered Japanese distribution system encouraged some foreign companies to go directly to consumers. The growth in direct marketing in Japan is supported by a number of demographic and technical factors. The dramatic increase in employed women from 50 percent to 75 percent has resulted in fewer available shopping hours. The introduction of toll-free telephone and cable has also made it easier to shop at home. One of the most successful direct-marketing companies in Japan is Amway. With sales of $6.2 billion, the company employs approximately three million independent distributors, using a direct-sales model.[49]

Direct marketing plays a role in emerging markets as well but faces a number of challenges. In Russia, direct marketing tends to be viewed negatively

A Mary Kay advertisement for the Chinese market. Direct marketers often find developing countries to be attractive markets.

as one of those newfangled Western business concepts. Bertelsmann, the German-based media company, put its planned Book Club India project on hold after realizing that a segmentation exercise on India's twenty-three largest urban markets yielded a total of only 297,000 potential club members, too small to pursue the opportunity.[50] The infrastructure in most developing countries in terms of delivery and telecommunications lags behind markets in the developed world. Still, urban consumers in Brazil receive an average of ten direct-mail pieces a month. Telemarketing is hampered by a lack of phones (only one in ten Brazilians has a phone), but Brazil is nevertheless a large market and tends to be ahead of the rest of Latin America in direct marketing.

Direct-sales firms such as Amway, Avon, and Mary Kay proved highly successful in many emerging markets. For Avon, Brazil is second only to the United States in volume sales. The success of these companies was due in large part to their ability to recruit independent salespersons to promote their products. Many people in developing countries saw this as an opportunity to supplement meager incomes. In addition, direct sales appeals to collectivist cultures where people often mix business and personal relationships. Many

Brazilian customers admit they will pay more to buy from someone they know rather than purchase the product cheaper at a store.[51]

Many local clones have emerged and flourished. Brazil's own Natura is seen as more upscale than Avon and has experienced phenomenal growth. However, in China, many local direct-sales companies proved fraudulent, cheating the salespeople they recruited of their investment. Overnight, the Chinese authorities denied the right to sell door-to-door. The only way for Amway, Avon, and Mary Kay to salvage their investments was to agree to market their products through regular retail stores. However, under pressure from the U.S. government, China agreed to lift sanctions on direct selling five years later.

Online Retailing

The Internet has opened an entirely new channel for retailers and manufacturers to sell their products. The United States is the undisputed leader in online retailing, or e-commerce. It still leads the world in low-cost Internet connections, and phone service in the United States can be unmeasured for local calls. In many other countries, this is not the case. A lengthy Internet connection can turn into an expensive shopping foray, particularly if nothing is purchased. U.S.-based online retailers, such as Amazon.com, have expanded abroad with specific "stores" in the United Kingdom and Germany. Most online retailing, however, crosses borders; consumers can reach any store anywhere with a legitimate Internet address.

In other countries, online retailing continues to expand. In Germany, surveys found that some 27 percent of all Internet users had ordered or purchased a product online by 1999.[52] However, Japan's estimated online revenue for 2000 was US$1.8 billion, only 6 percent of U.S. revenues. Sales in Japan continue to be crippled by consumers' security-conscious fears of purchasing by credit card online. E-tailers are further hit by exorbitant charges and cumbersome paperwork required of them by credit card companies. The Japanese also avoid credit cards because of the 10 to 14 percent charges on balances unpaid for more than 2 months. These charges appear outrageous compared to the 0.05 percent that the Japanese earn on savings accounts.[53]

Not deterred by these problems, start-up company Thinkamerican.com signed up several boutique brands in its bid to launch a cultural portal linking shoppers in Japan to American brands. One advantage of cyberspace sales in Japan is the opportunity to avoid having to buy or rent any of the country's prohibitively expensive real estate, while still tapping into the world's second-largest economy.[54]

Online retailing requires a large connected population. As many e-commerce executives know, online retailing also depends on a solid fulfillment cycle that delivers the ordered merchandise quickly into the hands of the consumer. When this is to take place across borders, issues of taxation and tariffs may still remain, slowing down delivery systems. Many foreign markets do not yet offer reliable fulfillment centers for use by small online retailers. However, the trend is clearly in the direction of resolving this problem. Once this has occurred, many more consumers will reach into online stores in faraway places, potentially turning every online marketer into an international retailer.

Information Technology

The worldwide retail industry is moving rapidly toward the use of electronic checkouts that scan the bar codes on products, speeding up checkout, reducing errors, and eliminating the need to put a price label on each item. Electronic checkout also improves a store's ability to keep track of inventory and of purchase behavior. Some stores are experimenting with self-scanning as a way to speed up checkout and reduce costs. Royal Ahold of Holland, the parent company of Stop & Shop in the United States, introduced this practice in Europe and is now experimenting with it in the U.S. market. The same applies to Shaw's, another U.S.-based supermarket chain that has a European parent, J. Sainsbury of the United Kingdom.[55] Modern retailing systems are clearly emerging in many parts of the world, and their diffusion takes place very rapidly. This pushes the retailing environment in many countries toward a world standard that is best in class wherever it evolves.

Smuggling

Smuggling has recently emerged as a serious challenge to many international marketers.[56] Indian customs has credited the smuggling of gold, silver, and consumer durables into India with supporting a black-market economy equivalent to 20 percent of the national gross domestic product (GDP). In a single year, about half of all computer sales in Brazil involved smuggled computers. Today, smuggling accounts for an estimated one-third of all cigarettes sold worldwide.

Smuggling is the illegal transport of products across national borders and may involve the distribution of illicit products such as illegal drugs and arms. It also encompasses the illegal distribution of products that are legal to sell and use, such as computers, cosmetics, and VCRs. In the 1990s, the products most commonly smuggled into Mexico were consumer electronics, food and alcohol, clothing, automobiles and auto parts, and toys and games. It is the smuggling of legal products that concerns us here.

Smuggling the illegal transport of products across national borders

Smuggling is most prevalent in developing countries and in the transitional economies of the former Soviet bloc. It arose in response to traditionally high tariffs and low quotas placed on imported goods. For example, a smuggled VCR in Mexico could sell for US$200, whereas its legally imported equivalent would sell for US$600. With the move toward trade liberalization in the emerging world, we would expect smuggling to fade as tariffs and quotas decline.

Although smuggling has decreased in some countries, it hasn't been eradicated. There are two main reasons for this. First, trade liberalization is not universal or complete. The tariff levels on many products in many countries still promote smuggling. Second, tariffs are not the only taxes that smugglers can avoid. They can also avoid sales taxes and value-added taxes. If smugglers are to become legitimate importers, they must declare themselves to customs. This enables governments to identify them and demand income taxes from them. Therefore, the lowering of tariffs decreases the cost advantage that smugglers previously enjoyed but doesn't completely remove it.

For many years, international marketers viewed smuggling as a benign and even positive phenomenon. In some cases, smugglers distributed products to otherwise inaccessible markets. In other cases, smugglers delivered products to consumers at a considerably lower price, supporting greater sales and market growth. In either case, the international firm stood to gain by realizing greater sales revenue as the result of the smuggling of its products.

A recent analysis of the records of major international cigarette companies reveals that many executives in these firms knew that certain international distributors were involved in large-scale smuggling operations and cooperated in some ways to assist them. Three managers of British American Tobacco pleaded guilty or were convicted of smuggling.[57] Several countries in Europe and the developing world have initiated lawsuits against cigarette companies to recover taxes lost as a result of smuggling. The behavior of the international cigarette industry is likely to make governments all the more skeptical of other international firms that claim ignorance of smuggling operations.[58]

Nevertheless, governments have sometimes exhibited ambivalent attitudes toward smuggling. Prior to Poland's joining the European Union (EU), 25 percent of liquor and 15 percent of cigarettes consumed in Poland were smuggled in from Russian, Belarus, or Ukraine. But patrolling the Polish border was stymied by a lack of money and agents, and custom inspectors often turned a blind eye to contraband. Officials who caught Russian smugglers just sent them back home. The Polish government also recognized that smuggling provided a livelihood to many in Poland's depressed eastern border economy where unemployment reached 35 percent.[59] But once Poland joined the EU, Brussels, afraid that the EU could be flooded with contraband goods smuggled in through Poland, moved to shut down the contraband trade. The EU insisted that fines be levied on smugglers and their cars impounded and Polish visas revoked. In addition, the EU assigned funds to ensure that Poland's customs department had the latest in detection equipment, such as state-of-the-art X-ray scanners.[60]

Furthermore, the darker side of smuggling is becoming apparent. In the past 10 years, smuggling has evolved along lines of traditional organized crime. It has become more centralized and violent. As margins are squeezed by trade liberalization, smugglers have sought ways to protect their cost advantage, such as counterfeiting the products they previously bought. Some smugglers who transport consumer goods into developing countries have allied themselves with drug cartels to launder drug money. This phenomenon has caused firms such as Hewlett-Packard, Ford, General Motors, Sony, Westinghouse, Whirlpool, and General Electric to be invited by the U.S. Attorney General to answer questions about how the distribution of their products may have become involved in the laundering of drug money.[61] In the future, both host and home governments may require international marketers to take more precautions to ensure that their products are not distributed through these illegal channels.

CONCLUSION

To be successful in the global marketplace, a company needs market acceptance among buyers and market access via distribution channels. To achieve access, the firm must select the most suitable channel members, keeping in mind that substantial differences exist among countries on both the wholesale and the retail levels. There are major differences among countries in distribution. Local habits and cultures, legal restrictions, and infrastructure can all affect the success of distribution in a new country.

Proper distribution policies have to allow for the local market's buying and shopping habits. A company should not expect the same distribution density, channel alignment, or channel length in all its markets. The logistics system must reflect both local market situations and the difficulties inherent in moving products longer distances. Finding willing and suitable channel members may prove extremely difficult. Access may be achieved only by forging special alliances with present channel members or local companies that have access to them. Once the distribution system has been designed, participants still need to be motivated and controlled to ensure that the firm's marketing strategy is properly executed. Increasingly, governments may hold international firms liable for smuggled products, forcing marketers to control their channels better.

A major technological revolution is taking place with online retailing and the widespread use of the Internet by consumers. These trends are likely to reshape the global distribution system and the way companies tap into markets all over the world. Access to the Internet makes it easier for business or household customers to tap into foreign suppliers. This has far-reaching consequences for all global marketers and needs to be considered as the new world economy adapts to the Internet challenge.

To assess distribution strategies for your product and explore local channels, continue with the *Country Market Report* **on our website (college.hmco.com/ business/).**

QUESTIONS FOR DISCUSSION

1. You have been assigned the task of selecting distributors in Malaysia to handle your firm's line of car batteries. What criteria will you use to select among the twelve possible distributors?

2. The performance of your agents and distributors in South America has been poor over the past 3 years. List possible ways in which to improve the management of these agents and distributors.

3. Given the trends in global retailing, what distribution strategies should a worldwide manufacturer of women's clothing consider?

4. Your firm has just entered the Polish market for bottled water. The major distributor is owned by a competitive producer of bottled water. What strategies can you use to gain access to this market?

5. Compare and contrast, from the manufacturer's point of view, the problems that parallel imports cause (Chapter 12) with those caused by smuggling. If governments increasingly restrict international marketers from stopping parallel imports, can these same marketers be held responsible for products' being smuggled? Explain your reasoning.

CASE 13.1
Giants in Asia

The world's two largest retailers have targeted Asia with varying results. U.S.-based Wal-Mart and France's Carrefour both offer large stores stocked with groceries and general merchandise. Their entry into new national markets is invariably a shock to local retailers, who suddenly see the status quo of decades upset by these international competitors.

Government officials in China have credited Wal-Mart with revitalizing the retail sector. For years, government-owned retailers offered the same limited products, while employees took naps on the counters. When Wal-Mart opened its new store underneath the soccer stadium in the city of Dalian, the store was soon packed to capacity. Still, Wal-Mart chose to enter China slowly in order to learn as it went along. When it opened its first stores, customers arrived on bicycles and made only small purchases. Wal-Mart also discovered that it couldn't sell a year's supply of soy sauce to customers who lived in small apartments. Furthermore, the firm faced a variety of government restrictions. Foreign retailers needed government-backed partners, and cities often restricted the size of stores. In response to these challenges, Wal-Mart invited government officials to visit its headquarters in the United States, donated to local charities, and even built a school. Wal-Mart sourced nearly all its products locally, and nearly all employees were Chinese. To understand Chinese consumption patterns better, Wal-Mart's American manager walked the streets to see what the Chinese were buying.

In 2002, Wal-Mart decided to enter Japan. Wal-Mart studied the Japanese market for four years and decided it needed a local partner. It agreed to buy 6 percent of Japan's fifth-largest supermarket chain, Seiyu, with the option to increase its share to 67 percent by 2007. Still, Wal-Mart faced challenges: Japanese consumers associated low prices with poor quality. If the price of fish was low, it must be old. And employees balked at the idea of approaching customers and asking them if they needed assistance. Traditionally employees waited for the customer to ask them for assistance. Perhaps the biggest challenge was the speed at which competition responded by slashing prices, building single-story supercenters, providing acres of parking, launching "Made in Japan" campaigns, and streamlining their logistics systems.

Carrefour, which had 9,000 stores in twenty-seven countries, began its Asian operation in Taiwan in 1989. Twelve years later, it had opened ninety-six hypermarkets in Asia, including stores in China and Korea. Carrefour entered Indonesia at the height of the Asian financial crisis in 1998, opening six stores in the capital city of Jakarta in just 2 years. The new stores compete on selection and low prices and challenge both open-air markets and the city's small, Chinese-owned neighborhood grocers. The 280-member Indonesian Retail Merchant Association has urged Jakarta to impose zoning restrictions on hypermarkets. Carrefour is also a threat to the larger, locally established grocery chains. One such chain, Hero supermarkets, admitted it couldn't compete with Carrefour on overall prices and chose instead to discount high-visibility products such as rice and to offer a variety of promotional specials. Hero also competes on freshness and has an excellent reputation among consumers for its produce.

In 2001, Carrefour entered the Japanese market, investing $150 million to set up its first three stores. Carrefour had avoided Japan previously because of its high land prices. Although a depressed Japanese economy had lowered land prices, it meant the stores were opening in a climate of slow retail sales. Like Wal-Mart in China, Carrefour found itself making adaptations to local culture. Within days of opening in Japan, the stores began selling more vegetables in packages of two or three, as other Japanese grocers do, instead of by weight. To provide competitive prices, Carrefour plans to buy 54 percent of its products directly from Japanese suppliers. This would circumvent the cumbersome wholesaling system of Japan, but it would require convincing Japanese producers to abandon long-standing relationships with their distributors—something that other foreign retailers have had difficulty doing. In the meantime, Japanese grocery chains are restructuring and moving more to direct sourcing themselves.

Both Indonesian and Japanese competitors can take some hope in the fact that Carrefour had to retreat from the Hong Kong market in September 2000. The company cited stiff competition and restrictive development laws. Analysts suggested that the hypermarkets were unable to attract enough customers, who were unwilling to go out of their way to do their daily shopping.

Discussion Questions

1. What competitive advantages do foreign retailers such as Wal-Mart and Carrefour enjoy when they enter Asian markets?
2. What are some possible competitive advantages of local retailers?
3. Why do you think governments regulate retailing practices?

Sources: David Kruger, "Retailing—Challenge at the Checkout," *Far Eastern Economic Review*, January 18, 2001, p. 38; Peter Wonacott, "Wal-Mart Finds Market Footing in China," *Wall Street Journal*, July 17, 2000, p. A31; Warren Caragata, "Attack of the Hypermarkets," *Business Week*, May 22, 2000, p. 104; and Ann Zimmerman and Martin Fackler, "Pacific Aisles," *Wall Street Journal*, September 19, 2003, p. A1.

CASE 13.2
Who's to Blame?

Several European countries, including Germany, Italy, France, Belgium, and Finland, filed suits against U.S. tobacco giants Philip Morris and R.J. Reynolds alleging that the two firms had cooperated with smugglers of cigarettes. The countries sought compensation for unpaid custom duties as well as unpaid value-added taxes. The EU estimated that these losses came to billions of dollars. European governments weren't the only losers. An estimated third of all cigarettes sold in the world are smuggled. Malaysia has estimated that its losses in taxes due to smuggled cigarettes amounted to US$1.3 billion in one year alone. These cigarettes arrived mainly from Indonesia and Thailand and were brought in under the aegis of crime syndicates. Malaysia, like most other countries, taxed cigarettes heavily not only as a source of revenue but also as a proven method for discouraging smoking.

At the same time in India, British American Tobacco (BAT) was facing an exposé resulting from the public examination of its internal communiqués. For example, BAT products were legally restricted in India to duty-free shops and

hotels but were in fact smuggled into India on an extensive scale from the United Arab Emirates. A memorandum issued by a top BAT executive discussed how the firm could advertise its brands without calling attention to the fact that most of the cigarettes were smuggled into the country. The memorandum went on to discuss contingency plans if any of the normal smuggling channels were shut down. When the *Business Standard* called BAT for comment, the company sent the following reply:

> where governments are not prepared to address the underlying causes of the smuggling problem (excessive tax on tobacco), businesses such as ours are faced with a dilemma. If the demand for our products [is] not met, consumers will either switch to our competitor brands or there will be the kind of dramatic growth in counterfeit products that we have seen in Asian markets. . . . [W]here any government is unwilling to act or their efforts are unsuccessful, we act, completely within the law, on the

basis that our brands will be available alongside those of our competitors in the smuggled as well as the legitimate market.

Fuji and Kodak, on the other hand, were dismayed at the smuggling of their film into China, where it sold for far less than it did through the firms' official channels. Photosensitive products were among the goods most commonly smuggled into China. Retailers carried the smuggled products to increase their margins and boost sales. The smuggled film was easily identifiable. No Chinese language, required by law, appeared on the package. Instead, the packages of film were labeled in English, Russian, Indonesian, Vietnamese, Korean, or Arabic. The Chinese government assured Fuji and Kodak that it was taking the situation seriously and was beginning to stem the tide of smuggling.

China recently introduced severe penalties for smuggling, including life sentences and even the death penalty. China's smuggling law not only targets smugglers but also encompasses anyone who buys from smugglers. They, too, can be charged with smuggling. Vietnam is another country that has taken serious steps against smugglers. The head of a private company and the chief of the smuggling investigation bureau of Ho Chi Minh City's customs department were sentenced to death for smuggling. The case involved seventy-four people who were charged with smuggling $71.3 million worth of electrical goods and home appliances into Vietnam.

Discussion Questions

1. Why would BAT cooperate with smugglers?
2. How could smuggling hurt Fuji and Kodak?
3. Why do you think some countries are introducing stiff penalties for smuggling?
4. Whom do you think should be held responsible for smuggling—the manufacturer, the smugglers themselves, the retailers, or the final consumer?

Sources: Associated Press, "Belgium, Finland Join EU Lawsuit Against U.S. Tobacco Companies," February 21, 2001; "Government Cracks Down on Smuggling Channels," *South China Morning Post*, October 16, 2000, p. 6; Surajeet Das Gupta, "Did BAT Organize Cigarette Smuggling into India?" *Business Standard*, December 4, 2000, p. 1; "Cigarette Smuggling Costs Malaysia $1.3 B a Year," *Times of India*, November 26, 2000; and "Vietnam Official to Stand Trial for Car Smuggling," Dow Jones International News, September 11, 2000.

NOTES

1. Marc Lifsher, "Will Venezuelans Shun Mom and Pop for the Hypermarket?" *Wall Street Journal*, June 28, 2001, p. A13.
2. Erick Schonfeld, "The World According to eBay," *Business 2.0* 6 (January/February 2005), pp. 76–84.
3. Ikechi Ekeledo and K. Sivakumar, "The Impact of E-Commerce on Entry-Mode Strategies of Service Firms," *Journal of International Marketing* 12, no. 4 (2004), p. 65.
4. Euromonitor International Global Information Database, 2005, http://www.euromonitor.com/GMID (accessed March 9, 2005).
5. "Overview of the Current State and Potential of China's Cosmetics and Toiletries Market," *Household and Personal Products Industry* 39, no. 2 (February 2002), p. 1.
6. Aimin Chen, "The Structure of Chinese Industry and the Impact from China's WTO Entry," *Comparative Economic Studies* 44, no. 1 (Spring 2002), p. 74.
7. "Tecnica Acquires Nordica," *Powder Magazine*, January 14, 2002, www.powdermag.com (accessed March 9, 2005).
8. Warren Keegan, *Global Marketing Management*, 7th edition (Englewood Cliffs, NJ: Prentice-Hall, 2001), p 183.
9. "Seiko Epson Clones Strategy of U.S. Rival," *Nikkei Weekly*, January 17, 1994, p. 8.
10. "Ding-Dong, It's Seat Calling," *The Age*, July 30, 1998, p. 9.
11. Rasul Bailay, "In India, Shopping Takes on a Whole New Meaning," *Wall Street Journal*, December 16, 2003, p. A15.
12. Richard C. Cheung, T.C. Chu, and Jacques Penhirin, "Wholesale Moves in China," *McKinsey Quarterly*, no. 3 (2002), pp. 16–18.
13. "Arbitrator Fines Vulcan $23 Million," *Chemical Week*, March 14, 2001, p.13.
14. "Delta Dairy Streamlined Food Producer," *Financial Times*, July 8, 1993, p. 11.
15. S. Tamer Cavusgil, "The Importance of Distributor Training at Caterpillar," *Industrial Marketing Management* 19 (1990), p. 5.
16. Preet S. Aulakh and Esra F. Gencturk, "International Principal-Agent Relationships," *Industrial Marketing Management* 29 (2000), pp. 521–538.

17. Allan J. Magrath and Kenneth G. Hardy, "Avoiding the Pitfalls in Managing Distribution Channels," *Business Horizons* (September–October 1987), p. 31.
18. Keysuk Kim and Changho Oh, "On Distributor Commitment in Marketing Channels for Industrial Products: Contrast Between the United States and Japan," *Journal of International Marketing* 10, no. 1 (2002), p. 89.
19. David Arnold, "Seven Rules of International Distribution," *Harvard Business Review* 78 (November–December 2000), pp. 132–133.
20. "Kodak Japan to Make Chinon Fully Owned Subsidiary," Knight-Ridder Tribune Business News, January 22, 2004, p. 1.
21. "American Standard Succeeds in Korea by Outflanking Local Firms' Lockout," *Financial Times*, August 26, 1993, p. A6.
22. Leslie Chang and Peter Wonacott, "Cracking China's Market," *Wall Street Journal*, January 9, 2003, p. B1.
23. "Two Drug Giants Are Expected to Set $70 Billion Merger," *New York Times*, November 4, 1999, p. C10.
24. Donald G. McNeil Jr., "Coca-Cola Joins AIDS Fight in Africa," *New York Times*, June 21, 2001, p. 8.
25. "Japan Drug Maker to Buy Rival for $7.7 Billion," *New York Times*, February 26, 2005, p. 3.
26. "M&S Distribution Deal Could Cut Costs by 20 Percent," *Supply Management*, June 24, 1999, p. 12.
27. "Brussels Proposes Rules to Harmonize Lorry Bans," *Financial Times*, March 11, 1998, p. 6.
28. Ben Dolven, "The Perils of Delivering the Goods," *Far Eastern Economic Review*, July 25, 2002, p. 29.
29. "Importing with a Little Help from Friends," *Modern Plastics* (February 1, 2005), p. 50.
30. "Toshiba Sets Fast-forward System," *Electronic Buyer's News*, August 2, 1999, p. 10.
31. "RFID Advances Worldwide," *Information Week*, March 7, 2005, p. 1.
32. "Microsoft Alters Distribution Chain for Europe," *Financial Times*, November 12, 1993, p. 20.
33. Ilan Greenberg, "UPS Targets Logistics Business in Asia," *Wall Street Journal*, April 26, 2001, p. A17.
34. Neil S. Novich, "Leading-Edge Distribution Strategies," *Journal of Business Strategy* 11 (November–December 1990), p. 49.
35. Masaaki Kotabe and Janet Murray, "Global Sourcing Strategy and Sustainable Competitive advantage," *Industrial Marketing Management* 33 (2004), pp. 7–14.
36. "Continental Divide: U.K. OK, but Germany Still Ailing," *DSN Retailing Today*, June 10, 2002, p. 118.
37. "IKEA to Build 10 China Stores," *Vietnam Investment Review*, September 24, 2004, p. 3.
38. Marcus Walter, "Cash Economy," *Wall Street Journal*, December 10, 2004, p. A1.
39. Cecilie Rohwedder, "Style and Substance, The Chic of Arabia," *Wall Street Journal*, January 23, 2004, p. A11.
40. Tesco.com (accessed March 14, 2005).
41. "Global Retailers at Home in China," *MMR, Racher Press*, February 21, 2005, p. 11.
42. David Luhnow, "Crossover Success," *Wall Street Journal*, August 31, 2001, p. A1.
43. "Shopping All Over the World," *The Economist*, June 19, 1999, p. 59.
44. Miriam Jordan, "Wal-Mart Gets Aggressive About Brazil," *Wall Street Journal*, May 25, 2001, p. A8.
45. Ernest Beck, "Stores Told to Lift Prices in Germany," *Wall Street Journal*, September 11, 2000, p. A27.
46. Miriam Jordan, "Penney Blends Two Business Cultures," *Wall Street Journal*, April 5, 2001, p. A15.
47. The section on replicators, performance managers, and reinventors is taken from Luciano Catoni, Nora F. Larssen, James Naylor, and Andrea Zocchi, "Travel Tips for Retailers," *MacKinsey Quarterly*, no. 3 (2002).
48. Irena Vida, James Reardon, and Ann Fairhurst, "Determinants of International Retail Involvement: The Case of Large U.S. Retail Chains," *Journal of International Marketing* 8, no. 4 (2000), pp. 37–60.
49. Amway.com (accessed March 14, 2005).
50. "International Direct Marketing in a Rapidly Changing World," *Direct Marketing*, March 1, 1999, p. 44.
51. Miriam Jordan, "Knock Knock," *Wall Street Journal*, February 19, 2003, p. A1.
52. "Germany: Europe's On-line Front Runner," *Communications Week International*, March 15, 1999, p. 6.
53. Ken Belson, "Net Shopping," *Business Week*, July 31, 2001, p. 64.
54. Lisa Vickery, "E-Business: 'Cultural Portal' Could Translate Way to Profit," *Wall Street Journal*, February 12, 2001, p. B6.
55. "New Concepts Check Out: Self-scanning Reduces Lines, Personal Scanning Checks Out," *Boston Herald*, January 25, 1999, p. O27.
56. This section is largely taken from Kate Gillespie and J. Brad McBride, "Smuggling in Emerging Markets: Global Implications," *Columbia Journal of World Business* 31 (Winter 1996), pp. 40–54.
57. Maud S. Beelman, Duncan Campbell, Maria Teresa Ronderos, and Erik J. Schelzig, "Major Tobacco Multinational Implicated in Cigarette Smuggling, Tax Evasion, Documents Show," Investigative Report, The Center for Public Integrity, www.public-i.org/story_01_013100.htm.
58. Kate Gillespie, "Smuggling and the Global Firm." *Journal of International Management* 9, no. 3 (2003), pp. 317–333.
59. Marek Strzelecki, " 'Ants' Carry Contraband into Poland," *Wall Street Journal*, October 9, 2002, p. B31.
60. Guy Chazan, "Suddenly Boxed In, Russian Smugglers Plot Their Next Move," *Wall Street Journal*, May 4, 2004, p. A1.
61. Lowell Bergman, "U.S. Companies Tangled in Web of Drug Dollars," *New York Times*, October 10, 2000, p. 1.

14 GLOBAL PROMOTION STRATEGIES

EACH YEAR THE GOLIATHS of the civil aircraft industry face off at the Paris Air Show. America's Boeing Company and Europe's Airbus Industrie attempt not only to make sales but also to capture the imaginations of potential clients. Company representatives meet with major customers to discuss current products and establish the leads that will eventually result in sales of these big-ticket items. But promoting current products is not enough. The Paris Air Show is a time to unveil new ideas and present the company's vision of the future of flight. This vision, as well as actual products, will help establish the image of each company. In this global industry, corporate image is very important. Can the firm deliver on its promises of speed, economy in-cabin amenities, and innovative ideas?[1] International marketers in civil aircraft must communicate to potential customers that the answer is yes.

Global promotion strategies encompass a firm's marketing communications and include personal selling, sales promotion, public relations, and advertising. Managing the communications process for a single market is no easy task. And the task is even more difficult for global marketers, who must communicate to prospective customers in many national markets. In the process, they struggle with different cultures, habits, and languages.

LEARNING OBJECTIVES

After studying this chapter, you should be able to

▶ List the major factors that determine a firm's ability to use a push or a pull promotion strategy in different national markets.

▶ Contrast the benefits to the international marketer of using an international sales force with those of using local sales forces.

▶ Describe the impact that different purchasing behaviors, buying criteria, languages, and negotiation styles can have on international selling.

▶ Explain the importance of global account management.

▶ Describe how global marketers can successfully utilize international trade fairs and consortia as well as manage the international bidding process.

▶ Cite examples of how sales promotions vary across cultures, and suggest reasons for these differences.

▶ Note recent international trends in sales promotions, sports sponsorships, telemarketing, product placement, and managing word of mouth.

▶ Give examples of international public relations disasters, and suggest ways in which global marketers can promote the goodwill of their firms.

We begin this chapter by examining the cross-cultural implications of push strategies and pull strategies. We proceed to the challenge of developing a personal-selling effort on both the international and the local level, discussing differing sales practices as well as issues of recruitment and compensation of sales forces. Other promotion issues involving business-to-business and government sales are then discussed. We continue by exploring other aspects of global promotion such as sales promotions, sports sponsorships, spam, product placements, buzz, and public relations. (Advertising, a key element of the promotion mix, will be covered in detail in Chapter 15.)

GLOBAL PROMOTION STRATEGIES

How to manage the promotion mix globally is a critical question for many companies. Some firms do business in a certain way and do not rethink their promotion decisions when they internationalize. However, many companies find themselves in countries or situations that require an adjustment or a substantial change in their promotion mix. This section and the ones that follow are devoted to understanding how different international environments affect promotion mix decisions.

Pull versus Push Strategies

Pull strategy a promotional strategy directed at the final buyer or end user of a product or service

A **pull strategy** is characterized by a relatively greater dependence on promotion, including sales promotions and advertising, directed at the final buyer or end user for a product or service. Pull campaigns are typical for consumer-goods firms that target a large number of consumers. Pull campaigns are usually advisable when the product is widely used by consumers, when the channel is long, when the product is not very complex, and when self-service is the predominant shopping behavior. Increased or decreased reliance on pull campaigns for global markets depends on a number of factors. Most important are access to advertising media, channel length, and the leverage the company has with the distribution channel.

Marketers accustomed to having a large number of media available may find the choices limited in overseas markets. For many products, pull campaigns that rely heavily on advertising work only if access to electronic media, particularly television, is available. In some other countries, access to those media is restricted through time limits imposed by governments. Consequently, companies find it difficult to duplicate their promotional strategies when moving from an unregulated environment to more restricted environments.

Channel length is another major determinant of the feasibility of a pull campaign. Companies in consumer markets often face long channels. As a result, they try to overcome channel inertia by aiming their promotion directly at end users. When a company markets overseas, it may face an even longer channel because local distribution arrangements are different. Such is the case in Japan, where channels tend to be much longer than those in the United States. As a result, a greater reliance on a pull strategy may be advisable or necessary.

Distribution leverage is also different for each company from market to market. Gaining cooperation from local selling points, particularly in the retail sector, may be more difficult than in the domestic market. The fight for shelf space can be very intensive; shelf space in most markets is limited. Under these more competitive situations, reliance on a pull campaign becomes more important. If consumers are demanding the company's product, retailers will make every effort to carry it.

Push strategy a promotional strategy directed at the distributors of a product

In contrast to a pull strategy, a **push strategy** focuses on the distributors of a product rather than on the end user or ultimate buyer. Incentives are offered to wholesalers or retailers to carry and promote a product. A company may have to resort to a push strategy when lack of access to advertising media makes

WORLD BEAT 14.1

Hindu Festival Attracts U.S. Marketers

AS MILLIONS OF HINDU PILGRIMS mass at the confluence of the Ganges and Yamuna rivers for a festival of ritual cleansing, many are grabbing a Coke or a Pepsi to quench their thirst. Those are just two of the companies moving beyond their traditional marketing venues of sporting events and movies in search of fresh ways to reach India's rural masses. Their latest venue is the Kumbh Mela—a Hindu festival that comes every 12 years and draws thirty million participants over a period of a month.

Better yet for marketers, many of the people come from remote villages and small towns. About 80 percent of India's one billion people live in rural areas, far from the reach of most modern media. Getting them to try a product while at the festival could be the start of potentially extensive word-of-mouth advertising.

The latest festival was particularly awash with marketers pushing bottled soft drinks. The industry expects consumption to rise rapidly as more Indians indulge in Western-style food and beverages amid a growing affluence. PepsiCo's Indian unit teamed up with the state tourism department to sell Pepsi at stalls and restaurants in addition to its own twenty exclusive vendors. Rival Coca-Cola was selling at 115 stalls. Coke also had 15,000 posters, as well as billboards, banners, and police assistance booths painted red with the famous logo.

Some criticize the commercialization of an ancient religious tradition. Still smarting from its colonial past, India is frequently suspicious of foreign products and ideas. Many nationalist Hindus frown upon foreign products and see Coke and Pepsi as symbols of economic imperialism.

Still, the marketers' strategy may be working among some. One medical-store owner from India's eastern state of Orissa swaggered up to a makeshift tent shop to treat himself to his fifth bottle of Pepsi in three days. So, what does he think? "I like it," he says.

Source: From Rasul Bailay, "A Hindu Festival Attracts the Faithful and U.S. Marketers," *Wall Street Journal*, February 12, 2001. Copyright © 2001 by Dow Jones & Co. Inc. Reproduced with permission of Dow Jones & Co. Inc., via Copyright Clearance Center.

a pull strategy less effective. Limited ability to transfer a pull strategy from a company's home market has other effects on the company's performance in foreign markets. Reduced advertising tends to slow the product adoption process in new markets, forcing the firm to accept slower growth. In markets crowded with existing competitors, newcomers may find it difficult to establish themselves when avenues for pull campaigns are blocked.

Consequently, a company entering a new market may want to consider such situations in its planning and to adjust its expected results accordingly. A company accustomed to a given type of communications mix usually develops an expertise or a distinctive competence in the media commonly used. When the firm is suddenly faced with a situation in which that competence cannot be fully applied, the risk of failure or underachievement multiplies. Such constraints can even affect entry strategies and the market selection process.

PERSONAL SELLING

Personal selling communication between a potential buyer and a salesperson to the end of understanding buyer needs, matching those needs to the supplier's products or services, and ultimately achieving a sale

Personal selling takes place whenever a customer is met in person by a representative of the marketing company. When doing business globally, companies must meet customers from different countries. These individuals may be used to different business customs and will often speak a different language. That is why personal selling is extremely complex and demands some very special skills on the part of the salesperson.

The complexity of a product usually influences how extensively personal selling is used. The level of complexity has to be compared with the product knowledge of the clients. A company selling the same products abroad as those sold domestically may find that more personal selling is necessary abroad if foreign clients are less sophisticated than domestic clients. A U.S. company may use the same amount of personal selling in Europe as it does in the United States but may need to put forth a greater personal-selling effort in developing countries if the product is new to those markets.

Although very effective as a promotion tool, personal selling requires the intensive use of a sales force and can be costly. Costs vary across countries. In the United States, a typical sales call is estimated to cost in excess of $300. This has motivated some companies to investigate other forms of promotion. Dell Computer considered sales calls too expensive in Brazil and instead mailed brochures to potential small-business clients. It took the company over a year to put together a list of names and addresses, because these were not readily available in Brazil. However, the mail campaign was a success in the end.

International selling selling that crosses national boundaries and utilizes salespersons who travel to different countries

Local selling selling that targets a single country

In this section, we differentiate between **international selling** and local selling. When a company's sales force travels across countries and meets directly with clients abroad, it is practicing international selling. This type of selling requires the special skill of being able to manage within several cultures. Much more often, however, companies engage in **local selling:** They organize and staff a local sales force made up of local nationals to do the selling in only one country. Different problems arise in managing and operating a local sales force than in managing multicountry salespersons.

International Selling (Multicountry Sales Force)

The job of the international salesperson seems glamorous. One imagines a professional who frequently travels abroad, visiting a large number of countries and meeting with businesspeople of various backgrounds. However, this type of work is quite demanding and requires a special set of skills.

International salespersons are needed only when companies deal directly with their clients abroad. This is usually the case for industrial equipment or business services but is rarely required for consumer products or services. Consequently, for our purposes, international sales will be described in the context of business-to-business selling.

Purchasing Behavior. In business-to-business selling, one of the most important parts of the job consists of identifying the buying unit in the client company. The buying unit consists of all persons who have input into the buying decision. The seller must locate and access the actual decision makers, who may hold different positions from company to company or from country to country. In different countries, the purchasing manager may have different responsibilities, and engineers may play a greater or a lesser role. Buying decisions are often more centralized in many Asian and Latin American firms. In many cases, the owner of the firm will make the final buying decision. Gaining access to top management may not be easy and may cause delays. Even in Europe, the time between a first sales call and a purchase can be 50 percent longer than in the United States. Sales times in Japan can also be longer because of the Japanese emphasis on consensus in the buying unit. The members of the buying unit will want to explore and debate alternatives, while striving for a sense of unity and collegiality among themselves.[2]

Buying Criteria. In addition to different purchasing patterns, the international salesperson may have to deal with different decision criteria or objectives on the part of the purchaser. Buyers or users of industrial products in different countries may expect to maximize different goals. For example, Sealed Air had difficulty convincing businesses in Taiwan to purchase more expensive packaging systems to protect their products during shipping, even though these systems had proved cost-effective in avoiding breakage. Unlike buyers in other markets, Taiwanese manufacturers focused almost exclusively on the purchase price of the packaging.[3]

Language. Overcoming the language barrier is an especially difficult task for the international salesperson. In Chapter 3, we discussed several issues related to culture and language that can affect international marketing in general and personal selling in particular. Different societies apply different forms of address, use or avoid certain body language, and feel differently about the appropriateness of showing emotion. Certain societies are low-context cultures wherein the meanings of words are explicit. Other societies are high-context cultures wherein the meanings of words are implicit and change according to who speaks them as well as when and where they are spoken. It is very difficult for a non-native speaker to become fluent in the language of a high-context culture.

Of course, the personal-selling effort is markedly enhanced if the salesperson speaks the language of the customer, but for many industries, dependence on the local language is not so strong today as it was just one or two decades ago. For many new and highly sophisticated products, such as electronics and aerospace, English is the language spoken by most customers. Consequently, with more and more executives speaking English in many countries, many firms can market their products directly without local intermediaries.

English is widely spoken in Europe and is the leading second language in Asia and Latin America. Consequently, the ability to speak a number of foreign languages is less of a necessity. Still, learning a foreign language can be an excellent way to understand a foreign culture, and language proficiency continues to have a very favorable impact on the sales process. Local customers often appreciate a sales representative who speaks their language; it indicates the company's commitment to their market as well as its appreciation of their people and culture.

In industries where knowledge of the local language is important, companies tend to assign sales territories to salespersons on the basis of language skills. A European multinational manufacturer of textile equipment assigns countries to its sales staff according to the languages they speak. This is more important in traditional industries such as textile manufacturing, where businesses are more local in orientation and where managers may not speak English well.

Even executives who speak fairly good English may not understand all the details of product descriptions or specifications. As a result, a company can make an excellent impression by having its sales brochures translated into some of the key languages. European companies routinely produce company publications in several languages. Translations from English may not be needed for Scandinavia, where English proficiency is common. However, they may be valuable for other parts of the world, where the level of English-language skills is not high.

Business Etiquette. Global marketers selling to many markets are likely to encounter a diverse set of business practices as they move from one country to another. Because interpersonal behavior is intensely culture-bound, this part of the salesperson's job will vary by country. Many differences exist in how an appointment is made, how (and whether) an introduction is made, and in how much lead time is needed for making appointments. Whereas it is acceptable for visitors to arrive late in China, India, or Indonesia, arriving late in Hong Kong is not acceptable. Lateness causes the visitor to "lose face," which is an extremely serious matter among Hong Kong businesspeople. In Switzerland, where punctuality is also highly valued, clients may be favorably impressed if the salesperson arrives 10 or 15 minutes early for an appointment.

The salesperson must also know whether or not gifts are expected or desired. In most Chinese cultures, gift giving is viewed as a sign that the vendor is committed to establishing or sustaining a relationship with the client.[4] Exchanging business gifts is popular in Taiwan but less common in Saudi Arabia. In Switzerland, it is better to wait until the sale is finalized before offering a gift to a client. Even then the gift should not be too expensive, or it may be construed as a bribe and thus give offense. In short, what is expected or tolerated in some markets may be taboo in others.

No manager can be expected to know the business customs of every country, so important information must be obtained from special sources. A company's own foreign market representatives or sales subsidiary can provide key information or suggestions. Also, governments tend to collect data on business practices through their commercial officers posted abroad. Some business service companies, such as global accounting firms or global banks, also provide customers with profiles of business practices in foreign countries.[5]

Check out our website (college.hmco.com/business/) for links to business etiquette sources.

Foreign businesspersons receiving visitors from the United States or any other foreign country rarely expect the foreign visitor to be familiar with all local customs. However, it is always appreciated when the visitor can exhibit familiarity with the most common practices and some willingness to try to conform. Learning some foreign customs helps to generate goodwill toward the company and can increase the chances of making a sale.

International Sales Negotiations

It is the ultimate job of most sales forces to make a sale. As we mentioned in Chapter 5, negotiations can play an important role in selling, especially to businesses and governments. The terms of a sale—price, delivery terms, and financing options—can all be negotiable. Negotiations in the global arena are complicated because the negotiating partners frequently come from different cultural backgrounds. As a result, misunderstandings or misjudgments can occur among them. To maximize their effectiveness in these often difficult and protracted negotiations, international sales personnel must be attuned to cultural differences.

Careful background preparation on the cultural norms prevalent in the foreign country is the starting point in successful negotiations and selling. As noted in Chapter 5, negotiation styles can vary considerably. A 15-year study of negotiation styles in seventeen cultures found significant differences from culture to culture. For example, the Japanese were the least aggressive, using few threats or warnings, whereas the French and Brazilians were considerably more aggressive, frequently employing threats and interruptions.[6]

Time orientation is an important aspect for negotiating abroad. In some countries, such as China, negotiations tend to take much more time than in the United States or some other Western countries. One European company that operated a joint venture in China observed that during one meeting, 2 weeks were spent in a discussion that elsewhere might have taken only a few hours. In this situation, however, much of the time was used for interdepartmental negotiations among various Chinese agencies rather than for face-to-face negotiations with the European company.

Another difference between cultures is their attitude toward the final negotiated contract. Managers from the United States like to "get it all in writing." Contracts often spell out many contingencies and establish the position of both sides in light of these contingencies. Americans believe that the business relationship will proceed more smoothly if this is all worked out ahead of time. Other cultures consider this insistence on elaborate written contracts a sign of inflexibility or even lack of trust on the part of Americans. In Brazil, even a written contract may not be regarded as binding but, rather, as open for continued renegotiation. In any case, an understanding of the prevailing cultural attitudes is necessary to successfully negotiate the final sale.

Local Selling (Single-Country Sales Force)

When a company is able to maintain a local sales force in the countries where it does business, many of the difficulties of bridging the cultural gap with clients are minimized. The local sales force can be expected to understand local customs, and the global company typically gains additional acceptance in the market. This is primarily because local sales forces are usually staffed with local nationals. However, many challenges remain, and managing a local sales force often requires different strategies from those used in running a sales force in the company's domestic market.

Role of Local Sales Force. For firms that still use distributor sales forces to a large extent, a missionary sales force with limited responsibilities may suffice. A **missionary sales force** concentrates on visiting clients together with the local distributor's sales force. Its focus is on promoting the product rather than distributing the product or even finalizing the sale. If the global company's sales

Missionary sales force salespersons who promote a firm and its products or services but do not close a sale

force needs to do the entire job, a much larger sales force will be necessary. The size of the local sales force depends to a large extent on the number of clients and the desired frequency of visits. This frequency may differ from country to country, which means that the size of the sales force will differ accordingly.

Control over a firm's sales activities is a frequently cited advantage of operating a company-owned local sales force. With its own sales force, the company can emphasize the products it wants to market at any time and can maintain better control over the way it is represented. In many cases, price negotiations, in the form of discounts or rebates, are handled uniformly rather than leaving these decisions to an independent distributor with different interests. Having a company sales force helps ensure that the personnel have the necessary training and qualifications. Control over all of these parameters usually means higher sales than those achieved with a distributor sales force.

Also, the local sales force can represent an important bridge to the local business community. For industries in which the buying process is local rather than global, the sales force speaks the language of the local customer. It can be expected to understand the local business customs and to bring the international firm closer to its end users. In many instances, local customers, although they may not object to buying from a foreign firm, may prefer to deal with local representatives of that firm.

The role of the local sales force needs to be coordinated with the promotion mix selected for each market. As many companies have learned, advertising and other forms of promotion can be used to make the function of the sales force more efficient. In many consumer-goods industries, companies prefer a pull strategy, concentrating their promotion budget on the final consumer. In such cases, the role of the sales force is restricted to gaining distribution access. However, as we have noted before, there are countries in which access to communications media is severely restricted. As a result, companies may place greater emphasis on a push strategy, relying heavily on the local sales force. This will affect both the role and the size of the firm's sales force.

Foreign Sales Practices. Although sales forces are employed virtually everywhere, the nature of their interaction with the local customer is unique to each market and may affect local sales operations. For most Westerners, Japanese practices seem substantially different. Here is an example reported by Masaaki Imai, president of Cambridge Corporation, a Tokyo management consulting and recruiting firm.

When Bausch & Lomb first introduced its then-new soft-lens line into Japan, the company targeted influential eye doctors in each sales territory for its introductory launch. The firm assumed that once these leading practitioners signed up for the new product, marketing to the majority of eye doctors would be easier. However, a key customer quickly dismissed one salesperson. The doctor said that he thought very highly of Bausch & Lomb equipment but preferred regular lenses for his patients. The salesperson did not even have a chance to respond. He decided, because it was his first visit to this clinic, to wait around for a while. He talked to several assistants at the clinic and to the doctor's wife, who was handling the administration of the practice.

The next morning, the salesperson returned to the clinic and observed that the doctor was very busy. He talked again with the assistants and joined the doctor's wife when she was cooking and talked with her about food. When the couple's young son returned from kindergarten, the salesperson played with him and even went out to buy him a toy. The wife was very pleased with the well-intentioned babysitter. She later explained to the salesperson that her husband had very little time to listen to any sales presentations during the day, so she invited him to come to their home in the evening. The doctor, obviously primed by his wife, received the man very warmly, and they enjoyed *sake* together. The doctor listened patiently to the sales presentation and responded that he did not want to use the soft lenses on his patients right away. However, he suggested that the salesperson try them on his assistants the next day. Therefore, on the third day, the salesperson returned to the clinic and fitted several of the clinic's assistants to soft lenses. The reaction was very favorable, and the doctor placed an order on the third day of the sales call.[7]

Japanese customers often judge whether a company really wants to do business by the frequency of the sales calls they receive. Salespeople who make more frequent calls to a potential customer than the competition makes may be regarded as more sincere. This means that companies doing business in Japan have to make frequent sales calls to their top customers, even if only for courtesy reasons. Although this contact may occasionally be just a telephone call, the need to make frequent visits significantly affects the staffing levels of the company-owned sales force.

Recruiting. Companies have often found recruiting sales professionals quite challenging in many global markets. Although the availability of qualified sales personnel is a problem even in developed countries, the scarcity of skilled personnel is even more acute in developing countries. Global companies, accustomed to having sales staff with certain standard qualifications, may not find it easy to locate the necessary salespeople in a short period of time. One factor that limits their availability in many countries is the local economic situation. A good economic climate will limit the number of people a company can expect to hire away from existing firms unless a substantial increase over their present compensation is offered.

Furthermore, sales positions don't enjoy uniformly high esteem from country to country. Typically, sales as an occupation or career has generally positive associations in the United States. This allows companies to recruit excellent talent, usually fresh from universities, for sales careers. These university recruits often regard sales as a relatively high-paying career or as a path to middle management. Such an image of selling is rare elsewhere in the world. In Europe, many companies continue to find it difficult to recruit university graduates into their sales forces, except in such highly technical fields as computers, where the recruits are typically engineers. When selling is a less desirable occupation, the quality of the sales force may suffer. The time it takes to fill sales positions can be expected to increase dramatically if the company wants to insist on top-quality recruits.

Compensation. In their home markets where they usually employ large sales forces, global companies become accustomed to handling and motivating their sales forces in a given way. In the United States, typical motivation programs include some form of commission or bonus for meeting volume or budget projections, as well as vacation prizes for top performers. When a global company manages local sales forces in various countries, the company must determine the best way to motivate them. Salespersons from different cultures may not all respond the same way. Motivating practices may need to differ from country to country.

Jorge Vergara joined U.S.-based Herbalife when it first entered the Mexican market, and he soon became a star salesman. Then he left to start his own nutritional supplements company, Omnilife. Breaking with Herbalife's sales practices, Mr. Vergara modified his compensation system. Instead of rewarding on the basis of sales volume, he rewarded salespersons who sold consistently. He also paid them every 2 weeks, which is customary in Latin America, instead of monthly. After only 8 years, Omnilife became one of Latin America's largest sellers of nutritional supplements, ahead of both Herbalife and Amway Corporation.[8] One of the frequently discussed topics in the area of motivating salespeople is the value of the commission or bonus structure. In countries that rate high on uncertainty avoidance, sales representatives may prefer to receive guaranteed salaries. U.S. companies, on the other hand, have tended to use some form of commission structure for their sales forces. Although this may fluctuate from industry to industry, U.S. firms tend to use a more flexible and volume-dependent compensation structure than European firms do. Japanese firms more often use a straight-salary type of compensation. To motivate the sales force to achieve superior performance, the global company may be faced with using different compensation practices depending on local customs.

GLOBAL ACCOUNT MANAGEMENT

Global account team a team dedicated to servicing a multinational global buyer

Traditionally, account management has been performed on a country-by-country basis. This practice invariably leads, even in large global firms, to a country-specific sales force. However, as we noted in Chapter 5, some companies organize their sales force into global account teams. The **global account team** services an entire customer globally, or in all countries where a customer relationship exists. Global account teams may comprise members in different parts of the world, all serving segments of a global account and coordinated through a global account management structure.

Global accounts arose in response to more centralized purchasing within global firms. Companies that purchase similar components, raw materials, or services in many parts of the world realized that by combining the purchasing function and managing it centrally, they could demand better prices and service from suppliers. Today, many companies search the globe for the best buy.

Siemens's Automotive Systems Division has tailored its sales structure to these new realities. The company maintains global account teams for key customers such as Volkswagen and Ford. The teams are in charge of the firm's entire business, regardless of where the components are sourced or used. From the customer's perspective, the advantage stems from the clear designation of a counterpart who will handle all aspects of their business relationship.[9] The system of global account management is also practiced widely in the professional-service sectors. Globally active banks such as Citibank have maintained global account structures for years. Likewise, advertising agencies offer global clients global account management with seamless coordination across many countries. The world's leading accounting firms, such as Deloitte Touche Tohmatsu International, have long-standing traditions of managing international clients from a single unit.[10]

Global account management is greatly enhanced by sophisticated information technology (IT). With members of the team dispersed around the globe, it becomes essential to coordinate all actions meticulously. The development and rapid spread of such tools as videoconferencing and e-mail have greatly extended the reach of a management team beyond the typical one-location office.

Nonetheless, global account management can present challenges to global marketers. A study of sixteen large multinational companies revealed that prices quoted to global accounts were more likely to fall than to rise. In 27 percent of cases, prices were assessed as becoming much lower within 3 years. Although global account management has been shown to be very effective in certain situations, it is a difficult and expensive structure to implement. Because of these concerns, many vendors set clear criteria as to which customers qualify as **worthwhile global accounts.** Potential global accounts may need to meet minimum revenue levels that will support the additional overhead required by global account management. Marriott International requires that potential global accounts purchase over $25 million annually in hotel services. While customers often desire to become a global account to obtain volume price discounts, vendors should expect a global account client to differentiate them as a vendor, resulting in increased sales volume.[11]

Worthwhile global account an account that meets minimum revenue levels that support the additional overhead required by global account management

Implementing Successful Global Account Programs[12]

To implement a successful global account program, vendor companies should be as global and as coordinated as their customers—or problems can arise. One firm was surprised to receive a call from a global customer demanding service for a plant in Indonesia. The vendor had no sales or service operation in Indonesia but felt obliged to respond. Someone was flown out from a neighboring country at considerable expense.[13] Senior management commitment is essential. Global customers will expect to meet with senior managers from their key vendors on a regular basis. Top management must also authorize the allocation of essential people and resources to global account teams. This may require moving personnel and resources from countries and regions to a unit located at central headquarters.

Global account management requires a robust IT system. Global IT systems can track the progress of a global account in such areas as orders, back orders, shipments, accounts payable, complaints, and returns. Most important, a robust IT system can create value for the customer as well as for the vendor. For example, at Marriott International, the global account manager for IBM was able to track IBM's conference cancellations globally. These were costing IBM over one million dollars annually. Marriott International's account managers created an internal electronic bulletin board for IBM employees to purchase cancelled space, thereby reducing IBM cancellation fees and substantially reducing IBM's cost.

Finally, global account managers must possess special skills. Many national account managers may not have sufficient cross-cultural skills or the broader business acumen required for the job. Required skills of global account managers are more aligned with those of a general manager than a senior salesperson. Global account managers may be called upon to analyze an industry, understand competitive strategies, and identify new ways in which their firm can contribute to a customer's strategy. Many companies with global account management programs will find that additional training may be necessary to managers assigned this task.

SELLING TO BUSINESSES AND GOVERNMENTS

Promotion methods that are oriented largely toward business or government markets can be important to international firms operating in those markets. In particular, the use of international trade fairs, bidding procedures for international projects, and consortium selling all need to be understood in their international context.

International Trade Fairs

Participation in international trade fairs has become an important aspect of business-to-business marketing abroad. Trade fairs are ideal for exposing new customers and potential distributors to a company's product range and have been used extensively by both newcomers and established firms. In the United States, business customers can be reached through a wide range of media, such as specialized magazines with a particular industry focus. In many overseas countries, the markets are too small to allow for the publication of such trade magazines for only one country. As a result, prospective customers usually attend these trade fairs on a regular basis. Trade fairs also offer companies a chance to meet with prospective customers in a less formal atmosphere. For a company that is new to a certain market and does not yet have any established contacts, participating in a trade fair may be the only way to reach potential customers.

There are an estimated six hundred trade shows in seventy countries every year. Germany's Hannover Fair is considered the largest industrial fair in the world, attracting approximately 6,000 exhibitors in engineering and technology from over sixty countries. Other large general fairs include the Canton Fair in China and the Milan Fair in Italy. Germany hosts the most trade fairs, drawing a total of about ten million visitors a year.[14] In addition to general trade fairs, specialized trade fairs concentrate on a certain segment of an industry or user group. Such fairs usually attract limited participation in terms of both exhibitors and visitors. Typically, they are more technical in nature. Some of the specialized trade fairs do not take place every year. One of the leading specialized fairs for the chemical industry is the Achema, which is held in Frankfurt, Germany, every 3 years. Other specialized fairs that enjoy an international reputation include the air shows of Paris and of Farnborough, England, where aerospace products are displayed.[15]

Participation in trade fairs can save both time and effort for a company that wants to break into a new market and does not yet have any contacts. For new product announcements or demonstrations, the trade fair offers an ideal showcase. Trade fairs are also used by competitors to check out one another's most recent developments. They can give a newcomer an idea of the potential competition in some foreign markets. Consequently, trade fairs are a means of both selling products and gathering important and useful market intelligence. Therefore, marketers with global aspirations will do well to seek out the trade fairs directed at their industry or customer segment and to schedule regular attendance.

International exhibiting may require more planning than is necessary for domestic shows. First, begin planning 12 to 18 months in advance, taking into account the fact that international shipping may involve delays. Second, check show attendance. Many shows allow the general public to attend, in which case

The Ambiente Fair in Frankfurt, Germany is the world's largest trade fair for consumer goods. In 2005, it hosted 4,605 exhibitors from 90 countries and welcomed 141,000 visitors from 136 countries.

you may want to arrange for a private area for meeting with viable prospects. Third, in the United States, a show may be staffed by salespeople and middle managers. At many international shows, however, customers expect to see the CEO and senior management. Finally, use a local distributor, consultant, or sales representative to help with the local logistics and acquaint you with the local culture.[16]

A number of virtual trade shows have recently appeared on the Internet. For example, WholesaleTradeshow.com launched the first online, global trade show for wholesale and off-price apparel, footwear, and team sports merchandise. Merchandise could be viewed and bought online. Buyers and sellers could transact business 24 hours a day, 7 days a week via the site, supported by a multilingual customer service team and optional export management services.[17]

Selling Through a Bidding Process

Global marketers of industrial products may become involved in a bidding process, particularly when major capital equipment is involved. Companies competing for such major projects must take a number of steps before negotiations for a specific purchase can begin. Typically, companies actively seek new projects and then move on to prequalify for the particular project(s) they locate before a formal project bid or tender is submitted. Each phase requires careful management and the appropriate allocation of resources.

During the **search phase,** companies want to make sure that they are informed of any project meriting their interest that is related to their product lines. For particularly large projects that are government sponsored, full-page advertisements may appear in leading international newspapers or may be posted

Search phase a phase in the bidding process in which potential suppliers identify projects of interest to them on government websites. Companies can also utilize their networks of agents, contacts, or former customers to inform them of any project being considered.

Prequalifying phase a phase in the bidding process in which prospective buyers ask for documentation from interested suppliers to verify that bidders are trustworthy and capable of handling the proposed project

In the **prequalifying phase,** the purchaser frequently asks for documentation from interested companies that wish to make a formal tender. No formal bidding or tender documents are submitted. Instead, the buyer is more interested in general company background and is likely to ask the firm to describe similar projects it has completed in the past. At this stage, the company will have to sell itself and its capabilities. A large number of companies may be expected to pursue prequalification.

Formal bid a phase in the bidding process in which a potential supplier states the price it will charge a client for a project and details the terms of the project

In the next phase, the customer selects the companies—usually only three or four—to be invited to submit a **formal bid.** Formal bids consist of a written proposal of how to solve the specific client problem and the price the firm would charge for the project. For industrial equipment, this usually requires personal visits on location, special design of some components, and the preparation of full documentation, including engineering drawings, for the client. The bid preparation costs can be enormous, running as high as several million dollars for some very large projects. The customer will select the winner from among those submitting formal proposals. Rarely is it simply the lowest bidder who obtains the order. Technology, the type of solution proposed, the financing arrangements, and the reputation and experience of the firm all play a role.

Performance bond money supplied by a supplier and held in escrow to guarantee that a buyer will be reimbursed if a project is not completed in accordance with agreed-upon specifications.

Once an order is obtained, the supplier company may be expected to insure its own performance. For that purpose, the company may be asked to post a **performance bond,** which is a guarantee that the company will pay certain specified damages to the customer if the job is not completed in accordance with the agreed-upon specifications. Performance bonds are usually issued by banks on behalf of the supplier. The entire process, from finding out about a new prospect until the order is actually in hand, may take from several months to several years, depending on the project size or industry.

Consortium Selling

Consortium a group of firms that participate in a project on a preagreed basis but act as one company toward the buyer

Because of the high stakes involved in marketing equipment or large projects, companies frequently band together to form a consortium. A **consortium** is a group of firms that share in a certain contract or project on a preagreed basis but act as one company toward the customer. Joining together in a consortium can help companies share the risk in some very large projects. A consortium can also enhance the competitiveness of the members if they are involved in turnkey projects. A **turnkey project** is one in which the supplier offers the buyer a complete solution so that the entire operation can commence "at the turn of a key."

Turnkey project a project in which the supplier provides the buyer with a complete solution for immediate use, occupation, or operation

Most consortia are formed on an ad hoc basis. For the job of creating a major steel mill, for example, companies supplying individual components might combine into a group and offer a single tender to the customer. The consortium members have agreed to share all marketing costs and can help one another with design and engineering questions. Similarly, a consortium could form to deliver a turnkey hospital to the Saudi Arabian government. This would involve building the physical facilities, installing medical equipment, recruiting doctors, and training staff—among other things. In either case, the customer gets a chance to deal with one supplier only, which substantially simplifies the process. Ad hoc consortia can be formed for very large projects that require unique skills from their members. In situations where the same set of skills or products is in frequent demand, companies may form a permanent consortium. Whenever an appropriate opportunity arises, the consortium members will immediately prepare to qualify for the bidding.

Consortium members frequently come from the same country. However, telecommunications consortia often combine a local firm, whose local connections are of great value, with one or two international telephone operating companies, which offer expertise in running a network. On occasion, these consortia include equipment suppliers that join to ensure that their equipment will be included in any eventual contract.

OTHER FORMS OF PROMOTION

So far, our discussion has focused on personal and industrial selling as key elements of a promotion mix. However, forms of promotion other than selling and advertising can play a key role in marketing. As we discussed in Chapter 13, direct sales is not only a distribution strategy but a promotion strategy as well, because it involves communicating directly with the consumer. Another form of global promotion is sales promotion, which can include such elements as in-store retail promotions and coupons. Many of these tools are consumer-goods-oriented and are used less often in the marketing of industrial goods. In this section, we look at sales promotion activities, sports sponsorships, direct sales promotions, product placements, management of word of mouth, and public relations.

Sales Promotion

Sales promotion encompasses marketing activities that generate sales by adding value to products in order to stimulate consumer purchasing and/or channel cooperation. Sales promotions such as coupons, gifts, and various types of reduced-priced labels are used in most countries. In some countries, free goods, double-pack promotions, and in-store displays are also important. Government regulations and different retailing practices, however, tend to limit the options for global firms.

The area of sales promotion is largely local in focus. For example, in Mexico, 85 percent of cement sales are to individuals. Millions of do-it-yourselfers buy bags of cement to build their own homes. Cemex, the market leader in cement sales, sometimes buys food for a block party when a house is finished. And the company's 5,000 distributors can earn points toward vacations by increasing sales.[18]

In the United States, coupons are the leading form of sales promotion. Consumers bring product coupons to the retail store and obtain a reduced price for the product. Companies such as ACNeilsen specialize in managing coupon redemption centers centrally so that consumer-goods firms can outsource the physical handling of these promotions. Second in importance are refund offers. Consumers who send a proof of purchase to the manufacturer receive a refund in the form of a check. Less frequently used are cents-off labels and factory bonus packs, which induce customers to buy large quantities via a price incentive.

Couponing—where consumers bring product coupons to a retail store and obtain a reduced price for a product—varies significantly from country to country. As mentioned, in the United States, coupons are the leading form of sales promotion. Coupon distribution is popular and growing in Italy, while in the

United Kingdom and Spain, couponing is declining. Couponing is relatively new in Japan, where restrictions on newspaper coupons were lifted only in 1991.

An example of a sales promotion aimed at distributors is the slotting allowance. This is a payment made to retailers in return for their agreeing to take a new product. A slotting allowance helps compensate them for the time and effort expended in finding a space for the new product on their shelves. As products proliferate, finding shelf space is increasingly difficult, and firms must compete for access to that space. Slotting allowances in Europe's increasingly concentrated supermarket industry have become quite costly.

Although most sales promotions are relatively short-term, some may continue indefinitely. Promotions that encourage customer loyalty and repeat purchases are being used increasingly worldwide. Loyalty programs, such as frequent-flyer awards, have proliferated in the former Soviet bloc since the 1990s. Not all frequent-flyer programs were well managed. Polish Airlines established three levels of awards and service for frequent flyers (blue, silver, and gold) but actually treated all customers the same. This resulted in customer dissatisfaction with the program and in a large defection of frequent flyers to competitor British Airways.[19]

Most countries impose restrictions on some forms of promotions. Games of chance are frequently regulated. When reductions are made available, they often are not allowed to exceed a certain percentage of the product's purchase price. Japan, for instance, limits the value of a promotional gift attached to a product to a maximum of 10 percent of the product's price. In addition, the value of free merchandise cannot exceed 50,000 yen, or about $425. Even the value of prizes awarded through lotteries is restricted to a maximum of ¥1 million for an open lottery available to everyone and to ¥50,000 for lotteries attached to the purchase of specific products. For global firms such as American Express, these limits cause difficulties. In the United States, American Express offers free trips from New York to London as prizes to qualifying customers. The company would like to offer similar promotions to its Japanese customers, but the limitation of ¥50,000 allows for only a 3-day package tour from Tokyo to Seoul.[20]

Historically, Germany has been among the most restrictive countries as far as most sales promotions are concerned. Laws enacted in the 1930s drastically restricted the use of discounts, rebates, and free offers that the Nazi government regarded as products of Marxist consumer cooperatives. Only a few years ago, a German court stopped a drugstore from giving away free shopping bags to celebrate the store's birthday. A large retailer was blocked from donating a small sum to AIDS research for each customer transaction using a Visa card. A court declared that this promotion unfairly exploited the emotions of customers.

In 2001, Germany decided to repeal its 70-year-old laws against promotions. A European directive on e-commerce necessitated this change. The directive required that the rules of the country in which the vendor was based be applied to promotions within Europe. Fewer than one in ten Germans had ever made a purchase over the Internet. Still, the German government feared that this directive would eventually put German competitors at a disadvantage by preventing them from offering promotions similar to those allowed in neighboring countries. Despite the repeal of the antipromotion laws, a broad law against unfair competition remains on the books in Germany. Some fear that certain competitors could still attempt to use it to block the promotions of others.[21]

Because global firms will encounter a series of regulations and restrictions on promotions that differ among countries, there is little opportunity to standardize sales promotion techniques across many markets. Sales promotion can also be influenced by local culture, as well as by the competitiveness of the marketplace. A study of consumer attitudes regarding sales promotions found significant differences even among Taiwan, Thailand, and Malaysia. The Taiwanese consumer preferred coupons to sweepstakes. The Malaysians and Thais both preferred sweepstakes to coupons.[22] In Europe, McDonald's discovered that children were content with a simple word puzzle on a menu tray or a small stuffed animal and did not require the more expensive Happy Meal promotions that the company used in the United States.[23] This variation among markets has caused most companies to make sales promotions the responsibility of local managers, who are expected to understand the local preferences and restrictions.

Nonetheless, a firm should make certain that there is adequate communication among its subsidiaries to ensure that the best practices and new promotion ideas are disseminated throughout the firm. Sometimes it is even critical to communicate problems associated with promotions so that they will not be repeated in other national markets. In 1992, Pepsi began an under-the-bottle-cap promotion in Chile, where a preselected number of customers were to win a significant prize. A garbled fax led to a wrong number being announced for the promotion on Chilean television. Public anger turned to vandalism against the company and severely damaged Pepsi's brand equity in Chile. Unfortunately, the lesson from the Chilean case—the need to administer award promotions very carefully—was not communicated well to Pepsi's other operations. A few months later, a promotion in the Philippines that was intended to award $37,000 to one lucky winner fell victim to a computer error that produced thousands of winners. When Pepsi refused to honor the claims of all these winners, thirty Pepsi delivery trucks were burned, and company officials were threatened. Tragically, a woman and child were killed when a grenade tossed at a Pepsi truck rolled into a nearby store.[24]

Sports Promotions and Sponsorships

Major sports events are increasingly being covered by the mass media worldwide. The commercial value of these events has soared over the last decade. Today, large sports events, such as the Olympics and world championships in specific sports, cannot exist in their present form without funding by companies.

For some events, companies can purchase space for signs along the stadiums or arenas where sports events take place. When the event is covered on television, the cameras automatically take in the signs as part of the regular coverage. Aside from purchasing advertising spots or signage space in broadcast programs, individual companies can also engage in sponsorship. Main sponsors for the Olympic Games pay a fee of $40 million to the International Olympic Committee.

To take advantage of global sports events, a company should have a logo or brand name that is worth exposing to a global audience. It is not surprising to find that the most common sponsors are companies that produce consumer goods with global appeal, such as soft-drink manufacturers, makers of consumer electronics products, and film companies. More recent global players, such as Samsung and Hyundai from Korea, often make extensive use of sports

Soccer's FIFA is increasingly alarmed by "ambushers" such as Chinese fans who showed up at the World Cup in South Korea wearing Samsung caps. Samsung was not an official sponsor of the games, but thanks to the caps, the company enjoyed free publicity from the television coverage of the games.

sponsorship abroad, especially in the emerging markets of Africa, East Europe, and Latin America.

A firm must consider the popularity of certain sports. Few sports have global appeal. Baseball and American football have little appeal in Europe or parts of Asia and Africa. However, football (soccer) is the number one spectator sport in much of the world. Nike spends an estimated 40 percent of its global sports advertising budget on soccer. The company entered into a multiyear, $429 million contract to outfit England's Manchester United football club. Nike has also sponsored the national soccer teams of six countries, including Brazil and the United States.

Through the intensive coverage of sports in the news media all over the world, many companies continue to use the sponsorship of sporting events as an important element in their global communications programs. Successful companies must exhibit both flexibility and ingenuity in the selection of available events or participants. In some parts of the world, sports sponsorship may continue to be the only available way to reach large numbers of prospective customers. However, in some cultures, global marketers must beware the backlash associated with a losing team. For example, fans called for a boycott of products such as Pepsi that were endorsed by the Indian cricket team following a humiliating loss against Australia.[25] Chinese fans are also fickle. When their teams lose, they stay at home—to the dismay of sponsors. Consequently, multinational firms in China are increasingly focusing on grass-roots programs. Pepsi sponsors teen soccer, Adidas funds soccer camps, and Nike has started a high school basketball league.[26]

WORLD BEAT 14.2

The Olympics versus the World Cup

DURING THE OLYMPIC GAMES, teams from over two hundred countries compete in almost every imaginable sport, hoping to bring home the gold, silver, or bronze medal. The Olympic Winter Games of 2006 will be held in Torino, Italy, and the 2008 Olympic Games will be held in Beijing, China. The sponsors of the 2008 Olympics include Coca-Cola, General Electric, Visa, Kodak, Swatch, Panasonic, Samsung, John Hancock, McDonald's, Schlumberger, and Lenovo.

The top sponsors of the 2004 Olympics paid an average of $75 million per four-year cycle to associate their communications with the Olympics. However, the 2004 Summer Olympics in Athens, Greece, faced a number of challenges that may have reduced the return on investment for sponsors. Construction delays, terrorism jitters, and the steroid scandal all resulted in reduced attendance of the Athens Games.

The World Cup of football (referred to as soccer in the United States) has only thirty-two qualifying teams, but in most corners of the world there is a much more emotion and viewership for the World Cup matches than for the Olympic Games. In the United States, soccer does not have the viewership of other major league sports such as baseball, American football, basketball and hockey, but the United States is not representative of the rest of the world. Football (soccer) reigns as the favorite TV sport in twenty-four of thirty-four countries surveyed in a study by British Columbia–based Ipsos-Reid Corporation. And the World Cup is a major media event around the rest of the world.

Adidas has extended its 35-year relationship with the World Cup, agreeing to sponsor the World Cup in 2010 and 2014. In a deal estimated to cost $350 million, Adidas will also sponsor all Federation Internationale of Football Association (Fifa) tournaments taking place from 2010 to 2014, including the Men's World Cup, the Women's World Cup, and the World Youth Championship—at a cost to the company of $35 million. World Cup sponsors get two on-field advertising boards in all twenty stadiums. MasterCard, which tracks its exposure, receives 10 minutes to 13 minutes of visibility per 90-minute World Cup match, which is seen by billions of spectators worldwide as well as many of the 250 million soccer players.

Anheuser-Busch paid $40 million to sponsor the 2006 World Cup. As a result, Germans became concerned that they could not buy German beer at the games. However, Anheuser-Busch agreed to allow German Brewer Bitburger to sell its beer at the twelve tournament stadiums in exchange for withdrawing a legal complaint against Anheuser-Busch: The "Bud" name could be confused with the "Bit" brand.

Sources: Normandy Madden, "GE Jump Starts Olympic Push," *Advertising Age* 76, no. 1 (January 3, 2005), p. 6; "Bud vs. Bit: World Cup Beer Battle Bottled Up," *Amusement Business* 117, no. 1 (January 2005), p. 4; "The World," *Campaign* (UK), January 28, 2005, p. 14.; Stefano Hatfield, "It's World's Beautiful Game, Except for Here in the U.S.," *Advertising Age* 73, no. 23 (June 10, 2002), p. 29; and Dana James, "World Cup Scores," *Marketing News*, February 18, 2002, pp. 1, 15, 18.

Telemarketing, Direct Mail, and Spam

Telemarketing can be used both to solicit sales and to offer enhanced customer service to current and potential customers. To make telemarketing effective, however, an efficient telephone system is required. Telephone sales for individual households may become practical when many subscribers exist and when their telephone numbers can be easily obtained. Because of the language problems involved, companies must make sure their telemarketing sales forces not only speak the language of the local customer but also do so fluently and with the correct local or regional accent.

However, not all countries accept the practice of soliciting business directly at home. A telemarketing directive in the European Union (EU) allows consumers to place their names on a telephone preference list to eliminate telemarketing calls to their homes. Any firm that continues to call potential customers can be fined.[27] Even so, telemarketing is already big business in Europe; total full-time employment in the field is estimated at 1.5 million.

Telemarketing has been intensifying elsewhere as well. In Latin America, growth has been substantial; thirty-six telemarketing firms have been reported to be active in Brazil, twenty-five in Argentina, and fifteen in Chile. Call centers have grown very rapidly in Brazil, where the market for telemarketing center software and hardware exceeds $500 million per year.[28] Still, many Brazilians can be more effectively reached by loudspeaker than by telephone. Wal-Mart successfully sent out green vans to roam modest neighborhoods in São Paulo inviting people, via loudspeaker, to apply for credit cards at the company's Todo Dia stores.[29]

On a global level, telephone sales may also be helpful for business-to-business marketing. Because costs for overseas travel are considerable, telemarketing across countries or on a global basis may prove very cost-effective. Similarly, the Internet can further decrease customer service costs by allowing firms to respond to customers' requests via e-mail.

Similar to phone campaigns, direct-mail campaigns are largely dependent on good infrastructure. However, creativity and perseverance can sometimes overcome the obstacle of a poor mail delivery system. When the Carsa Group launched its first direct-mail campaign for financial services in Peru, it faced a postal system that was essentially nonexistent. Even using private courier firms was problematic: Such firms were known to broker clients' mailing lists to their competitors. Provincial couriers delivered mail as a sideline to their main business focus, such as fertilizer sales. Nonetheless, the Carsa Group went forward with the campaign, designing its own catalogues and establishing a call center overnight to support the campaign. Response rates topped 26 percent—more than ten times what many U.S. campaigns would consider to be outstanding results. What was the reason for such a high response? In Peru, 69 percent of families received fewer than two pieces of mail monthly, so the impact of the campaign's personalized letters was amazing![30]

Spam unsolicited commercial bulk e-mail

With the advent of the Internet, many marketers saw an opportunity to reach many potential customers cheaply and efficiently via e-mail. However, their would-be targets rebelled against unsolicited commercial bulk e-mail, or **spam.** Although some emerging markets, such as those in Asia, have less strict regulations on spam, laws in developing countries discourage it—as do new technologies to block incoming spam. On October 31, 2003, an EU directive went into effect requiring its member states to implement legislation banning unsolicited commercial e-mail without consumer consent or, in some cases, without a prior business relationship. The EU rule covers e-mail, faxes, automated calling systems, and mobile messaging. National governments are allowed to determine enforcement, but consumers must be allowed to claim damages.[31] Europe now has stronger privacy laws than the United States. Still, an estimated 53 percent of all e-mail in the EU is unsolicited commercial bulk e-mail. Eighty percent is in English and claims to originate in North America.[32]

Product Placement

Marketers increasingly seek to have their products appear in television shows and motion pictures. Some even pay to have discussions of their products written into scripts that air. However, global marketers are discovering that different cultures and regulatory environments may restrict the international expansion of this practice. For example, a study has shown that Chinese consumers are less accepting of product placements than are Americans.[33] And placement faces tough regulations in the United Kingdom, a society that worries about the blurring between advertising and entertainment. A brand name can be mentioned, but only if it is "editorially justified" in the opinion of the U.K.'s Independent Television Commission, the agency that licenses and regulates commercial television. For example, when Heinz sponsored a cooking series entitled "Dinner Doctors," its name appeared only in the sponsorship credits. No Heinz product could be mentioned or shown anywhere in the content of the show.[34]

Managing Word of Mouth

When importer Piaggio USA wanted to revive stagnant sales of Vespa scooters, it hired extremely attractive young women to pose as motorbike riders and frequent trendy cafés in Los Angeles. The scooter-riding models would then strike up conversations with other patrons at the cafés. When anyone complimented their bikes, they would pull out a notepad and write down the name and phone number of the local Vespa dealer. In Canada, Procter & Gamble promoted Cheer detergent by having brightly outfitted shoppers break into impromptu fashion shows in supermarkets, mentioning to onlookers that their clothes were washed in Cheer. In both cases, the marketers were attempting to catch the attention of potential customers not only to promote a sale but also to get people talking about their product to their friends. This managed word of mouth is called **buzz marketing.**[35]

Buzz marketing managed word of mouth in which a firm attempts both to promote a sale and to encourage people to talk about the firm's product or service

Buzz can be cheap; there are no national media to buy and no costly price promotions. Instead, product recommendations appear to come from a customer's coolest friends. Still, experts suggest that buzz marketing can backfire if consumers feel it is subversive or if too many companies are trying to do it. Then buzz can become merely annoying.[36]

In an individualistic culture such as that which prevails in the United States and Canada, one's "coolest friend" can conceivably be a person one has just met. In more collectivist cultures, where people are more wary of outsiders, marketers may need to recruit members from each target in-group very carefully to play this role. An unknown actor may not do. In Kaler, a town of three hundred families in rural India, Hyundai reached out to the village headman whose advice is sought on marriage, crops, and, more recently, which TV or car to buy. Says the headman, "If I tell them I like a particular brand, they'll go out and get it."[37]

Word of mouth can also be important in business-to-business marketing, where referrals are often crucial. However, there appear to be cultural differences in how managers seek advice concerning potential purchases. A study of U.S. and Japanese corporate buyers of financial services revealed that the Japanese used referral sources—both business and personal—almost twice as often as did U.S. corporate buyers. This supported prior research that suggested that Japanese corporate buyers use a greater variety of referral sources than their American counterparts.[38]

Public Relations

A company's public relations function consists of marketing activities that enhance brand equity by promoting goodwill toward the organization. In turn, this goodwill can encourage consumers to trust a company and predispose them to buy its products. Tim Horton's is a chain of doughnut and coffee stores across Canada that has successfully fought off the world's largest doughnut chain, Dunkin Donuts Inc. After 30 years in Canada, Dunkin Donuts only holds a 6 percent share of the Canadian market. Among the things that Canadian customers like about Tim Horton's is its charity work operating camps for underprivileged children.[39]

Often international marketers find that public relations activities are necessary to defend the reputation of a brand against bad publicity. With millions of Europeans afraid of contracting mad-cow disease by eating beef, McDonald's Corporation began an unusual public relations campaign. Customers were invited to visit the McDonald's meatpacking plant in France, which supplies its 860 restaurants in that country. Touring visitors learned that ground meat was made of 100 percent muscle, not of the nerve tissue that caused the risk of disease.[40]

Public relations campaigns themselves can go wrong. Instead of neutralizing bad publicity, such campaigns can sometimes increase it. In our global society, such gaffes can be heard around the world. Philip Morris's subsidiary in the Czech Republic—in an attempt to bolster goodwill with the Czech government—commissioned a study to show that cigarettes have positive financial benefits to the state. In addition to benefiting from the taxes assessed on cigarette sales, the Philip Morris subsidiary maintained, the state saves a great deal of pension money when a citizen dies prematurely from diseases attributed to smoking. When the press heard of this study, outraged editorials appeared in newspapers around the world.

One of the best-known public relations crises arose from the promotion strategy for baby formula that Nestlé employed in developing countries in the 1970s. Thirty years later, the crisis still haunts the firm and its industry. In the 1970s, Nestlé and other producers of baby formula flooded maternity wards in less developed countries with free samples of their products. When new mothers ran out of the samples, they often discovered that their own breast milk had dried up. Few could afford the expensive formula. Some diluted it in an effort to make it last longer, and this sometimes resulted in the death of the baby. Activists organized a global boycott of Nestlé products, and UNICEF, the United Nations agency charged with protecting children, refused to accept cash contributions from the company.[41]

Major formula producers agreed to comply with a voluntary marketing code devised by UNICEF and the World Health Organization that practically forbids any distribution of free formula. But the controversy hasn't stopped there. The companies have always understood this code to apply to less developed countries only, whereas UNICEF has stated that it understands the code to apply to developed countries as well. Recently, the controversy has heated up in the shadow of the AIDS epidemic in Africa. Studies show that about 15 percent of women with HIV in Africa will transmit it to their children through breastfeeding. Nestlé claims it has received desperate pleas from African hospitals for free formula but is afraid to violate the code. Both Nestlé and Wyeth-Ayerst Laboratories Inc. have offered to donate tons of free formula to HIV-infected

United Colors of Benetton, the Italian clothing company, is one of many global firms that associate themselves with charitable causes.

women in Africa. UNICEF refuses to lend its approval because it doesn't want to appear to endorse an industry it has long accused of abusive practices.[42]

International marketers often are accused of promoting products that change consumption patterns to the detriment of local cultures. Proactive public relations campaigns can often help to offset this xenophobia. After the United States began bombing raids into Afghanistan in the fall of 2001, Muslim radicals in Indonesia bombed a Kentucky Fried Chicken store. No ill feeling was expressed at a McDonald's franchise in Indonesia that had established goodwill over the years in its surrounding Muslim community by donating food and dining facilities to Islamic institutions.[43] Many international firms become involved in charitable donations involving both money and employees' time. Others offer corporate-sponsored scholarships. Whatever the chosen venue, fostering goodwill for the corporation in local communities plays an increasing role in international promotion strategy.

CONCLUSION

Promotion in an international context is particularly challenging because managers are constantly faced with communicating to customers with different cultural backgrounds. This tends to add to the complexity of the communications task, which demands a particular sensitivity to culture, habits, manners, and ethics.

Aside from the cultural differences that affect the content and form of communications, international firms also encounter a different set of cost constraints for the principal elements of the promotion mix, such as selling and advertising. Given such diversity from country to country, international firms have to design their communications carefully to fit each individual market. Furthermore, the availability of any one element cannot be taken for granted. The absence of any one element of the promotion mix, as a consequence of either legal considerations or level of economic development, may force the international firm to compensate with a greater reliance on other promotion tools.

When designing effective sales forces, international marketers need to compare the challenges involved in international selling with those inherent in local selling. International sales efforts can usually be maintained for companies selling highly differentiated and complex products to a clearly defined target market. In most other situations, wherein products are targeted at a broader type of business or at end users, international firms will typically have to engage a local sales force for each market. Local sales forces are usually very effective in reaching their own market or country. Establishing a local sales force and managing it are challenging tasks in most foreign markets and require managers with a special sensitivity to local laws, regulations, and trade practices.

As we saw in Chapter 13 as well as in this chapter, all forms of direct and interactive marketing apply to the international market as well. Many firms have succeeded by adopting U.S.-based or U.S.-originated direct-marketing ideas and using them skillfully abroad. With the international telecommunications infrastructure developing rapidly, the applications for telemarketing as well as Internet-based interactive marketing will expand. These will undoubtedly become important elements of the communications mix for globally active firms large and small.

What aspects of promotion should you consider for your product overseas? Continue with *Country Market Report* on our website (college.hmco.com/business/).

QUESTIONS FOR DISCUSSION

1. What difficulties could arise if a U.S. salesperson expected to make a sale of industrial equipment during a 2-week visit in China?

2. Why do you think many countries restrict the promotional use of sweepstakes and other games of chance?

3. What types of companies would you suggest sponsor the next Olympic Games? How would such firms profit from their association with the Olympic Games?

4. What are the advantages and disadvantages of a virtual trade show compared with an actual one?

5. Do you support UNICEF's decision to oppose the donation of baby formula to African hospitals? Why or why not?

CASE 14.1
The South American Sales Dilemma

Shortly after his thirty-fourth birthday, Jay Bishop was promoted from director of North American sales to director of global sales at Intelicon, a worldwide provider of digital marketing services. Among the services Intelicon provided were customized e-mail campaigns, online surveys, and online customer loyalty and incentive programs. Jay moved into his new position in January. One of his first tasks was to review all global sales numbers in order to identify areas for growth and improvement. During this exercise, he noticed a number of discrepancies between the Latin American sales numbers and numbers for the rest of world. In particular, he noted that 420 sales calls in the United States had resulted in 180 actual sales, whereas in Latin America, only 40 sales had resulted from 200 such sales calls. Eager to make a good start in his new job (and under pressure from his superiors to fix the situation), Jay immediately scheduled a trip to visit offices in Brazil and Argentina in February. He was surprised, however, to receive calls from the country managers in both São Paulo and Buenos Aires telling him to put the trip off until March. Recognizing that he knew little about Latin American culture and not wanting to ignore the advice of his new subordinates early on, Jay followed their advice and rescheduled his trip for mid-March.

As often happens when one is busy, Jay's Latin American trip arrived quickly. Stepping off the plane in São Paulo after the 10-hour trip, he was exhausted but ready to work. Passing through customs and into the passenger arrival area, he looked furtively for Rivaldo Pessoa, the Brazilian country manager. Mr. Pessoa, however, was nowhere in sight and did not arrive for 30 minutes. Jay was quite frustrated, not to mention jet-lagged. Moreover, Mr. Pessoa did not seem very apologetic when he blamed his tardiness on traffic and rain.

Rather than stopping at the hotel so he could drop off his luggage, Jay insisted that they go straight to the office and start analyzing why sales were down in Brazil. He kept trying to bring the topic up on the long drive into the city, but Mr. Pessoa insisted on asking him questions about his family and pointing out landmarks in the city, this being Jay's first visit to Brazil. "Why does this guy want to know my life story? Doesn't he know his job is at stake?" thought Jay. Eventually resigning himself to the fact that nothing would get done until they got to the office, Jay tried to sit back and enjoy the ride.

When they arrived at the office, Mr. Pessoa ushered Jay into the small conference room and then left for 10 minutes before returning with coffee and his two salespeople, Renata Pinheiro and Joao Prestes. Both spoke English well and seemed eager to make a good impression. Jay felt that neither had any idea why he was in Brazil, other than that it might be a goodwill tour. He wanted to get to the point, so he came out and said, "The reason I'm here is that we are not meeting our sales numbers for Latin America, and we need to change that." Mr. Pessoa looked a bit surprised, as did Renata and Joao. Jay pressed on, "I need to run through a few analytical questions to determine the root causes of the challenges in the Brazilian market so that we can fix them and take some of the pressure off of you guys." All three seemed to relax at that.

"Okay, let's begin," said Jay. "First, I want to learn more about your backgrounds, what brought you to Intelicon." Mr. Pessoa began: "Well, before I joined Intelicom 3 years ago, I worked over 20 years in the banking sector, most recently in investment banking at BNP Paribas. I helped take a number of Brazilian companies public and worked on numerous bond issues." Impressed, Jay turned to Joao, who said, "I started in professional services at IBM and worked there for 6 years. As the Internet took off, I wanted to get involved in a smaller, more Web-based business, which is when I came to Intelicon." Renata finished: "I graduated from the Fundacao Getulio Vargas a year ago," she said, "and took a degree in marketing. My parents pressed me to go into the family business, but I wanted to make a name for myself and felt that consultative sales would be a great place to start. My parents, however, were shocked that I wanted to sell things rather than doing something they considered more respectable, like marketing or finance. I'm out to prove myself."

Needless to say, Jay was very impressed with his new staff and was even more confused about why they were having so much trouble selling Intelicon's services. He decided to move on to more probing questions. Looking to Mr. Pessoa, he asked, "How do you get your sales prospects? Do you cold-call? Is that successful?" Mr. Pessoa looked a bit perplexed. "I suppose," he said, "that we could probably cold-call more. Mostly we rely on personal contacts within the different organizations." Jay was puzzled. He had heard that this was a common practice in Latin America, but felt that it could be contributing to the long sales cycles that were causing the closing rates in Latin America to be so much lower than in the rest of the world.

Jay believed he was starting to fill in the picture. However, to understand thoroughly the challenges he was facing in Latin America, he knew he would have to attend some sales calls. Mr. Pessoa mentioned that he had two meetings scheduled later in the afternoon, one with Abril, a large media conglomerate in São Paulo, and the other with CVRD, a powerful mining concern. Jay said he would like to attend, and although Pessoa looked wary for an instant, he readily agreed.

The meeting with Abril started well. Mr. Pessoa clearly had a lot of experience presenting to an audience, and he seemed to know two of the four executives in the room as they caught up on family and friends for the first few minutes of the meeting. At the end of the presentation, Mr. Pessoa and Jay asked a number of probing questions and generally felt the meeting was going well. However, the executives kept raising objections. Eventually Mr. Pessoa folded, thanking them for their time and leaving. Once again, Jay was puzzled. He made a point of mentioning to Mr. Pessoa that sometimes getting a "no" was part of sales and that to be successful he needed to find ways to turn a "no" into a "yes." Mr. Pessoa looked a bit embarrassed but said that he did need to do more of this.

The traffic on the way to the meeting with CVRD was horrible, and much to Jay's chagrin, they arrived nearly an hour late. This did not seem to be a problem, however, because the vice president they were slated to meet was also running late. Once again, Pessoa did an excellent job in the presentation of products and services, and there was clear interest on the part of the vice president. Jay thought for sure they would close him on the spot and was getting that tingly feeling. Both sides went through the motions, discussing timelines and pricing structures, but just when Jay was ready to go in for the kill, Pessoa thanked the gentleman for his time, said he would send him a proposal, and scheduled lunch together the following week. Jay did not know what to say. He guessed that the sale would eventually happen, but he also knew he needed to get revenue as soon as possible.

Exhausted, Jay headed back to his hotel and fell fast asleep. He had learned a lot in one day but realized that he still had a long way to go if he wanted to succeed. Tomorrow, he would fly to Argentina and do it all over again.

Discussion Questions

1. What might explain the lower ratio of sales to sales calls in Latin America compared with the United States?
2. In what ways might cultural differences explain differences in personal selling between Brazil and the United States?
3. What advice would you give Jay?

Source: Case prepared by Michael Magers. Used by permission.

CASE 14.2
Flying to Armenia

British Airways (BA) is the world's biggest international airline, flying passengers to 535 destinations in 160 countries. One such destination is the Republic of Armenia, a small country at the crossroads of Europe and Asia. The whole territory of Armenia is only 11,506 square miles with a population of three million. However, an additional seven million ethnic Armenians live outside Armenia. This Armenian diaspora remains intimately tied to its homeland across generations. Armenian communities around the world attend Armenian churches, teach their children the Armenian language, and celebrate Armenian national and cultural days with great passion. Many Armenians live in various countries of the Middle East and Europe, and one of the largest Armenian communities resides in the United States.

Recently, Armenia has been undergoing a rapid but difficult transition from a Soviet, centrally planned economy to a democratic society with a market economy. The 1990s were particularly difficult for the country. Armenia shared all the economic problems that resulted from the breakup of established economic relations among what had been the Soviet republics. In addition, it faced an electricity crisis combined with a military territorial conflict with neighboring Azerbaijan. These problems led to a marked lowering of the standard of living of the population in the country and to overall economic difficulties.

However, with foreign aid from the International Monetary Fund (IMF), the World Bank, the EU, and the U.S. government, as well as substantial assistance from the diaspora, the economy began to stabilize. By the end of the decade, a legal and regulatory framework for the private sector was being created, and an increasing number of multinational corporations, including Coca-Cola, Adidas, Samsung Electronics, Mercedes-Benz, and Kodak, had established a presence in the country.

Armenia had attracted several international airlines that competed alongside its national carrier, Armenian Airlines. These carriers included BA, Swiss Air, Austrian Air, Russian Aeroflot, and Syrian Air. Although traveling was not something many Armenians could afford, it remained the only viable way to travel in and out of the country. Armenia was landlocked, and traveling through neighboring countries was not practical because of poor transportation infrastructure and intermittent political tensions. Most air travelers were employees of international aid organizations operating in Armenia, business travelers, or diaspora Armenians visiting their homeland.

British Airways first entered the Armenian market with twice-weekly service from London to Yerevan, the capital of Armenia. Along with Swiss Air and Austrian Air, BA charged higher prices than Armenian Airlines, Aeroflot, or Syrian Air.

BA embarked on several successful promotions to attract customers, to establish brand recognition in the market, and to enhance its international reputation as a caring company. To mark the second anniversary of its instituting flights between London and Yerevan, BA put together a program of events designed to support cultural and humanitarian programs in Armenia. For example, it supported the Third International Chamber Music Festival, which took place in Yerevan, by bringing two leading Armenian musicians—cellist Alexander Chaoshian and pianist Seda Danyel—from London to Yerevan to participate in the event.

The company also announced a special discount rate to about a dozen destinations, substantially increasing the number of tickets sold. During this campaign, BA contributed $10 from the price of each economy-class ticket and $50 from the price of each business-class ticket to one of Armenia's largest orphanages. (For comparison, per-capita spending for a child in such institutions was around $700 per year.) A special ceremony was held to bestow the funds on the orphanage. For that ceremony, the BA hot-air balloon, a familiar ambassador around the world, was brought to Armenia for the first time. The balloon was set to spend a day in Opera Square, the foremost center for cultural activities in Yerevan. Prior to that, BA ran a competition in which questions about BA were posed in the local media. People who phoned in with the right answers could meet the crew of the balloon and go for a short ride. This event was widely covered in the Armenian press and on the television news.

British Airways also introduced the Executive Club, BA's frequent-flyer program, to the Armenian market. As with other frequent-flyer programs, members of the Executive Club could earn free flight miles by traveling via BA as well as using certain hotels and car rentals. Club membership also offered a variety of other benefits, such as priority on flight waiting lists and a special agent to handle inquiries. British Airways ran a special promotion of the Executive Club at the elite Wheel Club, a favorite dining place of expatriates working in Armenia, especially English speakers. Any member of the Executive Club who ate at the Wheel received an entry into a prize drawing. Anyone who was not a member of the Executive Club could join at the Wheel. The top prize was a pair of tickets to any destination.

British Airways also ran a "Where in the World?" competition. People were invited to write in and say where in the world they dreamed of spending Valentine's Day with the person they loved and why they wanted to go there. The three most creative, funny, or touching entries won a pair of tickets to the dream destination. The event was announced on Hay FM, one of Armenia's most popular radio channels among young people. The event enjoyed a high response rate and engendered considerable word of mouth among Hay FM listeners, as well as publicity in the local press.

Discussion Questions

1. For each of the five promotions discussed in the case, identify the target market, explain the motivation behind the promotion, and suggest ways in which to measure the success of the promotion.
2. Why do you think each of these promotions worked well in the Armenian market?
3. Would these promotions be as successful in your country? Why or why not?

Source: Case prepared by Anna V. Andriasova. Used by permission.

NOTES

1. J. Lynn Lunsford, Daniel Michaels, and Andy Pasztor, "At the Paris Air Show, Boeing–Airbus Duel Has New Twist," *Wall Street Journal*, June 15, 2001, p. B4.
2. Paul Romani, "Selling in the Global Community: The Japanese Model," *American Salesman* (October 1998), pp. 21–25.
3. "Sealed Air Taiwan (A)." Harvard Business School, Case No. 9-399-058.
4. Michael Ewing, Albert Caruana, and Henry Wong, "Some Consequences of Guanxi: A Sino-Singaporian Perspective," *Journal of International Consumer Marketing* 12, no. 4 (2000), pp. 75–89.
5. "Culture of Commerce: US Executives, Foreigners Learn to Negotiate a Two-Way Street," *Atlanta Journal-Constitution*, April 3, 2002, p. E1.
6. William Briggs, "Next for Communicators: Global Negotiation," *Communication World*, December 1, 1998, pp. 1–3.
7. "Salesmen Need to Make More Calls Than Competitors to Be Accepted," *Japan Economic Journal*, June 26, 1979, p. 30.
8. Jonathan Friedland, "Sweet Solution," *Wall Street Journal*, March 2, 1999, p. A1.
9. Jean-Pierre Jeannet, "Siemens Automotive Systems: Brazil Strategy" (Lausanne: IMD Institute, European Case Clearinghouse).
10. Jean-Pierre Jeannet and Robert Collins, "Deloitte Touche Tohmatsu International Europe" (Lausanne: IMD Institute, European Case Clearinghouse).
11. H. David Hennessey, "Discovering the Hidden Value in Global Account Management," unpublished working paper, Babson College, 2004.
12. Except where otherwise noted, ideas from this section are taken from H. David Hennessey, "Discovering the Hidden Value in Global Account Management," and H. David Hennessey and Jean-Pierre Jeannet, *Global Account Management* (Chichester, United Kingdom: John Wiley & Sons, 2003).
13. David Arnold, Julian Birkinshaw, and Omar Toulan, "Can Selling Be Globalized?: The Pitfalls of Global Account Management," *California Management Review* 44, 1 (Fall 2001), pp. 8–20.
14. Roger Daniels, "MT Survey of Surveys: Trade Fairs," *Management Today* February 7, 2005, p. 62.
15. Jim Carlton, "Comdex Loses Appeal to Industry Players," *Wall Street Journal*, November 16, 1998. p. B6.
16. Iris Kapustein, "Selling and Exhibiting Across the Globe," *Doors and Hardware*, September 1, 1998, p. 34.
17. PR Newswire, "WholesaleTradeshow.com Launches First Online Tradeshow for Wholesale and Offprice Merchandise," March 14, 2000.
18. Peter Fritsch, "Hard Profits," *Wall Street Journal*, April 22, 2002, p. A1.
19. R. Bruce Money and Deborah Colton, "The Response of the 'New Consumer' to Promotion in the Transition Economies of the Former Soviet Bloc," *Journal of World Business* 35, no. 2 (2000), pp. 189–205.
20. "U.S. Urges Easing of Product-Promotion Rules," *Nikkei Weekly*, November 6, 1995, p. 3.
21. David Wessel, "Capital: German Shoppers Get Coupons," *Wall Street Journal*, April 5, 2001, p. A1.
22. Lenard C. Huff and Dana L. Alden, "An Investigation of Consumer Response to Sales Promotion in Developing Markets," *Journal of Advertising Research* 38 (May/June 1998), pp. 47–57.
23. Lisa Bertagnoli, "Continental Spendthrifts," *Marketing News*, October 22, 2001, p. 15.

24. David A. Griffith and John K. Ryans, Jr., "Organizing Global Communications to Minimize Private Spill-over Damage to Brand Equity," *Journal of World Business* 32, no. 3 (1997), pp. 189–202.

25. Arundhati Parmar, "Jiminy, Cricket!" *Marketing News*, March 17, 2003, pp. 4–5.

26. Frederik Balfour, "It's Time for a New Playbook," *Business Week*, September 15, 2003, p. 56.

27. Melinda Ligos, "Direct Sales Dies in China," *Sales and Marketing Management*, August 1, 1998, p. 14.

28. "Brazil: Boom in the Call Centers Market," *Gazeta Mercantil*, May 31, 1999, p. 1.

29. Miriam Jordan, "Wal-Mart Gets Aggressive About Brazil," *Wall Street Journal*, May 25, 2001, p. A8.

30. William A. Kotas, "Starting From Scratch," *Marketing News*, September 30, 2002, p. 16.

31. Catherine Arnold, "The Spam Update," *Marketing News*, December 8, 2003, p. 9.

32. Brandon Mitchener, "Europe Blames Weaker U.S. Law for Spam Surge," *Wall Street Journal*, February 3, 2004, p. B1.

33. Sally A. McKechnie and Jia Zhou, "Product Placement in Movies: A Comparison of Chinese and American Consumer Attitudes," *International Journal of Advertising* 22 (2003), pp. 349–374.

34. Erin White, "U.K. TV Can Pose Tricky Hurdles," *Wall Street Journal*, June 27, 2003, p. B7.

35. Gerry Khermouch and Jeff Green, "Buzz Marketing," *Business Week*, July 30, 2001, pp. 50–56.

36. Ibid.

37. Cris Prystay, "Companies Market to India's Have-Littles," *Wall Street Journal*, June 5, 2003, p. B1.

38. R. Bruce Money, "Word-of-Mouth Referral Sources for Buyers of International Corporate Financial Services," *Journal of World Business* 35, no. 3 (Fall 2000), pp. 314–329.

39. Joel Baglole, "War of the Doughnuts," *Wall Street Journal*, August 23, 2001, p. B1.

40. John Carreyrou and Geoff Winestock, "In France, McDonald's Takes Mad-Cow Fears by the Horns," *Wall Street Journal*, April 5, 2001, p. A17.

41. Alix M. Freedman and Steve Stocklow, "Bottled Up," *Wall Street Journal*, December 5, 2000, p. A1.

42. Ibid.

43. Jay Solomon, "How Mr. Bambang Markets Big Macs in Muslim Indonesia," *Wall Street Journal*, October 26, 2001, p. A1.

15 MANAGING GLOBAL ADVERTISING

SHORTLY AFTER THE EXXON MOBIL MERGER, the new company, based in Irving, Texas, announced plans to promote its four key brands—Exxon, Mobil, Esso, and General—with a global television advertising campaign.[1]

Global campaigns were not new to the company. Exxon's 1965 Esso tiger campaign, "Put a tiger in your tank," was launched in the United States, Europe, and the Far East.[2] However, the new campaign was aimed at a hundred countries at a cost of $150 million. Five hours of film footage were developed centrally to be accessed by the company's various national subsidiaries. Up to six different casts stood by

to act out essentially the same story line—with a few variations. The same scene could be shot with a Japanese man, a sub-Saharan African, a Northern European, or a Southern European. Actors varied the hand they used in a scene depicting eating. (In some cultures, food is customarily eaten only with the right hand.) A voice-over told the same story in twenty-five different languages. Centralized production saved considerable production costs for ExxonMobil and helped ensure that television spots would be consistent and of similar quality around the world. It also meant substantial business for the agency—in this case, Omnicon

After studying this chapter, you should be able to

▶ List both the advantages and the special requirements of standardized campaigns.

▶ Define the global theme approach to advertising, and explain how it differs from a totally standardized campaign.

▶ Explain the market and cultural limitations on the advertising message and on its execution.

▶ Identify key issues related to advertising that tend to be regulated by national governments.

▶ Cite ways to avoid faulty translations and ways to minimize the need to translate.

▶ Explain how media availability, media habits, and scheduling international advertising all affect the advertising campaign.

▶ Differentiate among the three options of utilizing domestic advertising agencies, using local advertising agencies, and using international advertising networks.

▶ List the external and internal factors that influence a firm's decision whether to centralize or localize its advertising efforts.

Group's DDB Worldwide—that landed the job. Not everyone agreed that centralization of advertising was a good idea. The CEO of a rival agency, Bcom3 Group's Leo Burnett Worldwide, noted that brands at different stages around the world require different messages and advertising campaigns.[3]

International marketers face an important question: Should advertising campaigns be local or global? The first part of this chapter is organized around key factors that impact this decision. The chapter continues with a discussion of the major issues relating to media choices and campaign implementation.

GLOBAL VERSUS LOCAL ADVERTISING

Standardizing advertising across all markets has received a considerable amount of attention and is considered the most controversial topic in international advertising. Table 15.1 lists a number of global accounts and the advertising agencies that handle them. One of the best—and earliest—examples of a successful standardized campaign was Philip Morris's Marlboro campaign in Europe. Marlboro's success as a leading brand began in the 1950s when the brand was repositioned to ensure smokers that the flavor would be unchanged

TABLE 15.1 SELECTED GLOBAL ACCOUNTS

ACCOUNT	AGENCY
American Express	Ogilvy & Mather
Australian Tourist Commission	Grey Worldwide/Grey Global
Colgate-Palmolive	Young & Rubicam
Eastman Kodak	Ogilvy & Mather
Federal Express	DDB/Omnicom
General Motors	McCann Erickson Worldwide
Gillette	BBDO Worldwide/Omnicom
GlaxcoSmith Kline	EuroRSCG Worldwide/Havas
IBM	Ogilvy & Mather
Kao	Scholz & Friends
Lego	Saatchi & Saatchi/Publicis
L'Oreal (Lancôme, Labs, Garnier)	Publicis
MasterCard International	McCann Erickson Worldwide
Mattel (Barbie)	Ogilvy & Mather
Nautilus	Foote, Cone, & Belding/Interpublic
Novartis	EuroRSCG Worldwide/Havas
Olympus	Springer & Jacoby/Interpublic
Procter & Gamble	Grey Worldwide
Samsung Electronics	J. Walter Thompson & Red Cell/WPP
Sanofi-Aventis	EuroRSCG Worldwide/Havas
Siemens	TBWA Worldwide/Omnicom
Siemens Mobile	McCann Erickson Worldwide/Interpublic
Singapore Airlines	TBWA Worldwide/Omnicom
SingTel	Young & Rubicam/WPP
Smirnoff Ice	Bartle Bogle Hegarty/Publicis
Tourism Ireland	J. Walter Thompson & Red Cell/WPP
Unilever	Bartle Bogle Hegarty/Publicis
Whirlpool	Publicis
Zurich Financial	Publicis

SOURCE: Data collected from "Global/Pan-Regional Account Wins by Creative Agencies," *Advertising Age,* January 1, 2005, p. 12 and "Global Marketing," *Advertising Age,* November 8, 2005, pp. 17–27.

by the effect of the filter. The theme "Come to where the flavor is. Come to Marlboro country" became an immediate success in the United States and abroad. Similarly, Patek Philippe, maker of prestige watches, supported its brand with a standardized television campaign utilizing the theme "You never actually own a Patek Philippe. You merely look after it for the next generation." The campaign has been successful in the United States, Europe, China, Japan, Singapore, and Taiwan.[4]

Standardized campaigns have increased over the years. Most studies of international advertising standardization in the 1970s and 1980s concluded that very little standardization was being used. However, a study of thirty-eight multinationals in the 1990s noted that about half of these companies employed extensive or total standardization when developing and executing their global advertising. Only a quarter stated that standardization was very limited or non-existent.[5] Still, many marketing executives remain skeptical of the value of global advertising campaigns. A study of European consumers revealed a strong preference for local advertisements, even when consumers preferred global products. In many cases, the most memorable ads proved to be those promoting local brands.[6]

DEVELOPING GLOBAL CAMPAIGNS

Of course, firms do not need to choose solely between totally standardized worldwide campaigns and totally localized ones. Similar to developing global products, many firms adopt a modularized approach to global advertising: A company may select some featues as standard for all its advertisements while localizing others features. Most common is the **global theme approach**, wherein the same advertising theme is used around the world but is varied slightly with each local execution. Coke's global campaign featuring "Coke Moments" was developed and shot in a number of the brand's top markets, including Brazil, Germany, Italy, France, and South Africa as well as the United States. In "Spanish Wedding," a demure young woman enjoys a Coke while dressing for the big day.[7] Furthermore, if a global campaign is not appropriate, a regional one might be.

Global theme approach the use of an advertising campaign in which a single advertising theme is utilized in all markets but is varied slightly with each local execution

When developing global (or regional) campaigns, a company should follow procedures that are similar to those utilized in developing global products. In other words, local adaptation should not be an afterthought. Input should be sought early from markets where the campaign will ultimately air and should be incorporated into the design of the campaign. This ensures that a message will indeed be appropriate for each market and that the media necessary for the campaign will be available. It also identifies what adaptations need to be made and usually shortens the time of making such adaptations.

For example, standardized campaigns launched by automaker Fiat were originally developed in Italy and adapted with minor changes (such as translation) by local agencies in different national markets. Subsequently the company allied with Publicis Groupe to establish a Fiat-specific advertising agency for all of Europe that would create pan-European campaigns. A key mandate for the new agency was to seek input early in the development of campaigns to determine if a marketing message could use a single campaign across Europe or whether it required different campaigns for different markets.[8]

Two advertisements—one in English and the other in Spanish—promote Armstrong flooring and point potential buyers to the company's website. Different decors reflect the different cultures.

THE GLOBAL-LOCAL DECISION

A number of cost, market, and regulatory factors influence the extent to which advertising can be standardized.

Cost Savings

One advantage of a more standardized approach to advertising involves the economics of a global campaign. To develop individual campaigns in many countries is to incur duplicate costs, such as those for photographs, layouts, and the production of television commercials. In a standardized approach, these production costs can be reduced, and more funds can be spent on purchasing media space. For example, Unilever paid $700,000 for one series of TV commercials to be used in eighteen Asian and European countries. By reusing its commercials in many countries, the company saved on production costs. Furthermore, the company was able to spend more on the original version and therefore produce a better advertisement.[9]

Branding

In Chapter 11 we discussed the increased interest in global branding by multinational firms. Many companies market products under a single brand name globally or regionally. With the substantial amount of international travel occurring today and the considerable overlap in media across national borders, companies are increasingly interested in creating a single brand image. This image can become confused if local campaigns are in conflict with each other. The following list shows some examples of companies' efforts to create a single brand image:

▶ H.J. Heinz developed a global campaign for Heinz ketchup to develop consistency in the brand image and advertising across its various national markets.[10]

▶ Jaguar found that its new S-type model appealed to similar customers around the world, so it launched the same campaign from "Chicago to Riyadh, Tokyo and Berlin." This allowed Jaguar to enjoy a consistent image worldwide and save money by not having to develop a different theme for each market.[11]

▶ Disney embarked on its first global advertising campaign for its theme parks. Previously, the company advertised each park regionally, Now, Disney wants to address travelers worldwide and pull them into any Disney theme park anywhere.[12]

Target Market

Global campaigns may be more successful if the target market is relatively narrowly defined. For example, Procter & Gamble doubled the sales of Pringles potato chips in 4 years to $1 billion. Now one of P&G's top three global brands, Pringles is sold in over forty countries. P&G attributes the global success of Pringles to a uniform advertising message aimed at young children and teens. The message used around the world is "Once you pop you can't stop." Although P&G allows some local differences in product market-to-market, such as flavor variations, the bulk of the advertising is standardized.[13]

Market Conditions

While cost savings, global branding, and focused target markets argue for more standardized advertising, varying market conditions may limit the utility of standardization.

Stage in Life Cycle. Because products may be at different stages of their product life cycles in different countries, different types of advertising may be necessary to take into account various levels of customer awareness. Typically, a campaign during the earlier stages of the product life cycle concentrates on familiarizing people with the product category, because many prospective customers may not have heard about it. In later stages, with more intensive competition, campaigns tend to shift toward emphasizing the product's advantages over competitors' products. Sometimes Frito-Lay's products are so unfamiliar in certain overseas

WORLD BEAT 15.1

China's New Women Consumers

AS CONSUMER-GOODS COMPANIES ENTER CHINA, the image of the typical Chinese woman may need updating. Linda Kovarik, associate director for strategic planning at Leo Burnett, noticed that most female office workers had nicely framed pictures on their desks, not of their family or husband, but of themselves. This focus on themselves reflects the rise in women's standard of living and personal development. Chinese women are earning more money and moving into more managerial positions, and consumer marketers—and advertisers—must be alert to their needs. For example, sales of cosmetics in China have increased from $24 million in 1982 to an estimated $21 billion in 2005, and many multinational firms have entered the market. Procter & Gamble ran an ad for Rejoice shampoo that featured an airline hostess. But the ad was later pulled and replaced with a woman working as an aircraft mechanical engineer.

It is not just female office workers and managers who want a better life. In December 2004, 12,000 woman workers in the Uniden Wal-Mart factory, which makes cell phones, went on strike for better pay, shorter workdays, and rules to protect workers with seniority.

Sources: Susan Jakes, "From Mao to Maybelline," *Time* (Notebook Section), Spring 2005, p. 22. Carol Anne Douglas et al., "China Woman Wal-Mart Workers Demand Union," *Off Our Backs* 35, no. 1 (January 2005), p. 6; Cris Prystay, "As China's Women Change, Marketers Notice," *Wall Street Journal*, May 30, 2002, p. A11.

---

markets that advertising campaigns focus on educating consumers with the goal of changing their consumption habits. For example, Chinese ads show potatoes actually being sliced so people know where potato chips come from. In Turkey, Frito-Lay distributed pamphlets suggesting new recipes and eating habits: "Try a tuna sandwich for lunch, and join it with a bag of chips."[14]

Perception of Product. Products may also face unique challenges in certain markets requiring nationally tailored advertising campaigns. For example, Skoda automobiles are sold throughout Europe and in parts of Asia and Latin America. But in Britain they acquired a deplorable reputation. In a consumer survey, 60 percent of respondents said they would never consider buying a Skoda—even after Volkswagen AG bought the Czech car company and vastly improved the models. The solution was an ad campaign exploiting British humor and Skoda's position as the butt of many jokes. Each self-deprecating advertisement ended with "It's a Skoda. Honest." This very successful campaign improved the acceptance of the car in the British market.[15]

Regulatory Environment

In many instances, the particular regulations of a country prevent firms from using standardized approaches to advertising even when these would appear desirable. Malaysia, a country with a large Muslim population, has prohibited ads showing women in sleeveless dresses and pictures showing underarms.[16] Malaysia also bans all profanity from television broadcasts. Television shows are subject to review by the country's Censorship Board. Events that are broadcast live, such as the World Cup, are aired with a few minutes delay in order to accommodate the censor.[17] In some European countries, candy advertisements must show a toothbrush symbol.

In China, advertising is subjected to substantial scrutiny and regulation. All outdoor advertisements have to be approved by multiple government organizations.[18] Superlative adjectives, such as "best quality" and "finest ingredients" are banned. Television advertisements for "offensive products" such as hemorrhoid medications and athlete's-foot ointments cannot be aired during the three daily meal times.[19] Children portrayed in commercials are required to show respect for their elders, and children's advertisement should not attempt to instill a sense of superiority for owning a certain product.

Certain industries face more regulation than others. Differing national rules govern the advertising of pharmaceuticals, alcohol, tobacco, and financial services. Advertising for cigarettes and tobacco products is strictly regulated in many countries. The European Union (EU) banned all advertising of tobacco on billboards and in print advertising. One of the few areas where cigarette and tobacco advertising is still relatively restriction free is Central Asia and the Caucasus, formerly part of the Soviet Union. Most of these countries permit cigarette advertising on radio and television, although some relegate it to late-night slots. Such freedoms, however, are rare, and global marketers are well advised to check the local regulations carefully before launching any type of advertising campaign.[20] A stunt pilot was arrested in Lithuania for illegally advertising cigarettes during his maneuvers. The national parliament had just recently banned tobacco ads.[21]

The EU is debating a series of rulings that could have great impact on advertising in Europe. The discussions involve efforts toward greater consistency of regulations. Such consistency is generally viewed as desirable throughout Europe and might eventually result in uniform regulations for advertising. This would greatly enhance the potential for pan-European marketing campaigns and make global advertising more efficient. However, many expect that more consistent advertising regulations will result in more restrictive regulations concerning pharmaceuticals, food, and advertising to children.

Cultural Differences

Cultural differences can also restrict the use of standardized advertising. Taco Bell, a U.S.-based chain with 7,000 restaurants, found that Gidget the talking Chihuahua dog used in advertisements in the United States could not be used in Asia, where many consider dogs a food delicacy, or in Muslim countries, where many consider it taboo to even touch a dog.[22] Cultural differences also stymie Western advertisers in Eastern Europe. One Western food company wanted to introduce bouillon cubes to Romania via ads featuring a happy family gathered around the dinner table. The campaign had to be changed because Romanian consumers were not familiar with the family dinner concept.[23]

Even if nudity in advertising is not prohibited by law, it can be controversial in many cultures. Sara Lee, the U.S.-based firm that owns such lingerie brands as Playtex, Cacharel, and Wonderbra, faced intense opposition to a series of billboards in Mexico. The company launched its global Wonderbra campaign, which, as part of its outdoor advertising, featured a Czech model posing in the bra. In several Mexican cities, citizens protested the ads as offensive. The company redesigned its billboards for Mexico, clothing the model in a suit.[24]

Land of the Soft Sell: Advertising in the Japanese Market. Japan is the world's second-largest advertising market, after the United States.[25] Many Western firms face special challenges when developing advertising themes for this important market. The dominant style of advertising in Japan is an image-oriented approach, or "soft sell." This contrasts sharply with the more factual approach, or "hard sell," typical in the United States and with the use of humor prevalent in the United Kingdom.

Because different cultural backgrounds yield varying consumer attitudes, it is quite reasonable to expect differences in advertising appeals. In Japan, consumers tend to be moved more by emotion than by logic, in contrast to North Americans or Europeans, and Japanese advertisements often have a strong non-verbal content. Consequently, consumers need to be emotionally convinced about a product. This leads to advertising that rarely mentions price, shies away from comparative advertising aimed at discrediting the products of competing firms, and occasionally even omits the distinctive features or qualities of a product. According to some experts, Western advertising is designed to make the product look superior, whereas Japanese advertising is designed to make it look desirable. The Japanese language even has a verb (*kawasarern*) to describe the process of being convinced to buy a product contrary to one's own rational judgment.

Nonetheless, the Japanese are interested in foreign countries and words, particularly those of the English language. Research conducted for the Nikkei Advertising Research Institute in Japan compared the number of foreign words appearing in advertising headlines. Japan, with 39.2 percent, used the highest number of foreign words, followed by Taiwan with 32.1 percent, Korea with 15.7 percent, and France with 9.1 percent. The United States used foreign words in only 1.8 percent of the headlines investigated.[26]

Japanese television commercials are full of U.S. themes. They frequently incorporate U.S. landscapes or backgrounds and often employ U.S. celebrities. Stars such as Meg Ryan, Brad Pitt, and Demi Moore can be seen in commercials featuring cosmetics, clothing, or drinks.[27] By using American actors in their commercials, Japanese companies give the impression that these products are very popular in the United States. Thanks to the Japanese interest in and positive attitudes toward many U.S. cultural themes, such strategies have worked out well for Japanese advertisers.

Credibility of Advertising. English secondary schools teach students how to be "responsible consumers." Among other things, the required curriculum encourages students to criticize corporate advertising.[28]

In addition to other cultural differences among markets, there are national differences as to the credibility of advertising. A comparative survey conducted by a marketing research company investigated advertising credibility in forty countries.[29] In the United States, 86 percent of consumers were eager to criticize advertising practices, particularly those aimed at children, whereas 75 percent of consumers praised advertising's creativity. In Asia, consumers were more positive. Forty-seven percent indicated that advertisements provided good product information, and 40 percent said that advertisers respected consumers' intelligence. Globally, the results were 38 percent and 30 percent, respectively. Consumers in the former Soviet Union were among the most skeptical. Only 9 percent of consumers there believed that advertising provided good information, and only 10 percent said it respected consumers' intelligence. Globally, 61 percent of consumers appreciated advertising for both its creativity and its entertainment value, but only 23 percent of consumers living in the former Soviet Union agreed.

Differences in the credibility of advertising in general, and in that of some media in particular, must be taken into consideration by the international firm. Companies may want to place greater reliance on advertising in countries where its credibility is very high. In other countries, the marketer should think seriously about using alternative forms of communication.

Addressing Cultural Differences. Global firms can take a proactive approach to cultural differences when employing the global theme approach. In a major rebranding campaign for the Mars candy bar, outdoor billboards ran phrases aimed to trigger feelings of pleasure in local audiences. In Britain, the slogan ran "Saturday 3 p.m.," referring to the much-anticipated soccer kickoff time. In France, the word *August* evoked the month when the whole country traditionally goes on vacation. In Germany, the words *the last parking space* were chosen for their particular national appeal.[30]

To ensure that a message is in line with the existing cultural beliefs of the target market, companies can turn to a variety of resources. Local subsidiary personnel or local distributors can judge the cultural content and acceptability of the message. Advertising agencies with local offices can be helpful as well. Whether considering a local or a global approach, it is the responsibility of the international marketer to make sure that knowledgeable local nationals have enough input so that the mistake of using an inappropriate appeal in any given market can be avoided.

OVERCOMING LANGUAGE BARRIERS

Even when employing global campaigns, the proper translation of advertisements remains a major cultural challenge to global marketers. Even among English-speaking peoples, common words can vary, as Table 15.2 illustrates. Most translation blunders that plagued global advertising in the past were the result of literal translations performed outside the target country. Today, faulty translations can be avoided by enlisting local nationals or language experts. Global marketers typically have translations checked by a local advertising agency, by their own local subsidiary, or by an independent distributor located in the target country.

These same rules apply when translations are needed within a single country or regional market to reach consumers who speak different languages. When the California Milk Processor Board decided to translate its popular "Got milk?" campaign into Spanish, an adwoman who had moved to Los Angeles from Caracas, Venezuela, warned the board members that the slogan took on the meaning "Are you lactating?" in Spanish. The board wisely decided to adapt the campaign to ask, "And you, have you given them milk today?"[31]

TABLE 15.2 ENGLISH VERSUS ENGLISH	
AMERICAN DIALECT	BRITISH DIALECT
Apartment	Flat
Appetizer	Starter
Attic	Loft
Baby carriage	Pram
Car trunk	Boot
College	University
Commercial	Advert
Cookie	Biscuit
Doctor's office	Surgery
Make a decision	Take a decision
Pantyhose	Tights
Paper towel	Kitchen towel
To rent	To let
Realtor	Estate agent
Stove	Cooker
Sweater	Jumper
Washcloth	Flannel
Yard	Garden

In the EU, nine official languages are spoken. As a result, many advertisers emphasize visual communication rather than attempting to communicate their message through the various languages. Visual ads that incorporate pictures rather than words can be more universally understood. Visuals have the advantage of being less culture-specific. For example, Cartier, the French luxury-products firm, launched a campaign in 123 countries The campaign used magazines only and featured minimal copy (words). It emphasized dramatic photography so that the same message could be conveyed in Brazil, Japan, Russia, and dozens of other countries.

Still, some managers of global brands are rethinking the power of local language. The Welsh Language Board encourages the use of the traditional language of Wales in advertisements. Although in decline through most of the twentieth century, Welsh is enjoying a renaissance. Today it is spoken by half a million people in Britain. Coke recently agreed to use Welsh in bilingual posters. [32]

GLOBAL MEDIA STRATEGY

Global marketers today account for major purchases of media space. Table 15.3 lists the top global marketers in media spending. A variety of media are available across the world. Difficulties arise because not all media are available in all countries. And if they are available, their technical capability to deliver a

TABLE 15.3 Top Global Marketers

Rank 2003	Rank 2002	Company	Home Country	Industry Type	Annual Expenditures Worldwide (in $million)
1	1	Procter & Gamble	United States	Cosmetics/Toiletries	$5,762
2	3	Unilever	United Kingdom	Cosmetics/Toiletries, Food/Beverages	3,540
3	2	General Motors	United States	Automotive	3,412
4	4	Toyota Motor	Japan	Automotive	2,669
5	5	Ford Motor	United States	Automotive	2,537
6	6	Time Warner	United States	Publishers, Printers, Engravers	2,378
7	7	DaimlerChrysler	United States/ Germany	Automotive	2,230
8	8	L'Oreal	France	Cosmetics	2,180
9	10	Nestlé	Switzerland	Food/Beverages	1,737
10	12	Sony Corp.	Japan	Electronics	1,684
11	14	Walt Disney	United States	Broadcasting, Cable, Film/Video	1,680
12	15	Nissan Motor	Japan	Automotive	1,674
13	9	Johnson & Johnson	United States	Cosmetics/Toiletries	1,665
14	11	Honda Motor	Japan	Automotive	1,542
15	13	Altria Group	United States	Tobacco Products/ Supplies	1,514
16	16	Volkswagen	Germany	Automotive	1,435
17	19	PepsiCo	United States	Food/Beverages	1,255
18	20	Pfizer	United States	Pharmaceuticals	1,229
19	18	McDonald's	United States	Fast Food	1,213
20	17	Coca-Cola	United States	Food/Beverages	1,195
21	21	GlaxoSmithKline	United Kingdom	Pharmaceuticals/ Health Care	1,176
22	22	General Electric	United States	Lighting/Utilities	1,107
23	28	Reckitt Benckiser	United Kingdom	Cosmetics/Toiletries, Food/Beverages	1,097
24	31	Danone Group	France	Food Processing/ Manufacturing	1,018
25	23	News Corporation	Australia	Holding Company	1,005
26	27	Mars	United States	Food/Beverages	981
27	26	Yum Brands	United States	Restaurants	911
28	29	Matsushita Electric Industrial	Japan	Computer/Electronics	903
29	30	PSA Peugeot Citroën	France	Automotive	867

(*continued*)

TABLE 15.3 TOP GLOBAL MARKETERS (CONTINUED)

RANK 2003	RANK 2002	COMPANY	HOME COUNTRY	INDUSTRY TYPE	ANNUAL EXPENDITURES WORLDWIDE (IN $MILLION)
30	25	Viacom	United States	Broadcasting, Cable, Film/Video	$847
31	37	Hewlett-Packard	United States	Computers/Electronics	812
32	32	Deutsche Telekom	Germany	Internet Service Provider	744
33	35	Renault	France	Automotive	724
34	34	Tchibo Holding	Germany	Holding Company	714
35	41	Microsoft	United States	Computer/Electronics	684
36	36	Kao	Japan	Industrial Chemicals	668
37	33	General Mills	United States	Food/Beverages	656
38	60	Canon	Japan	Computer/Electronics	641
39	51	Kellogg	United States	Food/Beverages	622
40	42	Colgate-Palmolive	United States	Cosmetics/Toiletries	621
41	39	Mazda Motor	Japan	Automotive	614
42	38	IBM Corp.	United States	Computer/Electronics	606
43	54	Gillette	United States	Cosmetics/Toiletries	600
44	40	Dell	United States	Computer/Electronics	597
45	44	Wal-Mart Stores	United States	Retail	597
46	46	France Telecom	France	Telecommunications	583
47	53	Vodafone Group	United Kingdom	Holding Company	557
48	47	Henkel	Germany	Industrial Chemicals	539
49	57	Hyundai Motor	Korea	Automotive	532
50	24	Mitsubishi Motors	Japan	Automotive	531
51	43	Clorox	United States	Cleaning Agents	521
52	75	Novartis	Switzerland	Pharmaceuticals/ Health Care	518
53	50	Fiat	Italy	Automotive	506
54	62	Ferrero	Italy	Food/Beverages	504
55	45	Anheuser-Busch Cos.	United States	Food/Beverages	496
56	58	Samsung Group	Korea	Computer/Electronics	489
57	59	Ito-Yokado	Japan	Food/Beverages	479
58	49	Wm. Wrigley Jr.	United States	Food/Beverages	474
59	52	Cadbury Schweppes	United Kingdom	Food/Beverages	466
60	71	Bertelsmann	Germany	Printing/Publishing, Television, Broadcasting/ Film Production	451
61	73	MasterCard International	United States	Financial Services	447

(continued)

TABLE 15.3 Top Global Marketers (continued)

Rank 2003	Rank 2002	Company	Home Country	Industry Type	Annual Expenditures Worldwide (in $million)
62	55	SC Johnson	United States	Cleaning Agents, Cosmetics/Toiletries	$445
63	72	American Express	United States	Financial Services	439
64	67	Visa International	United States	Financial Services	431
65	61	Kimberly-Clark	United States	Paper, Packaging/Container	430
66	48	Diageo	United Kingdom	Holding Company	428
67	64	Suzuki Motor	Japan	Automotive	424
68	84	Nokia	Finland	Telecommunications	417
69	69	Fuji Heavy Industries	Japan	Computer/Electronics	413
70	66	Kia Motors	Korea	Automotive	413
71	74	BMW	Germany	Automotive	408
72	68	Wyeth	United States	Pharmaceuticals/Health Care	405
73	78	Mattel	United States	Games/Toys	393
74	70	Sara Lee	United States	Food/Beverages	388
75	65	Campbell Soup	United States	Food/Beverages	367

SOURCES: Data collected from "Top 100 Global Marketers," *Advertising Age,* November 8, 2004, pp. 3–5 and the RedBooks.com online database.

message to the required audience may be limited. Therefore, global marketers must consider the availability of various media for advertisers as well as the media habits of the target country.

Media Availability

Advertisers in the United States and many European countries have become accustomed to the availability of a full range of media for advertising purposes. Aside from the traditional print media, consisting of newspapers and magazines, the U.S. advertiser has access to radio, television, billboards, cinemas, and the Internet. In addition, direct mail can be used with most prospective client groups. This wide choice among media is not available in every country. Therefore, a company marketing its products in several countries may find itself unable to apply the same media mix in all markets. Even when certain media are available, access may be partially restricted. In some countries, public and private television channels may devote no more than a small percentage of their airtime to advertising.

Regional distribution of the media spending of top global advertisers is shown in Table 15.4. Across regions, global firms often employ different media mixes for their advertising. These differences in global advertising spending partially reflect different media availability. In light of media differences, as

TABLE 15.4 WORLDWIDE REVENUE BY REGION OF TOP SIX ADVERTISING HOLDING COMPANIES

	REVENUE	PERCENT		REVENUE	PERCENT
PUBLICIS GROUPE			**INTERPUBLIC GROUP**		
United States	$1.98 billion	45.0%	**OF COMPANIES**		
Europe	1.76 billion	40.0	United States	$3.28 billion	56.0%
Asia	410.0 million	9.3	Europe	1.69 billion	28.9
Latin America	171.9 million	3.9	Asia and other	420.1 million	7.2
Other	79.4 million	1.8	Latin America	233.9 million	4.0
			Other	232.1 million	4.0
WPP GROUP			**DENTSU**		
North America	$2.76 billion	40.9%	United States	$49.0 million	1.9%
Europe	2.87 billion	42.5	Japan	2.39 billion	94.0
Other	1.12 billion	16.6	Other	104.3 million	4.1
OMNICOM GROUP			**HAVAS**		
United States	$4.72 billion	54.8%	North America	$789.8 million	42.1%
Europe	2.73 billion	31.7	Europe	948.4 million	50.5
Other	1.17 million	13.6	Asia	74.2 millino	4.0
			Latin America	65.1 million	3.5

SOURCE: "Agency Family Trees: 2004 Revenue Ranking for the Top Six Holding Companies." Reprinted with permission from *Advertising Age*. Copyright, Crain Communications, Inc. 2004.

well as market differences, global managers must remain flexible in crafting their media plans. A company cannot expect to use its preferred medium to the fullest extent everywhere. Consequently, global advertising campaigns must be flexible enough to adapt to local situations. For example, when international insurers recently entered India's life insurance market, they estimated that only a quarter of the market had been tapped. As a result, advertisements explaining the benefits of life insurance proliferated. The ubiquitous ads appeared on billboards, in newspapers, on colorful websites, and on posters decorating kiosks.[33]

Global marketers must also be aware of regional trends:

▶ In Latin America, television advertising has reached a higher percentage of gross domestic product (GDP) than in any other region in the developing world. The demand for television slots in Mexico has caused prices to surge there.

▶ Billboard advertising is growing in Europe. Outdoor advertisements account for about 6 percent of overall advertising expenditures, not counting classified ads. And in Belgium, France, and Switzerland, the contribution of billboard advertising was nearly double that figure. New technology and higher-quality images are credited with spurring this growth.[34]

▶ In India, television channels and newspapers are proliferating due to a wave of new advertisers such as cellular operators, banks, and automobile manufacturers as well as a regulatory change that allows foreigners to hold up to 26 percent of India's new media companies.

A giant billboard advertises Coca-Cola in Warsaw, Poland. Such billboards have become common in many cities of the former Soviet bloc.

Global Media

Marketers can also employ global media. Global television includes news networks, such as BBC World and CNN, and consumer channels, such as Animal Planet, Discovery, ESPN, and MTV. However, the global print media consist largely of magazines targeted at business executives, such as *Business Week*, *The Economist*, *Fortune*, and *Time*, along with only a few consumer magazines such as *Reader's Digest* and *Elle*.[35]

Satellite television channels, which are not subject to government regulations, have revolutionized television in many parts of the world. English is the common language of the majority of satellite channels. However, there is a trend toward local-language satellite broadcasts. Satellite channels are now available in several European languages, such as German, French, and Swedish.

One of the most successful global satellite ventures is MTV. This music channel, which was launched in 1981 in the United States, now reaches about one billion people in 18 different languages and in more than 164 countries, with 80 percent of viewers living outside the United States.[36] McDonald's strategy of engaging MTV globally in some 160 countries was aimed at taking advantage of its global reach and the young audience attracted everywhere. McDonald's has thus become the sole sponsor of MTV Advance Warning, its first truly global program. The program focuses on emerging new musical talent with potential for international success in a number of countries.[37]

The leader in this field of privately owned channels is Sky Channel, owned by Rupert Murdoch, who controls vast media interests in many countries. Murdoch's Star Satellite System serves millions of people from Egypt to Mongolia, China, India, and Japan.[38] With its transnational reach, Star System relies heavily on advertising revenue from international and global advertisers.

Most observers admit that the availability of satellite commercial networks has already had an impact on the national regulatory boards of countries that tended to restrict or limit commercial airtime. Most predict that less restricted commercial television will become the norm. Overall, satellite television is likely to enlarge the television advertising market substantially in Europe and in developing countries.

Media Habits

Besides being concerned with media availability, international marketers must also consider media habits in different national markets. Substantial differences in media habits exist worldwide. As we have already seen, the penetration of various media can differ substantially from one country to another. Different levels of literacy and different cultures may favor one medium over another, regardless of media penetration. Accurate data concerning media usage may be unavailable in many developing countries, thus adding to the challenge of choosing national media and planning global campaigns.

Both the ownership or usage of television and radio, and the readership of print media (newspapers and magazines) vary considerably from one country to another. The developed industrial nations show high penetration ratios for

WORLD BEAT 15.2

Battle of the Beer Ads

GLOBAL MARKETERS OF BEER around the world use advertising to win and keep their customers. Anheuser-Busch emphasizes its American roots to sell Budweiser around the globe. In the United Kingdom, Budweiser ads feature funny American bar scenes and pickup lines. In Brazil, the Canadian brewer Molson used the sex appeal of a bikini-clad ex-model turned MTV host, Daniella Cicarelli, to increase sales of Molson's Kaiser brand. The ad has helped build Molson's 15 percent share of the Brazilian market, but it could become illegal under new rules that forbid the use of actors who look younger than twenty-five years old.

When Japan's Asahi beer came to the United Kingdom, the company used posters and billboards that fea-

tured third-rate celebrities in tacky settings, with text that was a mix of Japanese ideograms and stilted English translations. The idea of the posters was to gently mock Japanese advertising with a sophisticated parody. But to many British consumers, the ads look like they came straight from Tokyo on the cheap. Nonetheless, the Asahi advertising efforts have helped double the volume of Asahi beer sold in Britain.

Sources: Andrea Welsh, "Brewers in Brazil May Water Down Their Sales Pitch," *Wall Street Journal,* September 24, 2003, p. B4 Dan Bilefsky and Christopher Lawton, "In Europe, Marketing Beer as 'American' May Not Be a Plus," *Wall Street Journal,* July 21, 2004, p. B1; Sarah Ellison, "Bad Beer Ads," *Wall Street Journal Europe,* May 15, 2000.

all these major media carriers. Banner advertising on the Internet is a more recently devised way to try to reach literate, online consumers. But media habits vary here as well. Hong Kong's Internet surfers' average click rate for advertising banners at the top of the page is 0.78 percent, compared with 0.45 in Britain and 0.31 percent in the United States.[39]

The literacy of a country's population can strongly influence a firm's media decisions. Although this is less of a concern for companies in the industrial-products market, it is a crucial factor in consumer-goods advertising. In countries where large portions of the population are illiterate, the use of print media is of limited value. Both radio and television have been used by companies to circumvent the literacy problem. Television and radio can be used to overcome this problem, but they cannot be used in areas where the penetration of such receivers is limited. However, over the past 20 years, the diffusion of electronic media in developing countries has spurred a surge in television and radio advertising. In Egypt, the second-largest advertising market in the Middle East after Saudi Arabia, television accounts for 50 percent of advertising expenditures.[40] Television advertising is thought to have overtaken print advertising in India.

In fact, modernization in developing countries has created media opportunities. Across Asia—where cell phones have proliferated and there is little regulation of spam—advertisers increasingly reach consumers via text messages to their phones, and in Beijing, Communication Radio serves the needs of China's new commuters. In addition to offering traffic updates, the station plays light pop music to calm the nerves of motorists stuck in traffic. Eighty percent of Beijing drivers tune in. As private car ownership surges in China, Communication Radio has become one of the country's highest-ranked stations for advertising revenues.[41]

Scheduling International Advertising

Media expenditures tend to peak before sales peak. How long before depends on the complexity of the consumers' buying decision and the length of their deliberation. This principle, though somewhat generalized here, applies to international markets as well as to domestic ones. Differences exist, however, because of varying sales peaks, national vacations, and religious holidays and because of differences in the deliberation time with regard to purchases.

Sales peaks are influenced both by climatic seasons and by customs and traditions. Winter months in North America and Europe are summer months in countries of the Southern Hemisphere, such as Australia, New Zealand, South Africa, Argentina, and Brazil. Of course, the season influences the purchase and consumption of many consumer goods, such as clothing, vacation services, travel, and soft drinks. Vacations are particularly important for some European countries. Religious holidays may also affect the placement or timing of advertising. During the Islamic Ramadan, some Muslim countries do not allow any advertising to be placed.

For industrial products, the timing of advertising in support of sales efforts may be affected by the budgetary cycles that prevail in a given country. For countries with large state-controlled sectors, heavy emphasis needs to be placed on the period before a new national or sector plan is developed. Private-sector companies tend to be more heavily influenced by their own budgetary cycles, which usually coincide with their fiscal years. In Japan, for example, many companies begin their fiscal year in June rather than in January. To the extent that capital budgets are completed before the new fiscal year commences, products that require budgetary approval will need advertising support in advance of budget completion.

The time needed to think about a purchase has been cited as a primary consideration in deciding how long it is appropriate for the advertising peak to precede the sales peak. In its domestic market, a company may be accustomed to a given deliberation time on the part of its customers. But because deliberation times may be determined by income level or other environmental factors, other markets may exhibit different patterns. The purchase or replacement of a small electrical household appliance may be a routine decision for a North American household, and the purchase may occur whenever the need arises. In a country with lower income levels, such a purchase may be planned several weeks or even months ahead. Consequently, a company engaged in international advertising needs to evaluate carefully the underlying assumptions of its domestic advertising policies and not automatically assume that they apply elsewhere.

Organizing the Global Advertising Effort

A major concern for global marketing executives revolves around the organization of the company's global advertising effort. Key concerns include the role of the head office versus the roles that subsidiaries and the advertising agency should play. Marketers are aware that a more harmonious approach to the international advertising effort may enhance both the quality and the efficiency of the total effort. Organizing the effort deserves as much time as individual advertising decisions about individual products or campaigns. In this section, we look in greater detail at the selection of an advertising agency and at the managerial issues that arise in running a global advertising effort in a multinational corporation.

Selection of an Advertising Agency

Global companies have a number of options with respect to working with advertising agencies. Many companies develop an agency relationship domestically and must decide whether they expect their domestic agency to handle their global advertising business as well. In some foreign markets, companies need to select foreign agencies to work with them—a decision that may be made by the head office alone or left to the local subsidiaries. Recently, some agencies have banded together to form international networks to attract more global business.

Working with Domestic Agencies. When a company starts to grow internationally, it is not unusual for the domestic advertising agency to handle the international business as well. However, this is possible only when the domestic agency has global experience and capability. Many smaller domestic agencies do not have international experience. Companies are then forced to make other arrangements. Frequently, the global company begins by appointing individual

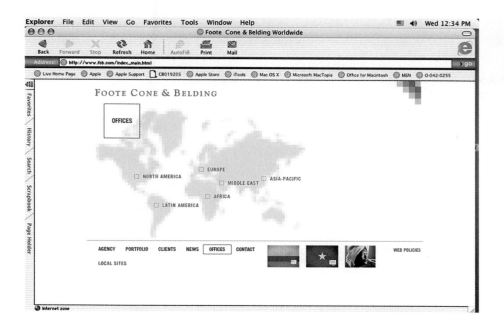

Foote Cone & Belding is one of the world's major advertising agency networks with offices and associates in 110 countries.

agencies in each of the various foreign markets where it is operating. This may be done with the help of the local subsidiaries or through the staff at the company's head office. Before long, however, the company will end up with a series of agency relationships that may make global coordination very difficult.

Working with Local Agencies Abroad. The local advertising agency is expected to understand the local environment fully and is in a position to create advertisements targeted to the local market. Although it markets one of the world's best-known brands, Mercedes-Benz is one of many firms that have chosen at times to utilize a variety of local agencies. Prior to 1980, the company did engage heavily in global advertising, using the Ogilvy & Mather Worldwide agency. When Ogilvy & Mather pursued the business of competitor Ford Motor Company, Mercedes fired the agency. Mercedes then adopted a policy of varying its brand image from country to country and employing the most creative agency in each country.

Working with International Advertising Networks. Many companies with extensive international operations find it too difficult and cumbersome to deal simultaneously with a large number of agencies, both domestic and international. For this reason, multinational firms have tended to concentrate their accounts with some large advertising agencies that operate their own global networks. Table 15.5 lists the world's top 50 marketing organizations/agencies.

The first generation of international networks was created by U.S.-based advertising agencies in the 1950s and 1960s when clients encouraged their U.S. agencies to move into local markets where the advertising agencies were weak. Leaders in this process were J. Walter Thompson, Ogilvy & Mather, BBDO, and Young & Rubicam. British entrepreneurs Saatchi & Saatchi and WPP dominated the second wave of international networks. Other networks were developed by

TABLE 15.5 WORLD'S TOP 50 MARKETING ORGANIZATIONS

RANK	AGENCY	HEADQUARTERS	WORLDWIDE REVENUE (IN MILLIONS OF U.S. DOLLARS)
1	Omnicom Group	USA	$9,747.2
2	WPP Group 1	U.K.	9,370.1
3	Interpublic Group of Cos.	USA	6,200.6
4	Publicis Groupe	France	4,777.3
5	Dentsu	Japan	2,851.0
6	Havas	France	1,866.0
7	Aegis Group	U.K.	1,373.6
8	Hakuhodo DY Holdings	Japan	1,372.4
9	Asatsu-DK	Japan	473.3
10	Carlson Marketing Group	USA	346.9
11	MDC Partners	Canada/USA	316.8
12	Incepta Group	U.K.	279.8
13	Monster Worldwide	USA	251.6
14	Digitas	USA	251.6
15	HealthSTAR Communications	USA	203.0
16	Alloy	USA	194.1
17	Cheil Communications	South Korea	185.9
18	Aspen Marketing Services	USA	180.0
19	G2R*2	South Korea	180.0
20	Tokyu Agency	Japan	176.0
21	George Johnson Co.	USA	172.9
22	aQuantive	USA	157.9
23	Doner	USA	155.7
24	Clemenger Communications	Australia	147.4
25	Select Communications	Germany	145.0
26	Epsilon	USA	144.4
27	Cossette Communication Group	Canada	140.1
28	Richards Group	USA	134.0
29	Bartle Bogle Hegarty	U.K.	115.9
30	M&C Saatchi	U.K.	114.3
31	PGI	USA	110.0
32	STW Group	Australia	107.0
33	RPA	USA	101.9
34	Marketing Store	USA	101.3
35	DVC Worldwide	USA	100.3
36	Cjime Communications	U.K.	99.2
37	inChord Communications	USA	98.5
38	Scholz & Friends	Germany	96.1
39	Armando Testa Group	Italy	96.0
40	HighCo	France	94.2

(continued)

TABLE 15.5 World's Top 50 Marketing Organizations (continued)			
Rank	Agency	Headquarters	Worldwide Revenue (in millions of U.S. dollars)
41	ChoicePoint Precision Marketing	USA	$93.4
42	Wieden & Kennedy	USA	92.6
43	SourceLink	USA	90.0
44	Asahi Advertising	Japan	88.2
45	Springer & Jacoby	Germany	86.0
46	Harte-Hanks Direct	USA	84.7
47	Cramer-Krasselt	USA	83.7
48	LB Icon	Sweden	82.7
49	Merkle	USA	78.7
50	Protocol Integrated Direct Marketing	USA	77.0

Source: Reprinted with permission from the May 2, 2005 issue of *Advertising Age.* Copyright, Crain Communications, Inc. 2005.

French and Japanese agencies.[42] The 1980s saw many mergers of medium-sized agencies around the world. In the 1990s, mergers and acquisitions occurred among even the largest global agencies. Some of these mergers utilized the umbrella of a holding company that allowed each agency to retain its brand identity while enjoying the advantages of greater size and the ability to access the full global reach of all alliance partners.[43]

Utilizing global advertising agencies or networks can be desirable in countries where advertising is not as developed as in the major markets of North America and Europe. For example, global agencies are favored in Eastern Europe, where up to 90 percent of the advertising in some markets is handled by affiliates of global agencies. They can leverage a vast knowledge within the agency network and transfer much-needed skills in order to attract business from such leading firms as Coca-Cola, Nestlé, and Unilever. When Vietnam opened to foreign advertising agencies—albeit those operating with a local, Vietnamese partner—nearly two dozen international agencies flooded into Vietnam, the world's thirteenth most populous country.[44]

International advertising networks are especially sought after because of their ability to execute global campaigns. Usually, one set of advertisements will be created and then circulated among the local affiliates. Working within the same agency or network guarantees consistency and a certain willingness among affiliate offices to accept direction from a central location. Therefore, as companies develop their global business and coordinate their global campaigns, they are likely to consolidate agencies. Colgate-Palmolive became the first packaged-goods company to consolidate its entire worldwide $500 million advertising budget in the hands of a single agency. In a similar vein, IBM selected Ogilvy & Mather to control its $450 million in billings, which had previously been scattered among forty different agencies. Procter & Gamble used nine core agencies for its U.S. business but placed its international advertising with only three global networks. Kraft Foods also moved to three networks to handle its advertising in more than thirty countries.[45]

Coordinating International Advertising

The role the international marketing executive plays in a company's international advertising effort may differ from firm to firm and depends on several factors. Outside factors, such as the nature of the market or of the competition, as well as internal factors, such as company culture or philosophy, may lead some firms to adopt a more centralized approach in international advertising. Other firms may prefer to delegate more authority to local subsidiaries and local agencies. Key factors that can cause a firm to either centralize or decentralize decision making for international advertising are reviewed in the sections that follow.

External Factors Affecting Advertising Coordination. One of the most important factors influencing how companies allocate decision making for international advertising is market diversity. For products or services where customer needs and interests are homogeneous across many countries, greater opportunities for standardization exist, and companies are more likely to centralize decision making. Companies operating in markets with very different customer needs or market systems are more likely to decentralize their international-advertising decision making. Local knowledge is more important to the success of these firms.

The nature of the competition can also affect the way an international firm plans for decision making related to advertising. Firms that essentially face local competition or different sets of competitors from country to country may find it more logical to delegate international advertising to local subsidiaries. On the other hand, if a company is competing everywhere against a small set of international firms, the company is more apt to centralize key marketing decisions in an attempt to coordinate its actions against its global competitors. In such cases, advertising decision making may be centralized as well.

Internal Factors Affecting Advertising Coordination. A company's own internal structure and organization can also greatly influence its options in terms of centralizing or decentralizing decision making about international advertising. The opportunities for centralizing are few when a company's approach is to customize advertising for each local market. However, when a company adheres to a standardized advertising format, a more centralized approach will be possible and probably even desirable.

Skill levels and efficiency concerns can also affect the level of centralization. Decentralization is possible only when the advertising skills of local subsidiaries and local agencies are sufficient for them to perform successfully. Decentralization is often believed to result in inefficiencies or decreased quality because a firm's budget may be spread over too many individual agencies. Instead of having a large budget in one agency, the firm has created mini-budgets that may not be adequate to attract the best creative talent to work on its products. Centralization often gives the firm access to better talent, though knowledge of the local markets may be sacrificed. On the other hand, international advertising cannot be centralized successfully in companies where the head-office staff does not possess a full appreciation of the international dimension of the firm's business.

The managerial style of the international company may also affect the centralization decision on advertising. Some companies pride themselves on giving considerable freedom to managers at their local subsidiaries. Under such circumstances, centralizing advertising decisions may be counterproductive. The general approach taken by the company's top management toward international markets is closely related to its desire to centralize or decentralize international advertising.

However, because the internal and external factors that characterize the company are subject to change over time, the decision to centralize or decentralize will never be a permanent one. For example, Coca-Cola shifted more advertising decision making to its subsidiaries. Then two years later, advertising oversight shifted back to headquarters in Atlanta. Lackluster sales and some embarrassing ads—an angry grandmother streaking down a beach in Italy—proved fatal to Coke's "think local" strategy.[46]

CONCLUSION

The complexity of dealing simultaneously with a large number of different customers in many countries, all speaking their own languages and subject to their own cultural heritage, presents a real challenge to the international marketer. Proponents of global advertising point to the convergence of customer needs and the emergence of "world consumers," customers who are becoming ever more homogeneous whether they live in Paris, London, New York, or Tokyo. However, many aspects of the advertising environment remain considerably diverse. Although English is rapidly becoming a global language, most messages still have to be translated into local languages. Widely differing regulations in many countries on the execution, content, and format of advertisements still make it very difficult to apply standardized solutions to advertising problems. Media availability to advertisers differs substantially in different parts of the world, so global companies still need to adapt their media mix to the local situation.

Most marketers realize that total customization is not desirable because it would require that each market create and implement its own advertising strategies. Top creative talent is scarce everywhere, and better creative solutions tend to be costlier ones. As a result, companies appear to be moving toward modularization, in which some elements of the advertising message are common to all advertisements whereas other elements are tailored to local requirements. Successful modularization requires that companies plan such an integration of responsibilities from the very outset, considering the full range of possibilities and the requirements that will need to be satisfied across their major markets. This is a considerable challenge to global marketing executives and their advertising partners.

Should advertising for your product be standardized, customized, or modularized? What adaptations might be necessary for your target market? Continue with *Country Market Report* on our website (college.hmco.com/business/).

QUESTIONS FOR DISCUSSION

1. What has motivated the apparent increase in the use of standardized advertising across national markets?

2. What do you think are the reasons that attitudes about the credibility of advertising vary among countries?

3. What advice would you give to a U.S. firm interested in advertising in Japan?

4. How will the advertising industry have to react to evolving conditions in developing countries and the former Soviet bloc?

5. How will increased Internet access affect international advertising?

CASE 15.1
Advertising to Kids

Children in the United States see an estimated 20,000 commercials a year. Marketers spend $5 billion a year directly targeting children. And much more advertising reaches children when they are not even the target audience.

An investigation by the U.S. Federal Trade Commission (FTC) discovered internal memos detailing how companies commonly target their marketing of violent games, music, and movies to children. This prompted lawmakers to reconsider tightening laws on advertising to children. In a follow-up study the next year, the FTC discovered that the movie and video-game industries had improved their practices but that the recording industry continued to show total disdain for public concerns about marketing violent and sexually explicit products to underage children. This encouraged the call for laws that would restrict advertisements—whether targeted directly to children or not—that reached large audiences under the age of seventeen.

A number of industries already set their own standards for advertising to children. The beer industry discourages placing ads on programs where half or more of the audience is under the age of eighteen. Several movie studios set their cutoff standard at 35 percent. Still, the Association of National Advertisers continues to lobby against any legislation that would restrict advertising for violent movies, video games, or music; it contends that such restrictions would curtail free speech, a fundamental American freedom enshrined in the American Bill of Rights. Ironically, a study conducted by the National Institute on Media and the Family discovered that 99 percent of students in

grades 7 through 12 could identify Budweiser as a brand of beer—significantly more students than could identify the purpose of the Bill of Rights. Nonetheless, advertisers won a legal victory when the Supreme Court struck down the state of Massachusetts's restrictions on billboard advertising of cigars and smokeless tobacco products. The law, aimed at protecting children, was deemed to violate the advertisers' freedom of speech.

The controversy over advertising to children is not restricted to the United States. In Britain, advertisements that provoke children to behave improperly are taboo. Regulators have no direct authority to ban advertisements, but they enjoy powerful influence with the nation's media. A television ad created by the Publicus Group for Hewlett-Packard featured children throwing snowballs at a passing train. Regulators considered this an incitement to antisocial behavior, and the spot was removed.

In Belgium, state broadcasters are forbidden to air advertisements aimed at children for 5 minutes on either side of a children's show. Greece bans toy advertising on television between 7:00 a.m. and 10:00 p.m. In Sweden, television advertising aimed at children has been illegal since 1991. Critics of the Swedish advertising ban are quick to point out that Swedish children have access to international channels that allow them to see ads from other countries. TV3, a Swedish channel that broadcasts from the United Kingdom, is free to advertise to children because of its British location. Even so, a number of European countries, including Greece, Belgium, Italy, and Poland, are debating tightening their restrictions. Advertisers argue that increased regulation across Europe could greatly curtail children's programming on the many private channels not subsidized by governments.

Across the world in Indonesia, a recent cigarette-advertising campaign came under attack by educators and politicians. The campaign featured animated characters, including ants, roosters, and snails, dancing to music. Critics believed that the ad encouraged children, who make up the majority of cartoon lovers, to think that smoking was a good thing. The company quickly removed the offending ad. In Indonesia, the penalty for marketers who target children is a hefty fine and a jail sentence of up to 5 years.

Discussion Questions

1. Why is advertising directed at children regulated in so many cultures? Why is there so much variation in these regulations?

2. Should the EU develop a common policy toward advertising that targets children? Why or why not? What barriers to such a policy might exist?

3. What restrictions on advertising directed at children would you favor? Why?

Sources: Suzanne Kapner, "Agencies Say British Regulators Are Too Quick to Ban Ads," *New York Times*, January 4, 2002, p. 4; Ronald Brownstein, "Targeting Kids," *Dallas Morning News*, May 6, 2001, p. 4J; Vanessa O'Connell, "Advertising Marketers to Attack Bills Restricting Ads," *Wall Street Journal*, July 25, 2001, p. B5; Sarah Ellision, "Marketing to Children Sparks Criticism in Europe," *Wall Street Journal*, December 18, 2000; "Kid Gloves: Banning Advertising to Children," *The Economist*, January 6, 2001; and "Cigarette Maker Pulls Ad Cartoon," *Jakarta Post*, December 14, 2001.

CASE 15.2
The Alliance

Dentsu, Japan's largest advertising agency, joined Leo Burnett and the MacManus Group, both headquartered in the United States, in an agreement to create one holding company, Bcom3, for the three agency networks. Although the three remained legally distinct companies, certain benefits were expected to arise from this new alliance. Leo Burnett and the MacManus Group hoped to cut costs by exploring ways to reduce redundant divisions and subsidiaries. Dentsu expected Bcom3 to expand its access to worldwide advertising networks for its clients, mainly Japanese companies. With a relatively small international presence, Dentsu could not currently serve a Japanese client in a foreign market as well as Leo Burnett or the MacManus Group could. By gaining the ability to tap into the international subsidiaries of Leo Burnett and the MacManus Group, Dentsu significantly enhanced its global presence virtually overnight.

But would this new alliance really be good for Dentsu? Dentsu Inc. was the largest independent advertising agency in the world. Founded in 1901 as a combination news and advertising agency, Dentsu evolved into a propaganda service known as Domei News Service during World War II. Dentsu was still 48 percent owned by Kyodo and Jiji, Japan's two major wire services. In the early postwar years, Dentsu helped launch Japanese commercial television and viewership rating services. Dentsu retained equity stakes in several television stations and helped conceive and market some programming. Of Dentsu's worldwide billings, about 5 percent came from its own overseas subsidiaries.

Dentsu dominated the Japanese advertising industry. Unlike the European and the American advertising industries, the industry in Japan had no taboo against an advertising agency representing competitors. Japanese clients were generally comfortable with different divisions or teams within the same ad agency handling competitor accounts. This was one reason why the biggest advertising agencies in Japan had become disproportionately large compared to agencies in Western markets. Dentsu itself handled ads for about 3,000 firms, including nearly all of Japan's major corporations. According to industry estimates, Dentsu booked on average 31 percent of all television commercials and 20 percent of newspaper ads in Japan.

However, the past decade had been problematic for Dentsu. A recession in Japan hurt profit margins, and growth had fallen to a 25-year low. Nissan Motor Company, Dentsu's long-term client, shocked management at Dentsu when it announced it was leaving to start a new relationship with Hakuhodo Inc. Hakuhodo, the second-largest advertising agency in Japan, was half Dentsu's size. Hakuhodo had formed an alliance with the U.S.-based multinational advertising agency TBWA and later bought 15 percent of TBWA's equity. Management at Nissan Motor explained that Nissan wanted to consolidate its marketing activities worldwide in cooperation with Hakuhodo and TBWA. Nissan Motor recognized that Dentsu was the number one agency in Japan, but the Japanese market alone was not big enough for Nissan Motor's profit objectives. The Nissan experience was a watershed. From then on, Dentsu was concerned that other "old friends" might defect.

Bcom3 also included two major media-buying firms, Starcom Worldwide and Mediavest. Media-buying firms exercise more power in negotiating with media companies, such as newspapers, television, and radio, because of their large purchases of media space and consequent market power. Dentsu performed media buying within its own organization but had never developed the size or market power of international firms such as Starcom or Mediavest. Therefore, Dentsu could profit from discounted media prices by working through these Bcom3 companies. In addition, these media-buying firms possessed advanced media-planning tools to help clients develop efficient and effective media portfolios, such as the means to determine what percentages of a campaign budget should go to national radio, newspaper, regional television, and so on.

Dentsu already was involved in a 50/50 joint venture with Young and Rubicam in Asian markets. It was the oldest surviving alliance between a Japanese and a U.S. advertising agency. Nonetheless, Dentsu's own subsidiaries in Asia competed with the joint venture. The relationship between the two partners was further strained when the WPP Group bought Young and Rubicam in 2000. Dentsu considered WPP a major competitor. WPP held a 20 percent stake in Japan's third-largest agency.

For Dentsu, an alliance with such firms as Leo Burnett and the MacManus Group offered a channel to service its clients better internationally, augmenting the business of its own overseas subsidiaries. After 2 years, however, management at Dentsu was reviewing the situation. The biggest advantage for Dentsu to date had been the cost savings associated with buying $100 million worth of advertising space each year in the United States for Japanese copier maker Canon. But Bcom3 was not yet capturing the many new global accounts that the partners had envisaged. Unlike Nissan Motor, most Japanese corporations had not consolidated their global advertising business within a few agencies. Most managers of Japanese subsidiaries in international markets were not Japanese. They often preferred to choose their own agencies, in spite of the relationship between headquarters in Japan and Dentsu. Furthermore, most Japanese multinational corporations had already built long-term relationships with Western advertising agencies.

Discussion Questions

1. Why was Dentsu interested in the Bcom3 alliance?
2. Why would Leo Burnett and the MacManus Group be interested in an alliance with Dentsu?
3. What problems can arise when two or more advertising agencies form an alliance? How might these problems be exacerbated if the agencies are from different cultures?
4. What recommendations would you give Dentsu?

Source: Case prepared by Jaeseok Jeong. Used by permission.

Notes

1. PR Newswire, "ExxonMobil Launches Advertising Campaign to Announce New Company," December 3, 1999.
2. Bill Chase, "Letters to the Editor," *Wall Street Journal* (Europe), July 24, 2001, p. 9.
3. Vanessa O'Connell, "Exxon 'Centralizes' New Global Campaign," July 7, 2001, *Wall Street Journal*, p. B6.
4. "Patek Philippe: Tradition Anyone?" *Ad Age International*, January 11, 1999, p. 9.
5. Greg Harris, "International Advertising Standardization: What Do Multinationals Actually Standardize?" *Journal of International Marketing* 12, no. 4 (1994), pp. 13–30.
6. Nancy Giges, "Europeans Buy Outside Goods, But Like Local Ads," *Advertising Age International*, April 27, 1992, p. I–1.
7. Hillary Chura and Richard Linnett, "Coca-Cola Readies Global Assault," *Advertising Age*, April 2, 2001, p. 1.
8. Erin White, "Publicis Groupe Creates Agency Dedicated Just to Serve Fiat," *Wall Street Journal*, July 11, 2003, p. B4.
9. "Ads Astride the World," *Financial Times*, April 13, 1989, p. 16.
10. Patricia Sabatini, "Heinz Re-enlists Leo Burnett for Global Campaign," *Pittsburgh Post-Gazette*, March 27, 1999, p. C1.
11. Bradford Wernie, "Jaguar Goes Global," *Automotive News Europe*, April 12, 1999, p. v.
12. Suzanne Vranica and Bruce Orwall, "Disney Will Launch Global Campaign to Boost Ailing Parks," *Asian Wall Street Journal*, December 30, 2004, p. A6.
13. Judann Pollack, "Pringles Wins Worldwide with One Message," *Ad Age International*, January 11, 1999, p. 14.
14. "Using Potato Chips to Spread the Spirit of Free Enterprise," ABCNEWS.com (accessed September 9, 2002).
15. Dana James, "Skoda Taken from Trash to Treasure," *Marketing News*, February 18, 2002, pp. 4–5.
16. Eirmalasare Bani, "Lipton Shoots Its Latest Commercial in Malaysia," *Business Times* (Malaysia), June 9, 1999, p. 15.
17. Deborah L. Vence, "Match Game," *Marketing News*, November 11, 2002, pp. 1, 12.
18. Philip J. Kitchen and Tao Li, "Perceptions of Integrated Marketing Communications: A Chinese Ad and PR Perspective," *International Journal of Advertising* 21, no. 1 (2005), p. 68.
19. Geoffrey A. Fowler, "Advertising: China Cracks Down on Commercials," *Wall Street Journal*, February 19, 2004, p. B7.
20. Melissa Akin, "Duma Smoking Bill Proves Nothing Is Sacred," *Moscow Times*, June 11, 1999, p. 1.
21. Associated Press, "Cigarette Stunt Pilot Fined for Airborne Cigarette Advertising," September 20, 2000.
22. Normandy Madden and Andrew Hornery, "As Taco Bell Enters Singapore, Gidget Avoids the Ad Limelight," *Ad Age International*, January 11, 1999, p. 13.
23. Ibid.
24. "Mexico Forces a Wonderbra Cover-Up," *Financial Times*, August 19, 1996, p. 4.
25. "Dentsu Ventures Abroad," *Asian Wall Street Journal*, March 29, 2001, p. N1.
26. Jae W. Hong, Aydin Muderrisoglu, and George M. Zinkhan, "Cultural Differences and Advertising Expression: A Comparative Content Analysis of Japanese and U.S. Magazine Advertising," *Journal of Advertising* 16, no. 1 (1987), pp. 55–62.
27. "Movie Stars Moonlight in Japan," *Forbes*, March 14, 2001.
28. Erin White, "U.K. Gives Lessons on Ad Messages," *Wall Street Journal*, December 2, 2002, p. B6.
29. Leah Rickard, "Ex-Soviet States Lead World in Ad Cynicism," *Advertising Age*, June 5, 1995, p. 3.
30. Dagmar Mussey, "Mars Goes Local," *Ad Age Global*, May 10, 2002.
31. Christopher Woodward, "Got Spanish? Anita Santiago Helps Advertisers Bridge the Gap Between Anglo and Latino Cultures," *Business Week*, August 14, 2000, p. F12.
32. Jim Pickard, "Coca-Cola to Use Welsh in Adverts," *Financial Times*, July 6, 2000.
33. Beverly Matthews, "Foreign Life Insurers Eye India," Reuters English News Service, April 3, 2001.
34. Alessandra Galloni, "Look Up," *Wall Street Journal* (Europe), April 4, 2001, p. 23.
35. Juliana Koranteng, "Global Media," *Ad Age International*, February 8, 1999, p. 23.
36. Kerry Capell, "MTV's World," *Business Week*, February 18, 2002, p. 81.
37. "McDonald's Strikes Sweeping International Music Deal," *Ad Age Online*, February 15, 2005.
38. "Phoenix Rising," *Newsweek*, November 12, 2001, p. 46. "HK Web Surfers Most Receptive to Banner Ads," Reuters News, April 4, 2001.
39. "Egyptian Spending on Advertising Growing 30% a Year," *Middle East Executive Reports*, August 1998, p. 10.
40. Kathy Chen, "Beyond the Traffic Report," *Wall Street Journal*, January 2, 2003, p. A9.
41. Andreas Grein and Robert Ducoffe, "Strategic Responses to Market Globalisation Among Advertising Agencies," *International Journal of Advertising* 17, no. 3 (1998), pp. 301–319.
42. Marye Tharp and Jaeseok Jeong, "The Global Network Communications Agency," *Journal of International Marketing* 9, no. 4 (2001), p. 113.
43. Michael Flagg, "Vietnam Opens Industry to Foreigners," *Wall Street Journal*, August 28, 2000, p. B8.
44. Mark Gleason and Pat Sloan, "$500 Million in Colgate Eggs in One Y&R Basket," *Advertising Age*, December 4, 1995, p. 1.
45. Betsy McKay, "Coke Hunts for Talent to Re-Establish Its Marketing Might," *Wall Street Journal*, March 6, 2002, p. B4.

Managing the Global Marketing Effort

PART 5

16 ORGANIZING FOR GLOBAL MARKETING

3M CREATED ITS INTERNATIONAL operations group in 1951, launching subsidiaries in Australia, Canada, France, Germany, Mexico, and the United Kingdom. Forty years later it became the first foreign firm to have a wholly owned subsidiary in China. Today, half of the company's sales are outside the United States, and three-quarters of its managers have worked in a foreign country. Yet despite its long history as an international firm, 3M still grapples with the question of how best to organize itself.

Over the years, 3M developed an organizational matrix—several structures superimposed on one another. Managers of country subsidiaries share responsibility with division managers located at headquarters in St. Paul, Minnesota. Disagreements over strategy some-

times arise. Subsidiary managers seek to maximize total sales and profits in their countries. Division managers seek to maximize the global sales and profits of their product lines. Despite the matrix, most concede that the country managers often exercise the greater power. In this respect, some are concerned that 3M has been left behind; most other global firms have centralized power over the past 20 years. However, running 3M's international business from St. Paul could prove too burdensome. The matrix allows the company to react quickly to local markets. Who better than the local manager to decide whether and how to raise prices in Germany? Thus the debate continues. Who is better qualified to decide how to market a product abroad—the person who best knows

After studying this chapter, you should be able to

▶ List and explain the internal and external factors that affect how global organizations are structured and managed.

▶ Note the advantages and disadvantages of the different ways of structuring a firm with international sales.

▶ Discuss global mandates, and note how global mandates can affect a firm's organization.

▶ Explain why organizational issues for born-global firms differ from those for traditional multinational companies.

▶ Give examples of how technology can be utilized to support internal global communications systems.

▶ List and explain the elements of an effective global control strategy.

▶ Discuss the conflicts that can arise between international headquarters and national subsidiaries.

▶ Consider a career in global marketing.

the product or the person who best knows the country?[1]

An important aspect of global marketing is the establishment of an appropriate organization. The organization must be able to formulate and implement strategies for each local market and for the global market as well. The objective is to develop a structure and control system that will enable the firm to respond to distinct variations in each market while applying the relevant experience that the company has gained in other markets and with other products. To be successful, companies need to find a proper balance between these two needs. A number of organizational structures are suitable for different internal and external environments. No one structure is best for all situations.

ELEMENTS THAT AFFECT A GLOBAL MARKETING ORGANIZATION

The success of a global strategy will be acutely influenced by the selection of an appropriate organization to implement that strategy. The structure of an international organization should be congruent with the tasks to be performed, the need for product knowledge, and the need for market knowledge. The ideal structure of such an organization should be a function of the products or services to be sold in the marketplace, as well as of the external and internal environments. Theoretically, the way to develop a global marketing organization is to analyze the specific tasks to be accomplished within an environment and then to design a structure that will support these tasks most effectively. A number of other factors complicate the selection of an appropriate organization, however. In most cases, a company already has an existing organizational structure. As the internal and external environments change, companies will need to reevaluate that structure. The search for an appropriate organizational structure must balance local responsiveness against global integration. It is important that global managers understand the strengths and weaknesses of different organizational structures as well as the factors that usually lead to change in the structure.

Corporate Goals

Every company needs a mission. The mission is the business's framework—the values that drive the company and the vision it has for itself. The mission statement is the glue that holds the company together. It asks four questions: (1) Why do we exist? (2) Where are we going? (3) What do we believe in? (4) What is our distinctive competence?[2]

After declaring its mission, no company should begin establishing an international organization until it has reviewed and established its strategies and objectives. Some global firms even include strategy statements in their missions. Corporate leaders develop strategic visions with slogans such as "Encircle Caterpillar" for Komatsu and "Beat Xerox" for Canon. If the head of a company can instill this sense of winning throughout the firm, it will inspire the organization to excel and achieve far greater goals.[3]

Corporate Worldview

Ethnocentric orientation a corporate worldview in which management is focused on the home market and considers ideas from the home market to be superior to those from foreign subsidiaries

Corporate management can adopt one of several worldviews concerning global markets. These worldviews, or orientations, will significantly affect the choice of organizational structure. Some firms adopt an **ethnocentric orientation.** Management is centered on the home market. Ideas that emanate from there are considered superior to those that arise from the foreign subsidiaries. Headquarters tells its subsidiaries what to do and solicits little or no input from the subsidiaries themselves. Top managers in the foreign subsidiaries are most often managers sent from headquarters on relatively short-term assignments. Alternatively, corporate management can take a

World Beat 16.1

America Meets the World

RESOLVING TENSIONS BETWEEN THE CENTER AND ITS OUTPOSTS is the essence of good organization according to the chief executive of British Airways. A successful global firm must have a culture that can accommodate the cultures of the world. The center must be strong without being crushing, the outposts true to themselves without losing their corporate identity. But to accommodate other cultures, you must first realize they exist.

European executives admire the financial results of American companies, but when they meet managers from the United States, they often find them to be monolingual and ignorant of geography and European history. One sales manager at a German manufacturer who traveled to Illinois to do business with a big client enjoyed the friendliness and openness of his customers and their ability to make quick decisions. Yet the manager, who was born and raised in France and spoke five languages fluently, was surprised to learn how few of them had traveled abroad and how personally nonglobal they

were. He was also taken aback when employees of his U.S. client called him by his first name. In Germany that would never happen until you knew someone for 10 years—and never when you are at a lower rank.

U.S. executives who have run businesses in Europe agree that Americans have to meet their foreign colleagues halfway. This is best done by educating oneself about European culture and by not assuming the American way is always the best. A U.S. manager who formerly ran General Electric's medical-equipment business in Europe notes that the first thing he did on arriving at his headquarters in Paris was to take a 4-week immersion course in French.

Sources: Julian Birkinshaw, "Intelligent Advice for Those Who Do Business Abroad," *Management Today*, November 5, 2004, p. 38; Rod Eddington, "Only the World's Favorite Empire's Will Last," *Financial Times*, July 14, 2003, p. 17; and Carol Hymowitz, "In the Lead," *Wall Street Journal*, August 15, 2000, p. B1.

---

polycentric orientation, wherein each market is considered unique. This is at the heart of the multidomestic strategies discussed in Chapter 1. Local subsidiaries are given great leeway to develop and implement their own strategies. Little or no interdependencies arise among subsidiaries. Management positions in local subsidiaries are usually filled by local nationals. Some polycentric firms evolve a focus that is regional rather than national. Geographic regions such as Europe and Latin America, rather than single national markets, are seen as possessing unique features that require separate marketing strategies. Decision making becomes centralized at the regional level, but regions still remain relatively independent of headquarters and of one another. A **geocentric orientation** returns power to global headquarters, but this orientation is very distinct from an ethnocentric orientation. A geocentric firm focuses on global markets as a whole rather than on its domestic market. Good ideas can come from any country, and the firm strives to keep communication lines open among its various units. Even top management at corporate headquarters is likely to come from many nations. Most important, all national units, including the domestic one, must consider what is best for the whole organization and act accordingly.

Polycentric orientation a corporate worldview in which each market is considered unique and local subsidiaries are given power to develop and implement independent strategies

Geocentric orientation a corporate worldview in which management pursues a global marketing strategy and decision making is shared by headquarters and subsidiaries

Headquartered in London, HSBC is one of the world's largest banking and financial services companies. With offices in over seventy-five countries, HSBC recognizes the importance of both local knowledge and global reach.

Other Internal Forces

Other internal factors often affect the international organization as well. These factors include the volume and diversity of the firm's international business, its economic commitment to international business, the available human resources, flexibility within the company, and home-country culture.

Importance of International Sales. The size and importance of a firm's international business affect its organizational structure. If only a small percentage of sales (1 to 10 percent) is international, a company will tend to have a simple organization such as an export department. As the proportion of international sales increases relative to total sales, a company is likely to evolve from having an export department to having an international division and then to having a worldwide organization. Companies may even consider moving global headquarters out of the home country when overseas sales become dominant. Japan's Sony Corporation, Nintendo Company, and Sega Enterprises have all considered moving their headquarters to the United States.[4]

Diversity of International Markets Served. As the number and diversity of international markets increase, it becomes necessary to have a more complex organization to manage the marketing effort, and it requires a larger number of people to understand the markets and implement the strategies.

Level of Economic Commitment. A company that is unwilling or unable to allocate adequate financial resources to its international efforts will not be able to sustain a complex or costly international structure. The less expensive organizational approaches to international marketing usually result in less control by the company at the local level. It is extremely important to build an organization that will provide the flexibility and resources to achieve the corporation's long-term goals for international markets.

Human Resources. Available and capable personnel are just as vital to a firm as financial resources. Some companies send top domestic executives to foreign operations only to find that these expatriates do not understand the nation's culture. The hiring of local executives is also difficult, because competition for such people can be extremely intense. Motorola puts hundreds of executives through workplace simulation exercises to try to identify the best candidates with the necessary international management skills to run a global business.[5] Because people are such an important resource in international organizations, a lack of appropriate personnel can constrain a firm's organizational growth.

Flexibility. When a company devises an organizational structure, it must build in some flexibility, especially to be prepared in case reorganization becomes necessary in the future. A study of the implementation of a global strategy for seventeen products found that organizational flexibility was one of the keys to success. The structure must be flexible enough to respond to the needs of consumers and the challenges of global competitors. Even companies that establish a perfect design for the present find themselves in trouble later on when the firm grows or declines.

Home-Country Culture and History. Siemens, the large German electronics and engineering conglomerate, does 80 percent of its business abroad, and 60 percent of its workforce is employed outside Germany. Managers of most local subsidiaries are local nationals.[6] However, like many German companies, Siemens has employed a more centralized management style when dealing with its important U.S. subsidiary, with power located at headquarters in Germany and a German citizen sent to oversee the U.S. market. Keeping close control over important markets and decisions has its roots in German history. Many day-to-day issues cannot be decided by an individual but must be approved by a management board in Germany, and a separate supervisory board consisting of shareholder and employee representatives has to approve major decisions. Some managers argue that Siemens won't truly change until Americans and Asians are on the board.[7]

However, appointing foreign managers to the position of chief executive is rare in continental Europe, as it is in Japan. It is more common in Great Britain and the United States. For example, in 2004, McDonald's appointed an Australian as CEO, and Coca-Cola appointed an Irishman as CEO. The foreign

CEO may be more common in the United States for several reasons. As we saw in Chapter 3, U.S. culture is more individualistic and, consequently, open to foreigners. Furthermore, foreign-born managers began seeking jobs in U.S. multinational corporations years ago as U.S. MNCs hired many foreigners to manage their many overseas subsidiaries. These managers often had to develop good English skills to advance, and many were willing to relocate overseas—including to the United States—in order to advance their careers. In contrast, American managers have tended to work for U.S. companies and don't develop foreign language skills. As a result, Americans rarely become CEOs of foreign companies.[8]

External Forces

A number of external factors can affect how global organizations are structured and managed. The most important of these are geographic distance, time zone differences, types of customers, and government regulations. In the international environment, each issue should be examined to determine its effect on the organization.

Geographic Distance. Technological innovations have somewhat eased the problems associated with physical distance. Companies, primarily in the United States and other developed countries, enjoy such conveniences as next-day mail and e-mail, facsimile machines, videoconferencing, mobile phones, mobile data transmissions, rapid transportation, and, of course, the Internet. However, these benefits cannot be taken for granted in international operations. Distance becomes a distinct barrier when operations are established in less developed countries, where the telecommunications infrastructure may be more primitive. Moreover, companies invariably find it necessary to have key personnel make trips to engage in face-to-face conversations. Organizations in the same region are often grouped together to help minimize travel costs and the travel time of senior executives. Technology has shortened, but not eliminated, the distance gap.

Time Zones. One problem even high technology cannot solve is time differences (see Figure 16.1). Managers in New York who reach an agreement over lunch will have a hard time finalizing the deal with their headquarters in London until the following day, because by that time, most executives in England will be on their way home for the evening. The 5-hour time difference results in lost communication time and impedes rapid results. E-mail has contributed substantially to the interaction among far-flung units, but adaptations still need to be made. Brady Corporation of Milwaukee produces industrial sign and printing equipment. About 45 percent of its sales are outside the United States. Managers in Milwaukee commonly take conference calls at 6 a.m. and place calls late at night to catch the company's Asian managers during their workdays.[9]

Types of Customers. Companies may need to take their "customer profiles" into account in structuring their global marketing organizations. Companies that serve a very few, geographically concentrated global customers will organize

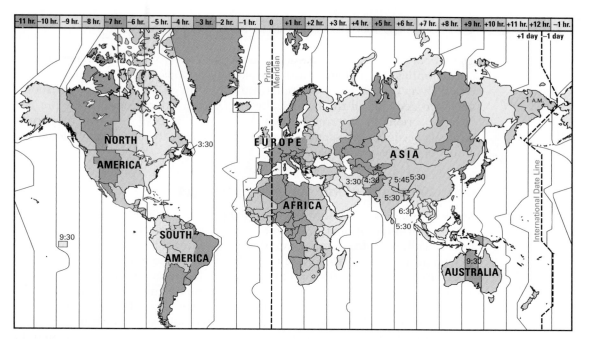

FIGURE 16.1
Time Zones of the World

their global marketing efforts differently from firms that serve a large number of small customers in country after country. For example, if a firm has key global customers, it may adjust its organization and select its office locations according to where its customers are located. Many companies that sell equipment or parts to automotive firms maintain marketing units near major concentrations of automotive activity, such as Detroit and Stuttgart, Germany. Supplier parks sit adjacent to Ford manufacturing sites in Spain, Germany, and Brazil and are increasingly planned for U.S. locations.[10] On the other hand, companies that sell to large numbers of customers tend to maintain more regional, or even country-specific, organizations, with relatively less centralization. Similarly, if customer needs or competition varies greatly from country to country, there is less impetus to centralize.

Government Regulations. How various countries attract or discourage foreign operations can affect the structure of the global organization. Laws involving imports, exports, taxes, and hiring differ from country to country. Local taxes, statutory holidays, and political risk can deter a company from establishing a subsidiary or management center in a country. Some countries require a firm that establishes plants on their territory to hire, train, and develop local employees and to share ownership with the government or local citizens. These requirements for local investment and ownership may dictate an organization that allows greater local decision making.

TYPES OF ORGANIZATIONAL STRUCTURES

The global marketplace offers many opportunities. To take advantage of these opportunities, a company must evaluate its options, develop a strategy, and establish an organization to implement the strategy. The organization should take into account all the factors affecting organizational design (see the preceding section) in determining which structure is best suited to its current strategic needs. In this section, we review the various types of international and global organizational structures.

Companies without International Specialists

Many companies, when they begin selling products to foreign markets, operate without an international organization or even an international specialist. A domestically oriented company may receive inquiries from foreign buyers who saw an advertisement in a trade magazine or attended a domestic trade show. The domestic staff will respond to the inquiry in the same way they respond to any other. Product brochures will be sent to the potential buyer for review. If sufficient interest exists on the part of both buyer and seller, then more communication (e-mails, faxes, telephone calls, personal visits) may transpire. With no specific individual designated to handle international business, it may be directed to a sales manager, an inside salesperson, a product manager, or an outside salesperson.

Companies without an international organization incur limited costs, but on the other hand, with no one responsible for international business, that business will probably provide little sales and profit. When the firm attempts to respond to the occasional inquiry, no one will understand the difficulties of translation into another language, the particular needs of the foreign customer, the transfer of funds, fluctuating exchange rates, shipping, legal liabilities, or the other many differences between domestic and international business. As the number of international inquiries grows or management recognizes the potential in international markets, international specialists will have to be added to the domestic organization.

International Specialists and Export Departments

The complexities of selling a product to a variety of different countries prompt most domestically oriented firms to establish some international expertise. This can vary from retaining a part-time international specialist to having a full complement of specialists organized into an export department. Figure 16.2 is a sample organization chart for an organization operating with an international specialist.

International specialists and export departments primarily perform a sales function. They respond to inquiries, manage exhibits at international trade shows, and handle export documentation, shipping, insurance, and financial matters. International specialists may also maintain contact with embassies, export financing agencies, and various departments of commerce. The international specialist or export department may use an export agent, an export management company, or import intermediaries to assist in the process.

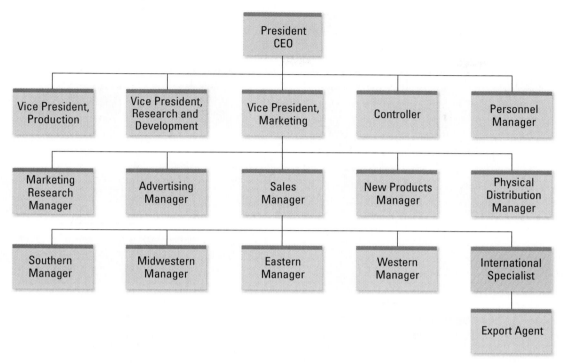

FIGURE 16.2
Organization with an International Specialist

Hiring international specialists gives firms the ability to respond to and process foreign business. The size of this type of organization will be directly related to the amount of international business handled. The costs should be minor when compared to the potential.

However, international specialists and export departments are often reactive rather than proactive in nature. They usually respond to inquiries. Few evaluate the worldwide demand for a product or service, identify opportunities, or develop a global strategy. Also, because international sales are so small, the international specialist may have little opportunity to modify current products or services to meet international market needs. In most cases, products are sold as is, with no modification.

International Divisions

As sales to foreign markets become more important to the company, and the complexity of coordinating the international effort extends beyond the capacity of a specialist or an export department, the firm may establish an international division. The international division normally reports to the president. This gives it equal status with other functions such as marketing, finance, and production. Figure 16.3 illustrates the organizational design of a firm using an international division.

International divisions are directly involved in the development and implementation of global strategy. Heads of international divisions have marketing

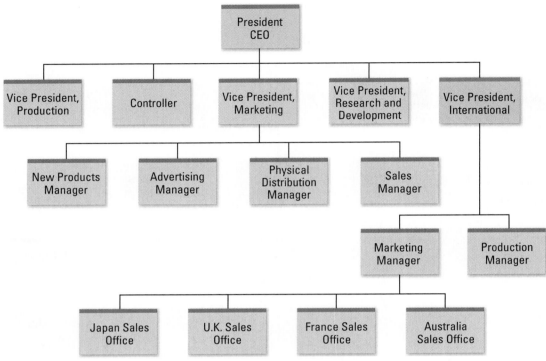

FIGURE 16.3
Organization with an International Division

managers, sales managers, and perhaps even production managers reporting to them. These divisions focus all their efforts on international markets. As a result, they are often successful at increasing international sales.

The international division actively seeks out market opportunities in foreign countries. The sales and marketing efforts in each country are supported through regional or local offices. These offices understand the local environments, including legal requirements, customer needs, and competition. This close contact with the market improves the organization's ability to perform successfully.

The use of international divisions is most common among large international firms with many different product lines or businesses. When none of the divisions has extensive international experience, all international business may be combined into the international division. For example, Alcon is a $1.5 billion U.S.-based company active in the ophthalmic area. Alcon's domestic business was organized along four product lines—equipment, pharmaceuticals, professional materials for surgeons, and over-the-counter eye-care products. Its international business, however, combined all products under an international division.

Worldwide or Global Organizations

As a firm recognizes the potential size of the global market, it begins to change from a domestic company with some business overseas to a worldwide company pursuing a global strategy. At this point, international divisions are superseded by new global structures. A company can choose to organize in terms of one of three dimensions: geography, function, or product. The matrix organization, another possible type of worldwide organization, combines two or more of these dimensions.

Geographic Organizational Structures. The geographic organizational design is appropriate when the company needs an intimate knowledge of its customers and their environments. Such a design gives the company an opportunity to understand the local culture, economy, politics, laws, and competitive situation. Geographic organizational structures can be either regionally focused or country-based structures.

▶ ***Regional Management Centers.*** Regional management centers enable an organization to focus on particular regions of the world, such as Europe, the Middle East, Latin America, North America, the Caribbean, or the Far East. Figure 16.4 illustrates the regional structure of a worldwide geographic organization.

The reasons for using a regional geographic approach to organizational design are related to market similarity and size. A group of countries that are

FIGURE 16.4
Geographic Organization by Regional Management Centers

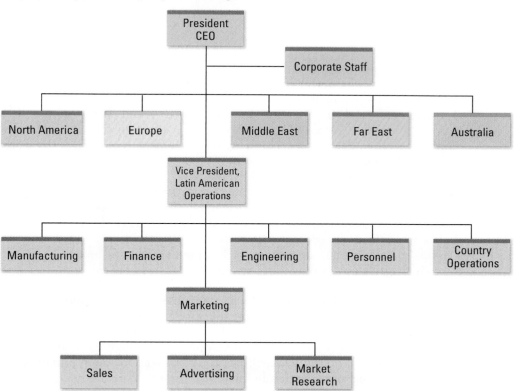

WORLD BEAT 16.2

Hong Kong Headquarters

HIGH COSTS AND POLLUTION haven't stopped Hong Kong from becoming the premier city in which to locate Asian headquarters. Hong Kong was home to nearly 1,000 headquarters in 2005. A study of more than 1,100 companies found that Hong Kong scored high in what companies see as most important when choosing a location for regional headquarters: political and legal stability, good infrastructure, professional services, and quality local managers.

Singapore, Hong Kong's nearest rival in terms of numbers of regional headquarters, is much farther from the key regional markets of China, Japan, and South Korea. However, many companies still seek out Singapore for their Asian headquarters. Borland Software shifted its Sydney headquarters to Singapore as a convenient location to service its growing markets in China and India.

Tokyo, which came in a distant third in the survey, may continue to lose position. Many respondents said that managers based there found themselves overwhelmed with managing their Japanese operations and unable to coordinate work effectively elsewhere in the region. In fact, the biggest threat to Hong Kong may be other cities in China. United Parcel Service is one of many firms that have decided to shift their Asian headquarters from Hong Kong to Beijing or Shanghai.

Sources: Rebecca Fannin, "The Three Capitals of China," *Chief Executive*, December 1, 2004, pp. 5–55; "United Parcel Service Inc.: Asian Headquarters Will Move to Shanghai from Hong Kong," *Asian Wall Street Journal*, July 7, 2003, p. M11; and Gren Manuel, "Hong Kong Tops the List in Asia for Business Location, Study Says," *Wall Street Journal*, January 10, 2001, p. A19.

located close together and have similar social and cultural histories, climates, resources, and (sometimes) languages may have many similar needs for products. Often these regional country groups have unified themselves for political and economic reasons. The European Union (EU) and Mercosur are such regional groupings. Also, once a market reaches a certain size, the firm must employ a staff dedicated to maximizing revenues from that area of the world and to protecting the firm's assets there.

The regional approach to a worldwide organization has a number of benefits. It allows a company to locate marketing and manufacturing efforts in such a way as to take advantage of regional agreements such as the North American Free Trade Agreement (NAFTA). Also, the regional approach puts the company in closer contact with distributors, customers, and subsidiaries. Regional management can respond to local conditions and react faster than a totally centralized organization wherein all decisions are made at the headquarters.

In Europe many large international companies were originally organized on a national basis. The national organizations, including those in France, Germany, Italy, and the United Kingdom, often were coordinated loosely through European headquarters. The development of a single European market caused companies to rethink their European organizations often to reduce the role of the national organization in favor of a stronger pan-European management. A study of twenty multinational companies found that a major benefit of

The skyline of Singapore. Whereas the nightlife of Hong Kong is popular with single expatriates, clean and orderly Singapore appeals to expatriates with families. That is one reason why Singapore remains competitive as a location for Asian headquarters of multinational firms.

a regional or pan-European structure was reduced operational costs. The study showed that by consolidating accounting services such as accounts payable, billings, and accounts receivable, firms could save 35–45 percent on these costs.[11] Another study of Western European and U.S.-based firms with significant operations in Central and Eastern Europe revealed that regional management centers were an attractive organizational device to exploit market similarities and supply local offices with support and expertise.[12]

Regional organizations have their disadvantages, however. First, regional organization implies that many functions are duplicated, either at regional head offices or in the countries. Such duplication, together with the need to rent offices in different locations, tends to add significantly to costs. A second, more serious disadvantage is that regional organizations inherently divide global authority. In a purely regionally organized company, only the CEO has true global responsibility. Developing global marketing strategies for products or services is difficult, because regional managers tend to focus on a limited regional perspective.

▶ *Country-Based Organizations.* The second type of geographic organization is the country-based organization, which utilizes a separate unit for each country. Figure 16.5 illustrates a simple country-based geographic organization.

A country-based organization resembles a regional structure, except that the focus is on single countries rather than on a group of countries. For example, instead of having a regional management center in Brussels overseeing all European sales and operations, the company has an organizational unit in each country. The country-based organization can be extremely sensitive to local

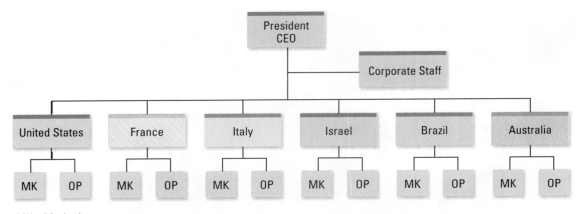

MK = Marketing
OP = Operations

FIGURE 16.5
Country-Based Geographic Organization

customs, laws, and needs, all of which may differ considerably even though the countries participate in a regional organization such as the EU or NAFTA.

One difficulty that plagues a country-based organization is its higher costs. Therefore, it is important to ensure that the benefits of a local organization offset its cost. Coordination with headquarters can also prove difficult. If a company is involved in forty countries, it can be cumbersome to have all forty country-based organizational units reporting to one or a few people in the company's headquarters. A final problem is that a country-based unit cannot take advantage effectively of regional groupings of countries, such as rationalizing production.

Country organizations are being phased out or reduced as regional organizations emerge. For example, in response to the signing of NAFTA, many firms began to integrate their separate organizations for Canada, the United States, and Mexico. Among these was Lego, the Danish toy maker. Lego reduced the responsibility of its Canadian operation and combined some executive positions at its Enfield, Connecticut, operation. At the same time, it decided to develop its Mexican market from the U.S. location as well. Other firms have chosen the same path, integrating their Canadian subsidiaries with their U.S. companies and developing their Mexican markets from the U.S. base.

To deal with the shortcomings of a country-based structure, many firms combine the concepts of regional and country-based organizations, as shown in Figure 16.6. Combining regional and country-based approaches minimizes many of the limitations of both designs, but it also adds an additional layer of management. Some executives think that superimposing a regional headquarters makes the country-level implementation of strategy more cumbersome rather than improving it. In order for the company to benefit from a regional center in such a combined approach, there must be some value in a regional strategy. Each company must reach its own decision regarding the proper geographic organization design, its cost, and its benefits.

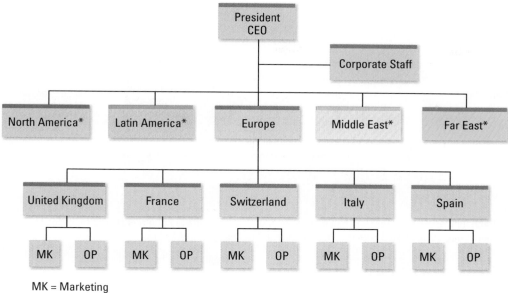

MK = Marketing
OP = Operations

* Country organizations similar to those shown for the European center would be under each regional office.

FIGURE 16.6
Organization Using Both Country-Based Units and Regionally Based Structure

Functional Organizational Structures. A second way of organizing a worldwide firm is by function. In such an organization, the top executives in marketing, finance, production, accounting, and research and development (R&D) all have worldwide responsibilities. For international companies, this type of organization is best for narrow or homogeneous product lines, with little variation between products or geographic markets. As shown in Figure 16.7, the functional organization has a simple structure. Each functional manager has worldwide responsibility for that function. Usually, the manager supervises people responsible for the function in regions or countries around the world.

Ford Motor Company abandoned its regional structure for a functional one. Previously, Ford had major operating units in North America, Europe, Latin America, Africa, and Asia. Each regional unit was responsible for its own operations, developing and producing cars for its regional markets. Faced with strong competition from its bigger rival, General Motors, and from the more efficient Japanese companies such as Toyota, Ford realized that under its regional setup it incurred a massive penalty for unnecessary duplication of key functions and efforts. Even though Ford served almost identical customer needs in many countries, the company was developing separate power trains and engines and was purchasing different component parts.[13]

The new organization of Ford Automotive called for four major functions—marketing and sales, manufacturing, and purchasing, and product development. The most important function was vehicle development, structured around five development centers in the United States and in Europe. The development center for small cars was located in Europe with locations in both Germany and

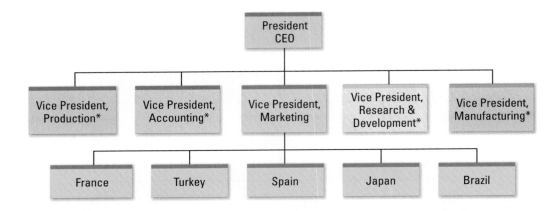

* Each functional vice president has managers of that function in the countries served reporting to him or her, as illustrated with the Vice President, Marketing.

FIGURE 16.7
Functional Global Organization

the United Kingdom. The United States received the development centers for rear-wheel-drive cars and commercial trucks, all with global development responsibility.[14] Some 25,000 Ford managers either moved from one location to another or were reassigned to report to new supervisors. The company expected to cut development costs by using fewer components, fewer engines, and fewer power trains, as well as by speeding up development cycles. As a result of this reorganization, Ford projected savings of $2–$3 billion per year.[15]

Still, the reorganization termed "Ford 2000" was undergoing modifications even before the arrival of the millennium. Ford's then chairman, Jacques Nasser, decided to return some power to Ford's regional business units. The move was made to enable Ford to respond more quickly to consumer trends. It would allow managers on the ground to respond quickly without waiting for direction from headquarters.

Product Organizational Structures. A third type of worldwide marketing organization is based on product line rather than on function or geographic area (see Figure 16.8). Under this structure, each product group is responsible for marketing, sales, planning, and (in some cases) production and R&D. Other functions, such as legal, accounting, and finance, can be included in the product group or performed by the corporate staff. Both Procter & Gamble, a leading global U.S. consumer products company, and Kraft Foods, a leading U.S. food company, have adopted the global product organization.

A firm may choose to organize by product line for several reasons. Structuring by product line is common for companies with several unrelated product lines. A product focus is also appropriate when the differences involved with marketing the various product lines are greater than the perceived differences between the geographic markets. Typically, the end users for a product organization vary by product line, so there is no advantage in having the same group handle marketing for the different product lines.

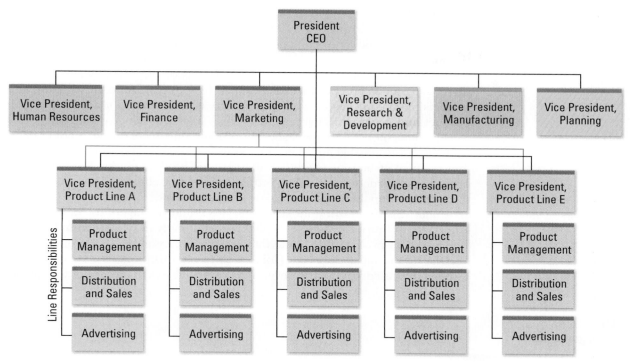

FIGURE 16.8
Global Product Organization

A product organization concentrates management on the product line, which is an advantage when the product line constantly changes with advancements in technology. Headquarters can develop global products and arrange global rollouts. A product organization is effective in monitoring competition that is globalized rather than localized. Also, the firm can add new product groups as it adds new, unrelated products through acquisition.

The product organization has limitations as well. Knowledge of specific geographic areas can be limited, because each product group may not be able to afford to maintain a large local presence in each market. Because decision making becomes more centrally located under a product structure, sensitivity to local market conditions can be diminished. This lack of knowledge and sensitivity may cause the company to miss local market opportunities. The top managers of international product divisions can themselves present a problem, particularly if they are promoted from the domestic side of the business. They can be ethnocentric and relatively uninterested in or uneasy with international markets.

Also, if each product group goes its own way, the company's international development may result in inefficiencies. For example, two product divisions may be purchasing advertising space independently in the same magazine. This will prove more expensive than combining the purchases. To offset the inefficiencies of a worldwide product organization, some companies provide for global coordination of activities such as advertising, customer service, and government relations.

Matrix Organizational Structures. As the Ford example suggests, some companies have grown frustrated with the limitations of a one-dimensional geographic, functional, or product organization structures. To overcome these drawbacks, the matrix organization was developed. As shown in Figure 16.9, the matrix organization allows for two or more dimensions of theoretically equal weight (here, geographic and product dimensions) in the organizational structure and in decision-making responsibility. A matrix organization often includes both product and geographic management components. Product management has worldwide responsibility for a specific product line, whereas geographic management is responsible for all product lines in a specific geographic area. These management structures overlap at the national product/market level. A matrix organization structure has a dual rather than a single chain of command, which means that many individuals will have two superiors.

Under this organizational structure, the brand managers for brands X, Y, and Z in any European country would report directly to two different bosses—vice president product line E and the director of marketing for Europe.

One of the most extensive global matrix organizations is that of ABB, a Swedish-Swiss company with several major businesses in electric power gener-

FIGURE 16.9
Matrix Organization

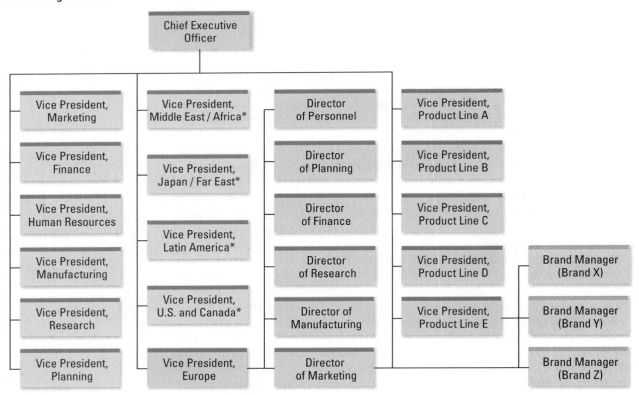

* Each regional vice president has functional managers reporting to him or her, as illustrated for the Vice President, Europe.

ation, railways, industry automation, and environmental equipment. Created as the result of a merger between Swedish-based Asea and Swiss-based Brown Boveri, the company operates worldwide in nearly sixty product areas. Each product division has global responsibility for strategy and is measured on the basis of its own profit-and-loss account. On the other side of the matrix are numerous country organizations responsible for implementing the global strategy in their assigned territories. Each local manager reports to a regional manager as well as to the assigned global product manager. For the matrix to work, both the regional manager and the product manager must jointly agree on the local strategy, budget, and business approach. The company has been structured into more than 3,000 units with this dual reporting arrangement. ABB has also promoted cooperation among its management to make the best of the matrix organization.[16]

Firms tend to adopt matrix organizations when they need to be highly responsive to two dimensions (such as product and geography). But matrix organizations are not without their challenges. Some critics of Unilever's matrix structure complained that its complexity—with some managers in charge of product categories, others in charge of brands, and still others in charge of geographic areas—resulted in duplication of authority and confusion of responsibility.[17] Power struggles are a common problem, especially when a matrix organization is first established. Relationships are tested as each side of the matrix attempts to "find its place" in the organization. In fact, the key to successful matrix management is the degree to which managers in an organization can resolve conflict and achieve the successful implementation of plans and programs. The matrix organization requires a change in management behavior from traditional authority to an influence system based on technical competence, interpersonal sensitivity, and leadership.

The matrix organization also requires a substantial investment in dual budgeting, accounting, transfer pricing, and personnel evaluation systems. Matrix structures may become even harder to manage as a result of corporate downsizing. Shrinking staffs add to the difficulties surrounding the multiplicity of bosses. Most companies have cut the assistants or liaison personnel who used to smooth things out and made sure everyone could get together on a certain day. As a result, some managers with more than one boss are now saddled with more work coordinating meetings and assignments, increasing their already heavy workloads.[18] Nonetheless, the additional complexity and cost of a matrix organization can sometimes be offset by the benefits of the dual focus. Overall, the matrix structure can permit an organization to function better in an uncertain and changing environment.

NEW TRENDS IN GLOBAL ORGANIZATIONS

Global companies must continually adapt their organizations to the needs of the marketplace. Bartlett and Ghoshal interviewed 236 managers in diverse groups of nine companies—Procter & Gamble, Kao, Unilever, ITT, Ericsson, NEC, General Electric, Philips, and Matsushita. Their responses suggest that the challenges of global efficiency, local responsiveness, and global learning have become so pervasive that the global organization of the future will have to contend with all of them simultaneously.[19]

As companies compete on a worldwide basis, they must develop global economies of scale. Instead of supporting manufacturing plants in each major market, they need to standardize products or components. Electrolux, Black & Decker, Unilever, and many other firms have rationalized their manufacturing to yield economies of scale. Although the washing machine or power tool may vary from country to country, the motors can be standardized and manufactured in large volume to reduce costs. The organizational structure needs in some way to encourage this trend toward efficiency.

The increased cost of R&D, shortened product life cycles, and consumer demand for the latest technology have increased the need for development and diffusion of worldwide learning. This learning is often related to R&D but can also include marketing or manufacturing learning. ITT's strategy of individually developing its telecommunication switch technology for each country, without gaining any global expertise, was one of the factors leading to the company's exit from that business. On the other hand, the culmination of P&G's 7 years of research to develop a heavy-duty, liquid laundry detergent in Europe was quickly and successfully transferred to the United States in the form of Liquid Tide.

Global Mandates

Global mandate a responsibility assigned to a manager or team within a firm to carry out a task on a global scale

As companies globalize their marketing organizations, the question of who should receive **global mandates** becomes an important concern. A global mandate is the expressed assignment to carry out a task on a global scale. Global mandates may be assigned to individual managers or to company teams. In either case, responsibility extends across all geographic locations, and the teams or marketing managers often make decisions that can affect all national subsidiaries. We have already discussed two types of global mandates—global brand management (Chapter 11) and global account management (Chapter 14). Global mandates can also be of a temporary nature.

Global team a task force established to address at the global level a particular issue facing a firm

Executives may be named to a task force or **global team** to deal with a particular global marketing issue, such as how to respond to a major change in product technology. Who should receive a global mandate is an important decision for all globally active firms. It would be difficult to implement a global marketing strategy if the company did not endow key marketing executives with global mandates.[20]

Organization of the Born-Global Firm

In Chapter 8 we introduced the concept of born-global firms. From their inception or very shortly thereafter, these new firms target global markets. Almost immediately, international sales account for a large proportion of their total sales. There are several explanations for this phenomenon. Entrepreneurs are increasingly exposed to global opportunities as a result of the communications revolution. Many global entrepreneurs have themselves worked or studied in foreign countries. Many realize that their customers and competition are global. A large number of global start-ups can be found in Silicon Valley, where rapidly changing technologies encounter worldwide demand.[21]

Born globals can benefit from the fact that they have no organizational history. Other firms have traditionally passed through several structural reorganizations as they evolved into global firms. Born-global firms can adopt global organizations from the start. This is enviable in that structural change can entail heavy costs and business disruptions. However, there is something to be said for the more traditional, gradual evolution of a global organization. Firms that move into international markets more slowly can build up market and cultural knowledge over time. They cultivate and support ever more extensive worldwide organizations by recruiting and training knowledgeable and experienced managers and staff. Born globals attempt to do this practically overnight and can find their managerial resources stretched to the limit. As is the case with other entrepreneurial ventures, they can find themselves with fewer assets than opportunities.[22]

CONTROLLING THE GLOBAL ORGANIZATION

As an international company becomes larger and more globally focused, maintaining control of international operations becomes increasingly important. Establishing a system to control marketing activities in numerous markets is not an easy job. However, if companies expect to implement their global strategies, they must establish a control system to regulate the many activities within their organizations.

Elements of a Control Strategy

Control is a cornerstone of organization. Control provides the means to direct, regulate, and manage business operations. The implementation of a global marketing program requires a significant amount of interaction not only among various national subsidiaries but also among the individual areas of marketing, such as product development and advertising, and among the other functional areas, such as production and R&D. The control system is used to measure these business activities along with competitive and market reactions. Deviations from the planned activities and results are analyzed and reported so that corrective action can be taken.

A control system has three basic elements: (1) the establishment of standards, (2) the measurement of performance against those standards, and (3) the analysis and correction of any deviations from the standards. Although control is a conceptually simple aspect of the organization process, a wide variety of problems arise in international situations, resulting in inefficiencies and intracompany conflict.

Developing Standards. Corporate goals are achieved through the effective implementation of a marketing strategy in the international firm's many national markets. Standard setting is driven by these corporate goals. Standards must be clearly defined, universally accepted, and understood by managers throughout the global organization. The standards should be set through joint deliberations involving corporate headquarters personnel and each local marketing organization. Normally, the standard setting is done annually when the operational business plan is established.

Firms can employ both behavioral and performance standards. **Behavioral standards** refer to actions taken within the firm. They can include the type and

Behavioral standards standards relating to actions taken within the firm

amount of advertising to be developed and utilized, the market research to be performed, and the prices to be charged for a product. **Performance standards** refer to market outcomes. They might include trial rates by customers or sales by product line. Recently, there has been a trend toward broadening the measures of business performance beyond financial data. More and more companies are measuring quality, customer satisfaction, innovation, and market share.[23]

Measuring and Evaluating Performance. After standards are set, performance must be monitored. In order to monitor performance against standards, management must be able to observe current performance. Much of the numerical information, such as sales and expenses, will be reported through the accounting system. Other items, such as the implementation of an advertising program, will be communicated through a report. At times, personal visits and meetings may be advisable when management is attempting to evaluate more complex issues, such as the success or failure of coordinated national actions against a global competitor.

Analyzing and Correcting Deviations from the Standards. The purpose of establishing standards and reporting performance is to ensure achievement of corporate goals. To achieve these goals, management must evaluate how well performance is living up to the standards the company has set and must initiate corrective action when performance is below those standards. As a consequence of distance, communication issues, and cultural differences, the control process can be difficult in the international setting.

Control strategy can be related to the principle of the carrot and the stick: using both positive and negative incentives. On the positive side, outstanding performance can be rewarded with increased independence, more marketing dollars, and salary increases or bonuses for the managers. On the negative side, unsatisfactory performance can mean reduction in all those items, as well as the threat that the managers responsible will lose their jobs. The key to correcting deviations is to get managers to understand and agree with the standards and then ensure that they have the means to correct the deficiencies. Hence the managers are often given some flexibility with resources. For example, if sales are down 10 percent, managers may need the authority to increase advertising or reduce prices to offset the sales decline.

Communication Systems

Effective communication systems facilitate control. Global strategies that require standardization and coordination across borders will need an effective communication system to support them. Headquarters staff will need to receive timely and accurate local input from national subsidiaries. Then decisions can be made quickly and transmitted back to the local management for rapid implementation.

As physical distances separating headquarters and national subsidiaries increase, the time and expense involved in communications increase, and so does the potential for error. Nonetheless, global communications are vastly improved over what they were only a few years ago. The quality of telecommunications has soared while its costs have plummeted. Today most countries have sufficient communications infrastructures. Still, communications infrastructures vary among countries, and problems can continue to arise in less developed countries.

Global information networks are now available that allow improved communication around the world. For example, the Internet links millions of computer users and gives them access to information, research, and services. These information superhighways are reducing many of the constraints imposed by geography. Increasingly, global businesses are harnessing the Internet for purposes of internal communications. Over the long term, these relatively inexpensive global networks will allow for better control. For example, Siemens operates in 190 countries and has instituted an internal system, or "sharenet," for posting knowledge throughout the global company. The sharenet came in handy when Siemens Malaysia wanted to bid on a high-speed data network linking Kuala Lumpur and its new airport. Lacking the know-how necessary for such a project, the subsidiary turned to the sharenet and discovered that Siemens was already working on a similar project in Denmark.[24]

Corporate Culture as Control

In addition to the processes we have described, many international firms attempt to establish cultural control. If an international firm can establish a strong corporate culture across its subsidiaries, then managers from its various units share a single vision and values. Some believe that this corporate socialization enables global firms to operate with less burdensome hierarchical structures and fewer time-consuming procedures.

Matsushita (Panasonic) provides managers with 6 months of cultural training, and Unilever's new hires go through corporate socialization as well. Such initiation programs help to build the vision and shared values of a strong corporate culture. Managers also receive ongoing training. For example, Unilever brings four hundred to five hundred international managers from around the world to its international management-training center. Unilever spends as much on training as it does on R&D, not only to upgrade skills but also to indoctrinate managers into the Unilever family. This helps build personal relationships and informal contacts that can be more powerful than any formal systems or structures.

However, we must remember that the corporate culture of a firm mirrors to a large extent the national culture of its homeland. When a U.S. multinational socializes its local managers to "think and act American," this can make communication and control within the multinational easier. However, it is still the case that local managers must operate within many national cultures that are different from the American culture. It is equally important that they maintain their local culture and remain capable of relating to local customers, competitors, and governments.

CONFLICT BETWEEN HEADQUARTERS AND SUBSIDIARIES

Despite attempts to build a transnational corporate culture within multinational firms, a universal problem facing international marketing managers is the internal conflict that arises between headquarters and subsidiaries. Table 16.1 summarizes several significant differences in perceptions of marketing issues between subsidiaries and home offices that emerged from a recent study

TABLE 16.1 PERCEPTIONS OF ISSUES RELATED TO MARKETING IN HOME OFFICE AND SUBSIDIARIES		
MARKETING ISSUE	HOME OFFICE	SUBSIDIARY
1. Visits from home office managers to subsidiaries are usually productive.	Agrees more	Agrees less
2. Problems come up frequently because the home office doesn't understand the variety of opinions that can exist at a subsidiary as a consequence of the more widely differing backgrounds there than at the home office.	Agrees less	Agrees more
3. Problems come up frequently because the home office doesn't understand that a subsidiary's culture can be different from that of the home office.	Agrees less	Agrees more
4. There is not enough emphasis at the subsidiaries on strategic thinking and long-term planning.	Agrees more	Agrees less
5. Subsidiaries are encouraged to suggest innovations to the home office.	Agrees more	Agrees less
6. The home office generally tries to change subsidiaries, rather than trying to understand and perhaps adapt to them.	Agrees less	Agrees more
7. Subsidiaries have enough flexibility to cope effectively with changing local conditions.	Agrees more	Agrees less
8. Knowledge is transmitted freely from the home office to subsidiaries.	Agrees more	Agrees less
9. There is a lack of carryover of marketing knowledge from one subsidiary to another.	Agrees more	Agrees less
10. The home office tries to involve subsidiaries' marketing managers meaningfully in decision making.	Agrees more	Agrees less

SOURCE: Reprinted from *Journal of World Business* 36, no. 2, Chi-Fai Chan and Neil Bruce Holbert, "Marketing Home and Away," p. 207. Copyright © 2001, with permission from Elsevier.

of U.S. companies with operations in Hong Kong. The study also identified four areas in which subsidiaries perceived their autonomy as significantly less than did headquarters—pricing, logo and name, and the choice of an advertising agency.[25] This is probably not surprising, given our prior discussion of the impact of global branding, increased price coordination worldwide, and the trend among multinationals to consolidate advertising within one or a few agency networks.

Conflicts between headquarters and subsidiaries are inevitable because of the natural differences in orientation and perception between the two groups. The subsidiary manager usually wants more authority and more local differentiation, whereas headquarters wants more detailed reporting and greater unification of geographically dispersed operations. The parent is usually the more powerful in the relationship, but sometimes a subsidiary can take over a parent company. Trendy U.S. retailer Esprit watched its sales in the United States decline while sales in Asia and Europe soared to over $1 billion a year. In 2002, its Hong Kong office bought full rights to the Esprit brand around the world for $150 million. Its first goal: Revamp strategy in the U.S. market.[26]

Conflict is not all bad. Conflict generates constant dialogue between different organizational levels during the planning and implementation of strategies. This dialogue can result in a balance between headquarters and subsidiary

Under its banner "Science for a Better Life," German-based Bayer is a major global player in health care, polymers, and crop science. It markets its products in over 120 countries. But all subsidiaries are not equal. Bayer's Brazilian subsidiary accounts for 43 percent of its Latin American sales. Its subsidiary in South Africa accounts for 78 percent of company sales in Africa.

authority, global and local perspective, and standardization and differentiation of the global marketing mix. And it can allow new and better ideas to surface from any part of the global organization.

CONSIDERING A GLOBAL MARKETING CAREER

A viable organizational structure, a unifying corporate culture, and effective control systems all enable a firm to compete in the global arena. Equally important are the individuals who manage the firm. Throughout this book, we have presented the argument that virtually all firms are affected by increased global competition. In turn, most firms not only will deal with competitors from other countries but also will depend on sales that are increasingly multinational. Many will need to adapt to buyers who are becoming increasingly global themselves. Because of this, firms will need managers who understand the issues we have discussed here: the impact of the global environment on marketing, global strategic planning, managing a marketing mix across cultures, and effectively managing relations between headquarters and subsidiaries to ensure that global strategy is well implemented. Any marketer who eventually reaches the upper echelons of management will need an understanding of the concepts we have covered in this book.

In many companies, global marketing is not always an entry-level job, especially for recent university graduates. Firms often choose to fill globally oriented positions with marketers who have first had domestic experience. A good career strategy is to join a company that has global operations and whose culture you admire. After proving yourself in the home market, you should be eligible for a global position in only a few years. This is especially true if you are assigned to the firm's headquarters. Informal networking with international executives can be a good way to broadcast your interest in international markets and global strategy—and companies are always in need of such motivated managers.

Besides this traditional route to a career in global marketing, there are other ways to go international—even at an entry level. Consider smaller companies that need help with international markets immediately. Export management companies are one option. For these types of firms, skills in the local language of a key target market can make you stand out. If you are an American citizen, you might join the Peace Corps. The Peace Corps offers positions that are business oriented, and you receive language and cultural training. Look for a job with a foreign multinational that operates in your country. Even if you don't work with foreign markets right away, you will gain the experience of working with different cultures within your organization. Or consider positions in purchasing with a company that deals extensively with foreign suppliers. Knowing about global marketing can make you a more sophisticated buyer. Many U.S. managers in entry-level positions in purchasing find themselves flying to Mexico or the Far East to help manage the buyer-supplier relationship. Finally, government positions such as those with local or national commerce departments can provide excellent experience and can put you in touch with many corporate executives working in international markets.

Whether you choose a more traditional route to a career in global marketing or find a particular niche that is right for you, the need for a global mindset and the numbers of challenging and exciting positions for global marketers will only increase in the future.

CONCLUSION

Organizing the marketing efforts of a company across a number of countries is a difficult process. As the scope of a company's international business changes, its organizational structure must be modified in accordance with the internal and external environments. In this chapter, we have reviewed the various types of organizations commonly used, showing the benefits of each. The dynamic nature of business requires that a company constantly reevaluate its organizational structure and processes and make any modifications necessary to meet the objectives of the firm.

The task of molding an organization to respond to the needs of a global marketplace also involves building a shared vision and developing human resources. A clear vision of the purpose of the company that is shared by everyone gives focus and direction to each manager. Managers can be a company's scarcest resource. A commitment to recruiting and developing managers who understand the complexities of the global marketplace and the importance of cross-cultural sensitivity should help the international firm build a common vision and values, which in turn facilitate the implementation of a global strategy.

QUESTIONS FOR DISCUSSION

1. How does a domestic organization evolve into an international organization? What type of international organization is likely to develop first? What type is likely to develop second? Why?

2. To achieve better international sales (which currently account for about 30 percent of total revenues), the U.S.-based toy manufacturer Mattel decided to put U.S. division heads in charge of international sales. Discuss the pros and cons of such a move in general and for a firm in the toy industry in particular.

3. Apart from its formal organizational structure, in what ways can the global company ensure that it is responding to the market and achieving efficiency, local responsiveness, and global learning?

4. What are the advantages and limitations of using the Internet as a means of internal communication within a global organization?

5. What suggestions would you propose to bridge the gaps between headquarters and subsidiaries that are noted in Table 16.1?

CASE 16.1
How Local Should Coke Be?

For twenty years, Coke had expanded its soft-drinks business rapidly overseas. It had consolidated its bottling networks to cover increasingly large territories in response to an increasingly centralized retail trade. Many decisions about advertising and packaging were dictated from Atlanta. With the purchase of Minute Maid orange juice in the late 1990s, Coke was hoping to gain economies of scale for global dominance in the juice business in addition to its presence in soft drinks.

By 2000, however, Coke was rethinking its U.S.-based centralized approach to running its global business. For the first time in its 114-year history, Coke's top executives met together outside Atlanta headquarters. It was a harbinger of things to come. From now on, the Coke board would meet outside the United States once a year. This change was one of many instigated by Coke's new CEO, Douglas Daft, who was attempting to turn the

company around after 2 years of poor profits. Daft himself was an Australian who had attracted attention with his successful management of Coke's Japanese subsidiary, where his localization approach had built a successful tea and coffee business. Under Daft, Atlanta was envisioned as a support to Coke's national subsidiaries, rather than as the traditional central headquarters that would mandate and direct the company's worldwide operations. Coke would cease to be big, slow, and out of touch and would instead be light on its feet and sensitive to local markets. One immediate effect of Daft's more localized strategy was the cutting of 2,500 jobs at Atlanta headquarters. Asian and Middle East operations, previously managed out of Atlanta, would be transferred to Hong Kong and London, respectively.

The backlash against Coke's centralized approach first emerged in Europe. Europe represented 20 percent of worldwide volume and 28 percent of worldwide profits. Two incidents caused Coke's new management to reconsider its European policy. In 1999, as a result of various court rulings across Europe, Coke had to scale back significantly its attempt to buy Cadbury Schweppes's beverage brands. A contamination scare also forced Coke to destroy 17 million cases of Coke at a cost of $200 million. Amid the bad publicity arising from this incident, Coke was accused of being evasive and arrogant and of delaying too long in its response while waiting for direction from Atlanta.

Daft decided to break up responsibility for Europe, which had long been handled by a single division that oversaw forty-nine markets. Ten new geographic groups were formed on the basis of culturally and economically clustered markets. After all, what did Finland and Italy have in common? In another break with the past, nine of the new groups were to be run by non-Americans. Previously, half of the top executives in Europe had been sent over from the United States. Europe would be the test case to see whether Coke could get closer to its consumers by altering its organization. The new European groups were still under orders to push Coke's four core brands—Coca-Cola, Fanta, Sprite, and Diet Coke—but they were encouraged to explore new products and develop flavors with local appeal. Germany responded with a berry-flavored Fanta, and Turkey developed a pear-flavored beverage.

Soon other changes were evident. The formal suits seen at headquarters in Atlanta were replaced by more informal attire. Local lawyers were employed instead of lawyers sent from the United States. Reporters seeking a Coke spokesperson could contact expanded communications offices in European countries instead of having to contact Atlanta. Previously, only a single global website had been allowed; now local subsidiaries could run their own websites. Coke's Belgian site—in Dutch, French, and English—received three million hits in its first month. One manager noted that developing the website took only a few weeks, whereas it would have taken 8 months under the old centralized system. Belgium was also the site for a new localized promotion idea. Coke hostesses were sent to discos at night to

hand out bottles of Coke and promote the idea of a "Coke pause" in a night of otherwise hard drinking. A local spokesman supported the new promotional idea, noting that Belgians were party animals—something Atlanta headquarters might have been slow to appreciate.

Although a euphoric freedom appeared to spread across Europe, the success of the new organizational structure was less clear when it came to the bottom line. Sales slipped slightly in Europe just as localization was being put in place. Some believed that Coke's restructuring of Europe was an overreaction to some bad publicity. They argued that Coke would always be a foreign target. McDonald's had tried to assuage French farmers with a local purchasing campaign, only to meet with indifference. Was Coke doomed to face similar indifference as it attempted to localize? As for the contaminated-bottles crisis, a year later in Belgium, sales had returned to normal levels, and schools where students had reported getting sick had renewed their contracts with Coke. And Atlanta was sending further messages that there would be limits to localization. One top executive at the German operations was fired for running television advertisements aimed at the radical youth movement.

Another early challenge to localization would likely be Coke's launch of its sports drink Powerade in Europe. The sports-drink market in Europe was only $1 billion, compared to $61 billion in the United States, but it was growing fast. Competition in Europe was fragmented but included Powerade's archrival Gatorade, owned by Coke's archrival PepsiCo. Gatorade held 78 percent of the U.S. market and was strong in Europe as well. Powerade would essentially retain its American formula but would taste slightly different because of ingredient regulations of the European Union. The new launch might possibly cannibalize Aquarius, Coke's other recent launch into the sports-drink market in Europe. However, a company spokesperson noted that Aquarius was meant to be drunk after exercising, whereas Powerade was to be drunk while exercising as well. At headquarters, managers envisioned the target market for their new introduction as European males age thirteen to twenty-nine. Powerade was scheduled to debut in

Europe in nine national markets—France, Germany, Greece, Hungary, Italy, Poland, Spain, Sweden, and Turkey.

Discussion Questions

1. What are the pros and cons of changing Coke's single European structure into ten different regional groups?
2. Do you agree with Coke's firing of the executive in Germany? Why or why not? How should Coke avoid incidents like this in the future?
3. If you were the manager of Coke in Germany or Turkey, where would you invest your greatest effort, behind the launch of Powerade or behind the launch of your locally developed fruit-flavored drinks? What factors would guide your decision?

4. What suggestions would you offer to Coke about its global organizational structure and control?

Sources: Chad Terhune and Betsy McKay, "Bottled Up," *Wall Street Journal*, May 4, 2004, p. A1; William Echikson and Dean Foust, "For Coke: Local Is It," *Business Week*, July 3, 2000, p. 122; Dean Foust and Gerry Khermouch, "Repairing the Coke Machine," *Business Week*, March 19, 2001, pp. 86–88; Bert Roughton Jr., "Independence Adds Marketing Oomph to Coke Abroad," *Atlanta Constitution*, June 11, 2000, p. 1G; Christopher Seward, "View from Top; Coke Wandered Off Its Path," *Atlanta Constitution*, March 28, 2000, p. 5D; Jabulani Sikhakhane, "Going Local in the Face of Globalization," *Financial Mail*, May 26, 2000, p. 28; Betsy McKay, "Coke Surprisingly Makes Minute Maid Its Unit of the Hour," *Wall Street Journal*, November 16, 2001, p. B3.; and Alessandra Galloni, "Coke to Launch Powerade Across Europe," *Wall Street Journal*, October 16, 2001, p. B11.

CASE 16.2

The Globalization of Indian IT

Wipro Ltd. originated as an Indian firm operating in the vegetable oils trade about half a century ago. By the beginning of the twenty-first century, it had evolved into one of India's largest software services companies, employing 6,700 software engineers. Located in India's high-tech city of Bangalore, Wipro began in the software business by writing code on contract, handling multimillion-dollar contracts with international companies such as General Electric, Nokia, and Home Depot. In 2001, however, its president, Vivek Paul, aspired to bring the company up the value-added chain to become one of the top ten information technology (IT) companies in the world. Instead of simply writing code, Wipro would expand into the more lucrative area of business process consulting, offering supply chain management and deciphering customer trends from sales data—and competing with the likes of IBM Global Services and Electronic Data Services. But was this vision viable? Could Wipro go from an Indian firm with overseas clients to a truly global corporation virtually overnight? One estimate suggested that Wipro would need to hire an additional 30,000 employees worldwide in order to accomplish this goal.

Key Indian software development companies such as Wipro Ltd. and Infosys Technologies Ltd. had already captured a lucrative market by handling code-writing jobs from larger international companies. Working from sites such as a high-technology industrial park in India's high-tech showcase Bangalore, Indian software companies could take advantage of both lower-paid Indian talent and the telecommunications revolution in order to service overseas markets quickly and effectively. Programmers in Bangalore earned only $800 a month, although salaries were rising at a rate of 15 percent a year. Western consulting companies, however, were beginning to challenge the competitive advantage of Indian firms by opening Asian software centers. Furthermore, India as a site for code writing was being challenged by such other low-cost countries as China, the Philippines, and Vietnam. Infrastructure problems such as electricity shortages and poor roads still plagued Bangalore—prompting companies such as Wipro to consider expanding elsewhere.

Moving into more sophisticated and higher-margin IT products meant both converting current clients and attracting new ones. Wipro convinced Thomas Cook Financial Services not only to use them for designing a system for automating Thomas Cook's foreign currency transactions but also to hire them to install the system within the British multinational. But new, smaller accounts would also be necessary if Indian firms were to carve out a significant global market share. VideosDotCom sent some work to Wipro when its Texas-based staff was too busy. Subsequently, it switched most of its development work to Bangalore, citing Wipro's extensive e-commerce experience, development skills, pricing, and overall quality. Infosys won a contract from EveryD.com, a Japanese online shopping and banking service for housewives. Its job encompassed developing the business plan, designing the portal, and writing the operational software. The Japanese customer noted that Infosys wasn't the cheapest of alternatives but that it had the necessary expertise and delivered the product on time.

In addition to these more established companies, Indian start-up software companies were developing their own products and taking them directly to the largest national market—the United States. Some executives of these Indian start-up companies found themselves moving overseas almost immediately. The chairman of Bombay-based I-Flex Solutions, a financial services software developer, moved to New Jersey in order to be able to call on potential clients personally. Over a period of just a few years, the company had posted 25 percent of its 1,425 employees to four continents. Despite being an Indian start-up, Talisma Corporation, a customer relations management software developer, was established and based in Seattle, where it could employ U.S. salespeople to promote its made-in-India product. One year later, Talisma had nineteen offices in seven countries.

Such IT start-ups contributed to the fact that India had become one of Asia's major destinations for venture capital. Still, Indian capital markets were generally noted for their conservatism. Firms were expected to post profits consistently. A loss of money, even in the short term, was considered unacceptable. Laying out large sums of money, such as those needed for the acquisition of other firms, was often judged to be very risky.

Some of the venture capital flowing into India came from expatriate Indians. Many Indian IT engineers worked or had worked in the United States. Silicon Valley's Indian high-tech population numbered around 200,000 and was considered to be the area's most successful immigrant community. Many Indians working in the IT industry in the United States believed that despite their technical expertise—or possibly because of it—they were being overlooked for management positions. Ironically, American companies considered their technical skills too valuable to lose by transferring them to management. Partially as a reaction to this, many Indians working in the United States considered starting their own businesses either in India or in the United States. Indians living in the United States often invested in each other's start-up companies, sat on each other's boards, and hired each other for key jobs. In fact, companies with Indian founders could often hire teams of developers more rapidly than the average U.S. company without the benefit of ethnic ties to the Indian community. IndUS Entrepreneurs (TIE) of Santa Clara emerged as one of the preeminent networking groups for Indian entrepreneurs. It hosted monthly Angel Forums at which entrepreneurs could pitch plans to potential investors. The IndUS Entrepreneurs website states as the group's goal the duplication of the Silicon Valley success story in India.

Discussion Questions

1. Why will Indian IT firms have to transform themselves into more global corporations in the future?
2. How will their internationalization experience differ from the experience of U.S.-based firms in the latter half of the twentieth century?

3. What unique advantages and disadvantages do these firms possess?
4. Which organizational structure do you think would be appropriate for a more global Wipro? Why?

Sources: S. Srinvasan, "Growth in India Bangalore's Plight," Associated Press, September 3, 2003; Robert D. Hof, "India and Silicon Valey," *Business Week*, December 8, 2003; Bruce Einhorn and Manjeet Kripalani, "India 3.0," *Business Week*, February 26, 2001, pp. 44–46; Julelcha Dash, "Indian Entrepreneurs Take Charge," *Computer World*, April 3, 2000, p. 39; and Mark Clifford, Manjeet Kripalani, and Heidi Dawley, "The 21st Century Corporation," *Business Week Online*, August 28, 2000.

Notes

1. Kevin Maler, "3M Looks to Expand Global Sales," Knight-Ridder Tribune Business News, June 17, 2001.
2. Andrew Campbell, Marion Devine, and David Young, *A Sense of Mission* (London: Economist Books, 1990), pp. 19–41.
3. Gary Hamel and C. K. Prahalad, "Strategic Intent," *Harvard Business Review* 67 (May–June 1989), pp. 63–68.
4. David P. Hamilton and Robert Steiner, "Sony's Idei Tightens Reins Again on Freewheeling U.S. Operations," *Wall Street Journal*, January 24, 1997, p. A10.
5. David Woodruff, "Your Career Matters," *Wall Street Journal*, November 11, 2000, p. B1.
6. Carol Hymowitz, "European Executives Give Some Advice on Crossing Borders," *Wall Street Journal*, December 2, 2003, p. B1.
7. Matthew Karnitschnig, "Identity Question," *Wall Street Journal*, September 8, 2003, p. A1.
8. Carol Hymowitz, "Foreign-Born CEOs are Increasing in U.S., Rarer Overseas," *Wall Street Journal*, May 25, 2004, p. B1.
9. Jason Gertzen, "Milwaukee-Based Manufacturer Seeks Overseas Expansion," Knight-Ridder Tribune Business News, June 11, 2001.
10. Will Pinkston, "Ford Mulls Suppliers Park Near Atlanta," *Wall Street Journal*, July 12, 2000, p. S1.
11. "European Study Finds Companies Can Save 35–45% by Moving to Financial Shared Services," *A. T. Kearney* (News Release), December 16, 1993, p. 1.
12. Arnold Schuh, "Global Standardization as a Success Formula for Marketing in Central Eastern Europe?" *Journal of World Business* 35, no. 2 (Summer 2000), pp. 133–148.
13. "Ford Maps Out a Global Ambition," *Financial Times*, April 3, 1995, p. 11.
14. James B. Treece, "Ford: Alex Trotman's Daring Global Strategy," *Business Week*, April 3, 1995, p. 94.
15. Keith H. Hammonds, "A Global Tune-up for Ford," *Business Week*, May 2, 1994, p. 38.
16. Christopher A. Bartlett, "ABB's Relays Business: Building and Managing a Global Matrix," Harvard Business School Case, 1993.
17. Ernest Beck, "Familiar Cry to Unilever: Split It Up!" *Wall Street Journal*, August 4, 2000, p. A7.
18. Carol Hymowitz, "In the Lead: Managers Suddenly Have to Answer to a Crowd of Bosses," *Wall Street Journal*, August 12, 2003, p. B1.
19. Christopher Bartlett and Sumantra Ghoshal, *Managing Across Borders* (London: Hutchinson Business Books, 1989), pp. 16–17.
20. Jean-Pierre Jeannet, *Managing with a Global Mindset* (London: Financial Times Pitman, 2000), p. 171.
21. Benjamin M. Oriatt and Patricia Phillips McDougall, "Global Startups," *Academy of Management Executive* 9, no. 2 (May 1995), p. 43.
22. Jean-Pierre Jeannet, "OnePIN Goes Global" (case), Babson College Glavin Center, 2004.
23. Michael Goold, *Strategic Control* (London: Economist Books, 1990), p. 120.
24. "Electric Glue," *The Economist*, June 2, 2001.
25. Chi-fai Chan and Neil Bruce Holbert, "Marketing Home and Away: Perceptions of Managers in Headquarters and Subsidiaries," *Journal of World Business* 36, 2 (Summer 2001): 205–221.
26. Sarah McBride, "Can Esprit Be Hip Again?" *Wall Street Journal*, June 17, 2002, p. B1.

Appendix: Cases

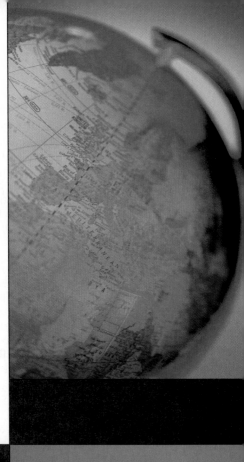

CASE 1   AGT, INC.

AGT, Inc. is a marketing research company located in the city of Karachi, Pakistan. Jeff Sons Trading Company (JST) has approached it to look at the potential market for an amusement park in Karachi. Because the city is crowded and real estate costs are high, it will be difficult to find a large enough piece of land on which to locate such a facility. Even if land is available, it will be expensive and that will have a detrimental effect on the overall costs of the project. JST needs to know the potential of this type of investment. They want the market research to identify if a need for the amusement park exists and, if it does, what the public's attitude toward that type of recreational facility might be. If a need is found and support is sufficient, then they want to know the type of amusement park required by potential customers. JST will make its investment decision based on the results of this study.

Background

Pakistan is a typical less developed country (LDC) of the Third World faced with the usual problems of rapidly increasing population, sizable government deficit, and heavy dependence on foreign aid. The country's economy has grown rapidly in the last decade, with GDP expanding at 6.7 percent annually, more than twice the population growth. Like any other LDC, it displays dualism in its economic system: the cities have modern facilities, the smaller towns have some or none. The same holds true for income distribution patterns. Real per capita GDP is Rupees 10,000, or US $400 annually. There is a small wealthy class (1 to 3%), a middle class consisting of another 20 percent, and the remainder of the population is poor. Half of the population lives below the poverty line. Most of the middle class is an urban working class.

Karachi, as the country's largest city and boasting a dense population of over 6 million, has been chosen as the site of the first large-scale amusement park in Pakistan. Current recreational facilities in Karachi, including a poorly maintained zoo, are modest, and people with families avoid visiting most facilities because of the crowds. There are other small parks, but they are not sufficient to cater to such a large population. The main place people go for recreation is the beach. The beaches near Karachi are not well developed and are regularly polluted by oil slicks from the port.

Our working hypothesis is that Karachi citizens have a growing need to spend their leisure time in recreational activities. (Indeed, many middle class and wealthy citizens already take vacations with their families and spend money on recreational activities abroad.) To determine whether there is a true need for this type of recreational facility, we propose to conduct a market research feasibility study.

Potential problems facing the construction of an amusement park in Karachi include:

- The communications infrastructure is poor.
- Only a small percentage of the people own their own transportation.
- Public and private transportation systems are not efficient.
- Maintaining law and order is a problem, said to be similar in scope to the crime problem in Los Angeles.

Research Objectives

To make an investment decision, JST outlined the research objectives necessary to design a marketing strategy that would accomplish the desired return on investment goals. These objectives were the following:

1. Identify the potential demand for this project.
2. Identify the primary target market and what they expect of an amusement park.

Information Needs

To fulfill their objectives, JST determined that they would need the following information:

Market

a. Is there a need for this project in this market?
b. How large is the potential market?
c. Is this market large enough to be profitable?

Consumers

a. Are the potential customers satisfied with the existing facilities in the city?
b. Will these potential consumers utilize an amusement park?
c. Which segment of the population is most interested in this type of facility?
d. Is the population ready to support this type of project?

e. What media could be used to promote the park successfully to potential customers?

Location

a. Where should this project be built to attract the most visitors?
b. How will consumers' existing attitudes on location influence the viability and cost of this project?
c. Will the company have to arrange for transportation to and from the facility if it is located outside the city area?
d. Is security a factor in determining the location of the facility?

Recreation Facilities

a. What type of attractions should the company provide at the park to attract customers?
b. Should there be overnight accommodations within the park?
c. Should the facility be available only to certain segments of the population or should it be open to all?

Proposal

With the objectives just outlined in mind, AGT, Inc. presented the following proposal:

The city of Karachi's population has its different economic clusters scattered haphazardly throughout the city. To conduct market research under these conditions and obtain accurate results will consequently be difficult. We recommend an extensive study to make sure we have an adequate sampling of opinion from the target market. Given these parameters, we recommend that the target market be defined as follows:

Desired Respondent Characteristics

- Upper Class: 1% (around 60,000)
- Middle Class: 15 to 20% (around 900,000 to 1,200,000)
- Male and female
- Age: 15 to 50 years (for survey; market includes all age groups)
- Income level: Rs 25,000 and above per year (Rs: 2000 per month)
- Household size: families will be better for the purposes of the sample
- Involved in entertainment activities
- Involved in recreational activities
- Actively participates in social activities
- Member of different clubs
- Involved in outdoor activities

To obtain accurate information regarding respondents' characteristics, we have to approach the market very carefully because of prevailing circumstances and existing cultural practices. People have little or no knowledge of market surveys. Obtaining their cooperation, even without cultural barriers, via a phone or mail survey will be difficult. In the following paragraphs we will discuss the negative and positive points of all types of surveys and select the appropriate form for our study.

The first, and possibly best, method for conducting the survey under these circumstances will be through the mail, which will not only be cheaper than other methods but can also cover all the population clusters easily. We cannot rely on a mail survey alone, however, because the mail system in Pakistan is unreliable and inefficient. We can go through courier services or registered mail, but doing so will cause the cost to skyrocket.

The other option is to conduct a survey by telephone. In this city of 6 million there are about 200,000 working telephones (one per 152 persons). Most of the telephones are in businesses or government offices. The problem is not that the citizens of Karachi cannot afford a telephone, but that they cannot get one because of the short supply. Another problem with a telephone survey is cultural; it is not considered polite in Pakistani society to call a stranger and start asking questions. It would be even more of a breach of etiquette if a male survey member were to reach a female household member. Because people are not familiar with marketing surveys, they would not be willing to volunteer the information we require on the telephone. The positive feature of a telephone survey is that most upper class women do not work and can be reached easily. To contact them, however, we would need to use a survey staff composed of females only. Overall, the chances of cooperation with a telephone survey are very low.

A mall/bazaar intercept could also be used. Again, however, we will face some cultural problems. It's not considered ethical for a male to approach a female in the mall. The only people willing to talk in public are likely to be men and we will thus miss female opinion.

To gather respondent data by survey in a country such as Pakistan, we will have to tailor our existing data collecting methods and make them fit the circumstances and cultural practices of that marketplace. As a company based in Pakistan with experience in living under these cultural practices, we propose the following design for the study and the questionnaire.

Design of the Study

Our study will contain a mixture of three types of survey, with each survey making use of a different method. We recommend the following types of surveys, tailored to fit the prevailing circumstances:

1. Mail Survey

We plan to modify this type of survey to fit the existing situation and to be maximally effi-cient. Specific changes have been made to counter the inefficient postal system and to generate a better percentage of response. We plan to deliver the surveys to respondents by the newspaper deliverymen rather than by mail. The average circulation of the various newspapers in Karachi ranges from 50,000 to 200,000 per day. The two dailies chosen have the largest circulation in the city.

A questionnaire will be placed in each newspaper delivered to respondents. This questionnaire will introduce us to the respondent and will ask for his cooperation, and it will include return postage and the firm's address. Identification of the firm will give respondents some confidence that they are not volunteering information to unknown parties. A small promotional gift will be promised for returning the completed survey. Since respondents who intend to claim the gift will give us their address, this will help us maintain a list of respondents for future surveys. Delivery with the daily newspaper will also allow us to focus easily on specific clusters.

We expect some loss in return mail because there is no acceptable way to get the questionnaires back except through the government postal system. Accordingly, we plan to deliver 5,000 questionnaires to counter the anticipated loss in return mail. The cost of this survey will be less than it would be if we mailed the questionnaires. Because this will be the first exposure for many respondents that allows them to give their views about an as yet nonexistent product, we do not have any return percentage on which to base our survey response expectations. In fact, this information may well provide the basis for future studies.

2. Door-to-Door Interviews

We will have to tailor the mall/bazaar intercept, as we did the mail survey, to get the highest possible response percentage. Instead of intercepting at malls, we believe it will be better to send surveyors door to door. This method can generate a better percentage of responses and also allows us to identify the respondents accurately. To conduct this survey, we will solicit the cooperation of the local business schools in providing us with students who will act as our surveyors. By using these young students we stand a better chance of generating a higher response than we would using older staff. We also plan to hire some additional personnel, mostly females, and train them to conduct this survey.

3. Additional Mail Survey

We plan to conduct this part of the survey to identify different groups of people already involved in similar types of recreational activity. There are eight to ten exclusive clubs in the city of Karachi. A few focus solely on some outdoor activity such as yachting and boating, golf, and the like. Their membership numbers vary from three to five thousand. The high cost of membership and monthly fees have restricted these clubs to the upper middle class and the wealthy. We can safely say that the people using these clubs belong to the 90th percentile of income level.

We propose to visit these clubs and personally ask for members' cooperation in participating in our survey. We also plan to obtain the clubs' membership list and have the questionnaire delivered to them. They will be asked to return the completed questionnaire to the club office or to mail it in the postage-paid reply envelope. We believe that this group will cooperate and give us high-quality feedback.

The second delivered survey will be to local schools. With the schools' cooperation, we will ask that this questionnaire be delivered by pupils to their parents. The cover letter will ask parents to fill out the questionnaire and return it to the school. This survey will provide a good sample of people who want outdoor activities for their children. We hope to generate a substantial response through this method.

Questionnaire Design

The type of questions asked should help our client make the decision about whether to invest in the project. (See proposed questionnaire.) Through the survey questionnaires we should be able to answer the question "Is the population ready for this project and are they willing to support it?" The questionnaire, a mixture of open-ended and close-ended questions, should also help to answer the following questions:

- Is there a market for this type of project?
- Is the market substantial?
- Is the market profitable?
- Will this project fill a real need?
- Will this project be only a momentary fad?
- Is the market evenly distributed in all segments/clusters, or is there a high demand in some segments?
- Is the population geared toward and willing to spend money on this type of entertainment facility? If so, how much?
- What is the best location for this project?
- Are people willing to travel some distance to reach this type of facility? Or do they want it within city limits?
- What types of entertainment/rides do people want in an amusement park?

- Through what type of media or promotion can prospective customers best be reached?

Discussion Questions

1. What are the objectives of the research project? Does the survey satisfy these objectives?
2. How do elements of culture affect the research design, collection of data, and analysis? Contrast this case with the design, collection of data, and analysis of a similar survey project in a more developed country such as the United States.
3. What alternative data collection methods might be useful to pursue? What are the strengths and weaknesses of these alternative methods?

Case prepared by William J. Carner. Used by permission.

QUESTIONNAIRE

1. Are there adequate recreational facilities in the city?
   Yes ☐   No ☐

2. How satisfied are you with the present recreational facilities?
   (Please rate from 0–10 degrees)

   0—1—2—3—4—5—6—7—8—9—10
   Poor   Excellent

3. How often do you visit the present recreational facilities? (Please check)
   Weekly ☐
   Fortnightly ☐
   Monthly ☐
   Once in two months ☐
   Yearly ☐
   More (indicate number)____ ☐
   Not at all ☐

4. Do you visit recreational areas with your family?
   Yes ☐   No ☐
   If no, why not?
   Security ☐
   Distance ☐
   Expense ☐
   Crowd (not family oriented) ☐
   Poor service ☐
   Other (Please specify) ☐
   _____

4a. Do you stay overnight?
    Yes ☐   No ☐
    If yes, how long? _____
    (Please indicate number of days)

4b. If no, would you have stayed if provided the right circumstances or facilities?
    Yes ☐   No ☐

5. Have you ever visited an amusement park?
   (Here in Pakistan ☐   Abroad ☐)
   Yes ☐ (Please go to question 5b)
   No ☐ (Please go to question 5a)

5a. If no, why not?
    Security ☐
    Distance ☐
    Expense ☐
    Crowd (not family oriented) ☐
    Poor service ☐
    Other (Please specify) _____ ☐
    _____

5b. If yes, when did you last visit an amusement park?
    Last month ☐
    Last six months ☐
    Within a year ☐
    More (specify number) ☐

    WHERE? _____

6. What did you enjoy most in that park?
   Roller coasters ☐
   Water slides ☐
   Children's play areas ☐
   Shows ☐
   Games ☐
   Simulators ☐
   Other_____ ☐

6a. How much did you spend in that park? (approximately)
   Rs 50 or less ☐
   51 to 100 ☐
   101 to 150 ☐
   151 to 200 ☐
   More than 200 ☐

   WHERE? _____

6b. How would you rate the value received? (Please rate from 0 – 10 degrees)

   0—1—2—3—4—5—6—7—8—9—10
   Poor   Excellent

7. Would you utilize an amusement park if one were built locally?
   Yes ☐   No ☐

8. What would you like to see in an amusement park? (Please give us your six best choices.)
   a._____   d._____
   b._____   e._____
   c._____   f._____

9. Where would you like its location to be?
   Within city area ☐
   Beach area ☐
   Suburbs ☐
   Outskirts of city ☐
   Indifferent ☐

10. How many kilometers will you be willing to travel to the park?
   Under 10 K ☐
   11 to 20 ☐
   21 to 35 ☐
   36 to 55 ☐
   56 to 65 ☐
   More than 65 ☐

11. How often do you take vacations for recreational purposes?
   Never ☐
   Once a year ☐
   Twice a year ☐
   More (please specify) _____ ☐

Please Tell Us About Yourself:

12. Please indicate your age.
   Under 15 ☐
   16 to 21 ☐
   22 to 29 ☐
   30 to 49 ☐
   50 to 60 ☐
   Over 60 ☐

13. Please indicate your gender:
   Male ☐   Female ☐

14. Are you married?
   Yes ☐   No ☐

15. How many children do you have?
   Please indicate number_____

16. Please indicate your total family income. (Yearly)
   Under 12,000 ☐
   Over 12,000 to 15,000 ☐
   Over 15,000 to 20,000 ☐
   Over 20,000 to 25,000 ☐
   Over 25,000 to 40,000 ☐
   Over 40,000 to 60,000 ☐
   Over 60,000 to 80,000 ☐
   Over 80,000 ☐

17. Do you own your own means of transport?
   Yes ☐   No ☐

18. Any other comments?
   (If you need more space, please attach an additional sheet.)
   _____
   _____
   _____
   _____
   _____

Thank you, we appreciate your time!

Important:
If you want us to contact you again in the later stages of this project, or if you are interested in its results, give us your name and address and we will be glad to keep you informed. Thank you.
_____
_____
_____
_____
_____

CASE 2   OUTBACK GOES INTERNATIONAL

In early 1995, Outback Steakhouse enjoyed the position as one of the most successful restaurant chains in the United States. Entrepreneurs Chris Sullivan, Bob Basham, and Tim Gannon, each with more than 20 years' experience in the restaurant industry, started Outback Steakhouse with just two stores in 1988. In 1995, the company was the fastest growing U.S. steakhouse chain with over 200 stores throughout the United States.

Outback achieved its phenomenal success in an industry that was widely considered as one of the most competitive in the United States. Fully 75 percent of entrants into the restaurant industry failed within the first year. Outback's strategy was driven by a unique combination of factors atypical of the foodservice industry. As Chairman Chris Sullivan put it, "Outback is all about a lot of different experiences that has been recognized as entrepreneurship." Within 6 years of commencing operations, Outback was voted as the best steakhouse chain in the country. The company also took top honors along with Olive Garden as America's favorite restaurant. In December 1994, Outback was awarded Inc.'s prestigious Entrepreneur of the Year award. In 1994 and early 1995, the business press hailed the company as one of the biggest success stories in corporate America in recent years

In late 1994, Hugh Connerty was appointed president of Outback International. In early 1995, Connerty, a highly successful franchisee for Outback, explained the international opportunities facing Outback Steakhouse as it considered its strategy for expansion abroad:

> *We have had hundreds of franchise requests from all over the world. [So] it took about two seconds for me to make that decision [to become president of Outback International]. . . . I've met with and talked to other executives who have international divisions. All of them have the same story. At some point in time the light goes off and they say, "Gee we have a great product. Where do we start?" I have traveled quite a bit on holiday. The world is not as big as you think it is. Most companies who have gone global have not used any set strategy.*

Despite his optimism, Connerty knew that the choice of targeted markets would be critical. Connerty wondered what strategic and operational changes the company would have to make to ensure success in those markets.

History of Outback Steakhouse, Inc.

Chris Sullivan, Bob Basham, and Tim Gannon met in the early 1970s shortly after they graduated from college. The three joined Steak & Ale, a Pillsbury subsidiary and restaurant chain, as management trainees as their first postcollege career positions. During the 1980s, Sullivan and Basham became successful franchisees of 17 Chili's restaurants in Florida and Georgia with franchise headquarters in Tampa, Florida.[1] Meanwhile, Tim Gannon played significant roles in several New Orleans restaurant chains. Sullivan and Basham sold their Chili's franchises in 1987 and used the proceeds to fund Outback, their start-from-scratch entrepreneurial venture. They invited Gannon to join them in Tampa in the fall of 1987. The trio opened their first two restaurants in Tampa in 1988.

The three entrepreneurs recognized that in-home consumption of meat, especially beef, had declined.[2] Nonetheless, upscale and budget steakhouses were extremely popular. The three concluded that people were cutting in-home red meat consumption but were still very interested in going out to a restaurant for a good steak. They saw an untapped opportunity between high-priced and budget steakhouses to serve quality steaks at an affordable price.

Using an Australian theme associated with the outdoors and adventure, Outback positioned itself as a place providing not only excellent food but also a cheerful, fun, and comfortable experience. The company's Statement of Principles and Beliefs referred to employees as "Outbackers" and highlighted the

---

1. All three Outback founders credited casual dining chain legend and mentor Norman Brinker with his strong mentoring role in their careers. Brinker played a key role in all the restaurant chains Sullivan and Basham were associated with prior to Outback.

2. American consumption of meat declined from the mid-1970s to the early 1990s primarily as a result of health concerns about red meat. In 1976, Americans consumed 131.6 pounds of beef and veal, 58.7 pounds of pork, and 12.9 pounds of fish. In 1990, the figures had declined to 64.9 pounds of beef and veal, 46.3 of pork, and 15.5 of fish. The dramatic decrease was attributed to consumer attitudes toward a lowfat, healthier diet. Menu items that gained in popularity were premium baked goods, coffees, vegetarian menu items, fruits, salsa, sauces, chicken dishes, salad bars, and spicy dishes. [George Thomas Kurian, *Datapedia of the United States 1790–10000* (Maryland: Bernan Press, 1994), p. 113.]

importance of hospitality, sharing, quality, fun, and courage.

Catering primarily to the dinner crowd,[3] Outback offered a menu that featured specially seasoned steaks and prime rib. The menu also included chicken, ribs, fish, and pasta entrees in addition to the company's innovative appetizers.[4] CFO Bob Merritt cited Outback's food as a prime reason for the company's success. As he put it:

One of the important reasons for our success is that we took basic American meat and potatoes and enhanced the flavor profile so that it fit with the aging population. . . . Just look at what McDonald's and Burger King did in their market segment. They [have] tried to add things to their menu that were more flavorful. [For example] McDonald's put the Big Mac on the menu. . . . as people age, they want more flavor . . . higher flavor profiles. It's not happenstance. It's a science. There's too much money at risk in this business not to know what's going on with customer taste preferences.

The company viewed suppliers as "partners" in the company's success and was committed to work with suppliers to develop and maintain long-term relationships. Purchasing was dedicated to obtaining the highest-quality ingredients and supplies. Indeed, the company was almost fanatical about quality. As Tim Gannon, vice president and the company's chief chef, put it, "We won't tolerate less than the best." One example of the company's quality emphasis was its croutons. Restaurant kitchen staff made the croutons daily on site. The croutons had 17 different seasonings, including fresh garlic and butter. The croutons were cut by hand into irregular shapes so that customers would recognize they were handmade. At about 40 percent of total costs, Outback had one of the highest food costs in the industry. On Friday and Saturday nights, customers waited up to 2 hours for a table. Most felt that Outback provided exceptional value for the average entree price of $15 to $16.

Outback focused not only on the productivity and efficiency of "Outbackers" but also on their long-term well-being. Executives referred to the company's employee commitment as "tough on results,

but kind with people." A typical Outback restaurant staff consisted of a general manager, an assistant manager, and a kitchen manager plus 50 to 70 mostly part-time hourly employees. The company used aptitude tests, psychological profiles, and interviews as part of the employee selection process. Every applicant interviewed with two managers. The company placed emphasis on creating an entrepreneurial climate where learning and personal growth were strongly emphasized. As Chairman Chris Sullivan explained:

I was given the opportunity to make a lot of mistakes and learn, and we try to do that today. We try to give our people a lot of opportunity to make some mistakes, learn, and go on.

In order to facilitate ease of operations for employees, the company's restaurant design devoted 45 percent of restaurant floor space to kitchen area. Wait staff were assigned only three tables at any time. Most Outback restaurants were only open 4:30 to 11:30 P.M. daily. Outback's wait staff enjoyed higher income from tips than in restaurants that also served lunch. Restaurant management staff worked 50 to 55 hours per week in contrast to the 70 or more common in the industry. Company executives felt that the dinner-only concept had led to effective utilization of systems, staff, and management. "Outbackers" reported that they were less worn out working at Outback and that they had more fun than when they worked at other restaurant companies.

Outback executives were proud of their "B-locations [with] A-demographics" location strategy. They deliberately steered clear of hightraffic locations targeted by companies that served a lunch crowd. Until the early 1990s, most of the restaurants were leased locations, retrofits of another restaurant location. The emphasis was on choosing locations where Outback's target customer would be in the evening. The overall strategy payoff was clear. In an industry where a sales-to-investment ratio of 1.2:1 was considered strong, Outback's restaurants generated $2.10 for every $1 invested in the facility. The average Outback restaurant unit generated $3.4 million in sales.

In 1995, management remained informal. Headquarters were located on the second floor of an unpretentious building near the Tampa airport. There was no middle management—top management selected the joint-venture partners and franchisees who reported directly to the president. Franchisees and joint-venture partners, in turn, hired the general managers at each restaurant.

---

3. Outback's original Henderson Blvd. (Tampa, Florida) restaurant was one of the few open for lunch. By 1995, the chain also had begun to open in some locations for Sunday lunch or for special occasions such as Mother's Day lunch.
4. Outback's signature trademark was its bestselling "Aussie-Tizer," the Bloomin' Onion. The company expected to serve 9 million Bloomin' Onions in 1995.

Outback provided ownership opportunities at three levels of the organization: at the individual restaurant level, though multiple-store arrangements (joint-venture and franchise opportunities), and through a stock ownership plan for every employee. Health insurance also was available to all employees, a benefit not universally available to restaurant industry workers. Outback's restaurant-level general managers' employment and ownership opportunities were atypical in the industry. A restaurant general manager invested $25,000 for a 10 percent ownership stake in the restaurant, a contract for 5 years in the same location, a 10 percent share of the cash flow from the restaurant as a yearly bonus, opportunity for stock options, and a 10 percent buyout arrangement at the end of the 5 years. Outback store managers typically earned an annual salary and bonus of over $100,000 as compared with an industry average of about $60,000 to $70,000. Outback's management turnover of 5.4 percent was one of the lowest in its industry, in which the average was 30 to 40 percent.

Community involvement was strongly encouraged throughout the organization. The corporate office was involved in several nonprofit activities in the Tampa area and also sponsored major national events such as the Outback Bowl and charity golf tournaments. Each store was involved in community participation and service. For example, the entire proceeds of an open house held just prior to every restaurant opening went to a charity of the store manager's choice.

Early in its history the company had been unable to afford any advertising. Instead, Outback's founders relied on their strong relationships with local media to generate public relations and promotional efforts. One early relationship developed with Nancy Schneid who had extensive experience in advertising and radio. Schneid later became Outback's first vice president of marketing. Under her direction, the company developed a full-scale national media program that concentrated on television advertising and local billboards. The company avoided couponing, and its only printed advertising typically came as part of a package offered by a charity or sports event.

Early financing for growth had come from limited-partnership investments by family members, close friends, and associates. The three founders' original plan did not call for extensive expansion or franchising. However, in 1990, some friends, disappointed in the performance of several of their Kentucky-based restaurants, asked to franchise the Outback concept. The converted Kentucky stores enjoyed swift success. Additional opportunities with other individuals experienced in the restaurant industry arose in various parts of the country. These multistore arrangements were in the form of franchises or joint ventures. Later in 1990, the company turned to a venture capital firm for financing for a $2.5 million package. About the same time, Bob Merritt joined the company as CFO. Merritt's previous IPO[5] experience helped the company undertake a quick succession of three highly successful public equity offerings. During 1994, the price of the company's stock ranged from $22.63 to a high of $32.00. The company's income statements, balance sheets, and a summary of the stock price performance appear as Exhibits A, B, and C, respectively.

Outback's International Rollout

Outback's management believed that the U.S. market could accommodate at least 550 to 600 Outback steakhouse restaurants. At the rate the company was growing (70 stores annually), Outback would near the U.S. market's saturation within 4 to 5 years. Outback's plans for longer-term growth hinged on a multipronged strategy. The company planned to roll out an additional 300 to 350 Outback stores, expand into the lucrative Italian dining segment through its joint venture with the successful Houston-based Carrabbas Italian Grill, and develop new dining themes.

At year-end 1994, Outback had 164 restaurants in which the company had direct ownership interest. The company had 6 restaurants that it operated through joint ventures in which the company had a 45 percent interest. Franchisees operated another 44 restaurants. Outback operated the company-owned restaurants as partnerships in which the company was general partner. The company owned from 81 to 90 percent. The remainder was owned by the restaurant managers and joint-venture partners. The 6 restaurants operated as joint ventures also were organized as partnerships in which the company owned 50 percent. The company was responsible for 50 percent of the costs of these restaurants.

The company organized the joint venture with Carrabbas in early 1993. The company was responsible for 100 percent of the costs of the new Carrabba's Italian Grills, although it owned a 50 percent share. As of yearend 1994, the joint venture operated 10 Carrabba's restaurants.

5. Merritt had worked as CFO for another company that had come to the financial markets with its IPO (initial public offering).

EXHIBIT A CONSOLIDATED STATEMENTS OF INCOME			
	Years Ended December 31,		
	1994	**1993**	**1992**
Revenues	$451,916,000	$309,749,000	$189,217,000
Costs and expenses			
Costs of revenues	175,618,000	121,290,000	73,475,000
Labor and other related expenses	95,476,000	65,047,000	37,087,000
Other restaurant operating expenses	93,265,000	64,603,000	43,370,000
General and administrative expenses	16,744,000	12,225,000	9,176,000
(Income) from oper. of unconsol. affl.	(1,269,000)	(333,000)	
	379,834,000	262,832,000	163,108,000
Income from operations	72,082,000	46,917,000	26,109,000
Nonoperating income (expense)			
Interest income	512,000	1,544,000	1,428,000
Interest expense	(424,000)	(369,000)	(360,000)
	88,000	1,175,000	1,068,000
Income before elimination			
Minority partners interest and income taxes	72,170,000	48,092,000	27,177,000
Elimination of minority partners' interest	11,276,000	7,378,000	4,094,000
Income before provision for income taxes	60,894,000	40,714,000	23,083,000
Provision for income taxes	21,602,000	13,922,000	6,802,000
Net income	$39,292,000	$26,792,000	$16,281,000
Earnings per common share	$0.89	$0.61	$0.39
Weighted average number of common shares outstanding	43,997,000	43,738,000	41,504,000
Pro forma:			
Provision for income taxes	22,286,000	15,472,000	8,245,000
Net income	$38,608,000	$25,242,000	$14,838,000
Earnings per common share	$0.88	$0.58	$0.36

The franchised restaurants generated 0.8 percent of the company's 1994 revenues as franchise fees. The portion of income attributable to restaurant managers and joint-venture partners amounted to $11.3 million of the company's $72.2 million 1994 income.

By late 1994, Outback's management also had begun to consider the potential of non-U.S. markets for the Outback concept. As Chairman Chris Sullivan put it:

> . . . we can do 500 to 600 [Outback] restaurants, and possibly more over the next 5 years. . . . [However] the world is becoming one big market, and we want to be in place so we don't miss that opportunity. There are some problems, some challenges with it, but at this point there have been some casual restaurant chains that have gone [outside the United States] and their average unit sales are

> way, way above the sales level they enjoyed in the United States. So the potential is there. Obviously, there are some distribution issues to work out, things like that. But we are real excited about the future internationally. That will give us some potential outside the United States to continue to grow as well.

In late 1994, the company began its international venture by appointing Hugh Connerty as president of Outback International. Connerty, like Outback's three founders, had extensive experience in the restaurant industry. Prior to joining Outback, he developed a chain of successful Hooter's restaurants in Georgia. He used the proceeds from the sale of these franchises to fund the development of his franchise at Outback restaurants in northern Florida and southern Georgia. Connerty's success as a franchisee was well recognized. Indeed, in

EXHIBIT B CONSOLIDATED BALANCE SHEETS

	December 31,				
	1994	1993	1992	1991	1990
Assets					
Current assets					
Cash and cash equivalents	$18,758,000	$24,996,000	$60,538,000	$17,000,700	$2,983,000
Short-term municipal securities	4,829,000	6,632,000	1,316,600		
Inventories	4,539,000	3,849,000	2,166,500	1,020,800	319,200
Other current assets	11,376,000	4,658,000	2,095,200	794,900	224,100
Total current assets	39,502,000	40,135,000	66,116,700	18,816,400	3,526,300
Long-term municipal securities	1,226,000	8,903,000	7,071,200		
Property, fixtures, and equipment, net	162,323,000	101,010,000	41,764,500	15,479,000	6,553,200
Investments in and advances to unconsolidated affiliates	14,244,000	1,000,000			
Other assets	11,236,000	8,151,000	2,691,300	2,380,700	1,539,600
	$228,531,000	$159,199,000	$117,643,700	36,676,100	11,619,100
Liabilities and stockholders' equity					
Current liabilities					
Accounts payable	$10,184,000	$1,053,000	$3,560,200	643,800	666,900
Sales taxes payable	3,173,000	2,062,000	1,289,500	516,800	208,600
Accrued expenses	14,961,000	10,435,000	8,092,300	2,832,300	954,800
Unearned revenue	11,862,000	6,174,000	2,761,900	752,800	219,400
Current portion of long-term debt	918,000	1,119,000	326,600	257,000	339,900
Income taxes payable			369,800	1,873,200	390,000
Total current liabilities	41,098,000	20,843,000	16,400,300	6,875,900	2,779,600
Deferred income taxes	568,000	897,000	856,400	300,000	260,000
Long-term debt	12,310,000	5,687,000	1,823,700	823,600	1,060,700
Interest of minority partners in consolidated partnerships	2,255,000	1,347,000	1,737,500	754,200	273,000
Total liabilities	56,231,000	28,774,000	20,817,900	8,753,700	4,373,300
Stockholders' equity					
Common stock, $0.01 par value, 100,000,000 shares authorized for 1994 and 1993; 50,000,000 authorized for 1992 42,931,344 and 42,442,800 shares issues and out standing as of December 31, 1994z and 1993, respectively. 39,645,995 shares issued and outstanding as of December 31, 1992.	429,000	425,000	396,500	219,000	86,300
Additional paid-in capital	83,756,000	79,429,000	74,024,500	20,296,400	4,461,100
Retained earnings	88,115,000	50,571,000	22,404,800	7,407,000	2,698,400
Total stockholders' equity	172,300,000	130,425,000	96,825,800	27,922,400	7,245,800
	$228,531,000	$159,199,000	$117,643,700	$36,676,100	$11,619,100

Year	**Systemwide Sales**	**Co. Revenues**	**Net Income**	**EPS**	**Co. Stores**	**Franchises and JVS**	**Total**
1988	2,731	2,731	47	0.01	2	0	2
1989	13,328	13,328	920	0.04	9	0	9
1990	34,193	34,193	2,260	0.08	23	0	23
1991	91,000	91,000	6,064	0.17	49	0	49
1992	195,508	189,217	14,838	0.36	81	4	85
1993	347,553	309,749	25,242	0.58	124	24	148
1994	548,945	451,916	38,608	0.88	164	50	214

EXHIBIT C SELECTED FINANCIAL AND STOCK DATA

OUTBACK Stock Data	High	Low
1991		
Second quarter	$4.67	$4.27
Third quarter	6.22	4.44
Fourth quarter	10.08	5.5
1992		
First quarter	13.00	9.17
Second quarter	11.41	8.37
Third quarter	16.25	10.13
Fourth quarter	19.59	14.25
1993		
First quarter	22.00	15.50
Second quarter	26.16	16.66
Third quarter	24.59	19.00
Fourth quarter	25.66	21.16
1994		
First quarter	29.50	23.33
Second quarter	28.75	22.75
Third quarter	30.88	23.75
Fourth quarter	32.00	22.63

1993 Outback began to award a large crystal trophy with the designation "Connerty Franchisee of the Year" to the company's outstanding franchisee.

Much of Outback's growth and expansion were generated through joint-venture partnerships and franchising agreements. Connerty commented on Outback's franchise system:

Every one of the franchisees lives in their areas. I lived in the area I franchised. I had relationships that helped with getting permits. That isn't any different than the rest of the world. The loyalties of individuals that live in their respective areas [will be important]. We will do the franchises one by one. The biggest decision we have to make is how we pick that franchise partner. . . . That is what we will concentrate on. We are going to select a person who has synergy with us, who thinks like us, who believes in the principles and beliefs.

Outback developed relationships very carefully. As Hugh Connerty explained:

. . . trust . . . is foremost and sacred. The trust between [Outback] and the individual franchisees is not to be violated.. . . Company grants franchises one at a time.[6] It takes a lot of trust to invest millions of

6. Outback did not grant exclusive territorial franchises. Thus, if an Outback franchisee did not perform, the company could bring additional franchisees into the area. Through 1994, Outback had not had territorial disputes between franchisees.

dollars without any assurance that you will be able to build another one.

However, Connerty recognized that expanding abroad would present challenges. He described how Outback would approach its international expansion:

We have built Outback one restaurant at a time. . . . There are some principles and beliefs we live by. It almost sounds cultish. We want international to be an opportunity for our suppliers. We feel strongly about the relationships with our suppliers. We have never changed suppliers. We have an undying commitment to them and in exchange we want them to have an undying commitment to us. They have to prove they can build plants [abroad]. . . .

He explained:

I think it would be foolish of us to think that we are going to go around the world buying property and understanding the laws in every country, the culture in every single country. So the approach that we are going to take is that we will franchise the international operation with company-owned stores here and franchises there so that will allow us to focus on what I believe is our pure strength, a support operation.

U.S. Restaurants in the International Dining Market

Prospects for international entry for U.S. restaurant companies in the early 1990s appeared promising. Between 1992 and 1993 alone, international sales for the top 50 restaurant franchisers increased from US$15.9 billion to US$17.5 billion. Franchising was the most popular means for rapid expansion. Exhibit D provides an overview of the top U.S. restaurant franchisers, including their domestic and international revenues and number of units in 1993 and 1994.

International expansion was an important source of revenues for a significant number of players in the industry. International growth and expansion in the U.S. restaurant industry over the 1980s and into the 1990s was driven largely by major fast-food restaurant chains. Some of these companies, for example, McDonald's, Wendy's, Dairy Queen, and Domino's Pizza, were public and freestanding. Others, such as Subway and Little Caesars, remained private and freestanding. Some of the largest players in international markets were subsidiaries of major consumer products firms such as PepsiCo[7]

and Grand Metropolitan PLC.[8] Despite the success enjoyed by fast-food operators in non-U.S. markets, casual dining operators were slower about entering the international markets. (See Appendix A for brief overviews of the publicly available data on the top 10 franchisers and casual dining chains that had ventured abroad as of early 1995.)

One of the major forces driving the expansion of the U.S. foodservice industry was changing demographics. In the United States, prepared foods had become the fastest-growing category because they relieved the cooking burdens on working parents. By the early 1990s, U.S. consumers were spending almost as much on restaurant fare as for prepared and nonprepared grocery store food. U.S. food themes were very popular abroad. U.S. food themes were common throughout Canada as well as western Europe and East Asia. As a result of the opening of previously inaccessible markets such as eastern Europe, the former Soviet Union, China, India, and Latin America, the potential for growth in U.S. food establishments abroad was enormous.

In 1992 alone, there were more than 3000 franchisers in the United States operating about 540,000 franchised outlets—a new outlet of some sort opened about every 16 minutes. In 1992, franchised business sales totaled $757.8 billion, about 35 percent of all retail sales. Franchising was used as a growth vehicle by a variety of businesses, including automobiles, petroleum, cosmetics, convenience stores, computers, and financial services. However, foodservice constituted the franchising industry's largest single group. Franchised restaurants generally performed better than free-standing units. For example, in 1991 franchised restaurants experienced perstore sales growth of 6.2 percent versus an overall restaurant industry growth of 3.0 percent. However, despite generally favorable sales and profits, franchisor-franchisee relationships often were difficult.

Abroad, franchisers operated an estimated 31,000 restaurant units. The significant increase in restaurant franchising abroad was driven by universal cultural trends, rising incomes, improved international transportation and communications, rising educational levels, increasing numbers of women entering the workforce, demographic concentrations of people in urban areas, and the willingness of younger generations to try new products.[9] However, there were substantial differences in these

---

7. PepsiCo owned Kentucky Fried Chicken, Taco Bell, and Pizza Hut.

8. Grand Met owned Burger King.

9. Ref. AME 76 (KR).

EXHIBIT D TOP 50 U.S. RESTAURANT FRANCHISES RANKED BY SALES

Rank	Firm	Total Sales		International Sales		Total Stores		International Stores	
		1994	1993	1994	1993	1994	1993	1994	1993
1	McDonald's	25986	23587	11046	9401	15205	13993	5461	4710
2	Burger King	7500	6700	1400	1240	7684	6990	1357	1125
3	KFC	7100	7100	3600	3700	9407	9033	4258	3905
4	Taco Bell	4290	3817	130	100	5615	4634	162	112
5	Wendy's	4277	3924	390	258	4411	4168	413	377
6	Hardee's	3491	3425	63	56	3516	3435	72	63
7	Dairy Queen	3170	2581	300	290	3516	3435	628	611
8	Domino's	2500	2413	415	275	5079	5009	840	550
9	Subway	2500	2201	265	179	9893	8450	944	637
10	Little Caesar	2000	2000	70	70	4855	4754	155	145
Average of firms 11–20		1222	1223	99	144	2030	1915	163	251
Average of firms 21–30		647	594	51	26	717	730	37	36
Average of firms 31–40		382	358	7	9	502	495	26	20
Average of firms 41–50		270	257	17	23	345	363	26	43

NonFast Food in Top 50

Rank	Firm	Total Sales		International Sales		Total Stores		International Stores	
		1994	1993	1994	1993	1994	1993	1994	1993
11	Denny's	1779	1769	63	70	1548	1515	58	63
13	Dunkin Donuts	1413	1285	226	209	3453	3047	831	705
14	Shoney's	1346	1318	0	0	922	915	0	0
15	Big Boy	1130	1202	100	0	940	930	90	78
17	Baskin-Robbins	1008	910	387	368	3765	3562	1300	1278
19	T.G.I. Friday's	897	1068	114	293	314	NA	37	NA
20	Applebee's	889	609	1	0	507	361	2	0
21	Sizzler	858	922	230	218	600	666	119	116
23	Ponderosa	690	743	40	38	380	750	40	38
24	Int'l House of Pancakes	632	560	32	29	657	561	37	35
25	Perkins	626	588	12	10	432	425	8	6
29	Outback Steakhouse	549	348	0	0	NA	NA	NA	NA
30	Golden Corral	548	515	1	0	425	425	2	1
32	TCBY Yogurt	388	337	22	15	2801	2474	141	80
37	Showbiz/Chuck E. Cheese	370	373	7	8	332	NA	8	NA
39	Round Table Pizza	357	340	15	12	576	597	29	22
40	Western Sizzlin	337	351	3	6	281	NA	2	NA
41	Ground Round	321	310	0	0	NA	NA	NA	NA
42	Papa John's	297	NA	0	NA	632	NA	0	NA
44	Godfather's Pizza	270	268	0	0	515	531	0	0
45	Bonanza	267	327	32	47	264	NA	30	NA
46	Village Inn	266	264	0	0	NA	NA	NA	NA
47	Red Robin	259	235	27	28	NA	NA	NA	NA
48	Tony Roma's	254	245	41	36	NA	NA	NA	NA
49	Marie Callender	251	248	0	0	NA	NA	NA	NA

NOTE: NA: Not ranked in the top 50 for that category.
SOURCE: "Top 50 Franchises," *Restaurant Business*, November 1, 1995, pp. 35–41.

changes between the United States and other countries and from country to country.

Factors Affecting Country Selection

Outback had not yet formed a firm plan for its international rollout. However, Hugh Connerty indicated the preliminary choice of markets targeted for entry:

> The first year will be Canada. . . . Then we'll go to Hawaii. . . . Then we'll go to South America and then develop our relationships in the Far East, Korea, Japan, . . . the Orient. At the second year we'll begin a relationship in Great Britain and from there a natural progression throughout Europe. But we view it as a very long-term project. I have learned that people think very different than Americans.

There were numerous considerations that U.S. restaurant chains had to take into account when determining which non-U.S. markets to enter. Some of these factors are summarized in Exhibit E. Issues regarding infrastructure and demographics are expanded below. Included are some of the difficulties that U.S. restaurant companies encountered in various countries. Profiles of Canada, South Korea, Japan, Germany, Mexico, and Great Britain appear as Appendix B.

Infrastructure

A supportive infrastructure in the target country is essential. Proper means of transportation, communication, basic utilities such as power and water, and locally available supplies are important elements in the decision to introduce a particular restaurant concept. A restaurant must have the ability to get resources to its location. Raw materials for food preparation, equipment for manufacture of food served, employees, and customers must be able to enter and leave the establishment. The network that brings these resources to a firm is commonly called a *supply chain*.

The level of economic development is closely linked to the development of a supportive infrastructure. For example, the U.S. International Trade Commission said:

> Economic conditions, cultural disparities, and physical limitations can have substantial impact on the viability of foreign markets for a franchise concept. In terms of economics, the level of infrastructure development is a significant factor. A

> weak infrastructure may cause problems in transportation, communication, or even the provision of basic utilities such as electricity. . . . International franchisers frequently encounter problems finding supplies in sufficient quantity, of consistent quality, and at stable prices. . . . Physical distance also can adversely affect a franchise concept and arrangement. Long distances create communication and transportation problems, which may complicate the process of sourcing supplies, overseeing operations, or providing quality management services to franchisees.[10]

Some food can be sourced locally, some regionally or nationally, and some must be imported. A country's transportation and distribution capabilities may become an element in the decision of the country's suitability for a particular restaurant concept.

Sometimes supply-chain issues require firms to make difficult decisions that affect the costs associated with the foreign enterprise. Family Restaurants, Inc., encountered problems providing brown gravy for its CoCo's restaurants in South Korea. "If you want brown gravy in South Korea," said Barry Krantz, company president, "you can do one of two things. Bring it over, which is very costly. Or, you can make it yourself. So we figure out the flavor profile, and make it in the kitchen." Krantz concedes that a commissary is "an expensive proposition but the lesser of two evils.[11]

In certain instances, a country may be so attractive for long-term growth that a firm dedicates itself to creating a supply chain for its restaurants. An excellent illustration is McDonald's expansion into Russia in the late 1980s:

> . . . supply procurement has proved to be a major hurdle, as it has for all foreign companies operating in Russia. The problem has several causes: the rigid bureaucratic system, supply shortages caused by distribution and production problems, available supplies not meeting McDonald's quality standards. . . . To handle these problems, McDonald's scoured the country for supplies, contracting for such items as milk, cheddar cheese, and beef. To help ensure ample supplies of the quality products it needed, it undertook to educate Soviet farmers and cattle ranchers on how to grow and raise those products. In addition, it built a $40 million food-processing center

10. "Industry and Trade Summary: Franchising," U.S. International Trade Commission, Washington, D.C., 1995, pp. 15–16.
11. "World Hunger," *Restaurant Hospitality,* November 1994, p. 97.

EXHIBIT E FACTORS AFFECTING COMPANIES' ENTRY INTO INTERNATIONAL MARKETS

External Factors

Country market factors
- Size of target market, competitive structure—atomistic, oligopolistic to monopolistic, local marketing infrastructure (distribution, etc.)

Country production factors
- Quality, quantity, and cost of raw materials, labor, energy, and other productive agents in the target country as well as the quality and cost of the economic infrastructure (transportation, communications, port facilities, and similar considerations)

Country environmental factors
- Political, economic, and sociocultural character of the target country—government policies and regulations pertaining to international business
- Geographic distance—impact on transportation costs
- Size of the economy, absolute level of performance (GDP per capita), relative importance of economic sectors—closely related to the market size for a company's product in the target country
- Dynamics including rate of investment, growth in GDP, personal income, changes in employment. Dynamic economies may justify entry modes with a high break-even point even when the current market size is below the break-even point.
- Sociocultural factors—cultural distance between home country and target country societies. Closer the cultural distance, quicker entry into these markets, e.g., Canada.

Home country factors
- Big domestic market allows a company to grow to a large size before it turns to foreign markets. Competitive structure. Firms in oligopolistic industries tend to imitate the actions of rival domestic firms that threatens to upset competitive equilibrium. Hence, when one firm invests abroad, rival firms commonly follow the lead. High production costs in the home country is an important factor.

Internal Factors

Company product factors
- Products that are highly differentiated with distinct advantages over competitive products give sellers a significant degree of pricing discretion.
- Products that require an array of pre- and postpurchase services makes it difficult for a company to market the product at a distance.
- Products that require considerable adaptation.

Company resource/commitment factors
- The more abundant a company's resources in management, capital, technology, production skills, and marketing skills, the more numerous its entry mode options. Conversely, a company with limited resources is constrained to use entry modes that call for only a small resource commitment. Size is therefore a critical factor in the choice of an entry mode. Although resources are an influencing factor, it must be joined with a willingness to commit them to foreign market development. A high degree of commitment means that managers will select the entry mode for a target from a wider range of alternative modes than managers with a low commitment.
- The degree of a company's commitment to international business is revealed by the role accorded to foreign markets in corporate strategy, the status of the international organization, and the attitudes of managers.

SOURCE: Franklin Root: Entry Strategies for International Markets. Lexington, MA: D.C. Heath (1987).

---

about 45 minutes from its first Moscow restaurant. And because distribution was [and still is] as much a cause of shortages as production was, McDonald's carried supplies on its own trucks.[12]

Changing from one supply chain to another can affect more than the availability of quality provisions—it can affect the equipment that is used to make the food served. For example:

. . . Wendy's nearly had its Korean market debut delayed by the belatedly discovered problem of thrice-frozen hamburger. After being thawed and frozen at each step of Korea's cumbersome three-company distribution channel, ground beef there takes on added water weight that threw off Wendy's patty specifications, forcing a hasty stateside retooling of the standard meat patty die used to massproduce its burgers.[13]

---

12. *International Business Environments and Operations,* 7th ed., 1995, pp. 117–119.

13. "U.S. Restaurant Chains Tackle Challenges of Asian Expansion," *Nation's Restaurant News,* February 14, 1994, p. 36.

Looking at statistics such as the number of ports, airports, quantity of paved roads, and transportation equipment as a percentage of capital stock per worker can give a bird's eye view of the level of infrastructure development.

Demographics

Just like the domestic market, restaurants in a foreign market need to know who their customers will be. Different countries will have different strata in age distribution, religion, and cultural heritage. These factors can influence the location, operations, and menus of restaurants in the country.

A popular example is India, where eating beef is contrary to the beliefs of the 80 percent of the population that is Hindu.[14] Considering that India's population is nearly 1 billion people, companies find it hard to ignore this market even if beef is a central component of the firm's traditional menu. "We're looking at serving mutton patties," says Ann Connolly, a McDonald's spokeswoman.[15]

Another area where religion plays a part in affecting the operation of a restaurant is the Middle East. Dairy Queen expanded to the region and found that during the Islamic religious observance of Ramadan, no business was conducted; indeed, the windows of shops were boarded up.[16]

Age distribution can affect who should be the target market. "The company [McDonald's in Japan] also made modifications [not long after entering the market], such as targeting all advertising to younger people, because the eating habits of older Japanese are very difficult to change."[17] Age distribution also can affect the pool of labor available. In some countries, over 30 percent of the population is under 15 years old; in other countries, over 15 percent is 65 or older. These varying demographics could create a change in the profile for potential employees in the new market.

Educational level may be an influence on both the buying public and the employee base. Literacy rates vary, and once again, this can change the profile of an employee as well as who comprises the buying public.

Statistics can help compare countries using demographic components such as literacy rates, total population and age distribution, and religious affiliations.

14. *CIA World Factbook*, India, 1995.
15. "Big McMuttons," *Forbes*, July 17, 1995, p. 18.
16. Interview with Cheryl Babcock, professor, University of St. Thomas, October 23, 1995.
17. "Franchise Management in East Asia," *Academy of Management Executive*, 4(2) (1990), p. 79.

Income

Buying power is another demographic that can provide clues to how the restaurant might fare in the target country, as well as how the marketing program should position the company's products or services. Depending on the country and its economic development, the firm may have to attract a different segment than in the domestic market. For example, in Mexico:

. . . major U.S. firms have only recently begun targeting the country's sizable and apparently burgeoning middle class. For its part, McDonald's as changed tactics from when it first entered Mexico as a prestige brand aimed almost exclusively at the upper class, which accounts for about 5 percent of Mexico's population of some 93 million. With the development of its own distribution systems and improved economies of scale, McDonald's lately has been slashing prices to aid its penetration into working-class population strongholds. "I'd say McDonald's pricing now in Mexico is 30 percent lower, in constant dollar terms, than when we opened in '85," says Moreno [Fernando Moreno, now international director of Peter Piper Pizza], who was part of the chain's inaugural management team there.[18]

There are instances where low disposable income does not translate to a disinterest in dining out in a Western-style restaurant. While Americans dine at a fast-food establishment such as McDonald's one or two times per week, lower incomes in the foreign markets make eating at McDonald's a special, once-a-month occurrence. "These people are not very wealthy, so eating out at a place like McDonald's is a dining experience."[19] China provides another example:

. . . at one Beijing KFC last summer, [the store] notched the volume equivalent of nine U.S. KFC branches in a single day during a $1.99 promotion of a two-piece meal with a baseball cap. Observers chalk up that blockbuster business largely to China's ubiquitous "spoiled-brat syndrome" and the apparent willingness of indulgent parents to spend one or two months' salaries on splurges for the only child the government allows them to rear.[20]

18. "U.S. Operators Flock to Latin America," *Nation's Restaurant News*, October 17, 1994, p. 47.
19. Interview with Cheryl Babcock, professor, University of St. Thomas, October 23, 1995.
20. "U.S. Restaurant Chains Tackle Challenges of Asian Expansion," *Nation's Restaurant News*, February 14, 1994, p. 36.

Statistics outlining the various indexes describing the country's gross domestic product, consumer spending on food, consumption and investment rates, and price levels can assist in evaluating target countries.

Trade Law

Trade policies can be friend or foe to a restaurant chain interested in expanding to other countries. Trade agreements such as NAFTA (North American Free Trade Agreement) and GATT (General Agreement on Tariffs and Trade) can help alleviate the ills of international expansion if they achieve their aims of "reducing or eliminating tariffs, reducing nontariff barriers to trade, liberalizing investment and foreign exchange policies, and improving intellectual property protection. . . . The recently signed Uruguay Round Agreements [of GATT] include the General Agreement on Trade in Services (GATS), the first multilateral, legally enforceable agreement covering trade and investment in the services sector. The GATS is designed to liberalize trade in services by reducing or eliminating governmental measures that prevent services from being freely provided across national borders or that discriminate against firms with foreign ownership.[21]

Franchising, one of the most popular modes for entering foreign markets, scored a win in the GATS agreement. For the first time, franchising was addressed directly in international trade talks. However, most countries have not elected to make their restrictions on franchising publicly known. The U.S. International Trade Commission pointed out:

Specific commitments that delineate barriers are presented in Schedules of Commitments [Schedules]. As of this writing, Schedules from approximately 90 countries are publicly available. Only 30 of these countries specifically include franchising in their Schedules. . . . The remaining twothirds of the countries did not schedule commitments on franchising. This means that existing restrictions are not presented in a transparent manner and additional, more severe restrictions may be imposed at a later date. . . . Among the 30 countries that addressed franchising in the Schedules, 25 countries, including the United States, have committed themselves to maintain no limitations on franchising except for restrictions on

the presence of foreign nationals within their respective countries.[22]

Despite progress, current international restaurant chains have encountered a myriad of challenges because of restrictive trade policies. Some countries make the import of restaurant equipment into their country difficult and expensive. The Asian region possesses "steep tariffs and [a] patchwork of inconsistent regulations that impede imports of commodities and equipment.[23]

Outback's Growth Challenge

Hugh Connerty was well aware that there was no mention of international opportunities in Outback's 1994 Annual Report. The company distributed that annual report to shareholders at the April 1995 meeting. More than 300 shareholders packed the meeting to standing room only. During the question and answer period, a shareholder had closely questioned the company's executives as to why the company did not pay a dividend. The shareholder pointed out that the company made a considerable profit in 1994. Chris Sullivan responded that the company needed to reinvest the cash that might be used as dividends in order to achieve the targeted growth. His response was a public and very visible commitment to continue the company's fastpaced growth. Connerty knew that international had the potential to play a critical role in that growth. His job was to help craft a strategy that would ensure Outback's continuing success as it undertook the new and diverse markets abroad.

This case was prepared by Marilyn L.Taylor, Gottlieb/ Missouri Chair of Strategic Management, Henry W. Bloch School of Business and Public Administration, University of Missouri at Kansas City; George M. Puia, Dow Chemical Centennial Chair in Global Business, College of Business Management, Saginaw Valley State University; and Madelyn Gengelbach, M.B.A., Henry W. Bloch School of Business and Public Administration, University of Missouri at Kansas City.

This case was developed with support from the Ewing Marion Kauffman Foundation and was presented to North American Case Research Association. Reprinted by permission of the authors.

---

21. "Industry and Trade Summary: Franchising," U.S. International Trade Commission, Washington, D.C., 1995, p. 30.

22. *Ibid.*
23. "U.S. Restaurant Chains Tackle Challenges of Asian Expansion," *Nation's Restaurant News,* February 14, 1994, p. 36.

APPENDIX A: PROFILES OF CASUAL DINING AND FAST-FOOD CHAINS*

This appendix provides summaries of the 1995 publicly available data on (1) the two casual dining chains represented among the top 50 franchisers that had operations abroad (Applebee's and T.G.I. Friday's/Carlson Companies, Inc.) and (2) the top ten franchisers in the restaurant industry, all of which are fastfood chains (Burger King, Domino's, Hardee's, International Dairy Queen, Inc., Little Caesar's, McDonald's, PepsiCo including KFC, Taco Bell and Pizza Hut, Subway, and Wendy's).

(1) Casual Dining Chains with Operations Abroad

Applebee's. Applebee's was one of the largest casual chains in the United States. It ranked twentieth in sales and thirty-sixth in stores for 1994. Like most other casual dining operators, much of the company's growth had been fueled by domestic expansion. Opening in 1986, the company experienced rapid growth and by 1994 had 507 stores. The mode of growth was franchising, but in 1992 management began a program of opening more company-owned sites and buying restaurants from franchisees. The company positioned itself as a neighborhood bar and grill and offered a moderately priced menu including burgers, chicken, and salads.

In 1995 Applebee's continued a steady program of expansion. Chairman and CEO Abe Gustin set a target of 1200 U.S. restaurants and also had begun a slow push into international markets. In 1994 the company franchised restaurants in Canada and Curacao and signed an agreement to franchise 20 restaurants in Belgium, Luxembourg, and the Netherlands.

	1989	1990	1991	1992	1993	1994[a]
Sales ($m)	29.9	38.2	45.1	56.5	117.1	208.5
Net income ($m)	0.0	1.8	3.1	5.1	9.5	16.9
EPS ($)	(0.10)	0.13	0.23	0.27	0.44	0.62
Stock price close ($)	4.34	2.42	4.84	9.17	232.34	13.38
Dividends ($)	0.00	0.00	0.01	0.02	0.03	0.04
No. of employees	1,149	1,956	1,714	2,400	46,600	8,700

[a]1994: Debt ratio 20.1%; R.O.E. 19.2; cash $17.2m; current ratio 1.13; LTD $23.7 .

T.G.I. Friday's/Carlson Companies, Inc. T.G.I. Friday's was owned by Carlson Companies, Inc., a large, privately held conglomerate that had interests in travel (65 percent of 1994 sales), hospitality (30 percent) plus marketing, employee training and incentives (5 percent). Carlson also owned a total of 345 Radisson Hotels and Country Inns plus 240 units of Country Kitchen International, a chain of family restaurants.

*Unless otherwise noted, the information from this Appendix was drawn from "Top 50 Franchisers," *Restaurant Business*, November 1, 1995, pp. 35–41; and Hoover's Company profile Database 1996, Reference Press, Inc., Austin, TX (from American Online Service), various company listings.

Most of Carlson's revenues came from its travel group. The company experienced an unexpected surprise in 1995 when U.S. airlines announced that it would put a cap on the commissions it would pay to book U.S. flights. Because of this change, Carlson decided to change its service to a fee-based arrangement and expected sales to drop by US$100 million in 1995. To make up for this deficit, Carlson began to focus on building its hospitality group of restaurants and hotels through expansion in the United States and overseas. The company experienced significant senior management turnover in the early 1990s, and founder Curtis Carlson, age 80, had announced his intention to retire at the end of 1996. His daughter was announced as next head of the company.

T.G.I. Friday's grew 15.7 percent in revenue and 19.4 percent in stores in 1994. With 37 restaurants overseas, international sales were 12.7 percent of sales and 11.8 percent of stores systemwide. Carlson operated a total of 550 restaurants in 17 countries. About onethird of overall sales came from activities outside the U.S.

	1985	1986	1987	1988	1989	1990	1991	1992	1993	1994
Sales[a]	.9	1.3	1.5	1.8	2.0	2.2	2.3	2.9	2.3	2.3

[a]$b; no data available on income; excludes franchisee sales.

(2) The Top Ten Franchisers in the Restaurant Industry

Burger King. In 1994, Burger King was number two in sales and number four in stores among the fast-food competitors. Burger King did not have the same presence in the global market as McDonald's and KFC. For example, McDonald's and KFC had been in Japan since the 1970s. Burger King opened its first Japanese locations in 1993. By that time, McDonald's already had over 1000 outlets there. In 1994, Burger King had 1357 non-U.S. stores (17.7 percent of systemwide total) in 50 countries, and overseas sales (18.7 percent) totaled US$1.4 billion.

Burger King was owned by the British food and spirits conglomerate Grand Metropolitan PLC. Among the company's top brands were Pillsbury, Green Giant, and Häagen-Dazs. Grand Met's situation had not been bright during the 1990s, with the loss of major distribution contracts like Absolut vodka and Grand Marnier liqueur, as well as sluggish sales for its spirits in major markets. Burger King was not a stellar performer either and undertook a major restructuring in 1993 to turn the tide including reemphasis on the basic menu, cuts in prices, and reduced overhead. After quick success, BK's CEO James Adamson left his post in early 1995 to head competitor Flagston Corporation.

	1985	1986	1987	1988	1989	1990	1991	1992	1993	1994
Sales[a]	5,590	5,291	4,706	6,029	9,298	9,394	8,748	7,913	8,120	7,780
Net income[a]	272	261	461	702	1,068	1,069	616	412	450	
EPS ($)	14	16	19	24	28	32	33	28	30	32
Stock price close ($)	199	228	215	314	329	328	441	465	476	407
Dividend/ share ($)	5.0	5.1	6.0	7.5	8.9	10.2	11.4	12.3	13.0	14.0
Employees (K) 137	131	129	90	137	138	122	102	87	64	

[a]Millions of Sterling; 1994: debt ratio 47.3%; R.O.E. 12.4%; Cash (Ster.) 986M; LTD (Ster.) 2322M. 1994 Segments sales (profit): North America: 62% (69%); U.K. & Ireland 10% (10%); Africa & Middle East 2% (1%); Other Europe: 21% (18%); Other Countries: 5% (2%). Segment sales (profits) by operating division: drinks 43% (51%); food 42% (26%); retailing 14% (22%); other 1% (1%).

Domino's. Domino's Pizza was eighth in sales and seventh in stores in 1994. Sales and store unit growth had leveled off; from 1993 to 1994 sales grew 3.6 percent and units only 1.4 percent. The privately held company registered poor performance in 1993, with a 0.6 percent sales decline from 1992. Observers suggested that resistance to menu innovations contributed to the share decline. In the early 1990s the company did add deep dish pizza and buffalo wings.

Flat company performances and expensive hobbies were hard on the owner and founder Thomas Monaghan. He attempted to sell the company in 1989 but could not find a buyer. He then replaced top management and retired from business to pursue a growing interest in religious activities. Company performance began to slide, and the founder emerged from retirement to retake the helm in the early 1990s. Through extravagant purchases of the Detroit Tigers, Frank Lloyd Wright pieces, and antique cars, Monaghan put the company on the edge of financial ruin. He sold off many of his holdings (some at a loss), reinvested the funds to stimulate the firm, and once again reorganized management.

Despite all its problems, Domino's had seen consistent growth in the international market. The company opened its first foreign store in 1983 in Canada. Primary overseas expansion areas were eastern Europe and India. By 1994, Domino's had 5079 stores, with 823 of these in 37 major international markets. International brought in 17 percent of 1994 sales. Over the next 10 to 15 years the company had contracts for 4000 additional international units. These units would give Domino's more international than domestic units. International sales were 16.6 percent of total, and international stores were 16.5 percent of total in 1994.

	1985	1986	1987	1988	1989	1990	1991	1992	1993	1994
Sales[a]	1,100	1,430	2,000	2,300	2,500	2,600	2,400	2,450	2,200	2,500
Stores	2,841	3,610	4,279	4,858	5,185	5,342	5,571	5,264	5,369	5,079
Employees (K)	na	na	na	na	na	100	na	na	na	115

[a]$000,000.

Hardee's. Hardee's was number 6 in sales and 11 in stores for 1994. In 1981, the large, diversified Canadian company Imasco purchased the chain. Imasco also owned Imperial Tobacco (Player's and du Maurier, Canada's top two sellers), Burger Chef, two drug store chains, the development company Genstar, and CT Financial.

Hardee's had pursued growth primarily in the United States. Of all the burger chains in the top 10 franchises, Hardee's had the smallest international presence, with 72 stores generating US$63 million (1.8 and 2.0 percent of sales and stores, respectively) in 1994.

Hardee's sales grew by about 2 percent annually for 1993 and 1994. A failed attempt by Imasco to merge its Roy Roger's restaurants into the Hardee's chain forced the parent company to maintain both brands. Hardee's attempted to differentiate from the other burger chains by offering an upscale burger menu, which received a lukewarm reception by consumers.

	1985	1986	1987	1988	1989	1990	1991	1992	1993	1994
Sales[a]	3,376	5,522	6,788	7,311	8,480	9,647	9,870	9,957	9,681	9,385
Net income[a]	262	184	283	314	366	205	332	380	409	506
EPS ($)	1.20	0.78	1.12	1.26	1.44	1.13	0.64	0.68	0.74	0.78
Stock price close ($)	13.94	16.25	12.94	14.00	18.88	13.81	18.25	20.63	20.06	19.88
Dividends ($)	0.36	0.42	0.48	0.52	0.56	0.64	0.64	0.68	0.74	0.78
Employees (K)	na	na	na	na	190	190	180	na	200	200

[a]$M—all $ in Canadian; 1994: debt ratio: 38.4%; R.O.E. 16.1%; current ratio: 1.37; LTD (M): $1927; 1994 Segment sales (operating income): CT Financial Services 47%; (28%); Hardee's 32% (11%); Imperial Tobacco 16% (50%); Shoppers Drug Mart 2% (9%); Genstar Development 1% (2%).

International Dairy Queen, Inc. Dairy Queen was one of the oldest fastfood franchises in the United States; the first store was opened in Joliet, Illinois, in 1940. By 1950, there were over 1100 stores, and by 1960, Dairy Queen had locations in 12 countries. Initial franchise agreements focused on the right to use the DQ freezers, an innovation that kept ice cream at the constant 23°F necessary to maintain the soft consistency. In 1970, a group of investors bought the franchise organization, but the group has been only partly successful in standardizing the fastfood chain. In 1994 a group of franchisees filed an antitrust suit in an attempt to get the company to loosen its control on food supply prices and sources. DQ franchises cost $30,000 initially plus continuing payments of 4 percent of sales.

The company's menu consisted of ice cream, yogurt, and brazier (hamburgers and other fast food) items. Menu innovations had included Blizzard (candy and other flavors mixed in the ice cream). The company also had acquired several companies, including the Golden Skillet (1981), Karmelkorn (1986), and Orange Julius (1987).

In 1994, Dairy Queen ranked number 7 in sales and 6 in stores. By that same year, the company had expanded its presence into 19 countries with 628 stores and US$300 million in international sales. 1994 was an excellent year for DQ; sales were up 22.8 percent over 1993. This dramatic change (1993 scored an anemic 3.0 percent gain) was fueled by technology improvements for franchisees and international expansion. In 1992 Dairy Queen opened company-owned outlets in Austria, China, Slovenia, and Spain. DQ announced in 1995 that they had a plan to open 20 stores in Puerto Rico over a 4-year period.

	1985	1986	1987	1988	1989	1990	1991	1992	1993	1994
Sales[a]	158	182	210	254	282	287	287	296	311	341
Net income[a]	10	12	15	20	23	27	28	29	30	31
EPS ($)	0.33	0.42	0.51	0.70	0.83	0.97	1.05	1.12	1.79	1.30
Stock price close ($)	5.20	7.75	8.00	11.50	14.75	16.58	21.00	20.00	18.00	16.25
Dividends ($)	0	0	0	0	0	0	0	0	0	0
Employees (K)	430	459	503	520	549	584	592	672	538	564

[a]$M; 1994: debt ratio 15.3%; R.O.E. 24.4%; current ratio 3.04; LTD $23M. 1994 restaurants: U.S. 87%; Canada 9%; other 4%; restaurants by type: DQs franchised by company, 62%; franchised by territorial operators, 27%; foreign, 3%; Orange Julius, 7%; Karmelkorn, 1%; Golden Skillet less than 1%; sales by source: good supplies and equipment to franchises, 78%; service fees, 16%; franchise sales and other fees, 3%; realestate finance and rental income, 3%.

Little Caesar's. Little Caesar's ranked 10 in sales and 8 in stores for 1994. Sales growth had slowed to a halt; a 1992–1993 increase of 12.2 percent evaporated into no increase for 1993–1994.

These numbers were achieved without a significant overseas presence. Of the top 10 franchises, only Hardee's had a smaller number of stores in foreign lands. Little Caesar's received 3.5 percent of sales from foreign stores. Only 3.2 percent of the company's stores were in non-U.S. locations, namely, Canada, Czech and Slovak Republics, Guam, Puerto Rico, and the United Kingdom.

	1985	1986	1987	1988	1989	1990	1991	1992	1993	1994
Sales	340	520	725	908	1,130	1,400	1,725	2,050	2,150	2,000
No. of stores	900	1,000	1,820	2,000	2,700	3,173	3,650	4,300	5,609	4,700
Employees	18,000	26,160	36,400	43,600	54,000	63,460	73,000	86,000	92,000	95,000

McDonald's. At the top in 1994 international sales and units, McDonald's, Inc., was the most profitable retailer in the United States during the 1980s and into the 1990s. The company opened its first store in California in 1948, went public in 1965, and by 1994 had over 20 percent of the U.S. fast-food business. McDonald's opened its first international store in Canada in 1967. Growing domestic competition in the 1980s gave impetus to the company's international expansion. By 1994 there were over 15,000 restaurants under the golden arches in 79 countries. The non-U.S. stores provided about onethird of total revenues and half the company's profits. McDonald's planned to open 1200 to 1500 new restaurants in 1995—most outside the United States. International markets had grown into an attractive venue for the burger giant because there was "less competition, lighter market saturation, and high name recognition" in international markets.

The company's growth was fueled by aggressive franchising. In the early 1990s, two-thirds of the McDonald's locations were franchised units, and franchisees remained with the company an average of 20 years. McDonald's used heavy advertising ($1.4 billion in 1994) and frequent menu changes and other innovations [1963, FiletOFish sandwich and Ronald McDonald; 1968, Big Mac and first TV ads; 1972, Quarter Pounder, Egg McMuffin (breakfast); 1974, Ronald McDonald House; 1975, drive thru; 1979, Happy Meals; 1983, Chicken McNuggets; 1986, provided customers with list of products' ingredients; 1987, salads; 1980s, "value menus"; 1991, McLean DeLuxe, a lowfat hamburger (not successful) and experimentation with decor and new menu items at local level; 1993; first restaurants inside another store (WalMart)]. The company planned to open its first restaurants in India in 1996 with menus featuring chicken, fish sandwiches, and vegetable nuggets. There would be no beef items.

From 1993–1994, McDonald's grew 10.2 percent in sales and 8.7 percent in stores. Because of its extensive experience in international markets, international sales had grown to 42.5 percent of total revenues and half its profits. Indeed, McDonald's was bigger than the 25 largest full-service chains put together.

	1985	1986	1987	1988	1989	1990	1991	1992	1993	1994
Sales[a]	3,695	4,144	4,894	5,566	6,142	6,640	6,695	7,133	7,408	8,321
Net income[a]	433	480	549	656	727	802	860	959	1,083	1,224
EPS ($)	0.56	0.63	0.73	0.86	0.98	1.10	1.18	1.30	1.46	1.68
Stock price close ($)	9.00	10.16	11.00	12.03	17.25	14.56	19.00	24.38	28.50	29.25
Dividends ($)	0.10	0.11	0.12	0.14	0.16	0.17	0.18	0.20	0.21	0.23
Employees (K)	148	159	159	169	176	174	168	166	169	183

[a]$M; 1994: debt ratio 41.2%; R.O.E. 20.7%; cash: $180M; current ratio: 0.31; LTD $2.9M; market value: $20B.

PepsiCo: KFC and Taco Bell (also Includes Pizza Hut; Latter Is Not in the Top 50).
Pepsico owned powerful brand names such as Pepsi-Cola and Frito-Lay and also was the world's no. 1 fast-food chain—with its ownership of KFC, Taco Bell, and Pizza Hut. KFC was third in sales and stores of the top 50 franchises in 1994. Active in the international arena since the late 1960s, KFC had been a major McDonald's competitor in non-U.S. markets. In 1994, the company had US$3.6 billion in sales and 4258 stores in other countries. McDonald's had been commonly number one in each country it entered, but KFC had been number two in international sales and had the number one sales spot in Indonesia. In 1994, KFC international revenues were 50.7 percent of sales with 45.3 percent of stores in international locations.

Taco Bell was fourth in sales and fifth in stores of the top 50 franchises in 1994. This ranking had been achieved with minimal international business to date. Taco Bell had US $130 million sales and 162 stores internationally. The company attempted to enter the Mexican market in 1992 with a kiosk and cart strategy in Mexico City. The venture did not fare well, and Taco Bell soon pulled out of Mexico. In 1994, international revenues were 3.0 percent of sales and 2.9 percent of stores were international locations.

	1985	1986	1987	1988	1989	1990	1991	1992	1993	1994
Sales[a]	8,057	9,291	11,485	13,007	15,242	17,803	19,608	21,970	25,021	28,474
Net income[a]	544	458	595	762	901	1,077	1,080	1,302	1,588	1,784
EPS ($)	0.65	0.58	0.76	0.97	1.13	1.35	1.35	1.61	1.96	2.22
Stock price close ($)	8.06	8.66	11.11	13.15	21.31	26.00	22.88	31.40	40.88	36.25
Div./share ($)	0.15	0.21	0.22	0.25	0.31	0.37	0.44	0.50	0.58	0.68
Employees (K)	150	214	225	235	266	308	338	372	423	471

[a]$M; 1994: debt ratio 48.1%, R.O.E. 27.0%; cash(M) $1,488; current ratio 0.96; LTD (M) $8.841. 1994 segment sales (operating income): restaurants: 37% (22%); beverages 34% (37%); snack foods 29% (41%).

Subway. Founded more than 29 years ago, Subway remained privately held in 1994. The company had experienced explosive growth during the 1990s. It ranked ninth in sales and second in stores for 1994. Sales grew 13.6 percent from 1993 to 1994 and 26 percent from 1992 to 1993. Stores grew 17.1 percent from 1993 to 1994 and 15.3 percent from 1992 to 1993. In 1994, Subway overtook KFC as the number two chain in number of stores behind McDonald's. The company attributed its growth at least partially to an exceptionally low-priced and well-structured franchise program. In addition, store sizes of 500 to 1500 square feet were small. Thus the investment for a Subway franchise was modest.

The company's growth involved a deliberate strategy. The formula involved no cooking on site, except for the baking of bread. The company promoted the "efficiency and simplicity" of its franchise and advertised its food as "healthy, delicious, [and] fast." The company advertised regularly on TV with a $25 million budget and planned to increase that significantly. All stores contributed 2.5 percent of gross sales to the corporate advertising budget. Subway's goal was to equal or exceed the number of outlets operated by the largest fast-food company in every market that it entered. In most cases the firm's benchmark was burger giant McDonald's.

International markets played an emerging role in Subway's expansion. In 1994, international sales were 10.6 percent of sales, compared with 8.9 percent the previous year. International stores were 9.5 percent of total in 1994 and 7.5 percent in 1993. Subway boasted a total of 9893 stores in all 50 states and 19 countries.

Wendy's. Wendy's was number five in sales and number nine in stores for 1994. In 1994, after 25 years of operation, Wendy's had grown to 4411 stores. This growth had been almost exclusively domestic until 1979, when Wendy's ventured out of the United States and Canada to open its first outlets in Puerto Rico, Switzerland, and West Germany. Wendy's granted J.C. Penney the franchise rights to France, Belgium, and Holland and had one store opened in Belgium by 1980.

Wendy's still saw opportunities for growth in the United States. Industry surveys had consistently ranked Wendy's burgers number one in quality but poor in convenience (Wendy's had one store for every 65,000 people, while McDonald's, in contrast, had one for every 25,000). Growth was driven primarily by franchising. In 1994, 71 percent of the stores were operated by franchisees and 29 percent by the company. Company restaurants provided 90 percent of total sales, while franchise fees provided 8 percent. The company had made menu and strategic changes at various points in history. For example, in 1977 the company first began TV advertising; 1979 introduced its salad bar; 1985 experimented with breakfast; 1986 and 1987 introduced Big Classic and SuperBar buffet (neither very successful); 1990 grilled chicken sandwich and 99 cent Super Value Menu items; and 1992 packaged salads.

Wendy's planned to add about 150 restaurants each year in foreign markets. With a presence of 236 stores in 33 countries in 1994, international was 9.1 percent of sales and 9.4 percent of stores in 1994.

	1985	1986	1987	1988	1989	1990	1991	1992	1993	1994
Sales[a]	1,126	1,140	1,059	1,063	1,070	1,011	1,060	1,239	1,320	1,398
Net income[a]	76	(5)	4	29	24	39	52	65	79	97
EPS ($)	0.82	(0.05)	0.04	0.30	0.25	0.40	0.52	0.63	0.76	0.91
Stock price close ($)	13.41	10.25	5.63	5.75	4.63	6.25	9.88	12.63	17.38	14.38
Div./share ($)	0.17	0.21	0.24	0.24	0.24	0.24	0.24	0.24	0.24	0.24
Employees (K)	40	40	45	42	39	35	39	42	43	44

[a]$M; 1994: debt ratio 36.6%; R.O.E. 5.2%; current ratio 0.98; LTD(M) $145.

APPENDIX B: COUNTRY SUMMARIES*

Canada

In the 1990s, Canada was considered an ideal first stop for U.S. business seeking to begin exporting. Per capita output, patterns of production, market economy, and business practices were similar to the United States. U.S. goods and services were well received in Canada; 70 percent of all Canadian imports were from the United States. Canada's market conditions were stable, and U.S. companies continued to see Canada as an attractive option for expansion.

Canada had one of the highest real growth rates among the OECD during the 1980s, averaging about 3.2 percent. The Canadian economy softened during the 1990s, but Canadian imports of U.S. goods and services were expected to increase about 5 percent in fiscal year 1996.

Although Canada sometimes mirrored the United States, there are significant cultural and linguistic differences from the United States and between the regional markets in Canada. These differences were evident in the mounting friction between the English- and French-speaking areas of Canada. The conflict had potential for splitting of territory between the factions, slicing Canada into two separate countries. The prospect of this outcome left foreign investors tense.

Germany

In the mid-1990s, Germany was the largest economy in Europe, and the fifth largest overall importer of U.S. goods and services. Since reunification in 1990, the eastern part of Germany had continued to receive extensive infusions of aid from western Germany, and these funds were only just beginning to show an impact. The highly urbanized and skilled western German population enjoyed a very high standard of living with abundant leisure time. In 1994, Germany emerged from a recession and scored a GDP of US$2 trillion.

A unique feature of Germany was the unusually even distribution of both industry and population— there was no single business center for the country. This was a challenge for U.S. firms. They had to establish distribution networks that adequately covered all areas of the country. In Germany there was little opportunity for regional concentration around major population centers as in the United States.

The country was a good market for innovative high-tech goods and high-quality food products. Germans expected high-quality goods and would reject a less expensive product if quality and support were not in abundance. Strongest competition for U.S. firms were the German domestic firms not only because of their home-grown familiarity of the market but also because of the consumers' widely held perception that German products were "simply the best."

A recurring complaint from Germans was the prevalent "here today, gone tomorrow" business approach of American firms. Germans viewed business as a longterm commitment to support growth in markets and did not always receive the level and length of attention necessary from U.S. companies to satisfy them.

*Note that the material in this Appendix is adapted from the Department of Commerce *Country Commercial Guides* and the *CIA World Fact Book*.

Conditions in the former area of East Germany were not the doomsday picture often painted, nor were they as rosy as the German government depicts. It would take 10 to 15 years for the eastern region of the country to catch up to the western region in terms of per capita income, standard of living, and productivity.

Japan

Japan had the second largest economy in the world. Overall economic growth in Japan over the past 35 years had been incredible: 10 percent average annual growth during the 1960s, 5 percent in the 1970s and 1980s. Growth ground to a halt during the 1990s due to tight fiscal policy. The government tightened fiscal constraints in order to correct the significant devaluation of the real estate markets. The economy posted a 0.6 growth in 1994 largely due to consumer demand. The overall economic outlook remained cloudy, but the outlook for exports to Japan remained positive.

Japan was a highly homogeneous society with business practices characterized by longstanding close relationships among individuals and firms. It took time for Japanese businessmen to develop relationships, and for non-Japanese businesspeople the task of relationship building in Japan was formidable. It was well known that Japan's market was not as open as the United States, but the U.S. government had mounted multifaceted efforts to help U.S. businesspeople to "open doors." While these efforts were helpful, most of the responsibility in opening the Japanese market to U.S. goods or services remained with the individual firm. Entering Japan was expensive and generally required four things: (1) financial and management capabilities and a Japanese-speaking staff residing within the country, (2) modification of products to suit Japanese consumers, (3) a longterm approach to maximizing market share and achieving reasonable profit levels, and (4) careful monitoring of Japanese demand, distribution, competitors, and government. Despite the challenges of market entry, Japan ranked as the second largest importer of U.S. goods and services.

Historically, Japanese consumers were conservative and brand conscious, although the recession during the 1990s nurtured opportunities for "value" entrants. Traditional conformist buying patterns were still prominent, but more individualistic habits were developing in the younger Japanese aged 18 to 21. This age cohort had a population of 8 million people and boasted a disposable income of more than US$35 billion.

Japanese consumers were willing to pay a high price for quality goods. However, they had a well-earned reputation for having unusually high expectations for quality. U.S. firms with high-quality, competitive products had to be able to undertake the high cost of initial market entry. For those who were willing, Japan could provide respectable market share and attractive profit levels.

Mexico

Mexico had experienced a dramatic increase in imports from the United States since the late 1980s. During 1994, the country experienced 20 percent growth over 1993. In 1994, Mexico's peso experienced a massive devaluation brought on by investor anxiety and capital flight. Although the Mexican government implemented tight fiscal measures to stabilize the peso, its efforts could not stop the country from plunging into a serious recession.

Inflation rose as a result of the austerity policies, and it was expected to be between 42 and 54 percent in 1995. Negative economic growth was anticipated in 1995 as well. The U.S. financial assistance package (primarily loans) provided Mexico with nearly US$50 billion and restored stability to the financial markets by mid-1995. The government was taking measures to improve the country's infrastructure. Mexico's problems mask that its government had, on the whole, practiced sound economic fundamentals.

Mexico was still committed to political reform despite the current economic challenges. After ruling the government uninterrupted for 60 years, the PRI party had begun to lose some seats to other political parties. Mexico was slowly evolving into a multiparty democracy.

Despite the economic misfortunes of recent years, Mexico remained the United States' third largest trading partner. Mexico still held opportunities for U.S. firms able to compete in the price-sensitive recessionary market. Mexico had not wavered on the NAFTA agreement since its ratification, and in the mid-1990s, 60 percent of U.S. exports to Mexico entered duty-free.

South Korea

South Korea had been identified as one of the U.S. Department of Commerce's 10 "Big Emerging Markets." The country's economy overcame tremendous obstacles after the Korean War in the 1950s left the country in ruins. The driving force behind South Korea's growth was export-led development and energetic emphasis on entrepreneurship. Annual real GDP growth from 1986 to 1991 was over 10 percent. This blistering pace created inflation, tight labor markets, and a rising current account deficit. Fiscal policy in 1992 focused on curbing inflation and reducing the deficit. Annual growth, reduced to a still enviable 5 percent in 1992, rose to 6.3 percent in 1993. Fueled by exports, 1994s growth was a heady 8.3 percent. South Korea's GDP was larger than those of Russia, Australia, and Mexico.

The American media had highlighted such issues as student demonstrations, construction accidents, and North Korean nuclear problem and trade disputes. Investors needed to closely monitor developments related to North Korea. However, the political landscape in South Korea had been stable enough over the 1980s to fuel tremendous economic expansion. The country was undertaking significant infrastructure improvements. Overall, South Korea was a democratic republic with an open society and a free press. It was a modern, cosmopolitan, fastpaced, and dynamic country with abundant business opportunities for savvy American businesses.

There had been staggering development of U.S. exports to South Korea: US$21.6 billion in 1994 and over US$30 billion expected in 1995. While South Korea was 22 times smaller than China in terms of population, it imported two times more U.S. goods and services than China in 1994.

Although South Korea ranked as the United States' sixth largest export market, obstacles for U.S. firms still remained. Despite participation in the Uruguay Round of GATT and related trade agreements, customs clearance procedures and regulations for labeling, sanitary standards, and quarantine often served as significant nontariff barriers.

United Kingdom (or Great Britain)

The United Kingdom (U.K.) was the United States' fourth largest trading partner and the largest market for U.S. exports in Europe. Common language, legal heritage, and business practices facilitated U.S. entry into the British market.

The United Kingdom had made significant changes to their taxation, regulation, and privatization policies that changed the structure of the British economy and increased its overall efficiency. The reward for this disciplined economic approach had been sustained, modest growth during the 1980s and early 1990s. GDP grew 4.2 percent in 1994, the highest level in 6 years. The United Kingdom trimmed its deficit from US$75 billion in fiscal 1994 to US$50 billion in fiscal 1995.

The United Kingdom had no restrictions on foreign ownership and movement of capital. There was a high degree of labor flexibility. Efficiencies had soared in the United Kingdom, and in the mid-1990s, the country boasted the lowest real per unit labor cost of the Group of Seven (G7) industrialized countries.

The United Kingdom's shared cultural heritage and warm relationship with the United States translated into the British finding U.S. goods and services as attractive purchases. These reasons, coupled with British policy emphasizing free enterprise and open competition, made the United Kingdom the destination of 40 percent of all U.S. investment in the EU.

The U.K. market was based on a commitment to the principles of free enterprise and open competition. Demand for U.S. goods and services was growing. The abolition of many internal trade barriers within the European Common market enabled European-based firms to operate relatively freely. As a result, U.S. companies used the United Kingdom as a gateway to the rest of the EU. Of the top 500 British companies, one in eight was a U.S. affiliate. Excellent physical and communications infrastructure combined with a friendly political and commercial climate were expected to keep the United Kingdom as a primary target for U.S. firms for years to come.

CASE 3   TONERNOW.COM: A DOTCOM GOES GLOBAL

Introduction

It was the second week in April 2000. Dotcom euphoria gripped the U.S. economy and venture capital was flowing everywhere. Henry Kasindorf and Rich Katz, young founders of a New Jersey-based brick-and-mortar company recently turned dotcom, had received communications from all over the world soliciting their participation in licensing agreements, partnerships, and other similar relationships. Serious offers had come from Australia, Brazil, South Africa, Central America, and Europe. Their company, tonernow.com, was hot.

Kasindorf and Katz were facing a big question: should operations remain focused on the U.S. or

This case was written by Martha Lanning, Research Associate, William F. Glavin Center for Global Entrepreneurial Leadership, under the direction of Jean-Pierre Jeannet, F.W. Olin Distinguished Professor of Global Business. This case was written as a basis for class discussion rather than to illustrate either effective or ineffective handling of a business situation. Copyright © 2000 by Babson College, William F. Glavin Center for Global Entrepreneurial Leadership. Not to be used or reproduced without written permission.

William F. Glavin Center for Global Entrepreneurial Leadership
Distributed by The European Case Clearing House, England and USA.
North America, phone: +1 781 239 5884, fax: +1 781 239 5885, e-mail: ECCHBabson@aol.com.
Rest of the World, phone:+44 (0)1234 750903, fax:+44 (0)1234 751125, e-mail:ECCH@cranfield.ac.uk.
All rights reserved. Printed in UKand USA. Website: http://www.ecch.cranfield.ac.uk.

should the company go global? The business was expanding and many issues required immediate attention. Globalization would inject even greater urgency into the situation.

tonernow.com was the e-commerce arm of IQ Computer Products, a company Kasindorf and Katz had founded in 1993. The brick-and-mortar segment of the business, not counting the website, was now selling approximately $5 million. Some two-thirds of this volume went to individual retail clients and one-third to wholesalers and distributors.

The tonernow.com website launched in beta format on September 15, 1999, now carried over 3,000 products at discounts of 30% to 70% off manufacturer list prices. The site also offered a proprietary line of compatible toner products.

Toner was a black, powdered, plastic substance contained in cartridges used in printers, copiers, and fax machines. Toner powder adhered to parts of a drum that had been properly charged for toner coverage. A fuser assembly within the printer or copier machine melted the toner to fuse it to the page, resulting in a sharp text that could not be smudged. When toner ran out, the machines could not function. Toner was critical for office productivity.

Company History

Kasindorf and Katz had met as freshmen undergraduates at Babson College in 1987, the year Kasindorf achieved recognition for his successful launch of a condom vending machine business. Kasindorf described his rocky beginning as an entrepreneur:

"I used all my professors. One in law helped me with the contracts, marketing helped me with the brochures. I was fascinated by all the resources that were available, some of the best in the world! I attended a student government meeting and brought the project up for approval, but the Assistant Dean shot me down. I stormed into the Dean's office and got it OK'd. That business was fun, it got my feet wet. There were a lot of legal issues, such as liability if one of the condoms broke. Also, I was a freshman and in the middle of finals I got 12 voice mails from reporters!"

Within months, Kasindorf had set up condom dispensers in college bathrooms throughout the Boston area. Two years later he sold the business for $25,000 and used the proceeds to start another venture. The partners laughed as they recalled their early collaboration:

KASINDORF: "We didn't take much of a liking to each other."

KATZ: "We didn't hit it off."

KASINDORF: "I needed a ride, I told him it would take five minutes, it took 40, and he liked me even less! Then we had a Human Communications class together. My only memory is that Rich got a 37 on the midterm and I got a 16.[1] We sort of bonded after that."

The T-Shirt Business

Kasindorf and Katz soon founded a screen-printed T-shirt company operating on campus. The shirts featured creative graphics using well-known consumer goods logos and sold like hotcakes. Kasindorf explained:

"The copyright hounds had their bounty hunters looking for us. You do have to change 20% of the design so you're not infringing on someone else's mark. We had friends at other schools who started selling the T-shirts for us. Then U.S. News & World Report *came out with the Babson ranking, and we launched a new T-shirt highlighting the No. 1 ranking during homecoming weekend.[2] In 1988–1989, our picture ran in the Babson College publication with the* U.S. News & World Report *ranking."*

IQ Computer Products

After graduating from Babson College, Kasindorf and Katz briefly went their separate ways, each working elsewhere. However, in May 1993, they teamed up again, this time purchasing two small manufacturing companies with combined revenues under $300,000. According to Katz, "One was a sole proprietorship, a guy was making toner products out of his garage."

Based on this purchase, Kasindorf and Katz opened business activity in Spring Valley, NY, some 45 miles from New York City. The new enterprise produced toner and employed four people in addition to Kasindorf and Katz: one in customer service, one to perform accounting and clerical tasks, and two in manufacturing. Operations included manufacturing, customer service, accounting, warehousing, and sales.

Recycling toner cartridges was encouraged on an industry-wide basis. The two partners saw this as an advantage, an aspect of the business that would aid

---

1. Out of a possible score of 100 on the midterm exam.
2. *U.S. News & World Report* ranked Babson College the No. 1 business school in the U.S. for entrepreneurial studies.

in cost control and make the product "recession-proof."

Funding came entirely from cash flow, profits, and a small bank loan. In 1993, the partners held notes to the two original owners. Within two years the notes were paid off.

By 1994, business was exploding out of the 900 square feet facility in Spring Valley. The young entrepreneurs consolidated the two original firms, named the new entity IQ Computer Products (IQCP), and moved the company to its present site in Englewood, NJ. Kasindorf discussed the decision to locate in Englewood:

"We wanted to stay in New York, and so did the employees. We took it to the State to inquire regarding subsidies and incentives, but they laughed at us because we were under one million dollars in sales. The next week I went to Trenton[3] to talk to the same department, but in New Jersey. They had a team of people assembled in a conference room. They offered training and incentives, and each one made a proposal to us on why we should locate in New Jersey. They welcomed us with open arms."

Growing the Business

During the period 1994–1998, the company added products and diversified as Kasindorf and Katz grew the business. They brought the repair division, previously subcontracted, in-house and hired their own technicians.

In 1994, IQCP sold in three states: New York, New Jersey, and Connecticut. IQCP also serviced a small number of other states by UPS.[4] In 1997, the company began using Federal Express to offer three-day delivery to California with standard ground rates. That same year, business expanded into Canada. By 1998, IQCP was selling in 14 states, mainly in the Northeast but also in California and Colorado.

The partners elaborated on the importance of building customer relationships.

KATZ: "We felt we could sell products other than those we manufactured. Our customers told us they wanted other products. Our customers asked <u>us</u> because the level of service we offered was so far above what other companies offered."

KASINDORF: "We hand-delivered the product, no matter how large or small the order. Our rep showed up with a nice shirt and our IQCP logo, offered to clean the printer and install the customer's cartridge so it would achieve optimal performance. People started to see the attention we gave."

KATZ: "When we started, quality was a major issue in the industry."

KASINDORF: "People are leery of this industry. Therefore, it's important for us to appear as legitimate as possible. We advertise in the *New York Times*, we bring large customers here to tour our facility."

KATZ: "We encourage people to call our reference list. We've had long-standing relationships with our customers, and they rave about us. We are very, very careful here. It's a 'razor blade' product, people come back and buy it again and again. We want people to have an experience second to none. If there's a problem, we replace it with no charge and we handle it quickly."

KASINDORF: "We sell to some of the largest law firms in New York City. We are right there when their laser printers need repair. They rely on us."

Website Launch

In 1998, Kasindorf and Katz made the decision to go dotcom. They looked at what was necessary for their company to remain successful and determined that it would be essential to develop an e-commerce strategy and get online. As Kasindorf put it, "We knew we had to now or we'd be left behind."

Kasindorf and Katz knew what was successful *offline*, and they wanted to translate that to *online*. They also wanted to avoid cannibalizing their existing business. The primary options were either to create online ordering for existing clients or to create an entirely new entity as the e-commerce solution.

Kasindorf and Katz decided to create a new entity. They would develop it as an e-commerce arm of the IQCP business. They needed to launch a website, and they would require it to be:

- Serious and straight forward
- User-friendly
- Easy to navigate
- Fun with a couple of unique twists

The partners hired a full-service PR firm. In addition, they hired a freelance media consultant to do media planning.

KASINDORF: "We knew we did not want to do this in-house. We met with a lot of big communications companies and realized the budget we had to develop the site was low. We also realized we'd probably get lost in some of these companies. So

---

3. Capital of the state of New Jersey.
4. United Parcel Service, a delivery service.

we decided to look for more of a boutique-type web developer. We found a great little company in Silicon Alley."

KATZ: "Henry really oversaw the process. We trust our vendors, but we really wanted to have a heavy hand in terms of how the site was developed. We knew how our customers wanted the experience to *feel*."

KASINDORF: "For eight months, it was all I did. It was tremendously stressful! Even as good as the developers were."

KATZ: "We had to develop all the relational links. It was 3,000 products!"

The staff in-house set about developing a large relational database that would allow prospective customers to shop four ways: by key word, brand, product type, or product number. The project took six months and thousands of "man-hours" with five people dedicated full-time. The complete project cost approximately $200,000, half of which went to development alone.

The team designed the database to cross-sell and up-sell each product so that when a prospective customer input a product specification, the website would automatically offer helpful suggestions. The up-sell offered suggestions such as "this printer also takes product so-and-so, we have these products at different prices, do you want to buy it/these also?" The cross-sell offered tonernow.com's own branded products once the customer had input a selection, for example a compatible or related product version, some manufactured on a private label basis and others by tonernow.com.[5] The cross-sell also offered incentives such as double points for a rewards program.

Kasindorf described the complexity of the project:

"We had fantastic developers, but they did not know anything about product. It was up to us to develop the back-end issues. We learned through focus groups that most people really don't know what they need. Also, product numbers are long, and there's no apparent connection between the number and the product. We wanted to make the site user-friendly, for people to get what they wanted in two clicks or less. Most competitor sites require five clicks or more. There is nothing out there like our proprietary database, it's unique to the industry. We have people who want to license use of the database because of how powerful it is."

The Ambush Campaign

The next task was to develop a budget for the first three months after launch. An important part of this step was to look at the different vehicles for advertising. The budget would allocate money for various types of advertising such as banner ads, email marketing, radio, TV, and billboard.

The partners examined many names for the new entity and finally found one they liked. It was owned by a cyber-squatter, so they bought it. The new name would be *tonernow.com*.

The original plan was to launch the website in June, but it quickly became apparent that June would be impossible.

KASINDORF: "There was no way for June to work. September 15 was Internet World at the Javits Center.[6] We decided on an ambush campaign. No display at the expo. We had men dressed in white jumpsuits with the tonernow.com logo, in front of a giant tonernow.com billboard, handing out shopping bags with T-shirts to each person."

KATZ (laughing): "We really used our T-shirt expertise!"

Dotcom Results

Once the website launched, resulting activity was entirely new business. No activity migrated from the brick-and-mortar operation to the website. Kasindorf and Katz had decided to maintain two separate profit centers and market to two separate databases. They would possibly migrate individual customers, two-thirds of the brick-and-mortar segment of the business, to the website at a later time. They had not publicized the website to their traditional customers in order to avoid cannibalization. Moreover, the website sold at lower margins, and significant customer migration would have reduced margins overall.

Gross sales rocketed upward. From initial sales volume of a few thousand dollars in December 1999, by January 2000 business had jumped 115%, by February 209%, and by March 118%.

Going for Venture Capital

The partners soon turned their attention to crafting a business plan.

KATZ: "Toward the end of the year was when we started to focus on VC. It had always been

---

5. As an input example, product EPS-SO2-0089.

6. The Jacob K. Javits Convention Center, New York's premier trade show and convention venue with more than 814,400 square feet of exhibit space.

understood that at some point, we'd get venture capital and take the company public."

KASINDORF: "We had first-mover advantage, we were more a 'click-and-mortar' rather than e-commerce. Very appealing to the VC people. We'd shown we could grow in a brick-and-mortar way. It was more a question of how much equity we'd have to give up and who we'd go with, not _if_ we'd go."

The partners expected to get exactly what they sought in the first round, but they were in for a few surprises. The first surprise was that profitability was not required.

KASINDORF: "In our projections we were showing profitability after two years. Investment bankers, consultants, and VC people told us we were not showing a loss!"

KATZ: "It just made sense to us, that we were in business to make a profit."

KASINDORF: "Another thing! We'd walk into a VC meeting wearing business suits, not ripped jeans, wearing tattoos and carrying our skateboards. The first meeting we ever had, we walked out of there with a $37 million valuation."

KATZ: "We began to get offers on the table. Then in spring the NASDAQ got hit hard."

The Toner Supplies Industry

The toner supplies industry was a highly fragmented segment within the larger office supplies industry. In 1999, the market for toner supplies was estimated at $30 billion. Players in the market included OEMs, office superstores, dealers of equipment such as copiers, printers and fax machines, catalog distributors, and re-manufacturers.

Customers were extremely sensitive to price and convenience. When toner ran out, the productivity of an office machine was placed on hold until new toner could be supplied. Thus, same day delivery was a key to success.

Laser copying and printing had dramatically changed the industry in recent years. Developments such as color printing had placed new demands on paper quality. Paper needed to be able to handle black and white toner printing as well as printing that used the newer four-color toner technology. Color toner particles had recently been made smaller in order to improve print quality.

Competition

Toner cartridges and inkjet cartridges formed a highly specialized niche segment of the office sup-

plies industry. Toner and other supplies carried a much higher margin than hardware. Within this segment there was no single dominant player. Several large companies held a major share of the toner supplies market: Hewlett-Packard (H-P), Lexmark, Xerox, IBM, Canon, and Ricoh, among other OEMs.

In early 2000, Konica Corp. and Minolta Co. both of Japan announced an agreement in the areas of information technology equipment and printer toner production. The agreement involved a joint venture to manufacture toner.

In 1999, H-P had launched a new line of toner supplies, eliptica, to compete with Xerox. Two years earlier Xerox had begun to offer H-P compatible laser printer cartridges, and the eliptica line was H-P's counterstrike response. After only eight months of operation, H-P surprised the industry in spring 2000 by announcing the end of the eliptica venture in order to re-focus on other strategic growth opportunities.

H-P was the world's largest maker of printers, and China was the world's fastest growing market. Printer sales in China totaled some $900 million in 1999. H-P had been selling printers in China since the mid-1980's and now controlled almost one quarter of the market.

Cartridge Recycling

The resale of toner and related products was highly profitable with gross margins ranging from 20% to 70%. Empty toner cartridges that had been used could be returned to be recycled. The process ideally involved cleaning and refitting the cartridge, as well as filling it with new toner. However, many "remanufacturers" used shortcuts and provided recycled cartridges of poor quality.

Industry Fraud

Fraud was a serious problem for the industry. Customers using counterfeit supplies risked poor equipment performance, low supply yields, inferior print quality, toner leakage, high cartridge failure rates, and increased equipment downtime.

Illegal operations typically contacted potential victims by telephone, misrepresenting themselves as having taken over the previous toner supplier's operation, or as a firm that worked in tandem with the legitimate supplier. These "telemarketers" sold low quality goods to unsuspecting customers. Advances in communications technology had increased the opportunity for this type of fraud.

Xerox had been working with federal authorities to crack down on counterfeit toner distributors. In 1999, federal agents raided a warehouse in

Milwaukee seizing 47,000 counterfeit supplies boxes estimated at a market value of $8 million.

Building a Strategy for the Future

In spring 2000, Kasindorf and Katz had been shopping their company to venture capital people with the expectation of increasingly lucrative offers. However, the valuation of tonernow.com had tanked when the NASDAQ plummeted.

The deals now on the table were lower than the partners had previously considered desirable. Moreover, taking one of the deals would force them to relinquish at least some measure of control to their funding source.

Overview of the Current Business

Since 1994, tonernow.com had grown significantly. The firm employed 30 people and sold in all 50 states. Over 3,000 different products were offered with approximately 40 manufactured in-house. Some 10% of the products covered 80% to 90% of the market. tonernow.com sourced OEM products from vendors and also provided 300 compatible products that were not OEM-branded. Compatibles were manufactured either by tonernow.com or by another firm and sold under the tonernow.com name.

The mission of tonernow.com was to become the best known brand in the imaging supplies industry. The objective was to deliver high-end value through e-commerce while offering the following service elements:

- The Web's largest selection of toner products
- A superior website with built-in guidance tools and support designed for cross-selling and up-selling to products with superior margins
- Discounts from 30% to 70% lower than manufacturer's prices
- Service and maintenance programs for business equipment
- A rewards program with incentives for return customers
- Free next-day shipping with Federal Express
- Email reminders and an auto-ship program
- Online and offline ordering options
- National advertising

Customer Service: A Key to Success

The company had retained many of its original customers as a result of superior customer service.

KASINDORF: "When we were just 23 and starting out, people saw the commitment we had to serving them. Among our customers we have very

low attrition rates. Companies we were doing business with in 1993 are still our customers."

KATZ: "We definitely benchmark other companies. We look at them to see if they're doing something right. And we learn from our customers."

KASINDORF: "As we've grown, there have been a lot of internal pressures. The ability to have two partners running the business is unique in that we're able to feed off each other in certain ways. We're able to do that in a way that has really contributed to our growth. Our roles are not completely pigeonholed, we have insight into each other's areas, and that's beneficial."

KATZ: "When we first started, we were both into selling, selling, selling. We had no idea how things would develop. As you grow, there's always the issue of costs getting out of control. As a result, I am now more involved with the operations. Henry is more the outside guy who handles sales and marketing. He instituted the procedures of how we deal with customer relations. I've kinda stayed inside and developed cost-cutting measures. We run a manufacturing operation, and neither of us had any manufacturing or engineering background. Also, we have some very big competitors. They've put obstacles in our way, and we've had to figure out how to get around them."

Changing Realities

By spring 2000, tonernow.com had attracted attention from outside the U.S. Katz remarked that the attention had been entirely unsolicited:

"We got noticed through trade shows. But as soon as we became a dotcom, it added instant credibility. When people saw the functionality of the site, they were just wowed by it. International contacts were also wowed by it. Once they got into our site, they saw we had a great deal to offer."

A number of deals had been proposed, and the partners were now considering options for international expansion. They would need to examine every aspect of the business: from legal to operational, from inquiry handling to delivery process, including customer relationships and confirmation of shipping dates. The move from small domestic player to globalization posed many challenges, among which might be any or all of the following:

- Licensing the technology
- Setting up licensing agreements
- Dealing with royalties
- Collecting payment via credit card
- Translating foreign currency into U.S. dollars
- Access to tonernow.com's proprietary database

- Restrictions to impose on website use run through other countries
- How to maintain control of the technology
- Cross-cultural revisions of the website to make it readily understandable
- Legal requirements of setting up business activity
- Same day delivery

Options on the Table

tonernow.com had received communications from Europe, Australia, Brazil, Central America, and South Africa (**Exhibits 1–3**). In some cases, a concrete business proposal had been offered. Suggestions included the following:

Gateway page: This element would enable a customer in a foreign country to log on to the tonernow.com website and then be directed to the specific site for his/her geographic region.

Localization: Making cultural and linguistic changes in the website or gateway page in order to give the look and feel of the local country.

Licensing: Making the website structure and content available in a non-U.S. setting, including templates, shipping, data base, product information, and costing data, among other elements. Specifically, licensing would provide website content, brand relationships, and alternative revenue through co-op funds available with the brands. In addition, a licensing agreement would include:

- International contacts for global contracts
- Comprehensive collateral materials
- Outbound marketing material (bulk email copy, promotions, online coupons)
- Launch support
- Development of local media affiliations
- Proprietary strategic information

The structure that would be required to handle business differed for each geography, and the partners did not want to undertake a different strategy for each region. Kasindorf saw this as a "monumental chore." He was also concerned about the level of service:

> *"Who would send the second confirmation that confirms the ship date? C.O.D. orders and credit card orders online are an issue, because some people don't want to input their credit cards online. Who will handle customer service inquiries? Certainly you want someone local to do this."*

Brazil: The contact company had connections with all the major players including the government.

They had come to CEBIT, the major industry trade show in Hanover, Germany, looking for opportunities. For tonernow.com to go into Brazil as an aftermarket supplier might make sense because entry barriers were high. Katz stated:

> *"We found there was only one licensee there for each manufacturer. To bring us in on a gray market basis would kill our margins. We would have to come in selling our own branded product because the distribution channels are so tight."*

Australia: tonernow.com had exhibited at a large print industry show in California where they met an Australian distributor of toner supplies. The partners recalled his offer:

> *"He told us 'we want to use your site in Australia, how can we do this?' Licensing the technology would result in people getting access to our proprietary database. The alternative would be to set them up as licensees of the technology to use the site in their restricted geographic territory. We did the analysis, to look into running the site for them, and also collecting payment with credit cards in Australian dollars."*

Conclusion

Conducting business internationally would require playing the game with more than one set of rules (**Exhibit 4**). Whether to globalize or remain domestic was the big question. tonernow.com was a small, new company. It shared little in common with firms running large global operations. The partners considered the ramifications of setting up business on an international scale:

KATZ: "In the U.S. when you shake on it, it's a done deal, but in other countries you're not sure. Also in some countries, to get a domain name is very expensive. Fraud overseas is a lot harder to combat than fraud in the U.S."

KASINDORF: "We've started to question everything. Sales are very strong, site revenues are growing, but we're bleeding because of the costs associated with doing business in this manner: advertising, overhead, promotions 'buy one get one free' to gain market share. We are about eight months late with what we were trying to do because the landscape has changed so much. We've gotten into a difficult financial situation thinking we did not *need* to be as profitable as we had planned."

KATZ: "A lot of dotcom casualties have already happened. We want to be very careful."

EXHIBIT 1
Europe

EMAIL FROM HENRY TO EUROPE

••• *I enjoyed meeting you and discussing our mutual e-commerce interests. At this point we are in discussions with firms in various regions who are interested in forming alliances to build the tonernow.com brand on a global level.*

It would be helpful if you could provide me with an understanding of your interest in working with tonernow.com and whether you are interested in pursuing further discussions. Many synergies exist between our firms, and a well thought out strategy of how we could work together would be mutually beneficial.

EMAIL FROM EUROPE BACK TO HENRY

••• *Further to our recent telephone conversations and meetings, I have thought long and hard about how we could take this opportunity forward. The opportunities I see are as follows:*

1. *We could fulfill tonernow.com orders to customers within their countries and also fulfill a manufacturing role for tonernow.com.*
2. *We could bring on other companies in Europe who can also fulfill customer requirements in both.*
3. *We could introduce various OEMs to the tonernow.com distribution model.*

I will call you tomorrow to discuss the above in more detail. I would like to work with you on these options but need to know whether they fit in with your plans. Other considerations are: languages for Europe, software compatibility (i.e. order processing and stock system reconciliation), and dealer blind shipping timescales.

EXHIBIT 2
Brazil

EMAIL FROM BRAZIL TO HENRY

••• *As we talked about in Germany, one of the product lines we have interest to work with, and have been talking about, is the ink jet cartridges. So far it looks to us like it would not be good in Brazil to work with remanufactured cartridges, and we are evaluating the possibilities for importing compatible ones. We have received several proposals for that, mainly from European and Asian companies. One has a strong capability to give huge discounts on their lines, and we are about to receive some samples from them in order to test quality matters.*

EMAIL FROM HENRY BACK TO BRAZIL

••• *In terms of your market analysis for Brazil, I believe that a strategy with compatible products would be very effective for you. Please understand that there are many companies in the market producing and distributing "compatible" toner cartridges that are "remanufactured." Our firm produces and distributes both types of products.*

I realize this may be a bit confusing, but packaging requirements enable us to use the term "compatible" if a certain amount of internal components are replaced during our production process. I realize that there are many companies throughout the world that would like to earn your business for the Brazil market, and I recommend that you proceed slowly and cautiously as this can be very complex.

We can develop a comprehensive user-friendly website for you specifically for your market. The website can be a useful marketing tool for your sales reps, and your customers will appreciate the fact that they can access the information online, order product or simply get product reference information. We can negotiate with the various suppliers on your behalf to produce products for your market under the brand name on a private label basis, therefore you will not be tied to any one manufacturer's brand except your own.

EXHIBIT 3
Central America

EMAIL FROM HENRY TO CENTRAL AMERICA

••• *We are currently undergoing our first round of venture capital financing. I have recruited some senior members for our senior management team and one of the first steps we are taking is to partner with a major distributor in the European market. I am currently analyzing the possibilities for Latin America and the Caribbean in this market.*

Currently the U.S. and European markets are highly fragmented and lack a dominant player. Our focus is to become the world leader in these markets via the Internet. We have relationships with many of the OEMs in each of the markets that we are targeting, and they will be working closely with us to achieve our objectives.

Please let me know if you have an interest in working with us, in what territories you can provide distribution, with which manufacturers you currently have relationships, and whether you have or are planning to implement an e-commerce strategy.

EMAIL FROM CENTRAL AMERICA BACK TO HENRY

••• *Thanks for your continued interest. The opportunity to distribute the recycled toners is not as clear-cut for us as it would be for other companies. Let me explain. We have been approved to distribute (product xyz) in several countries of Central America. We will be investing a lot to open operations in each of these countries.*

I know that some non-original supplies are being imported into these countries, and we certainly do not have 100% share of the original toner market, so there is room for growth. My main concern is that we may only substitute the (product xyz) toners for yours, thereby lowering our sales volumes and possibly the margin. The margin is the clincher.

I have no idea what your toners sell for and how much I can earn on each one. I'm sure you will have good news for me in this department. Please send me your price list and the credit terms we could work on. I'm sure we will be able to do something together.

EXHIBIT 4
Legal Advice
(Excerpt from an entity in Europe)

As you are aware, in many jurisdictions it is necessary to have some sort of local presence before a local domain name can be obtained. We can assist in helping you satisfy these local presence requirements, whether it be by setting up a branch office or a limited company, registering a trademark or in some cases just providing a local address. We hope to be able to provide a seamless service.

As you will appreciate, setting up said alliance will involve a lot of work on our part and although we are some way down the line, it will inevitably take some time, possibly another couple of months, to put in place all the necessary arrangements and set up the technology. However, in the meantime, we have been approached by a number of clients of (company name) who wish to proceed more quickly.

We have already gathered a substantial amount of information and made contacts in most jurisdictions. In many we are in a position to begin offering our services. If you provide us with a list of the jurisdictions in which you are interested, we will forward to you further information regarding whether there is a local presence requirement in those jurisdictions, and if there is, the easiest option for satisfying this requirement.

In setting up this project, one of the most difficult issues to date has been ascertaining the costs of setting up local entities in each jurisdiction. Where it is possible to determine the actual costs, it is apparent that there are significant differences in costs. Therefore to simplify matters to date we have been suggesting a fixed fee per country. This gives you as the client a greater degree of certainty and makes it easier for us to manage the process and achieve consistency in the services we are offering.

However, if there is a relatively small number of countries, you may prefer to work individual fees for each country. We can discuss this with you in more detail when your exact requirements are known.

CASE 4   DELISSA IN JAPAN (REVISED)

"We can maintain our presence in Japan or we can pull out . . ."

In the autumn of 1997, Bjorn Robertson, who had recently been named Managing Director of Agria, Sweden's leading dairy products cooperative, met with his team to review the international side of the business. The four men sat around a table piled high with thick reports, Nielsen audits, film storyboards, yogurt cups, and a mass of promotional material in Japanese. Agria's "Delissa" line of fresh dairy products was sold all over the world through franchise agreements. Several of these agreements were up for review, but the most urgent one was the agreement with Nikko of Japan.

"In the light of these results, there are several things we can do in Japan. We can maintain our presence and stay with our present franchisee, we can change our franchisee, or we can pull out. But, let's look first at how badly we are really doing in Japan." Bjorn Robertson looked across the conference table at Peter Borg, Stefan Gustafsson and Lars Karlsson, each of whom had been involved with Agria's Japanese business over the past few years.

Robertson read aloud to the others a list of Agria's major foreign ventures featuring the Delissa yogurt brand: "U.S.A. launch date 1977, market share is 12.5 percent; Germany launch 1980, market share is 14 percent; U.K. launch 1982, market share is 13.8 percent; France launch 1983, market share is 9.5 percent; Japan launch 1987, market share today is 2–3 percent." Robertson circled the figure with his marker and turned to look around at his team. "Under 3% after 10 years in the market! What happened?" he asked.

History

Agria was founded in 1973 when a group of Swedish dairy cooperatives decided to create a united organization that would develop and sell a line of fresh dairy products. The principal engineers of the organization were Rolf Anderen and Bo Ekman, who had established the group's headquarters in

Uppsala, near Stockholm. In 1980, after the individual cooperatives had been persuaded to drop their own trademarks, the Delissa line was launched. This was one of the few "national" lines of dairy products in Sweden. It comprised yogurts, desserts, fresh cheese, and fresh cream. In the two decades that followed, Agria's share rose from 3 percent to 25 percent of the Swedish fresh milk products market. Anderen's vision and the concerted efforts of 20,000 dairy farmer members of the cooperative had helped build Agria into a powerful national and international organization.

By 1997, more than 1.1 billion Delissa yogurts and desserts were being consumed per year worldwide. In fiscal year 1996, Delissa had sales of $2.1 billion and employed 4,400 people in and outside Sweden.

Industrial franchising was not very widespread in the 1980s, and few Swedish dairy products firms had invested money abroad. However, Ekman's idea of know-how transfer ventures, whereby a local license would manufacture yogurt using Swedish technology and then market and distribute the product using its own distribution network, had enabled Delissa to penetrate over thirteen foreign markets with considerable success and with a minimal capital outlay. In contrast, Delissa's biggest competitor worldwide, Danone—a French food conglomerate marketing a yogurt line under the "Danone" brand name—had gone into foreign markets, mainly by buying into or creating local companies, or by forming regular joint ventures.

By the time Bjorn Robertson took over as European marketing director in 1991, the Delissa trademark—with the white cow symbol so familiar in Sweden—was known in many different countries worldwide. Delissa was very active in sponsoring sports events, and Robertson—himself a keen cross-country skier and sailor—offered his personal support to Delissa's teams around the world.

When he reviewed the international business, Robertson had been surprised by the results of Agria's Japanese joint venture, which did not compare to those achieved in most foreign markets. Before calling together the international marketing team for a discussion, Robertson requested the files on Japan and spent some time studying the history of the alliance. He read:

Proposal for Entry into the Japanese Market

In early 1985, the decision was made to enter the Japanese market. Market feasibility research and a search for a suitable franchisee is underway, with an Agria team currently in Japan.

Objectives

The total yogurt market in Japan for 1986 is estimated at approximately 600 million cups (100mn ml). The market for yogurt is expected to grow at an average of at least 8% p.a. in volume for the next five years. Our launch strategy would be based on an expected growth rate of 10% or 15% for the total market. We have set ourselves the goal of developing a high quality range of yogurts in Japan, of becoming well known with the Japanese consumer. We aim to reach a 5% market share in the first year and 10% share of market within three years of launch. We plan to cover the three main metropolitan areas, Tokyo, Osaka, and Nagoya, within a two-year period, and the rest of the country within the next three years.

Robertson circled the 10 percent with a red pen. He understood that management would have hesitated to set too high a goal for market share compared to other countries since some executives felt that Japan was a difficult market to enter. But, in 1993, the Japanese operation had not reached its target. In 1997, Delissa's share of the total yogurt market had fallen to 2 percent, without ever reaching 3 percent. Robertson wrote a note to the Uppsala-based manager responsible for Far Eastern business stating that he felt Agria's record in Japan in no way reflected the type of success it had had elsewhere with Delissa. He began to wonder why Japan was so different.

The report continued with a brief overview of the Japanese yogurt market:

Consumption

Per capita consumption of yogurt in Japan is low compared to Scandinavian countries. It is estimated at around 5.3 cups per person per year in Japan, versus 110 in Sweden and 120 in Finland. Sales of yogurt in Japan are seasonal, with a peak period from March to July. The highest sales have been recorded in June, so the most ideal launch date would be at the end of February.

Types of Yogurt Available in Japan—1986

In Japan, yogurt sales may be loosely broken down into three major categories:

- Plain (39% of the market in volume): Called "plain" in Japan because the color is white, but it is really flavored with vanilla. Generally sold in 500 ml pure pack cups. Sugared or sometimes with a sugar bag attached.

- Flavored (45% of the market in volume): Differentiated from the above category by the presence of coloring and gelifiers.
  Not a wide range of varieties, mainly: vanilla, strawberry, almond, and citrus.
- Fruit (16% of the market in volume): Similar to the typical Swedish fruit yogurt but with more pulp than real fruit.
  Contains some coloring and flavoring.

Western-type yogurts also compete directly in the same price bracket with local desserts—like puddings and jellies—produced by Japanese competitors.

Competition

Three major Japanese manufacturers account for about half of the total real yogurt market:

Snow Brand Milk Products is the largest manufacturer of dairy products in Japan and produces drinking milk, cheeses, frozen foods, biochemicals and pharmaceuticals. Turnover in 1985 was 443.322 million yen ($1 = ¥234 in 1985).

Meiji Milk Products, Japan's second largest producer of dairy foods, particularly dried milk for babies, ice cream, cheese. Its alliance with the Bulgarian government helped start the yogurt boom in Japan. Turnover in 1985 was 410,674 million yen.

Morinaga Milk Industry, Japan's third largest milk products producer processes drinking milk, ice cream, instant coffee. It has a joint venture with Kraft U.S. for cheese. Turnover in 1985 was 301,783 million yen.

The share of these three producers has remained stable for years and is approximately: Yukijirushi (Snowbrand) 25%; Meiji 19%; Morinaga 10%.

The Japanese also consume a yogurt drink called "Yakult Honsha" which is often included in statistics on total yogurt consumption as it competes with normal yogurt. On a total market base for yogurts and yogurt drink, Yakult has 31%. Yakult drink is based on milk reconstituted from powder or fresh milk acidified with lactic acid and glucose. Yakult is not sold in shops, but through door-to-door sales and by groups of women who visit offices during the afternoon and sell the product directly to employees.

Along with some notes written in 1985 by Mr. Ole Bobek, Agria's Director of International Operations,

Robertson found a report on meetings held in Uppsala at which two members of Agria's negotiating team presented their findings to management.

Selecting a Franchisee

We have just returned from our third visit to Japan where we once again held discussions with the agricultural cooperative, Nikko. Nikko is the country's second largest association of agricultural cooperatives; it is the Japanese equivalent of Agria. Nikko is a significant political force in Japan but not as strong as Zennoh, the National Federation of Agricultural Cooperatives which is negotiating with Sodima, one of our French competitors. Nikko is price leader for various food products in Japan (milk, fruit juice, rice) and is active in lobbying on behalf of agricultural producers. Nikko is divided into two parts: manufacturing and distribution. It processes and distributes milk and dairy products, and it also distributes raw rice and vegetables.

We have seen several other candidates, but Nikko is the first one that seems prepared to join us. We believe that Nikko is the most appropriate distributor for Agria in Japan. Nikko is big and its credentials seem perfect for Agria, particularly since its strong supermarket distribution system for milk in the three main metropolitan areas is also ideally suited for yogurt. In Japan, 80% of yogurt is sold through supermarkets. We are, however, frustrated that, after prolonged discussions and several trips to Japan, Nikko has not yet signed an agreement with Agria. We sense that the management does want to go ahead but that they want to be absolutely sure before signing. We are anxious to get this project underway before Danone, Sodima or Chambourcy[1] enter Japan.

The same report also contained some general information on the Japanese consumer, which Robertson found of interest:

Some Background Information on the Japanese Consumer

Traditionally, Japan is not a dairy products consumer, although locally produced brands of yogurt are sold along with other milk-based items such as puddings and coffee cream.

---

[1]Chambourcy was a brand name for yogurt produced and distributed by Nestlé in various countries. Nestlé, with sales of $52 billion in 1996, was the world's largest food company; its headquarters are in Vevey (Switzerland).

Many aspects of life in Japan are miniaturized due to lack of space: 60% of the total population of about 120 million is concentrated on 3% of the surface of the islands. The rest of the land mass is mountainous. In Japan, 85% of the population live in towns of which over one third have more than half a million people. This urban density naturally affects lifestyle, tastes, and habits. Restricted living space and lack of storage areas mean that most Japanese housewives must shop daily and consequently expect fresh milk products in the stores every day as they rarely purchase long-life foods or drinks. The country is fairly homogeneous as far as culture and the distribution of wealth is concerned. Disposable income is high. The Japanese spend over 30% of their total household budget on food, making it by far the greatest single item, with clothing in second place (10%).

The market is not comparable to Scandinavia or to the United States as far as the consumption of dairy products is concerned. There are young housewives purchasing yogurt today whose mothers barely knew of its existence and whose grandmothers would not even have kept milk in the house. At one time it was believed that the Japanese do not have the enzymes to digest milk and that, only a generation ago, when children were given milk, it was more likely to be goat's milk than cow's milk. However, with the market evolving rapidly towards "Westernization," there is a general interest in American and European products, including yogurt.

Although consumption of yogurt per capita is still low in Japan at the moment, research shows that there is a high potential for growth. When we launch, correct positioning will be the key to Delissa's success as a new foreign brand. We will need to differentiate it from existing Japanese brands and go beyond the rather standardized "freshness" advertising theme.

Distribution

Traditionally, Japanese distribution methods have been complex; the chain tends to be many-layered, making distribution costs high. Distribution of refrigerated products is slightly simpler than the distribution of dry goods because it is more direct.

The Japanese daily-purchase habit means that the delivery system adopted for Delissa must be fast and efficient. Our basic distribution goal would be to secure mass sales retailer distribution. Initially, items would be sold through existing sales outlets that sell Nikko's drinking milk,

"Nikkodo." The milk-related products and dessert foods would be sold based on distribution to mass sales retailers. The objective would be to make efficient use of existing channels of distribution with daily delivery schedules and enjoy lower distribution costs for new products.

The Japanese Retail Market

The retail market is extremely fragmented with independent outlets accounting for 57% of sales (vs. 3% in the U.S.). With 1,350 shops for every 100,000 people, Japan has twice as many outlets per capita as most European countries. Tradition, economics, government regulations, and service demands affect the retail system in Japan. Housewives shop once a day on the average and most select the smaller local stores, which keep longer hours, deliver orders, offer credit, and provide a meeting place for shoppers. Opening a Western-style supermarket is expensive and complicated, so most retailing remains in the hands of the small, independent, or family business.

Japan has three major metropolitan areas: Tokyo, Osaka, and Nogaya, with a respective population of 11, 3, and 2 million inhabitants. Nikko's Nikkodo, with a 15% share of total, is market leader ahead of the many other suppliers. Nikko feels the distribution chain used for Nokkodo milk would be ideal for yogurt. Each metropolitan area has a separate distribution system, each one with several depots and branches. For instance, Kanto (Great Tokyo)—the largest area with over 40 million people—has five Nikko depots and five Nikko branches.

Most of the physical distribution (drivers and delivery vans) is carried out by a subsidiary of Nikko with support from the wholesalers. The refrigerated milk vans have to be fairly small (less than two tons) so that they can drive down the narrow streets. The same routes are used for milk delivery, puddings, and juices. Our initial strategy would be to accept Nikko's current milk distribution system as the basic system and, at the same time, adopt shifting distribution routes. Japan's complicated street identification system, whereby only numbers and no names are shown, makes great demands on the distribution system and the drivers.

The Franchise Contract

Robertson opened another report written by Ole Bobek, who had headed up the Japan project right from the start and had been responsible for the early years of the joint venture. He left the company in 1990. This report contained all the details concerning the contract between Agria and Nikko. In 1985, Nikko and Agria had signed an industrial franchise agreement permitting Nikko to manufacture and distribute Delissa products under license from Agria. The contract was Agria's standard Delissa franchisee agreement covering technology transfer associated with trademark exploitation. Agria was to provide manufacturing and product know-how, as well as marketing, technical, commercial, and sales support. Agria would receive a royalty for every pot of yogurt sold. The Nikko cooperative would form a separate company for the distribution, marketing, and promotion of Delissa products. During the pre-launch phase, Per Bergman, Senior Area Brand Manager, would train the sales and marketing team, and Agria's technicians would supply know-how to the Japanese.

By the end of 1986, a factory to produce Delissa yogurt, milk, and dairy products had been constructed in Mijima, 60 miles northwest of Tokyo. Agria provided Nikko with advice on technology, machinery, tanks, fermentation processes, and so forth. Equipment from the United States, Sweden, Germany, and Japan was selected. A European-style Erka filling machine was installed which would fill two, four, or six cups at a time, and was considered economical and fast.

Robertson opened another report by Bobek entitled "Delissa Japan—Pre-Launch Data." The report covered the market, positioning, advertising and media plan, minutes of the meetings with Nikko executives and the SRT International Advertising Agency that would handle the launch, analysis of market research findings, and competitive analysis. Robertson closed the file and thought about the Japanese market. During the planning phase before the launch, everything had looked so promising. In its usual methodical fashion, Agria had prepared its traditional launch campaign to ensure that the new Agria/Nikko venture guaranteed a successful entry into Japan for Delissa. "Why then," wondered Robertson, "were sales so low after nine years of business?" Robertson picked up the telephone and called Rolf Anderen, one of Agria's founders and former chairman of the company. Although retired, Anderen still took an active interest in the business he had created. The next day, Robertson and Anderen had lunch together.

The older man listened to the new managing director talking about his responsibilities, the Swedish headquarters, foreign licensees, new products in the pipeline, and so forth. Over coffee, Robertson

broached the subject of the Japanese joint venture, expressing some surprise that Delissa was so slow in taking off. Anderen nodded his understanding and lit his pipe:

Yes, it has been disappointing. I remember those early meetings before we signed up with Nikko. Our team was very frustrated with the negotiations. Bobek made several trips, and had endless meetings with the Japanese, but things still dragged on. We had so much good foreign business by the time we decided to enter Japan, I guess we thought we could just walk in wherever we wanted. Our Taiwanese franchise business had really taken off, and I think we assumed that Japan would do likewise. Then, despite the fact that we knew the Japanese were different, Wisenborn—our international marketing manager—and Bobek still believed that they were doing something wrong. They had done a very conscientious job, yet they blamed themselves for the delays. I told them to be patient and to remember that Asians have different customs and are likely to need some time before making up their minds. Our guys went to enormous pains to collect data. I remember when they returned from a second or third trip to Japan with a mass of information, media costs, distribution data, socioeconomic breakdowns, a detailed assessment of the competitive situation, positioning statements, etc. But no signed contract. [Anderen chuckled as he spoke.] Of course, Nikko finally signed, but we never were sure what they really thought about us, or what they really expected from the deal.

Robertson was listening intently, so Anderen continued:

The whole story was interesting. When you enter a market like Japan, you are on your own. If you don't speak the language, you can't find your way around. So you become totally dependent on the locals and your partner. I must say that, in this respect, the Japanese are extremely helpful. But, let's face it, the cultural gap is wide. Another fascinating aspect was the rite of passage. In Japan, as in most Asian countries, you feel you are observing a kind of ritual, their ritual. This can destabilize the solid Viking manager. Of course, they were probably thinking that we have our rituals, too. On top of that, the Nikko people were particularly reserved and, of course, few of them spoke anything but Japanese.

There was a lot of tension during those first months, partly because France's two major brands of yogurt, "Yoplait" and "Danone" were actually in the process of entering the Japanese market, confirming a fear that had been on Bobek's mind during most of the negotiation period.

Anderen tapped his pipe on the ashtray and smiled at Robertson.

If it's any consolation to you, Bjorn, the other two international brands are not doing any better than we are in Japan today.

What About These Other European Competitors?

The discussion with Anderen had been stimulating and Robertson, anxious to get to the bottom of the story, decided to speak to Peter Borg, a young Danish manager who had replaced Bergman and had been supervising Agria's business in Japan for several years. Robertson asked Borg for his opinion on why "Danone" and "Yoplait" were apparently not doing any better than Delissa in Japan. Borg replied:

I can explain how these two brands were handled in Japan, but I don't know whether this will throw any light on the matter as far as their performance is concerned. First, Sodima, the French dairy firm, whose Yoplait line is sold through franchise agreements all over the world, took a similar approach to ours. Yoplait is tied up with Zennoh, the National Federation of Agricultural Cooperative Association, the equivalent of Sodima in Japan. Zennoh is huge and politically very powerful. Its total sales are double those of Nikko. Yoplait probably has about 3% of the total Japanese yogurt market, which is of course a lot less than their usual 15–20% share in foreign markets. However, Zennoh had no previous experience in marketing yogurt.

Danone took a different approach. The company signed an agreement with a Japanese partner, Ajinomoto. Their joint venture, Ajinomoto-Danone Co. Ltd., is run by a French expatriate together with several Japanese directors. A prominent French banker based in Tokyo is also on the board. As you know, Ajinomoto is the largest integrated food processor in Japan, with sales of about $3 billion. About 45% of the company's business is in amino acids, 20% in fats, and 15% in oil. Ajinomoto has a very successful joint venture with General Foods for "Maxwell House," the instant coffee. However, Ajinomoto had had no experience at all in dealing with fresh dairy products before entering this joint venture with Danone. So, for both of the Japanese partners—Ajinomoto and Zennoh, this business was completely new and was probably part of a diversification move. I heard that the Danone joint venture had a tough time at the beginning. They had to build their dairy products distribution network

from scratch. By the way, I also heard from several sources that it was distribution problems that discouraged Nestlé from pursuing a plan to reintroduce its Chambourcy yogurt line in Japan. Japanese distribution costs are very high compared to those in Western countries. I suspect that the Danone-Ajinomoto joint venture probably only just managed to break even last year.

"Thanks, Peter," Robertson said. "It's a fascinating story. By the way, I hear that you just got married to a Japanese girl. Congratulations, lucky chap!"

After his discussion with Borg, Robertson returned to his Delissa-Nikko files. Delissa's early Japanese history intrigued him.

Entry Strategy

The SRT International Advertising Agency helped develop Delissa's entry into what was called the "new milk-related products" market. Agria and Nikko had approved a substantial advertising and sales promotion budget. The agency confirmed that, as Nikko was already big in the "drinking milk" market, it was a good idea to move into the processed milk or "eating milk" field, a rapidly growing segment where added value was high.

Bjorn Robertson studied the advertising agency's pre-launch rationale which emphasized the strategy suggested for Delissa. The campaign, which had been translated from Japanese into English, proposed:

Agria will saturate the market with the Delissa brand and establish it as distinct from competitive products. The concept "natural dairy food is good to taste" is proposed as the basic message for product planning, distribution, and advertising. Nikko needs to distinguish its products from those of early-entry dairy producers and other competitors by stressing that its yogurt is "new and natural and quite different from any other yogurts."

The core target group has been defined as families with babies. Housewives have been identified as the principal purchasers. However, the product will be consumed by a wider age bracket from young children to high school students.

The advertising and point-of-sale message will address housewives, particularly younger ones. In Japan, the tendency is for younger housewives to shop in convenience stores (small supermarkets), while the older women prefer traditional supermarkets. Housewives are becoming more and more insistent that all types of food be absolutely fresh, which means that Delissa should be perceived as coming directly from the manufacturer that very day. We feel that the "freshness" concept, which has been the main selling point of the whole Nikko line, will capture the consumers' interest as well as clearly differentiate Delissa from other brands. It is essential that the ads be attractive and stand out strikingly from the others, because Nikko is a newcomer in this competitive market. Delissa should be positioned as a luxurious mass communication product.

The SRT also proposed that, as Japanese housewives were becoming more diet conscious, it might be advisable to mention the dietary value of Delissa in the launch rationale. Agria preferred to stress the idea that Delissa was a Swedish product being made in Japan under license from Agria Co., Uppsala. They felt that this idea would appeal to Japanese housewives, who associated Sweden with healthy food and "sophisticated" taste. The primary messages to be conveyed would, therefore, be: "healthy products direct from the farm" and "sophisticated taste from Sweden." Although, it was agreed that being good for health and beauty could be another argument in Delissa's favor, this approach would not help differentiate Delissa from other brands, all of which project a similar image.

In order to reinforce the product's image and increase brand awareness, the SRT proposed that specific visual and verbal messages be used throughout the promotional campaign. A Swedish girl in typical folk costume would be shown with a dairy farm in the background. In the words of the agency, "We feel that using this scene as an eye-catcher will successfully create a warm-hearted image of naturalness, simplicity, friendliness, and fanciful taste for the product coming from Sweden." This image would be accompanied by the text: "Refreshing nature of Delissa Swedish yogurt: it's so fresh when it's made at the farm."

Also included in the SRT proposal:

Advertising

To maximize the advertising effort with the budget available, the campaign should be run intensively over a short period of time rather than successively throughout the year. TV ads will be used as they have an immediate impact and make a strong impression through frequent repetition. The TV message will then be reinforced in the press. The budget will be comparable to the one used for launching Delissa in the United States.

Pricing

Pricing should follow the top brands (Yukijirushi, Meiji, and Morinaga) so as to reflect a high-class image, yet the price should be affordable to the housewife. The price sensitivity analysis conducted last month showed that the Delissa could be priced at 15% above competitive products.

Launch

In January 1987, Delissa's product line was presented to distributors prior to launch in Tokyo, Osaka, and Nagoya. Three different types of yogurt were selected for simultaneous launch:

- Plain (packs of 2 and 4)
- Plain with sugar (packs of 2 and 4)
- Flavored with vanilla, strawberry, and pineapple (packs of 2). (Fruit yogurt, Delissa's most successful offering at home and in other foreign markets, would be launched a year or two afterwards.)

All three types were to be sold in 120 ml cups. A major pre-launch promotional campaign was scheduled for the month before launch with strong TV, newspaper, and magazine support, as well as street shows, in-store promotions, and test trials in and outside retail stores. On March 1, 1987, Delissa was launched in Tokyo, and on May 1 in Osaka and Nagoya.

1990: Delissa After Three Years in Japan

Three years after its launch, Delissa—with 2 percent of the Japanese yogurt market—was at a fraction of target. Concerned by the product's slow progress in Japan, Agria formed a special task force to investigate Delissa's situation and to continue monitoring the Japanese market on a regular basis. The results of the team's research now lay on Robertson's desk. The task force from Uppsala included Stefan Gustafsson (responsible for marketing questions), Per Bergman (sales and distribution), and Peter Borg (who was studying the whole operation as well as training the Nikko salesforce). The team spent long periods in Tokyo carrying out regular audits of the Delissa-Nikko operations, analyzing and monitoring the Japanese market, and generating lengthy reports as they did so, most of which Robertson was in the process of studying.

Borg, eager to excel on his new assignment, sent back his first report to headquarters:

Distribution/Ordering System

I feel that the distribution of Delissa is not satisfactory and should be improved. The ordering system seems overcomplicated and slow, and may very well be the cause of serious delivery bottle-necks. Whereas stores order milk and juice by telephone, Delissa products are ordered on forms using following procedure:

Day 1 A.M.: Each salesman sent an order to his depot.

Day 1 P.M.: Each depot's orders went to the Yokohama depot.

Day 2 P.M.: The Yokohama depot transmitted the order to the factory.

Day 2 P.M.: Yogurt was produced at Nikko Milk Processing.

Day 3: Delivery to each depot.

Day 4: Delivery to stores.

Gustafsson agrees with me that the delivery procedure is too long for fresh food products, particularly as the date on the yogurt cup is so important to the Japanese customer. The way we operate now, the yogurt arrives in the sales outlet two or three days after production. Ideally, the time should be shortened to only one day. We realize that, traditionally, Japanese distribution is much more complex and multilayered than in the West. In addition, Tokyo and Osaka, which are among the largest cities in the world, have no street names. So, a whole system of primary, secondary, and sometimes tertiary wholesalers is used to serve supermarkets and retailers. And, since the smaller outlets have very little storage space, wholesalers often have to visit them more than once a day.

I wonder if Nikko is seriously behind Delissa. At present, there are 80 Nikko salesmen selling Delissa, but they only seem to devote about 5 percent of their time to the brand, preferring to push other products. Although this is apparently not an uncommon situation in many countries, in Japan it is typical—as the high costs there prohibit having a separate salesforce for each line.

Borg's report continued:

Advertising

Since we launched Delissa in 1987, the advertising has not been successful. I'm wondering how well we pretested our launch campaign and follow-up. The agency seems very keen on Delissa as a product, but I wonder if our advertising messages are not too cluttered. Results of recent consumer research surveys showed only 4% unaided awareness and only 16% of interviewees had any recall at all; 55% of respondents did not know what our TV commercials were trying to say.

A survey by the Oka Market Research Bureau on advertising effectiveness indicated that we should stress the fact that Delissa tastes good . . . delicious. Agria's position maintains that according to the Oka survey, the consumer believes that all brands taste good, which means the message will not differentiate Delissa. Research findings pointed out that Delissa has a strong "fashionable" image. Perhaps this advantage could be stressed to differentiate Delissa from other yogurts in the next TV commercial.

Delissa in Japan: Situation in and Leading Up to 1997

In spite of all the careful pre-launch preparation, ten years after its launch in Japan, Delissa had only 3 percent of the total yogurt market in 1997. Although Agria executives knew the importance of taking a long-term view of their business in Japan, Agria's management in Sweden agreed that these results had been far below expectations.

A serious setback for Agria had been the discovery of Nikko's limited distribution network outside the major metropolitan areas. When Agria proposed to start selling Delissa in small cities, towns, and rural areas, as had been agreed in the launch plan, it turned out that Nikko's coverage was very thin in many of these regions. In the heat of the planning for the regional launch, had there been a misunderstanding on Nikko's range?

Robertson continued to leaf through Agria's survey of Japanese business, reading extracts as he turned the pages. A despondent Borg had written:

1994: The Japanese market is very tough and competition very strong. Consumers' brand loyalty seems low. But the market is large with high potential—particularly amongst the younger population—if only we could reach it. Nikko has the size and manpower to meet the challenges and to increase its penetration substantially by 1996. However, Nikko's Delissa organization needs strengthening quickly. Lack of a real marketing function in Nikko is a great handicap in a market as competitive as Japan.

Distribution is one of our most serious problems. Distribution costs are extremely high in Japan, and Delissa's are excessive (27% of sales in 1994 vs. 19% for the competition). Comparing distribution costs to production costs and to the average unit selling price to distributors of 54.86 yen, it is obvious that we cannot make money on the whole Delissa range in Japan. Clearly, these costs in Japan must be reduced while improving coverage of existing stores.

Distribution levels of about 40% are still too low, which is certainly one of the major contributing factors for Delissa's poor performance. Nikko's weak distribution network outside the metropolitan areas is causing us serious problems.

1995: Delissa's strategy in Japan is being redefined (once more). The Swedish image will be dropped from the advertising since a consumer survey has shown that some consumers believed that "fresh from the farm" meant that the yogurt was directly imported from Sweden—which certainly put its freshness into question! Ads will now show happy blond children eating yogurt . . .

Over time, the product line has grown significantly and a line of puddings has recently been added. Nikko asks us for new products every three months and blames their unsatisfactory results on our limited line.

By 1997, plain yogurt should represent almost half of Delissa's Japanese sales and account for about 43% of the total Japanese market. The plain segment has grown by almost 50% in the past three years. However, we feel that our real strength should be in the fruit yogurt segment, which has increased by about 25% since 1994 and should have about 23% of the market by next year. So far, Delissa's results in fruit yogurt have been disappointing. On the other hand, a new segment—yogurt with jelly—has been selling well: 1.2 million cups three months after introduction. Custard and chocolate pudding sales have been disappointing, while plain yogurt drink sales have been very good.

Robertson came across a more recent memo written by Stefan Gustafsson:

Mid-Year Results

Sales as of mid-year 1996 are below forecast, and we are unlikely to meet our objective of 55 million 120 ml cups for 1998. At the present rate of sales, we should reach just over 42 million cups by year-end.

Stores Covered

In 1997, Delissa yogurt was sold mainly in what Nielsen defined as large and super large stores. Delissa products were sold in about 71% of the total stores selling Nikko dairy products. We think that about 7,000 stores are covered in the Greater Tokyo area, but we have found that Nikko has been somewhat unreliable on retailer information.

Product Returns

The number of Delissa products returned to us is very high compared to other countries. The average return rate from April 1996 to March 1997 was 5.06% vs. almost 0% in Scandinavia and the international standard of 2–3%. The average shelf life of yogurt in Japan is fourteen days. Does the high level of returns stem from the Japanese consumer's perception of when a product is too old to buy (i.e., five–six days)? The level of return varies greatly with the type of product: "healthy mix" and fruit yogurt have the highest rate, while plain and yogurt with jelly have the lowest return rate.

Media Planning

Oka's latest results suggest that Delissa's primary target should be young people between thirteen and twenty-four and its secondary target: children. Budget limitations demand that money be spent on advertising addressed to actual consumers (children), rather than in trying to reach the purchasers (mothers) as well.

However, during our recent visit to Japan, we found that Nikko and the agency were running TV spots—that were intended for young people and children—*from 11:15 to 12:15 at night.* We pointed out that far more consumers would be reached by showing the spots earlier in the evening. With our limited budget, careful media planning is essential. Nikko probably was trying to reach both the consumer and distributor with these late-night spots. Why else would they run spots at midnight when the real target group is children? Another question is whether TV spots are really what we need.

Looking at some figures on TV advertising rates in Japan, Robertson found that the price of a 15-second spot in the Tokyo area was between 1,250,000 and 2,300,000 yen in 1997 depending on the time it was run, which seemed expensive compared to European rates ($1 = ¥121 in 1997).

Robertson continued to peruse the report prepared by Stefan Gustafsson:

Positioning

I'm seriously wondering whom we are trying to reach in Japan and with what product. The Nielsen and Oka research findings show that plain yogurt makes up the largest segment in Japan, with flavored and fruit in second and third positions. It is therefore recommended that regular advertising should concentrate on plain yogurt, with periodic spots for the second two categories.

However, according to Nikko, the company makes only a marginal profit on plain yogurt, thus they feel it would be preferable to advertise fruit yogurt.

In light of this particular situation and the results of the Oka studies, we suggest that plain yogurt be advertised using the existing "brand image" commercial (building up the cow on the screen) and to develop a new commercial for fruit yogurt based on the "fashion concept." We also believe that, if plain yogurt is clearly differentiated through its advertising, sales will improve, production costs will drop, and Nikko will start making money on the product.

Last year, to help us understand where we may have gone wrong with our positioning and promotional activities, which have certainly changed rather often, we requested the Oka agency to conduct a survey using in-home personal interviews with a structured questionnaire; 394 respondents in the Keihin (Tokyo-Yokohama) metropolitan area were interviewed between April 11 and April 27, 1997. Some of the key findings are as follows:

Brand Awareness

In terms of unaided brand awareness, Meiji Bulgaria yogurt had the highest level with 27% of all respondents recalling Bulgaria first and 47% mentioning the brand without any aid. Morinaga Bifidus was in second place. These two leading brands were followed by Yoplait and Danone with 4% unaided awareness and 14% and 16% recall at any time. For Delissa, the unaided awareness was 3% and 16% for recall. In a photo-aided test, Delissa plain yogurt was recognized by 71% of all respondents with a score closer to Bulgaria. In the case of fruit yogurt, 78% recognized Delissa, which had the same level as Bulgaria. Awareness of Delissa was higher than Bifidus and Danone but lower than Yoplait. In the case of yogurt drink, 99% of all respondents were aware of Yakult Joy and 44% recognized Delissa (close to Bulgaria).

Interestingly, the brand image of Meiji Bulgaria was the highest of the plain yogurt brands in terms of all attributes except for "fashionability." At the lower end of the scale (after Bulgaria, Bifidus, and Natulait), Delissa was close to Danone and Yoplait in brand image. Delissa was considered less desirable than the top three, especially as far as the following characteristics were concerned: taste, availability in stores for daily shoppers, frequency of price discounting, reliability of manufacturer, good for health. Delissa's image was "fashionable." ["Is this good or bad?"

Gustafsson had scribbled on the report. "Should this be our new platform??? We've tried everything else!"]

Advertising Awareness

In the advertising awareness test, half of all respondents reported that they had not noticed advertising for any brand of yogurt during the past six months. Of those who had, top ranking went to Bifidus with 43%, Bulgaria 41% and Delissa in third place with 36%. Danone was fifth with 28% and Yoplait sixth with 26%. Respondents noticed ads for Delissa mainly on TV (94%), followed by in-store promotion (6%), newspapers (4%), and magazines (4%); 65% of the people who noticed Delissa ads could recall something about the contents of the current ads, and 9% recalled previous ads. However, when asked to describe the message of the Delissa ads, 55% of the respondents replied that they did not know what the company was trying to say.

Consumption

77% of all respondents had consumed plain yogurt within the past month: 28% Bulgaria, 15% Bifidus, 5% Yoplait, 4% Danone, and 3% Delissa. The number of respondents who had at least tried Delissa was low (22%) vs. 66% for Bulgaria, the best scoring brand. In the plain category, Delissa was third of the brands mainly consumed by respondents. Bulgaria was number 1 and Bifidus number 2. In the fruit segment (under yogurt consumed with the past month), Delissa was in third place (5%) after Yoplait (10%) and Bulgaria (8%). Danone was in fourth place with 3%. ["So where do we go from here?" Gustafsson had scrawled across the bottom of the page.]

Robertson closed the file on Gustafsson's question.

Where Do We Go from Here?

Robertson looked around the table at the other members of his team and asked, "What happened? We still haven't reached 3 percent after ten years in Japan!" Bjorn knew that Borg, Gustafsson, and Karlsson all had different opinions as to why Delissa had performed badly, and each manager had his own ideas on what kind of action should be taken.

Gustafsson had spent months at Nikko, visiting retailers with members of the sales force, instigating new market research surveys and supervising the whole Nikko-Delissa team. Language problems had made this experience a frustrating one for Gustafsson, who had felt cut off from the rest of the Nikko staff in the office. He had been given a small desk in a huge room along with over 100 people with whom he could barely communicate. The Japanese politeness grated on him after a while and, as no one spoke more than a few words of anything but Japanese, Gustafsson had felt lonely and isolated. He had come to believe that Nikko was not committed to the development of the Delissa brand in Japan. He also felt that the joint venture's market share expectations had been absurd and was convinced the franchise misrepresented the situation to Agria. He felt that Nikko was using the Delissa brand name as a public relations gimmick to build itself an international image. When he spoke, Gustafsson's tone was almost aggressive:

I don't know what to think, Bjorn. I know I don't understand our Japanese friends and I was never quite sure that I trusted them, either. They had a disconcerting way of taking control right from the start. It's that extreme politeness. You can't argue with them, and then suddenly they're in command. I remember when the Nikko managers visited us here in Sweden . . . a busload of them smiling and bowing their way around the plant, and we were bowing and smiling back. This is how they get their way and this is why we had such mediocre results in Japan. Agria never controlled the business. Our distribution set-up is a perfect example. We could never really know what was going on out there because language problems forced us to count on them. The same with our positioning and our advertising, "We're selling taste; no, we're selling health; no, we're selling fashion—to babies, to grandmas, to mothers." We thought we were in control but we weren't, and half the time we were doing the opposite of what we really wanted.

Bjorn, the Japanese will kill Delissa once they've mastered the Swedish technology. Then, they'll develop their own brand. Get out of the joint venture agreement with Nikko, Bjorn. I'd say, get out of Japan altogether.

Robertson next turned his attention toward Borg, who had a different view of the problem. He felt that the Nikko people, trained to sell the drinking milk line, lacked specific knowledge about the eating milk or yogurt business. Borg—who had also taken over sales training in Japan after replacing Bergman—had made several trips a year to train the Nikko people both in marketing the Delissa brand, and in improving distribution and sales. He had also trained a marketing manager. Borg had worked closely with the Japanese at the Tokyo headquarters.

Borg said, "I understand how Stefan feels . . . frustrated and let down, but have we given these people enough time?"

"Enough time!" said Gustafsson, laughing. "We've been there for over ten years and, if you look at our target, we have failed miserably. My question is 'have they given us enough support?'" Turning to Gustafsson, Borg continued:

I know how you feel, Stefan, but is ten years that long? When the Japanese go into business abroad, they stay there until they get a hold on the market, however long it takes. They persevere. They seem to do things at their own speed and so much more calmly than we do. I agree on the question of autonomy. It's their very lack of Western aggressiveness that enables them to get the upper hand. Their apparent humility is disarming. But, Bjorn, should we really leave the joint venture now? When I first went to Japan and found fault with everything we were doing, I blamed the whole thing on Nikko. After nearly six years of visits, I think I have learned something. We cannot approach these people on our terms or judge them as we would judge ourselves. We cannot understand them any more than they can understand us. To me, the whole point is not to even try and understand them. We have to accept them and then to trust. If we can't, then perhaps we should leave. But, Bjorn, I don't think we should give up the Japanese market so easily. As Stefan says, they can be excruciatingly polite. I wonder—beneath that politeness—what they think of us.

Lars Karlsson, the product manager, had been looking after the Japanese market only a short time, having been recruited by Agria from Procter & Gamble 18 months earlier.

Bjorn, for me, perhaps the most serious defect in our Japanese operation has been the poor communication between the partners and a mass of conflicting data. I came into the project late and was amazed at the quantity of research and reporting that had taken place over the last ten years by everyone concerned. Many of the reports I saw were contradictory and confusing. As well, the frequent turnover of managers responsible for Japan has interrupted the continuity of the project. And, after all the research we did, has anyone really used the findings constructively? How much is our fault? And another thing, have we been putting enough resources into Japan?

There are so many paradoxes. The Japanese seem to be so keen on the idea of having things Western, yet the successful yogurts in Japan have been the ones with that distinctive Japanese flavor. Have we disregarded what this means? Agria people believe that we have a superior product and that the type of yogurt made by our Japanese competitors does not really taste so good. How can this be true when we look at the market shares of the top Japanese producers? It obviously tastes good to the Japanese. Can we really change their preferences? Or should we perhaps look at our flavor?

It's interesting. Yoplait/Zennoh and Ajinomoto/ Danone's joint ventures could be encountering similar problems to ours. Neither has more than 3% of the Japanese yogurt market and they have the same flavor that we do.

Robertson listened to the views and arguments of his team with interest. Soon, he would have to make a decision. Almost ten years after launching Delissa with Nikko, should Agria cancel its contract and find another distributor? Or should the company renew the arrangement with Nikko and continue trying to gain market share? Or should Agria admit defeat and withdraw from Japan completely? Or was it, in fact, defeat at all? Robertson was glad that he had gathered his team together to discuss Delissa's future; their thoughts had given him new insights on the Japanese venture.

This case was prepared by Research Assistant Juliet Burdet-Taylor and Professor Dominique Turpin as a basis for class discussion rather than to illustrate either effective or ineffective handling of an administrative situation. All names and figures have been disguised. "Delissa in Japan ®. Copyright © 2002 by IMD—International Institute for Management Development, Lausanne, Switzerland. All rights reserved. Not to be used or reproduced without written permission directly from IMD, Lausanne, Switzerland.

CASE 5   KENTUCKY FRIED CHICKEN AND THE GLOBAL FAST-FOOD INDUSTRY

Kentucky Fried Chicken Corporation (KFC) was the world's largest chicken restaurant chain and third largest fast-food chain. KFC held over 55 percent of the U.S. market in terms of sales and operated over 10,200 restaurants worldwide in 1998. It opened 376 new restaurants in 1997 (more than one restaurant a day) and operated in 79 countries. One of the first fast-food chains to go international during the late 1960s, KFC has developed one of the world's most recognizable brands.

Japan, Australia, and the United Kingdom accounted for the greatest share of KFC's international expansion during the 1970s and 1980s. During the 1990s, KFC turned its attention to other international markets that offered significant opportunities for growth. China, with a population of over one billion, and Europe, with a population roughly equal to the United States, offered such opportunities. Latin America also offered a unique opportunity because of the size of its markets, its common language and culture, and its geographic proximity to the United States. Mexico was of particular interest because of the North American Free Trade Agreement (NAFTA), a free-trade zone between Canada,

the United States, and Mexico that went into effect in 1994.

Prior to 1990, KFC expanded into Latin America primarily through company-owned restaurants in Mexico and Puerto Rico. Company-owned restaurants gave KFC greater control over its operations than franchised or licensed restaurants. By 1995, KFC also had established company-owned restaurants in Venezuela and Brazil. In addition, it had established franchised units in numerous Caribbean countries. During the early 1990s, KFC shifted to a two-tiered strategy in Latin America. First, it established 29 franchised restaurants in Mexico following enactment of Mexico's new franchise law in 1990. This allowed KFC to expand outside its company restaurant base in Mexico City, Guadalajara, and Monterrey. KFC was one of many U.S. fast-food, retail, and hotel chains to begin franchising in Mexico following the new franchise law. Second, KFC began an aggressive franchise building program in South America. By 1998, it was operating franchised restaurants in 32 Latin American countries. Much of this growth was in Brazil, Chile, Colombia, Ecuador, and Peru.

Company History

Fast-food franchising was still in its infancy in 1952 when Harland Sanders began his travels across the United States to speak with prospective franchisees about his "Colonel Sanders Recipe Kentucky Fried

This case was prepared by Jeffrey A. Krug of the Department of Business Administration, University of Illinois at Urbana-Champaign.
Reprinted by permission of the author, Jeffrey A. Krug, University of Illinois at Urbana-Champaign.

Chicken." By 1960, "Colonel" Sanders had granted KFC franchises to over 200 take-home retail outlets and restaurants across the United States. He had also succeeded in establishing a number of franchises in Canada. By 1963, the number of KFC franchises had risen to over 300, and revenues had reached $500 million.

By 1964, at the age of 74, the Colonel had tired of running the day-to-day operations of his business and was eager to concentrate on public relations issues. Therefore, he sought out potential buyers, eventually deciding to sell the business to two Louisville businessmen—Jack Massey and John Young Brown, Jr.—for $2 million. The Colonel stayed on as a public relations man and goodwill ambassador for the company.

During the next 5 years, Massey and Brown concentrated on growing KFC's franchise system across the United States. In 1966, they took KFC public, and the company was listed on the New York Stock Exchange. By the late 1960s, a strong foothold had been established in the United States, and Massey and Brown turned their attention to international markets. In 1969, a joint venture was signed with Mitsuoishi Shoji Kaisha, Ltd., in Japan, and the rights to operate 14 existing KFC franchises in England were acquired. Subsidiaries also were established in Hong Kong, South Africa, Australia, New Zealand, and Mexico. By 1971, KFC had 2450 franchises and 600 company-owned restaurants worldwide and was operating in 48 countries.

Heublein, Inc.

In 1971, KFC entered negotiations with Heublein, Inc., to discuss a possible merger. The decision to seek a merger candidate was partially driven by Brown's desire to pursue other interests, including a political career (Brown was elected governor of Kentucky in 1977). Several months later, Heublein acquired KFC. Heublein was in the business of producing vodka, mixed cocktails, dry gin, cordials, beer, and other alcoholic beverages. However, Heublein had little experience in the restaurant business. Conflicts quickly erupted between Colonel Sanders, who continued to act in a public relations capacity, and Heublein management. Colonel Sanders became increasingly distraught over quality control issues and restaurant cleanliness. By 1977, new restaurant openings had slowed to about 20 per year. Few restaurants were being remodeled, and service quality had declined.

In 1977, Heublein sent in a new management team to redirect KFC's strategy. A "back-to-the-basics" strategy was immediately implemented. New unit construction was discontinued until existing restaurants could be upgraded and operating problems eliminated. Restaurants were refurbished, an emphasis was placed on cleanliness and service, marginal products were eliminated, and product consistency was reestablished. By 1982, KFC had succeeded in establishing a successful strategic focus and was again aggressively building new units.

R. J. Reynolds Industries, Inc.

In 1982, R. J. Reynolds Industries, Inc. (RJR), merged Heublein into a wholly owned subsidiary. The merger with Heublein represented part of RJR's overall corporate strategy of diversifying into unrelated businesses, including energy, transportation, food, and restaurants. RJR's objective was to reduce its dependence on the tobacco industry, which had driven RJR sales since its founding in North Carolina in 1875. Sales of cigarettes and tobacco products, while profitable, were declining because of reduced consumption in the United States. This was mainly the result of an increased awareness among Americans about the negative health consequences of smoking.

RJR had no more experience in the restaurant business than did Heublein. However, it decided to take a hands-off approach to managing KFC. Whereas Heublein had installed its own top management at KFC headquarters, RJR left KFC management largely intact, believing that existing KFC managers were better qualified to operate KFC's businesses than were its own managers. In doing so, RJR avoided many of the operating problems that plagued Heublein. This strategy paid off for RJR as KFC continued to expand aggressively and profitably under RJR ownership. In 1985, RJR acquired Nabisco Corporation for $4.9 billion. Nabisco sold a variety of well-known cookies, crackers, cereals, confectioneries, snacks, and other grocery products. The merger with Nabisco represented a decision by RJR to concentrate its diversification efforts on the consumer foods industry. It subsequently divested many of its nonconsumer food businesses. RJR sold KFC to PepsiCo, Inc., one year later.

Pepsico, Inc.

Corporate Strategy

PepsiCo, Inc., was formed in 1965 with the merger of the Pepsi-Cola Co. and Frito-Lay, Inc. The merger of these companies created one of the largest consumer products companies in the United States. Pepsi-Cola's traditional business was the sale of soft drink concentrates to licensed independent and company-owned bottlers that manufactured, sold, and distributed Pepsi-Cola soft drinks. Pepsi-Cola's best known trademarks were Pepsi-Cola, Diet Pepsi, Mountain Dew, and Slice. Frito-Lay manufactured and sold a variety of snack foods, including Fritos Corn Chips, Lay's Potato Chips, Ruffles Potato Chips, Doritos, Tostitos Tortilla Chips, and Chee-tos Cheese Flavored Snacks. PepsiCo quickly embarked on an aggressive acquisition program similar to that pursued by RJR during the 1980s, buying a number of companies in areas unrelated to its major businesses. Acquisitions included North American Van Lines, Wilson Sporting Goods, and Lee Way Motor Freight. However, success in operating these businesses failed to live up to expectations, mainly because the management skills required to operate these businesses lay outside of PepsiCo's area of expertise.

Poor performance in these businesses led then-chairman and chief executive officer Don Kendall to restructure PepsiCo's operations in 1984. First, businesses that did not support PepsiCo's consumer product orientation, such as North American Van Lines, Wilson Sporting Goods, and Lee Way Motor Freight, were divested. Second, PepsiCo's foreign bottling operations were sold to local business-people who better understood the culture and business environment in their respective countries. Third, Kendall reorganized PepsiCo along three lines: soft drinks, snack foods, and restaurants.

Restaurant Business and Acquisition of KFC

PepsiCo first entered the restaurant business in 1977 when it acquired Pizza Hut's 3200-unit restaurant system. Taco Bell was merged into a division of PepsiCo in 1978. The restaurant business completed PepsiCo's consumer product orientation. The marketing of fast food followed many of the same patterns as the marketing of soft drinks and snack foods. Therefore, PepsiCo believed that its management skills could be easily transferred among its three business segments. This was compatible with PepsiCo's practice of frequently moving managers among its business units as a way of developing future top executives. PepsiCo's restaurant chains also provided an additional outlet for the sale of Pepsi soft drinks. Pepsi-Cola soft drinks and fast-food products also could be marketed together in the same television and radio segments, thereby providing higher returns for each advertising dollar.

To complete its diversification into the restaurant segment, PepsiCo acquired Kentucky Fried Chicken Corporation from RJR-Nabisco for $841 million in 1986. The acquisition of KFC gave PepsiCo the leading market share in chicken (KFC), pizza (Pizza Hut), and Mexican food (Taco Bell), three of the four largest and fastest-growing segments within the U.S. fast-food industry.

Management

Following the acquisition by PepsiCo, KFC's relationship with its parent company underwent dramatic changes. RJR had operated KFC as a semiautonomous unit, satisfied that KFC management understood the fast-food business better than they. In contrast, PepsiCo acquired KFC in order to complement its already strong presence in the fast-food market. Rather than allowing KFC to operate autonomously, PepsiCo undertook sweeping changes. These changes included negotiating a new franchise contract to give PepsiCo more control over its franchisees, reducing staff in order to cut costs, and replacing KFC managers with its own. In 1987, a rumor spread through KFC's headquarters in Louisville that the new personnel manager, who had just relocated from PepsiCo's headquarters in New York, was overheard saying that "there will be no more home grown tomatoes in this organization."

Such statements by PepsiCo personnel, uncertainties created by several restructurings that led to layoffs throughout the KFC organization, the replacement of KFC personnel with PepsiCo managers, and conflicts between KFC and PepsiCo's corporate cultures created a morale problem within KFC. KFC's culture was built largely on Colonel Sanders' laidback approach to management. Employees enjoyed relatively good employment stability and security. Over the years, a strong loyalty had been created among KFC employees and franchisees, mainly because of the efforts of Colonel Sanders to provide for his employees' benefits, pension, and other nonincome needs. In addition, the southern environment of Louisville resulted in a friendly, relaxed atmosphere at KFC's corporate offices. This corporate culture was left essentially unchanged during the Heublein and RJR years.

In stark contrast to KFC, PepsiCo's culture was characterized by a strong emphasis on performance. Top performers expected to move up through the ranks quickly. PepsiCo used its KFC, Pizza Hut, Taco Bell, Frito-Lay, and Pepsi-Cola divisions as training grounds for its top managers, rotating its best managers through its five divisions on average every 2 years. This practice created immense pressure on managers to continuously demonstrate their managerial prowess within short periods, in order to maximize their potential for promotion. This practice also left many KFC managers with the feeling that they had few career opportunities with the new company. One PepsiCo manager commented, "You may have performed well last year, but if you don't perform well this year, you're gone, and there are 100 ambitious guys with Ivy League MBAs at PepsiCo who would love to take your position." An unwanted effect of this performance-driven culture was that employee loyalty often was lost, and turnover tended to be higher than in other companies.

Kyle Craig, president of KFC's U.S. operations, was asked about KFC's relationship with its corporate parent. He commented:

The KFC culture is an interesting one because I think it was dominated by a lot of KFC folks, many of whom have been around since the days of the Colonel. Many of those people were very intimidated by the PepsiCo culture, which is a very high performance, high accountability, highly driven culture. People were concerned about whether they would succeed in the new culture. Like many companies, we have had a couple of downsizings which further made people nervous. Today, there are fewer old KFC people around and I think to some degree people have seen that the PepsiCo culture can drive some pretty positive results. I also think the PepsiCo people who have worked with KFC have modified their cultural values somewhat and they can see that there were a lot of benefits in the old KFC culture.

PepsiCo pushes its companies to perform strongly, but whenever there is a slip in performance, it increases the culture gap between PepsiCo and KFC. I have been involved in two downsizings over which I have been the chief architect. They have been probably the two most gutwrenching experiences of my career. Because you know you're dealing with peoples' lives and their families, these changes can be emotional if you care about the people in your organization. However, I do fundamentally believe that your first obligation is to the entire organization.

A second problem for PepsiCo was its poor relationship with KFC franchisees. A month after becoming president and chief executive officer in 1989, John Cranor addressed KFC's franchisees in Louisville in order to explain the details of the new franchise contract. This was the first contract change in 13 years. It gave PepsiCo greater power to take over weak franchises, relocate restaurants, and make changes in existing restaurants. In addition, restaurants would no longer be protected from competition from new KFC units, and it gave PepsiCo the right to raise royalty fees on existing restaurants as contracts came up for renewal. After Cranor finished his address, there was an uproar among the attending franchisees, who jumped to their feet to protest the changes. The franchisees had long been accustomed to relatively little interference from management in their day-to-day operations (a tradition begun by Colonel Sanders). This type of interference, of course, was a strong part of PepsiCo's philosophy of demanding change. KFC's franchise association later sued PepsiCo over the new contract. The contract remained unresolved until 1996, when the most objectionable parts of the contract were removed by KFC's new president and CEO, David Novak. A new contract was ratified by KFC's franchisees in 1997.

PepsiCo's Divestiture of KFC, Pizza Hut, and Taco Bell

PepsiCo's strategy of diversifying into three distinct but related markets—soft drinks, snack foods, and fast-food restaurants—created one of the world's largest consumer products companies and a portfolio of some of the world's most recognizable brands. Between 1990 and 1996, PepsiCo grew at an annual rate of over 10 percent, surpassing $31 billion in sales in 1996. However, PepsiCo's sales growth masked troubles in its fast-food businesses. Operating margins (profit as a percent of sales) at Pepsi-Cola and Frito-Lay averaged 12 and 17 percent between 1990 and 1996, respectively. During the same period, margins at KFC, Pizza Hut, and Taco Bell fell from an average of over 8 percent in 1990 to a little more than 4 percent in 1996. Declining margins in the fast-food chains reflected increasing maturity in the U.S. fast-food industry, more intense competition among U.S. fast-food competitors, and the aging of KFC and Pizza Hut's restaurant base. As a result, PepsiCo's restaurant chains absorbed nearly one-half of PepsiCo's annual capital spending during the 1990s. However, they generated less than one-third of PepsiCo's cash flows. Therefore, cash was diverted from PepsiCo's soft drink and snack food businesses to its restaurant businesses. This reduced PepsiCo's return on assets, made it more difficult to compete effectively with CocaCola, and hurt its stock price. In 1997, PepsiCo spun off its restaurant businesses into a new company called Tricon Global Restaurants, Inc. (see Exhibit A). The new company was based

Tricon Global Restaurants, Inc.
Corporate Offices
(Louisville, Kentucky)
Andrall Pearson, Chairman and CEO
David Novak, Vice Chairman and President

Kentucky Fried Chicken Corporation
(Louisville, Kentucky)
Jeffrey Moody, Chief Concept Officer
Charles Rawley, Chief Operating Officer

Pizza Hut, U.S.A.
(Dallas, Texas)
Michael Rawlings, President & CCO
Aylwin Lewis, Chief Operating Officer

Taco Bell Corp.
(Irvine, California)
Peter Waller, President & CCO
Thomas Darin, Chief Operating Officer

Tricon Restaurants International
(Dallas, Texas)
Peter Bassi, President

EXHIBIT A
Tricon Global Restaurants, Inc.—organizational chart (1998)

in KFC's headquarters in Louisville, Kentucky. PepsiCo's objective was to reposition itself as a packaged goods company, to strengthen its balance sheet, and to create more consistent earning growth. PepsiCo received a onetime distribution from Tricon of $4.7 billion, $3.7 billion of which was used to pay off short-term debt. The balance was earmarked for stock repurchases.

Fast-Food Industry

According to the National Restaurant Association (NRA), food-service sales topped $320 billion for the approximately 500,000 restaurants and other food outlets making up the U.S. restaurant industry in 1997. The NRA estimated that sales in the fast-food segment of the food-service industry grew 5.2 percent to $104 billion, up from $98 billion in 1996. This marked the fourth consecutive year that fast-food sales either matched or exceeded sales in full-service restaurants, which grew 4.1 percent to $104 billion in 1997. The growth in fast-food sales reflected the long, gradual change in the restaurant industry from an industry once dominated by independently operated sit-down restaurants to an industry fast becoming dominated by fast-food restaurant chains. The U.S. restaurant industry as a whole grew by approximately 4.2 percent in 1997.

Major Fast-Food Segments

Six major business segments made up the fast-food segment of the food service industry. Sales data for the leading restaurant chains in each segment are shown in Exhibit B. Most striking is the dominance of McDonald's, which had sales of over $16 billion in 1996. This represented 16.6 percent of U.S. fast-food sales, or nearly 22 percent of sales among the nation's top 30 fast-food chains. Sales at McDonald's restaurants average $1.3 million per year, compared with about $820,000 for the average U.S. fast-food restaurant. Tricon Global Restaurants (KFC, Pizza Hut, and Taco Bell) had U.S. sales of $13.4 billion in 1996. This represented 13.6 percent of U.S. fast-food sales and 17.9 percent of the top 30 fast-food chains.

Sandwich chains made up the largest segment of the fast-food market. McDonald's controlled 35 percent of the sandwich segment, while Burger King ran a distant second with a 15.6 percent market share. Competition had become particularly intense within the sandwich segment as the U.S. fast-food market became more saturated. In order to increase sales, chains turned to new products to win customers away from other sandwich chains, introduced products traditionally offered by nonsandwich chains (such as pizzas, fried chicken, and tacos), streamlined their menus, and upgraded product quality. Burger King recently introduced its Big King,

EXHIBIT B LEADING U.S. FAST-FOOD CHAINS (RANKED BY 1996 SALES, $000S)					
Sandwich Chains	**Sales**	**Share**	**Family Restaurants**	**Sales**	**Share**
McDonald's	16,370	35.0%	Denny's	1,850	21.2%
Burger King	7,300	15.6%	Shoney's	1,220	14.0%
Taco Bell	4,575	9.8%	Big Boy	945	10.8%
Wendy's	4,360	9.3%	Int'l House of Pancakes	797	9.1%
Hardee's	3,055	6.5%	Cracker Barrel	734	8.4%
Subway	2,700	5.8%	Perkins	678	7.8%
Arby's	1,867	4.0%	Friendly's	597	6.8%
Dairy Queen	1,225	2.6%	Bob Evans	575	6.6%
Jack-in-the-Box	1,207	2.6%	Waffle House	525	6.0%
Sonic Drive-In	985	2.1%	Coco's	278	3.2%
Carl's Jr.	648	1.4%	Steak 'n Shake	275	3.2%
Other chains	2,454	5.2%	Village Inn	246	2.8%
Total	46,745	100.0%	Total	8,719	100.0%
Dinner Houses	**Sales**	**Share**	**Pizza Chains**	**Sales**	**Share**
Red Lobster	1,810	15.7%	Pizza Hut	4,927	46.4%
Applebee's	1,523	13.2%	Domino's Pizza	2,300	21.7%
Olive Garden	1,280	11.1%	Little Caesars	1,425	13.4%
Chili's	1,242	10.7%	Papa John's	619	5.8%
Outback Steakhouse	1,017	8.8%	Sbarros	400	3.8%
T.G.I. Friday's	935	8.1%	Round Table Pizza	385	3.6%
Ruby Tuesday	545	4.7%	Chuck E. Cheese's	293	2.8%
Lone Star Steakhouse	460	4.0%	Godfather's Pizza	266	2.5%
Bennigan's	458	4.0%	Total	10,614	100.0%
Romano's Macaroni Grill	344	3.0%			
Other dinner houses	1,942	16.8%			
Total	11,557	100.0%			
Grilled Buffet Chains	**Sales**	**Share**	**Chicken Chains**	**Sales**	**Share**
Golden Corral	711	22.8%	KFC	3,900	57.1%
Ponderosa	680	21.8%	Boston Market	1,167	17.1%
Ryan's	604	19.4%	Popeye's Chicken	666	9.7%
Sizzler	540	17.3%	Chick-fil-A	570	8.3%
Western Sizzlin'	332	10.3%	Church's Chicken	529	7.7%
Quincy's	259	8.3%	Total	6,832	100.0%
Total	3,116	100.0%			

SOURCE: *Nation's Restaurant News.*

a direct clone of the Big Mac. McDonald's quickly retaliated by introducing its Big 'n Tasty, a direct clone of the Whopper. Wendy's introduced chicken pita sandwiches, and Taco Bell introduced sandwiches called "wraps," breads stuffed with various fillings. Hardee's successfully introduced fried chicken in most of its restaurants. In addition to new products, chains lowered pricing, improved customer service, cobranded with other fast-food chains, and established restaurants in nontraditional locations (e.g., McDonald's installed restaurants in Wal-Mart stores across the country) to beef up sales.

The second largest fast-food segment was dinner houses, dominated by Red Lobster, Applebee's, Olive Garden, and Chili's. Between 1988 and 1996, dinner houses increased their share of the fast-food market from 8 to over 13 percent. This increase came mainly at the expense of grilled buffet chains, such as Ponderosa, Sizzler, and Western Sizzlin'. The market share of steak houses fell from 6 percent in 1988 to under 4 percent in 1996. The rise of dinner houses during the 1990s was partially the result of an aging and wealthier population that increasingly demanded higher-quality food in more upscale settings. However, rapid construction of new restaurants, especially among relative newcomers, such as Romano's Macaroni Grill, Lone Star Steakhouse, and Outback Steakhouse, resulted in overcapacity within the dinner house segment. This reduced per-restaurant sales and further intensified competition. Eight of the sixteen largest dinner houses posted growth rates in excess of 10 percent in 1996. Romano's Macaroni Grill, Lone Star Steakhouse, Chili's, Outback Steakhouse, Applebee's, Red Robin, Fuddruckers, and Ruby Tuesday grew at rates of 82, 41, 32, 27, 23, 14, 11, and 10 percent, respectively.

The third largest fast-food segment was pizza, long dominated by Pizza Hut. While Pizza Hut controlled over 46 percent of the pizza segment in 1996, its market share has slowly eroded because of intense competition and its aging restaurant base. Domino's Pizza and Papa John's Pizza have been

particularly successful. Little Caesars is the only pizza chain to remain predominantly a takeout chain, although it recently began home delivery. However, its policy of charging customers $1 per delivery damaged its perception among consumers as a high-value pizza chain. Home delivery, successfully introduced by Domino's and Pizza Hut, was a driving force for success among the market leaders during the 1970s and 1980s. However, the success of home delivery drove competitors to look for new methods of increasing their customer bases. Pizza chains diversified into nonpizza items (e.g., chicken wings at Domino's, Italian cheese bread at Little Caesars, and stuffed crust pizza at Pizza Hut), developed nontraditional items (e.g., airport kiosks and college campuses), offered special promotions, and offered new pizza variations with an emphasis on highquality ingredients (e.g., Roma Herb and Garlic Crunch pizza at Domino's and Buffalo Chicken Pizza at Round Table Pizza).

Chicken Segment

KFC continued to dominate the chicken segment, with 1997 sales of $4 billion (see Exhibit C). Its

EXHIBIT C TOP U.S. CHICKEN CHAINS							
Sales ($ M)	**1992**	**1993**	**1994**	**1995**	**1996**	**1997**	**Growth Rate%**
KFC	3,400	3,400	3,500	3,700	3,900	4,000	3.3
Boston Market	43	147	371	754	1,100	1,197	94.5
Popeye's	545	569	614	660	677	727	5.9
Chick-fil-A	356	396	451	502	570	671	11.9
Church's	414	440	465	501	526	574	6.8
Total	4,758	4,952	5,401	6,118	6,772	7,170	8.5
U.S. restaurants							
KFC	5,089	5,128	5,149	5,142	5,108	5,120	0.1
Boston Market	83	217	534	829	1,087	1,166	69.6
Popeye's	769	769	853	889	894	949	4.3
Chick-fil-A	487	545	534	825	717	762	9.0
Church's	944	932	937	953	989	1,070	2.5
Total	7,372	7,591	8,007	8,638	8,795	9,067	4.2
Sales per unit ($000s)							
KFC	668	663	680	720	764	781	3.2
Boston Market	518	677	695	910	1,012	1,027	14.7
Popeye's	709	740	720	743	757	767	1.6
Chick-fil-A	731	727	845	608	795	881	3.8
Church's	439	472	496	526	531	537	4.1
Total	645	782	782	782	782	782	3.9

SOURCE: Tricon Global Restaurants, Inc., *1997 Annual Report*; Boston Chicken, Inc., *1997 Annual Report*; Chick-fil-A, corporate headquarters, Atlanta; AFC Enterprises, Inc., *1997 Annual Report*.

nearest competitor, Boston Market, was second with sales of $1.2 billion. KFC operated 5120 restaurants in the United States in 1998, eight fewer restaurants than in 1993. Rather than building new restaurants in the already saturated U.S. market, KFC focused on building restaurants abroad. In the United States, KFC focused on closing unprofitable restaurants, upgrading existing restaurants with new exterior signage, and improving product quality. The strategy paid off. While overall U.S. sales during the last 10 years remained flat, annual sales per unit increased steadily in 8 of the last 9 years.

Despite KFC's continued dominance within the chicken segment, it has lost market share to Boston Market, a new restaurant chain emphasizing roasted rather than fried chicken. Boston Market has successfully created the image of an upscale deli offering healthy, "home style" alternatives to fried chicken and other "fast foods." It has broadened its menu beyond rotisserie chicken to include ham, turkey, meat loaf, chicken pot pie, and deli sandwiches. In order to minimize its image as a fast-food restaurant, it has refused to put drive-thrus in its restaurants and has established most of its units in outside shopping malls rather than in free-standing units at intersections so characteristic of other fast-food restaurants.

In 1993, KFC introduced its own rotisserie chicken, called Rotisserie Gold, to combat Boston Market. However, it quickly learned that its customer base was considerably different from that of Boston Market's. KFC's customers liked KFC chicken despite the fact that it was fried. In addition, customers did not respond well to the concept of buying whole chickens for takeout. They preferred instead to buy chicken by the piece. KFC withdrew its rotisserie chicken in 1996 and introduced a new line of roasted chicken called Tender Roast, which could be sold by the piece and mixed with its Original Recipe and Extra Crispy Chicken.

Other major competitors within the chicken segment included Popeye's Famous Fried Chicken and Church's Chicken (both subsidiaries of AFC Enterprises in Atlanta), Chick-fil-A, Bojangle's, El Pollo Loco, Grandy's, Kenny Rogers Roasters, Mrs. Winner's, and Pudgie's. Both Church's and Popeye's had similar strategies—to compete head on with other "fried chicken" chains. Unlike KFC, neither chain offered rotisserie chicken, and nonfried chicken products were limited. Chick-fil-A focused exclusively on pressure-cooked and char-grilled skinless chicken breast sandwiches, which it served to customers in sit-down restaurants located predominantly in shopping malls. As many malls added food courts, often consisting of up to 15 fast-food units competing side by side, shopping malls became less enthusiastic about allocating separate store space to food chains. Therefore, in order to complement its existing restaurant base in shopping malls. Chick-fil-A began to open smaller units in shopping mall food courts, hospitals, and colleges. It also opened freestanding units in selected locations.

Demographic Trends

A number of demographic and societal trends contributed to increased demand for food prepared away from home. Because of the high divorce rate in the United States and the fact that people married later in life, singleperson households represented about 25 percent of all U.S. households, up from 17 percent in 1970. This increased the number of individuals choosing to eat out rather than eat at home. The number of married women working outside the home also has increased dramatically during the last 25 years. About 59 percent of all married women have careers. According to the Conference Board, 64 percent of all married households will be double-income families by 2000. About 80 percent of households headed by individuals between the ages of 25 and 44 (both married and unmarried) will be double-income. Greater numbers of working women increased family incomes. According to *Restaurants & Institutions* magazine, more than one-third of all households had incomes of at least $50,000 in 1996. About 8 percent of all households had annual incomes over $100,000. The combination of higher numbers of dual-career families and rising incomes meant that fewer families had time to prepare food at home. According to Standard & Poor's *Industry Surveys*, Americans spent 55 percent of their food dollars at restaurants in 1995, up from 34 percent in 1970.

Fast-food restaurant chains met these demographic and societal changes by expanding their restaurant bases. However, by the early 1990s, the growth of traditional free-standing restaurants slowed as the U.S. market became saturated. The major exception was dinner houses, which continued to proliferate in response to Americans' increased passion for beef. Since 1990, the U.S. population has grown at an average annual rate of about 1 percent and reached 270 million people in 1997. Rising immigration since 1990 dramatically altered the ethnic makeup of the U.S. population. According to the Bureau of the Census, Americans born outside the United States made up 10 percent of the population in 1997. About 40 percent were Hispanic, while 24 percent were Asian. Nearly 30 percent of Americans born outside the United States arrived since 1990.

As a result of these trends, restaurant chains expanded their menus to appeal to the different ethnic tastes of consumers, expanded into nontraditional locations such as department stores and airports, and made food more available through home delivery and takeout service.

Industry Consolidation and Mergers and Acquisitions

Lower growth in the U.S. fast-food market intensified competition for market share among restaurant chains and led to consolidation, primarily through mergers and acquisitions, during the mid-1990s. Many restaurant chains found that market share could be increased more quickly and cheaply by acquiring an existing company rather than building new units. In addition, fixed costs could be spread across a larger number of restaurants. This raised operating margins and gave companies an opportunity to build market share by lowering prices. An expanded restaurant base also gave companies greater purchasing power over supplies. In 1990, Grand Metropolitan, a British company, purchased Pillsbury Co. for $5.7 billion. Included in the purchase was Pillsbury's Burger King chain. Grand Met strengthened the franchise by upgrading existing restaurants and eliminated several levels of management in order to cut costs. This gave Burger King a longneeded boost in improving its position against McDonald's, its largest competitor. In 1988, Grand Met had purchased Wienerwald, a West German chicken chain, and the Spaghetti Factory, a Swiss chain.

Perhaps most important to KFC was Hardee's acquisition of 600 Roy Rogers restaurants from Marriott Corporation in 1990. Hardee's converted a large number of these restaurants to Hardee's units and introduced "Roy Rogers" fried chicken to its menu. By 1993, Hardee's had introduced fried chicken into most of its U.S. restaurants. Hardee's was unlikely to destroy the customer loyalty that KFC long enjoyed. However, it did cut into KFC's sales, because it was able to offer consumers a widened menu selection that appealed to a variety of family eating preferences. In 1997, Hardee's parent company, Imasco, Ltd., sold Hardee's to CKE Restaurants, Inc. CKE owned Carl's Jr., Rally's Hamburgers, and Checker's Drive-In. Boston Chicken, Inc., acquired Harry's Farmers Market, an Atlanta grocer that sold fresh quality prepared meals. The acquisition was designed to help Boston Chicken develop distribution beyond its Boston Market restaurants. AFC Enterprises, which operated Popeye's and Church's, acquired Chesapeake Bagel Bakery of McLean, Virginia, in order to diversify away from fried chicken and to strengthen its balance sheet.

The effect of these and other recent mergers and acquisitions on the industry was powerful. The top 10 restaurant companies controlled almost 60 percent of fast-food sales in the United States. The consolidation of a number of fast-food chains within larger, financially more powerful parent companies gave restaurant chains strong financial and managerial resources that could be used to compete against small chains in the industry.

International Quick-Service Market

Because of the aggressive pace of new restaurant construction in the United States during the 1970s and 1980s, opportunities to expand domestically through new restaurant construction in the 1990s were limited. Restaurant chains that did build new restaurants found that the higher cost of purchasing prime locations resulted in immense pressure to increase annual perrestaurant sales in order to cover higher initial investment costs. Many restaurants began to expand into international markets as an alternative to continued domestic expansion. In contrast to the U.S. market, international markets offered large customer bases with comparatively little competition. However, only a few U.S. restaurant chains had defined aggressive strategies for penetrating international markets by 1998.

Three restaurant chains that had established aggressive international strategies were McDonald's, KFC, and Pizza Hut. McDonald's operated the largest number of restaurants. In 1998, it operated 23,132 restaurants in 109 countries (10,409 restaurants were located outside the United States). In comparison, KFC, Pizza Hut, and Taco Bell together operated 29,712 restaurants in 79, 88, and 17 countries, respectively (9126 restaurants were located outside the United States). Of these four chains, KFC operated the greatest percentage of its restaurants (50 percent) outside the United States. McDonald's, Pizza Hut, and Taco Bell operated 45, 31, and 2 percent of their units outside the United States. KFC opened its first restaurant outside the United States in the late 1950s. By the time PepsiCo acquired KFC in 1986, KFC was already operating restaurants in 55 countries. KFC's early expansion abroad, its strong brand name, and its managerial experience

EXHIBIT D THE WORLD'S 30 LARGEST FAST-FOOD CHAINS (YEAR-END 1993, RANKED BY NUMBER OF COUNTRIES)

	Franchise	Location	Units	Countries
1	Pizza Hut	Dallas, Texas	10,433	80
2	McDonald's	Oakbrook, Illinois	23,132	70
3	KFC	Louisville, Kentucky	9,033	68
4	Burger King	Miami, Florida	7,121	50
5	Baskin Robbins	Glendale, California	3,557	49
6	Wendy's	Dublin, Ohio	4,168	38
7	Domino's Pizza	Ann Arbor, Michigan	5,238	36
8	TCBY	Little Rock, Arkansas	7,474	22
9	Dairy Queen	Minneapolis, Minnesota	5,471	21
10	Dunkin' Donuts	Randolph, Massachusetts	3,691	21
11	Taco Bell	Irvine, California	4,921	20
12	Arby's	Fort Lauderdale, Florida	2,670	18
13	Subway Sandwiches	Milford, Connecticut	8,477	15
14	Sizzler International	Los Angeles, California	681	14
15	Hardee's	Rocky Mount, North Carolina	4,060	12
16	Little Caesar's	Detroit, Michigan	4,600	12
17	Popeye's Chicken	Atlanta, Georgia	813	12
18	Denny's	Spartanburg, South Carolina	1,515	10
19	A&W Restaurants	Livonia, Michigan	707	9
20	T.G.I. Friday's	Minneapolis, Minnesota	273	8
21	Orange Julius	Minneapolis, Minnesota	480	7
22	Church's Fried Chicken	Atlanta, Georgia	1,079	6
23	Long John Silver's	Lexington, Kentucky	1,464	5
24	Carl's Jr.	Anaheim, California	649	4
25	Loterria	Tokyo, Japan	795	4
26	Mos Burger	Tokyo, Japan	1,263	4
27	Skylark	Tokyo, Japan	1,000	4
28	Jack in the Box	San Diego, California	1,172	3
29	Quick Restaurants	Berchem, Belgium	876	3
30	Taco Time	Eugene, Oregon	300	3

SOURCE: *Hotels,* May 1994; 1994 PepsiCo, Inc., *Annual Report.*

in international markets gave it a strong competitive advantage vis-à-vis other fast-food chains that were investing abroad for the first time.

Exhibit D shows *Hotels'* 1994 list of the world's 30 largest fast-food restaurant chains (*Hotels* discontinued reporting these data after 1994). Seventeen of the 30 largest restaurant chains (ranked by number of units) were headquartered in the United States. There were a number of possible explanations for the relative scarcity of fast-food restaurant chains outside the United States. First, the United States represented the largest consumer market in the world, accounting for over one-fifth of the world's gross domestic product (GDP). Therefore, the United States was the strategic focus of the largest restaurant chains. Second, Americans were more quick to accept the fast-food concept. Many other cultures had strong culinary traditions that were difficult to break down. Europeans, for example, had histories of frequenting more midscale restaurants, where they spent hours in a formal setting enjoying native dishes and beverages. While KFC was again building restaurants in Germany by the late 1980s, it previously failed to penetrate the German market, because Germans were not accustomed to takeout food or to ordering food over the counter. McDonald's had greater success penetrating the German market because it made a number of changes in its menu and operating procedures in order to better appeal to German culture.

For example, German beer was served in all of McDonald's German restaurants. KFC had more success in Asia and Latin America, where chicken was a traditional dish.

Aside from cultural factors, international business carried risks not present in the U.S. market.

Long distances between headquarters and foreign franchises often made it difficult to control the quality of individual restaurants. Large distances also caused servicing and support problems. Transportation and other resource costs were higher than in the domestic market. In addition, time, cultural, and language differences increased communication and operational problems. Therefore, it was reasonable to expect U.S. restaurant chains to expand domestically as long as they achieved corporate profit and growth objectives. As the U.S. market became saturated and companies gained expertise in international markets, more companies could be expected to turn to profitable international markets as a means of expanding restaurant bases and increasing sales, profits, and market share.

Kentucky Fried Chicken Corporation

KFC's worldwide sales, which included sales of both company-owned and franchised restaurants, grew to $8.0 billion in 1997. U.S. sales grew 2.6 percent over 1996 and accounted for about one-half of KFC's sales worldwide. KFC's U.S. share of the chicken segment fell 1.8 points to 55.8 percent (see Exhibit E). This marked the sixth consecutive year that KFC sustained a decline in market share. KFC's

market share has fallen by 16.3 points since 1988, when it held a 72.1 percent market share. Boston Market, which established its first restaurant in 1992, increased its market share from 0 to 16.7 percent over the same period. On the surface, it appeared as though Boston Market's market-share gain was achieved by taking customers away from KFC. However, KFC's sales growth has remained fairly stable and constant over the last 10 years. Boston Market's success was largely a function of its appeal to consumers who did not regularly patronize KFC or other chicken chains that sold fried chicken. By appealing to a market niche that was previously unsatisfied, Boston Market was able to expand the existing consumer base within the chicken segment of the fast-food industry.

Refranchising Strategy

The relatively low growth rate in sales in KFC's domestic restaurants during the 1992–1997 period was largely the result of KFC's decision in 1993 to begin selling company-owned restaurants to franchisees. When Colonel Sanders began to expand the Kentucky Fried Chicken system in the late 1950s, he established KFC as a system of independent franchisees. This was done in order to minimize his involvement in the operations of individual restaurants and to concentrate on the things he enjoyed the most—cooking, product development, and public relations. This resulted in a fiercely loyal and independent group of franchisees. PepsiCo's strategy when it acquired KFC in 1986 was to integrate KFC's operations in the PepsiCo system, in order to

EXHIBIT E TOP U.S. CHICKEN CHAINS—MARKET SHARE (%)						
	KFC	**Boston Market**	**Popeye's**	**Chick-fil-A**	**Church's**	**Total**
1988	72.1	0.0	12.0	5.8	10.1	100.0
1989	70.8	0.0	12.0	6.2	11.0	100.0
1990	71.3	0.0	12.3	6.6	9.8	100.0
1991	72.7	0.0	11.4	7.0	8.9	100.0
1992	71.5	0.9	11.4	7.5	8.7	100.0
1993	68.7	3.0	11.4	8.0	8.9	100.0
1994	64.8	6.9	11.3	8.4	8.6	100.0
1995	60.5	12.3	10.8	8.2	8.2	100.0
1996	57.6	16.2	10.0	8.4	7.8	100.0
1997	55.8	16.7	10.1	9.4	8.0	100.0
Change	−16.3	16.7	−1.9	3.6	−2.1	0.0

SOURCE: *Nation's Restaurant News.*

take advantage of operational, financial, and marketing synergies. However, such a strategy demanded that PepsiCo become more involved in decisions over franchise operations, menu offerings, restaurant management, finance, and marketing. This was met by resistance with KFC franchises, who fiercely opposed increased control by the corporate parent. One method for PepsiCo to deal with this conflict was to expand through company-owned restaurants rather than through franchising. PepsiCo also used its strong cash flows to buy back unprofitable franchised restaurants, which could then be converted into company-owned restaurants. In 1986, company-owned restaurants made up 26 percent of KFC's U.S. restaurant base. By 1993, they made up about 40 percent (see Exhibit F).

While company-owned restaurants were relatively easier to control compared with franchises, they also required higher levels of investment.This meant that high levels of cash were diverted from PepsiCo's soft drink and snack food businesses into its restaurant businesses. However, the fast-food industry delivered lower returns than the soft drink and snack foods industries. Consequently, increased investment in KFC, Pizza Hut, and Taco Bell had a negative effect on PepsiCo's consolidated return on assets. By 1993, investors became concerned that PepsiCo's return on assets did not match returns delivered by Coca-Cola. In order to shore up its re-

turn on assets, PepsiCo decided to reduce the number of company-owned restaurants by selling them back to franchisees. This strategy lowered overall company sales but also lowered the amount of cash tied up in fixed assets, provided PepsiCo with one-time cash flow benefits from initial fees charged to franchisees, and generated an annual stream of franchise royalties. Tricon Global continued this strategy after the spin off in 1997.

Marketing Strategy

During the 1980s, consumers began to demand healthier foods, greater variety, and better service in a variety of nontraditional locations such as grocery stores, restaurants, airports, and outdoor events. This forced fast-food chains to expand menu offerings and to investigate nontraditional distribution channels and restaurant designs. Families also demanded greater value in the food they bought away from home. This increased pressure on fast-food chains to reduce prices and to lower operating costs in order to maintain profit margins.

Many of KFC's problems during the late 1980s surrounded its limited menu and inability to quickly bring new products to market. The popularity of its Original Recipe Chicken allowed KFC to expand without significant competition from other chicken competitors through the 1980s. As a result, new

EXHIBIT F KFC RESTAURANT COUNT (U.S.)					
	Company-Owned	% Total	Franchised/Licensed	% Total	Total
1986	1,246	26.4	3,474	73.6	4,720
1987	1,250	26.0	3,564	74.0	4,814
1988	1,262	25.8	3,637	74.2	4,899
1989	1,364	27.5	3,597	72.5	4,961
1990	1,389	27.7	3,617	72.3	5,006
1991	1,836	36.6	3,186	63.4	5,022
1992	1,960	38.8	3,095	61.2	5,055
1993	2,014	39.5	3,080	60.5	5,094
1994	2,005	39.2	3,110	60.8	5,115
1995	2,026	39.4	3,111	60.6	5,137
1996	1,932	37.8	3,176	62.2	5,108
1997	1,850	36.1	3,270	63.9	5,120
1986–1993 Compounded annual growth rate					
	7.1%		−1.7%		1.1%
1993–1997 Compounded annual growth rate					
	−2.1%		1.5%		0.1%

SOURCE: Tricon Global Restaurants, Inc., *1997 Annual Report*; PepsiCo, Inc., *Annual Reports*, 1994, 1995, 1996, 1997.

product introductions were never an important element of KFC's overall strategy. One of the most serious setbacks suffered by KFC came in 1989 as KFC prepared to add a chicken sandwich to its menu. While KFC was still experimenting with its chicken sandwich, McDonald's test marketed its McChicken sandwich in the Louisville market. Shortly thereafter, it rolled out the McChicken sandwich nationally. By beating KFC to the market, McDonald's was able to develop strong consumer awareness for its sandwich. This significantly increased KFC's cost of developing awareness of its own sandwich, which KFC introduced several months later. KFC eventually withdrew its sandwich because of low sales.

In 1991, KFC changed its logo in the United States from Kentucky Fried Chicken to KFC in order to reduce its image as a fried chicken chain. It continued to use the Kentucky Fried Chicken name internationally. It then responded to consumer demands for greater variety by introducing several products that would serve as alternatives to its Original Recipe Chicken. These included Oriental Wings, Popcorn Chicken, and Honey BBQ Chicken. It also introduced a dessert menu that included a variety of pies and cookies. In 1993, it rolled out Rotisserie Chicken and began to promote its lunch and dinner buffet. The buffet, which included 30 items, was introduced into almost 1600 KFC restaurants in 27 states by year-end. In 1998, KFC sold three types of chicken—Original Recipe and Extra Crispy (fried chicken) and Tender Roast (roasted chicken).

One of KFC's most aggressive strategies was the introduction of its Neighborhood Program. By mid-1993, almost 500 company-owned restaurants in New York, Chicago, Philadelphia,Washington, D.C., St. Louis, Los Angeles, Houston, and Dallas had been outfitted with special menu offerings to appeal exclusively to the black community. Menus were beefed up with side dishes such as greens, macaroni and cheese, peach cobbler, sweet-potato pie, and red beans and rice. In addition, restaurant employees wore African-inspired uniforms.The introduction of the Neighborhood Program increased sales by 5 to 30 percent in restaurants appealing directly to the black community. KFC followed by testing Hispanic-oriented restaurants in the Miami area, offering side dishes such as fried plantains, flan, and tres leches.

One of KFC's most significant problems in the U.S. market was that overcapacity made expansion of free-standing restaurants difficult. Fewer sites were available for new construction, and those sites, because of their increased cost, were driving profit margins down. Therefore, KFC initiated a new three-pronged distribution strategy. First, it focused on building smaller restaurants in nontraditional outlets such as airports, shopping malls, universities, and hospitals. Second, it experimented with home delivery. Home delivery was introduced in the Nashville and Albuquerque markets in 1994. By 1998, home delivery was offered in 365 U.S. restaurants. Other nontraditional distribution outlets being tested included units offering drive-thru and carry-out service only, snack shops in cafeterias, scaled-down outlets for supermarkets, and mobile units that could be transported to outdoor concerts and fairs.

A third focus of KFC's distribution strategy was restaurant cobranding, primarily with its sister chain, Taco Bell. By 1997, 349 KFC restaurants had added Taco Bell to their menus and displayed both the KFC and Taco Bell logos outside their restaurants. Cobranding gave KFC the opportunity to expand its business dayparts.While about two-thirds of KFC's business was dinner, Taco Bell's primary business occurred at lunch. By combining the two concepts in the same unit, sales at individual restaurants could be increased significantly. KFC believed that there were opportunities to sell the Taco Bell concept in over 3900 of its U.S. restaurants.

Operating Efficiencies

As pressure continued to build on fast-food chains to limit price increases, restaurant chains searched for ways to reduce overhead and other operating costs in order to improve profit margins. In 1989, KFC reorganized its U.S. operations to eliminate overhead costs and increase efficiency. Included in this reorganization was a revision of KFC's crew training programs and operating standards. A renewed emphasis was placed on improving customer service, cleaner restaurants, faster and friendlier service, and continued high-quality products. In 1992, KFC reorganized its middle-management ranks, eliminating 250 of the 1500 management positions at KFC's corporate headquarters. More responsibility was assigned to restaurant franchisees and marketing managers and pay was more closely aligned with customer service and restaurant performance. In 1997, Tricon Global signed a 5-year agreement with PepsiCo Food Systems (which was later sold by PepsiCo to AmeriServe Food Distributors) to distribute food and supplies to Tricon's 29,712 KFC, Pizza Hut, and Taco Bell units. This provided KFC with significant opportunities to benefit from economies of scale in distribution.

International Operations

Much of the early success of the top 10 fast-food chains was the result of aggressive building strategies. Chains were able to discourage competition by building in low-population areas that could only support a single fast-food chain. McDonald's was particularly successful because it was able to quickly expand into small towns across the United States, thereby preempting other fast-food chains. It was equally important to beat a competitor into more largely populated areas where location was of prime importance. KFC's early entry into international markets placed it in a strong position to benefit from international expansion as the U.S. market became saturated. In 1997, 50 percent of KFC's restaurants were located outside the United States. While 364 new restaurants were opened outside the United States in 1997, only 12 new restaurants were added to the U.S. system. Most of KFC's international expansion was through franchises, although some restaurants were licensed to operators or jointly operated with a local partner. Expansion through franchising was an important strategy for penetrating international markets because franchises were owned and operated by local entrepreneurs with a deeper understanding of local language, culture, and customs, as well as local law, financial markets, and marketing characteristics. Franchising was particularly important for expansion into smaller countries such as the Dominican Republic, Grenada, Bermuda, and Suriname, which could only support a single restaurant. Costs were prohibitively high for KFC to operate company-owned restaurants in these smaller markets. Of the 5117 KFC restaurants located outside the United States in 1997, 68 percent were franchised, while 22 percent were company-owned, and 10 percent were licensed restaurants or joint ventures.

In larger markets such as Japan, China, and Mexico, there was a stronger emphasis on building company-owned restaurants. By coordinating purchasing, recruiting and training, financing, and advertising, fixed costs could be spread over a large number of restaurants, and lower prices on products and services could be negotiated. KFC also was better able to control product and service quality. In order to take advantage of economies of scale, Tricon Global Restaurants managed all the international units of its KFC, Pizza Hut, and Taco Bell

chains through its Tricon International Division located in Dallas, Texas. This enabled Tricon Global Restaurants to leverage its strong advertising expertise, international experience, and restaurant management experience across all its KFC, Pizza Hut, and Taco Bell restaurants.

Latin American Strategy

KFC's primary market presence in Latin America during the 1980s was in Mexico, Puerto Rico, and the Caribbean. KFC established subsidiaries in Mexico and Puerto Rico, from which it coordinated the construction and operation of company-owned restaurants. A third subsidiary in Venezuela was closed because of the high fixed costs associated with running the small subsidiary. Franchises were used to penetrate other countries in the Caribbean whose market size prevented KFC from profitably operating company restaurants. KFC relied exclusively on the operation of company-owned restaurants in Mexico through 1989. While franchising was popular in the United States, it was virtually unknown in Mexico until 1990, mainly because of the absence of a law protecting patents, information, and technology transferred to the Mexican franchise. In addition, royalties were limited. As a result, most fast-food chains opted to invest in Mexico using company-owned units.

In 1990, Mexico enacted a new law that provided for the protection of technology transferred into Mexico. Under the new legislation, the franchisor and franchisee were free to set their own terms. Royalties also were allowed under the new law. Royalties were taxed at a 15 percent rate on technology assistance and know-how and 35 percent for other royalty categories. The advent of the new franchise law resulted in an explosion of franchises in fast-food, services, hotels, and retail outlets. In 1992, franchises had an estimated $750 million in sales in over 1200 outlets throughout Mexico. Prior to passage of Mexico's franchise law, KFC limited its Mexican operations primarily to Mexico City, Guadalajara, and Monterrey. This enabled KFC to better coordinate operations and minimize costs of distribution to individual restaurants. The new franchise law gave KFC and other fast-food chains the opportunity to expand their restaurant bases more quickly into more rural regions of Mexico, where responsibility for management could be handled by local franchisees.

After 1990, KFC altered its Latin American strategy in a number of ways. First, it opened 29 franchises in Mexico to complement its company-owned restaurant base. It then expanded its company-owned restaurants into the Virgin Islands and reestablished a subsidiary in Venezuela. Third, it expanded its franchise operations into South America. In 1990, a franchise was opened in Chile, and in 1993, a franchise was opened in Brazil. Franchises were subsequently established in Colombia, Ecuador, Panama, and Peru, among other South American countries. A fourth subsidiary was established in Brazil, in order to develop company-owned restaurants. Brazil was Latin America's largest economy and McDonald's primary Latin American investment location. By June 1998, KFC operated 438 restaurants in 32 Latin American countries. By comparison, McDonald's operated 1091 restaurants in 28 countries in Latin America.

Exhibit G shows the Latin American operations of KFC and McDonald's. KFC's early entry into Latin America during the 1970s gave it a leadership position in Mexico and the Caribbean. It also had gained an edge in Ecuador and Peru, countries where McDonald's had not yet developed a strong presence. McDonald's focused its Latin American investment in Brazil, Argentina, and Uruguay, countries where KFC had little or no presence. McDonald's also was strong in Venezuela. Both KFC and McDonald's were strong in Chile, Colombia, Panama, and Puerto Rico.

Economic Environment and the Mexican Market

Mexico was KFC's strongest market in Latin America. While McDonald's had aggressively established restaurants in Mexico since 1990, KFC retained the leading market share. Because of its close proximity to the United States, Mexico was an attractive location for U.S. trade and investment. Mexico's population of 98 million people was approximately one-third as large as the United States and represented a large market for U.S. companies. In comparison, Canada's population of 30.3 million people was only one-third as large as Mexico's. Mexico's close proximity to the United States meant that transportation costs between the United States and Mexico were significantly lower than to Europe or Asia. This increased the competitiveness of U.S. goods in comparison with European and Asian goods, which had to be transported to Mexico across the Atlantic or Pacific Ocean at substantial cost. The United States was, in fact, Mexico's largest trading partner. Over 75 percent of Mexico's imports came from the United States, while 84 percent of its exports were to the United States (see Exhibit H). Many U.S. firms invested in Mexico in order to take advantage of lower wage rates. By producing goods in Mexico, U.S.

EXHIBIT G Latin American Restaurant Count: KFC and McDonald's (as of December 31, 1997)

	KFC Company Restaurants	KFC Franchised Restaurants	KFC Total Restaurants	McDonald's
Argentina	—	—	—	131
Bahamas	—	10	10	3
Barbados	—	7	7	—
Brazil	6	2	8	480
Chile	—	29	29	27
Columbia	—	19	19	18
Costa Rica	—	5	5	19
Ecuador	—	18	18	2
Jamaica	—	17	17	7
Mexico	128	29	157	131
Panama	—	21	21	20
Peru	—	17	17	5
Puerto Rico & Virgin Islands	67	—	67	115
Trinidad & Tobago	—	27	27	3
Uruguay	—	—	—	18
Venezuela	6	—	6	53
Other	—	230	230	2,259
Total	207	231	438	1,091

Source: Tricon Global Restaurants, Inc.; McDonald's, 1997 Annual Report.

EXHIBIT H Mexico's Major Trading Partners—% Total Exports and Imports						
	1992		1994		1996	
	Exports	Imports	Exports	Imports	Exports	Imports
U.S.	81.1	71.3	85.3	71.8	84.0	75.6
Japan	1.7	4.9	1.6	4.8	1.4	4.4
Germany	1.1	4.0	0.6	3.9	0.7	3.5
Canada	2.2	1.7	2.4	2.0	1.2	1.9
Italy	0.3	1.6	0.1	1.3	1.2	1.1
Brazil	0.9	1.8	0.6	1.5	0.9	0.8
Spain	2.7	1.4	1.4	1.7	1.0	0.7
Other	10.0	13.3	8.0	13.0	9.6	12.0
% Total	100.0	100.0	100.0	100.0	100.0	100.0
Value ($M)	46,196	62,129	60,882	79,346	95,991	89,464

SOURCE: International Monetary Fund, *Direction of Trade Statistics Yearbook*, 1997.

goods could be shipped back into the United States for sale or shipped to third markets at lower cost.

While the U.S. market was critically important to Mexico, Mexico still represented a small percentage of overall U.S. trade and investment. Since the early 1900s, the portion of U.S. exports to Latin America had declined. Instead, U.S. exports to Canada and Asia, where economic growth outpaced growth in Mexico, increased more quickly. Canada was the largest importer of U.S. goods. Japan was the largest exporter of goods to the United States, with Canada a close second. U.S. investment in Mexico also was small, mainly because of past government restrictions on foreign investment. Most U.S. foreign investment was in Europe, Canada, and Asia.

The lack of U.S. investment in and trade with Mexico during this century was mainly the result of Mexico's long history of restricting trade and foreign direct investment. The Institutional Revolutionary Party (PRI), which came to power in Mexico during the 1930s, had historically pursued protectionist economic policies in order to shield Mexico's economy from foreign competition. Many industries were governmentowned or controlled, and many Mexican companies focused on producing goods for the domestic market without much attention to building export markets. High tariffs and other trade barriers restricted imports into Mexico, and foreign ownership of assets in Mexico was largely prohibited or heavily restricted.

Additionally, a dictatorial and entrenched government bureaucracy, corrupt labor unions, and a long tradition of antiAmericanism among many government officials and intellectuals reduced the moti-

vation of U.S. firms for investing in Mexico. The nationalization of Mexico's banks in 1982 led to higher real interest rates and lower investor confidence. Afterward, the Mexican government battled high inflation, high interest rates, labor unrest, and lost consumer purchasing power. Investor confidence in Mexico, however, improved after 1988, when Carlos Salinas de Gortari was elected president. Following his election, Salinas embarked on an ambitious restructuring of the Mexican economy. He initiated policies to strengthen the free-market components of the economy, lowered top marginal tax rates to 36 percent (down from 60 percent in 1986), and eliminated many restrictions on foreign investment. Foreign firms can now buy up to 100 percent of the equity in many Mexican firms. Foreign ownership of Mexican firms was previously limited to 49 percent.

Privatization

The privatization of governmentowned companies came to symbolize the restructuring of Mexico's economy. In 1990, legislation was passed to privatize all governmentrun banks. By the end of 1992, over 800 of some 1200 government-owned companies had been sold, including Mexicana and AeroMexico, the two largest airline companies in Mexico, and Mexico's 18 major banks. However, more than 350 companies remained under government ownership. These represented a significant portion of the assets owned by the state at the start of 1988. Therefore, the sale of government-owned companies, in terms of asset value, was moderate. A large percentage of the remaining government-owned assets were controlled by government-run companies in certain strategic industries such as steel, electricity, and petroleum. These industries had long been protected by government ownership. As a result, additional privatization of government-owned enterprises until 1993 was limited. However, in 1993, President Salinas opened up the electricity sector to independent power producers, and Petroleos Mexicanos (Pemex), the staterun petrochemical monopoly, initiated a program to sell off many of its nonstrategic assets to private and foreign buyers.

North American Free Trade Agreement (NAFTA)

Prior to 1989, Mexico levied high tariffs on most imported goods. In addition, many other goods were subjected to quotas, licensing requirements, and other nontariff trade barriers. In 1986, Mexico joined the General Agreement on Tariffs and Trade (GATT), a world trade organization designed to eliminate barriers to trade among member nations. As a member of GATT, Mexico was obligated to apply its system of tariffs to all member nations equally. As a result of its membership in GATT, Mexico dropped tariff rates on a variety of imported goods. In addition, import license requirements were dropped for all but 300 imported items. During President Salinas' administration, tariffs were reduced from an average of 100 percent on most items to an average of 11 percent.

On January 1, 1994, the North American Free Trade Agreement (NAFTA) went into effect. The passage of NAFTA, which included Canada, the United States, and Mexico, created a trading bloc with a larger population and gross domestic product than the European Union. All tariffs on goods traded among the three countries were scheduled to be phased out. NAFTA was expected to be particularly beneficial for Mexican exporters because reduced tariffs made their goods more competitive in the United States compared with goods exported to the United States from other countries. In 1995, one year after NAFTA went into effect, Mexico posted its first balance of trade surplus in 6 years. Part of this surplus was attributed to reduced tariffs resulting from the NAFTA agreement. However, the peso crisis of 1995, which lowered the value of the peso against the dollar, increased the price of goods imported into Mexico and lowered the price of Mexican products exported to the United States. Therefore, it was still too early to assess the full effects of the NAFTA agreement. (See Exhibit I for further details.)

Foreign Exchange and the Mexican Peso Crisis of 1995

Between 1982 and 1991, a two-tiered exchange-rate system was in force in Mexico. The system consisted of a controlled rate and a freemarket rate. A con-

---

EXHIBIT I SELECTED ECONOMIC DATA FOR CANADA, THE UNITED STATES, AND MEXICO

Annual Change (%)	1993	1994	1995	1996	1997
GDP growth					
Canada	3.3	4.8	5.5	4.1	—
United States	4.9	5.8	4.8	5.1	5.9
Mexico	21.4	13.3	29.4	38.2	—
Real GDP growth					
Canada	2.2	4.1	2.3	1.2	—
United States	2.2	3.5	2.0	2.8	3.8
Mexico	2.0	4.5	−6.2	5.1	—
Inflation					
Canada	1.9	0.2	2.2	1.5	1.6
United States	3.0	2.5	2.8	2.9	2.4
Mexico	9.7	6.9	35.0	34.4	20.6
Depreciation against $U.S.					
Canada (C$)	4.2	6.0	−2.7	0.3	4.3
Mexico (NP)	−0.3	71.4	43.5	2.7	3.6

SOURCE: International Monetary Fund, *International Financial Statistics*, 1998.

trolled rate was used for imports, foreign debt payments, and conversion of export proceeds. An estimated 70 percent of all foreign transactions were covered by the controlled rate. A free-market rate was used for other transactions. In 1989, President Salinas instituted a policy of allowing the peso to depreciate against the dollar by one peso per day. The result was a grossly overvalued peso. This lowered the price of imports and led to an increase in imports of over 23 percent in 1989. At the same time, Mexican exports became less competitive on world markets.

In 1991, the controlled rate was abolished and replaced with an official free rate. In order to limit the range of fluctuations in the value of the peso, the government fixed the rate at which it would buy or sell pesos. A floor (the maximum price at which pesos could be purchased) was established at Ps 3056.20 and remained fixed. A ceiling (the maximum price at which the peso could be sold) was established at Ps 3056.40 and allowed to move upward by Ps 0.20 per day. This was later revised to Ps 0.40 per day. In 1993, a new currency, called the *new peso*, was issued with three fewer zeros. The new currency was designed to simplify transactions and to reduce the cost of printing currency.

When Ernesto Zedillo became Mexico's president in December 1994, one of his objectives was to continue the stability of prices, wages, and exchange rates achieved by ex-President Carlos Salinas de Gortari during his 5-year tenure as president. However, Salinas had achieved stability largely on the basis of price, wage, and foreign-exchange controls. While giving the appearance of stability, an overvalued peso continued to encourage imports, which exacerbated Mexico's balance of trade deficit. Mexico's government continued to use foreign reserves to finance its balance of trade deficits. According to the Banco de Mexico, foreign currency reserves fell from $24 billion in January 1994 to $5.5 billion in January 1995. Anticipating a devaluation of the peso, investors began to move capital into U.S. dollar investments. In order to relieve pressure on the peso, Zedillo announced on December 19, 1994 that the peso would be allowed to depreciate by an additional 15 percent per year against the dollar compared with the maximum allowable depreciation of 4 percent per year established during the Salinas administration. Within 2 days, continued pressure on the peso forced Zedillo to allow the peso to float freely against the dollar. By mid-January 1995, the peso had lost 35 percent of its value against the dollar, and the Mexican stock market plunged 20 percent. By November 1995,

the peso had depreciated from 3.1 pesos per dollar to 7.3 pesos per dollar.

The continued devaluation of the peso resulted in higher import prices, higher inflation, destabilization within the stock market, and higher interest rates. Mexico struggled to pay its dollar-based debts. In order to thwart a possible default by Mexico, the U.S. government, International Monetary Fund, and World Bank pledged $24.9 billion in emergency loans. Zedillo then announced an emergency economic package called the pacto that included reduced government spending, increased sales of government-run businesses, and a freeze on wage increases.

Labor Problems

One of KFC's primary concerns in Mexico was the stability of labor markets. Labor was relatively plentiful, and wages were low. However, much of the workforce was relatively unskilled. KFC benefited from lower labor costs, but labor unrest, low job retention, high absenteeism, and poor punctuality were significant problems. Absenteeism and punctuality were partially cultural. However, problems with worker retention and labor unrest also were the result of workers' frustration over the loss of their purchasing power due to inflation and government controls on wage increases. Absenteeism remained high at approximately 8 to 14 percent of the labor force, though it was declining because of job security fears. Turnover continued to be a problem and ran at between 5 and 12 percent per month. Therefore, employee screening and internal training were important issues for firms investing in Mexico.

Higher inflation and the government's freeze on wage increases led to a dramatic decline in disposable income after 1994. Further, a slowdown in business activity, brought about by higher interest rates and lower government spending, led many businesses to lay off workers. By the end of 1995, an estimated 1 million jobs had been lost as a result of the economic crisis sparked by the peso devaluation. As a result, industry groups within Mexico called for new labor laws giving them more freedom to hire and fire employees and increased flexibility to hire part-time rather than full-time workers.

Risks and Opportunities

The peso crisis of 1995 and resulting recession in Mexico left KFC managers with a great deal of uncertainty regarding Mexico's economic and political future. KFC had benefited from economic stability between 1988 and 1994. Inflation was brought down, the peso was relatively stable, labor unrest was relatively calm, and Mexico's new franchise law had enabled KFC to expand into rural areas using franchises rather than company-owned restaurants. By the end of 1995, KFC had built 29 franchises in Mexico. The foreign-exchange crisis of 1995 had severe implications for U.S. firms operating in Mexico. The devaluation of the peso resulted in higher inflation and capital flight out of Mexico. Capital flight reduced the supply of capital and led to higher interest rates. In order to reduce inflation, Mexico's government instituted an austerity program that resulted in lower disposable income, higher unemployment, and lower demand for products and services.

Another problem was Mexico's failure to reduce restrictions on U.S. and Canadian investment in a timely fashion. Many U.S. firms experienced problems getting required approvals for new ventures from the Mexican government. A good example was United Parcel Service (UPS), which sought government approval to use large trucks for deliveries in Mexico. Approvals were delayed, forcing UPS to use smaller trucks. This put UPS at a competitive disadvantage vis-à-vis Mexican companies. In many cases, UPS was forced to subcontract delivery work to Mexican companies that were allowed to use larger, more cost-efficient trucks. Other U.S. companies such as Bell Atlantic and TRW faced similar problems. TRW, which signed a joint-venture agreement with a Mexican partner, had to wait 15 months longer than anticipated before the Mexican government released rules on how it could receive credit data from banks. TRW claimed that the Mexican government slowed the approval process in order to placate several large Mexican banks.

A final area of concern for KFC was increased political turmoil in Mexico during the last several years. On January 1, 1994, the day NAFTA went into effect, rebels (descendants of the Mayans) rioted in the southern Mexican province of Chiapas on the Guatemalan border. After 4 days of fighting, Mexican troops had driven the rebels out of several towns earlier seized by the rebels. Around 150—mostly rebels—were killed. The uprising symbolized many of the fears of the poor in Mexico. While ex-President Salinas' economic programs had in-

creased economic growth and wealth in Mexico, many of Mexico's poorest felt that they had not benefited. Many of Mexico's farmers, faced with lower tariffs on imported agricultural goods from the United States, felt that they might be driven out of business because of lower priced imports. Therefore, social unrest among Mexico's Indians, farmers, and the poor could potentially unravel much of the economic success achieved in Mexico during the last 5 years.

Further, ex-President Salinas' handpicked successor for president was assassinated in early 1994 while campaigning in Tijuana. The assassin was a 23-year-old mechanic and migrant worker believed to be affiliated with a dissident group upset with the PRI's economic reforms. The possible existence of a dissident group raised fears of political violence in the future. The PRI quickly named Ernesto Zedillo, a 42-year-old economist with little political experience, as their new presidential candidate. Zedillo was elected president in December 1994. Political unrest was not limited to Mexican officials and companies. In October 1994, between 30 and 40 masked men attacked a McDonald's restaurant in the tourist section of Mexico City to show their opposition to California's Proposition 187, which would have curtailed benefits to illegal aliens (primarily from Mexico). The men threw cash registers to the floor, cracked them open, smashed windows, overturned tables, and spray-painted slogans on the walls such as "No to Fascism" and "Yankee Go Home."

KFC faced a variety of issues in Mexico and Latin America in 1998. Prior to 1995, few restaurants had been opened in South America. However, KFC was now aggressively building new restaurants in the region. KFC halted openings of franchised restaurants in Mexico, and all restaurants opened since 1995 were company-owned. KFC was more aggressively building restaurants in South America, which remained largely unpenetrated by KFC through 1995. Of greatest importance was Brazil, where McDonald's had already established a strong market-share position. Brazil was Latin America's largest economy and a largely untapped market for KFC. The danger in ignoring Mexico was that a conservative investment strategy could jeopardize its market-share lead over McDonald's in a large market where KFC long enjoyed enormous popularity.

Company and Name Index

SUBJECT INDEX

PHOTO AND AD CREDITS